해커스 지텔프

Level 2 실전 문제집 7회 | 구형

200% 활용법

무료 문제풀이 MP3

해커스인강(HackersIngang.com) 접속 ▶
상단 메뉴의 [G-TELP → MP3/자료 → 문제풀이 MP3] 클릭 ▶
본 교재의 [문제풀이 MP3] 클릭하여 이용하기

[문제풀이 MP3] 바로가기 ▶

무료 지텔프 기출 단어암기장(PDF)

해커스인강(HackersIngang.com) 접속 ▶
상단 메뉴의 [G-TELP → MP3/자료 → 무료 MP3/자료] 클릭 ▶
본 교재의 [지텔프 기출 단어암기장]
클릭하여 이용하기

[무료 MP3/자료] 바로가기 ▶

무료 자동 채점 및 성적 분석 서비스

교재 내 수록되어 있는 실전 TEST의 채점 및 성적 분석 서비스를 제공합니다.

[무료 자동 채점 및 성적 분석 서비스]
바로 이용하기 ▶

"딱 한 장에 담은 지텔프 문법 총정리" 무료 강의

딱 한 장에 담았다! 지텔프 문법 총정리 QR 강의!

1. 6개 문법 포인트 총정리!
2. 해커스 G-TELP 전문 선생님의 상세한 해설
3. G-TELP 최신 출제 경향을 반영한 강의

[지텔프 문법 총정리강의] 바로가기 ▶

G-TELP 무료 학습 콘텐츠

**지텔프 정답
실시간 확인**

**해커스 지텔프
적중예상특강**

**해커스 지텔프
무료 모의고사**

**매일 지텔프
문법 풀기**

방법 해커스영어(Hackers.co.kr) 접속 ▶ [공무원/지텔프] 메뉴 클릭하여 이용하기

* QR코드로 [해커스영어] 바로가기 ▶

해커스
지텔프 Level 2
최신기출유형 실전문제집이 특별한 이유!

최신 지텔프 시험을 그대로 담았으니까!

1

최근 3개년 시험의
기출 유형과 난이도를
100% 반영한 실전 문제

2

문제별 출제 의도를
빈틈없이 파고드는
지텔프 치트키

해커스 지텔프
Level 2

최신기출유형
실전 문제집
7회

문제집

실전 TEST + 정답 한눈에 보기
(OMR 답안지 수록)

해커스 어학연구소

해커스

지텔프
—— Level 2

최신기출^{유형}
실전문제집 7회

문제집

해커스 어학연구소

지텔프 한 번에
끝낼 수 있을까요 ?

만만치 않은 시험 응시료에,
따로 할 일도 산더미처럼 많고...

[해커스 지텔프 최신기출유형 실전문제집 7회 (Level 2)]는 자신 있게 말합니다.

지텔프, 한 번에 끝낼 수 있습니다.

실전에 최적화된 영역별 핵심 전략으로,
최신 출제 경향을 완벽 반영한 실전 TEST 7회분으로,
그리고 목표 달성을 돕는 무료 강의와 딱 한 장에 담은 지텔프 문법 총정리로,

[해커스 지텔프 최신기출유형 실전문제집 7회 (Level 2)]와 함께한다면

단기간에 확실하게 목표 점수를 달성할 수 있습니다.

"이미 수많은 사람들이 안전하게 지나간 길,
가장 확실한 길,
가장 빠른 길로 가면 돼요."

얼마 남지 않은 지텔프 시험,
해커스와 함께라면 한 번에 끝낼 수 있습니다!

: 목차

최신 출제 경향 완벽 반영! 실전완성 문제집 [책 속의 책]

명쾌한 해설로 점수 상승! 약점보완 해설집

<딱 한 장에 담은 지텔프 문법 총정리> 및 총정리강의

교재에 수록된 <딱 한 장에 담은 지텔프 문법 총정리> 및 QR코드를 찍어 무료로 볼 수 있는 총정리강의를 통해 시험장에 가기 전에 지텔프 문법을 총정리하세요!

<지텔프 기출 단어암기장> PDF

해커스인강(HackersIngang.com) 사이트에서 무료로 다운받을 수 있는 단어암기장을 통해 언제 어디서든 지텔프 필수 어휘를 암기하세요!

교재 구성 및 특징

최신 출제 경향을 완벽 반영한 7회분으로 실전 감각 완성!

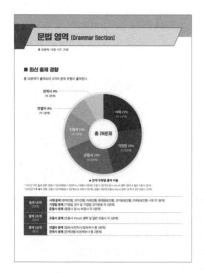

최신 지텔프 출제 경향 완벽 반영

실제 지텔프 시험과 가장 비슷한 난이도와 문제 유형으로 구성된 실전 TEST 7회분을 제공하였습니다.

자동 채점 및 성적 분석 서비스

타이머, 모바일 OMR, 자동 채점, 정답률 및 취약 유형 분석까지 제공하는 자동 채점 및 성적 분석 서비스를 통해 실전 감각을 키울 수 있습니다.

영역별 핵심 전략으로 빠른 실력 향상!

최신 출제 경향

최신 지텔프 시험의 문제 유형별 출제 비율을 제공하고 유형별 출제 형태를 우선순위에 따라 정리하여 목표 점수 달성을 위해 효과적으로 학습할 수 있게 하였습니다.

핵심 전략

각 영역의 유형별/파트별 핵심 전략을 제공하여 영역별 출제 공식과 정답의 단서를 찾는 방법을 한눈에 확인할 수 있게 하였습니다.

취약 유형 분석과 명쾌한 해설로 확실한 점수 상승!

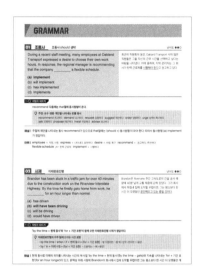

취약 유형 분석표

취약 유형 분석표를 통해 자신이 취약한 문제 유형을 스스로 확인할 수 있게 하였습니다.

지텔프 치트키

문제 풀이의 핵심이 되는 지텔프 치트키를 통해 문제를 쉽고 빠르게 푸는 전략을 제공하였습니다.

해설 & 오답분석

모든 문제에 대한 정확한 해석, 상세한 해설과 필수 학습 어휘를 제공하였습니다. 해설과 오답분석을 통해 정답이 되는 이유와 오답이 되는 이유를 확실히 파악할 수 있습니다.

풍부한 추가 학습 자료로 목표 점수 달성!

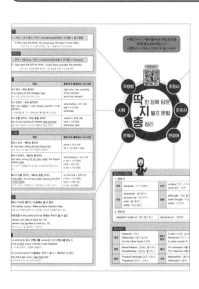

딱 한 장에 담은 지텔프 문법 총정리

지텔프 문법에서 출제되는 문법 포인트를 딱 한 장에 담은 총정리 자료를 통해 핵심만 빠르고 간단하게 정리할 수 있습니다.

총정리강의

QR코드를 찍어 무료로 볼 수 있는 총정리강의를 통해 지텔프 시험을 보는 데 꼭 필요한 문법만 효율적으로 학습할 수 있습니다.

지텔프 기출 단어암기장

지텔프 시험에 등장하는 빈출 어휘만 모은 단어암기장을 무료로 다운받아 이용할 수 있습니다.

* 지텔프 기출 단어암기장은 해커스인강(HackersIngang.com) 사이트에서 무료로 제공됩니다.

지텔프 시험 소개

■ 지텔프 시험은?

지텔프(G-TELP)란 General Tests of English Language Proficiency의 약자로 국제테스트 연구원(ITSC, International Testing Services Center)에서 주관하는 국제적 공인영어시험이며, 한국에서는 1986년에 지텔프 코리아가 설립되어 지텔프 시험을 운영 및 주관하고 있습니다. 현재 공무원, 군무원 등 각종 국가고시 영어대체시험, 기업체의 신입사원 채용 및 인사 · 승진 평가시험, 대학교 · 대학원 졸업 자격 및 논문 심사 영어대체시험 등으로 널리 활용되고 있습니다.

■ 지텔프 Level별 시험 구성

지텔프는 Level 1부터 5까지 다섯 가지 Level의 시험으로 구분됩니다. 한국에서는 다섯 가지 Level 중 Level 2 정기시험 점수가 활용되고 있습니다. 그 외 Level은 현재 수시시험 접수만 가능하며, 공인 영어 성적으로 거의 활용되지 않습니다.

구분	출제 방식 및 시간	평가 기준	합격자의 영어 구사 능력	응시 자격
Level 1	청취 30문항(약 30분) 독해 및 어휘 60문항(70분) 총 90문항(약 100분)	Native Speaker에 준하는 영어 능력: 상담, 토론 가능	외국인과 의사소통, 통역이 가능한 수준	Level 2 영역별 75점 이상 획득 시
Level 2	문법 26문항(20분) 청취 26문항(약 30분) 독해 및 어휘 28문항(40분) 총 80문항(약 90분)	다양한 상황에서 대화 가능: 업무 상담 및 해외 연수 등 가능	일상생활 및 업무 상담, 세미나 참석, 해외 연수 등이 가능한 수준	제한 없음
Level 3	문법 22문항(20분) 청취 24문항(약 20분) 독해 및 어휘 24문항(40분) 총 70문항(약 80분)	간단한 의사소통과 친숙한 상태에서의 단순 대화 가능	간단한 의사소통, 해외여행, 단순 업무 출장이 가능한 수준	제한 없음
Level 4	문법 20문항(20분) 청취 20문항(약 15분) 독해 및 어휘 20문항(25분) 총 60문항(약 60분)	기본적인 문장을 통해 최소한의 의사소통 가능	기본적인 어휘의 짧은 문장을 통한 최소한의 의사소통이 가능한 수준	제한 없음
Level 5	문법 16문항(15분) 청취 16문항(약 15분) 독해 및 어휘 18문항(25분) 총 50문항(약 55분)	극히 초보적인 수준의 의사소통 가능	영어 초보자로 일상의 인사, 소개 등을 듣고 이해 가능한 수준	제한 없음

■ 지텔프 Level 2의 구성

영역	내용	문항 수	시간	배점
문법	시제, 가정법, 준동사, 조동사, 연결어, 관계사	26문항 (1~26번)	영역별 시험 시간 제한 규정 폐지됨	100점
청취	PART 1 개인적인 이야기나 경험담에 관한 대화 PART 2 특정 주제에 대한 정보를 제공하는 공식적인 담화 PART 3 어떤 결정에 이르고자 하는 비공식적인 협상 등의 대화 PART 4 일반적인 어떤 일의 진행이나 과정에 대한 설명	7문항 (27~33번) 6문항 (34~39번) 6문항 (40~45번)* 7문항 (46~52번)*		100점
독해 및 어휘	PART 1 과거 역사 속의 인물이나 현시대 인물의 일대기 PART 2 최근의 사회적이고 기술적인 묘사에 초점을 맞춘 기사 PART 3 전문적인 것이 아닌 일반적인 내용의 백과사전 PART 4 어떤 것을 설명하거나 설득하는 상업 서신	7문항 (53~59번) 7문항 (60~66번) 7문항 (67~73번) 7문항 (74~80번)		100점
		80문항	약 90분	300점**

* 간혹 청취 PART 3에서 7문항, PART 4에서 6문항이 출제되는 경우도 있습니다.

** 각 영역 100점 만점으로 총 300점이며, 세 개 영역의 평균값이 공인 성적으로 활용되고 있습니다.

지텔프 시험 접수와 시험 당일 Tips

■ 시험 접수 방법

- **접수 방법** : 지텔프 홈페이지(www.g-telp.co.kr)에서 회원가입 후 접수할 수 있습니다.
- **시험 일정** : 매월 2~3회 일요일 오후 3시에 응시할 수 있습니다.

  * 정확한 날짜는 지텔프 홈페이지를 통해 확인할 수 있습니다.

■ 시험 당일 준비물

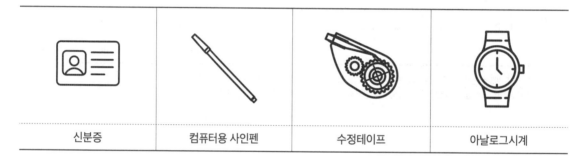

신분증	컴퓨터용 사인펜	수정테이프	아날로그시계

- 시험 당일 신분증이 없으면 시험에 응시할 수 없으므로, 반드시 신분증(주민등록증, 운전면허증, 공무원증 등)을 지참해야 합니다. 지텔프에서 인정하는 신분증 종류는 지텔프 홈페이지(www.g-telp.co.kr)에서 확인 가능합니다.

- 컴퓨터용 사인펜으로 마킹해야 하며 연필은 사용할 수 없습니다. 연필이나 볼펜으로 먼저 마킹한 후 사인펜으로 마킹하면 OMR 판독에 오류가 날 수 있으니 주의합니다.

- 마킹 수정 시, 수정테이프를 사용해야 하며 수정액은 사용할 수 없습니다. 다른 수험자의 수정테이프를 빌려 사용할 수 없으며, 본인의 것만 사용이 가능합니다.

- 대부분의 고사장에 시계가 준비되어 있지만, 자리에서 시계가 잘 보이지 않을 수도 있으니 개인 아날로그시계를 준비하면 좋습니다.

- 수험표는 별도로 준비하지 않아도 됩니다.

■ 시험 당일 Tips

① 고사장 가기 전
- 시험 장소를 미리 확인해 두고, 규정된 입실 시간에 늦지 않도록 유의합니다. 오후 2시 20분까지 입실해야 하며, 오후 2시 50분 이후에는 입실이 불가합니다.

② 고사장에서
- 1층 입구에 붙어 있는 고사실 배치표를 확인하여 자신이 배정된 고사실을 확인합니다.
- 고사실에는 각 응시자의 이름이 적힌 좌석표가 자리마다 놓여 있으므로, 자신이 배정된 자리에 앉으면 됩니다.

③ 시험 보기 직전
- 시험 도중에는 화장실에 다녀올 수 없고, 만약 화장실에 가면 다시 입실할 수 없으므로 미리 다녀오는 것이 좋습니다.
- 시험 시작 전에 OMR 카드의 정보 기입란에 올바른 정보를 기입해 둡니다.

④ 시험 시
- 답안을 따로 마킹할 시간이 없으므로 풀면서 바로 마킹하는 것이 좋습니다.
- 영역별 시험 시간 제한 규정이 폐지되었으므로, 본인이 취약한 영역과 강한 영역에 적절히 시간을 배분하여 자유롭게 풀 수 있습니다. 단, 청취 시간에는 다른 응시자에게 방해가 되지 않도록 주의해야 합니다.
- 시험지에 낙서를 하거나 다른 응시자들이 알아볼 수 있도록 큰 표시를 하는 것은 부정행위로 간주되므로 주의해야 합니다. 수험자 본인만 인지할 수 있는 작은 표시는 허용됩니다.
- OMR 카드의 정답 마킹란은 90번까지 제공되지만, 지텔프 Level 2의 문제는 80번까지만 있으므로 81~90번까지의 마킹란은 공란으로 비워두면 됩니다.

〈OMR 카드와 좌석표 미리보기〉

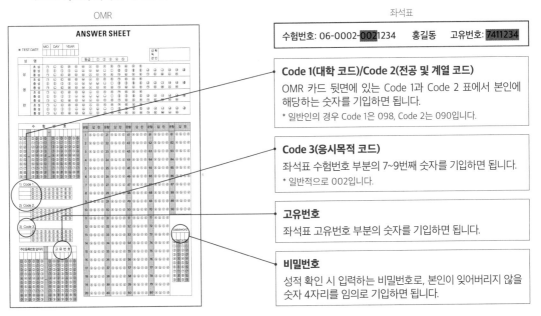

좌석표

수험번호: 06-0002-**002**1234   홍길동   고유번호: **7411234**

Code 1(대학 코드)/Code 2(전공 및 계열 코드)
OMR 카드 뒷면에 있는 Code 1과 Code 2 표에서 본인에 해당하는 숫자를 기입하면 됩니다.
* 일반인의 경우 Code 1은 098, Code 2는 090입니다.

Code 3(응시목적 코드)
좌석표 수험번호 부분의 7~9번째 숫자를 기입하면 됩니다.
* 일반적으로 002입니다.

고유번호
좌석표 고유번호 부분의 숫자를 기입하면 됩니다.

비밀번호
성적 확인 시 입력하는 비밀번호로, 본인이 잊어버리지 않을 숫자 4자리를 임의로 기입하면 됩니다.

지텔프 시험 미리보기

- 빈칸에 알맞은 문법 사항을 4개의 보기 중에서 고르는 영역입니다.
- 시제, 가정법, 준동사, 조동사, 연결어, 관계사 문제가 출제됩니다.
- 1번부터 26번까지 총 26문제가 출제됩니다.

---

1. In July, the James Webb telescope transmitted its first images back to Earth. According to the flight path, the telescope _____ the Sun when it takes the next set of photos.

   (a) will be orbiting
   (b) will orbit
   (c) is orbiting
   (d) orbits

해설 | 현재 동사로 미래의 의미를 나타내는 시간의 부사절 'when + 현재 동사'(when ~ takes)가 있고, 문맥상 미래 시점에 망원경이 다음 사진 세트를 찍을 때 그것(망원경)은 태양의 궤도를 돌고 있는 중일 것이라는 의미가 되어야 자연스럽다. 따라서 미래진행 시제 (a) will be orbiting이 정답이다.

---

2. It was a beautiful Saturday afternoon, but Stanley was inside tidying up his room. Once he finishes _____, he will embark on an adventure with his friends.

   (a) to clean
   (b) to have cleaned
   (c) cleaning
   (d) having cleaned

해설 | 빈칸 앞 동사 finish는 동명사를 목적어로 취하므로, 동명사 (c) cleaning이 정답이다.

청취 영역 · Listening Section

- 두 사람의 대화 혹은 한 사람의 담화를 듣고, 그와 관련된 6~7문제의 알맞은 정답을 4개의 보기 중에서 고르는 영역입니다.
- 4개 파트로 구성되며, PART 1/PART 3는 두 사람의 대화, PART 2/PART 4는 한 사람의 담화입니다.
- 27번부터 52번까지 총 26문제가 출제되며, 문제지에는 질문 없이 보기만 인쇄되어 있습니다.

PART 1. *You will hear a conversation between a man and a woman. You will hear questions 27 through 33 first, and then you will hear the conversation. Select the best answer to each question in the given time.*

27. (a) the deadline of a signup period
    (b) the availability of an activity center
    (c) the problem with planning committees
    (d) the awards for a sports competition

28. (a) by purchasing the prizes himself
    (b) by sharing his own experience
    (c) by offering to teach badminton
    (d) by recruiting talented players

[음성]

Twenty-seven. What are Jasmine and Dustin discussing?
Twenty-eight. How can Dustin probably assist Jasmine?

M: Hello, Jasmine! How are preparations for the bowling tournament coming along?
F: Hi, Dustin. Everything is almost ready to go! We reserved the bowling alley and opened registration for players to join. I just need to think of what prizes to give the winners.
M: Oh, I can help you come up with some ideas. My badminton league always provides great gifts to its tournament champions.

Twenty-seven. What are Jasmine and Dustin discussing?
Twenty-eight. How can Dustin probably assist Jasmine?

해설 | 27. 남자가 'How are preparations for the bowling tournament coming along?'이라며 볼링 대회 준비가 어떻게 되어가고 있는지 묻자, 여자가 'I just need to think of what prizes to give the winners.'라며 우승자에게 무슨 상을 줄지 생각하기만 하면 된다고 한 뒤, 볼링 대회 우승자를 위한 상에 관해 이야기하는 내용이 이어지고 있다. 따라서 (d)가 정답이다.

28. 남자가 'I can help you come up with some ideas'라며 그가 아이디어 내는 것을 도와줄 수 있다고 한 뒤, 'My badminton league always provides great gifts to its tournament champions.'라며 그의 배드민턴 대회는 대회 우승자에게 항상 좋은 선물을 제공한다고 한 것을 통해, Dustin이 그의 경험을 공유함으로써 Jasmine을 도울 수 있을 것임을 추론할 수 있다. 따라서 (b)가 정답이다.

독해 및 어휘 영역 — Reading & Vocabulary Section

- 지문을 읽고, 그와 관련된 7문제의 알맞은 정답을 4개의 보기 중에서 고르는 영역입니다. 7문제 중 마지막 2문제는 어휘 문제가 고정적으로 출제됩니다.
- 4개 파트로 구성되며, PART 1은 인물의 일대기, PART 2는 잡지 기사, PART 3는 지식 백과, PART 4는 비즈니스 편지 형태의 지문입니다.
- 53번부터 80번까지 총 28문제가 출제됩니다.

PART 1. Read the biography article below and answer the questions. The two underlined words are for vocabulary questions.

CLAIRE DENIS

Claire Denis is a French filmmaker most famous for her artistic style which favors visual components over dialogue. Her most successful film *Beau Travail*, which captures the human condition, is considered a masterpiece of modern cinema.

Claire Denis was born on April 21, 1946, in Paris, France. She spent much of her childhood traveling through Africa. Because her father was employed as a civil servant there during the colonial era, the family moved to a different country every two years. To pass the time, the young Denis read detective novels and watched old war movies. These were her first exposure to the narrative form. Due to concerns about her health after contracting polio, Denis returned to France where she eventually enrolled in a prestigious film school. After graduating, she had the opportunity to act as a production assistant under many influential directors. During this time, she not only developed her understanding of the movie-making process from the bottom up but also began to fall in love with film as an expression of art.

53. What is Clare Denis best known for?

    (a) her preference for illustrative elements

    (b) her stunning film backgrounds

    (c) her successful documentary movies

    (d) her crafting of realistic dialogues

해설 | 1단락의 'Claire Denis is ~ most famous for her artistic style which favors visual components over dialogue.'에서 클레르 드니는 대사보다 시각적 요소를 선호하는 그녀의 예술 스타일로 가장 유명하다고 했다. 따라서 (a)가 정답이다.

54. Why did Denis move back to her home country?

    (a) so that she could work as a civil servant

    (b) so that she could receive better medical treatment

    (c) so that she could shoot the film version of her novel

    (d) so that she could enter the next phase of her schooling

해설 | 2단락의 'Due to concerns about her health after contracting polio, Denis returned to France'에서 소아마비에 걸린 후 건강에 대한 우려 때문에 드니가 프랑스로 돌아왔다고 했다. 따라서 (b)가 정답이다.

55. How most likely did Denis learn the fundamentals of film production?

    (a) She took a cinema class in high school.

    (b) She gained experience on movie sets.

    (c) She interviewed influential scriptwriters.

    (d) She analyzed many prestigious films.

해설 | 2단락의 'she had the opportunity to act as a production assistant under many influential directors'에서 드니가 많은 영향력 있는 감독들 밑에서 조연출로 활동할 기회를 가졌다고 한 뒤, 'During this time, she ~ developed her understanding of the movie-making process from the bottom up'에서 이 시기에 그녀는 영화 제작 과정에 대한 이해를 기초부터 착실히 증진시켰다고 한 것을 통해, 드니가 영화 촬영장에서 경험을 쌓음으로써 영화 제작의 기초를 배웠던 것임을 추론할 수 있다. 따라서 (b)가 정답이다.

58. In the context of the passage, act means _____.

    (a) suffice

    (b) profit

    (c) work

    (d) appear

해설 | 2단락의 'the opportunity to act as a production assistant'는 조연출로 활동할 기회라는 뜻이므로, act가 '활동하다'라는 의미로 사용된 것을 알 수 있다. 따라서 '활동하다'라는 같은 의미의 (c) work가 정답이다.

지텔프 시험 성적 확인 및 활용처

■ 지텔프 성적 확인 방법

성적표는 온라인으로 출력(1회 무료)하거나 우편으로 수령할 수 있으며, 수령 방법은 접수 시 선택 가능합니다. (성적 발표일도 시험 접수 시 확인 가능)

〈성적표 미리보기〉

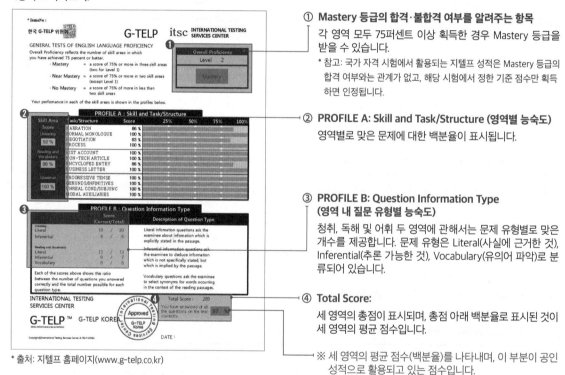

① **Mastery 등급의 합격·불합격 여부를 알려주는 항목**

각 영역 모두 75퍼센트 이상 획득한 경우 Mastery 등급을 받을 수 있습니다.

* 참고: 국가 자격 시험에서 활용되는 지텔프 성적은 Mastery 등급의 합격 여부와는 관계가 없고, 해당 시험에서 정한 기준 점수만 획득하면 인정됩니다.

② **PROFILE A: Skill and Task/Structure (영역별 능숙도)**

영역별로 맞은 문제에 대한 백분율이 표시됩니다.

③ **PROFILE B: Question Information Type
(영역 내 질문 유형별 능숙도)**

청취, 독해 및 어휘 두 영역에 관해서는 문제 유형별로 맞은 개수를 제공합니다. 문제 유형은 Literal(사실에 근거한 것), Inferential(추론 가능한 것), Vocabulary(유의어 파악)로 분류되어 있습니다.

④ **Total Score:**

세 영역의 총점이 표시되며, 총점 아래 백분율로 표시된 것이 세 영역의 평균 점수입니다.

※ 세 영역의 평균 점수(백분율)를 나타내며, 이 부분이 공인 성적으로 활용되고 있는 점수입니다.

* 출처: 지텔프 홈페이지(www.g-telp.co.kr)

■ 지텔프 점수 계산법

점수는 아래의 공식으로 산출할 수 있습니다. 총점과 평균 점수의 경우, 소수점 이하 점수는 올림 처리합니다.

각 영역 점수: 맞은 개수 × 3.75

평균 점수: 각 영역 점수 합계 ÷ 3

예) 문법 12개, 청취 5개, 독해 및 어휘 10개 맞혔을 시,

문법 12 × 3.75 = 45점 **청취** 5 × 3.75 = 18.75점 **독해 및 어휘** 10 × 3.75 = 37.5점

→ **평균 점수** (45 + 18.75 + 37.5) ÷ 3 = 34점

■ 지텔프 성적 활용처

국가 자격 시험	기준 점수
경찰공무원(경사, 경장, 순경)	43점
경찰간부 후보생	50점
소방공무원(소방장, 소방교, 소방사)	43점
소방간부 후보생	50점
군무원 9급	32점
군무원 7급	47점
군무원 5급	65점
호텔서비스사	39점
박물관 및 미술관 준학예사	50점
국가공무원 5급	65점
외교관후보자	88점
국가공무원 7급	65점
국가공무원 7급 외무영사직렬	77점
입법고시	65점
법원행정고시	65점
카투사	73점
기상직 7급	65점
국가정보원	공인어학성적 제출 필수
변리사	77점
세무사	65점
공인노무사	65점
관광통역안내사	74점
호텔경영사	79점
호텔관리사	66점
감정평가사	65점
공인회계사	65점
보험계리사	65점
손해사정사	65점

* 그 외 공공기관 및 기업체에서도 지텔프 성적을 활용하고 있으며 지텔프 홈페이지에서 모든 활용처를 확인할 수 있습니다.

수준별 맞춤 학습 플랜

TEST 1을 풀어본 후 결과에 맞는 학습 플랜을 선택하여 공부합니다.

1주 완성 학습 플랜

TEST 1 점수가 **60점 이상**인 학습자 또는 **32점을 목표로 단기간**에 점수를 얻고자 하는 학습자

- 1주 동안 매일 실전 TEST 1회분을 OMR 답안지를 활용하여 실전처럼 풀어본 후, 틀렸던 문제와 헷갈렸던 문제를 다시 한 번 풀어보며 완벽하게 이해합니다.

	Day 1	Day 2	Day 3	Day 4	Day 5	Day 6	Day 7
Week 1	TEST 1 문제풀이 및 오답분석	TEST 2 문제풀이 및 오답분석	TEST 3 문제풀이 및 오답분석	TEST 4 문제풀이 및 오답분석	TEST 5 문제풀이 및 오답분석	TEST 6 문제풀이 및 오답분석	TEST 7 문제풀이 및 오답분석

2주 완성 학습 플랜

TEST 1 점수가 **40점 이상**인 학습자 또는 **65점을 목표로 단기간**에 점수를 얻고자 하는 학습자

- 2주 동안 이틀에 한 번 실전 TEST 1회분을 OMR 답안지를 활용하여 실전처럼 풀어본 후, 틀렸던 문제와 헷갈렸던 문제를 다시 한번 풀어보며 완벽하게 이해합니다.
- 둘째 날 취약한 문제 유형을 파악하여 각 유형에서 등장하는 단서 및 paraphrasing된 표현을 정리합니다.

	Day 1	Day 2	Day 3	Day 4	Day 5	Day 6	Day 7
Week 1	TEST 1 문제풀이 및 오답분석	TEST 1 취약 유형 분석 및 정리	TEST 2 문제풀이 및 오답분석	TEST 2 취약 유형 분석 및 정리	TEST 3 문제풀이 및 오답분석	TEST 3 취약 유형 분석 및 정리	TEST 4 문제풀이 및 오답분석
Week 2	TEST 4 취약 유형 분석 및 정리	TEST 5 문제풀이 및 오답분석	TEST 5 취약 유형 분석 및 정리	TEST 6 문제풀이 및 오답분석	TEST 6 취약 유형 분석 및 정리	TEST 7 문제풀이 및 오답분석	TEST 7 취약 유형 분석 및 정리

3주 완성 학습 플랜

TEST 1 점수가 **40점 미만**인 학습자 또는 **시간이 걸리더라도 고득점**을 얻고자 하는 학습자

- 3주 동안 3일에 한 번 실전 TEST 1회분을 OMR 답안지를 활용하여 실전처럼 풀어본 후, 틀렸던 문제와 헷갈렸던 문제를 다시 한번 풀어보며 완벽하게 이해합니다.
- 둘째 날 취약한 문제 유형을 파악하여 각 유형에서 등장하는 단서 및 paraphrasing된 표현을 정리합니다.
- 셋째 날 <딱 한 장에 담은 지텔프 문법 총정리> 및 총정리강의를 통해 학습한 내용을 정리하고, <지텔프 기출 단어암기장>에 수록된 단어를 암기합니다.

	Day 1	**Day 2**	**Day 3**	**Day 4**	**Day 5**	**Day 6**	**Day 7**
Week 1	**TEST 1** 문제풀이 및 오답분석	**TEST 1** 취약 유형 분석 및 정리	**TEST 1** 총정리 및 어휘 암기	**TEST 2** 문제풀이 및 오답분석	**TEST 2** 취약 유형 분석 및 정리	**TEST 2** 총정리 및 어휘 암기	**TEST 3** 문제풀이 및 오답분석
Week 2	**TEST 3** 취약 유형 분석 및 정리	**TEST 3** 총정리 및 어휘 암기	**TEST 4** 문제풀이 및 오답분석	**TEST 4** 취약 유형 분석 및 정리	**TEST 4** 총정리 및 어휘 암기	**TEST 5** 문제풀이 및 오답분석	**TEST 5** 취약 유형 분석 및 정리
Week 3	**TEST 5** 총정리 및 어휘 암기	**TEST 6** 문제풀이 및 오답분석	**TEST 6** 취약 유형 분석 및 정리	**TEST 6** 총정리 및 어휘 암기	**TEST 7** 문제풀이 및 오답분석	**TEST 7** 취약 유형 분석 및 정리	**TEST 7** 총정리 및 어휘 암기

최신 출제 경향으로 보는
영역별 핵심 전략

문법 영역 (Grammar Section)

청취 영역 (Listening Section)

독해 및 어휘 영역 (Reading & Vocabulary Section)

문법 영역 (Grammar Section)

총 26문제 / 권장 시간: 20분

■ 최신 출제 경향

총 26문제가 출제되며, 6개의 문제 유형이 출제된다.

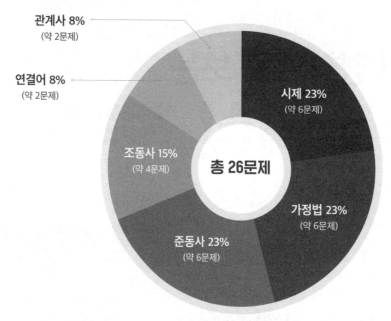

▲ 문제 유형별 출제 비율

* 2021년 이전 출제 경향: 준동사 5문제(동명사 3문제 & to 부정사 2문제), 조동사 5문제(조동사 should 생략 3문제 & 일반 조동사 2문제)
* 2022년 이후 출제 경향: 준동사 6문제(동명사 3문제 & to 부정사 3문제), 조동사 4문제(조동사 should 생략 2문제 & 일반 조동사 2문제)

출제 1순위 (23%)	**시제 문제** (현재진행, 과거진행, 미래진행, 현재완료진행, 과거완료진행, 미래완료진행 시제 각 1문제) **가정법 문제** (가정법 과거 및 가정법 과거완료 각 3문제) **준동사 문제** (동명사 및 to 부정사 각 3문제)
출제 2순위 (15%)	**조동사 문제** (조동사 should 생략 및 일반 조동사 각 2문제)
출제 3순위 (8%)	**연결어 문제** (접속사/전치사/접속부사 중 2문제) **관계사 문제** (관계대명사/관계부사 중 2문제)

■ 유형별 핵심 전략

보기의 구성이나 빈칸 문장을 통해 문제 유형을 확인한 후, 정답의 단서를 찾는다.

시제	**핵심 전략** 빈칸 주변이나 보기에 포함된 시간 표현 관련 단서를 파악한다. **빈출 단서** [현재진행] right now, now 등 [과거진행] while + 과거 동사 등 [미래진행] when + 현재 동사 등 [현재완료진행] since + 과거 동사 or 과거 시점 + (for + 기간 표현) 등 [과거완료진행] before / when + 과거 동사 + (for + 기간 표현) 등 [미래완료진행] by the time + 현재 동사 + (for + 기간 표현) 등	6문제
가정법	**핵심 전략** 빈칸이 if절에 있는 경우 주절의 시제, 빈칸이 주절에 있는 경우 if절의 시제를 파악한다. **빈출 단서** [가정법 과거] If + 주어 + 과거 동사, 주어 + would/could(조동사 과거형) + 동사원형 [가정법 과거완료] If + 주어 + had p.p., 주어 + would/could(조동사 과거형) + have p.p.	6문제
준동사	**핵심 전략** 빈칸 앞 동사 또는 문장 구조를 파악한다. **빈출 단서** [동명사를 목적어로 취하는 동사] enjoy, recommend, avoid, consider, imagine, prevent, keep, dread 등 [to 부정사를 목적어로 취하는 동사] decide, need, intend, promise, expect, wish, plan, hope 등 [to 부정사를 목적격 보어로 취하는 동사] require, ask, encourage, allow 등 [to 부정사의 역할] 명사 역할(~하는 것), 형용사 역할(~하는, ~할), 부사 역할(~하기 위해, ~하게 되다)	6문제
조동사	**핵심 전략** 빈칸 앞 당위성(주장·요구·명령·제안) 표현 또는 문맥을 파악한다. **빈출 단서** [조동사 should 생략] recommend, suggest, advise, essential, important, best, suggestion 등 [가능성/능력] can [허가] can, may [약한 추측] may, might [강한 확신] must [미래/예정] will [의지] will [의무/당위성] should, must [충고/조언] should	4문제
연결어	**핵심 전략** 문장 해석을 통해 앞뒤 문장의 관계를 파악한다. **빈출 단서** [접속사] because, although, while 등 [접속 부사] However, In fact, For example, Otherwise 등	2문제
관계사	**핵심 전략** 빈칸 앞 선행사와 그 선행사의 관계절 내 역할 및 콤마(,) 유무를 파악한다. **빈출 단서** [관계대명사] who, which, that 등 [관계부사] when, where 등	2문제

청취 영역 (Listening Section)

총 26문제 / 시험 시간: 약 30분

■ 최신 출제 경향

4개의 파트에서 총 26문제가 출제되며, 4개의 문제 유형이 출제된다.

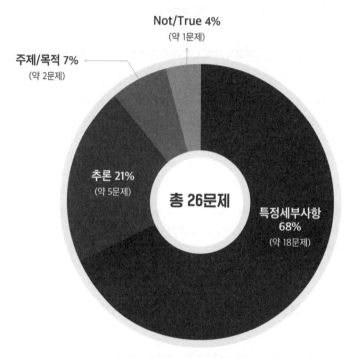

▲ 문제 유형별 출제 비율

출제 1순위 (68%)	**특정세부사항 문제** (의문사를 이용해 특정한 정보를 묻는 문제)
	ᴇx **What** caused the change in the city's air quality?
	ᴇx **How** does exercise help improve one's overall health?
출제 2순위 (21%)	**추론 문제** (화자가 다음에 할 일, 화자가 결정한 것, 추론 가능한 특정 사실 등을 묻는 문제)
	ᴇx What is Mark **most likely** to do following the conversation?
	ᴇx Why do people **probably** sleep less today than in the past?
출제 3순위 (7%)	**주제/목적 문제** (대화 또는 담화의 주제나 목적을 묻는 문제)
	ᴇx What is the talk **mainly** about?
	ᴇx What is the **purpose** of the talk?
출제 4순위 (4%)	**Not/True 문제** (대화 또는 담화에 언급된 것/언급되지 않은 것, 사실인 것/사실이 아닌 것을 묻는 문제)
	ᴇx What is **not** a recognized benefit of using electric cars?
	ᴇx Which is **true** about the recycling programs?

■ 파트별 핵심 전략

질문을 듣고 의문사와 키워드를 노트테이킹한 후 대화 또는 담화에서 키워드가 언급된 주변 내용을 주의 깊게 듣는다. 정답 단서가 그대로 언급되거나 올바르게 paraphrasing된 보기를 정답으로 선택한다.

PART 1 2인 대화	인사/안부 → 경험담 소개 → 몇 차례의 질문과 대답 → 마무리 인사 **핵심 전략** 실제로 경험한 사람의 발언에 주목한다. **빈출 주제** 파티 또는 행사에 다녀온 경험, 여행을 다녀온 경험, 동아리 활동 경험, 아르바이트 경험, 교환학생을 다녀온 경험, 취미 활동 소개 등	7문제
PART 2 1인 담화	인사/자기소개(소속·직책 등) → 대상 소개 → 세부사항 설명 → 마무리 인사 **핵심 전략** 소개/홍보 대상의 장점에 주목한다. **빈출 주제** 신기술을 접목한 신제품 홍보, 구독 서비스 홍보, 박람회·축제·이벤트 홍보, 기업 홍보 및 후원 요청 등	6문제
PART 3 2인 대화	인사/안부 → 두 가지 선택지 소개 → 장단점 비교 → 결정 및 추후 계획 암시 **핵심 전략** 최종 결정을 언급하는 마지막 발언에 주목한다. **빈출 주제** 아날로그 방식과 디지털 방식의 장단점 비교, 두 가지 전공의 장단점 비교, 두 가지 제품의 장단점 비교, 두 가지 주거 형태의 장단점 비교 등	6문제*
PART 4 1인 담화	인사/주의 환기 → 주제 소개 → 단계/항목별로 순차적 설명 **핵심 전략** 순서를 나타내는 말에 주목한다. **빈출 주제** 효율적인 업무 방법에 대한 조언, 환경을 보호하는 방법에 대한 조언, 건강을 관리하는 방법에 대한 조언, 동호회를 결성하는 절차 등	7문제*

* 간혹 청취 PART 3에서 7문제, PART 4에서 6문제가 출제되는 경우도 있다.

독해 및 어휘 영역 (Reading & Vocabulary Section)

총 28문제 / 권장 시간: 40분

■ 최신 출제 경향

4개의 파트에서 총 28문제가 출제되며, 5개의 문제 유형이 출제된다.

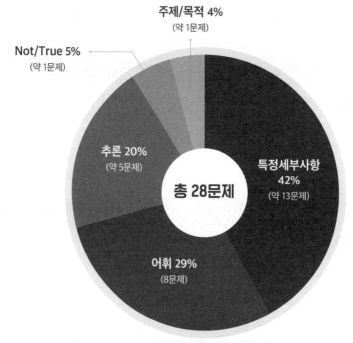

▲ 문제 유형별 출제 비율

출제 1순위 (42%)	**특정세부사항 문제** (의문사를 이용해 특정한 정보를 묻는 문제) ex **How** did Bell come up with the idea for the telephone? ex **What** did Dr. Evans say caused the tsunami?
출제 2순위 (29%)	**어휘 문제** (지문의 밑줄 친 어휘의 문맥상 유의어를 고르는 문제) ex In the context of the passage, cherish means _____.
출제 3순위 (20%)	**추론 문제** (지문에 명시적으로 언급되지는 않았으나 추론 가능한 것을 묻는 문제) ex What will Greta and Joe **probably** do about the problem? ex Why **most likely** did the wildfire spread more quickly than previous burns?
출제 4순위 (4~5%)	**주제/목적 문제** (지문의 주제나 목적을 묻는 문제) ex What is the article **mainly** about? ex **Why** did Lucas Berkley **write** a letter to Emily Nelson? **Not/True 문제** (지문에 언급된 것/언급되지 않은 것, 사실인 것/사실이 아닌 것을 묻는 문제) ex Which is **NOT** a part of the daily life of early settlers? ex According to the article, what is **true** about the Atkins diet?

■ 파트별 핵심 전략

질문을 읽고 의문사와 키워드를 파악한 후 지문에서 키워드가 언급된 주변 내용을 주의 깊게 읽는다. 정답 단서가 그대로 언급되거나 올바르게 paraphrasing된 보기를 정답으로 선택한다.

PART 1 인물의 일대기	인물 소개 → 어린 시절 및 진로 선택 계기 → 청년 시절 및 초기 활동 → 주요 업적 및 활동 → 근황 및 평가 **핵심 전략** 시기별로 인물에게 일어난 중요한 사건 및 업적에 주목한다. **빈출 주제** 예술가(가수·작곡가·화가 등)의 일대기 및 대표 작품들, 직업인(요리사·기업가 등)의 일대기 및 주요 업적 등	7문제
PART 2 잡지 기사	연구의 주제 → 연구의 계기 및 목적 → 연구의 결과 및 특징 → 연구의 의의 및 시사점 → 연구의 한계 및 추후 과제 **핵심 전략** 기사의 제목 및 기사에서 다루는 연구의 사회적 의의에 주목한다. **빈출 주제** 불치병의 치료법이나 신약 등의 발견 및 사회적 기대 효과, 첨단 기술의 발전 및 활용 방안, 새로운 동식물종의 발견 및 환경적 의의 등	7문제
PART 3 지식 백과	정의 → 기원/어원 → 여러 가지 특징 나열 → 현황 **핵심 전략** 소재의 정의 및 특징에 주목한다. **빈출 주제** 동물 혹은 식물의 종·생김새·서식 지역 소개, 최근 유행하고 있는 게임·SNS·취미 활동의 인기 요인 소개, 역사적으로 중요한 사건이나 장소의 의의 소개 등	7문제
PART 4 비즈니스 편지	편지의 목적 → 세부 사항 → 요청 사항 → 끝인사 및 연락처 전달 **핵심 전략** 발신자가 편지를 쓴 목적에 주목한다. **빈출 주제** 불친절한 응대에 항의하거나 친절한 서비스에 감사함을 전하는 편지, 새로운 정책이나 변경된 규정을 공지 혹은 안내하는 편지, 입사를 지원하는 편지 등	7문제

TEST 1

GRAMMAR

LISTENING

READING & VOCABULARY

테스트 전 확인사항

1. OMR 답안지를 준비하셨나요? ☐
2. 컴퓨터용 사인펜, 수정 테이프를 준비하셨나요? ☐
3. 음성을 들을 준비를 하셨나요? ☐

🎧 **TEST 1.mp3**
해커스인강(HackersIngang.com)에서 무료 다운로드
상단 메뉴 [MP3/자료 → 문제풀이 MP3]

TEST 1 음성 바로 듣기

📋 **자동 채점 및 성적 분석 서비스**
∨ 타이머, 모바일 OMR, 자동 채점
∨ 정답률 및 취약 유형 분석

자동 채점 및 성적 분석
서비스 바로 이용하기

시험 시간 : 90분

목표 점수 : _____점
시작 시간 : _____시 _____분 ~ 종료 시간 : _____시 _____분

General Tests of English Language Proficiency
G-TELP

Level 2

GRAMMAR SECTION

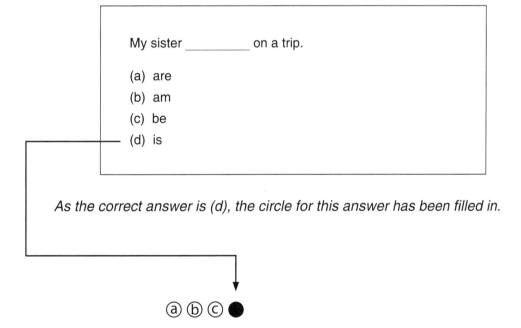

My sister _____ on a trip.

(a) are
(b) am
(c) be
(d) is

As the correct answer is (d), the circle for this answer has been filled in.

TURN THE PAGE TO BEGIN THE TEST

1. During a recent staff meeting, many employees at Oakland Transport expressed a desire to choose their own work hours. In response, the regional manager is recommending that the company _____ a flexible schedule.

   (a) implement
   (b) will implement
   (c) has implemented
   (d) implements

2. Brandon has been stuck in a traffic jam for over 40 minutes due to the construction work on the Riverview Interstate Highway. By the time he finally gets home from work, he _____ for an hour longer than normal.

   (a) has driven
   (b) will have been driving
   (c) will be driving
   (d) would have driven

3. SmartTune, an online audio distribution platform, has proven to be a powerful networking tool for songwriters. They _____ not only use it to collaborate with other artists but also to easily share their music with a wider audience.

   (a) must
   (b) would
   (c) might
   (d) can

4. Air pollution is worsening because many manufacturers refuse to limit the harmful emissions from their factories. If the government regulated the industry more strictly, fewer pollutants _____ our planet's atmosphere.

   (a) have entered
   (b) are entering
   (c) would have entered
   (d) would enter

5. During the first National Women's Rights Convention in 1850, the participants argued in favor of suffrage for all American citizens regardless of gender. This means that before women were allowed to vote in 1920, they _____ for the right for almost 70 years.

   (a) were struggling
   (b) struggle
   (c) had been struggling
   (d) have struggled

6. Eastern College has introduced a policy for its dormitories, as noise issues have led to frequent disputes among residents lately. Everyone living in the dorms is required to avoid _____ loud sounds in their rooms or the common areas after 10 p.m.

   (a) having made
   (b) to have made
   (c) to make
   (d) making

7. *Gardening Monthly* announced last week that it was shutting down on account of a sharp decline in subscriptions. Most experts in the publishing world agree that the magazine _____ many more readers if it had made its content available on the Internet.

(a) would have attracted
(b) attracted
(c) was attracting
(d) would attract

8. Local environmental groups are strongly opposed to the plan to build an industrial complex next to the Greenhill Wetlands. This marsh, _____, is populated by a large number of rare animals, including several endangered birds.

(a) what covers an area of over 25 square kilometers
(b) where it covers an area of over 25 square kilometers
(c) which covers an area of over 25 square kilometers
(d) that covers an area of over 25 square kilometers

9. It has always been my dream to visit the Great Barrier Reef in Australia. I like to imagine _____ through the crystal clear water while looking at the beautiful coral and the amazing marine life.

(a) swimming
(b) to swim
(c) having swum
(d) to have swum

10. Amelia is part of the music program at Miller University, which is home to the National A Cappella Championship. Since 1955, the school _____ the event, at which many aspiring singers are discovered.

(a) was hosting
(b) had been hosting
(c) will be hosting
(d) has been hosting

11. Bill Walton was one of the greatest college basketball players of all time, and he was becoming a dominant professional player when he broke both his ankle and wrist. If those injuries _____, he would have likely had a long and successful career.

(a) had never occurred
(b) never occurred
(c) would never occur
(d) never occur

12. There are various strategies job seekers can use to make their résumés appeal to potential employers. _____, they might focus on presenting their skills and experience in a way that shows a direct connection to the position being applied for.

(a) Likewise
(b) For example
(c) Meanwhile
(d) After all

TEST 1

TEST 2

TEST 3

TEST 4

TEST 5

TEST 6

TEST 7

해커스 지텔프 초신기출유형 실전문제집 7회 (Level 2)

13. The payroll deadline falls on a weekend this month. Accordingly, all employees are encouraged _____ their time cards and expense reports by June 25 so that their paychecks are not delayed.

    (a) to submit
    (b) submitting
    (c) to be submitting
    (d) having submitted

14. Professor Morris requested that the university's maintenance department send a technician to his classroom quickly. He _____ a lecture this morning when he noticed that the air conditioner had stopped working.

    (a) is delivering
    (b) was delivering
    (c) delivered
    (d) has been delivering

15. The Bow Valley Parkway, which winds through Banff National Park, closes from 8 p.m. until 8 a.m. in the spring. If it were to be open at night, animal populations _____ significant damage as a consequence of their migratory routes being obstructed.

    (a) would have suffered
    (b) suffer
    (c) are suffering
    (d) would suffer

16. Over the past year, Mica has rated highly on her monthly performance evaluations at Westport Advertising. As a result, the head of the marketing department will meet with her next week _____ a promotion to team leader.

    (a) to be conferring
    (b) to confer
    (c) will confer
    (d) conferring

17. Jeff has an appointment to take the road test to get his driver's license tomorrow. He feels confident that he will pass _____ he has taken lessons at Ace Driving Academy for weeks now.

    (a) as soon as
    (b) in case
    (c) because
    (d) even if

18. Please don't try to reach me unless there's an emergency. I _____ in the Ellen Banks Library this weekend to prepare for the final exam of my biology class, and I don't want to be distracted.

    (a) have studied
    (b) will be studying
    (c) will have been studying
    (d) was studying

19. The blog *Urban Scene* has released its annual list of the best restaurants in Portland. It includes details about the menus, prices, and facilities of 20 dining establishments. Readers appreciate _____ this useful information about where to eat out in the city.

   (a) being received
   (b) to receive
   (c) receiving
   (d) to be receiving

20. The dog my family adopted from the local animal shelter has serious health problems. Had we known about them sooner, we _____ her to the veterinarian to get treatment earlier.

   (a) would have taken
   (b) were taking
   (c) would take
   (d) took

21. Carson was confused by his employee review. According to his supervisor, Carson _____ work harder to ensure that his clients are satisfied with his service. This baffled him because he'd never received any direct complaints from customers.

   (a) will
   (b) may
   (c) would
   (d) should

22. Weston Incorporated's new Marvelous Meal Kits have packaging defects that prevent the food from staying fresh. The company has assured customers that it will take steps to keep this problem from reoccurring. However, customers are also demanding that it _____ their payments.

   (a) has refunded
   (b) refund
   (c) refunds
   (d) will refund

23. Shane didn't have enough money for a taxi ride to campus. Consequently, when he found out that the subway was delayed, he returned home to get his bike. He _____ on his way to school, and he's almost there.

   (a) will now cycle
   (b) is now cycling
   (c) has been now cycling
   (d) now cycles

24. Becky could tell that her parents were worried about her traveling abroad for a month. To ease their concerns, she promised _____ them every other day no matter what.

   (a) contacting
   (b) having contacted
   (c) to contact
   (d) to have contacted

해커스 지텔프 최신기출유형 실전문제집 7회 (Level 2)

25. MegaX Communications has found it difficult to hire experienced software programmers for an ongoing project. If the company were willing to offer better employee benefits, it _____ better-qualified applicants for the open positions.

(a) will draw
(b) would have drawn
(c) had drawn
(d) would draw

26. Psychologist Jean Piaget studied childhood intellectual development. However, some scholars question his theories because the individuals _____ were not randomly selected. To make matters worse, he usually relied on small sample sizes, so his findings may not apply to larger groups.

(a) which were the focus of his research
(b) what were the focus of his research
(c) who were the focus of his research
(d) whom were the focus of his research

THIS IS THE LAST PAGE OF THE GRAMMAR SECTION
DO NOT MOVE ON UNTIL DIRECTED TO DO SO

LISTENING SECTION

TEST 1

TEST 2

TEST 3

TEST 4

TEST 5

TEST 6

TEST 7

해커스 지털프 최신기출유형 실전문제집 7회 (Level 2)

DIRECTIONS:

The Listening Section has four parts. Each part contains a listening passage and multiple questions about the passage. You will hear the questions first, and then you will hear the passage. Select the best answer from the four choices provided for each question. Then, fill in the correct circle on your answer sheet.

Now you will hear an example question. You will then listen to a sample passage.

Now listen to the example question.

(a) San Francisco
(b) Los Angeles
(c) London
(d) Detroit

Brenda Kenwood was born in Detroit, so the best answer is (d). As the correct answer is (d), the circle for this answer has been filled in.

TURN THE PAGE TO BEGIN THE TEST

27. (a) She has been training for a horse race.
    (b) She is planning to build a stable.
    (c) She is learning to ride a horse.
    (d) She has been taking lessons for her work.

28. (a) because the sport involves lots of concentration
    (b) because players must be able to do two things at once
    (c) because the sport takes many years to master
    (d) because players must learn various riding styles

29. (a) She could barely control the horse.
    (b) She found cuts on her legs.
    (c) She was unable to stay balanced.
    (d) She had serious muscle pains.

30. (a) It helps one maintain good posture.
    (b) It increases one's self-control.
    (c) It works all parts of one's body.
    (d) It improves one's relationship to animals.

31. (a) because she cannot mount a horse safely
    (b) because she is worried about injuries
    (c) because she cannot jump over fences
    (d) because she is dedicated to racing

32. (a) by learning higher-level skills
    (b) by getting tips from his fellow students
    (c) by spending more time with his friend
    (d) by attaining insight from instructors

33. (a) visit a riding facility
    (b) take a placement test
    (c) drive a friend to his class
    (d) have a riding lesson

34. (a) the former players who teach music in school
    (b) the scholarships that the orchestra offers
    (c) the honors that the ensemble has earned
    (d) the international player who runs the program

35. (a) because it provides instruments for free
    (b) because it replaces its instruments each year
    (c) because it has a practice studio near the school
    (d) because it receives sufficient school funding

36. (a) to conduct themselves in a professional way
    (b) to practice for two hours daily
    (c) to be a positive example of their school
    (d) to travel to other states for performances

37. (a) by developing students' ability to focus
    (b) by providing extra time to study between shows
    (c) by tutoring students in a range of subjects
    (d) by promoting discussion between band members

38. (a) learning to accept failure as a part of life
    (b) mastering a skill with little difficulty
    (c) learning to speak in front of an audience
    (d) playing an instrument before a crowd

39. (a) She will let the students try out different instruments.
    (b) She will help students choose what instrument to play.
    (c) She will teach music to students in after-school classes.
    (d) She will share her musical interests with students.

40. (a) where to buy flight tickets
    (b) how to get travel information
    (c) the ideal time to visit Italy
    (d) the options for a trip

41. (a) It requires less effort to plan.
    (b) It provides well-located lodging.
    (c) It includes language learning opportunities.
    (d) It offers large discounts.

42. (a) They stay away from locations with mass appeal.
    (b) They decrease the chances of encountering other travelers.
    (c) They serve specific types of cuisines.
    (d) They reduce the occasions for spare time.

43. (a) by allowing one to avoid tourist areas
    (b) by making one seem approachable
    (c) by signaling a need for help
    (d) by showing familiarity with the native culture

44. (a) because they don't speak the local language
    (b) because their interactions are limited to individual activities
    (c) because their relationships don't last long
    (d) because they often have differing interests

45. (a) look for another destination
    (b) organize a trip of his own
    (c) invite Laura to join him
    (d) contact a tour operator

You will hear an explanation of a process. You will hear questions 46 through 52 first, and then you will hear the explanation. Select the best answer to each question in the given time.

46. (a) inspect the functions of the program
    (b) review the content of the presentation
    (c) adjust the equipment to the user's physique
    (d) examine the hardware of the device

47. (a) to prevent them from disrupting the meeting
    (b) to make them switch off the television sets
    (c) to have them prepare appropriate materials
    (d) to ask them to shut all the windows

48. (a) by viewing the shared calendar
    (b) by referring to the meeting plan
    (c) by requesting a reminder from the host
    (d) by reading over the invitation details

49. (a) It creates a professional setting.
    (b) It conveys a neutral disposition.
    (c) It encourages a sense of organization.
    (d) It presents a uniform appearance.

50. (a) when the chatbox is out of service
    (b) when the gathering has few attendees
    (c) when someone has an immediate question
    (d) when someone jumps in to make a comment

51. (a) looking at whoever is currently speaking
    (b) taking thorough notes while others talk
    (c) keeping one's eyes on the camera
    (d) maintaining an active use of gestures

52. (a) to suggest that a software update be installed
    (b) to recommend a virtual meeting tool
    (c) to emphasize the importance of the tips
    (d) to demonstrate the productivity of teleconferences

THIS IS THE LAST PAGE OF THE LISTENING SECTION
DO NOT MOVE ON UNTIL DIRECTED TO DO SO

READING AND VOCABULARY SECTION

TEST 1

TEST 2

TEST 3

TEST 4

TEST 5

TEST 6

TEST 7

DIRECTIONS:

You will now read four different passages. Comprehension and vocabulary questions follow every passage. Select the best answer from the four choices provided for each question. Then, fill in the correct circle on your answer sheet.

Read the following sample passage and example question.

Example:

> Brenda Kenwood was born in Detroit. After finishing university in Los Angeles, she settled in San Francisco.
>
> Where was Brenda Kenwood born?
>
> (a) San Francisco
> (b) Los Angeles
> (c) London
> (d) Detroit

As the correct answer is (d), the circle for this answer has been filled in.

TURN THE PAGE TO BEGIN THE TEST

해커스 지텔프 최신기출유형 실전문제집 7회 (Level 2)

MAX ERNST

Max Ernst was a German painter, sculptor, and poet. He is best known for inventing the artistic techniques frottage and grattage, which challenged the conventional standards of his time.

Ernst was born on April 2, 1891, in Brühl, Germany, into a middle-class Catholic family. His father was a teacher of the deaf and an amateur painter. Ernst became interested in art from a young age as a result of watching him paint. When Ernst entered the University of Bonn in 1909, he started painting as a hobby, producing portraits of his family and himself. Two years later, he joined a friend's expressionist art group and decided to become an artist. Ernst was affected by Pablo Picasso's Cubism and Vincent van Gogh's Expressionism. By 1913, his paintings were being <u>exhibited</u> alongside the works of other artists who influenced him.

Ernst was a leader in the Surrealist movement, an artistic and literary philosophy of the 1920s. This group of artists strived to generate works that reflected their unconscious thoughts and desires. This style of art would remain Ernst's focus throughout the rest of his career as it liberated him from the need to adhere to traditional figurative techniques. He also began a series of surrealist landscape paintings of forests, and depictions of different types of vegetation would be a recurring theme in his work.

The following year, Ernst invented frottage, which is the technique of creating a work of art on paper by taking a pencil rubbing from an object or uneven surface. With this, he combined impressions of shapes and textures to create images that one could not achieve through drawing alone. Ernst later utilized a similar technique in painting with grattage, which involves scraping applied paint off a canvas so the imprints of textured items placed under it are revealed. His famous painting *Forest and Dove* was produced using this method in 1927.

In 1941, after World War II broke out, Ernst fled to the United States, where his unique style was widely admired and inspired a new generation of artists, particularly Abstract Expressionists. Thanks to his extensive travels and his fierce <u>dedication</u> to his art, Ernst was a highly respected figure in critical circles with a strong following in Germany, France, and the United States. He eventually settled in France in the 1950s and stayed there until his death in 1976.

53. What is Max Ernst most famous for?

    (a) popularizing the techniques of German poetry

    (b) challenging the standards of a new artistic movement

    (c) imitating a highly popular style of painting

    (d) developing new methods for creating artwork

54. Why did Ernst take an interest in art as a child?

    (a) because he received painting lessons from a talented teacher

    (b) because he was given portrait assignments in school

    (c) because he was inspired by the work of celebrated artists

    (d) because he observed his father practicing art

55. What could be the reason that Ernst joined the Surrealist movement?

    (a) He wanted to avoid following convention.

    (b) He was encouraged by his friend's art group.

    (c) He needed a way to express his politics.

    (d) He was rejected by Expressionist artists.

56. How was Ernst's 1927 painting *Forest and Dove* created?

    (a) by rubbing a pencil drawing with objects

    (b) by lifting the texture of objects beneath a canvas

    (c) by applying unusual paint mixtures

    (d) by painting directly onto a textured canvas

57. How was Ernst's career affected by his move to America?

    (a) He changed his approach to painting.

    (b) He made art with violent themes.

    (c) He found a new audience for his work.

    (d) He sold paintings at galleries.

58. In the context of the passage, underline{exhibited} means _____.

    (a) shown
    (b) proven
    (c) disclosed
    (d) protected

59. In the context of the passage, underline{dedication} means _____.

    (a) achievement
    (b) devotion
    (c) capability
    (d) responsibility

PART 2. Read the magazine article below and answer the questions. The two underlined words are for vocabulary questions.

A POTENTIALLY GROUNDBREAKING SCREENING APP IS ON THE HORIZON

Researchers have developed a prototype for a new smartphone application that allows people to take a simple test to detect conditions like Alzheimer's at the earliest stages. The app, which tracks changes in the size of a person's pupils, is based on studies that have shown that increased pupil dilation can indicate neurological disease.

Researchers at the UC San Diego Center for Mental Health Technology (MHTech) collaborated with engineers to build the software. They were prompted to create this app in order to improve the availability of pupil response tests. Currently, these assessments can only be carried out in medical clinics using a specialized instrument called a pupilometer, the cost of which makes them unfeasible for the majority of people to own. According to Eric Granholm, a director at the MHTech Center, an accessible large-scale community screening tool like this one "could have a huge public health impact."

The app employs a near-infrared camera, a technology which most new smartphone models are equipped with. The user takes a recording of their eyes, and the app—which can differentiate between the iris and pupil no matter the eye color—calculates the size of their pupils to the submillimeter. The idea is that users who see their previous measurements change will be alerted to the potential onset of a cognitive disorder and seek treatment to manage the condition early.

As the app's pupil response check is meant to be a self-test, it was crucial that the app itself be easy to use. The researchers worked directly with elderly people to ensure that it could be used regardless of their familiarity with smartphones. The result of this approach is an interface that includes instructions with pictures and recorded commands. The developers believe that its ease of operation will help make the app a success.

Before the app's release, the researchers will conduct further studies to test its effectiveness as an examining tool especially for Alzheimer's disease, which is the most common cause of dementia. Specifically, they intend to work with people who are experiencing early-stage symptoms such as mild cognitive impairment. Their findings could be revolutionary as there are no definitive diagnostic tests for Alzheimer's disease at present.

60. What is the article mainly about?

    (a) a discovery about pupil dilation
    (b) the production of a diagnostic tool
    (c) the release of a new commercial app
    (d) a study on neurological disease progression

61. How do most people currently take a pupil response test?

    (a) by purchasing a piece of equipment
    (b) by undergoing a full medical examination
    (c) by attending a community screening assessment
    (d) by going to see a medical practitioner

62. Which of the following can probably be said about how the app works?

    (a) It is most effective on people with light eyes.
    (b) It is supposed to be used multiple times.
    (c) It works with any model of smartphone.
    (d) It requires users to differentiate the pupil and iris.

63. Why did researchers need elderly participants when designing the app?

    (a) to make audio recordings of instructions
    (b) to see whether it was easily usable
    (c) to assist with administering tests to elderly people
    (d) to make sure that phone technology was familiar

64. What is NOT true about Alzheimer's disease?

    (a) Its early signs include mental decline.
    (b) It can be difficult to diagnose conclusively.
    (c) Its symptoms may be eased by the app.
    (d) It is not the only cause of dementia.

65. In the context of the passage, prompted means _____.

    (a) motivated
    (b) requested
    (c) compelled
    (d) persuaded

66. In the context of the passage, further means _____.

    (a) spare
    (b) excessive
    (c) major
    (d) additional

TEST 1

TEST 2

TEST 3

TEST 4

TEST 5

TEST 6

TEST 7

해커스 지텔프 최신기출유형 실전문제집 7회 (Level 2)

PART 3. *Read the encyclopedia article below and answer the questions. The two underlined words are for vocabulary questions.*

VEGETABLE SHEEP

Vegetable sheep is the common name for a species of cushion plant that is native to New Zealand. The name comes from the plant's physical resemblance to a sheep when seen at a distance.

Vegetable Sheep's scientific name is *Raoulia eximia*. It is one of about 26 species of plants related to Compositae, which includes sunflowers and daisies. It was first identified by Joseph Hooker, a British botanist and explorer who visited New Zealand on duty in 1864. Hooker named the plant in honor of his colleague, French naturalist Étienne Raoul. The second half of the name means "strikingly unusual" in Latin.

Being a cushion plant, the vegetable sheep has a rounded shape and grows close to the ground. The largest specimens <u>reach</u> up to a meter or more in diameter and up to a meter tall. And although the plant may look soft, it is actually hard to the touch. Its exterior consists of a tight patchwork of tiny gray-green leaves, while fine white hairs give the plant its woolly appearance.

The roots of the vegetable sheep comprise a dense network of underground branches. The roots also extend over a wide mat above the surface of the ground. This mat forms a spongy material that sustains the plant by offering a mixture of raw soil and the rotted remains of dead leaves. However, the sponge-like mat, which <u>retains</u> moisture well, can be overwhelmed with excess humidity from regular rainfall, and this makes it acidic and generally low in nutrient content.

The plant's condensed shape and structure are suited to the alpine environment, which is frigid and barren due to elevation and constant exposure to high winds. They protect the plant against heavy snowfall, insulate it from the cold, and reflect bright sunlight.

Unlike related species that spread out across the ground, the vegetable sheep's small range leaves it vulnerable to the risk of habitat loss. Despite this, the plant's conservation status is listed as "not threatened" as of 2022, likely because it is inedible to potential predators.

67. According to the article, what is vegetable sheep?

    (a) a plant that looks like an animal
    (b) a food source for New Zealand livestock
    (c) a material used for making cushions
    (d) a vegetable that grows near sheep pastures

68. Why did Joseph Hooker visit New Zealand?

    (a) because he was searching for flower species
    (b) because he was traveling for his vocation
    (c) to meet a fellow explorer
    (d) to receive an honor in botany

69. Where does the vegetable sheep get most of its nutrition?

    (a) from an underground network of roots
    (b) from regular rainwater runoff
    (c) from waste matter on the ground
    (d) from acidic content of nearby plants

70. How did the vegetable sheep adapt to its environment?

    (a) by forming a dense structure
    (b) by altering its shape for cold weather
    (c) by maximizing exposure to sunlight
    (d) by dispersing its seeds to the wind

71. Why most likely will the vegetable sheep continue to survive as a species?

    (a) It has been adopted by farmers.
    (b) It is conserved by New Zealand's government.
    (c) It is unsuitable for consumption.
    (d) It can be grown in an artificial setting.

72. In the context of the passage, reach means _____.

    (a) arrive
    (b) live
    (c) span
    (d) cover

73. In the context of the passage, retains means _____.

    (a) holds
    (b) blocks
    (c) grabs
    (d) recalls

TEST 1

TEST 2

TEST 3

TEST 4

TEST 5

TEST 6

TEST 7

해커스 지텔프 최신기출유형 실전문제집 7회 (Level 2)

PART 4. *Read the business letter below and answer the questions. The two underlined words are for vocabulary questions.*

Kay Farrell
Aire Broadband Headquarters
7508 Market Lane
Paterson, NJ 07501

Dear Ms. Farrell:

This letter is about my TrueFiber Plus plan. I have been experiencing repeated problems with the Internet connection for months now.

I first signed up for the plan last June. I <u>concluded</u> it was a good deal since the company guaranteed speeds of up to 400 Mbps, a reliability rating of 99 percent, and protection from viruses and spyware.

However, a few months ago, the Internet speed began to fluctuate, and I rarely got more than 200 Mbps. I called your customer support team and allowed one of the staff to make changes to my computer remotely. This fixed the issue for a time, but it returned soon after.

Then, last month, my computer was infected with a virus from an unknown source, and some important files were lost. I find this puzzling because I remember that security against all viruses was included in the plan.

Finally, my connection dropped again last week, and this interrupted my work. I made a call to schedule a repair but was told that the earliest a technician could come was in two weeks. This is unacceptable because the outage is currently preventing me from doing my job from home.

Please send someone right away, or I will find another provider. If I have to end my contract, I don't think it's fair that I pay an early termination fee since all of these troubles have been caused by your company. I have been a good customer and never <u>missed</u> a payment. I look forward to your reply soon.

Sincerely,

Seth Gilmore

74. Why did Seth Gilmore write a letter to Kay Farrell?

    (a) to request a modification to his plan
    (b) to complain about an unreliable service
    (c) to inquire about fluctuating prices
    (d) to express his satisfaction with a service

75. When did Gilmore's problem improve temporarily?

    (a) when a company representative visited his home
    (b) after he removed a virus from his computer himself
    (c) when he followed instructions from a specialized site
    (d) after he authorized staff to access his device

76. How did the computer virus most likely cause damage?

    (a) by deleting some critical data files
    (b) by slowing down the performance of the device
    (c) by weakening the computer's virus protection
    (d) by revealing the user's personal information

77. Why is Gilmore dissatisfied with the repair schedule?

    (a) because he can't arrange for service during office hours
    (b) because he has to postpone the appointment time
    (c) because he doesn't yet have the money for repairs
    (d) because he requires immediate Internet access for work

78. What can be said about Aire Broadband?

    (a) It offers discounts on bundled services.
    (b) It is the cheapest Internet provider in Gilmore's area.
    (c) Its contract with Gilmore is still valid.
    (d) Its termination fee is equivalent to a monthly payment.

79. In the context of the passage, concluded means _____.

    (a) finished
    (b) collected
    (c) resolved
    (d) determined

80. In the context of the passage, missed means _____.

    (a) fallen
    (b) lost
    (c) neglected
    (d) canceled

THIS IS THE LAST PAGE OF THE TEST

TEST 2

GRAMMAR

LISTENING

READING & VOCABULARY

테스트 전 확인사항

1. OMR 답안지를 준비하셨나요? ☐
2. 컴퓨터용 사인펜, 수정 테이프를 준비하셨나요? ☐
3. 음성을 들을 준비를 하셨나요? ☐

🎧 **TEST 2.mp3**

해커스인강(HackersIngang.com)에서 무료 다운로드
상단 메뉴 [MP3/자료 → 문제풀이 MP3]

TEST 2 음성 바로 듣기

🗒 **자동 채점 및 성적 분석 서비스**

∨ 타이머, 모바일 OMR, 자동 채점
∨ 정답률 및 취약 유형 분석

자동 채점 및 성적 분석
서비스 바로 이용하기

시험 시간 : 90분

목표 점수 : _____점

시작 시간 : _____시 _____분 ~ 종료 시간 : _____시 _____분

General Tests of English Language Proficiency
G-TELP

Level 2

GRAMMAR SECTION

DIRECTIONS:

The following items need a word or words to finish the sentence. Select the best answer from the four choices provided for this item. Then, fill in the correct circle on your answer sheet.

Example:

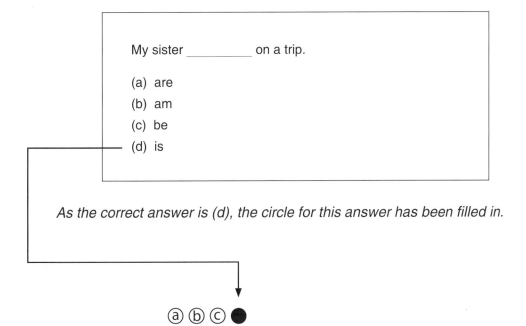

As the correct answer is (d), the circle for this answer has been filled in.

TURN THE PAGE TO BEGIN THE TEST

1. In spite of the convenience of self-checkout machines, most customers still prefer interacting with an actual person to using a touch screen. They do not mind _____ in line to be served by a cashier.

   (a) to have waited
   (b) to wait
   (c) waiting
   (d) being waited

2. The day was hot and humid, but now it is mild with a cool breeze. Laura and her husband _____ the pleasant evening outside while they watch the sun setting behind the mountains.

   (a) were enjoying
   (b) have enjoyed
   (c) will have enjoyed
   (d) are enjoying

3. The artist's latest paintings, though technically brilliant and visually appealing, don't get enough attention because they are only shown in small galleries. If his work _____ in bigger galleries, he would be quite famous today.

   (a) will be displayed
   (b) is displayed
   (c) were displayed
   (d) has been displayed

4. Alzheimer's disease is a neurological disorder that negatively affects the mental functioning of people. Scientists _____ on a vaccine to prevent this illness for decades, and they are optimistic that it will be available in the near future.

   (a) will be working
   (b) are working
   (c) had been working
   (d) have been working

5. The missed deliveries of snack foods were mainly due to supply chain issues outside of Tasty Treat's control. _____, the technical team managed to lessen the impact of the problem by improving the efficiency of the company's ordering system.

   (a) Otherwise
   (b) However
   (c) In fact
   (d) Thus

6. The West Coast fires that tore through Northern California, Oregon, and Washington were some of the worst in recorded history. New brush fires constantly broke out while firefighters _____ ones in other areas, making them nearly impossible to contain.

   (a) have been putting out
   (b) were putting out
   (c) are putting out
   (d) would put out

7. I don't think it's fair that the whole team has to stay late on account of Jack's poor planning and organizational skills! If he had just completed his work on time, we _____ our project by now.

   (a) would have finished
   (b) will be finished
   (c) have finished
   (d) would finish

8. A world-renowned composer heard Eleanor play the piano by chance and asked if she wanted to study under him. She was excited at the opportunity _____ at the feet of a master.

   (a) sitting
   (b) to sit
   (c) having sat
   (d) to have sat

9. Nut Explosion, a chocolate bar that includes peanuts and almonds, is one of the longest-running snacks sold by Weser Candies. In fact, the company will be celebrating a milestone next year. By then, it _____ the popular treat for 120 years.

   (a) will have been producing
   (b) is producing
   (c) has been producing
   (d) will be producing

10. The tote bags made by Lamak Sports are very trendy. Sales of these tote bags are projected _____ even more over the next two years as the products are introduced into new international markets.

   (a) having grown
   (b) growing
   (c) to grow
   (d) to have grown

11. Since Earth is not a perfect sphere, its gravitational force is distributed unequally. Glaciers _____ actually distorted Earth's crust, causing the planet's gravity to become irregular.

   (a) that melted thousands of years ago
   (b) which they melted thousands of years ago
   (c) what melted thousands of years ago
   (d) who melted thousands of years ago

12. Mr. Adams makes it a priority to teach his class how to explore topics without the Internet. He believes that if students keep _____ computers excessively, they will not be able to carry out some academic work.

   (a) to rely on
   (b) will rely on
   (c) relying on
   (d) having relied on

해커스 지텔프 최신기출유형 실전문제집 7회 (Level 2)

13. For firms that have access to confidential user data, a leak of private information can cause them to lose clients. Therefore, it is essential that such companies _____ comprehensive security protocols.

(a) execute
(b) to execute
(c) will execute
(d) executed

14. Yemen is entering the eighth year of a devastating war against Houthi rebels. As a consequence, more than 14 million citizens don't have enough food right now. The UN _____ more aid in the upcoming months to help them.

(a) sends
(b) will be sending
(c) sent
(d) was sending

15. Felix chose to install a new anti-virus program after his computer crashed for the third time. It _____ not make a difference, but he thinks it is worth a try.

(a) must
(b) could
(c) can
(d) may

16. An Ebola virus epidemic ravaged regions of West Africa from 2013 to 2016. Had it not been for the tireless service of international medical staff volunteering in the area, many more victims _____ to the disease.

(a) would succumb
(b) had succumbed
(c) have succumbed
(d) would have succumbed

17. Bentley's parents urged him to ask his aunt for a job at her company. But Bentley wanted to get a job on his own and wouldn't consider _____ a job he didn't earn himself.

(a) accepting
(b) to accept
(c) to have accepted
(d) having accepted

18. Duct tape was invented by Vesta Stoudt, a factory worker in Dixon, Illinois. She wrote to President Roosevelt about her idea after her superiors dismissed it. If she had not sent her letter, the product _____ to history decades ago.

(a) was lost
(b) would be lost
(c) would have been lost
(d) had been lost

19. Sophia couldn't believe her luck on the boat trip. She was shocked that she reeled in the biggest catch of the day. _____ she had gone fishing before, she had never caught anything.

(a) Unless
(b) Although
(c) Because
(d) Until

20. While practicing, Vancouver Bullets' star player Fran Allen sprained her ankle. Despite the severity of the injury, she expects _____ her team in time for the national soccer tournament next month.

(a) rejoining
(b) to rejoin
(c) to be rejoining
(d) having rejoined

21. Jessica sat down on the kitchen chair, annoyed because she would have to clean up all over again. She _____ the floors for 30 minutes before her kids ran through the house wearing their dirty shoes.

(a) has mopped
(b) was mopping
(c) will have been mopping
(d) had been mopping

22. The teacher is rather concerned about the students' level of preparation for the final examination next week. He assumes that if they were to take the test today, the majority of the students _____ completely.

(a) failed
(b) would fail
(c) will fail
(d) would have failed

23. After spending a long time exploring other media, Beth has returned to her original mode of creative expression. She has decided that she _____ dedicate the rest of the year to making sculptures in her workshop before she begins selling her pieces.

(a) can
(b) may
(c) might
(d) will

24. I wasn't sure whether to buy or rent a home. Thankfully, my coworker, _____ himself, gave me the phone number of his real estate agent so that I could ask any questions I might have.

(a) who is struggling with the dilemma
(b) how he is struggling with the dilemma
(c) that is struggling with the dilemma
(d) which is struggling with the dilemma

25. Several environmental organizations
    are dissatisfied with the slow rate of
    electric vehicle adoption. To accelerate
    the process, they request that the
    federal government _____ taxes on
    gasoline and other fossil fuels.

    (a) to raise
    (b) will raise
    (c) raise
    (d) raises

26. It's too bad that my niece Iris never has
    time to visit Central Park even though
    she lives nearby. If her job were to start
    in the afternoon, she _____ in a
    peaceful setting every morning!

    (a) jogged
    (b) is jogging
    (c) would jog
    (d) would have jogged

THIS IS THE LAST PAGE OF THE GRAMMAR SECTION
DO NOT MOVE ON UNTIL DIRECTED TO DO SO

LISTENING SECTION

DIRECTIONS:

The Listening Section has four parts. Each part contains a listening passage and multiple questions about the passage. You will hear the questions first, and then you will hear the passage. Select the best answer from the four choices provided for each question. Then, fill in the correct circle on your answer sheet.

Now you will hear an example question. You will then listen to a sample passage.

Now listen to the example question.

(a) San Francisco
(b) Los Angeles
(c) London
(d) Detroit

Brenda Kenwood was born in Detroit, so the best answer is (d). As the correct answer is (d), the circle for this answer has been filled in.

TURN THE PAGE TO BEGIN THE TEST

27. (a) because she has been out of the country
    (b) because she has been looking for work
    (c) because she has been on an extended vacation
    (d) because she has been busy with her job

28. (a) buying wooden statues as souvenirs
    (b) discovering an ancient stone pyramid
    (c) touring an old Indigenous historical site
    (d) attending a traditional temple service

29. (a) that it is made in an original manner
    (b) that it is inspired by various cuisines
    (c) that it is very expensive in restaurants
    (d) that it is too spicy for some travelers

30. (a) the quality of the hotel furniture
    (b) the size of the hotel room
    (c) the cleanliness of the facilities
    (d) the lack of room types available

31. (a) before she takes on a new position
    (b) when the summer holiday starts
    (c) after she completes her work project
    (d) once the flights are at a discount

32. (a) the reasonable price to travel overseas
    (b) the old buildings in the area
    (c) the beautiful beaches with clear turquoise waters
    (d) the taste of food prepared by professional cooks

33. (a) visit popular travel booking websites
    (b) text pictures from the trip to his family members
    (c) book a trip for Margaret on his computer
    (d) send his friend information to refer to

34. (a) He wanted to overcome his sedentary lifestyle.
    (b) Staying in good shape is hard for people.
    (c) He wished to make modern life more convenient.
    (d) Existing apps are too complicated.

35. (a) one's resting heart rate
    (b) one's style of living
    (c) one's level of activity
    (d) one's fitness objectives

36. (a) by listening to the advice of the on-site trainer
    (b) by familiarizing themselves with the equipment
    (c) by doing the same routines repeatedly
    (d) by viewing examples of good form

37. (a) to take the place of traditional progress graphs
    (b) to identify different members within a group
    (c) to take notice of exercise accomplishments
    (d) to designate user-specific workout goals

38. (a) foods bought at grocery stores
    (b) items without a valid barcode
    (c) meals consumed over the course of the day
    (d) recipes for low-calorie foods supplied by the app

39. (a) so one can develop a physically fit body
    (b) so one can be notified about calorie restrictions
    (c) so one can set limits on daily calorie intake
    (d) so one can lose weight in a short amount of time

40. (a) where to take his parents at the end of the week
    (b) what to have for dinner for the family gathering
    (c) when to talk to his parents about his trip to Italy
    (d) which day to see a new film

41. (a) the excitement of other people in the theater
    (b) the professional audio-visual quality
    (c) the convenience of the food service facilities
    (d) the wide selection of newly released movies

42. (a) because the process for making a payment had changed
    (b) because the variety of snacks offered was limited
    (c) because the price of tickets had risen significantly
    (d) because the cost of refreshments was high

43. (a) by wearing sleeping clothes
    (b) by having more seating options
    (c) by finding a movie everyone likes
    (d) by preparing food to enjoy

44. (a) Viewers tend to lose concentration easily.
    (b) Viewers can take lots of time to pick a movie.
    (c) Viewers may see inappropriate content.
    (d) Viewers must share financial details online.

45. (a) subscribe to a streaming service
    (b) stay in for the night
    (c) watch a movie at a cinema
    (d) go visit his parents

TEST 1
TEST 2
TEST 3
TEST 4
TEST 5
TEST 6
TEST 7

PART 4. *You will hear an explanation of a process. You will hear questions 46 through 52 first, and then you will hear the explanation. Select the best answer to each question in the given time.*

46. (a) traversing one time zone daily
    (b) passing many time zones quickly
    (c) waking up frequently during a flight
    (d) traveling for long stretches of time

47. (a) an inability to compromise with others
    (b) a lack of interest in local sights
    (c) a decreased capacity to focus
    (d) an excess of nighttime energy

48. (a) by staying awake the whole night before the flight
    (b) by gradually lengthening their normal rest cycle
    (c) by spending as much time as possible outdoors
    (d) by adjusting their bedtime to the final location

49. (a) when it is relatively short in length
    (b) when it is done within hours of landing
    (c) when it occurs in the late afternoon
    (d) when it is followed by a large meal

50. (a) They can cause dehydration.
    (b) They may prevent people from feeling rested.
    (c) They can reset one's sleeping schedule.
    (d) They may lead to serious health issues.

51. (a) by using comfortable bedding
    (b) by reducing the amount of light
    (c) by turning off electronic devices
    (d) by eliminating any sources of noise

52. (a) to inform them of flight discounts
    (b) to introduce lesser-known places
    (c) to urge them to take more trips
    (d) to point out a common problem

THIS IS THE LAST PAGE OF THE LISTENING SECTION
DO NOT MOVE ON UNTIL DIRECTED TO DO SO

READING AND VOCABULARY SECTION

DIRECTIONS:

You will now read four different passages. Comprehension and vocabulary questions follow every passage. Select the best answer from the four choices provided for each question. Then, fill in the correct circle on your answer sheet.

Read the following sample passage and example question.

Example:

Brenda Kenwood was born in Detroit. After finishing
university in Los Angeles, she settled in San Francisco.

Where was Brenda Kenwood born?

(a) San Francisco
(b) Los Angeles
(c) London
(d) Detroit

As the correct answer is (d), the circle for this answer has been filled in.

TURN THE PAGE TO BEGIN THE TEST

JULIA CHILD

Julia Child was an American chef and cookbook writer best known for teaching US audiences how to make French cuisine for the first time.

Julia Child was born in California on August 15, 1912, into a wealthy household. Because her family had a private chef, Child did not need to learn how to cook and showed no <u>particular</u> interest in it. While at school, she played various sports, which she excelled at.

When America entered the Second World War at the end of 1941, Child was employed as a research assistant at the Office of Strategic Services, which was in charge of developing underwater explosives. Curious sharks could set off the explosives, and it became Child's responsibility to prepare an effective shark repellent.

Child did not develop a real passion for food until 1946 when she married Paul Child, an enthusiastic food connoisseur. In 1948, the couple moved to Paris, where a meal at the restaurant La Couronne <u>sparked</u> Child's desire to take French cooking lessons. She studied at the prominent Le Cordon Bleu culinary school and graduated in 1951.

A short time later, she began giving French cooking classes to American women living in Paris. Encouraged by the positive reception, she, along with fellow cooking teachers Simone Beck and Louisette Bertholle, spent the next decade creating the recipes that would form the basis of her first book, *Mastering the Art of French Cooking*. The book, published in 1961, caused an instant sensation.

When Child returned to America in the 1960s, she starred in one of the first cooking shows on US television, *The French Chef.* There, she taught people how to make classic French dishes such as beef bourguignon at home. At the time, Americans considered French fare difficult to make and something they could only eat at fine dining establishments. Child's cheerful and authentic presentation style made certain that the show would remain on the air for a decade. It was recognized with prestigious television awards, such as a Peabody Award and an Emmy Award, for its entertainment value and educational content.

Child kept publishing cookbooks and making TV appearances through the 1990s, inspiring a generation of new cooks. In 1995, she established the Julia Child Foundation, which continues to provide grants to non-profit organizations related to food. She died of kidney failure on August 13, 2004, at the age of 91.

53. What is Julia Child best known for?

(a) introducing French cooking to the American public
(b) publishing the first English cookbook for an international audience
(c) hosting a television program about various countries' cuisines
(d) being the first American to appear on a French cooking show

54. When did Child first get interested in food?

(a) when she moved to Paris
(b) when she married her husband
(c) when she ate at a French restaurant
(d) when she enrolled in cooking school

55. How did living in France most likely influence the content of Child's first book?

(a) by encouraging her to read recipes in French
(b) by making her well-known among the French people
(c) by allowing her to collaborate with other teachers
(d) by giving her the experience of working in publishing

56. What did *The French Chef* probably accomplish?

(a) It taught people to focus on the quality of ingredients.
(b) It showed how to make home-cooked versions of restaurant dishes.
(c) It won the first Emmy Award for a female broadcaster.
(d) It popularized educational television programming in the U.S.

57. According to the passage, what did Child do through her foundation?

(a) She gave cooking classes.
(b) She appeared in instructional cooking videos.
(c) She made contributions to charity groups.
(d) She released follow-ups to her cookbook.

58. In the context of the passage, particular means _____.

(a) huge
(b) remarkable
(c) typical
(d) specific

59. In the context of the passage, sparked means _____.

(a) provoked
(b) beamed
(c) issued
(d) revived

RESEARCHERS TRAIN FISH TO ADD AND SUBTRACT

A study at the Institute of Zoology in the University of Bonn has revealed that two species of fish can do simple math. Led by zoology professor Dr. Vera Schluessel, the researchers showed that trained cichlids and stingrays have the ability to calculate sums and differences using the numbers one through five.

For the study, researchers used blue and yellow shapes to prompt the fish to add or subtract by one. The shapes <u>ranged</u> in size from small to large, which made calculation more difficult. To demonstrate their mathematical comprehension, the fish were expected to swim through a gate displaying one more or one less than the number of shapes on the card according to the color. Thus, if a researcher held up a card with four yellow shapes, the fish had to select a gate with three shapes.

Six cichlids and four stingrays successfully completed training and recognized specific colors as symbols for addition and subtraction. While cichlids learned faster than stingrays, and more cichlids carried out the task, the individual performances of stingrays exceeded those of cichlids. Cichlids achieved about a 78 percent and 69 percent correct answer rate for addition and subtraction, respectively. Meanwhile, stingrays were right about 94 percent and 89 percent of the time. Whenever the fish <u>executed</u> a task correctly, they were rewarded with food.

The researchers were surprised by the results of the experiment, as fish do not possess a cerebral cortex, which is the area of the brain responsible for complex reasoning. Moreover, according to Dr. Schluessel, it is odd that cichlids and stingrays have basic math skills because, unlike other species of fish, they do not rely on numbers when mating or laying eggs.

In general, the experiment suggests that the mathematical ability of fish is better than has long been assumed. People have considered fish to be relatively unintelligent with a memory span of only a few seconds, but there is increasing evidence that their cognitive abilities have been grossly underestimated.

60. What did researchers find out about certain fish species?

    (a) that they can perceive up to five objects at a time
    (b) that they can use mathematics to track prey
    (c) that they can recognize words for numbers
    (d) that they can perform basic calculations

61. How did the fish demonstrate their understanding of the task?

    (a) by swimming to a card displaying the previously seen color
    (b) by selecting a picture featuring colorful objects
    (c) by approaching a gate with identical geometric shapes
    (d) by choosing an entrance marked with the correct number of figures

62. Which of the following is NOT an outcome of the study?

    (a) Cichlids performed worse than stingrays overall.
    (b) Both species were better at subtraction than addition.
    (c) Both species exhibited an ability to make judgments.
    (d) Not all of the fish learned at the same speed.

63. According to the article, why were the findings of the experiment unanticipated?

    (a) because fish have an underdeveloped cerebral cortex
    (b) because fish cease complex reasoning after mating
    (c) because fish lack a part of an organ
    (d) because fish do not count their eggs

64. What is most likely true about the mental capacity of fish?

    (a) It exceeds people's expectations.
    (b) It is surpassed by other small animals.
    (c) It is restricted to counting capabilities.
    (d) It correlates directly with memory span.

65. In the context of the passage, ranged means _____.

    (a) included
    (b) varied
    (c) secured
    (d) reached

66. In the context of the passage, executed means _____.

    (a) gained
    (b) faced
    (c) ensured
    (d) did

해커스 지텔프 최신기출유형 실전문제집 7회 (Level 2)

PART 3. *Read the encyclopedia article below and answer the questions. The two underlined words are for vocabulary questions.*

TOAST

A toast is a gesture in which people at a gathering raise their glass as a sign of honor or friendliness. Toasts are most commonly made with alcoholic beverages during meaningful events, such as weddings and birthdays.

The exact origin of toasting is not known for certain. However, evidence of the practice can be found in many ancient cultures. The ancient Greeks, for example, poured out wine as a ritual offering to the gods and often drank to the health of others. The convention is frequently described in works of ancient literature such as Homer's *The Odyssey*.

The tradition of drinking to the health of others is thought to have arisen from concerns about poisoning, which was once a common way to eliminate rivals. Taking the first sip of a drink after wishing someone well was a way of letting them know it was safe to consume it. Also, there are stories suggesting that clinking glasses together <u>served</u> to build fellowship because this would cause the liquid from one glass to spill into the other.

Toasting spread throughout the continent of Europe, becoming so popular that in the 17th century it was necessary to invent the role of the toastmaster. Toastmasters were skilled public speakers who <u>oversaw</u> the practice of toasting at assemblies. They made sure that no one spoke for too long and that everyone who wished to deliver a toast had the opportunity to do so.

Today, various nations around the world have developed their own toasting customs. Some countries in Northeast Asia, for instance, use phrases that sound similar to begin a toast. However, in practice, the toasts follow different rules of etiquette depending on the culture of origin. For the Chinese, those with junior status will lower their cups to their seniors to show respect when clinking glasses. In Korea, a glass is refilled only after it is emptied, whereas in Japan, the glass is continuously refilled so that it never becomes empty.

67. According to the article, what do people do when they toast at an event?

(a) express goodwill toward others
(b) mark the beginning of a gathering
(c) encourage social drinking
(d) introduce a member of a group

68. What is the evidence that toasting is an ancient practice?

(a) It is shown in old paintings.
(b) It is written about in books.
(c) It is named after a figure from history.
(d) It is performed in various religious rituals.

69. Why most likely would someone take the first sip of a drink?

(a) to show appreciation for the host's generosity
(b) to improve a relationship with a rival
(c) to prove the harmlessness of the beverage
(d) to tell a story about building fellowship

70. How did toastmasters fulfill their duties?

(a) by planning regular gatherings
(b) by judging the quality of speeches
(c) by giving people a chance to speak
(d) by preparing lessons about public speaking

71. According to the passage, when should a glass be refilled in Japan?

(a) before it is given to a senior
(b) when it is raised for a toast
(c) when it is lowered to express politeness
(d) before it is completely drained

72. In the context of the passage, served means _____.

(a) acted
(b) offered
(c) believed
(d) provided

73. In the context of the passage, oversaw means _____.

(a) commanded
(b) supervised
(c) observed
(d) made

Edgar Agnello
Human Resources Director
Pierre Levine Museum
3390 E Lockett Rd
Flagstaff, AZ 86004

Dear Mr. Agnello:

I am writing to apply for the position of head curator at the Pierre Levine Museum, which was advertised in the August issue of the museum's newsletter. I am currently working as an assistant curator at the Tobin Clegg Art Gallery in New Mexico, a role I have held for the last four years.

I am drawn to the museum not only because I would like to play a part in preserving Pierre Levine's artistic legacy but also because I admire the museum's many philanthropic and educational contributions to society. If chosen for the position, I promise I will do everything I can to promote his creations and help the museum flourish.

I possess a bachelor's degree in fine arts and a master's degree in art history from Sutcliffe University. According to your ad, these qualifications are your main criteria for the curator job. In addition, at the Tobin Clegg Art Gallery, I acquire new paintings and sculptures for the gallery and conduct research in preparation for exhibitions and publications. Moreover, I keep track of acquisition schedules and help connect artists with collectors. I report directly to the head curator Mark Copeland, whose letter of reference I have enclosed along with my résumé.

My last day of work at the Tobin Clegg Art Gallery is September 5, and I am permanently relocating to Arizona on September 15. I'd love the chance for an in-person interview with you once I am settled. Until then, I can be reached via e-mail at d.Cobbett@fastmail.com. I appreciate your consideration and look forward to hearing from you.

Sincerely,

Diana Cobbett

74. What is the main purpose of the letter?

    (a) to ask for assistance with a search for artwork
    (b) to respond to an inquiry about an available position
    (c) to submit an application for a job opening
    (d) to ask about any employment opportunities

75. How does Cobbett think she can benefit the museum?

    (a) by spreading awareness about an individual's work
    (b) by organizing philanthropic events at the museum
    (c) by contributing to an artist's collection
    (d) by raising funds to expand the institution

76. How does Cobbett fulfill the core requirements for the position?

    (a) She is enrolled in a master's program.
    (b) She possesses work experience at a museum.
    (c) She has the desired educational background.
    (d) She studies art history at a university.

77. What can most likely be said about Mark Copeland?

    (a) He is preparing for a major exhibition.
    (b) He is unaware of Cobbett's resignation.
    (c) He is leaving for a new position.
    (d) He is supportive of Cobbett's future plans.

78. Why most likely does Cobbett mention her moving date?

    (a) because she will terminate her employment on this date
    (b) because she wants Agnello to contact her by this date
    (c) because she is available for interviews before this date
    (d) because she can meet Agnello after this date

79. In the context of the passage, drawn means _____.

    (a) carried
    (b) attracted
    (c) elicited
    (d) dictated

80. In the context of the passage, connect means _____.

    (a) associate
    (b) engage
    (c) assemble
    (d) grow

THIS IS THE LAST PAGE OF THE TEST

TEST 3

GRAMMAR

LISTENING

READING & VOCABULARY

테스트 전 확인사항

1. OMR 답안지를 준비하셨나요? ☐
2. 컴퓨터용 사인펜, 수정 테이프를 준비하셨나요? ☐
3. 음성을 들을 준비를 하셨나요? ☐

TEST 3 음성 바로 듣기

🎧 **TEST 3.mp3**

해커스인강(HackersIngang.com)에서 무료 다운로드
상단 메뉴 [MP3/자료 → 문제풀이 MP3]

자동 채점 및 성적 분석
서비스 바로 이용하기

 자동 채점 및 성적 분석 서비스

˅ 타이머, 모바일 OMR, 자동 채점
˅ 정답률 및 취약 유형 분석

시험 시간 : 90분

목표 점수 : _____ 점
시작 시간 : _____ 시 _____ 분 ~ 종료 시간 : _____ 시 _____ 분

General Tests of English Language Proficiency
G-TELP

Level 2

GRAMMAR SECTION

DIRECTIONS:

The following items need a word or words to finish the sentence. Select the best answer from the four choices provided for this item. Then, fill in the correct circle on your answer sheet.

Example:

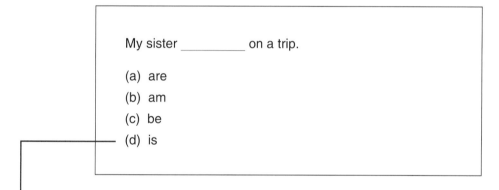

My sister _____ on a trip.

(a) are
(b) am
(c) be
(d) is

As the correct answer is (d), the circle for this answer has been filled in.

TURN THE PAGE TO BEGIN THE TEST

해커스 지텔프 최신기출유형 실전문제집 7회 (Level 2)

1. Today, the art program at Redwood High School officially shut down. When the administrators announced that it suffered from inadequate funding, some of the teachers admitted that they _____ for supplies with their own money for the last few months.

    (a) were shopping
    (b) had been shopping
    (c) shopped
    (d) would have shopped

2. Sandra is disappointed that she could only afford to buy her brother a small present for his birthday. If she had developed the habit of saving her allowance, she _____ him a video game console.

    (a) had gotten
    (b) would have gotten
    (c) would get
    (d) will have gotten

3. Scott tried to finalize the design plans, but he couldn't focus on his work. After one of his miscalculations had caused a weeklong delay in his firm's bridge-building project, he started to dread _____ his work to the senior architect.

    (a) to present
    (b) having presented
    (c) to be presenting
    (d) presenting

4. The city of Harrisburg has been having trouble with some local tour agencies that abandon tourists at random places. For visitors wishing to see the city, authorities suggest that they _____ the services of a reputable personal guide instead.

    (a) secured
    (b) are securing
    (c) will secure
    (d) secure

5. The writing structure of James Joyce's novel *Ulysses* is experimental, dense, and so confusing that most readers give up before concluding all 730 pages. _____, it is considered a masterpiece and Joyce's magnum opus.

    (a) Eventually
    (b) Nevertheless
    (c) Therefore
    (d) Similarly

6. Many of Courtney's friends wondered why she rarely bought new clothes or electronic devices. She told them that she avoided these items _____ a minimalist lifestyle.

    (a) maintaining
    (b) to have maintained
    (c) to maintain
    (d) having maintained

7. My friend Helen entrusted her two poodles to the staff at an expensive pet hotel when she went to her uncle's farm for a month. I _____ her pets if I had known she was going out of town!

(a) would have looked after
(b) would look after
(c) had looked after
(d) looked after

8. Manchester City fans have taken to the streets. They want to show their appreciation for the league-winning squad that inspired them all season. Therefore, the supporters _____ in front of the stadium since early this morning.

(a) are gathering
(b) gather
(c) have been gathering
(d) will be gathering

9. Shawn downloaded an incredibly effective application called Privacy Guard onto his laptop. It prevents _____ so he can protect the personal information that is stored on his computer.

(a) being hacked
(b) to be hacked
(c) having been hacked
(d) to have been hacked

10. Kellyanne was excited about lunch. She'd ordered her favorite curry and couldn't wait to dig in. But when she opened the bag, it was just an order of rice and roasted chicken. The driver _____ have delivered the wrong order.

(a) can
(b) must
(c) would
(d) should

11. Today, Michelle woke up before dawn and spent the whole morning baking for the family reunion. Fortunately, her efforts were not in vain because her treats, _____, were applauded by everyone.

(a) where they included pies and cakes
(b) what included pies and cakes
(c) that included pies and cakes
(d) which included pies and cakes

12. Professor Rogers took the semester off from teaching to dedicate all his time to finishing a paper for the October issue of an academic journal. At his current pace, however, he _____ it when graduates receive their diplomas next spring.

(a) will still write
(b) will still be writing
(c) has still written
(d) is still writing

해커스 지텔프 최신기출유형 실전문제집 7회 (Level 2)

13. After much deliberation, I decided to stick with my old cell phone even though all my coworkers were raving about the latest model released by Strata. Had it featured a cleaner interface, I _____ the device without hesitation.

   (a) would have purchased
   (b) will have purchased
   (c) would purchase
   (d) have purchased

14. Maria needed to cut back on her living expenses and figured that the best way to do it would be to stop eating out so often. As a result, she vowed _____ at home at least five days a week.

   (a) cooking
   (b) to be cooking
   (c) having cooked
   (d) to cook

15. Romance novels have been the most popular genre in the book market for a decade, and the demand for such stories has been increasing. This explains why publishers _____ to put out books about love these days.

   (a) are scrambling
   (b) scrambled
   (c) had scrambled
   (d) will have scrambled

16. Paul's final exam consisted of one question that asked about the second law of thermodynamics, which he had overlooked when cramming the night before. If he were to take the test again, he _____ all of his study time on that principle.

   (a) has concentrated
   (b) would have concentrated
   (c) concentrated
   (d) would concentrate

17. Exercise doesn't need to be done in a large time block to be beneficial to one's health. _____ working through your exercise routines all at once, you can break them up into multiple shorter sessions.

   (a) In case of
   (b) Despite
   (c) Rather than
   (d) Because of

18. Due to rising energy costs, Thimble Creek Manufacturing is enacting new policies at its factories to curb electricity consumption. For example, it ordered that machines _____ when not in use.

   (a) are disconnected
   (b) have been disconnecting
   (c) be disconnected
   (d) will be disconnected

19. I find it frustrating that our social media marketing team continues to release dull content that is full of grammatical errors. If we had hired a copy editor with more experience, we _____ this issue now.

(a) will not face
(b) would not have faced
(c) had not faced
(d) would not be facing

20. Marcus, a volunteer firefighter, was the first to respond to the blaze at the Walker Building downtown. When the emergency report appeared on the news, he _____ to the building to make sure that people there had evacuated safely.

(a) has already headed
(b) would already head
(c) already headed
(d) was already heading

21. Emmett is confident about getting the programming job since he passed the skills evaluation test and progressed through three stages of interviews with different employees of Smart Software, including the CEO. The offer _____ may arrive this week.

(a) whom he has been looking forward to receiving
(b) that he has been looking forward to receiving
(c) what he has been looking forward to receiving
(d) when he has been looking forward to receiving it

22. Adela has been planning a summer trip to Hawaii for ages and finally flies out next weekend. However, when she checked the weather forecast, she saw that it was likely _____ for most of her time there.

(a) to rain
(b) to have rained
(c) raining
(d) having rained

23. A lack of qualified teachers is a major factor affecting the quality of American schools. Indeed, few of those entering the workforce consider a career in education. If the nation's teachers were to receive higher compensation, the profession _____ more job seekers' attention.

(a) would grab
(b) has grabbed
(c) will grab
(d) would have grabbed

24. Sonya, the manager at Super Shoe Depot, notified the staff that she will hold a training session on the store's new inventory system tomorrow at 10 a.m. She clarified that the meeting is not optional, so all employees _____ be in attendance.

(a) can
(b) will
(c) may
(d) might

25. Fran requested leave for Thursday to spend time with her old friend Addison who came from Louisiana. Because they both enjoy _____ modern art, they spent the entire day at the opening of the World Abstract Art Exhibition.

(a) viewing
(b) to view
(c) will view
(d) to have viewed

26. The two presidential candidates strongly disagree about whether the country ought to accept more immigrants. By the end of the forthcoming election, they _____ this controversial issue publicly for over three months.

(a) have been debating
(b) will have been debating
(c) are debating
(d) will be debating

THIS IS THE LAST PAGE OF THE GRAMMAR SECTION
DO NOT MOVE ON UNTIL DIRECTED TO DO SO

LISTENING SECTION

DIRECTIONS:

The Listening Section has four parts. Each part contains a listening passage and multiple questions about the passage. You will hear the questions first, and then you will hear the passage. Select the best answer from the four choices provided for each question. Then, fill in the correct circle on your answer sheet.

Now you will hear an example question. You will then listen to a sample passage.

Now listen to the example question.

(a) San Francisco
(b) Los Angeles
(c) London
(d) Detroit

Brenda Kenwood was born in Detroit, so the best answer is (d). As the correct answer is (d), the circle for this answer has been filled in.

TURN THE PAGE TO BEGIN THE TEST

해커스 지텔프 최신기출유형 실전문제집 7회 (Level 2)

27. (a) She met Sam at a neighborhood meeting.
    (b) She attended a local event for residents.
    (c) She hosted a backyard party with her colleagues.
    (d) She joined a local association as an executive.

28. (a) introduce himself to the organization
    (b) try new cooking techniques
    (c) become acquainted with new neighbors
    (d) participate in some group activities

29. (a) by reading a neighborhood publication
    (b) by referring to an online calendar
    (c) by receiving a copy of an invitation
    (d) by signing up for a community website

30. (a) The fee is covered by a government grant.
    (b) The gatherings are hosted in a public space.
    (c) The gatherings are held by a charitable association.
    (d) The fee is included in residents' payments.

31. (a) when she visited a Lebanese bakery
    (b) when she lived in another country
    (c) when she went to the last neighborhood event
    (d) when she was on vacation abroad

32. (a) by making special local dishes for each other
    (b) by performing card tricks for the children
    (c) by playing various kinds of games together
    (d) by competing against one another in athletic events

33. (a) continue working on an agenda
    (b) select a host for the next event
    (c) send out invitations to a party
    (d) contact a neighbor living next door

34. (a) It is completely built.
    (b) It is currently available for activities.
    (c) It is open to people of all ages.
    (d) It is located near a park.

35. (a) They can learn how to be effective tutors.
    (b) They can study an array of subjects.
    (c) They can work with people from different regions.
    (d) They can do community service.

36. (a) to make useful everyday objects
    (b) to improve their critical thinking ability
    (c) to pick up new skills to use in the workplace
    (d) to create cooking vessels of professional quality

37. (a) performances by music students
    (b) social media courses for new users
    (c) celebrations for older individuals in the community
    (d) a wide variety of special monthly events

38. (a) plants that produce different colors
    (b) plants that have medicinal uses
    (c) plants that draw pollinating insects
    (d) plants that are grown without chemicals

39. (a) to view photographs of instructors
    (b) to learn about the cost to join
    (c) to read a list of frequently asked questions
    (d) to see a schedule of events

40. (a) because she wants to open a new business
    (b) because she cannot find workers to hire
    (c) because she cannot make her café successful
    (d) because her staff has been complaining a lot

41. (a) They can perform the work of multiple people.
    (b) They do not need worker's accident compensation insurance.
    (c) They are always fast when they complete tasks.
    (d) They are ready to work at all times.

42. (a) by avoiding causing problems with others
    (b) by having fewer visitors report poor experience
    (c) by helping resolve trouble between staff members
    (d) by lessening stress on human workers

43. (a) the time required to get a replacement
    (b) the limited number of functions
    (c) the possibility of a technology breakdown
    (d) the lack of trained repair technicians

44. (a) They cannot form personal connections with guests.
    (b) Customers would have difficulty operating them.
    (c) They would affect the restaurant's temperature.
    (d) Customers cannot ask them questions.

45. (a) install software updates on all of the computers in the café
    (b) test the functionality of the new machinery
    (c) continue to exclusively hire human workers
    (d) reduce the size of her staff

PART 4. *You will hear an explanation of a process. You will hear questions 46 through 52 first, and then you will hear the explanation. Select the best answer to each question in the given time.*

46. (a) the process to attain a state document
    (b) the way to get a business license
    (c) the significance of establishing state residency
    (d) the necessity of learning the basics of driving

47. (a) It can be used to prove U.S. citizenship.
    (b) The climate is too hot for walking.
    (c) It provides access to a discount on public transportation.
    (d) The state has a culture of personal automobile use.

48. (a) by checking an application form
    (b) by calling a government agency
    (c) by writing to a state representative
    (d) by referring to a posted list

49. (a) when the driver is unavailable for an eye exam
    (b) when the vision test was passed with corrective eyewear
    (c) when the application package was not submitted on time
    (d) when the applicant plans to wear sunglasses while driving

50. (a) because one cannot recognize the signs on it
    (b) because one has trouble with multiple-choice questions
    (c) because one is not comfortable with English
    (d) because one gets more than eight answers wrong

51. (a) confirm that a vehicle meets safety standards
    (b) check if a written examination was completed
    (c) verify that spoken instructions are followed
    (d) determine if a route was selected properly

52. (a) so it serves as proof of identity
    (b) so the owner can validate passing the test
    (c) so the owner can renew it after its expiration
    (d) so it matches records in a national database

THIS IS THE LAST PAGE OF THE LISTENING SECTION
DO NOT MOVE ON UNTIL DIRECTED TO DO SO

READING AND VOCABULARY SECTION

DIRECTIONS:

You will now read four different passages. Comprehension and vocabulary questions follow every passage. Select the best answer from the four choices provided for each question. Then, fill in the correct circle on your answer sheet.

Read the following sample passage and example question.

Example:

> Brenda Kenwood was born in Detroit. After finishing university in Los Angeles, she settled in San Francisco.
>
> Where was Brenda Kenwood born?
>
> (a) San Francisco
> (b) Los Angeles
> (c) London
> (d) Detroit

As the correct answer is (d), the circle for this answer has been filled in.

TURN THE PAGE TO BEGIN THE TEST

ERIN JACKSON

Erin Jackson is an American speed skater, inline skater, and roller derby player. She is famous for being the first Black woman to be awarded a gold medal in an individual Winter Olympic sport. She also became the first American woman to win a solo event since 2002 and a 500-meter race since 1994.

Erin Jackson was born on September 19, 1992 in Ocala, Florida to Tracy Jackson, a US Army veteran, and Rita Jackson, a pharmacy technician. Jackson was athletically gifted from a young age. Inspired by the artistic techniques used by figure skater Michelle Kwan at the Olympics, she joined a local inline skating team at the age of 10.

Jackson transitioned to the ice in 2017 because, like other inline skaters before her, she aspired to challenge herself at the highest level of speed skating. After only four months, Jackson skated at the 2017 Olympic trials to see where she stood. To her disbelief, she was among the fastest skaters—coming in third in the 500-meter sprint—and qualified for the 2018 Winter Olympics. Two years later, at the 2020 World Single Distances Speed Skating Championships, she came in 0.6 seconds behind winner Nao Kodaira, whom she later beat in several World Cup races.

Jackson improved her skills in preparation for the 2022 Winter Olympics and became the top-ranked 500-meter speed skater in the world. However, she fell and finished third at the US trials when she needed to be one of the top two finishers to be eligible for a spot. Fortunately, her teammate Brittany Bowe, who finished first in the trial and was set to compete in other events, decided to give her spot in the 500-meter event to Jackson. On February 13, 2022, Jackson finished the race in 37.04 seconds, becoming the first Black woman to win a gold medal in any non-team winter competition at the Olympics. This was only five years after Jackson switched from inline skating to ice.

Since her victory, Jackson has become a partner of Edge Sports, a non-profit organization that hopes to boost the participation of people of color in winter sports. She is collaborating with them to establish a chapter in Salt Lake City, Utah, where she is currently training for the 2026 Winter Olympics.

53. What is Erin Jackson best known for?

(a) holding an Olympic record for over 10 years
(b) being the first American to medal in speed skating
(c) winning an individual gold medal as a Black woman
(d) earning the most distinctions on the US skating team

54. According to the article, what most likely prompted Jackson's interest in skating?

(a) the encouragement of her parents
(b) the hosting of the Olympics by her town
(c) the formation of a local skating team
(d) the performance of an athlete

55. Why was Jackson probably surprised by the result of the 2017 Olympic trials?

(a) because her previous achievements were not considered
(b) because she succeeded despite a lack of experience
(c) because her competitors looked down on former inline skaters
(d) because she did not expect to take part in the qualifying race so early

56. How did Jackson make it to the 2022 Olympics?

(a) by agreeing to participate in longer races
(b) by finishing in third place at the US trials
(c) by taking a fellow athlete's place in an event
(d) by becoming the world's top 500-meter speed skater

57. What is the objective of Edge Sports?

(a) to use Jackson's celebrity status for exposure
(b) to increase ethnic diversity in a field dominated by white people
(c) to promote involvement in winter sports across the state of Utah
(d) to sponsor Jackson at the 2026 Winter Olympics

58. In the context of the passage, aspired means _____.

(a) desired
(b) required
(c) demanded
(d) claimed

59. In the context of the passage, improved means _____.

(a) fortified
(b) established
(c) broadened
(d) developed

PART 2. *Read the magazine article below and answer the questions. The two underlined words are for vocabulary questions.*

A ROBOT TO READ HUMAN EMOTIONS IS DEVELOPED

Pepper is a four-foot-tall humanoid robot that was introduced by SoftBank founder Masayoshi Son at a press conference on June 5, 2014. It has a tablet display on its chest and was the world's first robot designed to read emotions. This machine was the result of cooperation with Aldebaran Robotics, which was acquired by the Japanese company SoftBank in 2012 for $100 million.

Pepper was equipped with technology that allowed it to <u>gauge</u> people's emotions based on their tone of voice and facial expression. The more the robot interacted with humans, whether by making jokes, dancing, or communicating through its touchscreen, the more it understood about people. In fact, everything each robot learned was uploaded to a cloud-based system that other units could access, meaning the robots quickly grasped how to act naturally.

Although Aldebaran had previously produced other robots including the Noa and Romeo models, SoftBank was new to this field prior to Pepper. Regardless, the creation of a robot possessing the ability to recognize feelings was consistent with the company's mission to better people's lives through technology. When Pepper went on sale in Japan in 2015, priced at just under $2,000 per unit, 1,000 units sold out within a minute.

In addition to having been used in thousands of homes since then, Pepper was employed in offices, airports, restaurants, and banks. It performed a variety of functions including chatting with customers, offering menus, and making recommendations. Furthermore, in 2017, an international team received more than £2 million to fund a project using Pepper robots to help elderly individuals in hospitals and assisted living facilities feel less lonely. The team hoped that Pepper could alleviate some of the pressure faced by staff and <u>complement</u> existing care.

Nevertheless, despite Pepper's potential, SoftBank ceased production of the robot in June 2021, citing declining demand. In all, only 27,000 Pepper units were produced. According to industry sources familiar with Pepper's development, restarting production would be costly for the company. Instead, with its purchase of a 40 percent ownership stake in the industry leader AutoStore, SoftBank is shifting its robotics strategy to focus on storage automation.

60. What is the article mainly about?

(a) a joint effort to improve artificial intelligence
(b) the acquisition of a Japanese robotics firm
(c) a machine capable of understanding humans
(d) a tablet designed to enhance cooperation

61. According to the article, why do Pepper units learn how to behave so quickly?

(a) because they can access data uploaded online
(b) because they can recognize vocal tones with sensors
(c) because they are programmed to adjust to situations
(d) because they are equipped with advanced software

62. What can be said about Pepper's release in Japan?

(a) It was sold at a discounted price.
(b) It coincided with the sale of other robots.
(c) It created global demand for the technology.
(d) It was highly anticipated by the public.

63. Why were Pepper robots used in hospitals and assisted living facilities?

(a) to monitor elderly residents' bank accounts
(b) to assist individuals' psychological well-being
(c) to help an international team of doctors
(d) to replace the original staff members

64. How does SoftBank plan to move forward with its business?

(a) by reengaging in the production of Pepper units
(b) by moving its attention to another area of robotics
(c) by ceasing robotic development in the near future
(d) by offering an ownership stake to an industry leader

65. In the context of the passage, gauge means _____.

(a) collect
(b) reject
(c) assess
(d) quantify

66. In the context of the passage, complement means _____.

(a) enhance
(b) match
(c) instill
(d) complete

PART 3. *Read the encyclopedia article below and answer the questions. The two underlined words are for vocabulary questions.*

DERINKUYU UNDERGROUND CITY

The Derinkuyu underground city is an ancient, multi-level settlement located in Cappadocia, Turkey, which was carved from naturally occurring structures. Derinkuyu is notable because it extends 85 meters below the surface, making it the world's deepest subterranean city.

The creation of Derinkuyu, and the region's other underground settlements, was made possible by the area's geology. Prehistoric volcanic eruptions covered the landscape with ash, leaving formations of easy-to-carve rock. Initially, residents probably dug small underground rooms for food storage. As time passed, however, these rooms were underlined expanded and transformed into an intricate city which citizens could flee to in the event of invasion.

The settlement could accommodate up to 20,000 people and their livestock. It also featured amenities including chapels and schools. Ventilation chimneys distributed air throughout the city, while wells ensured a supply of water. Illumination, meanwhile, was done with torches.

It is uncertain who built this secret city. Some think the Hittites constructed it in the 15th century BC as they inhabited Cappadocia then and had many enemies. Others believe the Phrygians were responsible. In fact, the Phrygians overthrew the Hittites and dominated the region from the 12th to 6th centuries BC. They are also known to have erected other sophisticated structures like the fortress at Gordion.

Although there is no record of when the city was established, people continued to use it for centuries. Based on the discovery of artifacts, it was a place of refuge for citizens during the Arab-Byzantine wars. This is suggested by the heavy stone doors that closed from within and protected the city from potential threats. A passage connecting the city to a distinct community called Kaymakli indicates the two groups may have been allies.

In 1923, the Greek Christian refugees who had made their home in Derinkuyu were forcibly returned to Greece. For the next 40 years, the underground city remained undisturbed until a man carrying out repairs on his house knocked down a basement wall and accidentally found it. Then in 1969, Derinkuyu was partially opened to the public.

67. According to the article, what makes Derinkuyu noteworthy?

(a) its location in Turkey
(b) its great depth beneath the ground
(c) its multiple levels
(d) its construction from natural elements

68. Which of the following is true about Derinkuyu?

(a) It was used to escape dangerous volcanic eruptions.
(b) Its chambers were carved from hard stones.
(c) Its purpose changed with the passage of time.
(d) It was the only settlement of its kind in the region.

69. Why most likely do some experts believe the Phrygians designed Derinkuyu?

(a) because they were in power longer than the Hittites
(b) because they reigned over the region in the 15th century BC
(c) because they were constantly threatened by enemies
(d) because they built a complex fort in another area

70. Why probably was there a passage between Derinkuyu and Kaymakli?

(a) to accommodate a higher refugee population
(b) to serve as an escape route in case of earthquakes
(c) to prevent livestock from running away
(d) to facilitate cooperation between the cities

71. When did Derinkuyu become accessible to the general public?

(a) after a home was renovated
(b) after refugees returned to their home nation
(c) after authorities inspected a disturbance
(d) after a tourist attraction was planned

72. In the context of the passage, expanded means _____.

(a) limited
(b) amplified
(c) enlarged
(d) stretched

73. In the context of the passage, inhabited means _____.

(a) contained
(b) defended
(c) occupied
(d) fulfilled

해커스 지텔프 최신기출유형 실전문제집 7회 (Level 2)

Ms. Grace Adair
1414 Havenhurst Street
West Hollywood, CA 90046

Dear Ms. Adair:

I am writing from MCW Studios to tell you about a new competition show called *Make Me a Star*. Like other shows in this genre, the participants will be amateurs hoping to be discovered. It will air on television and later be uploaded to MCW's social media channel. There will be various types of acts, some of which will feature music. Since this is your area of expertise, we would like to know if you are interested in becoming a judge.

Your successful career as a recording artist makes you <u>ideal</u> for the role. While audiences mostly want to see contestants perform, they also tune in for the judges. I know people will appreciate what you have to say.

The judges will observe the contestants carefully. They will then vote for who will return in the show's next episode and who will leave. Throughout the process, the panel will comment on each act, either giving criticism or <u>praise</u>. Essentially, contestants will be eliminated until the season finale, when the winner and two runners-up will be chosen. You'd have to film two episodes a week from June to September and would be compensated accordingly.

If this opportunity appeals to you, please call me at 533-4679 so we can set up an appointment to meet at MCW Studios. Max Rasmussen, the show's creator, will be in attendance to discuss your duties more specifically.

Sincerely,

Darrel Cannon
Head of Programming
MCW Studios

74. Why did Darrel Cannon write a letter to Grace Adair?

    (a) to invite her to be a contestant on a show
    (b) to remark on her recent television appearance
    (c) to present her with a part in a competition
    (d) to ask her to play music of various genres on the air

75. Why do competition show audiences probably want to see Grace Adair?

    (a) because she has a positive personality
    (b) because she is a renowned celebrity
    (c) because she has released a new album
    (d) because she is experienced as a judge

76. When do contestants know if they will appear in the next episode?

    (a) after the judges cast their ballots
    (b) when they reach the end of an episode
    (c) when the audience votes for them
    (d) after they comment on each other

77. What happens leading up to the last episode of the season?

    (a) A contestant is chosen as the winner.
    (b) A contestant receives a cash prize.
    (c) Some participants compete in shorter rounds.
    (d) Some participants are cut from the show.

78. Why will Max Rasmussen attend a meeting?

    (a) so he can discuss changes to a show
    (b) so he can finalize a schedule with MCW Studios
    (c) so he can see the results of an audience survey
    (d) so he can talk about a project in detail

79. In the context of the passage, ideal means _____.

    (a) best
    (b) serious
    (c) specialized
    (d) preferred

80. In the context of the passage, praise means _____.

    (a) cheer
    (b) acclaim
    (c) devotion
    (d) honor

THIS IS THE LAST PAGE OF THE TEST

[해설집] 정답·스크립트·해석·해설 p.107 / 자동 채점 및 성적 분석 서비스 ▶

TEST 4

GRAMMAR

LISTENING

READING & VOCABULARY

테스트 전 확인사항

1. OMR 답안지를 준비하셨나요? ☐
2. 컴퓨터용 사인펜, 수정 테이프를 준비하셨나요? ☐
3. 음성을 들을 준비를 하셨나요? ☐

TEST 4 음성 바로 듣기

 TEST 4.mp3

해커스인강(HackersIngang.com)에서 무료 다운로드
상단 메뉴 [MP3/자료 → 문제풀이 MP3]

자동 채점 및 성적 분석
서비스 바로 이용하기

자동 채점 및 성적 분석 서비스

ⅴ 타이머, 모바일 OMR, 자동 채점
ⅴ 정답률 및 취약 유형 분석

시험 시간 : 90분

목표 점수 : _____점
시작 시간 : _____시 _____분 ~ 종료 시간 : _____시 _____분

General Tests of English Language Proficiency
G-TELP

Level 2

GRAMMAR SECTION

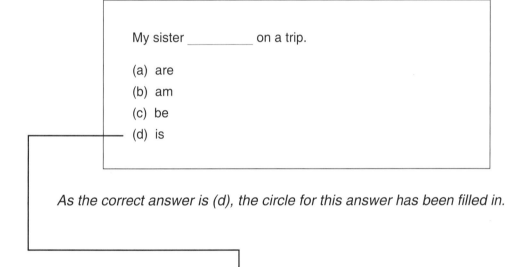

TURN THE PAGE TO BEGIN THE TEST

1. I'm sorry to say this, but I really must be going now. If I _____ about this get-together beforehand, I would have rescheduled my other engagement today.

   (a) were told
   (b) had been told
   (c) am told
   (d) would be told

2. The nuclear power plant in Bruno City had an accident that almost led to a massive radiation leak. Residents urged that the plant _____ to ensure that such a tragic incident would never happen.

   (a) be shut down
   (b) would be shut down
   (c) has been shut down
   (d) had been shut down

3. In times of inflation, consumers need to make an effort to differentiate between wants and needs. Once this is done, they _____ prioritize essential items when shopping and curtail unnecessary spending.

   (a) should
   (b) would
   (c) could
   (d) might

4. In psychology, the concept of introversion simply refers to a person's tendency to consider their inner thoughts over external factors. There are, however, plenty of introverts _____ to seek the safety of solitude.

   (a) which are motivated by social anxiety
   (b) who are motivated by social anxiety
   (c) whom are motivated by social anxiety
   (d) what are motivated by social anxiety

5. Paul Thomas Anderson burst onto the scene in the 1990s with hits like *Magnolia*. He _____ consistently well-regarded films featuring a bold visual style and strong acting performances since then.

   (a) would have directing
   (b) had been directing
   (c) was directing
   (d) has been directing

6. Apple is developing the first-ever fully autonomous vehicle that will require no input from a human driver. According to Apple analyst Ming-Chi Kuo, the company wishes _____ production by 2025 at the earliest.

   (a) starting
   (b) to be started
   (c) to start
   (d) will start

7. Dr. Lamar mentioned that Hannah's vitamin D deficiency had been present for some time. If she had gotten a checkup in the last two years, she _____ what was causing her fatigue much sooner.

(a) would find out
(b) found out
(c) had found out
(d) would have found out

8. Please be quiet. The writing examination is in progress. The students _____ on the test as hard as they can, and even the slightest noise will disturb them.

(a) are currently focusing
(b) were currently focusing
(c) have currently focused
(d) will currently focus

9. Joel moved from Los Angeles to Chicago with his family. While he likes his bigger room and the view from their house, he's worried about the winters because he has not experienced _____ extremely cold weather.

(a) being dealt with
(b) to deal with
(c) dealing with
(d) to have dealt with

10. Olsen hurt his back moving a sofa, so the doctor told him to rest for three days. However, he has to return to work immediately. If there were someone in the office to fill in for him, he _____ the doctor's instructions.

(a) does not ignore
(b) would not have ignored
(c) will not ignore
(d) would not ignore

11. Former colleagues at Prime Financial say that the new CFO of Southern Bank is an impressive young executive with fresh ideas. _____, some investors warn that she has too little know-how to meet the demands of the role.

(a) Similarly
(b) Besides
(c) Instead
(d) On the other hand

12. Ms. Jenkins ordered Kenny to stay after the period was over to have a chat about proper classroom behavior. He _____ at his smartphone for 30 minutes, up until she finally got his attention.

(a) would have stared
(b) is staring
(c) has stared
(d) had been staring

13. As cold fusion sounds like a shortcut to an unlimited supply of clean and safe energy, the idea will always seem appealing. Nevertheless, researchers have come to a consensus that it is impossible _____ a fusion reaction without a great deal of heat.

    (a) generating
    (b) having generated
    (c) to generate
    (d) to be generating

14. Parent-teacher conferences are important for establishing a clear communication channel that will ultimately benefit the children. Instructors ask that parents or guardians _____ any situations at home that might affect their child's conduct at school.

    (a) report
    (b) are reporting
    (c) reported
    (d) will report

15. Today, Naomi went for a 10-mile bike ride in the sweltering heat. She is supposed to have dinner with her friends at 5 p.m., but she is terribly exhausted. There's no doubt that she _____ on the couch tonight.

    (a) was relaxing
    (b) will be relaxing
    (c) will have been relaxing
    (d) has relaxed

16. Elaine knew she had other viral marketing projects that should take priority. Still, she was unable to resist _____ her coworkers for a meeting about the new PR campaign. She reasoned that this was a chance to grow as an employee.

    (a) to join
    (b) to have joined
    (c) being joined
    (d) joining

17. Marta took a deep breath and raised her hand to volunteer to give her presentation first. Even if the thought of speaking in front of the whole class made her nervous, she _____ more anxious waiting until later.

    (a) will only have felt
    (b) only felt
    (c) would only feel
    (d) had only felt

18. In the past, Danny had always been the last person picked when he played basketball on the playground. But now that he _____ perform a picture-perfect dunk as a result of persistent practice, the other players want to be on his team.

    (a) would
    (b) should
    (c) can
    (d) will

19. All newly hired staff members at Dresden Media participate in a three-hour orientation on their first day of work. They initially meet with the head of the personnel department, Ms. Reese, who gives a brief talk _____ the company's policies.

   (a) to have explained
   (b) having explained
   (c) will explain
   (d) to explain

20. Last Sunday morning, my friend Elliott was given two tickets to the Super Bowl, which started at 1 p.m. He decided to invite me, but he couldn't reach me on the phone. When he called, I _____ my lawn.

   (a) would be mowing
   (b) was mowing
   (c) had mown
   (d) mowed

21. Needing a pair of black shoes for a job interview, I asked my cousin if I could borrow hers. She agreed to lend them to me _____ I gave them back by the weekend because she wanted to wear them to a company dinner.

   (a) as long as
   (b) whereas
   (c) so that
   (d) unless

22. Ms. Leslie, the principal of Westwood High School, recently announced that funds had been set aside to expand the library's collection. Many of the books _____ were requested by students via a school survey.

   (a) how they have been selected for purchase
   (b) what have been selected for purchase
   (c) that have been selected for purchase
   (d) who have been selected for purchase

23. My teammate Norton often annoys me with his unsolicited advice. For example, he told me yesterday that if I had taken a different subway line, I _____ at work on time.

   (a) could have arrived
   (b) could arrive
   (c) arrived
   (d) will arrive

24. Mr. Connor is the longest-serving CEO in the history of Newport Restaurant Supplies. By the end of next month, he _____ the company for more than two decades, and he hopes to continue in his role for a few more years.

   (a) would have run
   (b) is running
   (c) will have been running
   (d) will be running

해커스 지텔프 최신기출유형 실전문제집 7회 (Level 2)

25. Although Tanya's little brother is having a hard time in university, she is no longer willing to give him suggestions for improving his grades. Why has she given up _____ to help him? It is because he never follows her counsel!

    (a) to try
    (b) trying
    (c) to be trying
    (d) having tried

26. The sales director of Aspen Plastics has delayed Friday's seminar until next week. If it _____ as originally scheduled, several employees would be absent because they would be taking part in a workshop in another city.

    (a) took place
    (b) had taken place
    (c) was taking place
    (d) has taken place

THIS IS THE LAST PAGE OF THE GRAMMAR SECTION
DO NOT MOVE ON UNTIL DIRECTED TO DO SO

LISTENING SECTION

DIRECTIONS:

The Listening Section has four parts. Each part contains a listening passage and multiple questions about the passage. You will hear the questions first, and then you will hear the passage. Select the best answer from the four choices provided for each question. Then, fill in the correct circle on your answer sheet.

Now you will hear an example question. You will then listen to a sample passage.

Now listen to the example question.

    (a) San Francisco

    (b) Los Angeles

    (c) London

    (d) Detroit

Brenda Kenwood was born in Detroit, so the best answer is (d). As the correct answer is (d), the circle for this answer has been filled in.

TURN THE PAGE TO BEGIN THE TEST

해커스 지텔프 최신기출유형 실전문제집 7회 (Level 2)

27. (a) where she lived during the summer
    (b) when her internship would end
    (c) how she enjoyed her final day at work
    (d) who attended the farewell party

28. (a) It reminds people of their needs.
    (b) It helps people learn about its features.
    (c) It makes advertisements easier to remember.
    (d) It generates public interest in it.

29. (a) because the writing must be technically correct
    (b) because copy must be translated to other languages
    (c) because they must develop interesting stories
    (d) because they must produce reference materials

30. (a) a web design firm
    (b) a medical clinic
    (c) a social media company
    (d) a travel agency

31. (a) by taking the same teacher's course
    (b) by supporting their efforts
    (c) by sharing the results of their research
    (d) by communicating with the same clients

32. (a) a high salary in the industry
    (b) a schedule with long vacations
    (c) the availability to select their own assignments
    (d) the freedom to choose their work locations

33. (a) go on a trip to the Caribbean
    (b) apply for a job at an advertising agency
    (c) ask her mentor for a reference letter
    (d) ask David about his work experience

34. (a) the popularity of a leisure activity
    (b) the lack of outdoor space in urban areas
    (c) a desire to spend more time outside
    (d) an event held in Santa Barbara

35. (a) It rents out clothes appropriate for the weather.
    (b) It offers tools for controlling the temperature.
    (c) It creates indoor backup plans for every picnic.
    (d) It hosts parties in an area with a mild climate.

36. (a) by using outdoor furniture
    (b) by setting up several lanterns around their tents
    (c) by bringing a variety of snacks from home
    (d) by asking for an alternative type of lighting

37. (a) to supply premium-quality desserts
    (b) to provide gourmet bread for appetizers
    (c) to keep the food fresher for longer
    (d) to lower their catering service prices

38. (a) putting together houses for birds
    (b) making a tool used to catch fish
    (c) assembling structures out of sand
    (d) building model accommodations

39. (a) leave their first review on the website
    (b) reserve the service over the Internet
    (c) submit a valid coupon
    (d) purchase a camping license

40. (a) She doesn't know where her classroom is.
    (b) She needs to choose the size of her class.
    (c) She wants to get information about her students.
    (d) She doesn't remember when the school year starts.

41. (a) They interact with the teacher more frequently.
    (b) They meet a similar group of peers.
    (c) They have more chances to work together.
    (d) They learn independently of each other.

42. (a) struggle with classroom management
    (b) complain to other teachers about student behavior
    (c) worry about the safety of students
    (d) devote a similar amount of effort to each pupil

43. (a) when activities are planned in advance
    (b) when teachers have individual time with students
    (c) when teachers organize group discussions
    (d) when the lessons are less difficult

44. (a) by making them less receptive to unfamiliar concepts
    (b) by causing them to ignore background information
    (c) by allowing them to change their point of view
    (d) by encouraging them to be more open-minded

45. (a) teach a large number of students
    (b) take breaks between classes
    (c) learn how to manage large classes
    (d) have a class with fewer students

46. (a) the unwelcome feelings at school
    (b) the fear of making bad choices
    (c) the new obligations they take on
    (d) the changes to their normal routine

47. (a) to avoid falling asleep
    (b) to help them stay organized
    (c) to improve the quality of their sleep
    (d) to prevent cognitive decline

48. (a) It may raise cortisol levels.
    (b) It causes damage to an empty stomach.
    (c) It may disrupt blood flow.
    (d) It slows the immune system's response time.

49. (a) a better grasp on time management
    (b) a lower degree of anxiety
    (c) a higher capacity for problem solving
    (d) an improved ability to wake up early

50. (a) It creates a routine activity to start the day.
    (b) It boosts energy until the next day.
    (c) It activates the memory structure in the brain.
    (d) It enhances performance in professional settings.

51. (a) finish a challenging word game
    (b) watch an educational movie
    (c) write a list of recent accomplishments
    (d) produce a thought-provoking puzzle

52. (a) by finishing small things daily
    (b) by allowing extra time for sleep
    (c) by encouraging each other
    (d) by making their schedule predictable

THIS IS THE LAST PAGE OF THE LISTENING SECTION
DO NOT MOVE ON UNTIL DIRECTED TO DO SO

READING AND VOCABULARY SECTION

DIRECTIONS:

You will now read four different passages. Comprehension and vocabulary questions follow every passage. Select the best answer from the four choices provided for each question. Then, fill in the correct circle on your answer sheet.

Read the following sample passage and example question.

Example:

Brenda Kenwood was born in Detroit. After finishing university in Los Angeles, she settled in San Francisco.

Where was Brenda Kenwood born?

(a) San Francisco
(b) Los Angeles
(c) London
(d) Detroit

As the correct answer is (d), the circle for this answer has been filled in.

TURN THE PAGE TO BEGIN THE TEST

PHIL KNIGHT

Phil Knight is an American businessman best known for cofounding the multinational athletic footwear and apparel company Nike, Inc. with Bill Bowerman. Despite never owning a sports team or being a professional athlete, Knight has been called "the most powerful person in sports."

Phil Knight was born in Portland, Oregon, on February 24, 1938. His father William Knight, the publisher of the *Oregon Journal*, was strict with his son, refusing to give him a job at his newspaper. Rather than becoming discouraged, Knight found a position at the rival paper the *Oregonian*. Around this time, Knight also developed a keen interest in running. He began running seven miles every morning and became a key member of his high school's track team.

Knight attended the University of Oregon, where he competed for the school's track and field team. He was mentored by Bill Bowerman, a legendary coach who trained numerous champion athletes during his career. After graduating with a journalism degree in 1959, Knight pursued an MBA from Stanford University. While writing a paper on the influence of Japanese imports, Knight started thinking about founding his own footwear business to sell Japanese running shoes.

Following his graduation, Knight gained the rights to distribute the running shoe brand Tiger in America. Knight mailed samples of the shoes to Bowerman, hoping he would buy some. In addition to making a purchase, Bowerman proposed that they become business partners. Together, they set up Blue Ribbon Sports on January 25, 1964.

In 1971, they did not renew their contract with Tiger and instead commenced designing their own products. The same year, they renamed the company Nike after the Greek goddess of victory and unveiled the iconic "swoosh" logo. As athletes began wearing its footwear at the Olympics, the company expanded rapidly. Throughout the 1980s and 1990s, Nike secured endorsements with some of the world's most famous athletes, including basketball player Michael Jordan. This increased the shoes' appeal among everyday sports enthusiasts. The company's "Just Do It" marketing campaign further amplified the exposure of the brand.

As of 2021, Knight's net worth was about $60.8 billion, and he has donated vast sums of money through the Philip H. Knight Charitable Foundation Trust since 1990. Knight was inducted into the Oregon Sports Hall of Fame in 2000 for contributing approximately $230 million to the University of Oregon, thereby advancing athletics in the state. In 2021, the Naismith Memorial Basketball Hall of Fame recognized him for Nike's substantial backing of US basketball.

53. Which of the following is probably true about Knight during his early years?

(a) He was encouraged to become a journalist.
(b) He benefited from his father's business connections.
(c) He was an intern at a publishing company.
(d) He learned to be independent.

54. What prompted Knight to start a footwear business?

(a) completing a university assignment
(b) running on a university's track team
(c) purchasing a pair of Japanese shoes
(d) finding out about the popularity of imported shoes

55. What can probably be said about Bill Bowerman?

(a) He bought shoes for the students he coached.
(b) He was impressed with the package he received.
(c) He had prior experience selling athletic footwear.
(d) He stopped coaching to go into business with Knight.

56. According to the article, when did Knight's company begin to grow fast?

(a) when he changed the name of the brand
(b) when his products were advertised through television commercials
(c) after he added a new logo to his products
(d) after his shoes were worn at an international event

57. Why was Phil Knight honored in 2000?

(a) because he established a charitable foundation
(b) because his donation helped to finance US basketball
(c) because his funding improved sports in Oregon
(d) because he was the most famous graduate of his university

58. In the context of the passage, gained means _____.

(a) introduced
(b) obtained
(c) supported
(d) enlarged

59. In the context of the passage, iconic means _____.

(a) elaborate
(b) dramatic
(c) sensational
(d) well-known

해커스 지텔프 최신기출유형 실전문제집 7회 (Level 2)

GREENERY MAY REDUCE DEPRESSION AND IMPROVE COGNITION

A new study has found that living in cities with more vegetation could be linked to lower rates of depression and, by extension, higher cognitive function.

To begin the study, researchers led by Dr. Marcia Pescador Jimenez of the Boston University School of Public Health used a satellite image-based tool called the Normalized Difference Vegetation Index (NDVI). This allowed them to <u>estimate</u> the amount of green space that could be found in selected residential neighborhoods. From 2014 to 2016, they then tested the cognitive function of 13,595 women whose average age was 61.

They established that while there were no differences in working memory, women in areas with more greenery had superior attention spans and faster mental processing speeds than those with less foliage. The researchers also examined whether air pollution or physical activity played a role in cognitive function, and they ultimately determined that neither did.

This study builds upon previous research that has shown that spending time in parks and community gardens is associated with lower levels of stress. This is important because people who experience less stress in their day-to-day life are not as likely to suffer from depression, which is considered a risk factor for dementia.

Given the findings, Pescador Jimenez believes that it may be possible to improve the cognitive function of the population as a whole by adding more greenery to urban environments. However, what types of vegetation could achieve this <u>result</u> is unknown as the NDVI is only able to detect the location of vegetation and not its variety. She plans to use Google Street View images to discover which kinds of plants correlate with higher levels of cognitive health. Once discovered, this information could be valuable to city planners as they work with local governments to design green spaces for the benefit of citizens.

Investigation into this topic is still ongoing, and the findings are not conclusive because the research subjects were primarily white. To get a more comprehensive understanding of how the amount of green space in an urban area impacts cognitive function, the researchers believe other racial and ethnic groups must also be studied.

60. What did the study find out about cognitive ability?

    (a) that it is impaired by intellectual disorders
    (b) that exposure to green space can improve cognition
    (c) that living in an urban area can negatively affect mental ability
    (d) that it is positively correlated to depression rates

61. How did the researchers measure the figures after analyzing the green space in residential areas?

    (a) They traveled to residential neighborhoods.
    (b) They interviewed public health experts.
    (c) They charted Boston's vegetation growth.
    (d) They conducted mental ability exams.

62. What do the researchers probably believe about women who experience daily stress?

    (a) They are more inclined to develop age-related illness.
    (b) They perform an inadequate amount of physical activity.
    (c) They fail to take steps to manage their depression.
    (d) They spend less time engaging in work activities.

63. Why does Pescador Jimenez intend to use Google Street View?

    (a) to find out where the most vegetation is located in cities
    (b) to discover areas where more trees can be planted
    (c) to find what plants contribute to better mental function
    (d) to determine which urban plant varieties are most common

64. According to the article, how can the conclusions of the study be improved?

    (a) by inspecting the amount of green space in different areas
    (b) by studying women living outside urban environments
    (c) by following up with the older subjects of the research
    (d) by including a more diverse range of participants

65. In the context of the passage, estimate means _____.

    (a) review
    (b) consider
    (c) guess
    (d) prove

66. In the context of the passage, result means _____.

    (a) outcome
    (b) triumph
    (c) account
    (d) reaction

GOLDENEYE 007

GoldenEye 007 is a video game of the late 90s based on the 1995 James Bond film *GoldenEye*. It is considered revolutionary and frequently called one of the greatest video games of all time, both for its realism and for bringing first-person shooter games to home consoles.

Nintendo and British video game company Rare first began discussing *GoldenEye 007* in November 1994. Earlier that year, Rare had made waves in the gaming world with its release of the highly successful *Donkey Kong Country*. As the game had been published for the Super Nintendo console, it was originally suggested that *GoldenEye 007* be produced for the same platform. However, the game's director Martin Hollis wanted to design the game for the Nintendo 64 console, which was still being worked on at the time.

The development team, including character artist B. Jones and background artist Karl Hilton, visited the set of *GoldenEye* many times during the film's production. Using reference materials they <u>garnered</u>, Jones replicated the appearance of characters, while Hilton planned levels on the basis of locations in the film. Later, programmer Steve Ellies contributed to this massive hit by adding a multiplayer mode to the primarily single-player game. This allowed up to four players to compete against each other in several deathmatch scenarios.

GoldenEye 007 requires players to complete each level by fulfilling various objectives. These include rescuing hostages and destroying objects using a variety of weapons that the player can pick up from defeated enemies. The signature James Bond weapons available to use in the game appealed to players, with many feeling they created a sense of realism. The high-quality animations, special effects, and music were also praised. Meanwhile, the multiplayer mode, three levels of difficulty, and unlockable secret levels and bonuses are cited as making the game more fun and replayable.

Expectations for *GoldenEye 007* were low, as it was launched two years after the film on which it was based. However, it was a <u>resounding</u> success. It received multiple awards and was the third-best-selling Nintendo 64 game ever, grossing $250 million worldwide.

67. What is the article mainly about?

(a) the release of a video game console
(b) a game adapted from a film of the same title
(c) a script influenced by the James Bond series
(d) the birth of first-person shooter video games

68. What did Hollis aim to do when he was directing the game?

(a) create a game for a new device
(b) develop a brand-new video game platform
(c) improve his original gaming console
(d) make a version of *Donkey Kong Country* for Nintendo 64

69. Why most likely did members of the development team visit the *GoldenEye* film set?

(a) to decide which characters to include in the game
(b) to get the rights to replicate scenes from the film
(c) to determine the best locations for deathmatch scenarios
(d) to have the game look as authentic as possible

70. According to the article, which of the following made users want to replay *GoldenEye 007*?

(a) the difficulty in completing objectives
(b) the ability to play with other people
(c) the chance to unlock secret weapons
(d) the high-quality soundtrack

71. Why were hopes for *GoldenEye 007* low?

(a) It was based on an unpopular series.
(b) It had to be remade multiple times.
(c) It came out a few years after the movie.
(d) It worked poorly on the Nintendo 64 console.

72. In the context of the passage, garnered means _____.

(a) saved
(b) collected
(c) processed
(d) deposited

73. In the context of the passage, resounding means _____.

(a) major
(b) loud
(c) repetitive
(d) initial

TEST 1
TEST 2
TEST 3
TEST 4
TEST 5
TEST 6
TEST 7

해커스 지텔프 최신기출유형 실전문제집 7회 (Level 2)

Kerry Johnson
Principal
St. Jerome Middle School

Dear Ms. Johnson,

I am writing to you as the chosen representative of the parents of St. Jerome students. We want to express our gratitude for the excellence you have shown as school principal. We are particularly grateful for your recent decision to <u>start</u> the school's athletics program.

The other parents and I agree that our children need greater opportunities to participate in sports. Too many of them are glued to their televisions, computers, and electronic devices most of the time. Adding organized team sports to the school's extracurricular programs will not only help them get moving but also instill in them important traits such as leadership, teamwork, and sportsmanship. We are also pleased with the selection of coaches, all of whom have impressive credentials.

St. Jerome has always been known for its exceptional academics. The fact that it now involves sports gives us confidence that our students will receive a more balanced education. Speaking personally, I have had two other children attend St. Jerome since it opened and only wish that an initiative like this had been introduced sooner. It is truly <u>encouraging</u> to see a meaningful effort to develop competitive student athletics.

In closing, we are aware of the significant resources that incorporating team sports at St. Jerome will entail. Therefore, we are prepared to offer any kind of assistance that the school might require when securing the gear needed for this program to be a success. We are at your disposal.

Sincerely,

Michael Davis

74. Why most likely is Michael Davis thanking Kerry Johnson in the letter?

(a) because she represented St. Jerome at an athletics event
(b) because she recommended an excellent school principal
(c) because she proposed a physical education program for parents
(d) because she recognized the importance of sports in education

75. What effect do the parents anticipate the new school program will have?

(a) There will be an improvement in grades.
(b) Students will be better prepared for high school.
(c) Students will be less sedentary.
(d) The school's reputation will be enhanced.

76. Which aspect of the selected coaches are parents pleased about?

(a) their strong professional qualifications
(b) their history of teamwork
(c) their good displays of sportsmanship
(d) their superior leadership skills

77. How can St. Jerome Middle School most likely be described?

(a) It has never added extra subjects to its school curriculum.
(b) It is experiencing a decline in academic rankings.
(c) It has never engaged in sports tournaments.
(d) It is planning to initiate a leadership development course.

78. How are the parents of students prepared to support the school?

(a) by helping manage financial resources
(b) by disposing of old programs
(c) by assisting to obtain sports equipment
(d) by raising awareness of its needs

79. In the context of the passage, start means _____.

(a) sponsor
(b) launch
(c) reform
(d) progress

80. In the context of the passage, encouraging means _____.

(a) inspiring
(b) provoking
(c) beneficial
(d) fortunate

THIS IS THE LAST PAGE OF THE TEST

TEST 5

GRAMMAR

LISTENING

READING & VOCABULARY

테스트 전 확인사항

1. OMR 답안지를 준비하셨나요? ☐
2. 컴퓨터용 사인펜, 수정 테이프를 준비하셨나요? ☐
3. 음성을 들을 준비를 하셨나요? ☐

TEST 5 음성 바로 듣기

🎧 **TEST 5.mp3**

해커스인강(HackersIngang.com)에서 무료 다운로드
상단 메뉴 [MP3/자료 → 문제풀이 MP3]

자동 채점 및 성적 분석
서비스 바로 이용하기

 자동 채점 및 성적 분석 서비스

∨ 타이머, 모바일 OMR, 자동 채점
∨ 정답률 및 취약 유형 분석

시험 시간 : 90분

목표 점수 : _____점
시작 시간 : _____시 _____분 ~ 종료 시간 : _____시 _____분

General Tests of English Language Proficiency
G-TELP

Level 2

GRAMMAR SECTION

DIRECTIONS:

The following items need a word or words to finish the sentence. Select the best answer from the four choices provided for this item. Then, fill in the correct circle on your answer sheet.

Example:

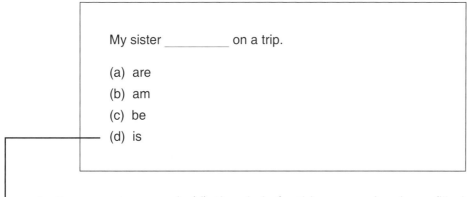

My sister _____ on a trip.

(a) are
(b) am
(c) be
(d) is

As the correct answer is (d), the circle for this answer has been filled in.

TURN THE PAGE TO BEGIN THE TEST

1. Mr. Coyle, the CEO of the travel agency Sterling Destinations, has decided to move its headquarters to a new location. Starting next week, his company _____ out of an office building right across the street from the Newton Subway Station.

   (a) has been operating
   (b) operates
   (c) is operating
   (d) will be operating

2. Dogwood Elementary School teacher Ms. Willis met with the principal to plan her class's upcoming field trip. They discussed _____ three hours at the National History Museum to give the children enough time to see all of the displays.

   (a) spending
   (b) to spend
   (c) to be spending
   (d) having spent

3. Daniel was frustrated with his academic advisor's habit of taking a long time to reply to emails. He could not begin researching, let alone writing his dissertation, _____ she approved his topic.

   (a) as soon as
   (b) until
   (c) after
   (d) when

4. When an individual visits a hospital because of an unidentified health problem, the doctor may arrange for a variety of medical tests. These provide the necessary information _____ the underlying cause of the patient's symptoms.

   (a) to diagnose
   (b) to be diagnosed
   (c) diagnosing
   (d) will diagnose

5. Mr. Weston, the chairperson of Lowden's public safety committee, is going to resign due to his deteriorating health. Considering Ms. Waters' contribution to the organization so far, he proposed that she _____ as his replacement.

   (a) serve
   (b) serves
   (c) is serving
   (d) will serve

6. When Louisa paid for admission to the impressionist exhibition, she didn't notice the sign about the 20 percent discount for university students. Had she shown her student ID at the ticket booth, she _____ $2 on her ticket.

   (a) had saved
   (b) could have saved
   (c) saved
   (d) could save

7. Despite his excellent academic record, Kyle is feeling uncertain about whether he will be accepted into Lethem University. He submitted his application, and he _____ a response from the school for the past month.

(a) would await
(b) is awaiting
(c) has been awaiting
(d) will have awaited

8. Amazing Adventure World is a popular tourist attraction that brings in many visitors from across the country. The amusement park, _____, includes Fun Scape, a roller coaster that reaches speeds of 65 miles per hour and features a 77-degree drop.

(a) which opened just last year
(b) when it opened just last year
(c) that opened just last year
(d) what opened just last year

9. Abigail became interested in learning Spanish after she joined a company that exports clothes to South America, but she doesn't have much time to study. If her work hours were reduced, she _____ in the language course offered at the Westlake Community Center.

(a) has enrolled
(b) would have enrolled
(c) enrolled
(d) would enroll

10. Greg was relieved when his coworker helped him with his report. He _____ on it for five hours since he came to work that morning and knew that he couldn't finish it by the end of the day without assistance.

(a) labored
(b) would have labored
(c) had been laboring
(d) was laboring

11. Residents of the Burnside Apartments wonder when the elevator will be repaired. The work is scheduled for completion on Sunday, but the building manager says he _____ definitely fix it by Friday because the problem isn't very serious.

(a) must
(b) would
(c) can
(d) might

12. Attractive Automobiles would like to expand into new markets in the following quarter. It plans _____ which demographic groups would be most likely to purchase its car cleaning services.

(a) researching
(b) to research
(c) to have researched
(d) having researched

해커스 지텔프 최신기출유형 실전문제집 7회 (Level 2)

13. Nancy called her boss to tell him that she would be late. It snowed heavily last night, and she is worried about driving. At the moment, the streets _____ of snow by city workers, and she will leave her home as soon as they finish.

    (a) will be cleared
    (b) have been cleared
    (c) were cleared
    (d) are being cleared

14. The local government intends to renovate the city's parks. While many are excited about this development, some question how the administration can justify _____ taxes next year to pay for this project. It's no secret that inhabitants are suffering from the recession.

    (a) to increase
    (b) to have increased
    (c) increasing
    (d) will increase

15. Gary was disappointed to hear that his history professor had rejected her students' request to push back the due date for the term paper. If the deadline had been extended, he _____ much less stress these days.

    (a) is having
    (b) has
    (c) would have
    (d) will have

16. Why do many independent stores in this area close during their first year of operation? Although there are a number of reasons, the most common is that these shops are set up in locations _____ to their potential consumers.

    (a) where they are not conveniently accessible
    (b) that they are not conveniently accessible
    (c) when they are not conveniently accessible
    (d) which they are not conveniently accessible

17. Ever since she started working at Wilson Marketing, Sally has never thought of changing jobs. If she signs another annual employment contract at the end of this month, she _____ a career there for eight years.

    (a) is building
    (b) will have been building
    (c) has been building
    (d) has built

18. Austin was worried about how long it would take for his injured knee to heal. But he is almost fully recovered thanks to his doctor's suggestion that he _____ to assist with rehabilitation.

    (a) exercise
    (b) exercising
    (c) exercised
    (d) to exercise

19. It's not fair that I'm getting blamed for the failure of the advertising campaign! If management had followed my recommendation, we _____ the trouble of alienating the target audience entirely.

(a) will have avoided
(b) had avoided
(c) would avoid
(d) would have avoided

20. John spent three years working as a real estate agent for Happy House. _____, he prepared a business plan and secured a commercial loan for a small office. Now, he can open up his own agency.

(a) Therefore
(b) In fact
(c) Meanwhile
(d) In contrast

21. Did you hear that Doug quit the school's baseball team? It turns out that he gave up all the other club activities he had been participating in _____ his time and attention to the theater group.

(a) to devote
(b) devoting
(c) having devoted
(d) to have devoted

22. Rebecca doesn't like her job at the restaurant, so she doesn't work very hard. If she _____ in an industry she had more passion for, she would perform her duties with a lot more effort.

(a) engages
(b) engaged
(c) has engaged
(d) had engaged

23. I have mastered as many types of sports as I could over the years. But most of all, I have to say that I felt the fittest while I _____ for a marathon. Furthermore, I was indescribably happy when I completed the race.

(a) would train
(b) was training
(c) had trained
(d) am training

24. Prime Electronics has received multiple complaints from clients regarding late product deliveries. Though last-minute issues are sometimes inevitable, the company _____ send shipments by the expected time to maintain a good relationship with its customers.

(a) would
(b) may
(c) can
(d) must

25. It wasn't easy for Samantha to move out of the city. At first, she missed the convenience of enjoying cultural facilities at any time and having a shopping mall close at hand. However, she absolutely adores _____ in the countryside now.

    (a) to have lived
    (b) to live
    (c) to be living
    (d) living

26. William couldn't believe that the school canceled the homecoming dance due to budget cuts. If the event had gone on as planned, he _____ his friends whom he graduated with last year.

    (a) would see
    (b) would have seen
    (c) was seeing
    (d) had seen

THIS IS THE LAST PAGE OF THE GRAMMAR SECTION
DO NOT MOVE ON UNTIL DIRECTED TO DO SO

LISTENING SECTION

DIRECTIONS:

The Listening Section has four parts. Each part contains a listening passage and multiple questions about the passage. You will hear the questions first, and then you will hear the passage. Select the best answer from the four choices provided for each question. Then, fill in the correct circle on your answer sheet.

Now you will hear an example question. You will then listen to a sample passage.

Now listen to the example question.

> (a) San Francisco
> (b) Los Angeles
> (c) London
> (d) Detroit

Brenda Kenwood was born in Detroit, so the best answer is (d). As the correct answer is (d), the circle for this answer has been filled in.

TURN THE PAGE TO BEGIN THE TEST

27. (a) that his song will be featured in a commercial
    (b) that his music will be in a film
    (c) that his writing has won a songwriting award
    (d) that his piece has been completed

28. (a) a horror movie
    (b) a romance movie
    (c) a suspense movie
    (d) a comedy movie

29. (a) by listening to somber music
    (b) by studying the movie's characters
    (c) by recording various sounds
    (d) by looking at the faces of the actors

30. (a) because it was expensive to use real instruments
    (b) because the tools sounded better
    (c) because the software was more professional
    (d) because it was easier to perform live

31. (a) when he finishes recording
    (b) when he signs a contract
    (c) before he starts recording
    (d) before he finalizes his pitch

32. (a) He thinks of the lyrics.
    (b) He comes up with the tune.
    (c) He talks to the producers.
    (d) He selects excerpts from films.

33. (a) She'll listen to music samples.
    (b) She'll watch a movie preview.
    (c) She'll go to a recording studio.
    (d) She'll meet with a songwriter.

You will hear a presentation to a group of people. You will hear questions 34 through 39 first, and then you will hear the talk. Select the best answer to each question in the given time.

34. (a) a way to develop an application
    (b) a summer photo-sharing contest
    (c) a new tool for managing pictures
    (d) a simple market research strategy

35. (a) They are approved by professional photo editors.
    (b) They are posted in their original forms.
    (c) They are converted to a specific file format.
    (d) They are scanned by an advanced algorithm.

36. (a) because they are easily encrypted
    (b) because they make chats more fun
    (c) because they express ideas that words cannot
    (d) because they connect users that speak different languages

37. (a) They hire creative software designers.
    (b) They allow anyone to edit the application.
    (c) They include tools to get feedback from users.
    (d) They modify the service regularly.

38. (a) having an app run more quickly
    (b) offering a personalized marketing platform
    (c) providing an uninterrupted user experience
    (d) reducing the overall memory usage

39. (a) those who need a limited number of stickers
    (b) those who need all of the photo editing tools
    (c) those who will upload up to 1,000 photos
    (d) those who will pay a $10 monthly subscription fee

You will hear a conversation between a man and a woman. You will hear questions 40 through 45 first, and then you will hear the conversation. Select the best answer to each question in the given time.

40. (a) She bought a new coffee maker.
    (b) She made a healthy meal.
    (c) She prepared a caffeinated beverage.
    (d) She washed a coffee cup.

41. (a) It enhances blood circulation.
    (b) It improves muscle strength.
    (c) It reinforces the immune system.
    (d) It eliminates a disease symptom.

42. (a) by decreasing the amount of sleep needed
    (b) by improving the ability to burn calories briefly
    (c) by providing extra energy for exercise
    (d) by reducing feelings of tiredness

43. (a) It decreases appetite.
    (b) It results in nervousness.
    (c) It leads to extreme diet changes.
    (d) It alters sleep patterns.

44. (a) because they may experience negative health issues
    (b) because they might develop unhealthy habits
    (c) because they may turn to alcohol
    (d) because they might worry about a productivity decline

45. (a) cut down on his caffeine consumption
    (b) drive to the grocery store
    (c) place an order for coffee beans online
    (d) postpone his plan to mow the lawn

46. (a) how to choose appropriate gifts
    (b) a do-it-yourself project
    (c) how to make aromas for candles
    (d) a home décor store

47. (a) They can tolerate high temperatures.
    (b) They are made of recycled materials.
    (c) They can be cleaned very easily.
    (d) They incorporate synthetic substances.

48. (a) the type of container
    (b) the volume of the vessel
    (c) the transfer rate of the water
    (d) the size of the measuring cup

49. (a) because its structure needs time to solidify
    (b) because it can cause a glass vessel to break
    (c) because its temperature can be dangerous
    (d) because it must simmer for a long time

50. (a) melting the candle's wax
    (b) fastening the burning element
    (c) preventing the wick from falling into the wax
    (d) securing the candle in the container

51. (a) because the fragrance is emitted by heated oil
    (b) because the ratio of fragrance has changed
    (c) because the temperature of the fragrance has cooled
    (d) because the fragrance is mixed with the wax

52. (a) when it is cooled to room temperature
    (b) when its temperature is over 55 degrees
    (c) when it is dried in a slow manner
    (d) when its vessel is filled too quickly

THIS IS THE LAST PAGE OF THE LISTENING SECTION
DO NOT MOVE ON UNTIL DIRECTED TO DO SO

READING AND VOCABULARY SECTION

DIRECTIONS:

You will now read four different passages. Comprehension and vocabulary questions follow every passage. Select the best answer from the four choices provided for each question. Then, fill in the correct circle on your answer sheet.

Read the following sample passage and example question.

Example:

Brenda Kenwood was born in Detroit. After finishing university in Los Angeles, she settled in San Francisco.

Where was Brenda Kenwood born?

(a) San Francisco
(b) Los Angeles
(c) London
(d) Detroit

As the correct answer is (d), the circle for this answer has been filled in.

TURN THE PAGE TO BEGIN THE TEST

PART 1. Read the biography article below and answer the questions. The two underlined words are for vocabulary questions.

AKON

Akon is a Senegalese-American singer, record producer, and entrepreneur known for combining his R&B-style vocals with hip-hop beats. He is the first solo artist to ever achieve the number one and number two spots simultaneously on the *Billboard* Hot 100.

Akon was born on April 16, 1973, in St. Louis, Missouri. His father Mor Thiam is a celebrated drummer, and his mother Kine Gueye Thiam is a dancer. Growing up in this environment, Akon was exposed to music from an early age. He learned to play five instruments including the guitar and the djembe, a traditional drum from West Africa. He lived in Dakar, Senegal until he was seven years old when his family returned to the US. There he heard hip-hop for the first time.

As a young man, Akon became involved in car theft and faced legal issues. While he was in jail, however, Akon rediscovered his interest in music and used the time to explore ideas for songs. Upon his release, he started recording tracks at home, and not long after, one of them was introduced to Devyne Stephens, the president of the record label Upfront Megatainment.

Stephens became Akon's friend and mentor, and Akon began producing songs at Stephens' studio. His demo tape fell into the hands of an executive at SRC Records, and Akon was signed on as an artist shortly thereafter. *Trouble*, Akon's debut album, came out in 2004. It contained the lead single "Locked Up," which reached number 8 on the *Billboard* Hot 100. The album also featured "Lonely," which became a worldwide sensation partially because it sampled Bobby Vinton's 1964 song "Mr. Lonely."

Since then, Akon has issued four other albums and also signed countless successful musicians to his own record label. He collaborated with legendary figures like Michael Jackson and co-wrote popular songs including Lady Gaga's Grammy Award-nominated "Just Dance." He has won numerous awards such as Favorite Soul/R&B Male Artist at the American Music Awards and was ranked number 6 on *Billboard*'s list of Top Digital Song Artists of the decade.

Beyond his career in entertainment, Akon works to improve the lives of underprivileged young people in West Africa and the United States through the Konfidence Foundation, an organization he started with his mother. In 2014, he launched Akon Lighting Africa, a project that has so far provided communities in 15 African countries with electricity via solar energy.

53. How most likely did Akon's parents influence him?

(a) by inspiring him to travel the world
(b) by encouraging him to listen to hip-hop
(c) by introducing him to famous musicians
(d) by giving him an appreciation of music

54. How did going to jail benefit Akon's career?

(a) It educated him about the law.
(b) He met the head of a record label.
(c) It rekindled his love for music-making.
(d) He made songs with other inmates.

55. When did Akon begin recording music for SRC Records?

(a) when his first single started to gain popularity in the US
(b) after he mentored an artist at the label
(c) when his first album became an international success
(d) after a music authority heard his samples

56. According to the article, what is true about Akon's record company?

(a) It became *Billboard*'s top label.
(b) It produced Grammy-winning songs.
(c) It represents popular acts.
(d) It develops Soul and R&B music.

57. What does Akon Lighting Africa do?

(a) supply energy to villages in Africa
(b) spread awareness of renewable energy
(c) replace traditional energy sources with solar panels
(d) provide youth in need with employment opportunities

58. In the context of the passage, celebrated means _____.

(a) sophisticated
(b) distinguished
(c) noticeable
(d) memorable

59. In the context of the passage, sensation means _____.

(a) hit
(b) impression
(c) impact
(d) sense

PART 2. Read the magazine article below and answer the questions. The two underlined words are for vocabulary questions.

HOW UGGS MADE A COMEBACK

The Ugg boot is a pull-on boot with fleece inside and a sheepskin exterior. It was a must-have item in the early 2000s and remained a wardrobe staple until the early 2010s when consumers started viewing them as unfashionable. In the 2020s, however, Uggs began making a comeback.

The style associated with Uggs originated in Australia. Boots similar to Uggs were worn during the 1920s by sheep shearers and during the 1960s by surfers for comfort and warmth. Entrepreneur Brian Smith helped popularize the footwear outside of Australia. In 1978, he established a California-based sheepskin boot company, which he trademarked "UGG." Sheepskin boots had always been referred to as "uggs" in Australia as they were thought to be ugly and only used for utilitarian purposes, but registering the name officially connected Smith to this particular style of boot.

In the 1990s, Smith began offering free Uggs to celebrities in the hope of gaining more exposure. By the early 2000s, famous American talk show host Oprah Winfrey was promoting them on her show and giving away hundreds of pairs. They were soon selling out, with prices being marked up by over 200 percent online. But, as is the case with all trends, the fervor eventually waned. Counterfeits entered the market, making the look less exclusive, and by 2010, they were <u>deemed</u> too sloppy to be worn in public.

Though they fell out of fashion for a decade, Deckers Outdoor Corporation, which had purchased the company from Smith, expanded the Ugg product line while maintaining the footwear's comfortable aesthetic. By the 2020s, consumer demand for nostalgic items from the 1990s and early 2000s surged, which prompted a revival of the brand. Moreover, since people were working from home due to the pandemic, comfort became more important than fashion.

Whether Uggs will ever reach their former <u>level</u> of popularity among celebrities and the general public remains to be seen. However, given that consumers today are placing more of an emphasis on the quality and longevity of goods and that Uggs are now available in various colors and styles, Uggs are likely to stay a part of the fashion landscape for the foreseeable future.

60. Which group first started wearing the Ugg-style of boot?

(a) those who got wool from sheep
(b) those who rode ocean waves
(c) those who had a sense of style
(d) those who lived in California

61. Where most likely does the term "ugg" come from?

(a) from a technique employed by Australian farmers
(b) from an expression denoting comfort
(c) from a trademark style of a company
(d) from an opinion about appearance

62. Why did the popularity of Uggs decrease?

(a) because their price went up dramatically
(b) because they stopped sales promotion activities
(c) because they were criticized by celebrities
(d) because their imitations became widely available

63. What probably prompted consumers to reconsider Uggs during the pandemic?

(a) People were pleased with the expanded product offerings.
(b) People prioritized comfort over style.
(c) Uggs had completely changed their look.
(d) Uggs appeared in fashion advertisements.

64. According to the article, what do consumers value nowadays?

(a) the durability of products
(b) views of famous people
(c) diversity in product lines
(d) the recognition of brands

65. In the context of the passage, deemed means _____.

(a) created
(b) considered
(c) announced
(d) allowed

66. In the context of the passage, level means _____.

(a) stage
(b) force
(c) amount
(d) peak

PART 3. Read the encyclopedia article below and answer the questions. The two underlined words are for vocabulary questions.

ZEIGARNIK EFFECT

The Zeigarnik effect is the tendency for people to have better recall of unfinished tasks than completed ones. Named after Lithuanian-Soviet psychologist Bluma Zeigarnik, the effect was first observed in waiters who were able to remember the pending orders but forgot them as soon as customers were served.

To back up her observation, Zeigarnik conducted experiments in 1927 with participants who were asked to work on short tasks like winding thread and constructing puzzles. Half of the participants were allowed to start an undertaking but then were ordered to move on to the next one when they were most <u>engrossed</u> in it. The other participants were not interrupted. When later asked to discuss the assignments, those who were stopped halfway recalled them twice as well as those who accomplished the objectives.

Zeigarnik concluded that as people approach the culmination of a job at hand, cognitive tension increases. In this state, the brain will remember the discontinued activity until it is resolved. Once completed, though, the strain is released and the pursuit fades from memory.

The Zeigarnik effect can be applied in a number of ways. For instance, television writers know that audiences are more likely to keep watching a show each week if an episode ends in a suspenseful way. Because a satisfying conclusion has not been reached, viewers recollect what happened until there is a resolution.

The Zeigarnik effect may also impact how people learn. If students split up their study sessions instead of going through all the material in one sitting, they will probably think about what they have already reviewed during their breaks. Furthermore, the effect could help people avoid procrastination in the sense that it is difficult to stop thinking about a chore once it has been started, increasing the likelihood of it getting finished.

While subsequent studies <u>support</u> Zeigarnik's findings, others refute them, suggesting that the effect cannot be reliably reproduced. Researchers who believe this claim that the effect depends on factors that change with each individual. These include how motivated they are to complete the task and how difficult they perceive it to be.

67. According to Bluma Zeigarnik's observations, what were the waiters able to do?

(a) They recalled the person who asked for the priciest dish.
(b) They recollected the uncompleted requests of customers.
(c) They remembered the details of completed orders.
(d) They fulfilled the orders in a timely manner.

68. Which of the following was included in Zeigarnik's experiments?

(a) assessing the quality of the participants' work
(b) timing the speed of the completed tasks
(c) interrupting participants from recounting assignments
(d) preventing participants from finishing jobs

69. According to the article, how is mental tension relieved?

(a) by forgetting a paused task
(b) by recalling important memories
(c) by reaching an activity's conclusion
(d) by continuing to decrease cognitive load

70. What probably explains why people watch weekly TV shows?

(a) the extensive discussion among viewers
(b) the satisfying endings featured in them
(c) the desire to see the solution to an issue
(d) the willingness to keep up with series

71. Why most likely do some researchers feel that Zeigarnik's experiments cannot be replicated?

(a) because participants find the tests difficult
(b) because participants have different skill sets
(c) because the public is aware of their findings
(d) because the original tasks no longer motivate people

72. In the context of the passage, engrossed means _____.

(a) directed
(b) entailed
(c) absorbed
(d) attracted

73. In the context of the passage, support means _____.

(a) endorse
(b) assist
(c) utilize
(d) cancel

해커스 지텔프 최신기출유형 실전문제집 7회 (Level 2)

Andrew Pacheco
Peacock Kitchen
174 Sandy Pines Road
East Montpelier, VT 05651

Dear Mr. Pacheco:

I'm pleased to inform you that we are opening our newest distribution center near your restaurant next Friday. Shephard Family Farm grows a wide variety of organic fruits and vegetables. In addition, we offer many other high-quality goods such as cheese, honey, and bread that you might be interested in using as ingredients at your establishment.

Shephard Family Farm began over 20 years ago with the mission to <u>minimize</u> the distance food travels and encourage people to buy from local suppliers. As you are aware, sourcing food from outside the region or other countries negatively impacts the environment since the fuel used in the transportation process adds to the overall carbon footprint.

Furthermore, fruits and vegetables begin losing nutrients not long after they are harvested. Therefore, eating produce that is transported thousands of miles over several days is not the healthiest option. That's why we drop off all customer orders within two business days.

We are committed to keeping our customers informed about what produce is available and discounted at our local retail partners through our monthly newsletter, *Shephard's Harvest*. That way, you can plan various seasonal menus throughout the year, which I <u>understand</u> is especially important in the restaurant business.

If you'd like to learn more about our farm, please visit our website at shephardfamilyfarm.com. I would also be happy to come to your restaurant to speak with you in person and give you a catalog of our products and rates. If you would like this, please let me know a day and time that works for you.

Best regards,

Eileen Shephard
Shephard Family Farm
1134 W Schultz Lane
Rutland, VT 03581

74. Why did Eileen Shephard write Andrew Pacheco a letter?

   (a) to congratulate him on starting a new business
   (b) to inquire about the food at his restaurant
   (c) to follow up on an order
   (d) to promote products to a potential client

75. According to the letter, what is the problem with non-local food?

   (a) Its shipping produces greenhouse gas emissions.
   (b) Its transportation costs vary depending on the region.
   (c) It is grown using environmentally irresponsible methods.
   (d) It hinders the development of the local economy.

76. Why does the Shephard Family Farm deliver produce within two business days?

   (a) so customers continue to use the service
   (b) so it can retain more of its nutritional value
   (c) so it can stay ripe when it arrives
   (d) so customers have time to explore order options

77. What will Pacheco probably do if he reads the farm's publication?

   (a) inform his customers where the goods come from
   (b) use different ingredients depending on the time of the year
   (c) enter into partnerships with other local businesses
   (d) plan a menu that includes seasonal special discounts

78. How can Pacheco find out about the products' prices?

   (a) by going to the store's website
   (b) by meeting with Shephard on her farm
   (c) by viewing a catalog on the Internet
   (d) by accepting Shephard's offer to visit him

79. In the context of the passage, minimize means _____.

   (a) control
   (b) ease
   (c) lessen
   (d) degrade

80. In the context of the passage, understand means _____.

   (a) grasp
   (b) reserve
   (c) settle
   (d) admit

THIS IS THE LAST PAGE OF THE TEST

TEST 6

GRAMMAR

LISTENING

READING & VOCABULARY

테스트 전 확인사항

1. OMR 답안지를 준비하셨나요?   ☐
2. 컴퓨터용 사인펜, 수정 테이프를 준비하셨나요?   ☐
3. 음성을 들을 준비를 하셨나요?   ☐

🎧 TEST 6.mp3

해커스인강(HackersIngang.com)에서 무료 다운로드
상단 메뉴 [MP3/자료 → 문제풀이 MP3]

TEST 6 음성 바로 듣기

▤ 자동 채점 및 성적 분석 서비스

ⅴ 타이머, 모바일 OMR, 자동 채점
ⅴ 정답률 및 취약 유형 분석

자동 채점 및 성적 분석
서비스 바로 이용하기

시험 시간 : 90분

목표 점수 : _____점
시작 시간 : _____시 _____분 ~ 종료 시간 : _____시 _____분

General Tests of English Language Proficiency
G-TELP

Level 2

GRAMMAR SECTION

DIRECTIONS:

The following items need a word or words to finish the sentence. Select the best answer from the four choices provided for this item. Then, fill in the correct circle on your answer sheet.

Example:

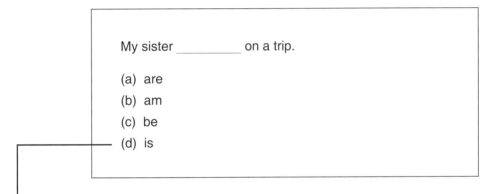

My sister _____ on a trip.

(a) are
(b) am
(c) be
(d) is

As the correct answer is (d), the circle for this answer has been filled in.

TURN THE PAGE TO BEGIN THE TEST

1. Perfect Programming's loss of revenue is affecting business operations. The board of directors recently decided _____ the development of its newest program until more funding could be secured.

   (a) suspending
   (b) to have suspended
   (c) to suspend
   (d) having suspended

2. Henry won a Paul Harrison Classical Music Scholarship and will start college next month. He began playing the violin at the age of five. When he finishes university, he _____ the violin for nearly 20 years.

   (a) will be learning
   (b) is learning
   (c) had learned
   (d) will have been learning

3. Urban farming has surprisingly strong yields of high-quality vegetables. Although it is not practical in every neighborhood, pick-your-own crops from urban farms _____ become a viable alternative to store-bought products.

   (a) can
   (b) must
   (c) would
   (d) should

4. The environmental group is having a hard time getting people to accept their proposal for reducing fine dust. If they were able to decrease the cost of the plan, many members of the public _____ it.

   (a) will welcome
   (b) had welcomed
   (c) would welcome
   (d) would have welcomed

5. Trade is commencing again between the two Asian nations after an intense storm made sea travel dangerous. Cargo ships from both countries departed this morning and will arrive soon. Before the weather cleared today, goods _____ at each nation's ports.

   (a) piled up
   (b) were piling up
   (c) have been piling up
   (d) had been piling up

6. Grayson is a heavy sleeper and always struggles with getting up early in the morning. A classmate who noticed his frequent tardiness recommended _____ only for afternoon courses.

   (a) to have registered
   (b) having registered
   (c) registering
   (d) to register

7. A national newspaper is being criticized by the CEO of AFC Industries for publishing an ad that misspelled the company's name. The paper publicly apologized and said that it _____ the ad if its editors had caught the mistake in time.

(a) would not print
(b) did not print
(c) would not have printed
(d) has not printed

8. Jackson City has large green spaces open to the public. People of all ages enjoy strolls in these areas. The leafy trees, _____, are appreciated by residents worn out by the heat.

(a) what provide plenty of shade to passerbys
(b) which provide plenty of shade to passerbys
(c) that provide plenty of shade to passerbys
(d) where they provide plenty of shade to passerbys

9. The firm had prepared the final documents to complete the merger, but it was not ready to release the news. When asked by a local reporter, the corporation's lawyer denied _____ the deal.

(a) being aware of
(b) to be aware of
(c) to have been aware of
(d) will be aware of

10. Discovered by a team of French scientists, the new bacteria are larger than anyone thought possible. The researchers _____ other microbes in the region for several years now, and they are hoping to continue their research.

(a) are investigating
(b) investigate
(c) have been investigating
(d) will investigate

11. Marcus doesn't think his team manager is using the right approach for the new content creation project. She is making all the members work on everything. If Marcus were to take charge of the team, he _____ individual tasks according to each employee's capabilities.

(a) assigned
(b) would assign
(c) would have assigned
(d) had assigned

12. Jessica finally heard back from the president of McMinnville Technologies. The executive stated that he was interested in the fintech application she has been developing. _____, he proposed meeting the very next day at the firm's headquarters.

(a) Nevertheless
(b) In fact
(c) Otherwise
(d) For example

해커스 지텔프 최신기출유형 실전문제집 7회 (Level 2)

13. Kristi is writing down a list of things to consider before she moves. It is important that she _____ in a quiet area that is close to her workplace and has good restaurants since she doesn't cook often.

    (a) dwelt
    (b) will dwell
    (c) dwells
    (d) dwell

14. The Davis High School graduation ceremony was a disaster because the administrators planned it as an outdoor event without checking the weather forecast in advance. The students _____ up to the stage to receive their diplomas when it began to pour.

    (a) were walking
    (b) walk
    (c) have walked
    (d) would walk

15. Yesterday, Nina's daughter suddenly went into labor. Nina had just visited her last week, and she wasn't due for another month. If Nina _____ the time was near, she would have stayed longer before flying home.

    (a) knew
    (b) would have known
    (c) had known
    (d) would know

16. Fuller Airlines introduced an additional nonstop flight from Atlanta to Rome, which is great news for passengers who are tired of lengthy layovers. The airline added the route _____ new customers, particularly business travelers.

    (a) having acquired
    (b) to be acquiring
    (c) acquiring
    (d) to acquire

17. Most cats hate being immersed in water, but that's not the case for Cooper, a three-year-old Bengal cat. He loves to swim and follows his owner _____ she heads into the backyard to take a dip in the pool.

    (a) because
    (b) whenever
    (c) since
    (d) unless

18. During the school announcements this morning, the principal talked about the upcoming Shakespeare Festival. The school plans to have various events related to his plays, and the drama club _____ Hamlet until the end of next week.

    (a) will be performing
    (b) was performing
    (c) will have performed
    (d) has performed

19. I have some exciting news! My boss doesn't want to risk _____ out on a potential partnership with a client in Vietnam, so he is sending me there on a business trip to close the deal.

(a) to miss
(b) missing
(c) having missed
(d) to have missed

20. Amanda was looking forward to making her first Thanksgiving dinner, but she ended up burning the turkey even though she adhered to her mother's directions carefully. Had she realized it was so difficult to cook a turkey properly, she _____ a precooked one.

(a) was buying
(b) would buy
(c) had bought
(d) would have bought

21. The city council is debating whether or not to approve funding for library renovations. The final decision is expected to be reached next Monday. Supporters of the expenditure claim that the facility _____ be remodeled because it is currently in terrible condition.

(a) must
(b) can
(c) would
(d) might

22. The Rover High School principal had a meeting with parents about getting rid of school uniforms owing to a petition signed by the students. While some parents agreed with this idea, the majority insisted that uniforms _____ mandatory.

(a) remain
(b) are remaining
(c) had remained
(d) remained

23. Anthony was selected to sing the national anthem at the memorial service for Veterans Day, which is only a week away. He cannot meet us right now because he _____ the song.

(a) practices
(b) practiced
(c) is practicing
(d) has been practicing

24. Cindy's boiler pipes froze during the snowstorm last night, so her house was very cold at dawn. She chose _____ a plumber before she left for work so that she wouldn't have to shiver in her bed tonight.

(a) calling
(b) to call
(c) to have called
(d) having called

25. Steps away from the finish line of the marathon, Victoria fell to the ground with an abrupt muscle spasm. After the competition, she told her family that she would have been all right if she _____ more prior to the race.

(a) is stretching
(b) would stretch
(c) stretched
(d) had stretched

26. The model of the human psyche consisting of the id, ego, and super-ego was postulated by the famous neurologist Sigmund Freud. Freud, _____, emphasized the importance of the unconscious mind.

(a) what scholars credit with the development of psychoanalysis
(b) which scholars credit with the development of psychoanalysis
(c) whom scholars credit with the development of psychoanalysis
(d) who credited with the development of psychoanalysis scholars

THIS IS THE LAST PAGE OF THE GRAMMAR SECTION
DO NOT MOVE ON UNTIL DIRECTED TO DO SO

LISTENING SECTION

DIRECTIONS:

The Listening Section has four parts. Each part contains a listening passage and multiple questions about the passage. You will hear the questions first, and then you will hear the passage. Select the best answer from the four choices provided for each question. Then, fill in the correct circle on your answer sheet.

Now you will hear an example question. You will then listen to a sample passage.

Now listen to the example question.

(a) San Francisco
(b) Los Angeles
(c) London
(d) Detroit

Brenda Kenwood was born in Detroit, so the best answer is (d). As the correct answer is (d), the circle for this answer has been filled in.

TURN THE PAGE TO BEGIN THE TEST

27. (a) when she visited a shopping mall last weekend
    (b) when she went to her first basketball game
    (c) when she attended a recent sporting event
    (d) when she traveled to the first ballfield ever built

28. (a) a voucher for a free trip
    (b) an extra ticket to a game
    (c) an invitation to a special match
    (d) a VIP coupon for an event

29. (a) It does not compare to anything else.
    (b) It is not very stimulating.
    (c) It is difficult to describe the energy.
    (d) It is full of loud noises.

30. (a) by talking to neighboring people
    (b) by using a chatting app between innings
    (c) by meeting fellow fans after the game
    (d) by sharing food with those nearby

31. (a) because it is a high-scoring game
    (b) because it involves constant changes
    (c) because it produces unexpected results
    (d) because it requires complex strategy

32. (a) She wasn't facing the right direction.
    (b) She didn't know it was allowed.
    (c) She wasn't sitting in the correct section.
    (d) She didn't have the proper equipment.

33. (a) go to the ballpark with his friend
    (b) join the Cubs' next training session
    (c) view a ball game on television
    (d) look for another baseball park

34. (a) introducing a new houseware manufacturer
    (b) promoting a piece of furniture
    (c) advocating for the purchase of handmade goods
    (d) discussing the home design industry

35. (a) by selecting expensive components
    (b) by forgoing multiple color options
    (c) by applying minimal hardware
    (d) by including contemporary style

36. (a) to offer the acoustics of a theater
    (b) to collect data from user experience
    (c) because it cannot connect to certain devices directly
    (d) because it does not have USB ports

37. (a) The company would be unable to inspect the chair.
    (b) The customer would be responsible for the repairs.
    (c) The company would issue a refund for the repair cost.
    (d) The customer would send it back to the manufacturer.

38. (a) limited use of fire retardants
    (b) recycled cotton fabric
    (c) sustainable manufacturing processes
    (d) fair pay for factory employees

39. (a) those who work in the home furnishings industry
    (b) those who buy a lot of home decorations
    (c) those who are unfamiliar with the brand's new product
    (d) those who subscribe to the newsletter

TEST 1 TEST 2 TEST 3 TEST 4 TEST 5 TEST 6 TEST 7 해커스 지텔프 최신기출유형 실전문제집 7회 (Level 2)

40. (a) how to buy a new camera
    (b) how to charge his phone quickly
    (c) what to use to take pictures
    (d) what to prepare for the architecture tour

41. (a) They have physical buttons.
    (b) They run advanced software.
    (c) They transfer images to storage quickly.
    (d) They work well from a distance.

42. (a) because his hands move too much
    (b) because he uses a phone to zoom
    (c) because his lens reflects light
    (d) because he crops his shots himself

43. (a) It can take less time.
    (b) It has a faster shutter speed.
    (c) It can capture anything in the frame.
    (d) It requires less prior knowledge.

44. (a) by purchasing an aftermarket accessory
    (b) by finding tips on social media sites
    (c) by utilizing professional editing software
    (d) by replacing the original lens

45. (a) bring a camera on his upcoming tour
    (b) employ a mobile phone for photography
    (c) buy a better pack for his gear
    (d) borrow lenses from his friend

46. (a) how to host a private website
    (b) the benefits of ballroom dancing
    (c) how to found a dance organization
    (d) the popularity of a web-based group

47. (a) It dictates the type of information posted.
    (b) It increases the public's interest in the group.
    (c) It gives members a sense of purpose.
    (d) It makes the group seem more professional.

48. (a) so the members can receive discounts
    (b) to help dancers become experts
    (c) to encourage more people to join the club
    (d) so the members can communicate easily

49. (a) when they decide the purpose of the group
    (b) when they outline the amendment process
    (c) when they address internal conflicts
    (d) when they produce a difficult dance

50. (a) limiting the number of members per class
    (b) establishing a set of behavioral standards
    (c) creating a strict reputation in the community
    (d) forming a powerful rules committee

51. (a) to sponsor a local competition
    (b) to promote their businesses
    (c) to gain access to foreign markets
    (d) to have dancers in advertisements

52. (a) by making more people aware of their events
    (b) by lowering the prices of classes permanently
    (c) by giving opportunities for beginners to perform
    (d) by reaching out to individuals through social media

THIS IS THE LAST PAGE OF THE LISTENING SECTION
DO NOT MOVE ON UNTIL DIRECTED TO DO SO

READING AND VOCABULARY SECTION

DIRECTIONS:

You will now read four different passages. Comprehension and vocabulary questions follow every passage. Select the best answer from the four choices provided for each question. Then, fill in the correct circle on your answer sheet.

Read the following sample passage and example question.

Example:

Brenda Kenwood was born in Detroit. After finishing university in Los Angeles, she settled in San Francisco.

Where was Brenda Kenwood born?

(a) San Francisco
(b) Los Angeles
(c) London
(d) Detroit

As the correct answer is (d), the circle for this answer has been filled in.

TURN THE PAGE TO BEGIN THE TEST

PART 1. *Read the biography article below and answer the questions. The two underlined words are for vocabulary questions.*

MARYAM MIRZAKHANI

Maryam Mirzakhani was a prominent Iranian mathematician and Stanford University professor. She is best known as the first Iranian and the only woman thus far to be awarded the Fields Medal, which is akin to a Nobel Prize as it is the highest honor a mathematician can receive.

Mirzakhani was born on May 12, 1977 in Tehran, Iran, to parents Ahmad Mirzakhani and Zahra Haghighi. She initially wanted to become a writer. She was not interested in mathematics due to a teacher's comment about her lack of talent in the subject, which shattered her confidence. It wasn't until another teacher later encouraged her that she decided to pursue math <u>seriously</u>. Participating in the International Mathematical Olympiad as a high school student in 1994, she was the first Iranian girl to win a gold medal. The following year, she achieved a perfect score in the same competition.

After studying mathematics at Sharif University of Technology, she earned a PhD from Harvard University, where she was recognized as an influential mathematician for her thesis titled *Simple Geodesics on Hyperbolic Surfaces and Volume of the Moduli Space of Curves*. Her thesis provided a new proof of the Witten conjecture on quantum gravity, which had long troubled mathematicians.

Mirzakhani continued focusing on the dynamics of moduli space after she became a professor at Stanford University in 2009. In 2014, Mirzakhani proved that complex geodesics in moduli space are regular rather than irregular. She made this breakthrough with mathematician Alex Eskin of the University of Chicago, with whom she had started working in 2006.

The International Mathematical Union presented Mirzakhani with the Fields Medal in Seoul, South Korea in 2014 for her contributions to the theory of moduli spaces of Riemann surfaces. In an interview, she said that she herself hoped to inspire other women to go after successful careers in science and mathematics.

While this was a <u>considerable</u> honor as she was the first woman to receive the famed medal, Mirzakhani won many other distinctions as well, including being admitted as a member of the Paris Academy of Sciences and the American Philosophical Society in 2015. After a four-year struggle against breast cancer, Mirzakhani died on July 14, 2017, at the age of 40. She is remembered today as a modest person whose enthusiasm and perseverance were unmatched.

53. What is Maryam Mirzakhani most famous for?

(a) being the first woman to win a prestigious award
(b) being the first Iranian to become a professor at an esteemed university
(c) teaching mathematics at a renowned Iranian educational institution
(d) getting a Nobel Prize for her work in mathematics

54. Why was Mirzakhani indifferent to mathematics at first?

(a) because her parents pressured her to master the subject
(b) because she dreamed of becoming a writing instructor
(c) because she participated in other academic competitions
(d) because an educator pointed out her insufficient ability

55. What best describes the Witten conjecture before Mirzakhani's proof?

(a) It had provided groundbreaking data on gravity.
(b) It had proven the existence of simple geodesics.
(c) It had been influential in the field of technology.
(d) It had lacked the information to be confirmed.

56. When did Mirzakhani prove an important fact about complex geodesics?

(a) when she collaborated with another scholar
(b) when she attended the University of Chicago
(c) when Eskin made a discovery concerning geodesics
(d) when Eskin started studying moduli space

57. Which of the following is NOT true about the later years of Mirzakhani's life?

(a) She contracted a deadly disease.
(b) She funded cancer research in Paris.
(c) She became a member of various scholarly organizations.
(d) She earned a reputation for being passionate.

58. In the context of the passage, seriously means _____.

(a) inevitably
(b) honestly
(c) intently
(d) rightly

59. In the context of the passage, considerable means _____.

(a) considerate
(b) necessary
(c) critical
(d) large

PART 2. Read the magazine article below and answer the questions. The two underlined words are for vocabulary questions.

AVOCADO: THE "GREEN GOLD" DESTROYING THE PLANET

The United States revoked a ban on the import of Mexican avocados in 1997, beginning what is now seemingly an obsession with the fruit. Since then, the Mexican state of Michoacán, the largest avocado producer in the world, has kept up with demand. However, Michoacán is currently facing resource depletion, extreme weather, soil degradation, and biodiversity loss.

Producing 80 percent of Mexico's avocados, the state is dependent on this fruit, which creates job opportunities in the region, generating about $3.1 billion annually for the nation. Given how vital its continued success is to the state, where 50.9 percent of people have an income below the poverty line, it is no wonder that there is little regard for the environmental damage it inflicts.

Large-scale deforestation has <u>passed</u> in the name of the lucrative industry. Because avocado trees require lots of sunlight to grow, taller trees nearby have been cut down. Furthermore, profit-seeking avocado producers are abusing a law designed to protect forest land. The law states that the land can be used for commercial agriculture only if it is lost to fire. However, avocado producers are burning it down instead of waiting for a forest fire caused by a natural event or an accident. The loss of forest land has depleted the soil of nutrients and led to habitat loss resulting in a decrease in biodiversity.

The weather in Michoacán has become hotter and drier, and hurricanes are more intense due to the reduction of forested land. In addition, the region is at a higher risk of earthquakes stemming from the frequent drilling of wells for agricultural water. In 2020, avocado farms drew approximately 9.5 billion liters of water a day from underground reservoirs, putting them in danger of being drained.

However, those involved in avocado production are not entirely responsible for the environmental damage. The strong demand for the fruit means that consumers are also at fault. To put an end to the <u>rampant</u> destruction, solutions such as expanding sustainable farming practices and revisions to trade agreements are being discussed.

60. What is the article mainly about?

    (a) the negative effects of avocado
        consumption on health
    (b) the cause of the rising demand for
        avocados
    (c) the environmental impact of avocado
        farming
    (d) the removal of a ban on avocado
        imports

61. According to the article, which is the
    result of the ongoing prosperity of the
    avocado industry?

    (a) Avocados are being grown in other
        parts of the nation.
    (b) Residents of Michoacán are
        becoming very rich.
    (c) Residents of Michoacán are ignoring
        the ecological consequences.
    (d) Avocados are getting more expensive
        in Mexico.

62. What can probably be said about
    avocado producers?

    (a) that they have their farmland legally
        protected
    (b) that they are planting avocado trees
        within dense forests
    (c) that they have changed a law
        regarding the use of forest land
    (d) that they are exploiting a gap in some
        legislation

63. Why has the chance of natural disasters
    increased in Michoacán?

    (a) because the land is being excavated
        often
    (b) because the temperature has
        decreased significantly
    (c) because there is little water left in
        surface-level reservoirs
    (d) because there is not as much wildlife
        due to deforestation

64. How are buyers responsible for the
    environmental destruction in Michoacán?

    (a) They promote the benefits of
        avocados.
    (b) They encourage the production of
        avocados.
    (c) They neglect to demand sustainable
        farming methods.
    (d) They violate amendments to trade
        agreements.

65. In the context of the passage, passed
    means _____.

    (a) occurred
    (b) delivered
    (c) approved
    (d) succeeded

66. In the context of the passage, rampant
    means _____.

    (a) lavish
    (b) robust
    (c) prolonged
    (d) uncontrolled

PART 3. *Read the encyclopedia article below and answer the questions. The two underlined words are for vocabulary questions.*

DUST BOWL

The Dust Bowl refers to a series of severe droughts and dust storms that took place in the Great Plains region of the United States during the 1930s. Its impact on the environment, the economy, and people was catastrophic and had long-lasting consequences.

In the decades prior to the Dust Bowl, migrants had been drawn to the Great Plains by legislation that promoted the settlement of the American West. They had no experience with the unique ecology and climate of the region, which are characterized by infrequent rain and high winds. Farmers therefore relied on methods they previously used to <u>cultivate</u> crops. This included digging up the native prairie grass before planting crops in the loose topsoil.

When the droughts arrived in the summer of 1931, the crops died and the dry topsoil blew away. This created thick dust storms that blocked out the sun and blanketed everything, rendering the land useless for farming. It is estimated that during the most devastating drought, which took place between 1934 and 1935, the region lost as much as 1.2 billion tons of soil.

Unable to produce food or earn an income, many families went bankrupt and had to leave their land. Approximately 2.5 million poverty-stricken people left states affected by the Dust Bowl in search of work. However, high unemployment resulting from the Great Depression made finding a job difficult. Many moved into homeless camps, where they continued to go hungry.

The establishment of the Soil Conservation Service by the Roosevelt administration helped cease soil erosion in the Great Plains, which had previously produced most of America's food supply. This service taught farmers agricultural techniques that would restore the land's fertility. For agreeing to <u>observe</u> the new approach in order to help address the nationwide hunger crisis, farmers were subsidized by the government.

Today, scientists speculate that temperature increases caused by climate change could lead to more droughts in the Great Plains. Despite this, agricultural crops will continue to be produced as irrigation is available via the Ogallala Aquifer. However, industrial farming operations are depleting the water within it faster than it can be replenished. When it runs out, the region may face another Dust Bowl.

67. Why most likely did people not realize the effect of removing the native grass?

(a) because they had no experience of farming
(b) because they were used to significant amounts of rain
(c) because they were unfamiliar with the region
(d) because they thought the wind would not affect the soil

68. According to the passage, what brought along the sandstorms?

(a) the beginning of a period of little rainfall
(b) the most severe drought in the history of the region
(c) the loss of more than a billion tons of soil
(d) the destruction of the land as a result of fire

69. When did people impacted by the Dust Bowl leave their homes?

(a) when out-of-state jobs became available
(b) after they encountered financial ruin
(c) when homeless camps began to open
(d) after the Great Depression ended

70. Why probably were farmers in the Great Plains provided with monetary support?

(a) The government wanted to prevent starvation in other nations.
(b) The farmers were still using outdated agricultural tools.
(c) The government wanted to increase food supplies in the country.
(d) The farmers were asked to plant new types of crops.

71. What do experts believe might happen to the Ogallala Aquifer?

(a) It will rely on industrial farming operations.
(b) It will be emptied from the overuse of water.
(c) It will be lost after the next Dust Bowl.
(d) It will dry up because of climate change.

72. In the context of the passage, cultivate means _____.

(a) nurture
(b) enrich
(c) support
(d) grow

73. In the context of the passage, observe means _____.

(a) detect
(b) practice
(c) monitor
(d) examine

Diane Orville
Chesapeake, Virginia

Dear Ms. Orville:

Following your recent interview and the verification of your work references, we are delighted to offer you the position of account executive within the sales and marketing department. As discussed, you will serve as a link between Shipspeed Logistics and its corporate clients. Your job will be to guarantee that our relationships with them are fruitful.

For this position, your annual salary will be $58,000 before taxes, with the possibility of an annual bonus subject to performance. You will also be entitled to our standard compensation package, which includes health insurance, 20 days of paid leave, and optional access to a pension plan.

After your first year of successful employment, you will be allowed to convert unused leave days into cash, attend professional training seminars off-site, and work remotely. You will also be given more opportunities for career advancement.

Should you accept, your first day of work will be on June 4 at our head office in Norfolk, Virginia. There will be a three-month trial period during which your job performance will be closely evaluated. Your hours will be from 8 a.m. to 5 p.m. daily from Monday to Friday. Occasional travel and overtime work may be required when your regular employment period begins.

Please sign the enclosed response form and return it to me by May 1 to signify your acceptance. If you have any questions, do not hesitate to contact me at wmeek@shipspeed.com. We look forward to welcoming you as the newest member of our company.

Sincerely,

Walter Meek
Human Resources Manager
Shipspeed Logistics

74. Why did Walter Meek write a letter to Diane Orville?

   (a) to confirm a scheduled interview
   (b) to make an offer of employment
   (c) to clarify a job description
   (d) to introduce a corporate client

75. According to the letter, how can Diane Orville earn extra money?

   (a) by securing her own health insurance
   (b) by opting out of a pension plan
   (c) by carrying out her job satisfactorily
   (d) by working additional hours

76. Based on the letter, what does an employee probably need to do to qualify for remote work?

   (a) submit a formal request
   (b) complete a year of labor
   (c) participate in a training seminar
   (d) advance to an executive position

77. What will happen during Orville's initial period of work?

   (a) She will attend a brief orientation.
   (b) She will work shorter hours than usual.
   (c) She will travel to a business event.
   (d) She will be carefully reviewed.

78. How is Orville asked to respond to the letter?

   (a) by sending back a document
   (b) by preparing a list of questions
   (c) by signing a contract electronically
   (d) by placing a call to a department

79. In the context of the passage, fruitful means _____.

   (a) fortunate
   (b) promising
   (c) productive
   (d) efficient

80. In the context of the passage, welcoming means _____.

   (a) accepting
   (b) releasing
   (c) persuading
   (d) entertaining

THIS IS THE LAST PAGE OF THE TEST

TEST 7

GRAMMAR

LISTENING

READING & VOCABULARY

테스트 전 확인사항

1. OMR 답안지를 준비하셨나요? ☐
2. 컴퓨터용 사인펜, 수정 테이프를 준비하셨나요? ☐
3. 음성을 들을 준비를 하셨나요? ☐

TEST 7 음성 바로 듣기

🎧 **TEST 7.mp3**

해커스인강(HackersIngang.com)에서 무료 다운로드
상단 메뉴 [MP3/자료 → 문제풀이 MP3]

자동 채점 및 성적 분석
서비스 바로 이용하기

📋 **자동 채점 및 성적 분석 서비스**

∨ 타이머, 모바일 OMR, 자동 채점
∨ 정답률 및 취약 유형 분석

시험 시간 : 90분

목표 점수 : _____ 점
시작 시간 : _____ 시 _____ 분 ~ 종료 시간 : _____ 시 _____ 분

General Tests of English Language Proficiency
G-TELP

Level 2

GRAMMAR SECTION

DIRECTIONS:

The following items need a word or words to finish the sentence. Select the best answer from the four choices provided for this item. Then, fill in the correct circle on your answer sheet.

Example:

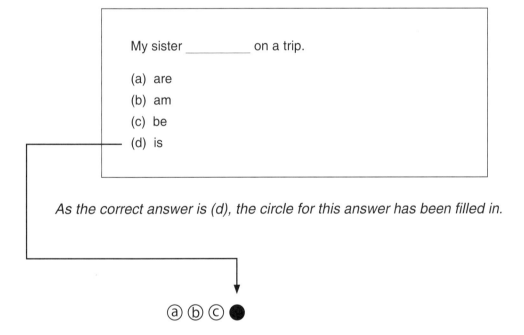

My sister _____ on a trip.

(a) are
(b) am
(c) be
(d) is

As the correct answer is (d), the circle for this answer has been filled in.

ⓐ ⓑ ⓒ ●

TURN THE PAGE TO BEGIN THE TEST

1. Of the almost 7,000 languages in the world, nearly half are at risk of vanishing. Endangered languages are crucial to understanding the cultures of indigenous groups, _____ efforts are being made to preserve these dialects through audio recordings and other methods.

   (a) so
   (b) but
   (c) since
   (d) while

2. Digital Design Incorporated experimented with a remote work system last year and discovered that workers were generally more productive at home. As a result, most employees _____ their tasks from home on a full-time basis nowadays.

   (a) will conduct
   (b) have conducted
   (c) conducted
   (d) are conducting

3. Dawson missed his daughter's school play as he had put off an assignment and had to work late to finish it, which upset his wife greatly. If he had managed his time more carefully, he _____ the performance.

   (a) had attended
   (b) could have attended
   (c) could attend
   (d) was attending

4. Steve was angry because the school bully kept calling him names. He was about to punch the bully when his friend Jenna stopped him, saying it was not worth _____. She told him that using violence would just cause more problems.

   (a) will fight over
   (b) fighting over
   (c) to fight over
   (d) having fought over

5. Coach Cartwright announced that the rookie player would be in the starting lineup. She _____ rapidly ever since she joined the team, and he feels that she can perform better than many of the veteran players.

   (a) improves
   (b) is improving
   (c) has been improving
   (d) will have been improving

6. For the first 32 years of his life, Thomas Davenport was known as a blacksmith, not an inventor. However, that all changed in 1837 _____ for the first-ever electric motor.

   (a) where he received an American patent
   (b) that he received an American patent
   (c) which he received an American patent
   (d) when he received an American patent

7. I heard that my favorite artist, Brandt Lars, will display his latest paintings at the Lyman Gallery. By the time the exhibit opens later this year, he _____ art for more than six decades!

   (a) has been creating
   (b) will be creating
   (c) will have been creating
   (d) is creating

8. Olivia's friends are always trying to get her to go out on her days off, but she prefers to spend time alone. If it were up to her, she _____ home watching movies every weekend.

   (a) will stay
   (b) has stayed
   (c) would stay
   (d) would have stayed

9. Awesome Outfits was planning to make a video that would play automatically on its website. Yet, the marketing director advised that the company _____ in this manner, since most of their target consumers find these types of ads intrusive.

   (a) not advertise
   (b) is not advertising
   (c) will not advertise
   (d) does not advertise

10. Luther's bicycle is a high-end model and is one of his most prized possessions. Even though he trusts his friends, he never lets them ride his bike because they _____ damage it by accident.

    (a) will
    (b) should
    (c) shall
    (d) might

11. This watercolor was only painted seven years ago, but some of the colors are already fading. The painting _____ in such poor condition if the museum took better care of it.

    (a) would not be
    (b) had not been
    (c) would have not been
    (d) will not be

12. The ownership association has voted to expand the apartment complex's fitness center. In order to cover the cost of the renovations, residents will be required _____ an additional $20 per month in condominium fees.

    (a) paying
    (b) to pay
    (c) to have paid
    (d) having paid

13. Parents love their children and want to give them everything, but this often leads to a fear of saying no. They believe a "no" will harm the relationship. _____, they are afraid of angering their children or falling out with them.

    (a) However
    (b) Instead
    (c) Regardless
    (d) Moreover

14. On account of the holiday, the postal service was suspended from Thursday to Sunday. This most likely means that next Monday postal workers _____ mail when their regular shifts end. Fortunately, they can collect overtime pay.

    (a) were still distributing
    (b) will still distribute
    (c) will still be distributing
    (d) have still distributed

15. Repusafe Financial experienced a security breach when hackers accessed its servers yesterday. The enterprise uses an outdated system that is more than a decade old. It _____ update to a newer one or else another attack is sure to occur.

    (a) can
    (b) must
    (c) will
    (d) might

16. When Gabriella picked zoology as her major, she didn't realize how many chemistry and math classes she would have to take. If she had been aware of these course requirements, she _____ to study something else.

    (a) would have chosen
    (b) would choose
    (c) was choosing
    (d) has chosen

17. Oscar's colleagues recommended that he use a professional cleaning service since he is too lazy to do housework. He objected because he dislikes _____ strangers into his house.

    (a) letting
    (b) to let
    (c) to have let
    (d) having let

18. Although we don't notice it, the Earth spins at a speed of roughly 1,000 miles per hour. If the planet were to suddenly stop turning, anything not firmly attached to the ground _____ into the atmosphere.

    (a) flies off
    (b) will fly off
    (c) would fly off
    (d) is flying off

19. It was becoming obvious that Becky wasn't going to make it to the airport in time for her flight. She still had two bags _____ before she could call a taxi.

(a) packing
(b) having packed
(c) to have packed
(d) to pack

20. According to the World Health Organization, only one infectious disease has ever been completely eradicated. Smallpox, _____ during the late 1970s, officially achieved this distinction in 1980.

(a) that had its last known case in Africa
(b) which had its last known case in Africa
(c) how it had its last known case in Africa
(d) who had its last known case in Africa

21. Journalists are finding it tougher to document stories these days due to a lack of confidence in the press. Good reporting involves _____ trust from sources who have inside information, but many people worry that their stories will not be reported accurately.

(a) to earn
(b) to have earned
(c) earning
(d) earn

22. Boston Rams fans were devastated to learn that Carl Ewing would be moving to a different team. Ewing _____ for the Rams for 14 years until he opted to take his talents to the New York Flames.

(a) competes
(b) has competed
(c) had been competing
(d) has been competing

23. Julia is writing a list of goals for her summer break. In addition to frequent exercise and hanging out with friends, she hopes _____ at least five works of literature.

(a) reading
(b) having read
(c) to have read
(d) to read

24. Riverside College aims to restructure its education model to increase class engagement. To accomplish this, experts on the school's steering committee state that it's necessary that the faculty _____ students more in the learning process.

(a) involve
(b) has involved
(c) will involve
(d) involves

25. Few investors doubted SkyTek's legitimacy when the firm was valued at $10 billion in 2020. But if they _____ its technological claims more closely, they probably would not have purchased a single stock.

    (a) were inspecting
    (b) inspected
    (c) had inspected
    (d) would inspect

26. It was a beautiful Saturday afternoon, and Lucy was enjoying relaxing in her room. She _____ whether or not to take a walk outside when her friend Alyssa called to invite her to a barbecue.

    (a) considered
    (b) was considering
    (c) is considering
    (d) has considered

THIS IS THE LAST PAGE OF THE GRAMMAR SECTION
DO NOT MOVE ON UNTIL DIRECTED TO DO SO

LISTENING SECTION

DIRECTIONS:

The Listening Section has four parts. Each part contains a listening passage and multiple questions about the passage. You will hear the questions first, and then you will hear the passage. Select the best answer from the four choices provided for each question. Then, fill in the correct circle on your answer sheet.

Now you will hear an example question. You will then listen to a sample passage.

Now listen to the example question.

(a) San Francisco

(b) Los Angeles

(c) London

(d) Detroit

Brenda Kenwood was born in Detroit, so the best answer is (d). As the correct answer is (d), the circle for this answer has been filled in.

TURN THE PAGE TO BEGIN THE TEST

27. (a) She is scared to work with dogs.
    (b) She is starting a new job.
    (c) She has never lived by herself.
    (d) She has to leave her pet alone.

28. (a) to give herself a chance to rest during the day
    (b) to be able to take better care of her dog
    (c) to have time to work out at the school gym
    (d) to visit her roommates before they went to school

29. (a) Her dog is shy around new people.
    (b) She doesn't want anyone in her house.
    (c) She can't trust an untested service.
    (d) Her dog is afraid of going outside.

30. (a) by buying him new toys to play with
    (b) by taking him on his normal walking route
    (c) by bringing him to the walker's house beforehand
    (d) by going with him to dog parks

31. (a) the duration of the walks being offered
    (b) the number of dogs on the walk
    (c) the size of the other dogs
    (d) the schedule of the service

32. (a) by walking along a longer path in the park
    (b) by working off excess energy before the evening
    (c) by interacting with a variety of unfamiliar people
    (d) by staying out of the house later in the afternoon

33. (a) try to make her workday shorter than it is
    (b) inquire about a size-specific group for her pet
    (c) ask a business to offer a service discount
    (d) begin training to be a professional dog walker

34. (a) to celebrate the expansion of the urban business community
    (b) to experiment with an array of cooking techniques
    (c) to unveil a newly renovated downtown music venue
    (d) to showcase desserts to local residents for the first time

35. (a) so they can try one of the vegan recipes
    (b) so they can follow a dietary requirement
    (c) so they can eat foods other than dessert
    (d) so they can order different kinds of chocolate

36. (a) The festival goers are going to evaluate the contestants' creations.
    (b) The competitors will each cast a vote for the highest-quality one.
    (c) The victors from previous contests will pick their favorite entries.
    (d) The bakers will determine the most creative one.

37. (a) the event's souvenir products
    (b) a free ticket for the following year's event
    (c) the opportunity to meet the vendors
    (d) a discount certificate for a cooking class

38. (a) by buying the most expensive admission ticket
    (b) by bringing a box from their home
    (c) by storing them in the provided container
    (d) by receiving extra samples from vendors

39. (a) reserving spots for vendors in advance
    (b) learning driving directions to the site's location
    (c) posting reviews of the event on a message board
    (d) registering online to participate in a festival

PART 3. *You will hear a conversation between a man and a woman. You will hear questions 40 through 45 first, and then you will hear the conversation. Select the best answer to each question in the given time.*

40. (a) moving to a nearby farm for their children's health
    (b) going on a weekend journey that is beneficial to kids
    (c) visiting their family members who live on rural farms
    (d) participating in a professional education program

41. (a) information on growing plants
    (b) how to look after animals
    (c) how to fix tractors
    (d) the origin of food

42. (a) The kids don't like touching plants.
    (b) It lacks sufficient indoor spaces for activities.
    (c) The kids fear the larger animals.
    (d) It comes with a risk of physical injury.

43. (a) They saw a film that took place on another planet.
    (b) They visited a famous observatory that had moon rocks.
    (c) They watched a shooting star through a telescope.
    (d) They took a science class during summer school.

44. (a) because the kids would prefer to go on an outing closer to home
    (b) because it costs a lot due to the large increase in gasoline prices
    (c) because the kids could become irritated
    (d) because it could be a waste of time

45. (a) book a trip to the observatory
    (b) make a hotel reservation
    (c) go through the options again
    (d) make a visit to the farm

PART 4. *You will hear an explanation of a process. You will hear questions 46 through 52 first, and then you will hear the explanation. Select the best answer to each question in the given time.*

46. (a) how to avoid using another person's work
    (b) personal opinions about plagiarism
    (c) how to get an author's permission
    (d) different types of plagiarism in college

47. (a) It makes it easier to forget important information.
    (b) It leads to poorly cited papers.
    (c) It diminishes the writing quality.
    (d) It causes more grammar mistakes.

48. (a) when they find it hard to meet their professors
    (b) when they fail to understand a topic
    (c) when they need additional views
    (d) when they have difficulty locating resources

49. (a) by referring to the endnotes in the syllabus
    (b) by searching the university's online library
    (c) by contacting other students in their class
    (d) by copying the quotes from the source material

50. (a) because professors are unconcerned with an outsider's ideas
    (b) because professors cannot evaluate works in a detached way
    (c) because it cannot convey complete comprehension
    (d) because it degrades the quality of a work

51. (a) use the best plagiarism checker available online
    (b) have an objective person thoroughly examine their work
    (c) employ more than one Internet-based checking program
    (d) review the citations before submitting the work

52. (a) to share their experiences with academic probation
    (b) to ask about the consequences of plagiarism
    (c) to receive notifications for future talks
    (d) to obtain an overview of the discussion

THIS IS THE LAST PAGE OF THE LISTENING SECTION
DO NOT MOVE ON UNTIL DIRECTED TO DO SO

READING AND VOCABULARY SECTION

DIRECTIONS:

You will now read four different passages. Comprehension and vocabulary questions follow every passage. Select the best answer from the four choices provided for each question. Then, fill in the correct circle on your answer sheet.

Read the following sample passage and example question.

Example:

> Brenda Kenwood was born in Detroit. After finishing university in Los Angeles, she settled in San Francisco.
>
> Where was Brenda Kenwood born?
>
> (a) San Francisco
> (b) Los Angeles
> (c) London
> (d) Detroit

As the correct answer is (d), the circle for this answer has been filled in.

TURN THE PAGE TO BEGIN THE TEST

ARTHUR READ

Arthur Read is the main character of the educational animated children's television series *Arthur*. It is based on the book series by Marc Brown, an American writer and illustrator. The series lasted for 25 seasons, making it the second longest-running animated series ever in the United States. It deals primarily with real-life issues that affect children and families. Arthur Read is listed as number 26 in *TV Guide*'s 50 greatest cartoon characters of all time.

Arthur is a light brown aardvark with small ears and brown glasses. He is most commonly portrayed as wearing a yellow sweater over a white collared shirt, blue jeans, and red and white sneakers. Arthur lives in Elwood City with his parents David and Jane, two younger sisters—a four-year-old nicknamed D.W. and an infant named Kate—and his dog Pal. He is a third-grade student in Mr. Ratburn's class at Lakewood Elementary School. In his free time, Arthur loves to read and hang out with his classmates, including his best friend Buster Baxter.

Arthur cares a lot about what his peers think of him. Like the celebrities he admires, he wants to be popular. In a conscious effort to gain favor with his fellow schoolmates, he sometimes laughs enthusiastically at their jokes, even when he doesn't understand them. His yearning for popularity stems from the fact that he was often teased when he was younger. For example, before getting glasses, he was made fun of by other students while playing basketball because he couldn't catch the ball.

While generally mild-mannered, Arthur lets his frustrations show from time to time. His annoyance is usually caused by his sister D.W., who has a habit of waking him up, interrupting his homework, and fighting with him over the television remote control. Despite this, Arthur for the most part tries his best to ignore D.W.'s irritating behavior and even begrudgingly does nice things for her at the request of his parents.

Arthur grows up to become an author. His childhood experiences and adventures with his friends and family in Elwood City help spawn a graphic novel, which earns him success as a professional writer. While the TV original series ended in 2022, fans of the show will be able to enjoy new content, as more episodes are expected to be released on an educational video platform.

53. What is the subject of the TV show *Arthur*?

  (a) problems that have an effect on real families
  (b) the life of an American author
  (c) techniques that are used for illustrations
  (d) the education of young children

54. Which of the following is NOT true about Arthur's life?

  (a) He is the youngest child in his family.
  (b) He dresses mostly in a layered outfit.
  (c) He is in the same class as his best friend.
  (d) He has a passion for books.

55. Why most likely was Arthur bad at playing basketball?

  (a) because he had no friends to practice with
  (b) because he was not interested in sports
  (c) because he had terrible eyesight
  (d) because he was shorter than other players

56. What does D.W. do that bothers Arthur?

  (a) She wishes to control him.
  (b) She disturbs his study time.
  (c) She watches TV too loudly.
  (d) She wakes up late at times.

57. How did Arthur achieve success as an author?

  (a) by writing about his younger days
  (b) by turning his stories into educational videos
  (c) by collaborating with a professional writer
  (d) by describing adventures with new friends

58. In the context of the passage, portrayed means _____.

  (a) imitated
  (b) interpreted
  (c) remembered
  (d) rendered

59. In the context of the passage, effort means _____.

  (a) desire
  (b) trial
  (c) contribution
  (d) endeavor

PEOPLE UNDER FINANCIAL STRESS REPORT LOWER PURCHASE HAPPINESS

A study published in the *Journal of Consumer Research* found that people's financial stress is related to "purchase happiness," which describes how satisfied a person is with a transaction.

Researchers from Duke University's Fuqua School of Business completed over 40 separate studies that evaluated people's understanding of their financial well-being and recent purchases. The results showed that people subject to financial constraints registered far lower levels of purchase happiness. This condition was evident regardless of whether a person bought an article of clothing, a piece of technology like a computer, or a vacation.

In addition, since the study measured how wealthy people believe themselves to be rather than their actual wealth, low purchase happiness was observed across different income levels. Perceptions of wealth were adversely impacted by growing price inflation throughout multiple economic sectors, including housing, energy, and consumer goods.

The researchers also revealed that low purchase happiness was closely correlated with notions surrounding opportunity cost. Opportunity cost represents the potential benefits that shoppers could have enjoyed if they had found other uses for their money. Due to financial pressure, people weighed opportunity costs more heavily, which caused them to harbor a greater sense of "buyer's remorse."

According to the study, feelings of dissatisfaction lead to a rise in negative customer reviews. The researchers examined online reviews for over 850 restaurants across the United States. Then, they took data collected from surveys and detected the zip codes in which residents experience financial stress. They found that restaurants in cities where people reported the highest financial stress tended to have a higher number of negative reviews. As these reviews accumulate, they pose risks for retailers who depend on positive reviews for sales, pushing them to find alternative approaches to receiving feedback.

Overall, the report strongly indicates that a perceived sense of low wealth, and not the actual level of prosperity, limits people's purchasing options and makes them less happy with their acquisitions. It supplements a growing body of research that is answering questions about the relationship between money and happiness. Future research will examine other factors, such as product quality and customer service, that influence purchase satisfaction.

60. When are people less satisfied with their consumption?

    (a) when the items are expensive
    (b) when they have insufficient funds
    (c) when companies sell inferior products
    (d) when they buy unnecessary merchandise

61. Why most likely were people across different income levels affected by the same condition?

    (a) They compared themselves to wealthier individuals.
    (b) They tracked their wealth using inaccurate indicators.
    (c) They based their status on a subjective measure.
    (d) They bought products that rose in price uniformly.

62. According to the article, when would consumers consider opportunity costs?

    (a) when they think they must maintain loyalty to one shop
    (b) when they feel pressured to conclude transactions
    (c) when they buy products that cost more than their actual worth
    (d) when they believe they could have made a better decision

63. What action will companies that value customer reviews take?

    (a) invest resources to improve the guest experience
    (b) adjust their methods to solicit customer comments
    (c) list client remarks on a larger number of review sites
    (d) relocate to more prosperous cities

64. What will upcoming analysis focus on?

    (a) additional drivers of consumer happiness
    (b) changing attitudes toward personal finances
    (c) the correlation of money with life satisfaction
    (d) the contribution of customer service to sales

65. In the context of the passage, completed means _____.

    (a) prepared
    (b) submitted
    (c) finished
    (d) monitored

66. In the context of the passage, accumulate means _____.

    (a) gather
    (b) unite
    (c) extend
    (d) develop

PART 3. Read the encyclopedia article below and answer the questions. The two underlined words are for vocabulary questions.

DUNG BEETLE

Dung beetles are insects that utilize the feces of animals for food and reproduction. They live in deserts, grasslands, and forests, and can be found almost everywhere on earth.

All dung beetles share a number of physical characteristics. Both males and females have large, horn-like structures on their heads or upper bodies as well as powerful front legs. The males use these to fight each other for mates, whereas the females employ them to keep others away from their dung. Dung beetles also have long flight wings that are protected by hardened outer wings called *elytra*. These increase lift and allow them to <u>travel</u> great distances when they detect manure with their antennae.

Depending on what dung beetles do with animal feces, they are classified into three groups: dwellers, tunnelers, and rollers. Dwellers lay their eggs on top of manure, with their larvae hatching and feeding there, while tunnelers burrow into the ground, taking pieces of the nearby excrement into the tunnels as needed. Rollers shape dung into a ball and push it to another location, where they use it as a food source and a place to breed. Rollers are known to use the band of light produced by clusters of stars as they transfer their perfectly round balls. By aligning themselves with it, they can proceed in a straight line and avoid getting lost.

Dung beetles play a <u>vital</u> role in the environment. They improve soil quality by digging tunnels and burying feces. They also inadvertently aid in the dispersal of seeds present in dung as they roam around. In agriculture, dung beetles are used by farmers to dispose of large amounts of livestock manure. Because these droppings are breeding grounds for pests, the beetles reduce pest populations that would otherwise harm farm animals.

Finally, dung beetles are regarded as organisms whose status in an environment is examined to determine the overall health of an ecosystem. They are widely used in ecological research monitoring the year-to-year changes to plant and animal life within nature.

67. What do male dung beetles use their horns for?

    (a) to protect their dung balls
    (b) to challenge others for partners
    (c) to dig long tunnels for mates
    (d) to detect fresh manure sources

68. Which of the following distinguishes the different types of dung beetles?

    (a) their methods of obtaining dung
    (b) their use of the dung they find
    (c) their means of transporting dung
    (d) their disposal of the dung they find

69. How do rollers navigate while moving a ball of dung?

    (a) by using their antennae to detect smells
    (b) by observing prominent landmarks
    (c) by rolling feces into a perfect sphere
    (d) by orienting themselves with starlight

70. When most likely do dung beetles help plants grow in other areas?

    (a) when they burrow underground to create home
    (b) when they disperse their own waste
    (c) when they transport feces to new locations
    (d) when they consume animal manure on farms

71. According to the article, what can researchers learn by studying dung beetles?

    (a) the condition of a natural environment
    (b) the causes of extreme natural disasters
    (c) the status of humans in an ecosystem
    (d) the impact of changes in livestock diets

72. In the context of the passage, travel means _____.

    (a) retain
    (b) convert
    (c) locate
    (d) move

73. In the context of the passage, vital means _____.

    (a) vibrant
    (b) unique
    (c) essential
    (d) best

해커스 지텔프 최신기출유형 실전문제집 7회 (Level 2)

Ronald Brewster
President
Brewster Construction

Dear Mr. Brewster:

I eagerly anticipate seeing you at our upcoming charity golf tournament, "Home in One." However, please be informed that the event will no longer be taking place at the Chandler Creek Golf Resort but at the Mesa Ranch Golf Course instead.

The management at Chandler Creek recently told us that they are closing earlier than planned to undertake important rehabilitation work. Meanwhile, Mesa Ranch has confirmed availability for the same date of Saturday, September 8.

As a result of this change, we have had to make other adjustments as well. First, the appreciation dinner for corporate sponsors is being moved inside. Since the outdoor veranda at Mesa Ranch is booked for a private event, we will use its main ballroom instead. Furthermore, the change of venue means that we will not be able to use hotel rooms. Therefore, we will be setting up a large, air-conditioned tent for VIP guests to relax in.

On a more positive note, catering and equipment rental costs are now significantly lower. For that reason, our executive committee is proposing that we add the excess funds to the event's charitable proceeds. They may be used alternatively to supplement cash prizes for the putting contest and raffle. We are looking forward to hearing your feedback on this matter. As you know, prizes have already been arranged for the winners of the golf tournaments. These include holiday packages, discount offers, and computing devices.

I hope that none of these changes causes you inconvenience. For other inquiries, you may contact our communications department at 602-657-6424. Thank you again for your support. This event will go a long way toward helping us realize the mission of "Home in One," which is to provide affordable housing for all.

Yours truly,

Wendy Simon
Communications director
Heart Homes, Inc.

74. Why did Wendy Simon write Ronald Brewster a letter?

(a) to request a different meeting time
(b) to ask for contributions for an event
(c) to mention a change of location
(d) to cancel an upcoming appointment

75. Why is Chandler Creek unavailable for the event?

(a) It will be going out of business shortly.
(b) It is starting repairs sooner than expected.
(c) It is undergoing an alteration to its management.
(d) It will host a social occasion on the same day.

76. Where will a meal for the benefactors take place?

(a) in a VIP lounge area
(b) in a hotel conference center
(c) in an indoor event room
(d) in an air-conditioned tent

77. What does Simon expect Brewster to do about the committee's proposal?

(a) contribute to the size of the donation
(b) review the list of contest prizes
(c) reconsider the catering options
(d) comment on the use of extra funds

78. What most likely is the goal of the fundraising event?

(a) helping individuals find inexpensive places to live
(b) thanking a developer for providing affordable housing
(c) marketing products to practitioners of golf
(d) raising money for the acquisition of a new property

79. In the context of the passage, confirmed means _____.

(a) selected
(b) verified
(c) explained
(d) proved

80. In the context of the passage, realize means _____.

(a) identify
(b) discover
(c) understand
(d) fulfill

THIS IS THE LAST PAGE OF THE TEST

정답 한눈에 보기 & OMR 답안지

정답 한눈에 보기

TEST 1

1	a	11	a	21	d	31	b	41	a	51	c	61	d	71	c
2	b	12	b	22	b	32	a	42	d	52	c	62	b	72	c
3	d	13	a	23	b	33	a	43	b	53	d	63	b	73	a
4	d	14	b	24	c	34	c	44	c	54	d	64	c	74	b
5	c	15	d	25	d	35	d	45	b	55	a	65	a	75	d
6	d	16	b	26	c	36	b	46	d	56	b	66	d	76	a
7	a	17	c	27	c	37	a	47	a	57	c	67	a	77	d
8	c	18	b	28	b	38	d	48	b	58	a	68	b	78	c
9	a	19	c	29	d	39	b	49	a	59	b	69	c	79	d
10	d	20	a	30	c	40	d	50	b	60	b	70	a	80	c

TEST 2

1	c	11	a	21	d	31	c	41	b	51	b	61	d	71	d
2	d	12	c	22	b	32	b	42	d	52	c	62	b	72	a
3	c	13	a	23	d	33	d	43	a	53	a	63	c	73	b
4	d	14	b	24	a	34	b	44	a	54	b	64	a	74	c
5	b	15	d	25	c	35	a	45	c	55	c	65	b	75	a
6	b	16	d	26	c	36	d	46	b	56	b	66	d	76	c
7	a	17	a	27	d	37	c	47	c	57	c	67	a	77	d
8	b	18	c	28	c	38	b	48	d	58	d	68	b	78	d
9	a	19	b	29	a	39	a	49	a	59	a	69	c	79	b
10	c	20	b	30	b	40	a	50	b	60	d	70	c	80	a

TEST 3

1	b	11	d	21	b	31	b	41	d	51	c	61	a	71	a
2	b	12	b	22	a	32	c	42	a	52	a	62	d	72	c
3	d	13	a	23	a	33	a	43	c	53	c	63	b	73	c
4	d	14	d	24	b	34	b	44	a	54	d	64	b	74	c
5	b	15	a	25	a	35	b	45	c	55	b	65	c	75	b
6	c	16	d	26	b	36	a	46	a	56	c	66	a	76	a
7	a	17	c	27	b	37	d	47	d	57	b	67	b	77	d
8	c	18	c	28	c	38	c	48	d	58	a	68	c	78	d
9	a	19	d	29	a	39	b	49	b	59	d	69	b	79	a
10	b	20	d	30	d	40	b	50	c	60	c	70	d	80	b

TEST 4

1	b	11	d	21	a	31	b	41	c	51	a	61	d	71	c
2	a	12	d	22	c	32	d	42	d	52	a	62	a	72	b
3	a	13	c	23	a	33	b	43	b	53	d	63	c	73	a
4	b	14	a	24	c	34	a	44	a	54	a	64	d	74	d
5	d	15	b	25	b	35	b	45	d	55	b	65	c	75	c
6	c	16	d	26	a	36	d	46	c	56	d	66	a	76	a
7	d	17	c	27	c	37	a	47	c	57	c	67	b	77	c
8	a	18	c	28	d	38	c	48	a	58	b	68	a	78	c
9	c	19	d	29	a	39	b	49	b	59	d	69	d	79	b
10	d	20	b	30	d	40	b	50	c	60	b	70	b	80	a

TEST 5

1	d	11	c	21	a	31	c	41	a	51	a	61	d	71	b
2	a	12	b	22	b	32	b	42	b	52	d	62	d	72	c
3	b	13	d	23	b	33	a	43	d	53	d	63	b	73	a
4	a	14	c	24	d	34	c	44	a	54	c	64	a	74	d
5	a	15	c	25	d	35	b	45	a	55	d	65	b	75	a
6	b	16	a	26	b	36	c	46	b	56	c	66	c	76	b
7	c	17	b	27	b	37	b	47	a	57	a	67	b	77	b
8	a	18	a	28	d	38	b	48	b	58	b	68	d	78	d
9	d	19	d	29	b	39	c	49	c	59	a	69	c	79	c
10	c	20	c	30	a	40	c	50	b	60	a	70	c	80	a

TEST 6

1	c	11	b	21	a	31	d	41	d	51	b	61	c	71	b
2	d	12	b	22	a	32	d	42	b	52	a	62	d	72	d
3	a	13	d	23	c	33	a	43	d	53	a	63	a	73	b
4	c	14	a	24	b	34	b	44	a	54	d	64	b	74	b
5	d	15	c	25	d	35	d	45	a	55	d	65	a	75	c
6	c	16	d	26	c	36	a	46	c	56	a	66	d	76	b
7	c	17	b	27	c	37	b	47	a	57	b	67	c	77	d
8	b	18	a	28	b	38	c	48	d	58	c	68	a	78	a
9	a	19	b	29	b	39	c	49	c	59	d	69	b	79	c
10	c	20	d	30	a	40	c	50	b	60	c	70	c	80	a

TEST 7

1	a	11	a	21	c	31	c	41	c	51	c	61	c	71	a
2	d	12	b	22	c	32	b	42	d	52	d	62	d	72	d
3	b	13	d	23	d	33	b	43	a	53	a	63	b	73	c
4	b	14	c	24	a	34	d	44	c	54	a	64	a	74	c
5	c	15	b	25	c	35	c	45	d	55	c	65	c	75	b
6	d	16	a	26	b	36	a	46	a	56	b	66	a	76	c
7	c	17	a	27	d	37	a	47	b	57	a	67	b	77	d
8	c	18	c	28	b	38	c	48	d	58	d	68	b	78	a
9	a	19	d	29	a	39	d	49	b	59	d	69	d	79	b
10	d	20	b	30	b	40	b	50	a	60	b	70	c	80	d

ANSWER SHEET

※ TEST DATE

MO.	DAY	YEAR

감독관인 확인

| 성 명 | | 등급 | ① ② ③ ④ ⑤ |

성 명 란

	초 성	ㄱ ㄴ ㄷ ㄹ ㅁ ㅂ ㅅ ㅇ ㅈ ㅊ ㅋ ㅌ ㅍ ㅎ
	중 성	ㅏ ㅑ ㅓ ㅕ ㅗ ㅛ ㅜ ㅠ ㅡ ㅣ ㅐ ㅒ ㅔ ㅖ ㅘ ㅙ ㅚ ㅝ ㅞ ㅟ ㅢ
	종 성	ㄱ ㄴ ㄷ ㄹ ㅁ ㅂ ㅅ ㅇ ㅈ ㅊ ㅋ ㅌ ㅍ ㅎ ㄲ ㄸ ㅃ ㅆ ㅉ

(초성/중성/종성 rows repeated)

수 험 번 호

(숫자 마킹란 0-9)

1) Code 1.
2) Code 2.
3) Code 3.

주민등록번호 앞자리 | 고 유 번 호

답 란

문항	답 란	문항	답 란	문항	답 란	문항	답 란	문항	답 란	문항	답 란
1	ⓐ ⓑ ⓒ ⓓ	21	ⓐ ⓑ ⓒ ⓓ	41	ⓐ ⓑ ⓒ ⓓ	61	ⓐ ⓑ ⓒ ⓓ	81	ⓐ ⓑ ⓒ ⓓ		
2	ⓐ ⓑ ⓒ ⓓ	22	ⓐ ⓑ ⓒ ⓓ	42	ⓐ ⓑ ⓒ ⓓ	62	ⓐ ⓑ ⓒ ⓓ	82	ⓐ ⓑ ⓒ ⓓ		
3	ⓐ ⓑ ⓒ ⓓ	23	ⓐ ⓑ ⓒ ⓓ	43	ⓐ ⓑ ⓒ ⓓ	63	ⓐ ⓑ ⓒ ⓓ	83	ⓐ ⓑ ⓒ ⓓ		
4	ⓐ ⓑ ⓒ ⓓ	24	ⓐ ⓑ ⓒ ⓓ	44	ⓐ ⓑ ⓒ ⓓ	64	ⓐ ⓑ ⓒ ⓓ	84	ⓐ ⓑ ⓒ ⓓ		
5	ⓐ ⓑ ⓒ ⓓ	25	ⓐ ⓑ ⓒ ⓓ	45	ⓐ ⓑ ⓒ ⓓ	65	ⓐ ⓑ ⓒ ⓓ	85	ⓐ ⓑ ⓒ ⓓ		
6	ⓐ ⓑ ⓒ ⓓ	26	ⓐ ⓑ ⓒ ⓓ	46	ⓐ ⓑ ⓒ ⓓ	66	ⓐ ⓑ ⓒ ⓓ	86	ⓐ ⓑ ⓒ ⓓ		
7	ⓐ ⓑ ⓒ ⓓ	27	ⓐ ⓑ ⓒ ⓓ	47	ⓐ ⓑ ⓒ ⓓ	67	ⓐ ⓑ ⓒ ⓓ	87	ⓐ ⓑ ⓒ ⓓ		
8	ⓐ ⓑ ⓒ ⓓ	28	ⓐ ⓑ ⓒ ⓓ	48	ⓐ ⓑ ⓒ ⓓ	68	ⓐ ⓑ ⓒ ⓓ	88	ⓐ ⓑ ⓒ ⓓ		
9	ⓐ ⓑ ⓒ ⓓ	29	ⓐ ⓑ ⓒ ⓓ	49	ⓐ ⓑ ⓒ ⓓ	69	ⓐ ⓑ ⓒ ⓓ	89	ⓐ ⓑ ⓒ ⓓ		
10	ⓐ ⓑ ⓒ ⓓ	30	ⓐ ⓑ ⓒ ⓓ	50	ⓐ ⓑ ⓒ ⓓ	70	ⓐ ⓑ ⓒ ⓓ	90	ⓐ ⓑ ⓒ ⓓ		
11	ⓐ ⓑ ⓒ ⓓ	31	ⓐ ⓑ ⓒ ⓓ	51	ⓐ ⓑ ⓒ ⓓ	71	ⓐ ⓑ ⓒ ⓓ				
12	ⓐ ⓑ ⓒ ⓓ	32	ⓐ ⓑ ⓒ ⓓ	52	ⓐ ⓑ ⓒ ⓓ	72	ⓐ ⓑ ⓒ ⓓ				
13	ⓐ ⓑ ⓒ ⓓ	33	ⓐ ⓑ ⓒ ⓓ	53	ⓐ ⓑ ⓒ ⓓ	73	ⓐ ⓑ ⓒ ⓓ	password			
14	ⓐ ⓑ ⓒ ⓓ	34	ⓐ ⓑ ⓒ ⓓ	54	ⓐ ⓑ ⓒ ⓓ	74	ⓐ ⓑ ⓒ ⓓ				
15	ⓐ ⓑ ⓒ ⓓ	35	ⓐ ⓑ ⓒ ⓓ	55	ⓐ ⓑ ⓒ ⓓ	75	ⓐ ⓑ ⓒ ⓓ				
16	ⓐ ⓑ ⓒ ⓓ	36	ⓐ ⓑ ⓒ ⓓ	56	ⓐ ⓑ ⓒ ⓓ	76	ⓐ ⓑ ⓒ ⓓ				
17	ⓐ ⓑ ⓒ ⓓ	37	ⓐ ⓑ ⓒ ⓓ	57	ⓐ ⓑ ⓒ ⓓ	77	ⓐ ⓑ ⓒ ⓓ				
18	ⓐ ⓑ ⓒ ⓓ	38	ⓐ ⓑ ⓒ ⓓ	58	ⓐ ⓑ ⓒ ⓓ	78	ⓐ ⓑ ⓒ ⓓ				
19	ⓐ ⓑ ⓒ ⓓ	39	ⓐ ⓑ ⓒ ⓓ	59	ⓐ ⓑ ⓒ ⓓ	79	ⓐ ⓑ ⓒ ⓓ				
20	ⓐ ⓑ ⓒ ⓓ	40	ⓐ ⓑ ⓒ ⓓ	60	ⓐ ⓑ ⓒ ⓓ	80	ⓐ ⓑ ⓒ ⓓ				

ANSWER SHEET

※ TEST DATE

MO.	DAY	YEAR

감독관 확인

| 성 명 | | 등급 | ① ② ③ ④ ⑤ |

성 명 란

초 성 ㉠ ㉡ ㉢ ㉣ ㉤ ㉥ ㉦ ㉧ ㉨ ㉩ ㉪ ㉫ ㉬ ㉭
중 성 ㅏ ㅑ ㅓ ㅕ ㅗ ㅛ ㅜ ㅠ ㅡ ㅣ ㅐ ㅒ ㅔ ㅖ ㅚ ㅟ ㅢ
종 성 ㄱ ㄴ ㄷ ㄹ ㅁ ㅂ ㅅ ㅇ ㅈ ㅊ ㅋ ㅌ ㅍ ㅎ ㄲ ㄸ ㅃ ㅆ ㅉ

(초성/중성/종성 rows repeated four times)

수 험 번 호

0	0		0	0	0	0		0	0	0	0	0	0	0
1	1		1	1	1	1		1	1	1	1	1	1	1
2	2		2	2	2	2		2	2	2	2	2	2	2
3	3		3	3	3	3		3	3	3	3	3	3	3
4	4		4	4	4	4		4	4	4	4	4	4	4
5	5		5	5	5	5		5	5	5	5	5	5	5
6	6		6	6	6	6		6	6	6	6	6	6	6
7	7		7	7	7	7		7	7	7	7	7	7	7
8	8		8	8	8	8		8	8	8	8	8	8	8
9	9		9	9	9	9		9	9	9	9	9	9	9

1) Code 1.

0 1 2 3 4 5 6 7 8 9
0 1 2 3 4 5 6 7 8 9
0 1 2 3 4 5 6 7 8 9

2) Code 2.

0 1 2 3 4 5 6 7 8 9
0 1 2 3 4 5 6 7 8 9
0 1 2 3 4 5 6 7 8 9

3) Code 3.

0 1 2 3 4 5 6 7 8 9
0 1 2 3 4 5 6 7 8 9
0 1 2 3 4 5 6 7 8 9

| 주민등록번호 앞자리 | 고 유 번 호 |

0	0	0	0	0	0		0	0	0	0	0	0	0
1	1	1	1	1	1		1	1	1	1	1	1	1
2	2	2	2	2	2		2	2	2	2	2	2	2
3	3	3	3	3	3		3	3	3	3	3	3	3
4	4	4	4	4	4		4	4	4	4	4	4	4
5	5	5	5	5	5		5	5	5	5	5	5	5
6	6	6	6	6	6		6	6	6	6	6	6	6
7	7	7	7	7	7		7	7	7	7	7	7	7
8	8	8	8	8	8		8	8	8	8	8	8	8
9	9	9	9	9	9		9	9	9	9	9	9	9

답 란

문항	답 란	문항	답 란	문항	답 란	문항	답 란	문항	답 란	문항	답 란
1	ⓐ ⓑ ⓒ ⓓ	21	ⓐ ⓑ ⓒ ⓓ	41	ⓐ ⓑ ⓒ ⓓ	61	ⓐ ⓑ ⓒ ⓓ	81	ⓐ ⓑ ⓒ ⓓ
2	ⓐ ⓑ ⓒ ⓓ	22	ⓐ ⓑ ⓒ ⓓ	42	ⓐ ⓑ ⓒ ⓓ	62	ⓐ ⓑ ⓒ ⓓ	82	ⓐ ⓑ ⓒ ⓓ
3	ⓐ ⓑ ⓒ ⓓ	23	ⓐ ⓑ ⓒ ⓓ	43	ⓐ ⓑ ⓒ ⓓ	63	ⓐ ⓑ ⓒ ⓓ	83	ⓐ ⓑ ⓒ ⓓ
4	ⓐ ⓑ ⓒ ⓓ	24	ⓐ ⓑ ⓒ ⓓ	44	ⓐ ⓑ ⓒ ⓓ	64	ⓐ ⓑ ⓒ ⓓ	84	ⓐ ⓑ ⓒ ⓓ
5	ⓐ ⓑ ⓒ ⓓ	25	ⓐ ⓑ ⓒ ⓓ	45	ⓐ ⓑ ⓒ ⓓ	65	ⓐ ⓑ ⓒ ⓓ	85	ⓐ ⓑ ⓒ ⓓ
6	ⓐ ⓑ ⓒ ⓓ	26	ⓐ ⓑ ⓒ ⓓ	46	ⓐ ⓑ ⓒ ⓓ	66	ⓐ ⓑ ⓒ ⓓ	86	ⓐ ⓑ ⓒ ⓓ
7	ⓐ ⓑ ⓒ ⓓ	27	ⓐ ⓑ ⓒ ⓓ	47	ⓐ ⓑ ⓒ ⓓ	67	ⓐ ⓑ ⓒ ⓓ	87	ⓐ ⓑ ⓒ ⓓ
8	ⓐ ⓑ ⓒ ⓓ	28	ⓐ ⓑ ⓒ ⓓ	48	ⓐ ⓑ ⓒ ⓓ	68	ⓐ ⓑ ⓒ ⓓ	88	ⓐ ⓑ ⓒ ⓓ
9	ⓐ ⓑ ⓒ ⓓ	29	ⓐ ⓑ ⓒ ⓓ	49	ⓐ ⓑ ⓒ ⓓ	69	ⓐ ⓑ ⓒ ⓓ	89	ⓐ ⓑ ⓒ ⓓ
10	ⓐ ⓑ ⓒ ⓓ	30	ⓐ ⓑ ⓒ ⓓ	50	ⓐ ⓑ ⓒ ⓓ	70	ⓐ ⓑ ⓒ ⓓ	90	ⓐ ⓑ ⓒ ⓓ
11	ⓐ ⓑ ⓒ ⓓ	31	ⓐ ⓑ ⓒ ⓓ	51	ⓐ ⓑ ⓒ ⓓ	71	ⓐ ⓑ ⓒ ⓓ		
12	ⓐ ⓑ ⓒ ⓓ	32	ⓐ ⓑ ⓒ ⓓ	52	ⓐ ⓑ ⓒ ⓓ	72	ⓐ ⓑ ⓒ ⓓ		
13	ⓐ ⓑ ⓒ ⓓ	33	ⓐ ⓑ ⓒ ⓓ	53	ⓐ ⓑ ⓒ ⓓ	73	ⓐ ⓑ ⓒ ⓓ		
14	ⓐ ⓑ ⓒ ⓓ	34	ⓐ ⓑ ⓒ ⓓ	54	ⓐ ⓑ ⓒ ⓓ	74	ⓐ ⓑ ⓒ ⓓ		
15	ⓐ ⓑ ⓒ ⓓ	35	ⓐ ⓑ ⓒ ⓓ	55	ⓐ ⓑ ⓒ ⓓ	75	ⓐ ⓑ ⓒ ⓓ		
16	ⓐ ⓑ ⓒ ⓓ	36	ⓐ ⓑ ⓒ ⓓ	56	ⓐ ⓑ ⓒ ⓓ	76	ⓐ ⓑ ⓒ ⓓ		
17	ⓐ ⓑ ⓒ ⓓ	37	ⓐ ⓑ ⓒ ⓓ	57	ⓐ ⓑ ⓒ ⓓ	77	ⓐ ⓑ ⓒ ⓓ		
18	ⓐ ⓑ ⓒ ⓓ	38	ⓐ ⓑ ⓒ ⓓ	58	ⓐ ⓑ ⓒ ⓓ	78	ⓐ ⓑ ⓒ ⓓ		
19	ⓐ ⓑ ⓒ ⓓ	39	ⓐ ⓑ ⓒ ⓓ	59	ⓐ ⓑ ⓒ ⓓ	79	ⓐ ⓑ ⓒ ⓓ		
20	ⓐ ⓑ ⓒ ⓓ	40	ⓐ ⓑ ⓒ ⓓ	60	ⓐ ⓑ ⓒ ⓓ	80	ⓐ ⓑ ⓒ ⓓ		

password

0	0	0	0
1	1	1	1
2	2	2	2
3	3	3	3
4	4	4	4
5	5	5	5
6	6	6	6
7	7	7	7
8	8	8	8
9	9	9	9

절취선

ANSWER SHEET

문항	답 란	문항	답 란	문항	답 란	문항	답 란	문항	답 란	문항	답 란
1	ⓐⓑⓒⓓ	21	ⓐⓑⓒⓓ	41	ⓐⓑⓒⓓ	61	ⓐⓑⓒⓓ	81	ⓐⓑⓒⓓ		
2	ⓐⓑⓒⓓ	22	ⓐⓑⓒⓓ	42	ⓐⓑⓒⓓ	62	ⓐⓑⓒⓓ	82	ⓐⓑⓒⓓ		
3	ⓐⓑⓒⓓ	23	ⓐⓑⓒⓓ	43	ⓐⓑⓒⓓ	63	ⓐⓑⓒⓓ	83	ⓐⓑⓒⓓ		
4	ⓐⓑⓒⓓ	24	ⓐⓑⓒⓓ	44	ⓐⓑⓒⓓ	64	ⓐⓑⓒⓓ	84	ⓐⓑⓒⓓ		
5	ⓐⓑⓒⓓ	25	ⓐⓑⓒⓓ	45	ⓐⓑⓒⓓ	65	ⓐⓑⓒⓓ	85	ⓐⓑⓒⓓ		
6	ⓐⓑⓒⓓ	26	ⓐⓑⓒⓓ	46	ⓐⓑⓒⓓ	66	ⓐⓑⓒⓓ	86	ⓐⓑⓒⓓ		
7	ⓐⓑⓒⓓ	27	ⓐⓑⓒⓓ	47	ⓐⓑⓒⓓ	67	ⓐⓑⓒⓓ	87	ⓐⓑⓒⓓ		
8	ⓐⓑⓒⓓ	28	ⓐⓑⓒⓓ	48	ⓐⓑⓒⓓ	68	ⓐⓑⓒⓓ	88	ⓐⓑⓒⓓ		
9	ⓐⓑⓒⓓ	29	ⓐⓑⓒⓓ	49	ⓐⓑⓒⓓ	69	ⓐⓑⓒⓓ	89	ⓐⓑⓒⓓ		
10	ⓐⓑⓒⓓ	30	ⓐⓑⓒⓓ	50	ⓐⓑⓒⓓ	70	ⓐⓑⓒⓓ	90	ⓐⓑⓒⓓ		
11	ⓐⓑⓒⓓ	31	ⓐⓑⓒⓓ	51	ⓐⓑⓒⓓ	71	ⓐⓑⓒⓓ				
12	ⓐⓑⓒⓓ	32	ⓐⓑⓒⓓ	52	ⓐⓑⓒⓓ	72	ⓐⓑⓒⓓ				
13	ⓐⓑⓒⓓ	33	ⓐⓑⓒⓓ	53	ⓐⓑⓒⓓ	73	ⓐⓑⓒⓓ				
14	ⓐⓑⓒⓓ	34	ⓐⓑⓒⓓ	54	ⓐⓑⓒⓓ	74	ⓐⓑⓒⓓ				
15	ⓐⓑⓒⓓ	35	ⓐⓑⓒⓓ	55	ⓐⓑⓒⓓ	75	ⓐⓑⓒⓓ				
16	ⓐⓑⓒⓓ	36	ⓐⓑⓒⓓ	56	ⓐⓑⓒⓓ	76	ⓐⓑⓒⓓ				
17	ⓐⓑⓒⓓ	37	ⓐⓑⓒⓓ	57	ⓐⓑⓒⓓ	77	ⓐⓑⓒⓓ				
18	ⓐⓑⓒⓓ	38	ⓐⓑⓒⓓ	58	ⓐⓑⓒⓓ	78	ⓐⓑⓒⓓ				
19	ⓐⓑⓒⓓ	39	ⓐⓑⓒⓓ	59	ⓐⓑⓒⓓ	79	ⓐⓑⓒⓓ				
20	ⓐⓑⓒⓓ	40	ⓐⓑⓒⓓ	60	ⓐⓑⓒⓓ	80	ⓐⓑⓒⓓ				

ANSWER SHEET

※ TEST DATE

MO.	DAY	YEAR

감독관인

성 명		

등급　① ② ③ ④ ⑤

성명란		초 성	ㄱ ㄴ ㄷ ㄹ ㅁ ㅂ ㅅ ㅇ ㅈ ㅊ ㅋ ㅌ ㅍ ㅎ
	성	중 성	ㅏ ㅑ ㅓ ㅕ ㅗ ㅛ ㅜ ㅠ ㅡ ㅣ ㅐ ㅒ ㅔ ㅖ ㅚ ㅟ ㅢ ㅝ
		종 성	ㄱ ㄴ ㄷ ㄹ ㅁ ㅂ ㅅ ㅇ ㅈ ㅊ ㅋ ㅌ ㅍ ㅎ ㄲ ㄸ ㅃ ㅆ ㅉ
	명	초 성	ㄱ ㄴ ㄷ ㄹ ㅁ ㅂ ㅅ ㅇ ㅈ ㅊ ㅋ ㅌ ㅍ ㅎ
		중 성	ㅏ ㅑ ㅓ ㅕ ㅗ ㅛ ㅜ ㅠ ㅡ ㅣ ㅐ ㅒ ㅔ ㅖ ㅚ ㅟ ㅢ ㅝ
		종 성	ㄱ ㄴ ㄷ ㄹ ㅁ ㅂ ㅅ ㅇ ㅈ ㅊ ㅋ ㅌ ㅍ ㅎ ㄲ ㄸ ㅃ ㅆ ㅉ
	란	초 성	ㄱ ㄴ ㄷ ㄹ ㅁ ㅂ ㅅ ㅇ ㅈ ㅊ ㅋ ㅌ ㅍ ㅎ
		중 성	ㅏ ㅑ ㅓ ㅕ ㅗ ㅛ ㅜ ㅠ ㅡ ㅣ ㅐ ㅒ ㅔ ㅖ ㅚ ㅟ ㅢ ㅝ
		종 성	ㄱ ㄴ ㄷ ㄹ ㅁ ㅂ ㅅ ㅇ ㅈ ㅊ ㅋ ㅌ ㅍ ㅎ ㄲ ㄸ ㅃ ㅆ ㅉ
		초 성	ㄱ ㄴ ㄷ ㄹ ㅁ ㅂ ㅅ ㅇ ㅈ ㅊ ㅋ ㅌ ㅍ ㅎ
		중 성	ㅏ ㅑ ㅓ ㅕ ㅗ ㅛ ㅜ ㅠ ㅡ ㅣ ㅐ ㅒ ㅔ ㅖ ㅚ ㅟ ㅢ ㅝ
		종 성	ㄱ ㄴ ㄷ ㄹ ㅁ ㅂ ㅅ ㅇ ㅈ ㅊ ㅋ ㅌ ㅍ ㅎ ㄲ ㄸ ㅃ ㅆ ㅉ

수 험 번 호

(digits 0–9 grids)

1) Code 1.
⓪①②③④⑤⑥⑦⑧⑨
⓪①②③④⑤⑥⑦⑧⑨
⓪①②③④⑤⑥⑦⑧⑨

2) Code 2.
⓪①②③④⑤⑥⑦⑧⑨
⓪①②③④⑤⑥⑦⑧⑨
⓪①②③④⑤⑥⑦⑧⑨

3) Code 3.
⓪①②③④⑤⑥⑦⑧⑨
⓪①②③④⑤⑥⑦⑧⑨
⓪①②③④⑤⑥⑦⑧⑨

주민등록번호 앞자리　고 유 번 호

(digits 0–9 grids)

답 란

문항	답 란	문항	답 란	문항	답 란	문항	답 란	문항	답 란	문항	답 란
1	ⓐⓑⓒⓓ	21	ⓐⓑⓒⓓ	41	ⓐⓑⓒⓓ	61	ⓐⓑⓒⓓ	81	ⓐⓑⓒⓓ		
2	ⓐⓑⓒⓓ	22	ⓐⓑⓒⓓ	42	ⓐⓑⓒⓓ	62	ⓐⓑⓒⓓ	82	ⓐⓑⓒⓓ		
3	ⓐⓑⓒⓓ	23	ⓐⓑⓒⓓ	43	ⓐⓑⓒⓓ	63	ⓐⓑⓒⓓ	83	ⓐⓑⓒⓓ		
4	ⓐⓑⓒⓓ	24	ⓐⓑⓒⓓ	44	ⓐⓑⓒⓓ	64	ⓐⓑⓒⓓ	84	ⓐⓑⓒⓓ		
5	ⓐⓑⓒⓓ	25	ⓐⓑⓒⓓ	45	ⓐⓑⓒⓓ	65	ⓐⓑⓒⓓ	85	ⓐⓑⓒⓓ		
6	ⓐⓑⓒⓓ	26	ⓐⓑⓒⓓ	46	ⓐⓑⓒⓓ	66	ⓐⓑⓒⓓ	86	ⓐⓑⓒⓓ		
7	ⓐⓑⓒⓓ	27	ⓐⓑⓒⓓ	47	ⓐⓑⓒⓓ	67	ⓐⓑⓒⓓ	87	ⓐⓑⓒⓓ		
8	ⓐⓑⓒⓓ	28	ⓐⓑⓒⓓ	48	ⓐⓑⓒⓓ	68	ⓐⓑⓒⓓ	88	ⓐⓑⓒⓓ		
9	ⓐⓑⓒⓓ	29	ⓐⓑⓒⓓ	49	ⓐⓑⓒⓓ	69	ⓐⓑⓒⓓ	89	ⓐⓑⓒⓓ		
10	ⓐⓑⓒⓓ	30	ⓐⓑⓒⓓ	50	ⓐⓑⓒⓓ	70	ⓐⓑⓒⓓ	90	ⓐⓑⓒⓓ		
11	ⓐⓑⓒⓓ	31	ⓐⓑⓒⓓ	51	ⓐⓑⓒⓓ	71	ⓐⓑⓒⓓ				
12	ⓐⓑⓒⓓ	32	ⓐⓑⓒⓓ	52	ⓐⓑⓒⓓ	72	ⓐⓑⓒⓓ				
13	ⓐⓑⓒⓓ	33	ⓐⓑⓒⓓ	53	ⓐⓑⓒⓓ	73	ⓐⓑⓒⓓ				
14	ⓐⓑⓒⓓ	34	ⓐⓑⓒⓓ	54	ⓐⓑⓒⓓ	74	ⓐⓑⓒⓓ				
15	ⓐⓑⓒⓓ	35	ⓐⓑⓒⓓ	55	ⓐⓑⓒⓓ	75	ⓐⓑⓒⓓ				
16	ⓐⓑⓒⓓ	36	ⓐⓑⓒⓓ	56	ⓐⓑⓒⓓ	76	ⓐⓑⓒⓓ				
17	ⓐⓑⓒⓓ	37	ⓐⓑⓒⓓ	57	ⓐⓑⓒⓓ	77	ⓐⓑⓒⓓ				
18	ⓐⓑⓒⓓ	38	ⓐⓑⓒⓓ	58	ⓐⓑⓒⓓ	78	ⓐⓑⓒⓓ				
19	ⓐⓑⓒⓓ	39	ⓐⓑⓒⓓ	59	ⓐⓑⓒⓓ	79	ⓐⓑⓒⓓ				
20	ⓐⓑⓒⓓ	40	ⓐⓑⓒⓓ	60	ⓐⓑⓒⓓ	80	ⓐⓑⓒⓓ				

password
(digits 0–9 grid)

절취선

ANSWER SHEET

※ TEST DATE

MO.	DAY	YEAR

감독	확인
관인	

성 명	

등급 ① ② ③ ④ ⑤

성 명 란	초 성	ㄱ ㄴ ㄷ ㄹ ㅁ ㅂ ㅅ ㅇ ㅈ ㅊ ㅋ ㅌ ㅍ ㅎ
	중 성	ㅏ ㅐ ㅑ ㅒ ㅓ ㅔ ㅕ ㅖ ㅗ ㅘ ㅙ ㅚ ㅛ ㅜ ㅝ ㅞ ㅟ ㅠ ㅡ ㅢ ㅣ
	종 성	ㄱ ㄴ ㄷ ㄹ ㅁ ㅂ ㅅ ㅇ ㅈ ㅊ ㅋ ㅌ ㅍ ㅎ ㄲ ㄳ ㄵ ㄶ ㄺ ㄻ ㄼ ㅄ ㅆ ㅉ

수 험 번 호

문항	답 란	문항	답 란	문항	답 란	문항	답 란	문항	답 란	문항	답 란
1	ⓐ ⓑ ⓒ ⓓ	21	ⓐ ⓑ ⓒ ⓓ	41	ⓐ ⓑ ⓒ ⓓ	61	ⓐ ⓑ ⓒ ⓓ	81	ⓐ ⓑ ⓒ ⓓ
2	ⓐ ⓑ ⓒ ⓓ	22	ⓐ ⓑ ⓒ ⓓ	42	ⓐ ⓑ ⓒ ⓓ	62	ⓐ ⓑ ⓒ ⓓ	82	ⓐ ⓑ ⓒ ⓓ
3	ⓐ ⓑ ⓒ ⓓ	23	ⓐ ⓑ ⓒ ⓓ	43	ⓐ ⓑ ⓒ ⓓ	63	ⓐ ⓑ ⓒ ⓓ	83	ⓐ ⓑ ⓒ ⓓ
4	ⓐ ⓑ ⓒ ⓓ	24	ⓐ ⓑ ⓒ ⓓ	44	ⓐ ⓑ ⓒ ⓓ	64	ⓐ ⓑ ⓒ ⓓ	84	ⓐ ⓑ ⓒ ⓓ
5	ⓐ ⓑ ⓒ ⓓ	25	ⓐ ⓑ ⓒ ⓓ	45	ⓐ ⓑ ⓒ ⓓ	65	ⓐ ⓑ ⓒ ⓓ	85	ⓐ ⓑ ⓒ ⓓ
6	ⓐ ⓑ ⓒ ⓓ	26	ⓐ ⓑ ⓒ ⓓ	46	ⓐ ⓑ ⓒ ⓓ	66	ⓐ ⓑ ⓒ ⓓ	86	ⓐ ⓑ ⓒ ⓓ
7	ⓐ ⓑ ⓒ ⓓ	27	ⓐ ⓑ ⓒ ⓓ	47	ⓐ ⓑ ⓒ ⓓ	67	ⓐ ⓑ ⓒ ⓓ	87	ⓐ ⓑ ⓒ ⓓ
8	ⓐ ⓑ ⓒ ⓓ	28	ⓐ ⓑ ⓒ ⓓ	48	ⓐ ⓑ ⓒ ⓓ	68	ⓐ ⓑ ⓒ ⓓ	88	ⓐ ⓑ ⓒ ⓓ
9	ⓐ ⓑ ⓒ ⓓ	29	ⓐ ⓑ ⓒ ⓓ	49	ⓐ ⓑ ⓒ ⓓ	69	ⓐ ⓑ ⓒ ⓓ	89	ⓐ ⓑ ⓒ ⓓ
10	ⓐ ⓑ ⓒ ⓓ	30	ⓐ ⓑ ⓒ ⓓ	50	ⓐ ⓑ ⓒ ⓓ	70	ⓐ ⓑ ⓒ ⓓ	90	ⓐ ⓑ ⓒ ⓓ
11	ⓐ ⓑ ⓒ ⓓ	31	ⓐ ⓑ ⓒ ⓓ	51	ⓐ ⓑ ⓒ ⓓ	71	ⓐ ⓑ ⓒ ⓓ		
12	ⓐ ⓑ ⓒ ⓓ	32	ⓐ ⓑ ⓒ ⓓ	52	ⓐ ⓑ ⓒ ⓓ	72	ⓐ ⓑ ⓒ ⓓ		
13	ⓐ ⓑ ⓒ ⓓ	33	ⓐ ⓑ ⓒ ⓓ	53	ⓐ ⓑ ⓒ ⓓ	73	ⓐ ⓑ ⓒ ⓓ		
14	ⓐ ⓑ ⓒ ⓓ	34	ⓐ ⓑ ⓒ ⓓ	54	ⓐ ⓑ ⓒ ⓓ	74	ⓐ ⓑ ⓒ ⓓ		
15	ⓐ ⓑ ⓒ ⓓ	35	ⓐ ⓑ ⓒ ⓓ	55	ⓐ ⓑ ⓒ ⓓ	75	ⓐ ⓑ ⓒ ⓓ		
16	ⓐ ⓑ ⓒ ⓓ	36	ⓐ ⓑ ⓒ ⓓ	56	ⓐ ⓑ ⓒ ⓓ	76	ⓐ ⓑ ⓒ ⓓ		
17	ⓐ ⓑ ⓒ ⓓ	37	ⓐ ⓑ ⓒ ⓓ	57	ⓐ ⓑ ⓒ ⓓ	77	ⓐ ⓑ ⓒ ⓓ		
18	ⓐ ⓑ ⓒ ⓓ	38	ⓐ ⓑ ⓒ ⓓ	58	ⓐ ⓑ ⓒ ⓓ	78	ⓐ ⓑ ⓒ ⓓ		
19	ⓐ ⓑ ⓒ ⓓ	39	ⓐ ⓑ ⓒ ⓓ	59	ⓐ ⓑ ⓒ ⓓ	79	ⓐ ⓑ ⓒ ⓓ		
20	ⓐ ⓑ ⓒ ⓓ	40	ⓐ ⓑ ⓒ ⓓ	60	ⓐ ⓑ ⓒ ⓓ	80	ⓐ ⓑ ⓒ ⓓ		

1) Code 1.

⓪ ① ② ③ ④ ⑤ ⑥ ⑦ ⑧ ⑨
⓪ ① ② ③ ④ ⑤ ⑥ ⑦ ⑧ ⑨
⓪ ① ② ③ ④ ⑤ ⑥ ⑦ ⑧ ⑨

2) Code 2.

⓪ ① ② ③ ④ ⑤ ⑥ ⑦ ⑧ ⑨
⓪ ① ② ③ ④ ⑤ ⑥ ⑦ ⑧ ⑨
⓪ ① ② ③ ④ ⑤ ⑥ ⑦ ⑧ ⑨

3) Code 3.

⓪ ① ② ③ ④ ⑤ ⑥ ⑦ ⑧ ⑨
⓪ ① ② ③ ④ ⑤ ⑥ ⑦ ⑧ ⑨
⓪ ① ② ③ ④ ⑤ ⑥ ⑦ ⑧ ⑨

password

주민등록번호 앞자리	고 유 번 호

절취선

ANSWER SHEET

※ TEST DATE

MO.	DAY	YEAR

등급　① ② ③ ④ ⑤

감독확인
관인

성　명		

성명란

초성 ㄱ ㄴ ㄷ ㄹ ㅁ ㅂ ㅅ ㅇ ㅈ ㅊ ㅋ ㅌ ㅍ ㅎ
중성 ㅏ ㅑ ㅓ ㅕ ㅗ ㅛ ㅜ ㅠ ㅡ ㅣ ㅐ ㅒ ㅔ ㅖ ㅘ ㅝ ㅚ ㅟ ㅢ ㅙ
종성 ㄱ ㄴ ㄷ ㄹ ㅁ ㅂ ㅅ ㅇ ㅈ ㅊ ㅋ ㅌ ㅍ ㅎ ㄲ ㄸ ㅃ ㅆ ㅉ

(성명 입력 초성·중성·종성 블록 4회 반복)

수 험 번 호

| | | | — | | | — | | | | | | | |

0 0 0 0 0 0 0 0 0 0 0 0 0 0
1 1 1 1 1 1 1 1 1 1 1 1 1 1
2 2 2 2 2 2 2 2 2 2 2 2 2 2
3 3 3 3 3 3 3 3 3 3 3 3 3 3
4 4 4 4 4 4 4 4 4 4 4 4 4 4
5 5 5 5 5 5 5 5 5 5 5 5 5 5
6 6 6 6 6 6 6 6 6 6 6 6 6 6
7 7 7 7 7 7 7 7 7 7 7 7 7 7
8 8 8 8 8 8 8 8 8 8 8 8 8 8
9 9 9 9 9 9 9 9 9 9 9 9 9 9

1) Code 1.

0 1 2 3 4 5 6 7 8 9
0 1 2 3 4 5 6 7 8 9
0 1 2 3 4 5 6 7 8 9

2) Code 2.

0 1 2 3 4 5 6 7 8 9
0 1 2 3 4 5 6 7 8 9
0 1 2 3 4 5 6 7 8 9

3) Code 3.

0 1 2 3 4 5 6 7 8 9
0 1 2 3 4 5 6 7 8 9
0 1 2 3 4 5 6 7 8 9

주민등록번호앞자리 ／ 고 유 번 호

0 0 0 0 0 0　0 0 0 0 0 0 0
1 1 1 1 1 1　1 1 1 1 1 1 1
2 2 2 2 2 2　2 2 2 2 2 2 2
3 3 3 3 3 3　3 3 3 3 3 3 3
4 4 4 4 4 4　4 4 4 4 4 4 4
5 5 5 5 5 5　5 5 5 5 5 5 5
6 6 6 6 6 6　6 6 6 6 6 6 6
7 7 7 7 7 7　7 7 7 7 7 7 7
8 8 8 8 8 8　8 8 8 8 8 8 8
9 9 9 9 9 9　9 9 9 9 9 9 9

답란

문항	답 란	문항	답 란	문항	답 란	문항	답 란	문항	답 란
1	ⓐ ⓑ ⓒ ⓓ	21	ⓐ ⓑ ⓒ ⓓ	41	ⓐ ⓑ ⓒ ⓓ	61	ⓐ ⓑ ⓒ ⓓ	81	ⓐ ⓑ ⓒ ⓓ
2	ⓐ ⓑ ⓒ ⓓ	22	ⓐ ⓑ ⓒ ⓓ	42	ⓐ ⓑ ⓒ ⓓ	62	ⓐ ⓑ ⓒ ⓓ	82	ⓐ ⓑ ⓒ ⓓ
3	ⓐ ⓑ ⓒ ⓓ	23	ⓐ ⓑ ⓒ ⓓ	43	ⓐ ⓑ ⓒ ⓓ	63	ⓐ ⓑ ⓒ ⓓ	83	ⓐ ⓑ ⓒ ⓓ
4	ⓐ ⓑ ⓒ ⓓ	24	ⓐ ⓑ ⓒ ⓓ	44	ⓐ ⓑ ⓒ ⓓ	64	ⓐ ⓑ ⓒ ⓓ	84	ⓐ ⓑ ⓒ ⓓ
5	ⓐ ⓑ ⓒ ⓓ	25	ⓐ ⓑ ⓒ ⓓ	45	ⓐ ⓑ ⓒ ⓓ	65	ⓐ ⓑ ⓒ ⓓ	85	ⓐ ⓑ ⓒ ⓓ
6	ⓐ ⓑ ⓒ ⓓ	26	ⓐ ⓑ ⓒ ⓓ	46	ⓐ ⓑ ⓒ ⓓ	66	ⓐ ⓑ ⓒ ⓓ	86	ⓐ ⓑ ⓒ ⓓ
7	ⓐ ⓑ ⓒ ⓓ	27	ⓐ ⓑ ⓒ ⓓ	47	ⓐ ⓑ ⓒ ⓓ	67	ⓐ ⓑ ⓒ ⓓ	87	ⓐ ⓑ ⓒ ⓓ
8	ⓐ ⓑ ⓒ ⓓ	28	ⓐ ⓑ ⓒ ⓓ	48	ⓐ ⓑ ⓒ ⓓ	68	ⓐ ⓑ ⓒ ⓓ	88	ⓐ ⓑ ⓒ ⓓ
9	ⓐ ⓑ ⓒ ⓓ	29	ⓐ ⓑ ⓒ ⓓ	49	ⓐ ⓑ ⓒ ⓓ	69	ⓐ ⓑ ⓒ ⓓ	89	ⓐ ⓑ ⓒ ⓓ
10	ⓐ ⓑ ⓒ ⓓ	30	ⓐ ⓑ ⓒ ⓓ	50	ⓐ ⓑ ⓒ ⓓ	70	ⓐ ⓑ ⓒ ⓓ	90	ⓐ ⓑ ⓒ ⓓ
11	ⓐ ⓑ ⓒ ⓓ	31	ⓐ ⓑ ⓒ ⓓ	51	ⓐ ⓑ ⓒ ⓓ	71	ⓐ ⓑ ⓒ ⓓ		
12	ⓐ ⓑ ⓒ ⓓ	32	ⓐ ⓑ ⓒ ⓓ	52	ⓐ ⓑ ⓒ ⓓ	72	ⓐ ⓑ ⓒ ⓓ		
13	ⓐ ⓑ ⓒ ⓓ	33	ⓐ ⓑ ⓒ ⓓ	53	ⓐ ⓑ ⓒ ⓓ	73	ⓐ ⓑ ⓒ ⓓ		
14	ⓐ ⓑ ⓒ ⓓ	34	ⓐ ⓑ ⓒ ⓓ	54	ⓐ ⓑ ⓒ ⓓ	74	ⓐ ⓑ ⓒ ⓓ		
15	ⓐ ⓑ ⓒ ⓓ	35	ⓐ ⓑ ⓒ ⓓ	55	ⓐ ⓑ ⓒ ⓓ	75	ⓐ ⓑ ⓒ ⓓ		
16	ⓐ ⓑ ⓒ ⓓ	36	ⓐ ⓑ ⓒ ⓓ	56	ⓐ ⓑ ⓒ ⓓ	76	ⓐ ⓑ ⓒ ⓓ		
17	ⓐ ⓑ ⓒ ⓓ	37	ⓐ ⓑ ⓒ ⓓ	57	ⓐ ⓑ ⓒ ⓓ	77	ⓐ ⓑ ⓒ ⓓ		
18	ⓐ ⓑ ⓒ ⓓ	38	ⓐ ⓑ ⓒ ⓓ	58	ⓐ ⓑ ⓒ ⓓ	78	ⓐ ⓑ ⓒ ⓓ		
19	ⓐ ⓑ ⓒ ⓓ	39	ⓐ ⓑ ⓒ ⓓ	59	ⓐ ⓑ ⓒ ⓓ	79	ⓐ ⓑ ⓒ ⓓ		
20	ⓐ ⓑ ⓒ ⓓ	40	ⓐ ⓑ ⓒ ⓓ	60	ⓐ ⓑ ⓒ ⓓ	80	ⓐ ⓑ ⓒ ⓓ		

password

0 0 0 0
1 1 1 1
2 2 2 2
3 3 3 3
4 4 4 4
5 5 5 5
6 6 6 6
7 7 7 7
8 8 8 8
9 9 9 9

절취선

ANSWER SHEET

※ TEST DATE | MO. | DAY | YEAR

| 성 명 | | 등급 | ① ② ③ ④ ⑤ |

감독확인관인

성명란

초성 / 중성 / 종성 (ㄱ ㄴ ㄷ ㄹ ㅁ ㅂ ㅅ ㅇ ㅈ ㅊ ㅋ ㅌ ㅍ ㅎ ...)

수 험 번 호

(0~9 digit bubbles)

1) Code 1.
(0 1 2 3 4 5 6 7 8 9)

2) Code 2.
(0 1 2 3 4 5 6 7 8 9)

3) Code 3.
(0 1 2 3 4 5 6 7 8 9)

| 주민등록번호 앞자리 | 고 유 번 호 |

(0~9 digit bubbles)

문항	답 란	문항	답 란	문항	답 란	문항	답 란	문항	답 란
1	ⓐ ⓑ ⓒ ⓓ	21	ⓐ ⓑ ⓒ ⓓ	41	ⓐ ⓑ ⓒ ⓓ	61	ⓐ ⓑ ⓒ ⓓ	81	ⓐ ⓑ ⓒ ⓓ
2	ⓐ ⓑ ⓒ ⓓ	22	ⓐ ⓑ ⓒ ⓓ	42	ⓐ ⓑ ⓒ ⓓ	62	ⓐ ⓑ ⓒ ⓓ	82	ⓐ ⓑ ⓒ ⓓ
3	ⓐ ⓑ ⓒ ⓓ	23	ⓐ ⓑ ⓒ ⓓ	43	ⓐ ⓑ ⓒ ⓓ	63	ⓐ ⓑ ⓒ ⓓ	83	ⓐ ⓑ ⓒ ⓓ
4	ⓐ ⓑ ⓒ ⓓ	24	ⓐ ⓑ ⓒ ⓓ	44	ⓐ ⓑ ⓒ ⓓ	64	ⓐ ⓑ ⓒ ⓓ	84	ⓐ ⓑ ⓒ ⓓ
5	ⓐ ⓑ ⓒ ⓓ	25	ⓐ ⓑ ⓒ ⓓ	45	ⓐ ⓑ ⓒ ⓓ	65	ⓐ ⓑ ⓒ ⓓ	85	ⓐ ⓑ ⓒ ⓓ
6	ⓐ ⓑ ⓒ ⓓ	26	ⓐ ⓑ ⓒ ⓓ	46	ⓐ ⓑ ⓒ ⓓ	66	ⓐ ⓑ ⓒ ⓓ	86	ⓐ ⓑ ⓒ ⓓ
7	ⓐ ⓑ ⓒ ⓓ	27	ⓐ ⓑ ⓒ ⓓ	47	ⓐ ⓑ ⓒ ⓓ	67	ⓐ ⓑ ⓒ ⓓ	87	ⓐ ⓑ ⓒ ⓓ
8	ⓐ ⓑ ⓒ ⓓ	28	ⓐ ⓑ ⓒ ⓓ	48	ⓐ ⓑ ⓒ ⓓ	68	ⓐ ⓑ ⓒ ⓓ	88	ⓐ ⓑ ⓒ ⓓ
9	ⓐ ⓑ ⓒ ⓓ	29	ⓐ ⓑ ⓒ ⓓ	49	ⓐ ⓑ ⓒ ⓓ	69	ⓐ ⓑ ⓒ ⓓ	89	ⓐ ⓑ ⓒ ⓓ
10	ⓐ ⓑ ⓒ ⓓ	30	ⓐ ⓑ ⓒ ⓓ	50	ⓐ ⓑ ⓒ ⓓ	70	ⓐ ⓑ ⓒ ⓓ	90	ⓐ ⓑ ⓒ ⓓ
11	ⓐ ⓑ ⓒ ⓓ	31	ⓐ ⓑ ⓒ ⓓ	51	ⓐ ⓑ ⓒ ⓓ	71	ⓐ ⓑ ⓒ ⓓ		
12	ⓐ ⓑ ⓒ ⓓ	32	ⓐ ⓑ ⓒ ⓓ	52	ⓐ ⓑ ⓒ ⓓ	72	ⓐ ⓑ ⓒ ⓓ		
13	ⓐ ⓑ ⓒ ⓓ	33	ⓐ ⓑ ⓒ ⓓ	53	ⓐ ⓑ ⓒ ⓓ	73	ⓐ ⓑ ⓒ ⓓ		
14	ⓐ ⓑ ⓒ ⓓ	34	ⓐ ⓑ ⓒ ⓓ	54	ⓐ ⓑ ⓒ ⓓ	74	ⓐ ⓑ ⓒ ⓓ		
15	ⓐ ⓑ ⓒ ⓓ	35	ⓐ ⓑ ⓒ ⓓ	55	ⓐ ⓑ ⓒ ⓓ	75	ⓐ ⓑ ⓒ ⓓ		
16	ⓐ ⓑ ⓒ ⓓ	36	ⓐ ⓑ ⓒ ⓓ	56	ⓐ ⓑ ⓒ ⓓ	76	ⓐ ⓑ ⓒ ⓓ		
17	ⓐ ⓑ ⓒ ⓓ	37	ⓐ ⓑ ⓒ ⓓ	57	ⓐ ⓑ ⓒ ⓓ	77	ⓐ ⓑ ⓒ ⓓ		
18	ⓐ ⓑ ⓒ ⓓ	38	ⓐ ⓑ ⓒ ⓓ	58	ⓐ ⓑ ⓒ ⓓ	78	ⓐ ⓑ ⓒ ⓓ		
19	ⓐ ⓑ ⓒ ⓓ	39	ⓐ ⓑ ⓒ ⓓ	59	ⓐ ⓑ ⓒ ⓓ	79	ⓐ ⓑ ⓒ ⓓ		
20	ⓐ ⓑ ⓒ ⓓ	40	ⓐ ⓑ ⓒ ⓓ	60	ⓐ ⓑ ⓒ ⓓ	80	ⓐ ⓑ ⓒ ⓓ		

password

(0~9 digit bubbles)

절취선

MEMO

한 권으로 지텔프를 완벽하게 끝낼 수 있으니까!

3

출제 포인트만 엄선해
빠르게 정리하는
무료 지텔프 문법 총정리강의

4

내 예상 점수와 취약 영역을
정확하게 진단하는
무료 자동 채점 및 성적 분석 서비스

해커스
지텔프
Level 2
최신기출유형
실전문제집 7회

해커스 어학연구소

TEST 1
정답·스크립트·해석·해설

GRAMMAR

LISTENING

READING & VOCABULARY

TEST 1 점수 확인하기

GRAMMAR _____ / 26 (점수 : _____ 점)
LISTENING _____ / 26 (점수 : _____ 점)
READING & VOCABULARY _____ / 28 (점수 : _____ 점)

TOTAL _____ / 80 **(평균 점수 : _____ 점)**

*각 영역 점수: 맞은 개수 × 3.75
*평균 점수: 각 영역 점수 합계 ÷ 3

정답 및 취약 유형 분석표

자동 채점 및 성적 분석 서비스 ▶

문제집 p.28

GRAMMAR

번호	정답	유형
01	a	조동사
02	b	시제
03	d	조동사
04	d	가정법
05	c	시제
06	d	준동사
07	a	가정법
08	c	관계사
09	a	준동사
10	d	시제
11	a	가정법
12	b	연결어
13	a	준동사
14	b	시제
15	d	가정법
16	b	준동사
17	c	연결어
18	b	시제
19	c	준동사
20	a	가정법
21	d	조동사
22	b	조동사
23	b	시제
24	c	준동사
25	d	가정법
26	c	관계사

LISTENING

PART	번호	정답	유형
PART 1	27	c	특정세부사항
	28	b	추론
	29	d	특정세부사항
	30	c	특정세부사항
	31	b	특정세부사항
	32	a	특정세부사항
	33	a	추론
PART 2	34	c	특정세부사항
	35	d	특정세부사항
	36	b	Not/True
	37	a	특정세부사항
	38	d	특정세부사항
	39	b	추론
PART 3	40	d	주제/목적
	41	a	특정세부사항
	42	d	특정세부사항
	43	b	특정세부사항
	44	c	특정세부사항
	45	b	추론
PART 4	46	d	특정세부사항
	47	a	특정세부사항
	48	b	특정세부사항
	49	a	특정세부사항
	50	b	특정세부사항
	51	c	특정세부사항
	52	c	추론

READING & VOCABULARY

PART	번호	정답	유형
PART 1	53	d	특정세부사항
	54	d	특정세부사항
	55	a	추론
	56	b	특정세부사항
	57	c	특정세부사항
	58	a	어휘
	59	b	어휘
PART 2	60	b	주제/목적
	61	d	특정세부사항
	62	b	추론
	63	b	특정세부사항
	64	c	Not/True
	65	a	어휘
	66	d	어휘
PART 3	67	a	특정세부사항
	68	b	특정세부사항
	69	c	특정세부사항
	70	a	특정세부사항
	71	c	추론
	72	c	어휘
	73	a	어휘
PART 4	74	b	주제/목적
	75	d	특정세부사항
	76	a	추론
	77	d	특정세부사항
	78	c	추론
	79	d	어휘
	80	c	어휘

유형	맞힌 개수
시제	/ 6
가정법	/ 6
준동사	/ 6
조동사	/ 4
연결어	/ 2
관계사	/ 2
TOTAL	/ 26

유형	맞힌 개수
주제/목적	/ 1
특정세부사항	/ 19
Not/True	/ 1
추론	/ 5
TOTAL	/ 26

유형	맞힌 개수
주제/목적	/ 2
특정세부사항	/ 12
Not/True	/ 1
추론	/ 5
어휘	/ 8
TOTAL	/ 28

01 조동사 　조동사 should 생략 　　　　　　　　　　　　　　　　　　　　　난이도 ●●○

During a recent staff meeting, many employees at Oakland Transport expressed a desire to choose their own work hours. In response, the regional manager is recommending that the company _____ a flexible schedule.

(a) **implement**
(b) will implement
(c) has implemented
(d) implements

최근의 직원회의 동안, Oakland Transport 사의 많은 직원들은 그들 자신의 근무 시간을 선택하고 싶다는 바람을 나타냈다. 이에 응하여, 지역 관리자는 그 회사가 탄력 근로제를 <u>시행해야 한</u>다고 권고하고 있다.

─○ 지텔프 치트키

recommend 다음에는 that절에 동사원형이 온다.

☼ **주장·요구·명령·제안을 나타내는 빈출 동사**
　recommend 권고하다　demand 요구하다　request 요청하다　suggest 제안하다　order 명령하다　urge 강력히 촉구하다
　ask 요청하다　propose 제안하다　insist 주장하다　advise 권고하다

해설 | 주절에 제안을 나타내는 동사 recommend가 있으므로 that절에는 '(should +) 동사원형'이 와야 한다. 따라서 동사원형 (a) implement 가 정답이다.

어휘 | employee n. 직원, 사원　express v. 나타내다, 표현하다　desire n. 바람, 욕구　recommend v. 권고하다, 추천하다
　flexible schedule phr. 탄력 근로제　implement v. 시행하다

---

02 시제 　미래완료진행 　　　　　　　　　　　　　　　　　　　　　　　　난이도 ●●○

Brandon has been stuck in a traffic jam for over 40 minutes due to the construction work on the Riverview Interstate Highway. By the time he finally gets home from work, he _____ for an hour longer than normal.

(a) has driven
(b) **will have been driving**
(c) will be driving
(d) would have driven

Brandon은 Riverview 주간 고속도로의 건설 공사 때문에 40분 넘게 교통 체증에 갇혀 있었다. 그가 회사에서 마침내 집에 <u>도착할</u> 무렵이면, 그는 평소보다 한 시간 더 오랫동안 <u>운전해오고 있는 중일 것이다</u>.

─○ 지텔프 치트키

'by the time + 현재 동사'와 'for + 기간 표현'이 함께 오면 미래완료진행 시제가 정답이다.

☼ **미래완료진행과 자주 함께 쓰이는 시간 표현**
　· by the time / when / if + 현재 동사 + (for + 기간 표현)　~할 무렵이면 / ~할 때 / 만약 ~한다면 (~ 동안)
　· by / in + 미래 시점 + (for + 기간 표현)　~ 즈음에는 / ~에 (~ 동안)

해설 | 현재 동사로 미래의 의미를 나타내는 시간의 부사절 'by the time + 현재 동사'(By the time ~ gets)와 지속을 나타내는 'for + 기간 표현'(for an hour longer)이 있고, 문맥상 미래 시점에 Brandon이 회사에서 집에 도착할 무렵이면 그는 평소보다 한 시간 더 오랫동안 계

속해서 운전해오고 있는 중일 것이라는 의미가 되어야 자연스럽다. 따라서 미래완료진행 시제 (b) will have been driving이 정답이다.

오답분석
(c) 미래진행 시제는 특정 미래 시점에 한창 진행 중일 일을 나타내므로, 과거 또는 현재에 시작해서 특정 미래 시점까지 계속해서 진행되고 있을 일을 표현할 수 없어 오답이다.

어휘 | stuck adj. 갇힌, 빠져나갈 수 없는 traffic jam phr. 교통 체증 construction n. 건설 interstate highway phr. 주간 고속도로

---

03 조동사　조동사 can

난이도 ●●●

SmartTune, an online audio distribution platform, has proven to be a powerful networking tool for songwriters. They _____ not only use it to collaborate with other artists but also to easily share their music with a wider audience.

(a) must
(b) would
(c) might
(d) can

온라인 오디오 유통 플랫폼인 SmartTune은 작곡가들을 위한 강력한 네트워킹 도구임이 입증되어왔다. 그들은 그것을 다른 예술가들과 협업하는 데뿐만 아니라 그들의 음악을 더 다양한 청중들과 쉽게 공유하는 데 또한 사용할 수 있다.

─○ 지텔프 치트키

'~할 수 있다'라고 말할 때는 can을 쓴다.

해설 | 문맥상 강력한 네트워킹 도구임이 입증된 SmartTune을 작곡가들이 다른 예술가들과 협업하는 데뿐만 아니라 그들의 음악을 더 다양한 청중들과 쉽게 공유하는 데 또한 사용할 수 있다는 의미가 되어야 자연스러우므로, '~할 수 있다'를 뜻하면서 가능성을 나타내는 조동사 (d) can이 정답이다.

오답분석
(c) 빈칸 앞 문장에서 SmartTune은 작곡가들을 위한 강력한 네트워킹 도구임이 이미 입증되어왔다고 했으므로, '~할지도 모른다'를 뜻하면서 약한 추측을 나타내는 조동사 might는 문맥에 적합하지 않아 오답이다.

어휘 | distribution n. 유통, 배포 prove v. 입증되다, 판명되다 collaborate v. 협업하다 share v. 공유하다 wide adj. 다양한

---

04 가정법　가정법 과거

난이도 ●●○

Air pollution is worsening because many manufacturers refuse to limit the harmful emissions from their factories. If the government regulated the industry more strictly, fewer pollutants _____ our planet's atmosphere.

(a) have entered
(b) are entering
(c) would have entered
(d) would enter

많은 제조사들이 그것들의 공장에서 나오는 해로운 배기가스를 제한하기를 거부하기 때문에 대기 오염이 악화되고 있다. 만약 정부가 산업을 더 엄격하게 규제한다면, 더 적은 오염 물질이 지구의 대기로 유입될 것이다.

'if + 과거 동사'가 있으면 'would/could + 동사원형'이 정답이다.

> 💡 **가정법 과거**
> If + 주어 + 과거 동사, 주어 + would/could(조동사 과거형) + 동사원형

해설 | If절에 과거 동사(regulated)가 있으므로, 주절에는 이와 짝을 이루어 가정법 과거를 만드는 'would(조동사 과거형) + 동사원형'이 와야 한다. 따라서 (d) would enter가 정답이다.

어휘 | pollution n. 오염 worsen v. 악화되다 manufacturer n. 제조사 emission n. 배기가스 regulate v. 규제하다 strictly adv. 엄격하게 pollutant n. 오염 물질 atmosphere n. 대기

---

05 시제   과거완료진행   난이도 ●●○

During the first National Women's Rights Convention in 1850, the participants argued in favor of suffrage for all American citizens regardless of gender. This means that before women were allowed to vote in 1920, they _____ for the right for almost 70 years.

(a) were struggling
(b) struggle
(c) had been struggling
(d) have struggled

1850년 최초의 전국여성인권협약에서, 참가자들은 성별에 상관없이 모든 미국 시민들을 위한 참정권을 지지한다는 주장을 했다. 이것은 1920년에 여성들이 투표하도록 허용되기 전까지, 그들이 거의 70년 동안 그 권리를 위해 투쟁해오고 있던 중이었다는 것을 의미한다.

'before + 과거 동사'가 있으면 과거완료진행 시제가 정답이다.

> 💡 **과거완료진행과 자주 함께 쓰이는 시간 표현**
> • before / when / since + 과거 동사 + (for + 기간 표현) ~하기 전에 / ~했을 때 / ~ 이래로 (~ 동안)
> • (for + 기간 표현) + (up) until + 과거 동사 (~ 동안) ~했을 때까지

해설 | 과거완료진행 시제와 함께 쓰이는 시간 표현 'before + 과거 동사'(before ~ were allowed)와 'for + 기간 표현'(for almost 70 years)이 있고, 문맥상 대과거(1850년에 최초의 전국여성인권협약에서 참가자들이 모든 미국 시민들을 위한 참정권을 지지한 시점)부터 과거(1920년에 여성들이 투표하도록 허용된 시점)까지 거의 70년 동안 여성들이 그 참정권을 위해 계속해서 투쟁해오고 있던 중이었다는 의미가 되어야 자연스럽다. 따라서 과거완료진행 시제 (c) had been struggling이 정답이다.

> 오답분석
> (a) 과거진행 시제는 특정 과거 시점에 한창 진행 중이었던 일을 나타내므로, 대과거에 시작해서 특정 과거 시점까지 계속해서 진행되고 있었던 일을 표현할 수 없어 오답이다.

어휘 | convention n. 협약, 조약 participant n. 참가자 argue v. 주장하다 in favor of phr. ~을 지지하는 suffrage n. 참정권, 투표권 regardless of phr. ~에 상관없이 vote v. 투표하다 struggle v. 투쟁하다

---

06 준동사   동명사를 목적어로 취하는 동사   난이도 ●○○

Eastern College has introduced a policy for its dormitories, as noise issues have led to frequent disputes among

Eastern 대학은 기숙사를 위한 한 정책을 도입했는데, 이는 최근에 소음 문제가 거주자들 간의 잦은 분쟁

residents lately. Everyone living in the dorms is required to avoid _____ loud sounds in their rooms or the common areas after 10 p.m.

(a) having made
(b) to have made
(c) to make
(d) making

으로 이어졌기 때문이다. 기숙사에 사는 모든 사람들은 밤 10시 이후에 그들의 방이나 공용 공간에서 시끄러운 소리를 내는 것을 피하도록 요구된다.

⟶○ 지텔프 치트키

avoid는 동명사를 목적어로 취한다.

> 💡 **동명사를 목적어로 취하는 빈출 동사**
> avoid 피하다 imagine 상상하다 mind 개의하다 keep 계속하다 consider 고려하다 prevent 방지하다 enjoy 즐기다
> recommend 권장하다 risk 위험을 무릅쓰다 involve 포함하다

해설 | 빈칸 앞 동사 avoid는 동명사를 목적어로 취하므로, 동명사 (d) making이 정답이다.

> 오답분석
>
> (a) having made도 동명사이기는 하지만, 완료동명사(having made)로 쓰일 경우 '피하는' 시점보다 '(소리를) 내는' 시점이 앞선다는 것을 나타내므로 문맥에 적합하지 않아 오답이다.

어휘 | policy n. 정책 dormitory n. 기숙사 frequent adj. 잦은 dispute n. 분쟁 resident n. 거주자 avoid v. 피하다
common adj. 공용의, 공동의

---

07 가정법   가정법 과거완료   난이도 ●●○

Gardening Monthly announced last week that it was shutting down on account of a sharp decline in subscriptions. Most experts in the publishing world agree that the magazine _____ many more readers if it had made its content available on the Internet.

(a) would have attracted
(b) attracted
(c) was attracting
(d) would attract

「Gardening Monthly」지는 구독의 급격한 감소로 인해 폐간한다고 지난주에 발표했다. 출판업계의 전문가들 대부분은 만약 이 잡지사가 인터넷상에서 그것의 콘텐츠를 이용할 수 있게 했다면 그것이 더 많은 독자들을 끌어들였을 것이라는 데 동의한다.

⟶○ 지텔프 치트키

'if + had p.p.'가 있으면 'would/could + have p.p.'가 정답이다.

> 💡 **가정법 과거완료**
> If + 주어 + had p.p., 주어 + would/could(조동사 과거형) + have p.p.

해설 | if절에 'had p.p.' 형태의 had made가 있으므로, 주절에는 이와 짝을 이루어 가정법 과거완료를 만드는 'would(조동사 과거형) + have p.p.'가 와야 한다. 따라서 (a) would have attracted가 정답이다.

어휘 | announce v. 발표하다 shut down phr. 폐간하다, 문을 닫다 on account of phr. ~으로 인하여, ~ 때문에 sharp adj. 급격한
decline n. 감소, 하락 subscription n. 구독 expert n. 전문가 publishing n. 출판업 attract v. 끌어들이다

08 관계사　주격 관계대명사 which　　　　난이도 ●●○

Local environmental groups are strongly opposed to the plan to build an industrial complex next to the Greenhill Wetlands. This marsh, _____, is populated by a large number of rare animals, including several endangered birds.

(a) what covers an area of over 25 square kilometers
(b) where it covers an area of over 25 square kilometers
(c) which covers an area of over 25 square kilometers
(d) that covers an area of over 25 square kilometers

지역 환경 단체들이 Greenhill 습지 옆에 산업 단지를 조성하려는 계획에 강력히 반대하고 있다. 이 습지는, <u>25제곱킬로미터가 넘는 면적</u>을 차지하는데, 몇몇 멸종 위기에 처한 조류를 포함해 다수의 희귀 동물들이 서식하고 있다.

◦─○ 지텔프 치트키

사물 선행사가 관계절 안에서 주어 역할을 하고, 빈칸 앞에 콤마(,)가 있으면 주격 관계대명사 which가 정답이다.

해설 | 사물 선행사 This marsh를 받으면서 콤마(,) 뒤에 올 수 있는 주격 관계대명사가 필요하므로, (c) which covers an area of over 25 square kilometers가 정답이다.

오답분석
(d) 관계대명사 that도 사물 선행사를 받을 수 있지만, 콤마 뒤에 올 수 없으므로 오답이다.

어휘 | be opposed to phr. ~에 반대하다　industrial complex phr. 산업 단지　wetland n. 습지　marsh n. 습지　populate v. 서식하다, 살다　rare adj. 희귀한, 드문　endangered adj. 멸종 위기에 처한

09 준동사　동명사를 목적어로 취하는 동사　　　　난이도 ●●○

It has always been my dream to visit the Great Barrier Reef in Australia. I like to imagine _____ through the crystal clear water while looking at the beautiful coral and the amazing marine life.

(a) swimming
(b) to swim
(c) having swum
(d) to have swum

호주의 그레이트배리어리프를 방문하는 것은 항상 나의 꿈이었다. 나는 아름다운 산호와 놀라운 해양 생물을 보면서 맑고 투명한 물속을 <u>헤엄치는 것</u>을 상상하는 걸 좋아한다.

◦─○ 지텔프 치트키

imagine은 동명사를 목적어로 취한다.

해설 | 빈칸 앞 동사 imagine은 동명사를 목적어로 취하므로, 동명사 (a) swimming이 정답이다.

오답분석
(c) having swum도 동명사이기는 하지만, 완료동명사(having swum)로 쓰일 경우 '상상하는' 시점보다 '헤엄치는' 시점이 앞선다는 것을 나타내므로 문맥에 적합하지 않아 오답이다.

어휘 | crystal clear phr. 맑고 투명한　coral n. 산호　marine adj. 해양의

10 시제 현재완료진행

Amelia is part of the music program at Miller University, which is home to the National A Cappella Championship. Since 1955, the school _____ the event, at which many aspiring singers are discovered.

(a) was hosting
(b) had been hosting
(c) will be hosting
(d) has been hosting

Amelia는 Miller 대학의 음악 프로그램에 속해 있는데, 이것은 전국 아카펠라 챔피언전의 본고장이다. 1955년 이래로, 그 학교가 이 행사를 주최해오고 있는 중이며, 그곳에서 장차 가수가 되려는 많은 사람들이 발굴된다.

지텔프 치트키

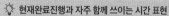

'since + 과거 시점'이 있으면 현재완료진행 시제가 정답이다.

💡 **현재완료진행과 자주 함께 쓰이는 시간 표현**
- (ever) since + 과거 시점 + (for + 기간 표현) ~한 이래로 (줄곧) (~ 동안)
- lately / for + 기간 표현 + now 최근에 / 현재 ~ 동안

해설| 현재완료진행 시제와 함께 쓰이는 시간 표현 'since + 과거 시점'(Since 1955)이 있고, 문맥상 과거 시점인 1955년부터 현재까지 계속해서 Miller 대학이 행사를 주최해오고 있는 중이라는 의미가 되어야 자연스럽다. 따라서 현재완료진행 시제 (d) has been hosting이 정답이다.

어휘| aspiring adj. 장차 ~이 되려는 host v. 주최하다

11 가정법 가정법 과거완료

Bill Walton was one of the greatest college basketball players of all time, and he was becoming a dominant professional player when he broke both his ankle and wrist. If those injuries _____, he would have likely had a long and successful career.

(a) had never occurred
(b) never occurred
(c) would never occur
(d) never occur

빌 월턴은 역대 가장 위대한 대학 농구 선수들 중 한 명이었으며, 그의 발목과 손목이 둘 다 골절되었을 때 그는 가장 유력한 프로 선수가 되고 있던 중이었다. 만약 그러한 부상이 발생하지 않았었다면, 그는 아마 길고 성공적인 경력을 쌓았을 것이다.

지텔프 치트키

if와 'would/could + have p.p.'가 있으면 had p.p.가 정답이다.

해설| 주절에 'would(조동사 과거형) + have p.p.' 형태의 would have ~ had가 있으므로, If절에는 이와 짝을 이루어 가정법 과거완료를 만드는 과거완료 동사가 와야 한다. 따라서 (a) had never occurred가 정답이다.

어휘| dominant adj. 가장 유력한 break v. 골절되다, 부러지다 ankle n. 발목 wrist n. 손목 injury n. 부상 occur v. 발생하다, 일어나다

TEST 1

TEST 2

TEST 3

TEST 4

TEST 5

TEST 6

TEST 7

해커스 지텔프 최신기출유형 실전문제집 7회 (Level 2)

12 연결어 접속부사

There are various strategies job seekers can use to make their résumés appeal to potential employers. _____, they might focus on presenting their skills and experience in a way that shows a direct connection to the position being applied for.

(a) Likewise
(b) For example
(c) Meanwhile
(d) After all

구직자들이 그들의 이력서가 잠재적 고용주들의 관심을 끌도록 만들기 위해 사용할 수 있는 여러 가지 전략들이 있다. 예를 들어, 그들은 지원하려는 직무와 직접적인 연관성을 보여 주는 방식으로 그들의 기량과 경험을 나타내는 데 집중할 수 있다.

⊶○ 지텔프 치트키

'예를 들어'라는 의미의 예시를 나타낼 때는 For example을 쓴다.

💡 예시를 나타내는 빈출 접속부사
For example 예를 들어 For instance 예를 들어

해설 | 빈칸 앞 문장은 구직자들이 그들의 이력서가 잠재적 고용주들의 관심을 끌도록 만들기 위해 사용할 수 있는 여러 가지 전략들이 있다는 일반론적인 내용이고, 빈칸 뒤 문장은 지원하려는 직무와 직접적인 연관성을 보여 주는 방식으로 그들의 기량과 경험을 나타내는 데 집중할 수 있다는 구체적인 내용으로서 빈칸 앞 문장에서 언급한 전략의 예를 들고 있다. 따라서 '예를 들어'라는 의미의 예시를 나타내는 접속부사 (b) For example이 정답이다.

오답분석
(a) Likewise는 '마찬가지로', (c) Meanwhile은 '그동안에', (d) After all은 '결국'이라는 의미로, 문맥에 적합하지 않아 오답이다.

어휘 | strategy n. 전략 job seeker phr. 구직자 résumé n. 이력서 appeal v. 관심을 끌다; n. 관심 potential adj. 잠재적인 employer n. 고용주 present v. 나타내다 apply v. 지원하다

13 준동사 to 부정사를 목적격 보어로 취하는 동사

The payroll deadline falls on a weekend this month. Accordingly, all employees are encouraged _____ their time cards and expense reports by June 25 so that their paychecks are not delayed.

(a) to submit
(b) submitting
(c) to be submitting
(d) having submitted

이번 달에는 급여 대상자 명단의 마감일이 주말에 해당된다. 이에 따라, 모든 직원들은 그들의 월급이 체불되지 않도록 6월 25일까지 근무 시간 기록표와 경비 보고서를 제출할 것이 권장된다.

⊶○ 지텔프 치트키

encourage는 to 부정사를 목적격 보어로 취한다.

💡 to 부정사를 목적격 보어로 취하는 빈출 동사
encourage 권장하다 require 요구하다 urge 강력히 촉구하다 allow 허락하다 ask 요청하다

해설 | 빈칸 앞 동사 encourage는 'encourage + 목적어 + 목적격 보어'의 형태로 쓰일 때 to 부정사를 목적격 보어로 취하여, '-에게 ~할 것을 권장하다'라는 의미로 사용된다. 따라서 to 부정사 (a) to submit이 정답이다. 참고로, 'all employees are encouraged to submit'은 'encourage(동사) + all employees(목적어) + to submit(목적격 보어)'에서 변형된 수동태 구문이다.

어휘 | payroll n. 급여 대상자 명단 deadline n. 마감일, 기한 fall on phr. (어떤 날짜가) ~에 해당되다 time card phr. 근무 시간 기록표
expense n. 경비, 비용 paycheck n. 월급, 급료 submit v. 제출하다

---

14 시제 과거진행   난이도 ●●○

Professor Morris requested that the university's maintenance department send a technician to his classroom quickly. He _____ a lecture this morning when he noticed that the air conditioner had stopped working.

(a) is delivering
(b) was delivering
(c) delivered
(d) has been delivering

Morris 교수는 대학의 관리부가 그의 강의실로 기술자를 빨리 보내 줘야 한다고 요청했다. 그가 오늘 아침에 에어컨이 작동을 멈췄다는 것을 알아차렸을 때 그는 강의를 하고 있던 중이었다.

⊶○ 지텔프 치트키

'for + 기간 표현' 없이 'when + 과거 동사'만 있으면 과거진행 시제가 정답이다.

> 💡 **과거진행과 자주 함께 쓰이는 시간 표현**
> • when / while + 과거 동사 ~했을 때 / ~하던 도중에
> • last + 시간 표현 / yesterday 지난 ~에 / 어제

해설 | 과거진행 시제와 함께 쓰이는 시간 표현 '과거 시점'(this morning)과 'when + 과거 동사'(when ~ noticed)가 있고, 문맥상 Morris 교수가 과거 시점인 오늘 아침에 에어컨 작동이 멈췄다는 것을 알아차렸을 때 그는 강의를 하고 있던 중이었다는 의미가 되어야 자연스럽다. 따라서 과거진행 시제 (b) was delivering이 정답이다.

오답분석

(c) 특정 과거 시점에 한창 진행 중이었던 행동을 표현하기에는 과거 시제보다 과거진행 시제가 더 적절하므로, 과거 시제는 오답이다.

어휘 | request v. 요청하다 maintenance n. 관리, 정비 notice v. 알아차리다 deliver v. (연설·강연 등을) 하다

---

15 가정법 가정법 과거   난이도 ●●○

The Bow Valley Parkway, which winds through Banff National Park, closes from 8 p.m. until 8 a.m. in the spring. If it were to be open at night, animal populations _____ significant damage as a consequence of their migratory routes being obstructed.

(a) would have suffered
(b) suffer
(c) are suffering
(d) would suffer

보우 밸리 파크웨이는, 밴프 국립공원을 관통하여 구불구불 나 있는데, 봄철에는 오후 8시부터 오전 8시까지 폐쇄된다. 만약 그것이 밤에 개방된다면, 동물 개체군은 그들의 이동 경로가 방해되는 결과로 상당한 피해를 입을 것이다.

'if + were to + 동사원형'이 있으면 'would/could + 동사원형'이 정답이다.

> ☀ **가정법 과거(were to)**
> If + 주어 + were to + 동사원형, 주어 + would/could(조동사 과거형) + 동사원형

해설 | If절에 과거 동사(were to be)가 있으므로, 주절에는 이와 짝을 이루어 가정법 과거를 만드는 'would(조동사 과거형) + 동사원형'이 와야 한다. 따라서 (d) would suffer가 정답이다.

어휘 | wind v. 구불구불하다 significant adj. 상당한, 중요한 damage n. 피해 consequence n. 결과 migratory adj. 이동하는 route n. 경로 obstruct v. 방해하다 suffer v. (피해 등을) 입다, 겪다

---

16 준동사 to 부정사의 부사 역할 난이도 ●●●

Over the past year, Mica has rated highly on her monthly performance evaluations at Westport Advertising. As a result, the head of the marketing department will meet with her next week _____ a promotion to team leader.

(a) to be conferring
(b) to confer
(c) will confer
(d) conferring

지난 한 해 동안, Mica는 Westport 광고사의 월례 인사 고과에서 높이 평가되어 왔다. 그 결과, 마케팅 부서장은 팀장으로의 승진을 <u>논의하기 위해</u> 다음 주에 그녀를 만날 것이다.

'~하기 위해'라고 말할 때는 to 부정사를 쓴다.

해설 | 빈칸 앞에 주어(the head of the marketing department), 동사(will meet)가 갖춰진 완전한 절이 있으므로, 부사(next week) 다음에 위치한 빈칸 이하는 문장의 필수 성분이 아닌 수식어구이다. 따라서 목적을 나타내며 수식어구를 이끌 수 있는 to 부정사 (b) to confer가 정답이다.

어휘 | rate v. 평가되다 performance evaluation phr. 인사 고과 promotion n. 승진 confer v. 논의하다

---

17 연결어 접속사 난이도 ●●○

Jeff has an appointment to take the road test to get his driver's license tomorrow. He feels confident that he will pass _____ he has taken lessons at Ace Driving Academy for weeks now.

(a) as soon as
(b) in case
(c) because
(d) even if

Jeff는 내일 운전면허를 따기 위한 도로 주행 시험 응시가 예약되어 있다. 그는 현재 몇 주째 Ace 운전 학원에서 강습을 받아 왔<u>기 때문에</u> 그가 합격할 것이라고 확신한다.

'~이기 때문에'라는 의미의 이유를 나타낼 때는 because를 쓴다.

> 💡 이유를 나타내는 빈출 접속사
> because ~이기 때문에 since ~이기 때문에 as ~이기 때문에

해설 | 문맥상 Jeff가 현재 몇 주째 운전 학원에서 강습을 받아 왔기 때문에 내일 응시가 예약되어 있는 도로 주행 시험에 합격할 것이라고 확신한다는 의미가 되어야 자연스럽다. 따라서 '~이기 때문에'라는 의미의 이유를 나타내는 부사절 접속사 (c) because가 정답이다.

> 오답분석
>
> (a) as soon as는 '~ 하자마자', (b) in case는 '~할 경우에 대비하여', (d) even if는 '~에도 불구하고'라는 의미로, 문맥에 적합하지 않아 오답이다.

어휘 | appointment n. 예약, 약속 confident adj. 확신하는, 자신감 있는

---

18 시제 　미래진행 　　　　　　　　　　　　　　　　난이도 ●●○

Please don't try to reach me unless there's an emergency. I _____ in the Ellen Banks Library this weekend to prepare for the final exam of my biology class, and I don't want to be distracted.

긴급한 일이 아니라면 내게 연락하려고 하지 말아 줘. 나는 생물학 수업의 기말고사를 준비하기 위해 이번 주말에 Ellen Banks 도서관에서 공부하고 있는 중일 것이고, 방해받고 싶지 않아.

(a) have studied
(b) will be studying
(c) will have been studying
(d) was studying

'for + 기간 표현' 없이 특정 미래 시점을 나타내는 표현만 있으면 미래진행 시제가 정답이다.

> 💡 미래진행과 자주 함께 쓰이는 시간 표현
> • when / if + 현재 동사 ~할 때 / 만약 ~한다면 　　• until / by + 미래 시점 ~까지
> • next + 시간 표현 다음 ~에 　　　　　　　　　　• starting + 미래 시점 / tomorrow ~부터 / 내일

해설 | 미래진행 시제와 함께 쓰이는 시간 표현 this weekend가 있고, 문맥상 미래 시점인 이번 주말에 화자가 Ellen Banks 도서관에서 공부하고 있는 중일 것이라는 의미가 되어야 자연스럽다. 따라서 미래진행 시제 (b) will be studying이 정답이다.

어휘 | reach v. 연락하다 emergency n. 긴급한 일 biology n. 생물학 distract v. 방해하다, 혼란하게 하다

---

19 준동사 　동명사를 목적어로 취하는 동사 　　　　　　　　난이도 ●○○

The blog *Urban Scene* has released its annual list of the best restaurants in Portland. It includes details about the menus, prices, and facilities of 20 dining establishments. Readers appreciate _____ this useful information about where to eat out in the city.

'Urban Scene' 블로그는 포틀랜드 내 최고 식당들의 연례 목록을 공개해 왔다. 그것은 20개 음식점의 메뉴, 가격, 그리고 시설에 관한 자세한 정보를 담고 있다. 독자들은 그 도시에서 외식할 장소에 관한 유용한 정보를 얻는 것을 고마워한다.

(a) being received
(b) to receive
(c) receiving
(d) to be receiving

──○ 지텔프 치트키

appreciate는 동명사를 목적어로 취한다.

해설 | 빈칸 앞 동사 appreciate는 동명사를 목적어로 취하므로, 동명사 (c) receiving이 정답이다.

어휘 | release v. 공개하다, 발표하다 annual adj. 연례의 facility n. 시설 dining establishment phr. 음식점 appreciate v. 고마워하다 eat out phr. 외식하다

20 가정법 가정법 과거완료

난이도 ●●●

The dog my family adopted from the local animal shelter has serious health problems. Had we known about them sooner, we _____ her to the veterinarian to get treatment earlier.

나의 가족이 지역 동물 보호소에서 입양한 개는 심각한 건강 문제들을 가지고 있다. 우리가 그것들에 대해 더 일찍 알았다면, 우리는 더 빨리 치료받도록 그녀를 수의사에게 데려갔을 것이다.

(a) would have taken
(b) were taking
(c) would take
(d) took

──○ 지텔프 치트키

Had p.p.가 있으면 'would/could + have p.p.'가 정답이다.

💡 가정법 과거완료(도치)

Had + 주어 + p.p., 주어 + would/could(조동사 과거형) + have p.p.

해설 | if가 생략되어 도치된 절에 'had p.p.'형태의 Had ~ known이 있으므로, 주절에는 이와 짝을 이루어 가정법 과거완료를 만드는 'would(조동사 과거형) + have p.p.'가 와야 한다. 따라서 (a) would have taken이 정답이다. 참고로, 'Had we known ~'은 'If we had known ~'으로 바꿔 쓸 수 있다.

어휘 | adopt v. 입양하다 shelter n. 보호소 veterinarian n. 수의사 treatment n. 치료

21 조동사 조동사 should

난이도 ●●○

Carson was confused by his employee review. According to his supervisor, Carson _____ work harder to ensure that his clients are satisfied with his service. This baffled him because he'd never received any direct complaints from customers.

Carson은 그의 직원 평가로 인해 혼란스러웠다. 그의 관리자에 따르면, Carson은 그의 고객들이 그의 서비스에 반드시 만족하도록 하기 위해 더 열심히 일해야 한다. 이것은 그를 몹시 당황하게 했는데 왜냐하면 그는 고객들로부터 어떠한 직접적인 불만도 받은 적이 없었기 때문이다.

(a) will

TEST 1

TEST 2

TEST 3

TEST 4

TEST 5

TEST 6

TEST 7

해커스 지텔프 최신기출유형 실전문제집 7회 (Level 2)

(b) may
(c) would
(d) should

'~해야 한다'라고 말할 때는 should를 쓴다.

해설 | 문맥상 Carson은 그동안 고객들로부터 어떠한 직접적인 불만도 받은 적이 없었기 때문에 그의 고객들이 그의 서비스에 반드시 만족하도록 하기 위해 더 열심히 일해야 한다는 그의 관리자의 말에 몹시 당황했다는 의미가 되어야 자연스러우므로, '~해야 한다'를 뜻하면서 당위성을 나타내는 조동사 (d) should가 정답이다. 참고로, should와 must 모두 '~해야 한다'를 뜻하지만, should는 must보다 약한 어조로 충고나 권유를 할 때 쓴다.

어휘 | supervisor n. 관리자, 감독관   baffle v. 몹시 당황하게 하다

---

22 조동사   조동사 should 생략   난이도 ●●○

Weston Incorporated's new Marvelous Meal Kits have packaging defects that prevent the food from staying fresh. The company has assured customers that it will take steps to keep this problem from reoccurring. However, customers are also demanding that it _____ their payments.

(a) has refunded
(b) refund
(c) refunds
(d) will refund

Weston 주식회사의 새로운 Marvelous 식자재 세트에는 음식이 신선함을 유지하지 못하게 하는 포장 결함이 있다. 그 회사는 이 문제가 재발하지 않도록 조치를 취할 것을 고객들에게 확언했다. 하지만, 고객들은 또한 그것이 그들의 지불금을 <u>환불해야 한다</u>고 요구하고 있다.

demand 다음에는 that절에 동사원형이 온다.

해설 | 주절에 요구를 나타내는 동사 demand가 있으므로 that절에는 '(should +) 동사원형'이 와야 한다. 따라서 동사원형 (b) refund가 정답이다.

어휘 | Incorporated adj. 주식회사   meal kit phr. 식자재 세트   defect n. 결함   prevent v. ~하지 못하게 하다   assure v. 확언하다, 보장하다   payment n. 지불금   refund v. 환불하다

---

23 시제   현재진행   난이도 ●●○

Shane didn't have enough money for a taxi ride to campus. Consequently, when he found out that the subway was delayed, he returned home to get his bike. He _____ on his way to school, and he's almost there.

(a) will now cycle
(b) is now cycling

Shane은 캠퍼스까지 택시를 타고 갈 충분한 돈이 없었다. 따라서, 지하철이 지연되었다는 것을 알게 됐을 때, 그는 그의 자전거를 가지러 집으로 돌아왔다. 그는 <u>지금 자전거를 타고</u> 학교로 가는 길이고, 거의 다 도착했다.

(c) has been now cycling

(d) now cycles

─○ 지텔프 치트키

보기에 now가 있으면 현재진행 시제가 정답이다.

> ☆ 현재진행과 자주 함께 쓰이는 시간 표현
> • right now / now / currently / at the moment 바로 지금 / 지금 / 현재 / 바로 지금
> • these days / nowadays 요즘

해설│ 보기에 현재진행 시제와 함께 쓰이는 시간 표현 now가 있고, 문맥상 말하고 있는 현재 시점에 자전거를 타고 학교로 가는 길이며 거의 다 도착했다는 의미가 되어야 자연스럽다. 따라서 현재진행 시제 (b) is now cycling이 정답이다.

오답분석

(d) 현재 시제는 반복되는 일이나 습관, 일반적인 사실을 나타내므로, 현재 시점에 한창 진행 중인 일을 표현하기에는 현재진행 시제보다 부적절하므로 오답이다.

어휘│ consequently adv. 따라서, 그 결과 find out phr. 알게 되다, 발견하다 delay v. 지연시키다 cycle v. 자전거를 타다

---

24 준동사   to 부정사를 목적어로 취하는 동사   난이도 ●●○

Becky could tell that her parents were worried about her traveling abroad for a month. To ease their concerns, she promised _____ them every other day no matter what.

(a) contacting

(b) having contacted

(c) to contact

(d) to have contacted

Becky는 부모님이 그녀가 한 달 동안 해외로 여행하는 것에 대해 걱정하고 있다는 것을 알 수 있었다. 그들의 걱정을 덜어 주기 위해, 그녀는 무슨 일이 있어도 하루 걸러 그들에게 연락할 것을 약속했다.

─○ 지텔프 치트키

promise는 to 부정사를 목적어로 취한다.

> ☆ to 부정사를 목적어로 취하는 빈출 동사
> promise 약속하다 expect 예상하다 vow 맹세하다 wish 희망하다 plan 계획하다 decide 결정하다 hope 바라다 agree 동의하다
> intend 계획하다 prepare 준비하다

해설│ 빈칸 앞 동사 promise는 to 부정사를 목적어로 취하므로, to 부정사 (c) to contact가 정답이다.

오답분석

(d) to have contacted도 to 부정사이기는 하지만, 완료부정사(to have contacted)로 쓰일 경우 '약속하는' 시점보다 '연락하는' 시점이 앞선다는 것을 나타내므로 문맥에 적합하지 않아 오답이다.

어휘│ tell v. 알다, 판단하다 abroad adv. 해외로 ease v. (걱정을) 덜어 주다 concern n. 걱정, 우려 no matter what phr. 무슨 일이 있어도

25 가정법   가정법 과거 난이도 ●●○

MegaX Communications has found it difficult to hire experienced software programmers for an ongoing project. If the company were willing to offer better employee benefits, it _____ better-qualified applicants for the open positions.

(a) will draw
(b) would have drawn
(c) had drawn
(d) would draw

MegaX 정보 통신사는 진행 중인 프로젝트를 위한 숙련된 소프트웨어 프로그래머들을 고용하는 것이 어렵다는 것을 알게 되었다. 만약 그 회사가 더 나은 직원 혜택을 제공할 의향이 있다면, 그것은 공석에 더 좋은 자격을 갖춘 지원자들을 끌어들일 것이다.

⊶─○ 지텔프 치트키

'if + 과거 동사'가 있으면 'would/could + 동사원형'이 정답이다.

해설 | If절에 과거 동사(were)가 있으므로, 주절에는 이와 짝을 이루어 가정법 과거를 만드는 'would(조동사 과거형) + 동사원형'이 와야 한다. 따라서 (d) would draw가 정답이다.

어휘 | ongoing adj. 진행 중인   be willing to phr. ~할 의향이 있다   qualified adj. 자격을 갖춘   applicant n. 지원자   open position phr. 공석   draw v. 끌어들이다

26 관계사   주격 관계대명사 who 난이도 ●●●

Psychologist Jean Piaget studied childhood intellectual development. However, some scholars question his theories because the individuals _____ were not randomly selected. To make matters worse, he usually relied on small sample sizes, so his findings may not apply to larger groups.

(a) which were the focus of his research
(b) what were the focus of his research
(c) who were the focus of his research
(d) whom were the focus of his research

심리학자 장 피아제는 아동기의 지능 발달에 대해 연구했다. 그러나, 일부 학자들은 그의 연구의 대상이었던 사람들이 무작위로 선정된 것이 아니었기 때문에 그의 이론에 의문을 제기한다. 설상가상으로, 그는 보통 작은 표본 크기에 의존했으므로, 그의 연구 결과가 더 큰 집단에는 적용될 수 없을지도 모른다.

⊶─○ 지텔프 치트키

사람 선행사가 관계절 안에서 주어 역할을 하면 주격 관계대명사 who가 정답이다.

해설 | 사람 선행사 the individuals를 받으면서 보기의 관계절 내에서 주어 역할을 할 수 있는 주격 관계대명사가 필요하므로, (c) who were the focus of his research가 정답이다.

어휘 | psychologist n. 심리학자   intellectual adj. 지능의, 지적인   scholar n. 학자   randomly adv. 무작위로   select v. 선정하다   sample n. 표본   apply v. 적용되다

LISTENING

음성 바로 듣기

안부 인사	M: Hey, Sandra. You haven't been around much lately. How's everything going?
주제 제시: 승마 배우기	F: Hi, Franklin. ²⁷I've been busy. I started horseback riding lessons recently, and I'm spending all my time outside of work at the stables nowadays. M: Oh, how fun! I wasn't aware that you were interested in horses. F: In truth, I've always been scared of them. I decided to learn to ride so I could get over my fear.
폴로 배우기	M: That's interesting. Have you considered learning to play polo? You know, the sport of hitting a ball into a goal with a stick as you ride a horse. F: Ha-ha. No. I'm concentrating on the basics. It would take years for my skills to get good enough to take on polo. M: Well, ²⁸horseback riding alone is already difficult without trying to hit a ball while doing it. Anyway, are you enjoying the lessons?
승마가 어려운 이유	F: They're great, but I had no idea how challenging horseback riding was. ²⁹I was shocked when I woke up the day after my first lesson. My arms, legs, and core muscles were all hurting so much. M: ³⁰Staying balanced while controlling the horse really stimulates those muscle groups. That's why horseback riding is a great exercise for the entire body.
승마의 장점	F: Totally. I've seen an incredible improvement in my fitness levels since I started riding. I've also heard it gives you quite the aerobic workout. Apparently, a one-hour ride burns more calories than jogging for the same amount of time! M: That's amazing. And I bet competitive riding consumes even more calories because you have to work harder just to keep yourself in the proper position. F: Yes, that's right. Our instructor had us race around the track one day. It was so hard to stay on.
장애물 경마	M: Imagine riding on an obstacle course where you have to jump over fences and ditches! F: ³¹I doubt I'll ever be up for that. I've fallen off my horse just walking on flat ground and that left me

남: 안녕, Sandra. 너는 최근에 잘 나타나지 않더라. 어떻게 지내?

여: 안녕, Franklin. ²⁷난 바빴어. 나는 최근에 승마 강습을 시작했고, 요즘 직장 밖에서의 모든 시간을 승마 교습장에서 보내고 있어.

남: 오, 정말 재미있겠다! 나는 네가 말에 관심이 있었는지 몰랐어.

여: 사실, 나는 항상 그것들이 무서웠어. 나는 승마를 배우기로 결심했고 두려움을 극복할 수 있었지.

남: 흥미롭네. 폴로를 하는 것을 배우는 걸 고려해 본 적 있어? 너도 알잖아, 말을 타면서 막대기로 공을 쳐서 골대에 넣는 스포츠 말이야.

여: 하하. 아니. 난 기초에 집중하고 있어. 폴로에 도전할 만큼 내 실력이 좋아지려면 몇 년은 걸릴 거야.

남: 하긴, ²⁸그것을 하면서 공을 치려고 노력하는 것 없이도 승마는 그 자체로 이미 어렵지. 그나저나, 수업은 즐겁니?

여: 그것은 훌륭하지만, 나는 승마가 얼마나 어려운지 몰랐어. ²⁹첫 수업 다음 날 일어났을 때 나는 충격을 받았지. 내 팔, 다리, 그리고 코어근육들이 모두 너무 많이 아팠거든.

남: ³⁰말을 통제하면서 균형을 유지하는 것은 그 근육 부위들을 굉장히 자극해. 그것이 승마가 훌륭한 전신 운동인 이유야.

여: 맞아. 나는 말을 타기 시작한 이후로 내 체력 수준의 엄청난 향상을 봤어. 나는 그것이 또한 상당한 유산소 운동이 된다고 들었어. 듣자 하니, 한 시간 동안의 승마는 같은 양의 시간 동안 조깅하는 것보다 더 많은 열량을 태운대!

남: 굉장하구나. 그리고 나는 경쟁을 벌이는 승마가 훨씬 더 많은 열량을 소모한다고 확신하는데 이는 단지 스스로 제대로 된 자세를 유지하기 위해 더 열심히 노력해야 하기 때문이야.

여: 응, 맞아. 우리 강사가 어느 날은 우리를 트랙을 돌며 경주하게 했어. 버티는 게 너무 힘들었지.

남: 울타리와 도랑을 뛰어넘어야 하는 장애물 코스에서 말을 타는 것을 상상해봐!

여: ³¹난 내가 그걸 할 의향이 생길지 의문이야. 그냥 평지를 걷다가도 말에서 떨어진 적이 있고 그것은 나

해커스 지텔프 최신기출유형 실전문제집 7회 (Level 2)

bruised up. [31]The injuries would be much worse if I took a spill jumping through the air.

M: I agree. That is far more dangerous.

F: [32]Why don't you join my riding class? You might like it!

M: I was just thinking about the same thing. But I've ridden before, so I know the basics. [32]I'd like to learn some more advanced riding techniques.

F: No wonder! I thought you knew a lot about horseback riding. There is an intermediate-level class that meets at the same time as my beginner's class. Maybe you could take that one.

M: That could be an option. When is your next class? [33]I could go with you and talk to the instructors to find out which would be better for me.

F: [33]It's tomorrow at 2 p.m. If you're free, I can pick you up on my way there.

M: That's perfect. I'm off all day. Come by around noon and we can have lunch before heading to the stables.

남자가 다음에 할 일

를 멍들게 했어. [31]만약 내가 공중에서 점프를 하다가 떨어졌다면 부상이 훨씬 더 심각했을 거야.

남: 동의해. 그건 훨씬 더 위험하지.

여: [32]내 승마 수업에 함께하지 않을래? 네가 마음에 들어 할지도 몰라!

남: 나도 마침 같은 생각을 하고 있었어. 하지만 나는 전에 말을 타본 적이 있어서, 기본은 알고 있어. [32]나는 조금 더 고급 승마 기술을 배워보고 싶어.

여: 어쩐지! 나는 네가 승마에 대해 많이 안다고 생각했어. 내 초급반과 같은 시간에 진행되는 중급반이 있어. 아마 넌 그 수업을 수강할 수 있을 거야.

남: 그게 하나의 선택지가 될 수 있겠다. 너의 다음 수업은 언제야? [33]너와 함께 가서 어느 것이 나에게 더 좋을지 알아보기 위해 강사들과 이야기할 수 있을 것 같아.

여: [33]내일 오후 2시야. 네가 시간이 되면, 내가 그곳에 가는 길에 널 태우러 갈게.

남: 완벽해. 나는 하루 종일 쉬어. 정오쯤 오면 승마 교습장으로 향하기 전에 같이 점심을 먹을 수 있겠다.

어휘 | horseback riding 승마 stable[stéibəl] 승마 교습장 get over ~을 극복하다 concentrate[kάːnsəntreit] 집중하다 take on ~에 도전하다
challenging[tʃǽləndʒiŋ] 어려운 stimulate[stímjəleit] 자극하다 fitness[fítnəs] 체력 aerobic[eróubik] 유산소의
apparently[əpǽrəntli] 듣자 하니 competitive[kəmpétətiv] 경쟁을 벌이는 proper[prάːpər] 제대로 된 obstacle[άːbstəkəl] 장애물
fence[fens] 울타리 ditch[ditʃ] 도랑 be up for ~할 의향이 있다 bruise[bruːz] 멍이 들게 하다 take a spill 떨어지다

---

27 특정세부사항   What   난이도 ●○○

What is the reason that Sandra has been so busy lately?	Sandra가 최근에 매우 바빴던 이유는 무엇인가?
(a) She has been training for a horse race.	(a) 경마에 대비해 훈련을 해오고 있었다.
(b) She is planning to build a stable.	(b) 승마 교습장을 지을 계획을 하고 있다.
(c) She is learning to ride a horse.	**(c) 말 타는 법을 배우고 있다.**
(d) She has been taking lessons for her work.	(d) 그녀의 업무를 위한 수업을 받아오고 있었다.

━○ 지텔프 치트키

질문의 키워드 busy가 그대로 언급된 주변 내용을 주의 깊게 듣는다.

해설 | 여자가 'I've been busy.'라며 바빴다고 한 뒤, 'I started horseback riding lessons recently'라며 그녀가 최근에 승마 강습을 시작했다고 했다. 따라서 (c)가 정답이다.

Paraphrasing
lately 최근에 → recently 최근에
started horseback riding lessons 승마 강습을 시작했다 → learning to ride a horse 말 타는 법을 배우고 있는

어휘 | horse race 경마

TEST 1

TEST 2

TEST 3

TEST 4

TEST 5

TEST 6

TEST 7

해커스 지텔프 최신기출유형 실전문제집 7회 (Level 2)

28 추론　특정사실　　　　　　　　　　　　　　　　　　　　　난이도 ●●●

Why most likely is polo considered difficult?

(a) because the sport involves lots of concentration
(b) because players must be able to do two things at once
(c) because the sport takes many years to master
(d) because players must learn various riding styles

폴로가 왜 어렵다고 여겨지는 것 같은가?

(a) 그 스포츠가 많은 집중력을 수반하기 때문에
(b) 선수들이 한 번에 두 가지 일을 할 수 있어야 하기 때문에
(c) 그 스포츠는 숙달하는 데 수년이 걸리기 때문에
(d) 선수들이 다양한 승마 방식들을 배워야 하기 때문에

🎧 지텔프 치트키

질문의 키워드 polo가 그대로 언급된 주변 내용을 주의 깊게 듣는다.

해설 | 남자가 'horseback riding alone is already difficult without trying to hit a ball while doing it'이라며 승마를 하면서 공을 치려고 노력하는 것 없이도 승마는 그 자체로 이미 어렵다고 한 것을 통해, 선수들이 한 번에 두 가지 일을 할 수 있어야 하기 때문에 폴로가 어렵다고 여겨지는 것임을 추론할 수 있다. 따라서 (b)가 정답이다.

29 특정세부사항　What　　　　　　　　　　　　　　　　　　　난이도 ●●○

What surprised Sandra after her first class?

(a) She could barely control the horse.
(b) She found cuts on her legs.
(c) She was unable to stay balanced.
(d) She had serious muscle pains.

첫 수업 후 Sandra를 놀라게 한 것은 무엇인가?

(a) 말을 거의 통제할 수 없었다.
(b) 그녀의 다리에서 상처를 발견했다.
(c) 균형을 유지할 수 없었다.
(d) 심각한 근육통이 있었다.

🎧 지텔프 치트키

질문의 키워드 surprised가 shocked로 paraphrasing되어 언급된 주변 내용을 주의 깊게 듣는다.

해설 | 여자가 'I was shocked ~ the day after my first lesson.'이라며 첫 수업 다음 날 충격을 받았다고 한 뒤, 'My arms, legs, and core muscles were all hurting so much.'라며 자신의 팔, 다리, 그리고 코어근육들이 모두 너무 많이 아팠다고 했다. 따라서 (d)가 정답이다.

Paraphrasing
muscles were ~ hurting so much 근육들이 너무 많이 아팠다 → had serious muscle pains 심각한 근육통이 있었다

30 특정세부사항　Which　　　　　　　　　　　　　　　　　　난이도 ●●○

According to Franklin, which is a benefit of horseback riding?

(a) It helps one maintain good posture.
(b) It increases one's self-control.
(c) It works all parts of one's body.
(d) It improves one's relationship to animals.

Franklin에 따르면, 승마의 이점은 무엇인가?

(a) 좋은 자세를 유지하는 데 도움이 된다.
(b) 자기 통제력을 높인다.
(c) 신체의 모든 부분들을 움직인다.
(d) 동물들과의 관계를 향상시킨다.

질문의 키워드 horseback riding과 관련된 긍정적인 흐름을 파악한다.

해설 | 남자가 'Staying balanced while controlling the horse ~ stimulates those muscle groups.'라며 말을 통제하면서 균형을 유지하는 것이 근육 부위들을 자극한다고 한 뒤, 'That's why horseback riding is a great exercise for the entire body.'라며 그것이 승마가 훌륭한 전신 운동인 이유라고 했다. 따라서 (c)가 정답이다.

Paraphrasing
exercise for the entire body 전신 운동 → works all parts of one's body 신체의 모든 부분들을 움직인다

---

31 특정세부사항 Why
난이도 ●●○

Why is Sandra not up for trying an obstacle course?

(a) because she cannot mount a horse safely
(b) because she is worried about injuries
(c) because she cannot jump over fences
(d) because she is dedicated to racing

Sandra는 왜 장애물 코스를 시도할 의향이 없는가?

(a) 안전하게 말에 올라탈 수 없기 때문에
(b) 부상이 걱정되기 때문에
(c) 울타리를 뛰어넘을 수 없기 때문에
(d) 경주에 전념하고 있기 때문에

○ 지텔프 치트키

질문의 키워드 obstacle course가 그대로 언급된 주변 내용을 주의 깊게 듣는다.

해설 | 여자가 'I doubt I'll ever be up for that.'이라며 자신이 장애물 코스를 할 의향이 생길지 의문이라고 한 뒤, 'The injuries would be much worse if I took a spill jumping through the air.'라며 만약 공중에서 점프를 하다가 떨어졌다면 부상이 훨씬 더 심각했을 것이라고 했다. 따라서 (b)가 정답이다.

어휘 | mount[maunt] 올라타다 dedicated[dédikeitid] 전념하는, 헌신하는

---

32 특정세부사항 How
난이도 ●●○

How does Franklin hope to gain from riding lessons?

(a) by learning higher-level skills
(b) by getting tips from his fellow students
(c) by spending more time with his friend
(d) by attaining insight from instructors

Franklin은 어떻게 승마 수업으로부터 이득을 얻기를 바라는가?

(a) 더 높은 수준의 기술을 배움으로써
(b) 그의 동료 학생들로부터 조언을 받음으로써
(c) 그의 친구와 더 많은 시간을 보냄으로써
(d) 강사들로부터 통찰력을 얻어냄으로써

○ 지텔프 치트키

질문의 키워드 riding lessons가 riding class로 paraphrasing되어 언급된 주변 내용을 주의 깊게 듣는다.

해설 | 여자가 'Why don't you join my riding class?'라며 자신의 승마 수업에 함께할 것을 제안하자, 남자가 'I'd like to learn ~ more advanced riding techniques.'라며 더 고급 승마 기술을 배워보고 싶다고 했다. 따라서 (a)가 정답이다.

Paraphrasing
advanced ~ techniques 고급 기술 → higher-level skills 더 높은 수준의 기술

어휘 | attain[ətéin] 얻어내다, 획득하다 insight[ínsait] 통찰력, 이해

TEST 1
TEST 2
TEST 3
TEST 4
TEST 5
TEST 6
TEST 7

해커스 지텔프 최신기출유형 실전문제집 7회 (Level 2)

33 추론 다음에 할 일

난이도 ●●○

Based on the conversation, what will Franklin most likely do tomorrow?

(a) visit a riding facility
(b) take a placement test
(c) drive a friend to his class
(d) have a riding lesson

대화에 따르면, Franklin이 내일 할 일은 무엇일 것 같은가?

(a) 승마 시설을 방문한다
(b) 배치 시험을 본다
(c) 친구를 그의 수업에 차로 데려다준다
(d) 승마 강습을 받는다

지텔프 치트키

다음에 할 일을 언급하는 후반을 주의 깊게 듣는다.

해설 | 남자가 'I could go with you and talk to the instructors to find out which would be better for me.'라며 여자와 함께 가서 어느 것이 자신에게 더 좋을지 알아보기 위해 강사들과 이야기할 수 있을 것 같다고 하자, 여자가 'It's tomorrow at 2 p.m.'이라며 다음 수업이 내일 오후 2시라고 한 것을 통해, Franklin이 내일 승마 시설을 방문할 것임을 추론할 수 있다. 따라서 (a)가 정답이다.

PART 2 [34~39] 발표 학교 오케스트라 홍보

음성 바로 듣기

주제 제시: 학교 동아리 홍보

Hello, I have been working as the musical director of Red Grove High School's Maple Orchestra for the last six years. Starting today, we are accepting sign-ups for new members who want to join.

동아리 소개

Over the years, ³⁴the Maple Orchestra has been a major point of pride for our school. It has won several awards, with the most notable being the prize for best youth ensemble in the nation. Also, numerous players have gone on to earn music scholarships from prestigious universities and some even play for international orchestras.

연습 공간과 충분한 예산

³⁵Our orchestra is in a fortunate position. We have a dedicated on-campus music room where we can practice uninterrupted. In addition, ³⁵the school provides an adequate budget that we use to keep a supply of quality instruments on hand. For a small fee, any orchestra member can rent an instrument for the entire school year.

보유 악기 종류

Speaking of instruments, let me tell you what we have available. You can pick a string or brass, a woodwind, a keyboard, or even a percussion instrument. We possess everything from violins and flutes to harps and timpani which are rare to come across in your daily life.

안녕하세요, 저는 지난 6년 동안 Red Grove 고등학교 Maple 오케스트라의 지휘자로 일해 왔습니다. 오늘부터, 저희는 가입하기를 원하는 신규 단원들의 신청을 받을 것입니다.

수년 동안, ³⁴Maple 오케스트라는 우리 학교의 주요 자랑거리였습니다. 그것은 여러 상들을 받아 왔으며, 가장 주목할 만한 것은 전국 최우수 청소년 합주단 상입니다. 또한, 많은 연주자들이 명문 대학에서 음악 장학금을 받아 왔고 일부는 국제적인 오케스트라에서도 연주하고 있습니다.

³⁵저희 오케스트라는 운이 좋은 상황에 있습니다. 저희는 방해받지 않고 연습할 수 있는 교내 전용 음악실이 있습니다. 게다가, 저희가 보유하고 있는 질 좋은 악기들의 공급을 유지하는 데 사용할 ³⁵충분한 예산을 학교가 제공합니다. 적은 회비로, 어떤 오케스트라 단원이라도 학기 내내 악기를 빌릴 수 있습니다.

악기에 대해 말씀드리자면, 저희가 사용할 수 있는 것에 대해 알려 드리겠습니다. 여러분은 현악기나 금관 악기, 목관 악기, 건반, 혹은 심지어 타악기도 고를 수 있습니다. 저희는 바이올린과 플루트부터 일상생활에서 접하기 힘든 하프와 팀파니까지 모든 것을 보유하고 있습니다.

동아리 일정

What you need to know is that being a member of the Maple Orchestra can be a serious commitment. [36(b)]We practice three times a week in two-hour-long sessions. I expect all players to arrive on time and [36(a)]to act in a professional manner. We are currently [36(d)]scheduled for eight performances this year, including two out-of-state trips. On those outings, we will compete against other schools from around the country. While performing and traveling, keep in mind that [36(c)]we must always respectfully represent our school.

장점1: 인지 및 사교 능력 향상

Now, why should you join the orchestra? For starters, [37]playing music can boost your grades. Learning to read music, concentrating for long periods, and developing a sense of self-discipline have been shown to improve cognitive abilities. You will also have the opportunity to strengthen your social skills. This will come as a result of communicating with your fellow bandmates and meeting other students from different schools.

장점2: 자신감 향상

Furthermore, participating in the orchestra can build your confidence. It's no secret that learning to play an instrument is difficult. But through persistence and hard work, you will no doubt become adept at your instrument. You can then apply this lesson to other areas of life. Whenever I face a challenge, I feel secure in my ability to overcome it because of the work ethic I have developed through music. And, of course, [38]performing in front of audiences will make you more self-confident as well.

장점3: 악기 연주의 기쁨

I haven't even mentioned the sheer joy that accompanies playing an instrument. The skill you gain in the Maple Orchestra will stay with you for the rest of your life. Playing can be a fun hobby and an outlet to express your creativity.

가입 안내

As I mentioned, the sign-up period opens today and will close at the end of the week. If you're interested, please head over to the music room to add your name and your top two preferred instruments to the list. [39]Don't worry if you're unsure of which instrument you should play. I will be there to help you decide.

여러분이 아셔야 할 것은 Maple 오케스트라의 단원이 되는 것이 상당한 헌신이 될 수 있다는 것입니다. [36(b)]저희는 2시간씩 일주일에 3번 연습합니다. 저는 모든 연주자들이 제시간에 도착하여 [36(a)]전문가적인 태도로 행동하기를 기대합니다. 저희는 현재 [36(d)]두 차례 다른 주로 출장 가는 것을 포함하여, 올해 8번의 공연이 계획되어 있습니다. 그 출장들에서, 저희는 전국에서 온 타 학교들과 경쟁할 것입니다. 공연과 여행을 하는 동안, [36(c)]저희는 항상 학교를 공손하게 대표해야 한다는 것을 명심하십시오.

자, 여러분은 왜 오케스트라에 가입해야 할까요? 우선, [37]음악을 연주하는 것은 여러분의 성적을 높일 수 있습니다. 악보 읽는 것을 배우고, 오랜 시간 동안 집중하며, 자기 수양 의식을 기르는 것이 인지 능력을 향상시키는 것으로 밝혀졌습니다. 여러분에게 또한 사교 능력을 강화할 기회가 있을 것입니다. 이것은 동료 단원들과 의사소통하고 다양한 학교에서 온 다른 학생들을 만나는 것의 결과로 나타날 것입니다.

나아가, 오케스트라에 참여하는 것은 여러분의 자신감을 키워 줄 수 있습니다. 악기 연주를 배우는 것이 어렵다는 것은 누구나 아는 사실입니다. 그러나 끈기와 노력을 통해, 여러분은 틀림없이 여러분의 악기에 능숙해질 것입니다. 그런 다음 여러분은 이 교훈을 삶의 다른 영역에 적용할 수 있습니다. 저는 어려운 일에 직면할 때마다, 음악을 통해 길러온 근면 덕분에 그것을 극복하는 제 능력에 확신을 느낍니다. 그리고, 물론, [38]청중 앞에서 공연하는 것은 또한 여러분을 더욱 자신감 있게 만들어 줄 것입니다.

악기를 연주하는 것에 수반되는 순수한 기쁨에 대해서는 심지어 언급하지도 않았습니다. Maple 오케스트라에서 쌓은 능력은 평생 여러분과 함께할 것입니다. 악기 연주는 재미있는 취미이자 창의력을 표현하는 배출구가 될 수 있습니다.

제가 언급했듯이, 신청 기간은 오늘 시작되며 이번 주 말에 마감될 것입니다. 만약 관심이 있으시면, 음악실로 오셔서 명단에 여러분의 이름과 선호하는 상위 두 개의 악기를 기재하십시오. [39]어떤 악기를 연주해야 할지 잘 모르겠더라도 걱정하지 마세요. 제가 여러분이 결정하는 것을 돕기 위해 그곳에 있을 것입니다.

어휘 | notable[nóutəbəl] 주목할 만한 scholarship[skάːlərʃip] 장학금 prestigious[prestídʒəs] 명문의 adequate[ǽdikwət] 충분한 brass[bræs] 금관 악기 woodwind[wúdwìnd] 목관 악기 percussion[pərkʌ́ʃən] 타악기 commitment[kəmítmənt] 헌신 outing[áutiŋ] 출장, 여행 respectfully[rispéktfəli] 공손하게 represent[rèprizént] 대표하다 boost[buːst] 높이다 self-discipline 자기 수양 cognitive[kάːgnətiv] 인지의 persistence[pərsístəns] 끈기 adept[ədépt] 능숙한 secure[sikjúr] 확신하는 overcome[òuvərkʌ́m] 극복하다 sheer[ʃir] 순수한 accompany[əkʌ́mpəni] 수반되다 outlet[áutlet] 배출구

34 특정세부사항 What

난이도 ●●○

What makes the orchestra a source of pride for the school?

(a) the former players who teach music in school
(b) the scholarships that the orchestra offers
(c) the honors that the ensemble has earned
(d) the international player who runs the program

무엇이 오케스트라를 학교의 자랑거리로 만드는가?

(a) 학교에서 음악을 가르치는 이전 연주자들
(b) 오케스트라가 제공하는 장학금들
(c) 합주단이 받아 온 상들
(d) 프로그램을 운영하는 국제적인 연주자

─○ 지텔프 치트키

질문의 키워드 a source of pride가 point of pride로 paraphrasing되어 언급된 주변 내용을 주의 깊게 듣는다.

해설 | 화자가 'the Maple Orchestra has been a major point of pride for our school'이라며 Maple 오케스트라가 학교의 주요 자랑거리였다고 한 뒤, 'It has won several awards, with the most notable being the prize for best youth ensemble in the nation.'이라며 오케스트라가 여러 상들을 받아 왔으며, 가장 주목할 만한 것은 전국 최우수 청소년 합주단 상이라고 했다. 따라서 (c)가 정답이다.

Paraphrasing
It has won ~ awards 그것이 상들을 받아 왔다 → the honors that the ensemble has earned 합주단이 받아 온 상들

35 특정세부사항 Why

난이도 ●●○

Why does the speaker say that the Maple Orchestra is in a favorable situation?

(a) because it provides instruments for free
(b) because it replaces its instruments each year
(c) because it has a practice studio near the school
(d) because it receives sufficient school funding

화자는 왜 Maple 오케스트라가 좋은 상황에 있다고 말하는가?

(a) 악기를 무료로 제공하기 때문에
(b) 매년 그것의 악기를 교체하기 때문에
(c) 학교 근처에 연습실이 있기 때문에
(d) 학교의 충분한 재정 지원을 받기 때문에

─○ 지텔프 치트키

질문의 키워드 favorable situation이 fortunate position으로 paraphrasing되어 언급된 주변 내용을 주의 깊게 듣는다.

해설 | 화자가 'Our orchestra is in a fortunate position.'이라며 오케스트라가 운이 좋은 상황에 있다고 한 뒤, 'the school provides an adequate budget'이라며 학교가 충분한 예산을 제공한다고 했다. 따라서 (d)가 정답이다.

Paraphrasing
the school provides an adequate budget 학교가 충분한 예산을 제공한다 → sufficient school funding 학교의 충분한 재정 지원

오답분석
(c) 화자가 오케스트라가 방해받지 않고 연습할 수 있는 전용 음악실이 교내에 있다고 했으므로 오답이다.

어휘 | favorable[féivərəbəl] 좋은, 호의적인 replace[ripléis] 교체하다 sufficient[səfíʃənt] 충분한 funding[fʌ́ndiŋ] 재정 지원, 자금

36 Not/True Not 문제

난이도 ●●●

Which is not a requirement for members of the Maple Orchestra?

Maple 오케스트라 단원들에게 요구되는 것이 아닌 것은 무엇인가?

해커스 지텔프 최신기출유형 실전문제집 7회 (Level 2)

(a) to conduct themselves in a professional way

(b) to practice for two hours daily

(c) to be a positive example of their school

(d) to travel to other states for performances

(a) 전문가적인 태도로 행동하는 것

(b) 매일 2시간 동안 연습하는 것

(c) 학교에 긍정적인 본보기가 되는 것

(d) 공연을 위해 다른 주로 이동하는 것

⊶○ 지텔프 치트키

보기의 키워드와 담화의 내용을 대조하며 듣는다.

해설 | (b)는 화자가 'We practice three times a week in two-hour-long sessions.'라며 오케스트라 단원들은 2시간씩 일주일에 3번 연습한다고 언급했으므로 담화의 내용과 일치하지 않는다. 따라서 (b)가 정답이다.

>   오답분석
>
>   (a) 화자가 모든 연주자들이 전문가적인 태도로 행동하기를 기대한다고 언급하였다.
>   (c) 화자가 연주자들이 항상 학교를 공손하게 대표해야 한다고 언급하였다.
>   (d) 화자가 두 차례 다른 주로 출장 가는 것을 포함하여 8번의 공연이 계획되어 있다고 언급하였다.

---

37 특정세부사항 How   난이도 ●●○

According to the speaker, how does playing in the orchestra help improve grades?

(a) by developing students' ability to focus

(b) by providing extra time to study between shows

(c) by tutoring students in a range of subjects

(d) by promoting discussion between band members

화자에 따르면, 오케스트라에서 연주하는 것이 성적을 올리는 데 어떻게 도움이 되는가?

(a) 학생들의 집중력을 발달시킴으로써

(b) 공연들 사이에 공부할 별도의 시간을 제공함으로써

(c) 다양한 과목들을 학생들에게 개인 지도함으로써

(d) 악단원들 사이의 토론을 촉진함으로써

⊶○ 지텔프 치트키

질문의 키워드 improve grades가 boost ~ grades로 paraphrasing되어 언급된 주변 내용을 주의 깊게 듣는다.

해설 | 화자가 'playing music can boost ~ grades'라며 음악을 연주하는 것이 성적을 높일 수 있다고 한 뒤, 'Learning to read music, concentrating for long periods ~ have been shown to improve cognitive abilities.'라며 오랜 시간 동안 집중하는 것 등이 인지 능력을 향상시키는 것으로 밝혀졌다고 했다. 따라서 (a)가 정답이다.

Paraphrasing

concentrating for long periods 오랜 시간 동안 집중하는 것 → students' ability to focus 집중력

---

38 특정세부사항 What   난이도 ●●○

Based on the talk, what can strengthen a student's sense of confidence?

(a) learning to accept failure as a part of life

(b) mastering a skill with little difficulty

(c) learning to speak in front of an audience

(d) playing an instrument before a crowd

담화에 따르면, 학생의 자신감을 강화할 수 있는 것은 무엇인가?

(a) 실패를 삶의 일부로 받아들이는 법을 배우는 것

(b) 별 어려움 없이 기술을 숙달하는 것

(c) 청중 앞에서 말하는 법을 배우는 것

(d) 군중 앞에서 악기를 연주하는 것

🔑—○ 지텔프 치트키

질문의 키워드 sense of confidence가 self-confident로 paraphrasing되어 언급된 주변 내용을 주의 깊게 듣는다.

해설 | 화자가 'performing in front of audiences will make you more self-confident as well'이라며 청중 앞에서 공연하는 것이 학생을 더욱 자신감 있게 만들어 줄 것이라고 했다. 따라서 (d)가 정답이다.

Paraphrasing
strengthen a ~ sense of confidence 자신감을 강화하다 → make you more self-confident 더욱 자신감 있게 만들어 주다
performing in front of audiences 청중 앞에서 공연하는 것 → playing an instrument before a crowd 군중 앞에서 악기를 연주하는 것

| 39 | **추론** | 특정사실 | 난이도 ●●○ |

Why most likely will the speaker be in the music room during the enrollment period?

(a) She will let the students try out different instruments.
(b) She will help students choose what instrument to play.
(c) She will teach music to students in after-school classes.
(d) She will share her musical interests with students.

왜 화자는 등록 기간 동안 음악실에 있을 것 같은가?

(a) 학생들이 다양한 악기들을 시도하게 할 것이다.
(b) 학생들이 어떤 악기를 연주할지 선택하는 것을 도울 것이다.
(c) 방과 후 수업에서 학생들에게 음악을 가르칠 것이다.
(d) 그녀의 음악적 관심사를 학생들과 공유할 것이다.

해설 | 화자가 'Don't worry if you're unsure of which instrument you should play.'라며 어떤 악기를 연주해야 할지 잘 모르겠더라도 걱정하지 말라고 한 뒤, 'I will be there to help you decide.'라며 학생들이 결정하는 것을 돕기 위해 자신이 그곳(음악실)에 있을 것이라고 한 것을 통해, 학생들이 어떤 악기를 연주할지 선택하는 것을 돕기 위해 화자가 등록 기간 동안 음악실에 있을 것임을 추론할 수 있다. 따라서 (b)가 정답이다.

Paraphrasing
enrollment period 등록 기간 → sign-up period 신청 기간

PART 3[40~45] 장단점 논의 가이드가 있는 여행과 혼자 하는 여행의 장단점 비교

음성 바로 듣기

| 안부
인사 | F: Hi, Victor. Summer break is right around the corner. Have you finalized the plans for your trip to Italy?
M: Hey, Laura. Unfortunately, I haven't. I keep going back and forth about the type of vacation I want to take. | 여: 안녕, Victor. 여름방학이 바로 코앞에 와 있네. 이 탈리아 여행 계획은 마무리했어?
남: 안녕, Laura. 유감스럽게도, 아직 못 했어. 나는 내가 가고 싶은 휴가의 유형에 대해 계속 갈팡질팡하고 있거든. |
| 주제
제시:
장단점
비교 | F: What do you mean? I thought you'd already decided to spend six weeks in Italy.
M: Oh, yes. The destination and time frame are all set. I mean ⁴⁰I'm not sure if I should join a guided tour or if I should just go alone. | 여: 무슨 말이야? 나는 네가 이미 이탈리아에서 6주를 보내기로 결정했다고 생각했어.
남: 오, 맞아. 목적지와 기간은 모두 정해졌어. 내 말은 ⁴⁰가이드가 있는 여행에 합류할지 아니면 그냥 혼자 가야 할지 잘 모르겠다는 뜻이야. |

	F: Ah, gotcha. That's a big decision. I've gone on both types of trips and they're so different that the one you choose can totally change your experience.
	M: Is that so? Maybe you can tell me what you thought about each and help me figure out which one would best suit my needs.
가이드 있는 여행의 장점	F: I can try. Probably [41]the best thing about taking a guided tour is that it's much more convenient. Once you've selected a tour package, you don't have to do anything else.
	M: That's true. [41]The tour would all be planned out, including accommodations, meals, and transportation.
	F: Not to mention the fact that you'd have a guide who knows the area inside out and can speak the local language fluently. That would give you the opportunity to learn things that solo tourists would miss.
가이드 있는 여행의 단점	M: That sounds ideal. Was there anything you didn't like about going on an organized tour?
	F: Well, [42]it is kind of rigid. You don't have a lot of free time to explore or meet local people.
	M: Hmm . . . That doesn't appeal to me. Getting to know people of different cultures is one of my favorite parts of traveling.
혼자 하는 여행의 장점	F: In that case, a solo trip would be best for you then. [43]It's much easier to go out and make friends with locals when you're on your own. Others are also more likely to approach you if they see that you're alone.
	M: Ha-ha. I understand how that would be true. It might even give me a chance to practice speaking Italian a little since I won't have a guide to talk for me.
	F: Yes, you'd definitely pick up quite a bit of the language that way. You'd also be able to save tons of money. If you know how to stretch your budget, traveling by yourself can actually be the more affordable option. You can stay in hostels and eat at local shops instead of going to places for tourists.
혼자 하는 여행의 단점	M: All of that sounds great. Did you come across any downsides to planning your own trip?
	F: Yeah, there were a few things. [44]The worst is that it gets lonely. You meet many interesting people from the area but most of them are only around for a few hours and then you're alone again.

여: 아, 알겠어. 그건 중요한 결정이지. 나는 두 가지 유형의 여행을 모두 가 봤는데 그것들은 너무 달라서 네가 선택하는 것이 너의 경험을 완전히 바꿀 수 있어.

남: 그래? 어쩌면 네가 나에게 각각에 대해 어떻게 생각했는지 이야기해주고 어느 것이 내 요구를 가장 잘 만족시킬지를 찾는 데 도움을 줄 수 있을 거야.

여: 해 볼게. 아마도 [41]가이드가 있는 여행을 하는 것의 가장 좋은 점은 그게 훨씬 더 편하다는 거야. 일단 네가 여행 패키지를 선택하면, 그 밖의 다른 일은 할 필요가 없어.

남: 맞아. [41]그 여행은 숙소, 식사, 그리고 교통수단을 포함한 모든 것이 계획되어 있을 거야.

여: 그 지역을 환히 알고 있고 현지 언어를 유창하게 구사할 수 있는 가이드가 있다는 사실은 말할 것도 없어. 그것은 너에게 혼자 여행하는 사람들이 놓칠 수 있는 것들을 배울 기회를 줄 거야.

남: 이상적인 것 같네. 단체 여행을 하는 것에 관해 마음에 들지 않았던 점은 없었어?

여: 음, [42]그건 조금 융통성이 없어. 답사하거나 현지 사람들을 만날 자유 시간이 많지 않거든.

남: 흠... 그 점은 내게 매력적이지 않네. 다른 문화의 사람들을 알아가는 것은 여행에서 내가 가장 좋아하는 부분 중 하나야.

여: 그 경우에는, 그럼 혼자 하는 여행이 가장 좋을 것 같아. [43]혼자 있으면 밖에 나가서 현지인들과 친구가 되는 것이 훨씬 더 쉬워. 다른 사람들 또한 네가 혼자인 것을 보면 너에게 다가갈 가능성이 더 크거든.

남: 하하. 어떻게 그게 진짜일지 알겠어. 나를 위해 말을 해 줄 가이드가 없을 테니 그것이 나에게 이탈리아어 말하기를 조금 연습할 기회를 줄 수도 있겠다.

여: 응, 그런 식으로 너는 분명 언어를 꽤 많이 배울 거야. 넌 또한 아주 많은 돈을 절약할 수 있을 거야. 만약 네가 예산을 절약하는 방법을 알고 있다면, 혼자 여행하는 것이 사실상 더 저렴한 선택지가 될 수 있어. 너는 관광객들을 위한 장소에 가는 것 대신에 호스텔에 머물고 현지 가게에서 식사하면 돼.

남: 모두 훌륭한 것 같네. 혼자 하는 여행을 계획하는 데 있어 어떤 단점이라도 발견했어?

여: 응, 몇 가지가 있었어. [44]가장 안 좋은 점은 외로워진다는 거야. 너는 그 지역에서 많은 흥미로운 사람들을 만나겠지만 그들 대부분은 단지 몇 시간 동안만 주위에 있을 거고 그런 다음 너는 다시 혼자일 거야.

M: That could be a problem. Also, I wouldn't have anyone to share the experience with.

F: Right. And not knowing anyone might expose you to dangerous situations like tourist scams.

M: That's something I hadn't thought about before.

F: You would be okay, but it's something to consider.

남: 그게 문제가 될 수 있겠네. 또한, 경험을 공유할 사람도 없을 거야.

여: 맞아. 그리고 아무도 모르는 것은 너를 관광 사기와 같은 위험한 상황에 노출시킬지도 몰라.

남: 그건 내가 전에는 생각해보지 못했던 점이야.

여: 아마 별일 없겠지만, 고려해야 할 사항이야.

남자의 결정

M: Thanks for talking this through with me, Laura.

F: No problem. Has it helped you make a decision?

M: Yes. ⁴⁵I'm going to go for the option that will allow me to become more acquainted with the local residents.

남: 이것에 관해 나와 끝까지 이야기를 나눠줘서 고마워, Laura.

여: 고맙기는. 네가 결정하는 데 도움이 되었니?

남: 응. ⁴⁵나는 현지 주민들과 더 친해지게 할 선택지를 택할 것 같아.

어휘 | around the corner 코앞에 와 있는 accommodation[əkàːmədéiʃən] 숙소 inside out 환히, 구석구석까지 fluently[flúːəntli] 유창하게 ideal[àidíəl] 이상적인 rigid[rídʒid] 융통성이 없는 pick up 배우다 stretch one's budget 예산을 절약하다 affordable[əfɔ́ːrdəbəl] 저렴한 expose[ikspóuz] 노출시키다 scam[skæm] 사기 go for ~을 택하다 acquainted[əkwéintid] 친한

---

40 주제/목적   대화의 주제   난이도 ●○○

What are Victor and Laura discussing?

(a) where to buy flight tickets
(b) how to get travel information
(c) the ideal time to visit Italy
(d) the options for a trip

Victor와 Laura는 무엇에 관해 논의하고 있는가?

(a) 비행기 표를 사는 곳
(b) 여행 정보를 얻는 방법
(c) 이탈리아를 방문하기에 이상적인 시기
(d) 여행의 선택지들

지텔프 치트키

대화의 주제를 언급하는 초반을 주의 깊게 듣고 전체 맥락을 파악한다.

해설 | 남자가 'I'm not sure if I should join a guided tour or if I should just go alone'이라며 가이드가 있는 여행에 합류할지 아니면 혼자 가야 할지 잘 모르겠다고 한 뒤, 대화 전반에 걸쳐 어떤 유형의 여행을 선택할지를 논의하는 내용이 이어지고 있다. 따라서 (d)가 정답이다.

---

41 특정세부사항   장·단점   난이도 ●●○

According to Laura, what is the best part about traveling with a guide?

(a) It requires less effort to plan.
(b) It provides well-located lodging.
(c) It includes language learning opportunities.
(d) It offers large discounts.

Laura에 따르면, 가이드와 함께 여행하는 것에 관해 가장 좋은 점은 무엇인가?

(a) 계획하는 데 더 적은 노력이 요구된다.
(b) 위치가 좋은 숙소를 제공한다.
(c) 언어 학습 기회를 포함한다.
(d) 큰 할인을 제공한다.

지텔프 치트키

질문의 키워드 traveling with a guide와 관련된 긍정적인 흐름을 파악한다.

해커스 지텔프 최신기출유형 실전문제집 7회 (Level 2)

해설 | 여자가 'the best thing about taking a guided tour is that it's much more convenient'라며 가이드가 있는 여행을 하는 것의 가장 좋은 점은 그것이 훨씬 더 편하다는 것이라고 하자, 남자가 'The tour would all be planned out, including accommodations, meals, and transportation.'이라며 그 여행은 숙소, 식사, 그리고 교통수단을 포함한 모든 것이 계획되어 있을 것이라고 했다. 따라서 (a)가 정답이다.

Paraphrasing
much more convenient 훨씬 더 편한 → requires less effort 더 적은 노력이 요구된다

어휘 | well-located 위치가 좋은 lodging[láːdʒiŋ] 숙소 discount[dískaunt] 할인

---

42 특정세부사항 How   난이도 ●●○

How are organized tours more restrictive than solo travel?	어떻게 단체 여행이 혼자 하는 여행보다 더 제한적인가?
(a) They stay away from locations with mass appeal.	(a) 대중성이 있는 장소에 접근하지 않는다.
(b) They decrease the chances of encountering other travelers.	(b) 다른 여행자들을 마주칠 기회를 감소시킨다.
(c) They serve specific types of cuisines.	(c) 특정한 종류의 요리를 제공한다.
(d) They reduce the occasions for spare time.	**(d) 여유 시간의 기회를 줄인다.**

⟲○ 지텔프 치트키
질문의 키워드 restrictive가 rigid로 paraphrasing되어 언급된 주변 내용을 주의 깊게 듣는다.

해설 | 여자가 'it is ~ rigid'라며 단체 여행은 융통성이 없다고 한 뒤, 'You don't have a lot of free time to explore or meet local people.'이라며 답사하거나 현지 사람들을 만날 자유 시간이 많지 않다고 했다. 따라서 (d)가 정답이다.

Paraphrasing
free time 자유 시간 → spare time 여유 시간

어휘 | restrictive[ristríktiv] 제한적인 stay away ~에 접근하지 않다 mass[mæs] 대중의 encounter[inkáuntər] 마주치다

---

43 특정세부사항 How   난이도 ●●○

How does traveling alone make it easier to meet local people?	혼자 여행하는 것이 어떻게 현지 사람들을 만나는 것을 더 쉽게 만드는가?
(a) by allowing one to avoid tourist areas	(a) 관광지들을 피할 수 있게 함으로써
(b) by making one seem approachable	**(b) 다가가기 쉬워 보이게 함으로써**
(c) by signaling a need for help	(c) 도움이 필요하다는 신호를 보냄으로써
(d) by showing familiarity with the native culture	(d) 고유문화를 잘 알고 있음을 보여줌으로써

⟲○ 지텔프 치트키
질문의 키워드 local people이 locals로 paraphrasing되어 언급된 주변 내용을 주의 깊게 듣는다.

해설 | 여자가 'It's much easier to ~ make friends with locals when you're on your own.'이라며 혼자 있으면 현지인들과 친구가 되는 것이 훨씬 더 쉽다고 한 뒤, 'Others are ~ more likely to approach you if they see that you're alone.'이라며 다른 사람들이 여행자가 혼자인 것을 보면 여행자에게 다가갈 가능성이 더 크다고 했다. 따라서 (b)가 정답이다.

TEST 1

TEST 2

TEST 3

TEST 4

TEST 5

TEST 6

TEST 7

해커스 지텔프 최신기출유형 실전문제집 7회 (Level 2)

Paraphrasing

more likely to approach 다가갈 가능성이 더 큰 → approachable 다가가기 쉬운

어휘 | signal[sígnəl] 신호를 보내다　familiarity[fəmìliǽrəti] 잘 알고 있음　native[néitiv] 고유의

---

44 특정세부사항　Why

난이도 ●●○

Why do solo travelers get lonely even when they come across others?

(a) because they don't speak the local language
(b) because their interactions are limited to individual activities
(c) because their relationships don't last long
(d) because they often have differing interests

왜 혼자 여행하는 사람들은 심지어 다른 사람들을 만날 때에도 외로워지는가?

(a) 현지 언어를 구사하지 못하기 때문에
(b) 교류가 개별적인 활동으로 제한되기 때문에
(c) 관계가 오래 지속되지 않기 때문에
(d) 종종 서로 다른 관심사를 가지고 있기 때문에

── ○ 지텔프 치트키

질문의 키워드 lonely가 그대로 언급된 주변 내용을 주의 깊게 듣는다.

해설 | 여자가 'The worst is that it gets lonely.'라며 혼자 하는 여행의 가장 안 좋은 점은 외로워진다는 것이라고 한 뒤, 'You meet many interesting people ~ but most of them are only around for a few hours and then you're alone again.'이라며 많은 흥미로운 사람들을 만나겠지만 그들 대부분은 단지 몇 시간 동안만 주위에 있을 것이고 여행자는 다시 혼자일 것이라고 했다. 따라서 (c)가 정답이다.

Paraphrasing

most of them are only around for a few hours 그들 대부분은 단지 몇 시간 동안만 주위에 있을 것이다 → their relationships don't last long 관계가 오래 지속되지 않다

어휘 | interaction[ìntərǽkʃən] 교류, 상호 작용　last[læst] 지속되다

---

45 추론　다음에 할 일

난이도 ●●○

What has Victor probably decided to do about his summer vacation?

(a) look for another destination
(b) organize a trip of his own
(c) invite Laura to join him
(d) contact a tour operator

Victor는 여름휴가에 관해 무엇을 하기로 결정한 것 같은가?

(a) 또 다른 행선지를 찾는다
(b) 자신만의 여행을 계획한다
(c) Laura를 그와 함께하자고 초대한다
(d) 패키지여행 전문 여행업자에게 연락한다

── ○ 지텔프 치트키

다음에 할 일을 언급하는 후반을 주의 깊게 듣는다.

해설 | 남자가 'I'm going to go for the option that will allow me to become more acquainted with the local residents.'라며 현지 주민들과 더 친해지게 할 선택지를 택할 것이라고 한 것을 통해, Victor는 여름휴가에 관해 가이드 없이 혼자 하는 자신만의 여행을 계획하기로 결정한 것임을 추론할 수 있다. 따라서 (b)가 정답이다.

인사 + 주제 제시

Good afternoon, everyone. As we all know, it's becoming more common to hold online work meetings from home nowadays. That's why I've prepared several tips that will facilitate these virtual gatherings. Whether you are the host or simply an attendee, following this advice will make your meetings more efficient and productive.

조언1: 장비 확인 + 자료 준비

[46]First, check the technology. Before the work session, test out the camera and microphone on your computer to make sure you can be seen and heard properly. After completing the inspection, familiarize yourself with how the video conferencing program works. If you plan on giving a presentation, have your files open so you can display them without delay.

조언2: 방해 요소 제거

Second, eliminate distractions. Like the previous tip, take care of this prior to the meeting. [47]Notify others in your home about the conference and let them know how long you will be unavailable. [47]This will keep them from interrupting you while you're working. Also, limit surrounding noise by turning off nearby televisions and closing windows. And shut the door of the room you're in to create a quiet space where you can focus.

조언3: 체계화

Third, stay organized. Schedule calls on a shared calendar and send invitations to the relevant parties well in advance. As the appointment date approaches, leave them a friendly reminder. For the meeting itself, [48]arrange an agenda that details the items to discuss and the goals of the gathering. This will let everyone know what to expect and prepare, while also making certain that no one's time is wasted.

조언4: 업무 환경 조성

Fourth, despite the comfort of being home, [49]try to foster a professional atmosphere. We can accomplish this by wearing work-appropriate attire that conveys a business-like attitude and also demonstrates etiquette to colleagues. Being dressed in casual clothes can signal that you're not ready to work. Similarly, find a neutral background. I recommend a blank wall or an orderly bookshelf. If neither of these options is available, then consider downloading a plain virtual backdrop. Backgrounds crowded with clutter make it hard for others to focus and get into work mode.

Fifth, listen more than you speak. In general, it's best to leave the microphone on mute. Doing so removes background noise and decreases the likelihood of

안녕하세요, 여러분. 우리 모두 알다시피, 요즘은 집에서 온라인 업무 회의를 주최하는 것이 더 보편화되고 있습니다. 그래서 저는 이러한 가상 모임을 용이하게 할 몇 가지 조언들을 준비했습니다. 여러분이 주최자이든 혹은 그저 참석자이든, 이 조언을 따르는 것은 여러분의 회의를 더욱 효율적이고 생산적이게 만들 것입니다.

[46]첫째, 장비를 확인하십시오. 업무 시간 전에, 여러분이 제대로 보이고 들릴 수 있는지 확실히 하기 위해 컴퓨터의 카메라와 마이크를 점검하십시오. 점검을 마친 후, 화상 회의 프로그램이 어떻게 작동하는지 숙지하십시오. 만약 여러분이 발표할 계획이시라면, 그것(파일)을 지체 없이 보여줄 수 있도록 파일을 열어 두십시오.

둘째, 방해 요소를 제거하십시오. 앞선 조언과 마찬가지로, 회의 전에 이것을 처리하십시오. [47]집에 있는 다른 사람들에게 회의에 대해 알리고 여러분이 얼마나 오래 부재할지를 알려 주십시오. [47]이것은 여러분이 일하고 있는 동안 그들이 여러분을 방해하는 것을 방지할 것입니다. 또한, 근처에 있는 텔레비전을 끄고 창문을 닫음으로써 주변 소음을 제한하십시오. 그리고 여러분이 집중할 수 있는 조용한 공간을 만들기 위해 여러분이 있는 방의 문을 닫으십시오.

셋째, 체계화 해 두십시오. 공유 달력에서 소집 일정을 잡고 관련 당사자들에게 제대로 미리 초대장을 보내십시오. 약속 날짜가 다가오면, 그들에게 친절한 알림을 남기십시오. 회의 자체에 관해서는, [48]논의할 항목과 모임의 목표를 자세히 설명하는 의사일정을 마련하십시오. 이것은 모든 사람에게 무엇을 예상하고 준비해야 하는지 알려주는 동시에, 누구의 시간도 낭비되지 않음을 확실히 할 것입니다.

넷째, 집에 있는 것의 편안함에도 불구하고, [49]전문적인 분위기를 조성하려고 노력하십시오. 우리는 사무적인 태도를 보여 주고 또한 동료들에게 예절을 표하는 [49]업무에 적합한 옷을 착용함으로써 이를 해낼 수 있습니다. 평상복을 입는 것은 여러분이 일할 준비가 되지 않았다는 신호를 줄 수 있습니다. 마찬가지로, 특성 없는 배경을 찾으십시오. 저는 빈 벽이나 정돈된 책장을 추천합니다. 만약 이 선택지들 중 어느 것도 이용할 수 없는 경우, 무늬가 없는 가상 배경을 다운로드하는 것을 고려하십시오. 잡동사니로 어수선한 배경은 다른 사람들이 집중하고 업무 상태로 들어가는 것을 어렵게 만듭니다.

다섯째, 말하기보다는 귀를 기울이십시오. 일반적으로, 마이크는 음 소거 상태로 두는 것이 가장 좋습니다. 그렇게 하는 것은 잡음을 제거하고 기침이나 재

TEST 1

TEST 2

TEST 3

TEST 4

TEST 5

TEST 6

TEST 7

해커스 지텔프 최신기출유형 실전문제집 7회 (Level 2)

조언5:
경청

accidental interruptions brought on by coughs or sneezes. Furthermore, instead of jumping in while someone else is talking, utilize the chat box to indicate that you have a question or comment you would like to voice at the next opportunity. As a rule of thumb, only unmute yourself when you have something meaningful to contribute. However, ⁵⁰for smaller sessions with no more than five participants, muting may be unnecessary. These tend to be more collaborative, and participants benefit from open communication.

조언6:
시선
처리

Finally, show that you're paying attention. Rather than concentrating on maintaining eye contact, as we would in person, ⁵¹look at your camera, not the computer screen. This will convey your active engagement. Likewise, avoid looking down or away for too long when writing or typing notes. This is because others can perceive these actions as a lack of interest.

끝인사

⁵²I hope these pieces of advice can help you get the most out of your teleconferences. From my experience, ⁵²they are just as important as the image and audio quality of your video conferencing software. Thank you so much for listening.

채기로 인해 초래되는 돌발적인 중단의 가능성을 줄입니다. 나아가, 다른 사람이 이야기하고 있는 도중에 끼어드는 대신, 채팅창을 활용하여 다음 차례에 언급하고 싶은 질문이나 의견이 있음을 나타내십시오. 경험에 근거한 규칙에 따르면, 도움이 될 의미 있는 무언가가 있을 때만 음 소거를 해제하십시오. 그러나, ⁵⁰참여자가 5명 이하인 소규모 회의의 경우, 음 소거가 필요하지 않을 수 있습니다. 이것은 더욱 협력적인 경향이 있으며, 참여자들은 개방된 의사소통의 덕을 봅니다.

마지막으로, 여러분이 집중하고 있음을 보여 주십시오. 직접 만났을 때처럼 시선을 마주치는 것을 유지하는 데 집중하기보다는, ⁵¹컴퓨터 화면이 아닌 카메라를 바라보십시오. 이것은 여러분의 적극적인 참여를 보여 줄 것입니다. 마찬가지로, 메모를 작성하거나 입력할 때 너무 오랫동안 아래를 내려다보거나 시선을 돌리지 마십시오. 이는 다른 사람들이 이러한 행동들을 관심 부족으로 인식할 수 있기 때문입니다.

⁵²저는 이 몇 가지 조언이 원격 회의를 최대한 활용하는 데 도움이 되기를 바랍니다. 제 경험에 따르면, ⁵²그것들은 화상 회의 소프트웨어의 이미지 및 오디오 품질만큼이나 정말 중요합니다. 들어 주셔서 대단히 감사합니다.

어휘 | virtual[və́:rtʃuəl] 가상의 inspection[inspékʃən] 점검 eliminate[ilíməneit] 제거하다 distraction[distrǽkʃən] 방해 요소 notify[nóutifai] 알리다 party[pá:rti] 당사자 arrange[əréindʒ] 마련하다 foster[fá:stər] 조성하다 attire[ətáiər] 옷, 복장 convey[kənvéi] 보여 주다 neutral[njú:trəl] 특성 없는 clutter[klʌ́tər] 잡동사니 accidental[æ̀ksədéntəl] 돌발적인 indicate[índikeit] 나타내다 a rule of thumb 경험에 근거한 규칙 engagement[ingéidʒmənt] 참여 perceive[pərsí:v] 인식하다

---

46 특정세부사항 What   난이도 ●●○

What is the first thing one should do before an online meeting?

(a) inspect the functions of the program
(b) review the content of the presentation
(c) adjust the equipment to the user's physique
(d) **examine the hardware of the device**

온라인 회의 전에 가장 먼저 해야 할 일은 무엇인가?

(a) 프로그램의 기능을 점검한다
(b) 발표 내용을 복습한다
(c) 장비를 사용자의 체격에 맞춘다
(d) **기기의 하드웨어를 점검한다**

지텔프 치트키

질문의 키워드 first가 그대로 언급된 주변 내용을 주의 깊게 듣는다.

해설 | 화자가 'First, check the technology.'라며 첫째로 장비를 확인하라고 한 뒤, 'Before the work session, test out the camera and microphone on your computer to make sure you can be seen and heard properly.'라며 업무 시간 전에 본인이 제대로 보이고 들릴 수 있는지 확실히 하기 위해 컴퓨터의 카메라와 마이크를 점검하라고 했다. 따라서 (d)가 정답이다.

Paraphrasing
test out the camera and microphone on your computer 컴퓨터의 카메라와 마이크를 점검하다 → examine the hardware of the device 기기의 하드웨어를 점검하다

(b) 화자가 발표할 계획이라면 파일을 지체 없이 보여줄 수 있도록 열어 두라고 언급하기는 했지만, 발표 내용을 복습하라고 한 것은 아니므로 오답이다.

어휘 | adjust[ədʒʌ́st] 맞추다, 조정하다 physique[fəzíːk] 체격 examine[igzǽmin] 점검하다

---

47 특정세부사항   Why   난이도 ●●○

Why should people tell the others in the house about the meeting?	왜 사람들은 집에 있는 다른 사람들에게 회의에 대해 말해야 하는가?
(a) to prevent them from disrupting the meeting	**(a) 그들이 회의를 방해하는 것을 막기 위해서**
(b) to make them switch off the television sets	(b) 그들이 텔레비전을 끄게 하기 위해서
(c) to have them prepare appropriate materials	(c) 그들이 적절한 자료를 준비하게 하기 위해서
(d) to ask them to shut all the windows	(d) 그들에게 모든 창문을 닫으라고 부탁하기 위해서

지텔프 치트키

질문의 키워드 others in the house가 others in ~ home으로 paraphrasing되어 언급된 주변 내용을 주의 깊게 듣는다.

해설 | 화자가 'Notify others in your home about the conference'라며 집에 있는 다른 사람들에게 회의에 대해 알리라고 한 뒤, 'This will keep them from interrupting you while you're working.'이라며 이것은 일하고 있는 동안 그들이 방해하는 것을 방지할 것이라고 했다. 따라서 (a)가 정답이다.

Paraphrasing
keep ~ from interrupting 방해하는 것을 방지하다 → prevent ~ from disrupting 방해하는 것을 막다

어휘 | disrupt[disrʌ́pt] 방해하다 material[mətíəriəl] 자료

---

48 특정세부사항   How   난이도 ●●●

How can attendees learn what they need to do to prepare for a conference?	참석자들은 회의를 준비하기 위해 무엇을 해야 하는지 어떻게 알 수 있는가?
(a) by viewing the shared calendar	(a) 공유 달력을 봄으로써
(b) by referring to the meeting plan	**(b) 회의 계획을 참고함으로써**
(c) by requesting a reminder from the host	(c) 주최자로부터의 알림을 요청함으로써
(d) by reading over the invitation details	(d) 초대장의 세부 사항을 읽음으로써

지텔프 치트키

질문의 키워드 prepare가 그대로 언급된 주변 내용을 주의 깊게 듣는다.

해설 | 화자가 'arrange an agenda that details the items to discuss and the goals of the gathering'이라며 논의할 항목과 모임의 목표를 자세히 설명하는 의사일정을 마련하라고 한 뒤, 'This will let everyone know what to ~ prepare'라며 이것은 모든 사람에게 무엇을 준비해야 하는지 알려줄 것이라고 했다. 따라서 (b)가 정답이다.

Paraphrasing
an agenda 의사일정 → the meeting plan 회의 계획

(a) 화자가 공유 달력에서 소집 일정을 잡으라고 언급한 것이지 공유 달력에 회의 준비 내용이 포함되어 있다고 한 것은 아니므로 오답이다.

49 특정세부사항 Why
난이도 ●●○

Why is it important to dress in formal attire for a video meeting?	화상 회의를 위해 격식 차린 옷을 입는 것이 왜 중요한가?
(a) It creates a professional setting.	**(a) 전문적인 환경을 조성한다.**
(b) It conveys a neutral disposition.	(b) 중립적인 성향을 보여 준다.
(c) It encourages a sense of organization.	(c) 조직감을 고취시킨다.
(d) It presents a uniform appearance.	(d) 획일적인 겉모습을 보여 준다.

지텔프 치트키

질문의 키워드 attire가 그대로 언급된 주변 내용을 주의 깊게 듣는다.

해설 | 화자가 'try to foster a professional atmosphere'라며 전문적인 분위기를 조성하려고 노력하라고 한 뒤, 'We can accomplish this by wearing work-appropriate attire'라며 업무에 적합한 옷을 착용함으로써 이를 해낼 수 있다고 했다. 따라서 (a)가 정답이다.

Paraphrasing

foster a professional atmosphere 전문적인 분위기를 조성하다 → creates a professional setting 전문적인 환경을 조성한다

어휘 | disposition[dìspəzíʃən] 성향   uniform[júːnəfɔːrm] 획일적인

50 특정세부사항 When
난이도 ●○○

When does the meeting participant keep the mute function turned off?	회의 참여자는 언제 음 소거 기능이 꺼진 상태를 유지하는가?
(a) when the chatbox is out of service	(a) 채팅창이 작동하지 않을 때
(b) when the gathering has few attendees	**(b) 모임에 참석자가 적을 때**
(c) when someone has an immediate question	(c) 누군가가 즉각적인 질문이 있을 때
(d) when someone jumps in to make a comment	(d) 누군가가 논평하려고 끼어들 때

지텔프 치트키

질문의 키워드 mute function이 muting으로 paraphrasing되어 언급된 주변 내용을 주의 깊게 듣는다.

해설 | 화자가 'for smaller sessions with no more than five participants, muting may be unnecessary'라며 참여자가 5명 이하인 소규모 회의의 경우 음 소거가 필요하지 않을 수 있다고 했다. 따라서 (b)가 정답이다.

Paraphrasing

smaller sessions 소규모 회의 → the gathering has few attendees 모임에 참석자가 적다

어휘 | out of service 작동하지 않는   immediate[imíːdiət] 즉각적인

According to the talk, what is one way of expressing engagement in a teleconference?

(a) looking at whoever is currently speaking
(b) taking thorough notes while others talk
(c) keeping one's eyes on the camera
(d) maintaining an active use of gestures

담화에 따르면, 원격 회의에서의 참여를 표현하는 한 가지 방법은 무엇인가?

(a) 누구든 현재 말하고 있는 사람을 보는 것
(b) 다른 사람이 말하는 동안 꼼꼼한 메모를 하는 것
(c) 시선을 카메라에 두는 것
(d) 적극적인 몸짓의 사용을 유지하는 것

─○ 지텔프 치트키

질문의 키워드 engagement가 그대로 언급된 주변 내용을 주의 깊게 듣는다.

해설 | 화자가 'look at your camera, not the computer screen'이라며 컴퓨터 화면이 아닌 카메라를 바라보라고 한 뒤, 'This will convey your active engagement.'라며 이것은 적극적인 참여를 보여 줄 것이라고 했다. 따라서 (c)가 정답이다.

Paraphrasing
look at your camera 카메라를 바라보다 → keeping one's eyes on the camera 시선을 카메라에 두는 것

어휘 | thorough[θʌ́rou] 꼼꼼한, 빈틈없는

---

52 추론   특정사실   난이도 ●●●

Why most likely does the speaker mention the features of a video conference program?

(a) to suggest that a software update be installed
(b) to recommend a virtual meeting tool
(c) to emphasize the importance of the tips
(d) to demonstrate the productivity of teleconferences

화자가 왜 화상 회의 프로그램의 기능을 언급하는 것 같은가?

(a) 소프트웨어 업데이트가 설치되어야 한다고 제안하기 위해서
(b) 가상 회의의 수단을 추천하기 위해서
(c) 조언의 중요성을 강조하기 위해서
(d) 원격 회의의 생산성을 입증하기 위해서

─○ 지텔프 치트키

질문의 키워드 video conference program이 video conferencing software로 paraphrasing되어 언급된 주변 내용을 주의 깊게 듣는다.

해설 | 화자가 'I hope these pieces of advice can help you get the most out of your teleconferences.'라며 이 몇 가지 조언들이 원격 회의를 최대한 활용하는 데 도움이 되기를 바란다고 한 뒤, 'they are just as important as the image and audio quality of your video conferencing software'라며 그 조언들은 화상 회의 소프트웨어의 이미지 및 오디오 품질만큼이나 정말 중요하다고 한 것을 통해, 화자가 조언의 중요성을 강조하기 위해 화상 회의 프로그램의 기능을 언급한 것임을 추론할 수 있다. 따라서 (c)가 정답이다.

어휘 | feature[fí:tʃər] 기능 emphasize[émfəsaiz] 강조하다

PART 1 [53~59] 인물의 일대기 초현실주의의 거장 막스 에른스트

인물 이름

MAX ERNST

소개 + 유명한 이유

Max Ernst was a German painter, sculptor, and poet. He is [53]best known for inventing the artistic techniques frottage and grattage, which challenged the conventional standards of his time.

어린 시절 + 업적 시작 계기

Ernst was born on April 2, 1891, in Brühl, Germany, into a middle-class Catholic family. His father was a teacher of the deaf and an amateur painter. [54]Ernst became interested in art from a young age as a result of watching him paint. When Ernst entered the University of Bonn in 1909, he started painting as a hobby, producing portraits of his family and himself. Two years later, he joined a friend's expressionist art group and decided to become an artist. Ernst was affected by Pablo Picasso's Cubism and Vincent van Gogh's Expressionism. By 1913, [58]his paintings were being exhibited alongside the works of other artists who influenced him.

주요 업적1: 초현실 주의 운동의 선도자

Ernst was a leader in the Surrealist movement, an artistic and literary philosophy of the 1920s. This group of artists strived to generate works that reflected their unconscious thoughts and desires. [55]This style of art would remain Ernst's focus throughout the rest of his career as it liberated him from the need to adhere to traditional figurative techniques. He also began a series of surrealist landscape paintings of forests, and depictions of different types of vegetation would be a recurring theme in his work.

주요 업적2: 예술 기법 발명

The following year, Ernst invented frottage, which is the technique of creating a work of art on paper by taking a pencil rubbing from an object or uneven surface. With this, he combined impressions of shapes and textures to create images that one could not achieve through drawing alone. Ernst later utilized a similar technique in painting with grattage, [56]which involves scraping applied paint off a canvas so the imprints of textured items placed under it are revealed. His famous painting *Forest and Dove* was produced using this method in 1927.

In 1941, after World War II broke out, [57]Ernst fled to the United States, where his unique style was widely admired and inspired a new generation of artists,

막스 에른스트

막스 에른스트는 독일의 화가이자, 조각가이자, 시인이었다. 그는 [53]예술 기법인 프로타주와 그라타주를 고안한 것으로 가장 잘 알려져 있으며, 그것들은 당대의 전통적 기준에 도전했다.

에른스트는 1891년 4월 2일에 독일 브륄에서, 중산층의 가톨릭 가정에서 태어났다. 그의 아버지는 청각 장애인을 가르치는 교사이자 아마추어 화가였다. [54]에른스트는 그가 그림을 그리는 것을 지켜본 결과로 어린 시절부터 미술에 관심을 갖게 되었다. 1909년에 에른스트가 본 대학에 입학했을 때, 그는 취미로 그림을 그리기 시작했고, 가족과 그 자신의 초상화를 그렸다. 2년 후에, 그는 친구의 표현주의 미술 단체에 가입했고 예술가가 되기로 결심했다. 에른스트는 파블로 피카소의 입체파와 빈센트 반 고흐의 표현주의의 영향을 받았다. 1913년에, [58]그의 그림들은 그에게 영향을 준 다른 화가들의 작품들과 나란히 전시되어 있었다.

에른스트는 1920년대의 예술적, 문학적 철학인 초현실주의 운동의 선도자였다. 이 예술가들의 단체는 그들의 무의식적인 생각과 욕망을 반영하는 작품들을 창조하기 위해 노력했다. [55]이러한 예술 양식이 전통적인 조형 기법을 고수할 필요로부터 그를 벗어나게 했기 때문에 그것은 에른스트의 남은 화가 생활 내내 그의 주안점으로 남아 있을 수 있었다. 그는 또한 숲에 대한 일련의 초현실주의 풍경화를 시작했으며, 다양한 종류의 초목에 대한 묘사는 그의 작품에서 반복되는 주제가 되곤 했다.

그다음 해에, 에른스트는 프로타주를 발명했는데, 그것은 물체나 울퉁불퉁한 표면을 연필로 탁본을 떠서 종이 위에 예술 작품을 만드는 기법이다. 이것으로, 그는 형태와 질감의 자국을 결합하여 소묘만으로는 이룰 수 없는 그림을 만들어 냈다. 후에 에른스트는 그라타주로 그림을 그리는 데 비슷한 기법을 사용했는데, [56]그것은 캔버스 아래에 놓인 질감이 있는 물체의 모습들이 드러나도록 캔버스로부터 칠해져 있는 물감을 긁어내는 것을 수반한다. 그의 유명한 그림인 「숲과 비둘기」가 1927년에 이 방법을 사용하여 만들어졌다.

1941년에, 제2차 세계 대전이 발발한 후, [57]에른스트는 미국으로 피난을 갔고, 그곳에서 그의 독특한 화풍은 널리 존경을 받았으며 새로운 세대의 예술가들,

<table>
<tr>
<td>후기
업적
+
죽음</td>
<td>particularly Abstract Expressionists. Thanks to his extensive travels and [59]his fierce <u>dedication</u> to his art, Ernst was a highly respected figure in critical circles with a strong following in Germany, France, and the United States. He eventually settled in France in the 1950s and stayed there until his death in 1976.</td>
<td>특히 추상 표현주의자들에게 영감을 주었다. 그의 광범위한 여행과 [59]그의 예술에 대한 맹렬한 <u>헌신</u> 덕분에, 에른스트는 독일, 프랑스, 그리고 미국의 강력한 추종자 무리와 함께 비평가들 집단에서 매우 높이 평가되는 인물이었다. 그는 결국 1950년대에 프랑스에 정착하였으며 그가 사망한 1976년까지 그곳에 머물렀다.</td>
</tr>
</table>

어휘 | challenge v. 도전하다 **conventional** adj. 전통적인 **standard** n. 기준 **enter** v. 입학하다 **portrait** n. 초상화 **expressionist** adj. 표현주의의 **Cubism** n. 입체파 **alongside** prep. ~과 나란히 **surrealist** adj. 초현실주의의 **literary** adj. 문학적인 **philosophy** n. 철학 **strive** v. 노력하다 **generate** v. 창조하다 **unconscious** adj. 무의식적인 **liberate** v. 벗어나게 하다 **adhere** v. 고수하다 **figurative** adj. 조형의 **vegetation** n. 초목 **recurring** adj. 반복되는 **uneven** adj. 울퉁불퉁한 **impression** n. 자국, 흔적 **scrape** v. 긁어내다 **imprint** n. 모습, 자국 **reveal** v. 드러나다, 누출하다 **flee** v. 피난을 가다 **extensive** adj. 광범위한 **fierce** adj. 맹렬한 **critical** adj. 비평가의 **following** n. 추종자 무리

---

53 특정세부사항   유명한 이유   난이도 ●○○

What is Max Ernst most famous for?	막스 에른스트는 무엇으로 가장 유명한가?
(a) popularizing the techniques of German poetry	(a) 독일 시의 기법들을 대중화한 것으로
(b) challenging the standards of a new artistic movement	(b) 새로운 예술 운동의 기준에 도전한 것으로
(c) imitating a highly popular style of painting	(c) 매우 대중적인 화풍을 모방한 것으로
(d) developing new methods for creating artwork	**(d) 예술 작품을 만드는 새로운 방법을 개발한 것으로**

━○ 지텔프 치트키

질문의 키워드 most famous가 best known으로 paraphrasing되어 언급된 주변 내용을 주의 깊게 읽는다.

해설 | 1단락의 'best known for inventing the artistic techniques frottage and grattage'에서 막스 에른스트는 예술 기법인 프로타주와 그라타주를 고안한 것으로 가장 잘 알려져 있다고 했다. 따라서 (d)가 정답이다.

Paraphrasing
inventing the artistic techniques 예술 기법을 고안한 것 → developing new methods for creating artwork 예술 작품을 만드는 새로운 방법을 개발한 것

어휘 | popularize v. 대중화하다 **imitate** v. 모방하다

---

54 특정세부사항   Why   난이도 ●●○

Why did Ernst take an interest in art as a child?	왜 에른스트는 어렸을 때 미술에 관심을 가졌는가?
(a) because he received painting lessons from a talented teacher	(a) 유능한 교사로부터 그림 수업을 받았기 때문에
(b) because he was given portrait assignments in school	(b) 학교에서 초상화 과제를 받았기 때문에
(c) because he was inspired by the work of celebrated artists	(c) 유명한 예술가들의 작품으로부터 영감을 받았기 때문에
(d) because he observed his father practicing art	**(d) 그의 아버지가 미술을 하는 것을 지켜보았기 때문에**

TEST 1

TEST 2

TEST 3

TEST 4

TEST 5

TEST 6

TEST 7

해커스 지텔프 최신기출유형 실전문제집 7회 (Level 2)

○— **지텔프 치트키**

질문의 키워드 take an interest가 became interested로 paraphrasing되어 언급된 주변 내용을 주의 깊게 읽는다.

해설 | 2단락의 'Ernst became interested in art from a young age as a result of watching him paint.'에서 에른스트는 그의 아버지가 그림을 그리는 것을 지켜본 결과로 어린 시절부터 미술에 관심을 가지게 되었다고 했다. 따라서 (d)가 정답이다.

Paraphrasing
watching him paint 그림을 그리는 것을 지켜보는 → observed his father practicing art 미술을 하는 것을 지켜보았다

어휘 | celebrated adj. 유명한 observe v. 지켜보다

---

55 추론 특정사실 난이도 ●●●

What could be the reason that Ernst joined the Surrealist movement?

(a) **He wanted to avoid following convention.**
(b) He was encouraged by his friend's art group.
(c) He needed a way to express his politics.
(d) He was rejected by Expressionist artists.

에른스트가 초현실주의 운동에 참여한 이유는 무엇이었을 것 같은가?

(a) **관행을 따르는 것을 피하고 싶었다.**
(b) 친구의 예술 단체에 의해 용기를 얻었다.
(c) 그의 정견을 표현할 방법이 필요했다.
(d) 표현주의 예술가들에게 거절당했다.

○— **지텔프 치트키**

질문의 키워드 Surrealist movement가 그대로 언급된 주변 내용을 주의 깊게 읽는다.

해설 | 3단락의 'This style of art would remain Ernst's focus ~ as it liberated him from the need to adhere to traditional figurative techniques.'에서 초현실주의라는 예술 양식이 전통적인 조형 기법을 고수할 필요로부터 에른스트를 벗어나게 했기 때문에 그 예술 양식이 그의 주안점으로 남아 있을 수 있었다고 한 것을 통해, 에른스트는 전통적인 조형 기법을 고수하는 관행을 따르는 것을 피하고 싶었기 때문에 초현실주의 운동에 참여한 것임을 추론할 수 있다. 따라서 (a)가 정답이다.

어휘 | convention n. 관행, 관습

---

56 특정세부사항 How 난이도 ●●●

How was Ernst's 1927 painting *Forest and Dove* created?

(a) by rubbing a pencil drawing with objects
(b) **by lifting the texture of objects beneath a canvas**
(c) by applying unusual paint mixtures
(d) by painting directly onto a textured canvas

에른스트의 1927년 그림인 「숲과 비둘기」는 어떻게 만들어졌는가?

(a) 연필화를 물건들로 문지름으로써
(b) **캔버스 아래 물체의 질감을 보이게 함으로써**
(c) 특이한 물감의 혼합물을 칠함으로써
(d) 질감이 있는 캔버스에 직접 그림을 그림으로써

○— **지텔프 치트키**

질문의 키워드 *Forest and Dove*가 그대로 언급된 주변 내용을 주의 깊게 읽는다.

해설 | 4단락의 'which involves scraping applied paint off a canvas so the imprints of textured items placed under it are revealed'에서 그라타주는 캔버스 아래에 놓인 질감이 있는 물체의 모습들이 드러나도록 캔버스로부터 칠해져 있는 물감을 긁어내는 것을 수반한다고 한 뒤, 'His famous painting *Forest and Dove* was produced using this method in 1927.'에서 에른스트의 유명한 그림인 「숲과 비둘기」가 1927년에 이 방법을 사용하여 만들어졌다고 했다. 따라서 (b)가 정답이다.

Paraphrasing

created 만들어진 → produced 만들어진

the imprints of textured items ~ are revealed 질감이 있는 물체의 모습들이 드러나다 → lifting the texture of objects 물체의 질감을 보이게 함

어휘 | rough adj. 거친 lift v. 보이게 하다, 들어올리다 press v. 찍다, 누르다

---

57 특정세부사항   How   난이도 ●●○

How was Ernst's career affected by his move to America?	에른스트의 경력이 미국으로의 이주에 어떻게 영향을 받았는가?
(a) He changed his approach to painting.	(a) 그림에 대한 그의 접근법을 바꾸었다.
(b) He made art with violent themes.	(b) 폭력적인 주제를 가진 예술 작품을 만들었다.
(c) He found a new audience for his work.	**(c) 그의 작품의 새로운 관객을 찾았다.**
(d) He sold paintings at galleries.	(d) 미술관에서 그림을 팔았다.

◉─○ 지텔프 치트키

질문의 키워드 America가 United States로 paraphrasing되어 언급된 주변 내용을 주의 깊게 읽는다.

해설 | 5단락의 'Ernst fled to the United States, where his unique style ~ inspired a new generation of artists, particularly Abstract Expressionists'에서 에른스트는 미국으로 피난을 갔고, 그곳에서 그의 독특한 화풍이 새로운 세대의 예술가들, 특히 추상 표현주의자들에게 영감을 주었다고 했다. 따라서 (c)가 정답이다.

Paraphrasing

his move to America 미국으로의 이주 → fled to the United States 미국으로 피난을 갔다

inspired a new generation of artists 새로운 세대의 예술가들에게 영감을 주었다 → found a new audience 새로운 관객을 찾았다

어휘 | violent adj. 폭력적인

---

58 어휘   유의어   난이도 ●○○

In the context of the passage, <u>exhibited</u> means _____.	지문의 문맥에서, 'exhibited'는 -을 의미한다.
(a) shown	**(a) 전시된**
(b) proven	(b) 증명된
(c) disclosed	(c) 폭로된
(d) protected	(d) 보호된

◉─○ 지텔프 치트키

밑줄 친 어휘의 유의어를 찾는 문제이므로, exhibited가 포함된 구절을 읽고 문맥을 파악한다.

해설 | 2단락의 'his paintings were being exhibited alongside the works of other artists who influenced him'은 에른스트의 그림들이 그에게 영향을 준 다른 화가들의 작품들과 나란히 전시되어 있었다는 뜻이므로, exhibited가 '전시된'이라는 의미로 사용된 것을 알 수 있다. 따라서 '전시된'이라는 같은 의미의 (a) shown이 정답이다.

In the context of the passage, <u>dedication</u> means _____.

(a) achievement
(b) devotion
(c) capability
(d) responsibility

지문의 문맥에서, 'dedication'은 -을 의미한다.

(a) 달성
(b) 헌신
(c) 능력
(d) 책임

━━○ 지텔프 치트키

밑줄 친 어휘의 유의어를 찾는 문제이므로, dedication이 포함된 구절을 읽고 문맥을 파악한다.

해설 | 5단락의 'his fierce dedication to his art'는 그의 예술에 대한 맹렬한 헌신이라는 뜻이므로, dedication이 '헌신'이라는 의미로 사용된 것을 알 수 있다. 따라서 '헌신'이라는 같은 의미의 (b) devotion이 정답이다.

PART 2[60~66] **잡지 기사** 신경 질환을 조기에 발견하는 스마트폰 애플리케이션의 개발

| 기사 제목 | **A POTENTIALLY GROUNDBREAKING SCREENING APP IS ON THE HORIZON** |

잠재적으로 획기적인 건강 검진 앱이 곧 본격화될 것이다

연구 소개

[60]Researchers have developed a prototype for a new smartphone application that allows people to take a simple test to detect conditions like Alzheimer's at the earliest stages. The app, which tracks changes in the size of a person's pupils, is based on studies that have shown that increased pupil dilation can indicate neurological disease.

[60]연구원들은 알츠하이머와 같은 질환을 초기 단계에 발견하기 위한 간단한 검사를 사람들이 받을 수 있게 하는 새로운 스마트폰 앱의 원형을 개발했다. 이 앱은, 사람의 동공 크기 변화를 추적하는데, 증가된 동공 확장이 신경 질환을 나타낼 수 있다는 것을 증명한 연구들에 바탕을 두고 있다.

연구 배경

Researchers at the UC San Diego Center for Mental Health Technology (MHTech) collaborated with engineers to build the software. [65]They were <u>prompted</u> to create this app in order to improve the availability of pupil response tests. [61]Currently, these assessments can only be carried out in medical clinics using a specialized instrument called a pupilometer, the cost of which makes them unfeasible for the majority of people to own. According to Eric Granholm, a director at the MHTech Center, an accessible large-scale community screening tool like this one "could have a huge public health impact."

정신 건강 기술(MHTech)을 위한 캘리포니아대학교 샌디에이고 캠퍼스 센터의 연구원들은 이 소프트웨어를 만들기 위해 공학자들과 협력했다. 그들은 동공 반응 검사의 유용성을 향상하기 위하여 [65]이 앱을 만들도록 <u>유도되었다</u>. [61]현재, 이러한 측정은 동공 측정계라고 불리는 특수한 기구를 사용하는 병원에서만 실행될 수 있는데, 이것의 가격은 대다수의 사람들이 그것들을 소유하는 것을 불가능하게 한다. MHTech 센터의 책임자인 에릭 그랜홀름에 따르면, 이것처럼 사용하기 쉬운 대규모의 집단검사 도구는 '큰 공공 보건 효과를 가질 수 있을 것이다'.

작동 원리

The app employs a near-infrared camera, a technology which most new smartphone models are equipped with. The user takes a recording of their eyes, and the app—which can differentiate between the iris and pupil no matter the eye color—calculates the size of their pupils to the submillimeter. The idea is that [62]users who see

그 앱은 근적외선 카메라를 활용하는데, 이 기술은 대부분의 새로운 스마트폰 모델들이 탑재하고 있는 것이다. 이용자는 그들의 눈을 촬영하고, 눈 색깔에 상관없이 홍채와 동공을 구별할 수 있는 그 앱은 그들의 동공 크기를 1밀리미터 이하의 단위까지 측정한다. 그 목적은 [62]이전의 측정값이 달라진 것을 확인한 이용자

their previous measurements change will be alerted to the potential onset of a cognitive disorder and seek treatment to manage the condition early.

유용성
연구

As the app's pupil response check is meant to be a self-test, it was crucial that the app itself be easy to use. [63]The researchers worked directly with elderly people to ensure that it could be used regardless of their familiarity with smartphones. The result of this approach is an interface that includes instructions with pictures and recorded commands. The developers believe that its ease of operation will help make the app a success.

추가
연구
+
의의

Before the app's release, the researchers [66]will conduct further studies to test its effectiveness as an examining tool especially for Alzheimer's disease, [64(d)]which is the most common cause of dementia. Specifically, they intend to work with people who are experiencing [64(a)]early-stage symptoms such as mild cognitive impairment. Their findings could be revolutionary as [64(b)]there are no definitive diagnostic tests for Alzheimer's disease at present.

들이 인지 장애의 잠재적인 발병에 대해 경고를 받고 조기에 그 질환을 관리하기 위해 치료를 모색하는 것이다.

그 앱의 동공 반응 검사는 자가 검사가 되도록 의도되었기 때문에, 앱 자체가 사용하기 쉬워야 한다는 것은 매우 중요했다. [63]연구원들은 이것이 스마트폰에 익숙한 것과 관계없이 사용될 수 있다는 것을 확실히 하기 위해 노년층의 사람들과 직접 작업했다. 이 접근법의 결과는 그림과 녹음된 명령어로 이루어진 사용 설명서를 포함한 인터페이스이다. 개발자들은 그것의 사용 용이성이 이 앱을 성공작으로 만드는 것을 도울 것이라고 여긴다.

이 앱의 출시 전에, 연구원들은 특히 알츠하이머병에 대한 검사 도구로서의 그 앱의 실효성을 시험하기 위하여 [66]추가적인 연구를 수행할 것인데, [64(d)]이것(알츠하이머병)은 치매의 가장 흔한 원인이다. 구체적으로, 그들은 [64(a)]가벼운 인지 장애와 같은 초기 단계의 증상들을 겪고 있는 사람들과 함께 작업할 계획이다. 그들의 연구 결과는 [64(b)]현재 알츠하이머병에 대한 확실한 진단 검사가 없기 때문에 획기적일 수 있다.

어휘 | groundbreaking adj. 획기적인 screening n. 건강 검진, 의학 검사 prototype n. 원형 condition n. 질환, 병 track v. 추적하다 pupil n. 동공 dilation n. 확장 neurological adj. 신경의 availability n. 유용성 assessment n. 측정, 평가 instrument n. 기구 unfeasible adj. 불가능한 majority n. 대다수 accessible adj. 사용하기 쉬운 equip v. 탑재하다 differentiate v. 구별하다 iris n. 홍채 calculate v. 측정하다 measurement n. 측정값 onset n. 발병, 시작 cognitive adj. 인지의 treatment n. 치료 crucial adj. 매우 중요한 familiarity n. 익숙함, 친숙함 instruction n. 사용 설명서 operation n. 사용, 작동 effectiveness n. 실효성 dementia n. 치매 impairment n. 장애 revolutionary adj. 획기적인 definitive adj. 확실한, 결정적인 diagnostic adj. 진단의

---

60 **주제/목적**   기사의 주제   난이도 ●○○

What is the article mainly about?

(a) a discovery about pupil dilation
(b) the production of a diagnostic tool
(c) the release of a new commercial app
(d) a study on neurological disease progression

기사의 주제는 무엇인가?

(a) 동공 확장에 관한 발견
(b) 진단 도구의 제작
(c) 새로운 상업용 앱의 출시
(d) 신경 질환 경과에 관한 연구

지텔프 치트키

지문의 초반을 주의 깊게 읽고 전체 맥락을 파악한다.

해설 | 1단락의 'Researchers have developed a prototype for a new smartphone application that allows people to take a simple test to detect conditions like Alzheimer's at the earliest stages.'에서 연구원들이 알츠하이머와 같은 질환을 초기 단계에 발견하기 위한 간단한 검사를 사람들이 받을 수 있게 하는 새로운 스마트폰 앱의 원형을 개발했다고 한 뒤, 지문 전반에 걸쳐 신경 질환을 진단하는 앱의 제작을 설명하는 내용이 이어지고 있다. 따라서 (b)가 정답이다.

어휘 | discovery n. 발견 commercial adj. 상업용의 progression n. 경과

해커스 지텔프 최신기출유형 실전문제집 7회 (Level 2)

61 특정세부사항   How   난이도 ●●○

How do most people currently take a pupil response test?

(a) by purchasing a piece of equipment
(b) by undergoing a full medical examination
(c) by attending a community screening assessment
(d) by going to see a medical practitioner

현재 대부분의 사람들은 어떻게 동공 반응 검사를 받는가?

(a) 설비를 구입함으로써
(b) 정밀 건강 검진을 받음으로써
(c) 의학 검사 측정을 수행함으로써
(d) 의사를 만나러 감으로써

━○ 지텔프 치트키

질문의 키워드 pupil response test가 pupil response tests로 언급된 주변 내용을 주의 깊게 읽는다.

해설 | 2단락의 'Currently, these assessments can only be carried out in medical clinics using a specialized instrument called a pupilometer'에서 현재 동공 반응 검사는 동공 측정계라고 불리는 특수한 기구를 사용하는 병원에서만 실행될 수 있다고 했다. 따라서 (d)가 정답이다.

어휘 | undergo v. 받다, 겪다   attend v. 수행하다   medical practitioner phr. 의사

62 추론   특정사실   난이도 ●●●

Which of the following can probably be said about how the app works?

(a) It is most effective on people with light eyes.
(b) It is supposed to be used multiple times.
(c) It works with any model of smartphone.
(d) It requires users to differentiate the pupil and iris.

다음 중 그 앱이 어떻게 작동하는지에 관해 말해질 수 있는 것은 무엇인 것 같은가?

(a) 밝은 눈을 가진 사람들에게 가장 효과적이다.
(b) 여러 번 사용되어야 한다.
(c) 어떤 스마트폰 모델에서든지 작동한다.
(d) 이용자들에게 동공과 홍채를 구별하도록 요구한다.

━○ 지텔프 치트키

질문의 키워드 how the app works와 관련된 주변 내용을 주의 깊게 읽는다.

해설 | 3단락의 'users who see their previous measurements change will be alerted to the potential onset of a cognitive disorder and seek treatment to manage the condition early'에서 이전의 측정값이 달라진 것을 확인한 이용자들이 인지 장애의 잠재적인 발병에 대해 경고를 받고 조기에 그 질환을 관리하기 위해 치료를 모색한다고 한 것을 통해, 측정값이 달라진 것을 확인하기 위해서 그 앱이 여러 번 사용되어야 함을 추론할 수 있다. 따라서 (b)가 정답이다.

오답분석
(c) 3단락에서 앱이 대부분의 새로운 스마트폰 모델들이 탑재하고 있는 기술을 활용한다고 했지만, 어떤 스마트폰 모델에서든지 작동한다고 한 것은 아니므로 오답이다.
(d) 3단락에서 앱이 이용자들의 홍채와 동공을 구별할 수 있다고 했으므로 오답이다.

63 특정세부사항   Why   난이도 ●●○

Why did researchers need elderly participants when designing the app?

(a) to make audio recordings of instructions

왜 연구원들은 그 앱을 설계할 때 노년층 참가자들을 필요로 했는가?

(a) 사용 설명서의 음성 녹음본을 만들기 위해서

(b) **to see whether it was easily usable**
(c) to assist with administering tests to elderly people
(d) to make sure that phone technology was familiar

(b) **쉽게 사용할 수 있는지 확인하기 위해서**
(c) 노년층의 사람들이 검사를 시행하는 것을 돕기 위해서
(d) 전화 기술에 익숙한 것을 확인하기 위해서

─○ 지텔프 치트키

질문의 키워드 elderly participants가 elderly people로 paraphrasing되어 언급된 주변 내용을 주의 깊게 읽는다.

해설 | 4단락의 'The researchers worked directly with elderly people to ensure that it could be used regardless of their familiarity with smartphones.'에서 연구원들은 그 앱이 스마트폰에 익숙한 것과 관계없이 사용될 수 있다는 것을 확실히 하기 위해 노년층의 사람들과 직접 작업했다고 했다. 따라서 (b)가 정답이다.

Paraphrasing
could be used regardless of ~ familiarity 익숙한 것과 관계없이 사용될 수 있다 → easily usable 쉽게 사용할 수 있는

어휘 | administer v. 시행하다

---

64 Not/True   Not 문제   난이도 ●●○

What is NOT true about Alzheimer's disease?

(a) Its early signs include mental decline.
(b) It can be difficult to diagnose conclusively.
(c) **Its symptoms may be eased by the app.**
(d) It is not the only cause of dementia.

알츠하이머병에 관해 사실이 아닌 것은 무엇인가?

(a) 그것의 초기 징후는 정신 쇠약을 포함한다.
(b) 확정적으로 진단하는 것이 어려울 수 있다.
(c) **앱에 의해 그것의 증상들이 완화될 수 있다.**
(d) 치매의 유일한 원인은 아니다.

─○ 지텔프 치트키

질문의 키워드 Alzheimer's disease가 그대로 언급된 주변 내용을 주의 깊게 읽고, 보기의 키워드와 지문 내용을 대조하며 언급되는 것을 하나씩 소거한다.

해설 | (c)는 지문에 언급되지 않았으므로, (c)가 정답이다.

오답분석
(a) 보기의 키워드 mental decline이 cognitive impairment로 paraphrasing되어 언급된 5단락에서 가벼운 인지 장애가 알츠하이머병의 초기 단계의 증상이라고 언급되었다.
(b) 보기의 키워드 conclusively가 definitive로 paraphrasing되어 언급된 5단락에서 현재 알츠하이머병에 대한 확실한 진단 검사가 없다고 언급되었다.
(d) 보기의 키워드 cause가 그대로 언급된 5단락에서 알츠하이머병이 치매의 가장 흔한 원인이라고 언급되었다.

어휘 | conclusively adv. 확정적으로 ease v. 완화하다

---

65 어휘   유의어   난이도 ●●○

In the context of the passage, prompted means _____.

(a) **motivated**
(b) requested

지문의 문맥에서, 'prompted'는 -을 의미한다.

(a) **유도된**
(b) 요청받은

(c) compelled

(d) persuaded

(c) 강요받은

(d) 권유받은

해설 | 2단락의 'They were prompted to create this app'은 그들은 이 앱을 만들도록 유도되었다는 뜻이므로, prompted가 '유도된'이라는 의미로 사용된 것을 알 수 있다. 따라서 '유도된'이라는 같은 의미의 (a) motivated가 정답이다.

66 어휘   유의어   난이도 ●●○

In the context of the passage, further means _____.

(a) spare

(b) excessive

(c) major

(d) additional

지문의 문맥에서, 'further'는 -을 의미한다.

(a) 여분의

(b) 과도한

(c) 주요한

(d) 추가적인

해설 | 5단락의 'will conduct further studies'는 추가적인 연구를 수행할 것이라는 뜻이므로, further가 '추가적인'이라는 의미로 사용된 것을 알 수 있다. 따라서 '추가적인'이라는 같은 의미의 (d) additional이 정답이다.

PART 3⁽⁶⁷⁻⁷³⁾ 지식 백과   베지터블 시프의 정의 및 특징

표제어	**VEGETABLE SHEEP**	**베지터블 시프**

정의

Vegetable sheep is the common name for a species of cushion plant that is native to New Zealand. [67]The name comes from the plant's physical resemblance to a sheep when seen at a distance.

이름의 유래

Vegetable Sheep's scientific name is *Raoulia eximia*. It is one of about 26 species of plants related to Compositae, which includes sunflowers and daisies. It was first identified by [68]Joseph Hooker, a British botanist and explorer who visited New Zealand on duty in 1864. Hooker named the plant in honor of his colleague, French naturalist Étienne Raoul. The second half of the name means "strikingly unusual" in Latin.

Being a cushion plant, the vegetable sheep has a rounded shape and grows close to the ground. The

베지터블 시프는 뉴질랜드가 원산지인 방석식물의 한 종에 대한 일반적인 이름이다. [67]그 이름은 멀리서 보았을 때 양과 이 식물의 물리적 유사성에서 비롯되었다.

베지터블 시프의 학명은 '라울리아 엑시미아'이다. 그것은 국화과와 관련된 26여 종의 식물 중 하나인데, 이것은 해바라기와 데이지를 포함한다. 그것은 1864년에 [68]임무 수행차 뉴질랜드를 방문한 영국의 식물학자이자 탐험가인 조지프 후커에 의해 처음 발견되었다. 후커는 그의 동료인 프랑스의 박물학자 에티엔 라울을 기리며 이 식물에 이름을 붙였다. 이름의 뒷부분은 라틴어로 '굉장히 특이한'이라는 뜻이다.

방석식물로서, 베지터블 시프는 둥근 모양을 하고 있고 땅 가까이에서 자란다. 가장 큰 표본은 [72]지름이

특징1: 외형	largest specimens ⁷²reach up to a meter or more in diameter and up to a meter tall. And although the plant may look soft, it is actually hard to the touch. Its exterior consists of a tight patchwork of tiny gray-green leaves, while fine white hairs give the plant its woolly appearance.

largest specimens ^{72}reach up to a meter or more in diameter and up to a meter tall. And although the plant may look soft, it is actually hard to the touch. Its exterior consists of a tight patchwork of tiny gray-green leaves, while fine white hairs give the plant its woolly appearance.

1미터 혹은 그 이상까지 그리고 높이가 1미터까지 이른다. 또한 비록 그 식물이 부드러워 보일지라도, 그것은 실제로 촉감이 단단하다. 그것의 외관은 작은 회녹색 잎의 촘촘한 쪽모이 모양으로 이루어져 있으며, 가는 흰 털이 그 식물을 양털로 덮인 듯한 겉모습을 제공한다.

특징2: 뿌리

The roots of the vegetable sheep comprise a dense network of underground branches. ^{69}The roots also extend over a wide mat above the surface of the ground. This mat forms a spongy material that sustains the plant by offering a mixture of raw soil and the rotted remains of dead leaves. However, the sponge-like mat, which ^{73}retains moisture well, can be overwhelmed with excess humidity from regular rainfall, and this makes it acidic and generally low in nutrient content.

베지터블 시프의 뿌리는 땅속 나뭇가지들의 조밀한 망을 구성한다. ^{69}뿌리는 또한 땅 표면 위로 광범위하게 엉겨 붙은 덩어리에 걸쳐 뻗어 있다. 이 엉겨 붙은 덩어리는 생흙과 죽은 잎의 썩은 잔여물의 혼합물을 제공함으로써 식물을 지탱하는 흡수력 있는 물질을 형성한다. 그러나, 이 스펀지 같은 엉겨 붙은 덩어리는, ^{73}습기를 잘 머금는데, 잦은 강우에 따른 과도한 습도에 뒤덮일 수 있으며, 이는 그것을 산성이 강하고 전반적으로 영양소 함량이 낮게 만든다.

서식 환경

^{70}The plant's condensed shape and structure are suited to the alpine environment, which is frigid and barren due to elevation and constant exposure to high winds. ^{70}They protect the plant against heavy snowfall, insulate it from the cold, and reflect bright sunlight.

^{70}이 식물의 응축된 모양과 구조는 고산 환경에 적합한데, 이것(고산 환경)은 고도와 강풍에 대한 지속적인 노출 때문에 몹시 춥고 척박하다. ^{70}그것들(응축된 모양과 구조)은 폭설로부터 그 식물을 보호하고, 추위로부터 그것을 보온하며, 밝은 햇빛을 반사한다.

보존 상태

Unlike related species that spread out across the ground, the vegetable sheep's small range leaves it vulnerable to the risk of habitat loss. Despite this, ^{71}the plant's conservation status is listed as "not threatened" as of 2022, likely because it is inedible to potential predators.

땅 전체에 퍼져 있는 관련 종들과는 달리, 베지터블 시프의 작은 영역은 그것을 서식지 상실의 위험에 취약하게 한다. 이것에도 불구하고, ^{71}그 식물의 보존 상태는 2022년 기준으로 '멸종 위기에 놓이지 않음'으로 등록되어 있는데, 이는 아마 잠재적 포식자가 그것을 먹을 수 없기 때문일 것이다.

어휘 | resemblance n. 유사성 Compositae n. 국화과 identify v. 발견하다 botanist n. 식물학자 naturalist n. 박물학자 strikingly adv. 굉장히 unusual adj. 특이한 specimen n. 표본, 견본 exterior n. 외관 patchwork n. 쪽모이 모양 fine adj. 가는, 미세한 woolly adj. 양털로 덮인 dense adj. 조밀한 extend v. 뻗다 mat n. 엉겨 붙은 덩어리 spongy adj. 흡수력 있는 sustain v. 지탱하다 moisture n. 습기 overwhelm v. ~에 뒤덮이다 humidity n. 습도 acidic adj. 산성이 강한 condensed adj. 응축된 alpine adj. 고산의 frigid adj. 몹시 추운 barren adj. 척박한 elevation n. 고도 insulate v. 보온하다, 단열하다 vulnerable adj. 취약한 habitat n. 서식지 conservation n. 보존 threatened adj. 멸종 위기에 놓인 inedible adj. 먹을 수 없는

---

67 특정세부사항   What

난이도 ●○○

According to the article, what is vegetable sheep?

(a) a plant that looks like an animal
(b) a food source for New Zealand livestock
(c) a material used for making cushions
(d) a vegetable that grows near sheep pastures

기사에 따르면, 베지터블 시프는 무엇인가?

(a) 동물처럼 생긴 식물
(b) 뉴질랜드 가축의 식량원
(c) 방석을 만드는 데 쓰이는 재료
(d) 양 목장 근처에서 자라는 채소

◆─○ 지텔프 치트키

표제어 vegetable sheep의 정의를 설명하는 1단락을 주의 깊게 읽는다.

TEST 1
TEST 2
TEST 3
TEST 4
TEST 5
TEST 6
TEST 7

해커스 지텔프 최신기출유형 실전문제집 7회 (Level 2)

해설 | 1단락의 'The name comes from the plant's physical resemblance to a sheep when seen at a distance.'에서 베지터블 시프의 이름은 멀리서 보았을 때 양과 이 식물의 물리적 유사성에서 비롯되었다고 했다. 따라서 (a)가 정답이다.

Paraphrasing
the ~ physical resemblance to a sheep 양과의 물리적 유사성 → looks like an animal 동물처럼 생기다

어휘 | livestock n. 가축 pasture n. 목장

---

68 **특정세부사항** Why 난이도 ●●○

Why did Joseph Hooker visit New Zealand?

(a) because he was searching for flower species
(b) **because he was traveling for his vocation**
(c) to meet a fellow explorer
(d) to receive an honor in botany

조지프 후커는 왜 뉴질랜드를 방문했는가?

(a) 꽃의 종을 찾고 있었기 때문에
(b) **그의 직업을 위해 여행하고 있었기 때문에**
(c) 동료 탐험가를 만나기 위해서
(d) 식물학에서의 상을 받기 위해서

◯ 지텔프 치트키
질문의 키워드 Joseph Hooker가 그대로 언급된 주변 내용을 주의 깊게 읽는다.

해설 | 2단락의 'Joseph Hooker, a British botanist and explorer who visited New Zealand on duty'에서 조지프 후커는 임무 수행 차 뉴질랜드를 방문한 영국의 식물학자이자 탐험가라고 했다. 따라서 (b)가 정답이다.

Paraphrasing
visited ~ on duty 임무 수행차 방문했다 → was traveling for his vocation 직업을 위해 여행하고 있었다

어휘 | vocation n. 직업, 천직 honor n. 상, 훈장

---

69 **특정세부사항** Where 난이도 ●●○

Where does the vegetable sheep get most of its nutrition?

(a) from an underground network of roots
(b) from regular rainwater runoff
(c) **from waste matter on the ground**
(d) from acidic content of nearby plants

베지터블 시프는 어디에서 대부분의 영양분을 얻는가?

(a) 땅속에 있는 뿌리의 망으로부터
(b) 잦은 빗물의 범람으로부터
(c) **땅 위에 있는 노폐물로부터**
(d) 인근 식물들의 산성 함량으로부터

◯ 지텔프 치트키
질문의 키워드 nutrition이 material that sustains the plant로 paraphrasing되어 언급된 주변 내용을 주의 깊게 읽는다.

해설 | 4단락의 'The roots ~ extend over a wide mat above the surface of the ground.'에서 베지터블 시프의 뿌리가 땅 표면 위로 광범위하게 엉겨 붙은 덩어리에 걸쳐 뻗어 있다고 한 뒤, 'This mat forms a ~ material that sustains the plant by offering a mixture of raw soil and the rotted remains of dead leaves.'에서 이 엉겨 붙은 덩어리가 생흙과 죽은 잎의 썩은 잔여물의 혼합물을 제공함으로써 베지터블 시프를 지탱하는 물질을 형성한다고 했다. 따라서 (c)가 정답이다.

Paraphrasing
above the surface of the ground 땅 표면 위 → on the ground 땅 위에
the rotted remains 썩은 잔여물 → waste matter 노폐물

어휘 | runoff n. 범람, 유수

How did the vegetable sheep adapt to its environment?	베지터블 시프는 어떻게 그것의 환경에 적응했는가?
(a) by forming a dense structure	**(a) 조밀한 구조를 형성함으로써**
(b) by altering its shape for cold weather	(b) 추운 날씨에 대비해 그것의 형태를 바꿈으로써
(c) by maximizing exposure to sunlight	(c) 햇빛에 대한 노출을 극대화함으로써
(d) by dispersing its seeds to the wind	(d) 그것의 씨앗을 바람에 퍼뜨림으로써

━○ 지텔프 치트키

질문의 키워드 environment가 그대로 언급된 주변 내용을 주의 깊게 읽는다.

해설 | 5단락의 'The plant's condensed shape and structure are suited to the alpine environment'에서 베지터블 시프의 응축된 모양과 구조가 고산 환경에 적합하다고 한 뒤, 'They protect the plant against heavy snowfall, insulate it from the cold, and reflect bright sunlight.'에서 그 응축된 모양과 구조가 폭설로부터 그 식물을 보호하고, 추위로부터 그것을 보온하며, 밝은 햇빛을 반사한다고 했다. 따라서 (a)가 정답이다.

Paraphrasing
The ~ condensed ~ structure 응축된 구조 → a dense structure 조밀한 구조

어휘 | alter v. 바꾸다 maximize v. 극대화하다 disperse v. 퍼뜨리다

Why most likely will the vegetable sheep continue to survive as a species?	왜 베지터블 시프가 하나의 종으로서 계속 살아남을 것 같은가?
(a) It has been adopted by farmers.	(a) 농부들에 의해 채택되었다.
(b) It is conserved by New Zealand's government.	(b) 뉴질랜드 정부에 의해 보호받는다.
(c) It is unsuitable for consumption.	**(c) 먹기에 적합하지 않다.**
(d) It can be grown in an artificial setting.	(d) 인공적인 환경에서 자랄 수 있다.

━○ 지텔프 치트키

질문의 키워드 continue to survive가 not threatened로 paraphrasing되어 언급된 주변 내용을 주의 깊게 읽는다.

해설 | 6단락의 'the plant's conservation status is listed as "not threatened" as of 2022, likely because it is inedible to potential predators'에서 베지터블 시프의 보존 상태가 2022년 기준으로 '멸종 위기에 놓이지 않음'으로 등록되어 있는데 이는 아마 잠재적 포식자가 그것을 먹을 수 없기 때문일 것이라고 한 것을 통해, 베지터블 시프는 먹기에 적합하지 않기 때문에 하나의 종으로서 계속 살아남을 것임을 추론할 수 있다. 따라서 (c)가 정답이다.

어휘 | adopt v. 채택하다 unsuitable adj. 적합하지 않은 artificial adj. 인공적인

In the context of the passage, <u>reach</u> means _____.	지문의 문맥에서, 'reach'는 -을 의미한다.
(a) arrive	(a) 도착한다

(b) live
(c) span
(d) cover

(b) 산다
(c) 이른다
(d) 덮는다

━○ **지텔프 치트키**

밑줄 친 어휘의 유의어를 찾는 문제이므로, reach가 포함된 구절을 읽고 문맥을 파악한다.

해설 | 3단락의 'reach up to a meter or more in diameter and up to a meter tall'은 지름이 1미터 혹은 그 이상까지 그리고 높이가 1미터까지 이른다는 뜻이므로, reach가 '이른다'라는 의미로 사용된 것을 알 수 있다. 따라서 '이른다'라는 같은 의미의 (c) span이 정답이다.

오답분석

(a) '도착하다'라는 의미의 arrive도 reach의 사전적 유의어 중 하나이다. 하지만 문맥상 베지터블 시프의 가장 큰 표본의 지름과 높이가 일정 수치까지 이른다는 의미가 되어야 적절하므로 문맥에 어울리지 않아 오답이다.

73 어휘   유의어   난이도 ●●○

In the context of the passage, retains means _____.

(a) holds
(b) blocks
(c) grabs
(d) recalls

지문의 문맥에서, 'retains'는 -을 의미한다.

(a) 보유한다
(b) 막는다
(c) 붙잡는다
(d) 상기한다

━○ **지텔프 치트키**

밑줄 친 어휘의 유의어를 찾는 문제이므로, retains가 포함된 구절을 읽고 문맥을 파악한다.

해설 | 4단락의 'retains moisture well'은 습기를 잘 머금는다는 뜻이므로, retains가 '머금는다'라는 의미로 사용된 것을 알 수 있다. 따라서 '보유한다'라는 비슷한 의미의 (a) holds가 정답이다.

PART 4 [74~80]   비즈니스 편지   인터넷 연결 서비스에 관해 불만을 제기하는 편지

수신인 정보	Kay Farrell Aire Broadband Headquarters 7508 Market Lane Paterson, NJ 07501 Dear Ms. Farrell:
편지의 목적: 불만 제기	This letter is about my TrueFiber Plus plan. [74]I have been experiencing repeated problems with the Internet connection for months now.
요금제 가입 배경	I first signed up for the plan last June. I [79]concluded it was a good deal since the company guaranteed speeds of up to 400 Mbps, a reliability rating of 99 percent, and

Kay Farrell
Aire Broadband 본사
마켓로 7508번지
07501 뉴저지주 패터슨

Ms. Farrell께:

이 편지는 저의 TrueFiber Plus 요금제에 관한 것입니다. [74]저는 지금 몇 달째 인터넷 연결에 관해 반복되는 문제를 겪어 오고 있습니다.

저는 지난 6월에 그 요금제에 처음 가입했습니다. 저는 [79]이것이 좋은 계약이라는 판단을 내렸는데 이는 귀사가 최대 400Mbps의 속도, 99퍼센트의 신뢰성 평가,

	protection from viruses and spyware.	그리고 바이러스 및 스파이웨어로부터의 보호를 보장했기 때문입니다.

<table>
<tr><td>불만1:
인터넷
속도</td><td>However, a few months ago, the Internet speed began to fluctuate, and I rarely got more than 200 Mbps. I called your customer support team and ⁷⁵allowed one of the staff to make changes to my computer remotely. This fixed the issue for a time, but it returned soon after.</td><td>하지만, 몇 달 전, 인터넷 속도가 수시로 변하기 시작했고, 200Mbps의 속도를 넘는 경우가 거의 없었습니다. 저는 귀사의 고객 지원팀에 전화를 걸었고 ⁷⁵직원 중 한 명이 원격으로 제 컴퓨터를 손볼 수 있도록 했습니다. 이것은 잠시 문제를 해결하였지만, 얼마 지나지 않아 이전 상태로 되돌아갔습니다.</td></tr>
<tr><td>불만2:
바이
러스
감염</td><td>Then, last month, ⁷⁶my computer was infected with a virus from an unknown source, and some important files were lost. I find this puzzling because I remember that security against all viruses was included in the plan.</td><td>그리고 나서, 지난달에, ⁷⁶제 컴퓨터가 출처를 알 수 없는 바이러스에 감염되었고, 몇몇 중요한 파일들이 유실되었습니다. 모든 바이러스들에 대비한 보안이 그 요금제에 포함된 것으로 기억하기 때문에 저는 이것이 당혹스러웠습니다.</td></tr>
<tr><td>불만3:
인터넷
연결
불량</td><td>Finally, my connection dropped again last week, and this interrupted my work. I made a call to schedule a repair but was told that the earliest a technician could come was in two weeks. ⁷⁷This is unacceptable because the outage is currently preventing me from doing my job from home.</td><td>결국, 지난주에 연결이 다시 끊겼고, 이것은 제 업무를 중단시켰습니다. 수리 일정을 잡으려고 전화했지만 기술자가 방문할 수 있는 가장 이른 시간이 2주 후라고 들었습니다. ⁷⁷그 고장이 현재 제가 집에서 일을 하지 못하게 하고 있기 때문에 이를 받아들일 수 없습니다.</td></tr>
<tr><td>해결책
제시</td><td>Please send someone right away, or I will find another provider. ⁷⁸If I have to end my contract, I don't think it's fair that I pay an early termination fee since all of these troubles have been caused by your company. I have been a good customer and ⁸⁰never <u>missed</u> a payment. I look forward to your reply soon.</td><td>지금 당장 누군가를 보내주시지 않는다면, 다른 제공업체를 찾아보겠습니다. ⁷⁸만약 제가 계약을 종료해야 한다면, 이 모든 문제들이 귀사에 의해 야기되었기 때문에 조기 해지 수수료를 지불하는 것은 공정하다고 생각하지 않습니다. 저는 좋은 고객이었고 ⁸⁰요금 납부를 빼먹은 적이 없습니다. 귀사의 빠른 회신을 기다리겠습니다.</td></tr>
<tr><td>발신인
정보</td><td>Sincerely,
Seth Gilmore</td><td>Seth Gilmore 드림</td></tr>
</table>

어휘 | connection n. 연결 deal n. 계약, 거래 guarantee v. 보장하다 reliability n. 신뢰성 fluctuate v. 수시로 변하다 remotely adv. 원격으로 infect v. 감염시키다 puzzling adj. 당혹스러운 drop v. 끊기다, 중단되다 interrupt v. 중단시키다 unacceptable adj. 받아들일 수 없는 outage n. 고장, 사용 불능 provider n. 제공업체 contract n. 계약 termination n. 해지

74	**주제/목적**	편지의 목적	난이도 ●●○

Why did Seth Gilmore write a letter to Kay Farrell?	왜 Seth Gilmore는 Kay Farrell에게 편지를 썼는가?
(a) to request a modification to his plan	(a) 그의 요금제 변경을 요청하기 위해서
(b) to complain about an unreliable service	**(b) 부실한 서비스에 대해 불평하기 위해서**
(c) to inquire about fluctuating prices	(c) 수시로 변하는 가격에 대해 문의하기 위해서
(d) to express his satisfaction with a service	(d) 서비스에 대한 그의 만족을 표현하기 위해서

지텔프 치트키

지문의 초반을 주의 깊게 읽고 전체 맥락을 파악한다.

해설 | 1단락의 'I have been experiencing repeated problems with the Internet connection for months now.'에서 Seth Gilmore는 지금 몇 달째 인터넷 연결에 관해 반복되는 문제를 겪어 오고 있다고 한 뒤, 자신이 사용하고 있는 인터넷 서비스에 대해 불평

하는 내용이 이어지고 있다. 따라서 (b)가 정답이다.

어휘ㅣ modification n. 변경 unreliable adj. 부실한, 의지할 수 없는 satisfaction n. 만족

---

75 특정세부사항 When
난이도 ●●○

When did Gilmore's problem improve temporarily?

(a) when a company representative visited his home
(b) after he removed a virus from his computer himself
(c) when he followed instructions from a specialized site
(d) after he authorized staff to access his device

Gilmore의 문제는 언제 일시적으로 개선되었는가?

(a) 회사 대표가 그의 집을 방문했을 때
(b) 그의 컴퓨터에서 스스로 바이러스를 제거한 후에
(c) 전문 사이트의 지시를 따랐을 때
(d) 그의 장치에 접근하도록 직원에게 권한을 부여한 후에

⌐O 지텔프 치트키

질문의 키워드 temporarily가 for a time으로 paraphrasing되어 언급된 주변 내용을 주의 깊게 읽는다.

해설ㅣ 3단락의 'allowed one of the staff to make changes to my computer remotely'에서 Gilmore가 직원 중 한 명이 원격으로 자신의 컴퓨터를 손볼 수 있도록 했다고 한 뒤, 'This fixed the issue for a time'에서 이것이 잠시 문제를 해결하였다고 했다. 따라서 (d)가 정답이다.

Paraphrasing
allowed ~ staff to make changes to my computer 직원이 컴퓨터를 손볼 수 있도록 했다 → authorized staff to access his device 장치에 접근하도록 직원에게 권한을 부여했다

어휘ㅣ temporarily adv. 일시적으로 representative n. 대표 remove v. 제거하다 instruction n. 지시 authorize v. 권한을 부여하다

---

76 추론 특정사실
난이도 ●●○

How did the computer virus most likely cause damage?

(a) by deleting some critical data files
(b) by slowing down the performance of the device
(c) by weakening the computer's virus protection
(d) by revealing the user's personal information

컴퓨터 바이러스가 어떻게 피해를 야기했을 것 같은가?

(a) 몇몇 중요한 데이터 파일들을 삭제함으로써
(b) 장치의 성능을 저하시킴으로써
(c) 컴퓨터의 바이러스 보호 기능을 약화시킴으로써
(d) 사용자의 개인 정보를 누출함으로써

⌐O 지텔프 치트키

질문의 키워드 virus가 그대로 언급된 주변 내용을 주의 깊게 읽는다.

해설ㅣ 4단락의 'my computer was infected with a virus from an unknown source, and some important files were lost'에서 Gilmore의 컴퓨터가 출처를 알 수 없는 바이러스에 감염되었고 몇몇 중요한 파일들이 유실되었다고 한 것을 통해, 컴퓨터 바이러스가 Gilmore의 몇몇 중요한 데이터 파일들을 삭제함으로써 피해를 야기했을 것임을 추론할 수 있다. 따라서 (a)가 정답이다.

Paraphrasing
important 중요한 → critical 중요한

어휘ㅣ critical adj. 중요한 weaken v. 약화시키다

해커스 지텔프 최신기출유형 실전문제집 7회 (Level 2)

Why is Gilmore dissatisfied with the repair schedule?	왜 Gilmore는 수리 일정에 불만이 있는가?
(a) because he can't arrange for service during office hours	(a) 영업시간에 서비스 일정을 잡을 수 없기 때문에
(b) because he has to postpone the appointment time	(b) 약속 시간을 미뤄야 하기 때문에
(c) because he doesn't yet have the money for repairs	(c) 아직 수리할 돈이 없기 때문에
(d) because he requires immediate Internet access for work	**(d) 업무를 위해 즉각적인 인터넷 접속이 필요하기 때문에**

◆──○ 지텔프 치트키

질문의 키워드 repair schedule이 schedule a repair로 paraphrasing되어 언급된 주변 내용을 주의 깊게 읽는다.

해설 | 5단락의 'This is unacceptable because the outage is currently preventing me from doing my job from home.'에서 Gilmore는 인터넷 연결 고장이 현재 그가 집에서 일을 하지 못하게 하고 있기 때문에 2주 후에나 가능한 수리 일정을 받아들일 수 없다고 했다. 따라서 (d)가 정답이다.

Paraphrasing
my job 일 → work 업무

어휘 | postpone v. 미루다　immediate adj. 즉각적인

What can be said about Aire Broadband?	Aire Broadband 사에 관해 말해질 수 있는 것은 무엇인가?
(a) It offers discounts on bundled services.	(a) 묶어서 파는 서비스에 할인을 제공한다.
(b) It is the cheapest Internet provider in Gilmore's area.	(b) Gilmore가 사는 지역에서 가장 저렴한 인터넷 제공업체이다.
(c) Its contract with Gilmore is still valid.	**(c) 그것의 Gilmore와의 계약은 여전히 유효하다.**
(d) Its termination fee is equivalent to a monthly payment.	(d) 그것의 해지 수수료는 월정액과 같다.

◆──○ 지텔프 치트키

질문의 키워드 Aire Broadband가 your company로 paraphrasing되어 언급된 주변 내용을 주의 깊게 읽는다.

해설 | 6단락의 'If I have to end my contract, I don't think it's fair that I pay an early termination fee since ~ troubles have been caused by your company.'에서 만약 자신이 계약을 종료해야 한다면 문제들이 Aire Broadband 사에 의해 야기되었기 때문에 조기 해지 수수료를 지불하는 것이 공정하다고 생각하지 않는다고 한 것을 통해, Aire Broadband 사와 Gilmore 사이의 계약이 아직 해지되지 않았으며 여전히 유효함을 추론할 수 있다. 따라서 (c)가 정답이다.

어휘 | bundle v. 묶어서 팔다　valid adj. 유효한　equivalent adj. 동등한

79 어휘 유의어

In the context of the passage, <u>concluded</u> means _____.

(a) finished
(b) collected
(c) resolved
(d) determined

지문의 문맥에서, 'concluded'는 -을 의미한다.

(a) 끝냈다
(b) 수집했다
(c) 해결했다
(d) 판단을 내렸다

🔑 지텔프 치트키

밑줄 친 어휘의 유의어를 찾는 문제이므로, concluded가 포함된 구절을 읽고 문맥을 파악한다.

해설 | 2단락의 'concluded it was a good deal'은 이것이 좋은 계약이라는 판단을 내렸다는 뜻이므로, concluded가 '판단을 내렸다'라는 의미로 사용된 것을 알 수 있다. 따라서 '판단을 내렸다'라는 같은 의미의 (d) determined가 정답이다.

오답분석

(a) '끝내다'라는 의미의 finish도 conclude의 사전적 유의어 중 하나이다. 하지만 문맥상 요금제가 다양한 혜택을 제공했기 때문에 이것이 좋은 계약이라는 판단을 내렸다는 의미가 되어야 적절하므로 conclude가 '끝내다'라는 의미가 아닌 '판단을 내리다'라는 의미로 사용된 것을 알 수 있다. 따라서 문맥에 어울리지 않아 오답이다.

80 어휘 유의어

In the context of the passage, <u>missed</u> means _____.

(a) fallen
(b) lost
(c) neglected
(d) canceled

지문의 문맥에서, 'missed'는 -을 의미한다.

(a) 넘어뜨린
(b) 잃은
(c) 빼먹은
(d) 취소한

🔑 지텔프 치트키

밑줄 친 어휘의 유의어를 찾는 문제이므로, missed가 포함된 구절을 읽고 문맥을 파악한다.

해설 | 6단락의 'never missed a payment'는 요금 납부를 빼먹은 적이 없다는 뜻이므로, missed가 '빼먹은'이라는 의미로 사용된 것을 알 수 있다. 따라서 '빼먹은'이라는 같은 의미의 (c) neglected가 정답이다.

오답분석

(b) '잃다'라는 의미의 lose도 miss의 사전적 유의어 중 하나이다. 하지만 문맥상 인터넷 서비스에 대한 요금 납부를 빼먹은 적이 없다는 의미가 되어야 적절하므로 miss가 '잃다'라는 의미가 아닌 '빼먹다'라는 의미로 사용된 것을 알 수 있다. 따라서 문맥에 어울리지 않아 오답이다.

해커스 지텔프 최신기출유형 실전문제집 7회 (Level 2)

TEST 2

정답·스크립트·해석·해설

GRAMMAR

LISTENING

READING & VOCABULARY

TEST 2 점수 확인하기

GRAMMAR _____ / 26 (점수 : _____ 점)
LISTENING _____ / 26 (점수 : _____ 점)
READING & VOCABULARY _____ / 28 (점수 : _____ 점)

TOTAL _____ / 80 (평균 점수 : _____ 점)

*각 영역 점수: 맞은 개수 × 3.75
*평균 점수: 각 영역 점수 합계 ÷ 3

정답 및 취약 유형 분석표

자동 채점 및 성적 분석 서비스 ▶

문제집 p.52

GRAMMAR

번호	정답	유형
01	c	준동사
02	d	시제
03	c	가정법
04	d	시제
05	b	연결어
06	b	시제
07	a	가정법
08	b	준동사
09	a	시제
10	c	준동사
11	a	관계사
12	c	준동사
13	a	조동사
14	b	시제
15	d	조동사
16	d	가정법
17	a	준동사
18	c	가정법
19	b	연결어
20	b	준동사
21	d	시제
22	b	가정법
23	d	조동사
24	a	관계사
25	c	조동사
26	c	가정법

유형	맞힌 개수
시제	/ 6
가정법	/ 6
준동사	/ 6
조동사	/ 4
연결어	/ 2
관계사	/ 2
TOTAL	/ 26

LISTENING

PART	번호	정답	유형
PART 1	27	d	특정세부사항
	28	c	특정세부사항
	29	a	특정세부사항
	30	b	특정세부사항
	31	c	특정세부사항
	32	b	특정세부사항
	33	d	추론
PART 2	34	b	특정세부사항
	35	a	Not/True
	36	d	특정세부사항
	37	c	특정세부사항
	38	b	특정세부사항
	39	a	추론
PART 3	40	a	주제/목적
	41	b	특정세부사항
	42	d	특정세부사항
	43	a	특정세부사항
	44	a	특정세부사항
	45	c	추론
PART 4	46	b	특정세부사항
	47	c	특정세부사항
	48	d	특정세부사항
	49	a	특정세부사항
	50	b	추론
	51	b	특정세부사항
	52	c	특정세부사항

유형	맞힌 개수
주제/목적	/ 1
특정세부사항	/ 20
Not/True	/ 1
추론	/ 4
TOTAL	/ 26

READING & VOCABULARY

PART	번호	정답	유형
PART 1	53	a	특정세부사항
	54	b	특정세부사항
	55	c	추론
	56	b	추론
	57	c	특정세부사항
	58	d	어휘
	59	a	어휘
PART 2	60	d	특정세부사항
	61	d	특정세부사항
	62	b	Not/True
	63	c	특정세부사항
	64	a	추론
	65	b	어휘
	66	d	어휘
PART 3	67	a	특정세부사항
	68	b	특정세부사항
	69	c	추론
	70	c	특정세부사항
	71	d	특정세부사항
	72	a	어휘
	73	b	어휘
PART 4	74	c	주제/목적
	75	a	특정세부사항
	76	c	특정세부사항
	77	d	추론
	78	d	추론
	79	b	어휘
	80	a	어휘

유형	맞힌 개수
주제/목적	/ 1
특정세부사항	/ 12
Not/True	/ 1
추론	/ 6
어휘	/ 8
TOTAL	/ 28

GRAMMAR

01 준동사   동명사를 목적어로 취하는 동사   난이도 ●●○

In spite of the convenience of self-checkout machines, most customers still prefer interacting with an actual person to using a touch screen. They do not mind _____ in line to be served by a cashier.

(a) to have waited
(b) to wait
(c) waiting
(d) being waited

셀프 계산기의 편리함에도 불구하고, 대부분의 고객들은 여전히 터치스크린을 사용하는 것보다 실제 사람과 소통하는 것을 선호한다. 그들은 점원에게 도움을 받기 위해 줄을 서서 <u>기다리는 것</u>을 개의치 않는다.

◁─○ 지텔프 치트키

mind는 동명사를 목적어로 취한다.

해설 | 빈칸 앞 동사 mind는 동명사를 목적어로 취하므로, 동명사 (c) waiting이 정답이다.

어휘 | convenience n. 편리함   customer n. 고객   prefer v. 선호하다   interact v. 소통하다   mind v. 개의하다, 상관하다

02 시제   현재진행   난이도 ●○○

The day was hot and humid, but now it is mild with a cool breeze. Laura and her husband _____ the pleasant evening outside while they watch the sun setting behind the mountains.

(a) were enjoying
(b) have enjoyed
(c) will have enjoyed
(d) are enjoying

그날은 덥고 습했지만, 지금은 시원한 산들바람 때문에 온화하다. Laura와 그녀의 남편은 산 너머로 지고 있는 해를 바라보면서 밖에서 즐거운 저녁 시간을 <u>즐기고 있는 중이다.</u>

◁─○ 지텔프 치트키

now와 'while + 현재 동사'가 함께 오면 현재진행 시제가 정답이다.

해설 | 현재진행 시제와 함께 쓰이는 시간 표현 now와 'while + 현재 동사'(while ~ watch)가 있고, 문맥상 말하고 있는 현재 시점에 Laura와 그녀의 남편이 즐거운 저녁 시간을 즐기고 있는 중이라는 의미가 되어야 자연스럽다. 따라서 현재진행 시제 (d) are enjoying이 정답이다.

어휘 | humid adj. 습한   mild adj. 온화한, 포근한   breeze n. 산들바람   pleasant adj. 즐거운

해커스 지텔프 최신기출유형 실전문제집 7회 (Level 2)

The artist's latest paintings, though technically brilliant and visually appealing, don't get enough attention because they are only shown in small galleries. If his work _____ in bigger galleries, he would be quite famous today.

(a) will be displayed
(b) is displayed
(c) were displayed
(d) has been displayed

그 예술가의 최근 그림들은, 기술적으로 훌륭하고 시각적으로 매력적이긴 하지만, 작은 미술관들에서만 전시되기 때문에 충분한 관심을 받지 못한다. 만약 그의 작품이 더 큰 미술관들에서 <u>전시된다면</u>, 그는 오늘날 꽤 유명할 것이다.

◀━○ 지텔프 치트키

if와 'would/could + 동사원형'이 있으면 과거 동사가 정답이다.

> ☀ **가정법 과거**
> If + 주어 + 과거 동사, 주어 + would/could(조동사 과거형) + 동사원형

해설 | 주절에 'would(조동사 과거형) + 동사원형' 형태의 would be가 있으므로, If절에는 이와 짝을 이루어 가정법 과거를 만드는 과거 동사가 와야 한다. 따라서 (c) were displayed가 정답이다.

어휘 | technically adv. 기술적으로   visually adv. 시각적으로   appealing adj. 매력적인   famous adj. 유명한   display v. 전시하다

---

04 **시제** 현재완료진행   난이도 ●●○

Alzheimer's disease is a neurological disorder that negatively affects the mental functioning of people. Scientists _____ on a vaccine to prevent this illness for decades, and they are optimistic that it will be available in the near future.

(a) will be working
(b) are working
(c) had been working
(d) have been working

알츠하이머병은 사람들의 정신적 기능에 부정적으로 영향을 미치는 신경 질환이다. 과학자들은 이 질환을 예방하기 위한 백신에 수십 년 동안 공을 들여오고 있는 중이며, 그들은 가까운 미래에 그것이 이용 가능할 것이라고 낙관한다.

◀━○ 지텔프 치트키

'for + 기간 표현'과 현재 동사가 함께 오면 현재완료진행 시제가 정답이다.

해설 | 빈칸 문장에 현재 동사가 사용되었고, 지속을 나타내는 시간 표현 'for + 기간 표현'(for decades)이 있다. 또한, 문맥상 과학자들이 알츠하이머병을 예방하기 위한 백신에 과거(공을 들이기 시작했던 시점)부터 현재까지 수십 년 동안 계속해서 공을 들여오고 있는 중이라는 의미가 되어야 자연스럽다. 따라서 현재완료진행 시제 (d) have been working이 정답이다.

오답분석

(b) 현재진행 시제는 특정 현재 시점에 한창 진행 중인 일을 나타내므로, 과거에 시작해서 현재 시점까지 계속해서 진행되고 있는 일을 표현할 수 없어 오답이다.

어휘 | neurological disorder phr. 신경 질환   negatively adv. 부정적으로   mental adj. 정신적인   functioning n. 기능, 작용   prevent v. 예방하다   optimistic adj. 낙관하는, 낙관적인   work v. 공을 들이다

The missed deliveries of snack foods were mainly due to supply chain issues outside of Tasty Treat's control. _____, the technical team managed to lessen the impact of the problem by improving the efficiency of the company's ordering system.

(a) Otherwise
(b) However
(c) In fact
(d) Thus

간식용 음식의 누락된 배달은 주로 Tasty Treat 사의 통제 밖에 있는 공급망 문제 때문이었다. <u>그러나</u>, 기술팀은 회사 주문 시스템의 효율성을 개선함으로써 그 문제의 영향을 용케 줄였다.

—○ 지텔프 치트키

'그러나'라는 의미의 대조를 나타낼 때는 However를 쓴다.

> ☀ **대조를 나타내는 빈출 접속부사**
> However 그러나　On the other hand 반면에　Otherwise 그렇지 않으면　In contrast 그에 반해

해설 | 빈칸 앞 문장은 간식용 음식의 누락된 배달은 주로 Tasty Treat 사의 통제 밖에 있는 공급망 문제 때문이었다는 내용이고, 빈칸 뒤 문장은 기술팀이 회사 주문 시스템의 효율성을 개선함으로써 그 문제의 영향을 줄였다는 대조적인 내용이다. 따라서 '그러나'라는 의미의 대조를 나타내는 접속부사 (b) However가 정답이다.

오답분석
(a) Otherwise는 '그렇지 않으면', (c) In fact는 '사실은', (d) Thus는 '그러므로'라는 의미로, 문맥에 적합하지 않아 오답이다.

어휘 | delivery n. 배달　technical adj. 기술의　manage v. 용케 해내다　lessen v. 줄이다　improve v. 개선하다　efficiency n. 효율성

The West Coast fires that tore through Northern California, Oregon, and Washington were some of the worst in recorded history. New brush fires constantly broke out while firefighters _____ ones in other areas, making them nearly impossible to contain.

(a) have been putting out
(b) were putting out
(c) are putting out
(d) would put out

북부 캘리포니아주, 오리건주, 그리고 워싱턴주를 강타한 서부 해안 화재는 기록된 역사상 최악의 화재 중 하나였다. 소방관들이 다른 지역에서 불을 <u>끄고 있던</u> 동안에 새로운 소규모 화재들이 끊임없이 발화했고, 이는 그것들을 진압하는 것을 거의 불가능하게 만들었다.

—○ 지텔프 치트키

'과거 동사 + while절'이 있으면 과거진행 시제가 정답이다.

해설 | 과거진행 시제와 함께 쓰이는 시간 표현 '과거 동사 + while절'(broke out while ~)이 있고, 문맥상 소규모 화재들이 끊임없이 발화했던 과거 시점에 소방관들은 다른 지역에서 불을 끄고 있던 도중이었다는 의미가 되어야 자연스럽다. 따라서 과거진행 시제 (b) were putting out이 정답이다.

어휘 | tear through phr. ~을 강타하다　constantly adv. 끊임없이　break out phr. 발화하다, 발생하다　contain v. 진압하다, 억제하다　put out phr. (불을) 끄다

I don't think it's fair that the whole team has to stay late on account of Jack's poor planning and organizational skills! If he had just completed his work on time, we _____ our project by now.

(a) **would have finished**
(b) will be finished
(c) have finished
(d) would finish

Jack의 형편없는 계획력과 조직력 때문에 팀 전체가 늦게까지 남아 있어야 하는 것은 타당하다고 생각하지 않는다! 만약 그가 그저 제때에 그의 일을 끝마쳤다면, 우리는 지금쯤 프로젝트를 끝냈을 것이다.

◆○ 지텔프 치트키

'if + had p.p.'가 있으면 'would/could + have p.p.'가 정답이다.

💡 **가정법 과거완료**
If + 주어 + had p.p., 주어 + would/could(조동사 과거형) + have p.p.

해설 | If절에 'had p.p.' 형태의 had ~ completed가 있으므로, 주절에는 이와 짝을 이루어 가정법 과거완료를 만드는 'would(조동사 과거형) + have p.p.'가 와야 한다. 따라서 (a) would have finished가 정답이다.

어휘 | fair adj. 타당한, 공평한　on account of phr. ~ 때문에　organizational adj. 조직적인　complete v. 끝마치다, 완료하다

A world-renowned composer heard Eleanor play the piano by chance and asked if she wanted to study under him. She was excited at the opportunity _____ at the feet of a master.

(a) sitting
(b) **to sit**
(c) having sat
(d) to have sat

세계적으로 유명한 한 작곡가가 우연히 Eleanor가 피아노를 연주하는 것을 듣고 그녀가 그의 밑에서 배우고 싶은지를 물었다. 그녀는 대가의 가르침을 받을 기회에 흥분했다.

◆○ 지텔프 치트키

'~(해야) 할', '~하는'이라고 말할 때는 to 부정사를 쓴다.

해설 | 빈칸 앞에 명사(the opportunity)가 있고 문맥상 '가르침을 받을 기회'라는 의미가 되어야 자연스러우므로, 빈칸은 명사를 수식하는 형용사의 자리이다. 따라서 명사를 꾸며주는 형용사적 수식어구를 이끌 수 있는 to 부정사 (b) to sit이 정답이다.

어휘 | world-renowned adj. 세계적으로 유명한　composer n. 작곡가　by chance phr. 우연히　sit at the feet of phr. ~의 가르침을 받다

Nut Explosion, a chocolate bar that includes peanuts and almonds, is one of the longest-running snacks sold by

땅콩과 아몬드가 들어 있는 초콜릿 바인 Nut Explosion은 Weser Candies 사에 의해 판매되는 가장 오래된

Weser Candies. In fact, the company will be celebrating a milestone next year. By then, it _____ the popular treat for 120 years.

(a) **will have been producing**
(b) is producing
(c) has been producing
(d) will be producing

간식들 중 하나다. 사실, 그 회사는 내년에 중대 시점을 기념할 것이다. 그쯤에, 그것은 그 인기 있는 간식을 120년 동안 <u>생산해오고 있는 중일 것이다</u>.

━○ 지텔프 치트키

'by then'과 'for + 기간 표현'이 함께 오면 미래완료진행 시제가 정답이다.

해설 | 미래완료진행 시제와 함께 쓰이는 시간 표현 'by + 미래 시점'(By then)과 'for + 기간 표현'(for 120 years)이 있고, 문맥상 미래 시점인 내년쯤에 Weser Candies 사가 인기 있는 초콜릿 바인 Nut Explosion을 120년 동안 계속해서 생산해오고 있는 중일 것이라는 의미가 되어야 자연스럽다. 따라서 미래완료진행 시제 (a) will have been producing이 정답이다.

> **오답분석**
> (d) 미래진행 시제는 특정 미래 시점에 진행 중일 일을 나타내므로, 과거 또는 현재에 시작해서 특정 미래 시점까지 계속해서 진행되고 있을 일을 표현할 수 없어 오답이다.

어휘 | celebrate v. 기념하다 milestone n. 중대 시점

---

10 **준동사**   to 부정사를 목적어로 취하는 동사   난이도 ●●○

The tote bags made by Lamak Sports are very trendy. Sales of these tote bags are projected _____ even more over the next two years as the products are introduced into new international markets.

(a) having grown
(b) growing
(c) **to grow**
(d) to have grown

Lamak Sports 사에 의해 제조된 토트백이 매우 유행하고 있다. 그 제품이 새로운 해외 시장에 도입됨에 따라 이 토트백의 매출은 향후 2년 동안 훨씬 더 <u>증가할 것</u>으로 예상된다.

━○ 지텔프 치트키

project는 to 부정사를 목적어로 취한다.

> ☼ **to 부정사를 목적어로 취하는 빈출 동사**
> project 예상하다 promise 약속하다 expect 예상하다 vow 맹세하다 wish 희망하다 plan 계획하다 decide 결정하다 hope 바라다
> agree 동의하다 intend 계획하다 prepare 준비하다

해설 | 빈칸 앞 동사 project는 to 부정사를 목적어로 취하므로, to 부정사 (c) to grow가 정답이다.

> **오답분석**
> (d) to have grown도 to 부정사이기는 하지만, 완료부정사(to have grown)로 쓰일 경우 토트백의 매출이 '예상되는' 시점보다 '증가하는' 시점이 앞선다는 것을 나타내므로 문맥에 적합하지 않아 오답이다.

어휘 | trendy adj. 유행하는 sale n. 매출 project v. 예상하다 introduce v. 도입하다, 소개하다 international adj. 해외의

11 관계사   주격 관계대명사 that

Since Earth is not a perfect sphere, its gravitational force is distributed unequally. Glaciers _____ actually distorted Earth's crust, causing the planet's gravity to become irregular.

(a) that melted thousands of years ago
(b) which they melted thousands of years ago
(c) what melted thousands of years ago
(d) who melted thousands of years ago

지구는 완벽한 구체가 아니기 때문에, 그것의 중력은 고르지 않게 분포되어 있다. 수천 년 전에 녹았던 빙하들이 실제로 지구의 지각을 일그러뜨렸으며, 이는 그 행성의 중력이 고르지 않게 만들었다.

━○ 지텔프 치트키

사물 선행사가 관계절 안에서 주어 역할을 하면 주격 관계대명사 that이 정답이다.

해설 | 사물 선행사 Glarciers를 받으면서 보기의 관계절 내에서 동사 melted의 주어가 될 수 있는 주격 관계대명사가 필요하므로, (a) that melted thousands of years ago가 정답이다.

어휘 | sphere n. 구체   gravitational force phr. 중력   distribute v. 분포하다   unequally adv. 고르지 않게   distort v. 일그러뜨리다   crust n. 지각   gravity n. 중력   irregular adj. 고르지 않은, 불규칙한

---

12 준동사   동명사를 목적어로 취하는 동사

Mr. Adams makes it a priority to teach his class how to explore topics without the Internet. He believes that if students keep _____ computers excessively, they will not be able to carry out some academic work.

(a) to rely on
(b) will rely on
(c) relying on
(d) having relied on

Mr. Adams는 그의 학급에 인터넷 없이 주제를 탐구하는 방법을 가르치는 것을 우선순위로 삼는다. 그는 만약 학생들이 지나치게 컴퓨터에 의존하는 것을 계속한다면, 그들이 일부 학업을 수행할 수 없을 것이라고 믿는다.

━○ 지텔프 치트키

keep은 동명사를 목적어로 취한다.

해설 | 빈칸 앞 동사 keep은 동명사를 목적어로 취하므로, 동명사 (c) relying on이 정답이다.

    오답분석

    (d) having relied on도 동명사이기는 하지만, 완료동명사(having relied on)로 쓰일 경우 '계속하는' 시점보다 '의존하는' 시점이 앞선다는 것을 나타내므로 문맥에 적합하지 않아 오답이다.

어휘 | priority n. 우선순위   explore v. 탐구하다   excessively adv. 지나치게, 과도하게   carry out phr. 수행하다   academic adj. 학업의   rely on phr. ~에 의존하다

For firms that have access to confidential user data, a leak of private information can cause them to lose clients. Therefore, it is essential that such companies _____ comprehensive security protocols.

(a) execute
(b) to execute
(c) will execute
(d) executed

이용자의 기밀 데이터에 접근 권한을 가지고 있는 기업들의 경우, 개인 정보의 유출은 그들이 고객들을 잃게 할 수 있다. 따라서, 그러한 회사들이 종합 보안 프로토콜을 <u>시행해야 하는</u> 것은 필수적이다.

🔑 지텔프 치트키

essential 다음에는 that절에 동사원형이 온다.

> 💡 주장·요구·명령·제안을 나타내는 빈출 형용사
> essential 필수적인　important 중요한　best 제일 좋은　necessary 필요한　mandatory 의무적인

해설 | 주절에 주장을 나타내는 형용사 essential이 있으므로 that절에는 '(should +) 동사원형'이 와야 한다. 따라서 동사원형 (a) execute가 정답이다.

어휘 | confidential adj. 기밀의　leak n. 유출　private adj. 개인의　client n. 고객　essential adj. 필수적인　comprehensive adj. 종합적인　security n. 보안　protocol n. 프로토콜, 통신 규약　execute v. 시행하다

Yemen is entering the eighth year of a devastating war against Houthi rebels. As a consequence, more than 14 million citizens don't have enough food right now. The UN _____ more aid in the upcoming months to help them.

(a) sends
(b) will be sending
(c) sent
(d) was sending

예멘이 후티 반군과의 파괴적인 전쟁의 8년째에 접어들고 있다. 결과적으로, 1,400만 명 이상의 시민들이 현재 충분한 식량을 가지고 있지 않다. 유엔은 그들을 돕기 위해 앞으로 몇 달 후에 더 많은 원조를 <u>보내고 있는 중일 것이다.</u>

🔑 지텔프 치트키

'for + 기간 표현' 없이 특정 미래 시점을 나타내는 표현만 있으면 미래진행 시제가 정답이다.

해설 | 미래진행 시제와 함께 쓰이는 시간 표현 'in + 미래 시점'(in the upcoming months)이 있고, 문맥상 미래 시점인 앞으로 몇 달 후에 유엔이 더 많은 원조를 보내고 있는 중일 것이라는 의미가 되어야 자연스럽다. 따라서 미래진행 시제 (b) will be sending이 정답이다.

어휘 | devastating adj. 파괴적인　rebel n. 반군　upcoming adj. 앞으로의, 다가오는

Felix chose to install a new anti-virus program after his computer crashed for the third time. It _____ not make a difference, but he thinks it is worth a try. (a) must (b) could (c) can **(d) may**	Felix는 그의 컴퓨터가 세 번째로 고장 난 후 새로운 바이러스 백신 프로그램을 설치하기로 결정했다. 그것이 변화를 가져오지 <u>않을지도 모르지만</u>, 그는 시도해 볼 가치가 있다고 생각한다.

▶◀◎ 지텔프 치트키

'~할지도 모른다'라고 말할 때는 may를 쓴다.

해설 | 문맥상 새로운 바이러스 백신 프로그램을 설치하는 것이 변화를 가져오지 않을지도 모르지만 시도해 볼 가치가 있다는 의미가 되어야 자연스러우므로, '~할지도 모른다'를 뜻하면서 약한 추측을 나타내는 조동사 (d) may가 정답이다. 참고로, may와 might 모두 '~할지도 모른다'를 뜻하지만, may는 might보다 일어날 가능성이 조금 더 큰 경우에 쓴다.

어휘 | install v. 설치하다   crash v. 고장 나다   worth adj. 가치가 있는

---

16 가정법   가정법 과거완료   난이도 ●●○

An Ebola virus epidemic ravaged regions of West Africa from 2013 to 2016. Had it not been for the tireless service of international medical staff volunteering in the area, many more victims _____ to the disease. (a) would succumb (b) had succumbed (c) have succumbed **(d) would have succumbed**	에볼라 바이러스 전염병은 2013년부터 2016년까지 서아프리카의 지역들을 황폐하게 만들었다. 그 지역에서 봉사하는 국제 의료진의 끊임없는 활동이 없었었다면, 더 많은 환자들이 이 병으로 <u>죽었을 것이다</u>.

▶◀◎ 지텔프 치트키

Had p.p.가 있으면 'would/could + have p.p.'가 정답이다.

> ☼ **가정법 과거완료(도치)**
> Had + 주어 + p.p., 주어 + would/could(조동사 과거형) + have p.p.

해설 | if가 생략되어 도치된 절에 'had p.p.' 형태의 Had ~ not been이 있으므로, 주절에는 이와 짝을 이루어 가정법 과거완료를 만드는 'would(조동사 과거형) + have p.p.'가 와야 한다. 따라서 (d) would have succumbed가 정답이다. 참고로 'Had it not been for ~'는 'If it had not been for ~'로 바꿔 쓸 수 있다.

어휘 | epidemic n. (유행성의) 전염병   ravage v. 황폐하게 만들다   tireless adj. 끊임없는   service n. 활동, 봉사   medical adj. 의료의   volunteer v. 봉사하다   victim n. 환자   succumb v. (병으로) 죽다, 쓰러지다

TEST 1
TEST 2
TEST 3
TEST 4
TEST 5
TEST 6
TEST 7

17 준동사　동명사를 목적어로 취하는 동사　난이도 ●○○

Bentley's parents urged him to ask his aunt for a job at her company. But Bentley wanted to get a job on his own and wouldn't consider _____ a job he didn't earn himself.

(a) **accepting**
(b) to accept
(c) to have accepted
(d) having accepted

Bentley의 부모는 이모에게 그녀 회사의 일자리를 요구해 보라고 그를 설득했다. 하지만 Bentley는 혼자 힘으로 직장을 얻기를 원했으며 그가 스스로 얻지 않은 일자리를 받아들이는 것을 고려하지 않을 것이다.

지텔프 치트키

consider는 동명사를 목적어로 취한다.

해설 | 빈칸 앞 동사 consider는 동명사를 목적어로 취하므로, 동명사 (a) accepting이 정답이다.

　오답분석
　(d) having accepted도 동명사이기는 하지만, 완료동명사(having accepted)로 쓰일 경우 '고려하는' 시점보다 '받아들이는' 시점이 앞선다는 것을 나타내므로 문맥에 적합하지 않아 오답이다.

어휘 | urge v. 설득하다, 권고하다　on one's own phr. 혼자 힘으로

18 가정법　가정법 과거완료　난이도 ●●○

Duct tape was invented by Vesta Stoudt, a factory worker in Dixon, Illinois. She wrote to President Roosevelt about her idea after her superiors dismissed it. If she had not sent her letter, the product _____ to history decades ago.

(a) was lost
(b) would be lost
(c) **would have been lost**
(d) had been lost

강력 접착테이프는 일리노이주 딕슨의 공장 노동자 베스타 스타우트에 의해 발명되었다. 그녀는 상사들이 그녀의 아이디어를 일축한 후에 루스벨트 대통령에게 그것에 대해 편지를 썼다. 만약 그녀가 그녀의 편지를 보내지 않았었다면, 그 제품은 수십 년 전에 역사 속으로 사라졌을 것이다.

지텔프 치트키

'if + had p.p.'가 있으면 'would/could + have p.p.'가 정답이다.

해설 | If절에 'had p.p.' 형태의 had not sent가 있으므로, 주절에는 이와 짝을 이루어 가정법 과거완료를 만드는 'would(조동사 과거형) + have p.p.'가 와야 한다. 따라서 (c) would have been lost가 정답이다.

어휘 | invent v. 발명하다　superior n. 상사　dismiss v. 일축하다, 무시하다

19 연결어　접속사　난이도 ●●●

Sophia couldn't believe her luck on the boat trip. She was shocked that she reeled in the biggest catch of the day.

Sophia는 보트 여행에서의 그녀의 행운을 믿을 수 없었다. 그녀는 그녀가 그날의 가장 큰 어획물을 낚았다

_____ she had gone fishing before, she had never caught anything.

(a) Unless
(b) Although
(c) Because
(d) Until

는 것에 깜짝 놀랐다. 그녀는 이전에 낚시하러 간 적이 있었음에도 불구하고, 그 어떤 것도 잡아본 적이 없었다.

지텔프 치트키

'~에도 불구하고'라는 의미의 양보를 나타낼 때는 although를 쓴다.

💡 **양보를 나타내는 빈출 접속사**
although ~에도 불구하고 even though ~에도 불구하고 while ~이긴 하지만

해설 | 문맥상 Sophia가 이전에 낚시하러 간 적이 있었음에도 불구하고 지금까지 그 어떤 것도 잡아본 적이 없었다는 의미가 되어야 자연스럽다. 따라서 '~에도 불구하고'라는 의미의 양보를 나타내는 부사절 접속사 (b) Although가 정답이다.

오답분석
(a) Unless는 '~하지 않는 한', (c) Because는 '~이기 때문에', (d) Until은 '~할 때까지'라는 의미로, 문맥에 적합하지 않아 오답이다.

어휘 | reel in phr. ~을 낚다

---

20 준동사 to 부정사를 목적어로 취하는 동사 난이도 ●○○

While practicing, Vancouver Bullets' star player Fran Allen sprained her ankle. Despite the severity of the injury, she expects _____ her team in time for the national soccer tournament next month.

(a) rejoining
(b) to rejoin
(c) to be rejoining
(d) having rejoined

연습 도중에, Vancouver Bullets 팀의 인기 선수인 Fran Allen이 발목을 삐었다. 부상의 심각성에도 불구하고, 그녀는 다음 달에 있을 전국 축구 경기를 위해 조만간 팀에 다시 합류하기를 바라고 있다.

지텔프 치트키

expect는 to 부정사를 목적어로 취한다.

해설 | 빈칸 앞 동사 expect는 to 부정사를 목적어로 취하므로, to 부정사 (b) to rejoin이 정답이다.

어휘 | sprain v. 삐다 severity n. 심각성 injury n. 부상 rejoin v. 다시 합류하다

---

21 시제 과거완료진행 난이도 ●●○

Jessica sat down on the kitchen chair, annoyed because she would have to clean up all over again. She _____ the floors for 30 minutes before her kids ran through the house wearing their dirty shoes.

Jessica는 처음부터 다시 청소해야 했기 때문에 화가 난 채로 부엌 의자에 앉았다. 그녀는 아이들이 더러운 신발을 신고 집안을 뛰어다니기 전에 30분 동안 바닥을 닦아오고 있던 중이었다.

(a) has mopped
(b) was mopping
(c) will have been mopping
(d) had been mopping

'before + 과거 동사'가 있으면 과거완료진행 시제가 정답이다.

해설 | 과거완료진행 시제와 함께 쓰이는 시간 표현 'for + 기간 표현'(for 30 minutes)과 'before + 과거 동사'(before ~ ran)가 있고, 문맥상 Jessica가 대과거(바닥을 닦기 시작한 시점)부터 과거(아이들이 집안을 뛰어다닌 시점)까지 30분 동안 계속해서 바닥을 닦아오고 있던 중이었다는 의미가 되어야 자연스럽다. 따라서 과거완료진행 시제 (d) had been mopping이 정답이다.

오답분석
(b) 과거진행 시제는 특정 과거 시점에 한창 진행 중이었던 일을 나타내므로, 대과거에 시작해서 특정 과거 시점까지 계속해서 진행되고 있었던 일을 표현할 수 없어 오답이다.

어휘 | annoyed adj. 화가 난 mop v. 닦다, 청소하다

22 가정법   가정법 과거   난이도 ●●○

The teacher is rather concerned about the students' level of preparation for the final examination next week. He assumes that if they were to take the test today, the majority of the students _____ completely.

(a) failed
(b) would fail
(c) will fail
(d) would have failed

그 교사는 학생들의 다음 주 기말고사 준비 수준에 대해 상당히 걱정이다. 그는 만약 그들이 오늘 시험을 본다면, 대다수의 학생들이 완전히 <u>낙제할 것이라고</u> 생각한다.

'if + were to + 동사원형'이 있으면 'would/could + 동사원형'이 정답이다.

💡 가정법 과거(were to)
  If + 주어 + were to + 동사원형, 주어 + would/could(조동사 과거형) + 동사원형

해설 | if절에 과거 동사(were to take)가 있으므로, 주절에는 이와 짝을 이루어 가정법 과거를 만드는 'would(조동사 과거형) + 동사원형'이 와야 한다. 따라서 (b) would fail이 정답이다.

어휘 | preparation n. 준비 final examination phr. 기말고사 assume v. 생각하다 majority n. 대다수 fail v. 낙제하다

23 조동사   조동사 will   난이도 ●●●

After spending a long time exploring other media, Beth has returned to her original mode of creative expression. She has decided that she _____ dedicate the rest of the

다른 표현 수단들을 조사하는 데 오랜 시간을 보낸 뒤, Beth는 그녀의 기존의 창조적인 표현 방식으로 되돌아왔다. 그녀는 작품들을 파는 것을 시작하기 전에 그

year to making sculptures in her workshop before she begins selling her pieces.

(a) can
(b) may
(c) might
(d) will

이녀의 작업장에서 조각품들을 만드는 것에 올해의 남은 시간을 바칠 <u>것으로</u> 결정했다.

── ○ 지텔프 치트키

'~할 것이다'라고 말할 때는 will을 쓴다.

해설 | 문맥상 기존의 창조적인 표현 방식으로 되돌아온 Beth가 조각품들을 만드는 것에 올해의 남은 시간을 바칠 것으로 결정했다는 내용이 되어야 자연스러우므로, '~할 것이다'를 뜻하면서 의지를 나타내는 조동사 (d) will이 정답이다.

어휘 | medium n. 표현 수단, 매체   original adj. 기존의, 독창적인   creative adj. 창조적인, 창의적인   expression n. 표현 방식   dedicate v. 바치다   sculpture n. 조각품

---

24 관계사   주격 관계대명사 who   난이도 ●●○

I wasn't sure whether to buy or rent a home. Thankfully, my coworker, _____ himself, gave me the phone number of his real estate agent so that I could ask any questions I might have.

(a) who is struggling with the dilemma
(b) how he is struggling with the dilemma
(c) that is struggling with the dilemma
(d) which is struggling with the dilemma

나는 집을 사야 할지 임차해야 할지 확신이 서지 않았다. 고맙게도, 나의 동료는, 그 자신도 이 난제로 고심하고 있는데, 내가 궁금해할지도 모르는 어떤 질문이든 할 수 있도록 그의 부동산 중개인의 전화번호를 나에게 알려줬다.

── ○ 지텔프 치트키

사람 선행사가 관계절 안에서 주어 역할을 하고, 빈칸 앞에 콤마(,)가 있으면 주격 관계대명사 who가 정답이다.

해설 | 사람 선행사 my coworker를 받으면서 콤마(,) 뒤에 올 수 있는 주격 관계대명사가 필요하므로, (a) who is struggling with the dilemma가 정답이다.

오답분석

(c) 관계대명사 that도 사람 선행사를 받을 수 있지만, 콤마 뒤에 올 수 없으므로 오답이다.

어휘 | thankfully adv. 고맙게도   real estate agent phr. 부동산 중개인   struggle v. 고심하다   dilemma n. 난제

---

25 조동사   조동사 should 생략   난이도 ●●○

Several environmental organizations are dissatisfied with the slow rate of electric vehicle adoption. To accelerate the process, they request that the federal government _____ taxes on gasoline and other fossil fuels.

몇몇 환경 단체들은 전기 자동차의 느린 채택 속도에 불만을 느끼고 있다. 그 과정을 가속화하기 위해, 그들은 연방 정부가 휘발유와 다른 화석 연료에 대한 세금을 <u>인상해야 한다</u>고 요청한다.

(a) to raise
(b) will raise
(c) **raise**
(d) raises

TEST 1   TEST 2   TEST 3   TEST 4   TEST 5   TEST 6   TEST 7

지텔프 치트키

request 다음에는 that절에 동사원형이 온다.

> 🔅 **주장·요구·명령·제안을 나타내는 빈출 동사**
> request 요청하다   recommend 권고하다   demand 요구하다   suggest 제안하다   order 명령하다   urge 강력히 촉구하다   ask 요청하다
> propose 제안하다   insist 주장하다   advise 권고하다

해설 | 주절에 요구를 나타내는 동사 request가 있으므로 that절에는 '(should +) 동사원형'이 와야 한다. 따라서 동사원형 (c) raise가 정답이다.

어휘 | environmental adj. 환경의   organization n. 단체   dissatisfied adj. 불만을 느끼는   adoption n. 채택, 입양   accelerate v. 가속화하다
federal government phr. 연방 정부   gasoline n. 휘발유   fossil fuel phr. 화석 연료

---

26   가정법   가정법 과거   난이도 ●●○

It's too bad that my niece Iris never has time to visit Central Park even though she lives nearby. If her job were to start in the afternoon, she _____ in a peaceful setting every morning!

(a) jogged
(b) is jogging
(c) **would jog**
(d) would have jogged

나의 조카 Iris가 근처에 살고 있음에도 불구하고 센트럴 파크에 갈 시간이 전혀 없다는 것은 너무 안타까운 일이다. 만약 그녀의 일이 오후에 시작된다면, 그녀는 매일 아침 평화로운 환경에서 조깅할 것이다!

지텔프 치트키

'if + were to + 동사원형'이 있으면 'would/could + 동사원형'이 정답이다.

해설 | If절에 과거 동사(were to start)가 있으므로, 주절에는 이와 짝을 이루어 가정법 과거를 만드는 'would(조동사 과거형) + 동사원형'이 와야 한다. 따라서 (c) would jog가 정답이다.

어휘 | nearby adv. 근처에   peaceful adj. 평화로운   setting n. 환경

해커스 지텔프 최신기출유형 실전문제집 7회 (Level 2)

음성 바로 듣기

안부 인사	**M:** Hey, Margaret. How've you been? ²⁷I haven't seen you in forever. **F:** Hi, Trevor. ²⁷Work has been overwhelming lately. I've been spending extra time at the office.
주제 제시: 여행 경험	**M:** Oh, sounds like you need a break. I just came back from a stay in Cancun. The beaches and historical sites in southeast Mexico were even more spectacular than I expected. **F:** Wow! I've always wanted to see Cancun's white-sand beaches and clear blue waters. Did you travel alone? **M:** Actually, it was a family trip. I went with my parents and my sisters. We were celebrating my parents' 20th wedding anniversary.
여행 기간	**F:** I want to hear all about it! How long were you there? I imagine it would take a long time to see everything. **M:** We landed in Mexico early Friday morning and flew back home late on Monday. We did a lot of activities in one weekend, though.
유적지 탐방	**F:** Oh, really? Can you tell me about some of the places you visited? **M:** Well, my family loves history, so ²⁸the ruins of the Mayan civilization were at the top of our sightseeing list. We went to Chichen Itza, an ancient city in which a stone pyramid more than 1,000 years old is located. The other temples and statues were incredible too. **F:** Cool! I wish I could visit a place like that. You must have been exhausted after exploring the archaeological sites.
정통 음식	**M:** That's right! We were tired and hungry. Luckily, ²⁹Cancun is the ideal place for authentic Mexican cuisine. I never knew I could eat so much! **F:** Sounds wonderful! I've heard that there are many restaurants with talented chefs there. What was your favorite dish? **M:** Well, it's hard to choose only one. The duck tacos and corn pancakes were delicious, but the slow-roasted pork leg was the best.
	F: Oh, that must've been amazing. How was the hotel you stayed at? Did it have good rooms and facilities?

남: 안녕, Margaret. 어떻게 지냈어? ²⁷정말 오랜만에 본다.

여: 안녕, Trevor. ²⁷요즘 일이 너무 벅찼어. 사무실에서 추가적인 시간을 보내오고 있어.

남: 오, 너에게 휴식이 필요할 것 같네. 나는 칸쿤에서 머물다가 얼마 전에 돌아왔어. 멕시코 남동부의 해변들과 유적지들은 내가 기대했던 것보다 훨씬 더 장관이었어.

여: 와! 난 항상 칸쿤의 백사장과 맑고 푸른 바다를 보고 싶었어. 너 혼자 여행했니?

남: 사실, 가족 여행이었어. 부모님과 누나들이랑 같이 갔지. 우린 부모님의 결혼 20주년을 축하했어.

여: 그것에 관한 모든 것을 듣고 싶어! 그곳에 얼마 동안 있었어? 모든 것을 보는 데 오랜 시간이 걸릴 것 같아.

남: 우리는 금요일 아침 일찍 멕시코에 도착해서 월요일 늦게 비행기로 귀국했어. 그래도, 우리는 한 주말 동안 많은 활동들을 했어.

여: 오, 정말? 네가 방문했던 몇몇 장소들에 관해 말해 줄 수 있어?

남: 음, 우리 가족은 역사를 좋아해서, ²⁸마야 문명의 유적지가 우리 관광 목록의 가장 위에 있었어. 우리는 치첸 이트사에 갔는데, 이 고대 도시는 1,000년 이상 된 석조 피라미드가 있는 곳이야. 다른 사원들과 조각상들 또한 굉장했어.

여: 멋지다! 나도 그런 곳에 가보고 싶어. 그 고고학 유적지들을 탐방하고 나서 넌 매우 지쳤겠는걸.

남: 맞아! 우리는 피곤하고 배고팠어. 다행히도, ²⁹칸쿤은 정통 멕시코 요리를 위한 최적의 장소야. 난 내가 그렇게 많이 먹을 수 있는지 몰랐어!

여: 놀라운걸! 그곳에는 유능한 요리사들이 있는 식당들이 많다고 들었어. 넌 어떤 음식이 제일 맛있었어?

남: 음, 딱 하나만 고르기가 어렵네. 오리 타코와 옥수수 팬케이크도 맛있었지만, 천천히 구운 돼지 다리가 최고였어.

여: 오, 굉장했을 것 같아. 네가 묵은 호텔은 어땠어? 방과 시설이 좋았니?

숙소	M: ³⁰That was my only disappointment. The room was clean and modern, but ³⁰there was barely enough space for all of us to sit down.	남: ³⁰그게 내 유일한 실망스러운 점이었어. 방은 깨끗하고 현대적이었지만, ³⁰우리 모두가 앉을 충분한 공간이 거의 없었어.
여행 경비	F: That's too bad. But how much does a trip like that cost? It's probably an expensive destination. M: Actually, it's not as costly as you might think. We could do all the things I told you about for a reasonable price. If you travel alone, some things would be even cheaper.	여: 그거참 안됐다. 근데 그런 여행은 비용이 얼마나 들어? 돈이 많이 드는 여행지일 것 같아. 남: 사실, 네가 생각하는 것만큼 비싸지 않아. 우리는 내가 네게 말한 모든 것들을 합리적인 가격에 할 수 있었어. 만약 네가 혼자 여행한다면, 어떤 것들은 훨씬 더 저렴할 거야.
여자의 연휴 계획	F: You've convinced me, Trevor. ³¹I think I'll head to Cancun for the long weekend next month. I should be finished with my current work assignment at that time. M: I'm glad I could help, Margaret. ³²What made you finally decide to visit Cancun? F: The food sounds great, but ³²it was your description of the ancient architecture that most influenced my decision. I can't wait to see it! By the way, could you tell me how you booked your trip? M: Yes, I used a website that my sister showed me. I don't remember the name, but it's on my computer at home.	여: 설득력 있는걸, Trevor. ³¹난 다음 달에 긴 주말 연휴 동안 칸쿤에 갈 것 같아. 그때 난 현재의 업무를 끝냈을 거야. 남: 내가 도움이 될 수 있어서 기뻐, Margaret. ³²결정적으로 왜 칸쿤을 방문하기로 결심한 거야? 여: 음식도 훌륭할 것 같지만, ³²나의 결정에 가장 영향을 미친 건 바로 고대 건축물에 대한 너의 묘사였어. 그것을 빨리 보고 싶어! 그나저나, 네가 어떻게 여행을 예약했는지 알려줄 수 있어? 남: 응, 나의 누나가 보여준 웹 사이트를 이용했어. 이름은 기억이 안 나는데, 집에 있는 내 컴퓨터에 있어.
남자가 다음에 할 일	F: ³³Can you send it to me later? I want to reserve a flight tonight. M: Of course. ³³I'll text it to you as soon as I get home. F: Thanks so much.	여: ³³그것을 나중에 나에게 보내줄 수 있어? 난 오늘 밤에 항공편을 예약하고 싶어. 남: 물론이지. ³³집에 도착하자마자 문자로 보낼게. 여: 정말 고마워.

어휘 | overwhelming [òuvərwélmiŋ] 너무 벅찬 historical site 유적지 spectacular [spektǽkjələr] 장관인 celebrate [séləbreit] 축하하다 ruin [rúːin] 유적지 civilization [sìvəlaizéiʃən] 문명 sightseeing [sáitsìːiŋ] 관광 ancient [éinʃənt] 고대의 explore [iksplɔ́ːr] 탐방하다 archaeological [àːrkiəláːdʒikəl] 고고학적인 ideal [àidíəl] 최적의, 이상적인 authentic [ɔːθéntik] 정통의 cuisine [kwizíːn] 요리 facility [fəsíləti] 시설 destination [dèstənéiʃən] 여행지, 목적지 reasonable [ríːzənəbəl] 합리적인 convince [kənvíns] 설득하다 description [diskrípʃən] 묘사 influence [ínfluəns] 영향을 미치다 book [buk] 예약하다 reserve [rizə́ːrv] 예약하다

---

27 특정세부사항   Why   난이도 ●○○

Why has Margaret been unable to see Trevor in a while?	왜 Margaret은 한동안 Trevor를 볼 수 없었는가?
(a) because she has been out of the country (b) because she has been looking for work (c) because she has been on an extended vacation **(d) because she has been busy with her job**	(a) 그녀가 외국에 있었기 때문에 (b) 그녀가 일자리를 찾고 있었기 때문에 (c) 그녀가 장기 휴가를 갔었기 때문에 **(d) 그녀가 그녀의 일로 바빴기 때문에**

○─ 지텔프 치트키

질문의 키워드 unable to see가 haven't seen으로 paraphrasing되어 언급된 주변 내용을 주의 깊게 듣는다.

해설 | 남자가 'I haven't seen you in forever.'라며 여자에게 정말 오랜만에 본다고 하자, 여자가 'Work has been overwhelming lately.'

라며 요즘 일이 너무 벅찼다고 했다. 따라서 (d)가 정답이다.

Paraphrasing
Work has been overwhelming 일이 너무 벅찼다 → has been busy with her job 일로 바빴다

어휘 | extended[iksténdid] 장기간의

---

28 특정세부사항　What　　　　　　　　　　　　　　　난이도 ●●○

What was the highlight of the family trip to Cancun?	칸쿤으로의 가족 여행 중 가장 중요한 부분은 무엇이었는가?
(a) buying wooden statues as souvenirs	(a) 기념품으로 나무 조각상들을 산 것
(b) discovering an ancient stone pyramid	(b) 고대 석조 피라미드를 발견한 것
(c) touring an old Indigenous historical site	**(c) 고대 토착 유적지를 관광한 것**
(d) attending a traditional temple service	(d) 전통적인 사원 예배에 참석한 것

○ 지텔프 치트키
질문의 키워드 highlight가 top of ~ list로 paraphrasing되어 언급된 주변 내용을 주의 깊게 듣는다.

해설 | 남자가 'the ruins of the Mayan civilization were at the top of our sightseeing list'라며 마야 문명의 유적지가 관광 목록의 가장 위에 있었다고 했다. 따라서 (c)가 정답이다.

Paraphrasing
the ruins of the Mayan civilization 마야 문명의 유적지 → an old Indigenous historical site 고대 토착 유적지
sightseeing 관광 → touring 관광하는 것

어휘 | highlight[háilait] 가장 중요한 부분; 강조하다　souvenir[sùːvəníə] 기념품　indigenous[indídʒənəs] 토착의　service[sə́ːrvis] 예배

---

29 특정세부사항　What　　　　　　　　　　　　　　　난이도 ●●○

What does Trevor think about the food in Cancun?	Trevor는 칸쿤의 음식에 관해 어떻게 생각하는가?
(a) that it is made in an original manner	**(a) 정통적인 방식으로 만들어졌다고**
(b) that it is inspired by various cuisines	(b) 다양한 요리들에 의해 영감을 받았다고
(c) that it is very expensive in restaurants	(c) 식당에서 매우 비싸다고
(d) that it is too spicy for some travelers	(d) 일부 관광객들에게 너무 맵다고

○ 지텔프 치트키
질문의 키워드 food가 cuisine으로 paraphrasing되어 언급된 주변 내용을 주의 깊게 듣는다.

해설 | 남자가 'Cancun is the ideal place for authentic Mexican cuisine'이라며 칸쿤은 정통 멕시코 요리를 위한 최적의 장소라고 했다. 따라서 (a)가 정답이다.

Paraphrasing
authentic 정통의 → original 정통적인

TEST 1
TEST 2
TEST 3
TEST 4
TEST 5
TEST 6
TEST 7

30 특정세부사항　What

난이도 ●○○

According to Trevor, what was disappointing about the accommodation?

(a) the quality of the hotel furniture
(b) the size of the hotel room
(c) the cleanliness of the facilities
(d) the lack of room types available

Trevor에 따르면, 숙소에 대해 실망스러웠던 점은 무엇인가?

(a) 호텔 가구의 품질
(b) 호텔 방의 크기
(c) 시설의 청결도
(d) 이용 가능한 객실 종류의 부족

─○ 지텔프 치트키

질문의 키워드 disappointing이 disappointment로 언급된 주변 내용을 주의 깊게 듣는다.

해설 | 남자가 'That was my only disappointment.'라며 호텔이 그의 유일한 실망스러운 점이었다고 한 뒤, 'there was barely enough space for all of us to sit down'이라며 방에는 그의 가족 모두가 앉을 충분한 공간이 거의 없었다고 했다. 따라서 (b)가 정답이다.

Paraphrasing
space 공간 → size 크기

어휘 | cleanliness[klénlinəs] 청결도

31 특정세부사항　When

난이도 ●●○

When will Margaret take a vacation?

(a) before she takes on a new position
(b) when the summer holiday starts
(c) after she completes her work project
(d) once the flights are at a discount

Margaret은 언제 휴가를 갈 것인가?

(a) 그녀가 새 직책을 맡기 전에
(b) 여름 연휴가 시작될 때
(c) 그녀가 그녀의 프로젝트 업무를 완수한 후에
(d) 항공편이 할인할 때

─○ 지텔프 치트키

질문의 키워드 vacation이 long weekend로 paraphrasing되어 언급된 주변 내용을 주의 깊게 듣는다.

해설 | 여자가 'I think I'll head to Cancun for the long weekend next month.'라며 다음 달에 긴 주말 연휴 동안 캉쿤에 갈 것 같다고 한 뒤, 'I should be finished with my current work assignment at that time.'이라며 그때 여자가 현재의 업무를 끝냈을 것이라고 했다. 따라서 (c)가 정답이다.

Paraphrasing
be finished with ~ work assignment 업무를 끝낸 → completes ~ work project 프로젝트 업무를 완수한다

32 특정세부사항　Which

난이도 ●●○

Which aspect of Cancun that Trevor mentioned affected Margaret's decision?

(a) the reasonable price to travel overseas
(b) the old buildings in the area

Trevor가 언급한 캉쿤의 어떤 면이 Margaret의 결정에 영향을 미쳤는가?

(a) 해외여행을 하기에 합리적인 가격
(b) 그 장소에 있는 고대 건축물들

(c) the beautiful beaches with clear turquoise waters

(d) the taste of food prepared by professional cooks

(c) 맑은 청록색 바다가 있는 아름다운 해변

(d) 전문 요리사들에 의해 준비된 음식의 맛

해설 | 남자가 'What made you finally decide to visit Cancun?'이라며 결정적으로 여자가 왜 칸쿤을 방문하기로 결심했는지를 묻자, 여자가 'it was your description of the ancient architecture that most influenced my decision'이라며 Margaret의 결정에 가장 영향을 미친 것은 바로 고대 건축물에 대한 남자의 묘사였다고 했다. 따라서 (b)가 정답이다.

Paraphrasing

the ancient architecture 고대 건축물 → the old buildings 고대 건축물들

어휘 | overseas[òuvərsíːz] 해외에 turquoise[tə́ːrkwɔiz] 청록색의

---

33 추론   다음에 할 일   난이도 ●●○

What will Trevor most likely do when he returns home?	Trevor가 집에 돌아오면 무엇을 할 것 같은가?
(a) visit popular travel booking websites	(a) 유명한 여행 예약 웹 사이트들을 방문한다
(b) text pictures from the trip to his family members	(b) 여행에서 찍은 사진들을 그의 가족들에게 문자로 보낸다
(c) book a trip for Margaret on his computer	(c) Margaret을 위해 그의 컴퓨터로 여행을 예약한다
(d) send his friend information to refer to	**(d) 그의 친구에게 참고할 수 있는 정보를 보낸다**

해설 | 여자가 'Can you send it to me later?'라며 여행을 예약하는 웹 사이트를 보내줄 수 있는지를 묻자, 남자가 'I'll text it to you as soon as I get home.'이라며 집에 도착하자마자 문자로 보내겠다고 했다. 따라서 (d)가 정답이다.

Paraphrasing

returns home 집에 돌아온다 → get home 집에 도착한다

PART 2^[34~39]   발표   새롭게 출시된 건강 애플리케이션의 홍보

음성 바로 듣기

주제 제시: 앱 출시	Good afternoon! I am the lead programmer behind Complete Wellness. It is a comprehensive health tracking mobile application that was just released last month.	안녕하세요! 저는 Complete Wellness의 주요 프로그래머입니다. 그것은 지난달에 막 출시된 종합 건강 추적 모바일 애플리케이션입니다.
개발 동기	³⁴I developed Complete Wellness because so many people struggle to stay fit nowadays due to the conveniences of modern life and our more sedentary lifestyles. Every day, fitness beginners start new programs that fail since they are complicated and	³⁴요즘 너무나도 많은 사람들이 현대 생활의 편리함과 몸의 움직임이 더 적은 생활 방식으로 인해 건강을 유지하는 데 어려움을 겪기 때문에 전 Complete Wellness를 개발했습니다. 매일, 운동 초보자 분들은 복잡하고 재미없어서 실패하는 새로운 프로그램들을

unenjoyable. On the other hand, those with more experience become bored and unmotivated due to less noticeable results over time. Complete Wellness is a platform that is not only easy and fun to use but also effective in helping users reach their dream state of health.

장점1:
맞춤형
목표
설정

Getting started is simple. After downloading the app, you will be asked to complete a short survey about your ³⁵⁽ᵈ⁾health goals. Do you want to burn fat, build muscle, or improve endurance and mobility? Next, you will be prompted to describe your current ³⁵⁽ᵇ⁾lifestyle, ³⁵⁽ᶜ⁾activity level, and exercise experience. These answers will enable Complete Wellness to customize the best plan for your specific fitness targets.

장점2:
전문적
프로
그램

Whether it's a high-intensity cardio workout circuit or a muscle-building routine, all of the recommended programs are created by certified personal trainers. The workouts can also be done conveniently at home with no additional equipment. ³⁶There are demonstration videos of each exercise that help users complete movement patterns with proper form. Moreover, we add to our library of health content every month, so you will never get tired repeating the same exercise routines.

주요
기능

In addition to calculating the duration of your workouts and how many calories you've burned, the app monitors your heart rate. However, I've found that simply recording data is not motivating enough. That's why Complete Wellness is outfitted with several engaging features. Attractive graphs show your progress, and ³⁷you will receive badges each time you reach a new milestone. For users that have a hard time working out alone, they can join and communicate with wellness groups that work together toward a common goal.

추가
기능1:
식단
기록

Of course, exercise is only one component of enhancing your overall well-being. Complete Wellness also has a Food Journal that suggests healthy recipes and logs your diet. Scan the barcode of any packaged product and the nutritional information will be appended to the journal. This is particularly well-suited for trips to the grocery store because it assures you that you're purchasing items that align with your aims. ³⁸You can make manual entries if something is not scannable or if you can't find it in our searchable database.

The Food Journal has two extra monitoring functions. It notifies you if you're approaching the calorie limit

시작하죠. 반면에, 더 많은 경험이 있는 분들은 시간이 지나면서 덜 눈에 띄는 결과 때문에 지루해하고 의욕을 잃습니다. Complete Wellness는 사용하기 쉽고 재미있을 뿐만 아니라 사용자들의 이상적인 건강 상태에 도달하는 것을 돕는 데 효과적이기도 한 플랫폼입니다.

시작하는 것은 간단합니다. 앱을 다운로드 받으신 후에, 여러분은 ³⁵⁽ᵈ⁾건강 목표에 관한 간단한 설문조사를 완료하라고 요청받으실 겁니다. 지방을 태우거나, 근육을 만들거나, 지구력과 기동성을 향상시키고 싶으신가요? 그런 다음, 여러분의 현재 ³⁵⁽ᵇ⁾생활 방식, ³⁵⁽ᶜ⁾활동 수준, 그리고 운동 경험을 설명하라고 요구받으실 겁니다. 이 답변들은 Complete Wellness로 하여금 여러분의 구체적인 운동 목표들을 위한 최고의 계획을 개개인에 맞게 설정할 수 있도록 할 겁니다.

고강도의 심장 강화 운동 서킷이든 혹은 근육을 키우는 루틴이든, 모든 추천 프로그램들은 공인된 개인 트레이너들에 의해 만들어집니다. 또한 운동을 별도의 장비 없이 집에서 편리하게 하실 수 있습니다. ³⁶사용자들이 올바른 자세로 운동 패턴을 완성하도록 돕는 각 운동의 시연 영상이 있습니다. 게다가, 저희는 매달 건강 콘텐츠 자료실을 확장하고 있어서, 여러분이 같은 운동 루틴을 반복하며 싫증이 나는 일은 결코 없을 것입니다.

여러분의 운동 시간과 얼마나 많은 칼로리를 소모했는지를 계산하는 것 외에도, 그 앱은 심장 박동수를 측정합니다. 그러나, 저는 단순히 데이터를 기록하는 것은 충분한 동기부여가 되지 않는다는 것을 알게 되었습니다. 이게 바로 Complete Wellness가 여러 가지 매력적인 기능들을 갖추고 있는 이유입니다. 흥미로운 그래프들이 여러분의 진행 상황을 보여주며, ³⁷여러분은 새로운 단계에 도달할 때마다 배지를 받으실 겁니다. 혼자 운동하는 데 어려움을 겪는 사용자들의 경우, 공동의 목표를 향해 협력하는 건강 그룹에 가입하시고 소통하실 수 있습니다.

물론, 운동은 여러분의 전반적인 건강을 증진하는 한 가지 요소일 뿐입니다. Complete Wellness에는 또한 건강한 요리법들을 제안하고 여러분의 식단을 기록하는 Food Journal이 있습니다. 포장 제품의 바코드를 스캔하시면 영양 정보가 그 일지에 추가될 것입니다. 이것(포장 제품의 바코드를 스캔하면 영양 정보가 일지에 추가되는 것)은 여러분이 목표와 일치하는 품목들을 구매하고 있음을 확인하기 때문에 특히 식료품점 방문에 적합합니다. ³⁸무언가를 스캔할 수 없거나 저희의 검색 가능한 데이터베이스에서 찾을 수 없는 경우에 수동으로 입력하실 수 있습니다.

Food Journal에 2개의 추가적인 추적 기능이 있습니다. 그것은 여러분이 하루 단위로 설정된 칼로리

<table>
<tr>
<td>추가 기능2: 칼로리 및 영양소 조절</td>
<td>that was set for the day so that you don't exceed it. Furthermore, the Food Journal highlights your consumption of macronutrients, such as protein, carbohydrates, and fats. ³⁹Optimally adjusting the ratio of these nutrients is a key factor in weight loss and muscle building.</td>
<td>제한에 가까워지고 있으면 이를 초과하지 않도록 여러분에게 알려줍니다. 게다가, Food Journal은 단백질, 탄수화물, 그리고 지방과 같은 대량영양소의 섭취를 강조합니다. ³⁹이러한 영양소들의 비율을 최적으로 조절하는 것은 체중 감량과 근육 형성의 핵심 요소입니다.</td>
</tr>
<tr>
<td>끝인사</td>
<td>If Complete Wellness sounds like it can be a useful tool for you, I invite you to stay behind for a few moments after my talk. I will be giving out vouchers for a free one-month subscription trial to the app, which includes total access to all of our workouts, diet plans, and analytic options. Thank you, and I hope you decide to join us.</td>
<td>만약 Complete Wellness가 여러분에게 유용한 도구가 될 수 있을 것 같다면, 제 강연 후에 잠시 자리에 남아계시길 바랍니다. 저는 앱의 무료 1개월 구독 체험권을 위한 쿠폰을 제공해 드릴 것이며, 이것은 저희의 모든 운동, 식단 계획, 그리고 분석 옵션을 포함합니다. 여러분께 감사드리며, 여러분이 저희와 함께하기로 결정하시길 바랍니다.</td>
</tr>
</table>

어휘 | comprehensive[kàːmprihénsiv] 종합적인　release[rilíːs] 출시하다　sedentary[sédənteri] 몸의 움직임이 적은, 앉아서 생활하는　complicated[kάːmplikeitid] 복잡한　effective[iféktiv] 효과적인　endurance[indúrəns] 지구력　prompt[prɑːmpt] 요구하다, 유도하다　customize[kʌ́stəmaiz] 개개인에 맞게 설정하다　equipment[ikwípmənt] 장비　demonstration[dèmənstréiʃən] 시연　duration[djuréiʃən] (지속) 시간　monitor[mάːnitər] 측정하다, 추적하다　outfit[áutfit] 갖추어 주다　engaging[ingéidʒiŋ] 매력적인　feature[fíːtʃər] 기능　milestone[máilstoun] 단계　nutritional[njuːtríʃənəl] 영양의　append[əpénd] 추가하다　align[əláin] 일치하다　exceed[iksíːd] 초과하다　consumption[kənsʌ́mpʃən] 섭취　macronutrient[mǽkrounjúːtriənt] 대량영양소(열량이 있는 영양소)　optimally[άːptəməli] 최적으로　voucher[váutʃər] 쿠폰　subscription[səbskrípʃən] 구독

---

34 특정세부사항　Why

난이도 ●●○

Why did the speaker create the application?	왜 화자는 그 애플리케이션을 만들었는가?
(a) He wanted to overcome his sedentary lifestyle. **(b) Staying in good shape is hard for people.** (c) He wished to make modern life more convenient. (d) Existing apps are too complicated.	(a) 몸의 움직임이 적은 그의 생활 방식을 극복하고 싶었다. **(b) 건강을 유지하는 것이 사람들에게 힘들다.** (c) 현대 생활을 더 편리하게 만들고 싶었다. (d) 기존의 앱들이 너무 복잡하다.

━○ 지텔프 치트키

질문의 키워드 create가 developed로 paraphrasing되어 언급된 주변 내용을 주의 깊게 듣는다.

해설 | 화자가 'I developed Complete Wellness because ~ people struggle to stay fit nowadays due to the conveniences of modern life and our more sedentary lifestyles.'라며 요즘 너무나도 많은 사람들이 현대 생활의 편리함과 몸의 움직임이 더 적은 생활 방식으로 인해 건강을 유지하는 데 어려움을 겪기 때문에 Complete Wellness를 개발했다고 했다. 따라서 (b)가 정답이다.

Paraphrasing
struggle to stay fit 건강을 유지하는 데 어려움을 겪는다 → staying in good shape is hard 건강을 유지하는 것이 힘들다

어휘 | overcome[òuvərkʌ́m] 극복하다

35 Not/True — Not 문제

Which of the following is not mentioned in the survey?

(a) one's resting heart rate
(b) one's style of living
(c) one's level of activity
(d) one's fitness objectives

다음 중 설문조사에 언급되지 않은 것은 무엇인가?

(a) 안정 시 심박수
(b) 생활 방식
(c) 활동 수준
(d) 건강 목표

─○ 지텔프 치트키

질문의 키워드 survey가 그대로 언급된 주변 내용을 주의 깊게 들으며 언급되는 것을 하나씩 소거한다.

해설 | (a)는 언급되지 않았으므로, (a)가 정답이다.

> 오답분석
> (b) 화자가 설문조사에서 생활 방식을 설명하라고 요구받을 것이라고 언급하였다.
> (c) 화자가 설문조사에서 활동 수준을 설명하라고 요구받을 것이라고 언급하였다.
> (d) 화자가 건강 목표에 관한 설문조사를 완료하라고 요청받을 것이라고 언급하였다.

어휘 | objective[əbdʒéktiv] 목표

---

36 특정세부사항 — How

How can users perform the workouts correctly?

(a) by listening to the advice of the on-site trainer
(b) by familiarizing themselves with the equipment
(c) by doing the same routines repeatedly
(d) by viewing examples of good form

사용자들은 어떻게 운동을 올바르게 할 수 있는가?

(a) 현장 강사의 조언을 들음으로써
(b) 그들 자신을 장비에 익숙하게 만듦으로써
(c) 같은 루틴을 반복적으로 수행함으로써
(d) 바른 자세의 예시를 봄으로써

─○ 지텔프 치트키

질문의 키워드 correctly가 proper로 paraphrasing되어 언급된 주변 내용을 주의 깊게 듣는다.

해설 | 화자가 'There are demonstration videos ~ that help users complete movement patterns with proper form.'이라며 사용자들이 올바른 자세로 운동 패턴을 완성하도록 돕는 각 운동의 시연 영상이 있다고 했다. 따라서 (d)가 정답이다.

Paraphrasing
perform the workouts 운동을 하다 → complete movement patterns 운동 패턴을 완성하다
demonstration 시연 → examples 예시

---

37 특정세부사항 — What

According to the speaker, what is the function of the badges?

(a) to take the place of traditional progress graphs
(b) to identify different members within a group
(c) to take notice of exercise accomplishments
(d) to designate user-specific workout goals

화자에 따르면, 배지의 기능은 무엇인가?

(a) 기존의 진행 그래프를 대체하는 것
(b) 집단 내 다양한 구성원들을 식별하는 것
(c) 운동 성과에 주의를 기울이는 것
(d) 사용자별 운동 목표를 지정하는 것

해설 | 화자가 'you will receive badges each time you reach a new milestone'이라며 사용자들이 새로운 단계에 도달할 때마다 배지를 받을 것이라고 했다. 따라서 (c)가 정답이다.

Paraphrasing
reach a new milestone 새로운 단계에 도달한다 → accomplishments 성과

어휘 | take the place of ~을 대체하다 identify[aidéntifai] 식별하다 take notice of ~에 주의를 기울이다
accomplishment[əká:mpliʃmənt] 성과 designate[dézigneit] 지정하다

38　**특정세부사항**　　What　　　　　　　　　　　　　　　　　　　　　　　난이도 ●●○

What must app users input by hand into the Food Journal?	앱 사용자들이 Food Journal에 수작업으로 입력해야 하는 것은 무엇인가?
(a) foods bought at grocery stores	(a) 식료품점에서 구매된 식품들
(b) items without a valid barcode	**(b) 유효한 바코드가 없는 물품들**
(c) meals consumed over the course of the day	(c) 하루 동안 섭취되는 식사들
(d) recipes for low-calorie foods supplied by the app	(d) 앱에서 제공되는 저칼로리 음식의 요리법들

■──○ 지텔프 치트키

질문의 키워드 by hand가 manual로 paraphrasing되어 언급된 주변 내용을 주의 깊게 듣는다.

해설 | 화자가 'You can make manual entries if something is not scannable or if you can't find it in our searchable database.'라며 무언가를 스캔할 수 없거나 검색 가능한 데이터베이스에서 찾을 수 없는 경우에는 Food Journal에 수동으로 입력할 수 있다고 했다. 따라서 (b)가 정답이다.

Paraphrasing
something is not scannable 무언가를 스캔할 수 없다 → items without a valid barcode 유효한 바코드가 없는 물품들

어휘 | valid[vǽlid] 유효한 supply[səplái] 제공하다

39　**추론**　　특정사실　　　　　　　　　　　　　　　　　　　　　　　　난이도 ●●●

Based on the talk, why most likely is watching macronutrients important for the body?	담화에 따르면, 왜 대량영양소에 유의하는 것이 신체에 중요한 것 같은가?
(a) so one can develop a physically fit body	**(a) 신체적으로 건강한 몸을 발달시킬 수 있게 하기 위해서**
(b) so one can be notified about calorie restrictions	(b) 칼로리 제한에 관한 알림을 받을 수 있게 하기 위해서
(c) so one can set limits on daily calorie intake	(c) 일일 칼로리 섭취에 제한을 설정할 수 있게 하기 위해서
(d) so one can lose weight in a short amount of time	(d) 짧은 시간 안에 체중을 감량할 수 있게 하기 위해서

해설 | 화자가 'Optimally adjusting the ratio of these nutrients is a key factor in weight loss and muscle building.'이라며 대량 영양소들의 비율을 최적으로 조절하는 것은 체중 감량과 근육 형성의 핵심 요소라고 한 것을 통해, 대량영양소에 유의하는 것은 신체적으로 건강한 몸을 발달시킬 수 있게 하기 때문에 신체에 중요한 것임을 추론할 수 있다. 따라서 (a)가 정답이다.

<u>오답분석</u>

(d) 대량 영양소들의 비율을 최적으로 조절하는 것이 체중 감량의 핵심 요소라고는 언급했지만, 짧은 시간 안에 체중을 감량할 수 있게 한 다고 한 것은 아니므로 오답이다.

어휘 | restriction[ristríkʃən] 제한 intake[ínteik] 섭취

음성 바로 듣기

PART 3 (40~45) 장단점 논의 영화관에서의 영화 관람과 집에서의 영화 관람의 장단점 비교

안부 인사	F: Hi, Carter. Have you decided how to entertain your parents when they visit this weekend? M: Hey, Beth. We are planning on visiting a new Italian restaurant that opened near my apartment building for dinner. Then, we will watch a movie together.
주제 제시: 장단점 비교	F: That sounds like a lot of fun. Are you going to a movie theater? M: I haven't decided yet. ⁴⁰I don't know if we should go out to the cinema or just stay at home and use a streaming service. F: I see. It can be hard to pick between two good options like those. Do your parents have a preference for one over the other? M: They wouldn't really care, but I want to do what's best for them. F: Haha . . . okay. In that case, let's go over the pros and cons of each individually. That might help you make a decision. What's the biggest plus of going out to the cinema?
영화관 에서의 영화 관람 장점	M: Well, ⁴¹the movie experience is better in theaters. They always have massive screens and great sound systems. F: That's true. Some of them even include features to stimulate all of your senses, such as motion seats, simulated weather, and aromas. These bring films to life! M: Yes. Also, going out is more of a special occasion. You have to put in some work to select when and where to see a movie. That's what makes a night at the cinema so memorable. F: Oh, yeah. It's also usually the only way that you can see the newest movies. They normally aren't available for home viewing for a few months after their release.

여: 안녕, Carter. 이번 주말에 너의 부모님께서 방문하실 때 어떻게 즐겁게 해 드릴지 결정했어?

남: 안녕, Beth. 우린 저녁을 먹으러 내 아파트 건물 근처에 개업한 새로운 이탈리아 식당을 방문할 계획이야. 그러고 나서, 우린 함께 영화를 볼 거야.

여: 정말 재밌겠다. 영화관에 갈 거야?

남: 아직 결정하지 못했어. ⁴⁰나는 우리가 영화관에 가야 할지 아니면 그냥 집에 있으면서 스트리밍 서비스를 이용해야 할지 모르겠어.

여: 그렇구나. 그것들같이 좋은 두 선택지 중에서 선택하는 것은 어려울 수 있지. 부모님이 둘 중 더 선호하시는 게 있어?

남: 그들은 별로 신경 쓰지 않겠지만, 나는 그들에게 가장 좋은 것을 하고 싶어.

여: 하하... 알았어. 그렇다면, 각각의 장단점을 하나하나 짚어보자. 그건 네가 결정을 내리는 데 도움을 줄지 몰라. 영화관에 가는 것의 가장 큰 장점은 뭐야?

남: 음, ⁴¹영화 경험은 영화관에서 더 훌륭해. 그것들에는 항상 거대한 스크린과 정말 좋은 음향 장치가 있지.

여: 맞아. 그것들 중 일부는 심지어 너의 모든 감각들을 자극하는 특징들을 포함하는데, 예를 들어 움직이는 좌석, 진짜처럼 꾸며낸 날씨, 그리고 향이 있어. 이것들은 영화에 생명을 불어넣어!

남: 응. 또한, 외출하는 것이 더 특별한 경우라고 할 수 있어. 너는 영화를 볼 시간과 장소를 선택하기 위해 어느 정도의 공을 들여야 해. 그것이 바로 영화관에서 보내는 밤을 정말 기억에 남게 만드는 거야.

여: 오, 맞아. 그것은 게다가 일반적으로 최신 영화들을 볼 수 있는 유일한 방법이기도 해. 그것들은 보통 개봉 후 몇 달 동안은 집에서 볼 수 없잖아.

해커스 지텔프 최신기출유형 실전문제집 7회 (Level 2)

영화관에서의 영화 관람 단점

M: That's a good point. But, on the other hand, it's a lot more expensive. For the three of us, it would be $30 just for the tickets.

F: And don't forget about snacks. They keep increasing in price, and they now cost more than the tickets do. [42]The last time I went to the movies, a small popcorn was nearly $10 and my drink was over $5. It was quite surprising. A night at the movies can easily end up costing you more than $100.

집에서의 영화 관람 장점

M: I guess it would be cheaper to stay home. I already pay for streaming services, so there wouldn't be any additional cost.

F: Instead of spending money on movie tickets, you could buy snacks at the supermarket to enjoy at home.

M: You're right. The streaming services also provide a lot more choices. It might be easier to find something that we'd all enjoy than it would be with the cinema's limited options.

F: [43]It's easy to get comfortable at home, too, because you can wear your pajamas.

집에서의 영화 관람 단점

M: That is an important consideration. However, we have to remember that [44]it's much harder to focus on a film at home because there are so many more distractions.

F: Hmm. . . After talking about both options, I can understand why you're having trouble with this. They both have positive and negative aspects.

남자의 결정

M: Yes, but I think our talk has really helped. I hadn't fully laid out the two alternatives before.

F: Oh, does that mean you've made a decision?

M: I think so. I only get to see my parents a few times a year. [45]It would be best to make an effort to create an evening they will remember.

F: That's very thoughtful of you. I think you've made the right choice.

남: 좋은 지적이야. 하지만, 다른 한편으로는, 그것은 훨씬 더 비싸. 우리 세 명에, 영화표 값만 30달러일 거야.

여: 그리고 간식에 대해서도 잊으면 안 돼. 그것들의 가격이 계속 오르고 있고, 지금은 그것들이 푯값보다 더 비싸. [42]내가 지난번에 영화를 보러 갔을 때, 작은 팝콘이 거의 10달러였고 음료는 5달러가 넘었어. 그건 상당히 놀라웠지. 영화관에서의 밤은 아마 틀림없이 결국 100달러 이상의 비용이 들게 될 수 있어.

남: 집에 있는 게 더 저렴할 것 같네. 스트리밍 서비스는 사전에 결제하니, 그 어떤 추가 비용도 없을 거야.

여: 영화표에 돈을 쓰는 것 대신에, 넌 슈퍼마켓에서 집에서 즐길 간식을 살 수 있어.

남: 네 말이 맞아. 스트리밍 서비스는 또한 훨씬 더 많은 선택지들을 제공해. 우리 모두가 즐길 것을 찾는 것이 영화관의 제한된 선택지들에서 찾는 것보다 더 쉬울지도 몰라.

여: [43]네가 잠옷을 입을 수 있기 때문에 집에서는 편안함도 느끼기 쉬워.

남: 그건 중요한 고려 사항이야. 하지만, [44]집중을 방해하는 것들이 너무나도 많기 때문에 집에서 영화에 집중하는 것이 훨씬 더 어렵다는 것을 기억해야 해.

여: 흠... 두 선택지에 관해 이야기를 해 보니, 왜 네가 이걸로 어려움을 겪고 있는지 이해할 수 있어. 그것들은 둘 다 긍정적인 면과 부정적인 면을 가지고 있어.

남: 맞아, 하지만 우리의 대화가 정말 도움이 된 것 같아. 나는 이전에 이 두 가지 대안을 충분히 정리해 본 적이 없었어.

여: 오, 그건 네가 결정을 내렸다는 뜻이야?

남: 그런 것 같아. 나는 일 년에 부모님을 몇 번밖에 만나지 못해. [45]그들이 기억할 저녁 시간을 만들기 위해 노력을 기울이는 것이 가장 좋을 것 같아.

여: 너 정말 사려 깊구나. 네가 옳은 선택을 한 것 같아.

어휘 | entertain [èntərtéin] 즐겁게 하다   preference [préfərəns] 선호   individually [ìndəvídʒuəli] 하나하나, 개별적으로   massive [mǽsiv] 거대한   stimulate [stímjəleit] 자극하다   simulated [símjəleitid] 진짜처럼 꾸며낸, 가상의   occasion [əkéiʒən] 경우, 날   memorable [mémərəbəl] 기억에 남는   release [rilí:s] 개봉   consideration [kənsìdəréiʃən] 고려 사항   distraction [distrǽkʃən] 집중을 방해하는 것   alternative [ɔ:ltə́:rnətiv] 대안   thoughtful [θɔ́:tfəl] 사려 깊은

TEST 1

TEST 2

TEST 3

TEST 4

TEST 5

TEST 6

TEST 7

해커스 지텔프 최신기출유형 실전문제집 7회 (Level 2)

40 **주제/목적** 대화의 주제   난이도 ●●○

What are Carter and Beth discussing in the conversation?

(a) where to take his parents at the end of the week
(b) what to have for dinner for the family gathering
(c) when to talk to his parents about his trip to Italy
(d) which day to see a new film

대화에서 Carter와 Beth는 무엇에 관해 논의하고 있는가?

(a) 주말에 그의 부모님을 어디로 모시고 갈지
(b) 가족 모임의 저녁 식사로 무엇을 먹을지
(c) 그의 이탈리아 여행에 관해 부모님께 언제 이야기할지
(d) 신작 영화를 무슨 요일에 볼지

━━○ 지텔프 치트키

대화의 주제를 언급하는 초반을 주의 깊게 듣고 전체 맥락을 파악한다.

해설 | 남자가 'I don't know if we should go out to the cinema or just stay at home and use a streaming service.'라며 그의 부모님과 영화관에 가야 할지 아니면 집에 있으면서 스트리밍 서비스를 이용해야 할지를 모르겠다고 한 뒤, 대화 전반에 걸쳐 부모님과 영화를 볼 장소에 관해 논의하는 내용이 이어지고 있다. 따라서 (a)가 정답이다.

41 **특정세부사항** What   난이도 ●●○

What makes going to the cinema a better experience?

(a) the excitement of other people in the theater
(b) the professional audio-visual quality
(c) the convenience of the food service facilities
(d) the wide selection of newly released movies

무엇이 영화관에 가는 것을 더 좋은 경험으로 만드는가?

(a) 영화관에 있는 다른 사람들의 즐거움
(b) 전문적인 시청각적 품질
(c) 음식 서비스 시설들의 편의성
(d) 새로 개봉한 영화들에 대한 폭넓은 선택

━━○ 지텔프 치트키

질문의 키워드 better experience가 experience is better로 언급된 주변 내용을 주의 깊게 듣는다.

해설 | 남자가 'the movie experience is better in theaters'라며 영화 경험은 영화관에서 더 훌륭하다고 한 뒤, 'They always have massive screens and great sound systems.'라며 영화관에는 항상 거대한 스크린과 정말 좋은 음향 장치가 있다고 했다. 따라서 (b)가 정답이다.

Paraphrasing
the cinema 영화관 → theaters 영화관
screens and ~ sound systems 스크린과 음향 장치 → audio-visual 시청각적인

42 **특정세부사항** Why   난이도 ●●○

Why was Beth surprised when she last visited a theater?

(a) because the process for making a payment had changed
(b) because the variety of snacks offered was limited
(c) because the price of tickets had risen significantly
(d) because the cost of refreshments was high

Beth는 지난번에 극장에 갔을 때 왜 놀랐는가?

(a) 결제하는 절차가 바뀌었었기 때문에
(b) 제공되는 간식의 종류가 제한적이었기 때문에
(c) 표의 가격이 상당히 올랐었기 때문에
(d) 간식의 가격이 비쌌기 때문에

해설 | 여자가 'The last time I went to the movies, a small popcorn was nearly $10 and my drink was over $5.'라며 지난번에 영화를 보러 갔을 때 작은 팝콘이 거의 10달러였고 음료는 5달러가 넘었다고 한 뒤, 'It was quite surprising.'이라며 그것은 상당히 놀라웠다고 했다. 따라서 (d)가 정답이다.

어휘 | make a payment 결제하다 variety[vəráiəti] 종류, 다양성 significantly[signífikəntli] 상당히 refreshment[rifréʃmənt] 간식

---

43 특정세부사항 How   난이도 ●○○

How can one get more comfortable while watching a movie at home?

(a) by wearing sleeping clothes
(b) by having more seating options
(c) by finding a movie everyone likes
(d) by preparing food to enjoy

집에서 영화를 보는 동안 어떻게 더 편안해질 수 있는가?

(a) 잠옷을 입음으로써
(b) 더 많은 좌석 선택지를 가짐으로써
(c) 모두가 좋아하는 영화를 찾음으로써
(d) 즐길 음식을 준비함으로써

해설 | 여자가 'It's easy to get comfortable at home, ~, because you can wear your pajamas.'라며 잠옷을 입을 수 있기 때문에 집에서는 편안함을 느끼기가 쉽다고 했다. 따라서 (a)가 정답이다.

Paraphrasing
your pajamas 잠옷 → sleeping clothes 잠옷

---

44 특정세부사항 장·단점   난이도 ●●●

According to the conversation, what is the disadvantage of using a streaming service?

(a) Viewers tend to lose concentration easily.
(b) Viewers can take lots of time to pick a movie.
(c) Viewers may see inappropriate content.
(d) Viewers must share financial details online.

대화에 따르면, 스트리밍 서비스를 이용하는 것의 단점은 무엇인가?

(a) 시청자들이 쉽게 집중력을 잃는 경향이 있다.
(b) 시청자들이 영화를 고르는 데 오랜 시간이 걸릴 수 있다.
(c) 시청자들이 부적절한 내용물을 시청할 수 있다.
(d) 시청자들이 재정 정보를 온라인으로 공유해야 한다.

해설 | 남자가 'it's much harder to focus on a film at home because there are so many more distractions'라며 집중을 방해하는 것들이 너무나도 많기 때문에 집에서 영화에 집중하는 것이 훨씬 더 어렵다고 했다. 따라서 (a)가 정답이다.

Paraphrasing
harder to focus 집중하는 것이 더 어려운 → lose concentration easily 쉽게 집중력을 잃다

어휘 | concentration[kàːnsəntréiʃən] 집중력 inappropriate[ìnəpróupriət] 부적절한

45 추론　다음에 할 일

난이도 ●●○

Based on the conversation, what has Carter probably decided to do?

(a) subscribe to a streaming service
(b) stay in for the night
(c) watch a movie at a cinema
(d) go visit his parents

대화에 따르면, Carter는 무엇을 하기로 결정한 것 같은가?

(a) 스트리밍 서비스를 구독한다
(b) 그날 밤에 집에 있는다
(c) 영화관에서 영화를 본다
(d) 그의 부모님을 뵈러 간다

◉── 지텔프 치트키

다음에 할 일을 언급하는 후반을 주의 깊게 듣는다.

해설 | 남자가 'It would be best to make an effort to create an evening they will remember.'라며 부모님이 기억할 저녁 시간을 만들기 위해 노력을 기울이는 것이 가장 좋을 것 같다고 한 것을 통해, Carter가 영화를 볼 시간과 장소를 선택하기 위해 어느 정도의 공을 들여야 하는 영화관에서 영화를 볼 것임을 추론할 수 있다. 따라서 (c)가 정답이다.

어휘 | stay in 집에 있다

PART 4 (46~52)　설명　시차증을 완화하기 위한 4가지 조언

음성 바로 듣기

| 인사 + 주제 제시 | Welcome, everyone! I am the founder and CEO of Top Air. Anyone who has taken a long flight has likely experienced jet lag. Unfortunately, there's no way to prevent it, but I'd like to share some tips for mitigating its effects. |

환영합니다, 여러분! 저는 Top Air 사의 설립자이자 최고 경영자입니다. 장거리 비행을 해본 분이라면 누구나 시차증을 경험해 보셨을 것입니다. 불행하게도, 그것을 막을 방법은 없지만, 전 그것의 영향을 완화하기 위한 몇 가지 조언을 공유하고 싶습니다.

| 시차증 정의 | What exactly is jet lag? Well, our internal clocks match the time zone we are in. Long-distance air travel disrupts this balance. Our bodies can easily handle a single zone change, but more than two in a single day causes jet lag. Therefore, [46]the more time zones we cross in a short amount of time, the more severe our symptoms will be. Once in a new location, fatigue overwhelms us, and we lack the energy to properly enjoy the local sights on our vacation. Or, [47]our ability to concentrate is compromised, so it becomes difficult to pay attention to the important matters of a business trip. And then at night, we are unable to fall asleep, which means that we will be exhausted the next day too. |

시차증이란 정확히 무엇인가요? 음, 우리의 체내 시계는 우리가 있는 시간대와 일치합니다. 장거리 비행이 이 균형을 방해하죠. 우리의 몸은 단 한 번의 시간대 변화는 쉽게 다룰 수 있지만, 하루에 두 번 이상의 변화는 시차증을 일으킵니다. 따라서, [46]우리가 짧은 시간 안에 더 많은 시간대를 가로지를수록, 우리의 증상은 더 극심해질 겁니다. 일단 새로운 장소에 가면, 피로가 우리를 엄습하고, 우린 휴가 때 지역 명소들을 제대로 즐기기 위한 에너지가 부족합니다. 혹은, [47]집중력이 떨어져서, 출장의 중요한 사안들에 주의를 기울이기 어려워집니다. 그리고 밤이 되면, 우리는 잠이 들 수 없는데, 이것은 우리가 그다음 날도 피곤할 것이라는 것을 의미합니다.

| 조언 제시 | Luckily, however, there are some ways to reduce jet lag's impact. |

하지만, 다행히도, 시차증의 영향을 줄일 수 있는 몇 가지 방법이 있습니다.

| 조언1: 수면 일정 조정 | First, [48]modify your sleep schedule to match your destination. If you do this a few days before your trip, your body will be able to adapt more easily once you |

첫 번째로, [48]목적지에 맞게 여러분의 수면 일정을 바꾸십시오. 만약 여러분이 여행 며칠 전에 이것을 한다면, 도착했을 때 여러분의 몸이 더 쉽게 적응할 수

touch down. For example, when you're traveling east, go to bed earlier than normal. If you're headed west, stay up past your usual bedtime.

Second, take extra care when you have a daytime arrival. If you arrive while the sun is up, it's important to stay awake. You can do some simple exercises to boost your energy levels or get exposure to sunlight. Your body will recognize the daylight and produce serotonin, a chemical that makes you feel alert. [49]Naps can be beneficial when you are feeling too worn out due to jet lag, but use them cautiously. [49]While taking a 20-minute nap upon reaching your new location is fine, it's best to avoid naps that are several hours long. Sleeping that much during the day will make it nearly impossible to sleep at night and thus will worsen your jet lag symptoms.

Third, watch your diet. For passengers who land in the evening, managing what you consume is essential to ensure that you get a good night's rest. For instance, [50]drinking beverages with caffeine or alcohol can inhibit deep sleep. By the same token, try to eat light and stay away from heavy or overly spicy foods in the few hours before bed. In addition, drink lots of water as it's common for travelers to suffer from dehydration, which will impact the quality of your recovery.

Fourth, prepare a suitable sleeping environment. The first night in a new location is critical because it helps to reset your internal clock. That's why it's crucial that you maintain a good sleep environment. [51]Draw the curtains of the room and wear a sleep mask to make sure you can be in total darkness. Set the room to a cool, comfortable temperature. Also, limit screen time during late hours because the use of electronic devices can interfere with your ability to sleep.

Those are a few tips to lessen the effects of jet lag. While I know they will benefit world travelers, [52]I hope they encourage people who seldom travel to visit the amazing destinations our world has to offer.

있을 것입니다. 예를 들어, 동쪽으로 여행할 때, 평소보다 일찍 잠자리에 드세요. 만약 서쪽으로 간다면, 평소의 취침 시간 이후까지 깨어 있으십시오.

두 번째로, 여러분이 낮에 도착할 때 좀 더 주의하십시오. 만약 여러분이 해가 떠 있을 때 도착한다면, 깨어 있는 것이 중요합니다. 여러분은 에너지 수준을 높이거나 햇빛에 노출되기 위해 몇 가지 간단한 운동을 하실 수 있습니다. 여러분의 몸은 햇빛을 인식하며 세로토닌을 생성할 것인데, 이 화학 물질은 여러분이 맑은 정신을 느끼게 하는 것입니다. [49]낮잠은 시차증 때문에 여러분이 너무 피곤할 때 도움이 될 수 있지만, 신중하게 활용하십시오. [49]새로운 장소에 도착하여 20분 동안 낮잠을 자는 것은 괜찮지만, 몇 시간이나 되는 낮잠은 피하는 것이 좋습니다. 낮에 그렇게 많이 자는 것은 밤에 자는 것을 거의 불가능하게 만들고 따라서 여러분의 시차증 증상들을 악화시킬 것입니다.

세 번째로, 식단에 주의하세요. 저녁에 착륙하는 승객들의 경우, 먹는 것을 관리하는 것은 여러분이 밤에 푹 쉬는 것을 확실히 하기 위해 필수적입니다. 예를 들어, [50]카페인이나 알코올이 든 음료를 마시는 것은 숙면을 방해할 수 있습니다. 같은 맥락에서, 잠자기 전 몇 시간 동안은 가볍게 먹고 소화가 잘 안되거나 지나치게 매운 음식을 멀리하도록 하십시오. 게다가, 여행자들이 탈수증으로 고생하는 것은 흔한 일이기 때문에 물을 많이 마셔야 하며, 이것은 회복의 질에 영향을 줄 것입니다.

네 번째로, 알맞은 수면 환경을 조성하세요. 새로운 장소에서의 첫날 밤은 여러분의 체내 시계를 재설정하는 데 도움이 되기 때문에 매우 중요합니다. 그것이 바로 좋은 수면 환경을 유지하는 것이 중대한 이유입니다. [51]방의 커튼을 치고 완전한 어둠 속에 있을 수 있도록 수면 안대를 착용하십시오. 방을 시원하고, 편안한 온도로 설정하십시오. 또한, 전자 기기의 사용이 여러분의 수면 능력을 방해할 수 있기 때문에 늦은 시간에는 전자 기기를 보는 시간을 제한하십시오.

이것들은 시차증의 영향을 줄이기 위한 몇 가지 조언들입니다. 그것들이 세계 여행자들에게 도움이 되리라는 것은 알고 있지만, [52]저는 그것들이 여행을 잘 하지 않는 사람들에게도 우리 세계가 제공하는 놀라운 여행지들을 방문할 것을 장려하길 바랍니다.

어휘 | founder[fáundər] 설립자 jet lag 시차증 prevent[privént] 막다, 방지하다 mitigate[mítigeit] 완화하다, 덜어주다
internal clock 체내 시계 severe[səvír] 극심한 symptom[símptəm] 증상 fatigue[fətíːg] 피로
compromise[káːmprəmaiz] 떨어지게 하다, 타협하다 touch down 도착하다, 착륙하다 exposure[ikspóuʒər] 노출
chemical[kémikəl] 화학 물질 alert[əláːrt] 맑은 정신의 cautiously[kɔ́ːʃəsli] 신중하게 worsen[wə́ːrsən] 악화시키다
manage[mǽnidʒ] 관리하다 inhibit[inhíbit] 방해하다 by the same token 같은 맥락에서 dehydration[dìːhaidréiʃən] 탈수증
recovery[rikʌ́vəri] 회복 suitable[súːtəbəl] 알맞은 maintain[meintéin] 유지하다 interfere[ìntərfír] 방해하다
encourage[inkə́ːridʒ] 장려하다

46 특정세부사항　What
난이도 ●●○

What makes jet lag worse?

(a) traversing one time zone daily
(b) passing many time zones quickly
(c) waking up frequently during a flight
(d) traveling for long stretches of time

무엇이 시차증을 더 악화시키는가?

(a) 매일 하나의 시간대를 가로지르는 것
(b) 많은 시간대를 빠르게 통과하는 것
(c) 비행 중에 자주 깨는 것
(d) 장기간에 걸쳐 여행하는 것

⊸○ 지텔프 치트키

질문의 키워드 worse가 more severe로 paraphrasing되어 언급된 주변 내용을 주의 깊게 듣는다.

해설 | 화자가 'the more time zones we cross in a short amount of time, the more severe our symptoms will be'라며 짧은 시간 안에 더 많은 시간대를 가로지를수록 시차증의 증상은 더 극심해질 것이라고 했다. 따라서 (b)가 정답이다.

Paraphrasing
cross in a short amount of time 짧은 시간 안에 가로지른다 → passing ~ quickly 빠르게 통과하는 것

오답분석
(a) 화자가 우리 몸이 단 한 번의 시간대 변화는 쉽게 다룰 수 있다고 언급했으므로 오답이다.

어휘 | traverse[trǽvə:rs] 가로지르다, 통과하다　stretch[stretʃ] 기간, 시간

47 특정세부사항　Which
난이도 ●●○

Which of the following is a symptom of jet lag?

(a) an inability to compromise with others
(b) a lack of interest in local sights
(c) a decreased capacity to focus
(d) an excess of nighttime energy

다음 중 시차증의 증상은 무엇인가?

(a) 타인과 타협하는 것에 대한 무능력
(b) 지역 명소들에 대한 흥미 부족
(c) 저하된 집중력
(d) 과도한 야간 에너지

⊸○ 지텔프 치트키

질문의 키워드 symptom이 symptoms로 언급된 주변 내용을 주의 깊게 듣는다.

해설 | 화자가 'our ability to concentrate is compromised'라며 시차증으로 인해 집중력이 떨어진다고 했다. 따라서 (c)가 정답이다.

Paraphrasing
our ability to concentrate is compromised 집중력이 떨어진다 → a decreased capacity to focus 저하된 집중력

오답분석
(b) 화자가 시차증으로 인해 지역 명소를 제대로 즐기기 위한 에너지가 부족하다고는 언급했지만, 지역 명소들에 대한 흥미 부족을 경험한 다고 한 것은 아니므로 오답이다.

어휘 | inability[ìnəbíləti] 무능력

How can passengers reduce the effects of jet lag before a trip?

(a) by staying awake the whole night before the flight
(b) by gradually lengthening their normal rest cycle
(c) by spending as much time as possible outdoors
(d) by adjusting their bedtime to the final location

승객들은 어떻게 여행 전에 시차증의 영향을 줄일 수 있는가?

(a) 비행 전에 밤새 깨어있음으로써
(b) 그들의 평상시 휴식 주기를 점진적으로 늘림으로써
(c) 가능한 한 많은 시간을 야외에서 보냄으로써
(d) 그들의 취침 시간을 최종 장소에 맞춤으로써

◦━○ 지텔프 치트키

질문의 키워드 reduce ~ effects가 reduce ~ impact로 paraphrasing되어 언급된 주변 내용을 주의 깊게 듣는다.

해설 | 화자가 'modify your sleep schedule to match your destination'이라며 시차증의 영향을 줄일 수 있는 첫 번째 방법으로 목적지에 맞게 수면 일정을 바꾸라고 했다. 따라서 (d)가 정답이다.

Paraphrasing
modify your sleep schedule to match your destination 목적지에 맞게 수면 일정을 바꾸다 → adjusting their bedtime to the final location 취침 시간을 최종 장소에 맞춤

어휘 | gradually [grǽdʒuəli] 점진적으로

When is it advisable to take a nap at the new location?

(a) when it is relatively short in length
(b) when it is done within hours of landing
(c) when it occurs in the late afternoon
(d) when it is followed by a large meal

새로운 장소에서 언제 낮잠을 자는 것이 바람직한가?

(a) 길이가 비교적 짧을 때
(b) 착륙 후 몇 시간 이내에 행해질 때
(c) 늦은 오후에 발생할 때
(d) 과식이 뒤따를 때

◦━○ 지텔프 치트키

질문의 키워드 nap이 그대로 언급된 주변 내용을 주의 깊게 듣는다.

해설 | 화자가 'Naps can be beneficial when you are feeling too worn out due to jet lag'라며 낮잠은 시차증 때문에 너무 피곤할 때 도움이 될 수 있다고 한 뒤, 'While taking a 20-minute nap ~ is fine, it's best to avoid naps that are several hours long.'이라며 20분 동안 낮잠을 자는 것은 괜찮지만 몇 시간이나 되는 낮잠은 피하는 것이 좋다고 했다. 따라서 (a)가 정답이다.

어휘 | advisable [ədváizəbəl] 바람직한 relatively [rélətivli] 비교적

Why most likely should certain foods be avoided before bedtime?

(a) They can cause dehydration.
(b) They may prevent people from feeling rested.

왜 취침 시간 전에 특정 음식이 피해져야 하는 것 같은가?

(a) 탈수증을 일으킬 수 있다.
(b) 사람들이 휴식을 느끼는 것을 방해한다.

(c) They can reset one's sleeping schedule.
(d) They may lead to serious health issues.

(c) 수면 일정을 초기 상태로 되돌릴 수 있다.
(d) 심각한 건강 문제를 야기할 수 있다.

지텔프 치트키

질문의 키워드 avoided가 stay away로 paraphrasing되어 언급된 주변 내용을 주의 깊게 듣는다.

해설 | 화자가 'drinking beverages with caffeine or alcohol can inhibit deep sleep'이라며 카페인이나 알코올이 든 음료를 마시는 것은 숙면을 방해할 수 있다고 한 뒤, 'By the same token, try to ~ stay away from heavy or overly spicy foods in the few hours before bed.'라며 같은 맥락에서 잠자기 전 몇 시간 동안은 소화가 잘 안되거나 지나치게 매운 음식을 멀리하라고 한 것을 통해, 사람들이 휴식을 느끼는 것을 방해하기 때문에 취침 시간 전에 특정 음식이 피해져야 하는 것임을 추론할 수 있다. 따라서 (b)가 정답이다.

---

51 특정세부사항 How 난이도 ●○○

Based on the talk, how should a good sleep environment be arranged?

(a) by using comfortable bedding
(b) by reducing the amount of light
(c) by turning off electronic devices
(d) by eliminating any sources of noise

담화에 따르면, 어떻게 좋은 수면 환경이 마련되어야 하는가?

(a) 편안한 침구를 이용함으로써
(b) 빛의 양을 줄임으로써
(c) 전자 기기를 끔으로써
(d) 모든 소음의 원천을 제거함으로써

지텔프 치트키

질문의 키워드 good sleep environment가 그대로 언급된 주변 내용을 주의 깊게 듣는다.

해설 | 화자가 'Draw the curtains of the room and wear a sleep mask to make sure you can be in total darkness.'라며 좋은 수면 환경을 마련하는 방법 중 하나로 방의 커튼을 치고 완전한 어둠 속에 있을 수 있도록 수면 안대를 착용하라고 했다. 따라서 (b)가 정답이다.

Paraphrasing
be in total darkness 완전한 어둠 속에 있다 → reducing the amount of light 빛의 양을 줄임

어휘 | arrange[əréindʒ] 마련하다 bedding[bédiŋ] 침구 eliminate[ilíməneit] 제거하다

---

52 특정세부사항 Why 난이도 ●●○

Why does the speaker mention those who rarely travel?

(a) to inform them of flight discounts
(b) to introduce lesser-known places
(c) to urge them to take more trips
(d) to point out a common problem

왜 화자는 여행을 거의 하지 않는 사람들을 언급하는가?

(a) 그들에게 항공편 할인을 알리기 위해서
(b) 덜 알려진 장소들을 소개하기 위해서
(c) 그들이 더 많은 여행을 하도록 설득하기 위해서
(d) 공통적인 문제점을 지적하기 위해서

지텔프 치트키

질문의 키워드 rarely travel이 seldom travel로 paraphrasing되어 언급된 주변 내용을 주의 깊게 듣는다.

해설 | 화자가 'I hope they encourage people who seldom travel to visit the amazing destinations our world has to offer'라

TEST 1 TEST 2 TEST 3 TEST 4 TEST 5 TEST 6 TEST 7

해커스 지텔프 최신기출유형 실전문제집 7회 (Level 2)

며 그것들(조언들)이 여행을 잘 하지 않는 사람들에게도 우리 세계가 제공하는 놀라운 여행지들을 방문할 것을 장려하기를 바란다고 했다. 따라서 (c)가 정답이다.

Paraphrasing
encourage ~ to visit ~ destinations 여행지들을 방문할 것을 장려한다 → urge ~ to take ~ trips 여행을 하도록 설득하다

어휘 | inform[infɔ́ːrm] 알리다   urge[əːrdʒ] 설득하다   point out 지적하다

READING & VOCABULARY

PART 1^(53~59) 인물의 일대기 미국에서 프랑스 요리를 대중화한 요리사 줄리아 차일드

인물 이름	**JULIA CHILD**	**줄리아 차일드**

**인물
소개**

Julia Child was an American chef and cookbook writer ⁵³best known for teaching US audiences how to make French cuisine for the first time.

줄리아 차일드는 ⁵³최초로 미국 청중들에게 프랑스 요리를 만드는 방법을 가르쳐준 것으로 가장 잘 알려져 있는 미국의 요리사이자 요리책 작가였다.

**어린
시절**

Julia Child was born in California on August 15, 1912, into a wealthy household. Because her family had a private chef, Child did not need to learn how to cook and ⁵⁸showed no <u>particular</u> interest in it. While at school, she played various sports, which she excelled at.

줄리아 차일드는 캘리포니아주에서 1912년 8월 15일에 부유한 가정에서 태어났다. 그녀의 가족에게는 개인 요리사가 있었기 때문에, 차일드는 요리하는 법을 배울 필요가 없었고 그것에 ⁵⁸특별한 관심을 보이지 않았다. 학창 시절에, 그녀는 다양한 스포츠를 했으며, 그것들에 뛰어났다.

**초기
활동**

When America entered the Second World War at the end of 1941, Child was employed as a research assistant at the Office of Strategic Services, which was in charge of developing underwater explosives. Curious sharks could set off the explosives, and it became Child's responsibility to prepare an effective shark repellent.

1941년 말 미국이 제2차 세계 대전에 참전했을 때, 차일드는 전략사무국의 연구 보조원으로 고용되었는데, 그것은 수중 폭발물 개발을 담당했다. 호기심 많은 상어들이 폭발물을 터뜨릴 수 있었고, 효과적인 상어 퇴치제를 조제하는 것은 차일드의 책무가 되었다.

**업적
시작
계기**

⁵⁴Child did not develop a real passion for food until 1946 when she married Paul Child, an enthusiastic food connoisseur. In 1948, the couple moved to Paris, where a meal at the restaurant La Couronne ⁵⁹<u>sparked</u> Child's desire to take French cooking lessons. She studied at the prominent Le Cordon Bleu culinary school and graduated in 1951.

⁵⁴차일드는 1946년에 열성적인 음식 감정가인 폴 차일드와 결혼하고 나서야 비로소 음식에 대한 진정한 열정을 키웠다. 1948년에, 부부는 파리로 이사했고, 그곳에 있는 레스토랑 La Couronne에서의 식사가 ⁵⁹프랑스 요리 수업을 듣고자 하는 차일드의 욕구를 불러일으켰다. 그녀는 유명한 르 코르동 블루 요리 학교에서 공부했고 1951년에 졸업했다.

**초기
업적**

A short time later, she began giving French cooking classes to American women living in Paris. Encouraged by the positive reception, ⁵⁵she, along with fellow cooking teachers Simone Beck and Louisette Bertholle, spent the next decade creating the recipes that would form the basis of her first book, *Mastering the Art of French Cooking*. The book, published in 1961, caused an instant sensation.

얼마 후, 그녀는 파리에 살고 있는 미국 여성들에게 프랑스 요리 수업을 하기 시작했다. 긍정적인 반응에 용기를 얻어, ⁵⁵그녀는, 동료 요리 강사 시몬 베크와 루이제트 베르톨과 함께, 그녀의 첫 번째 책인 『프랑스 요리의 기술』의 토대를 이루는 요리법들을 고안하는 데 다음 10년을 보냈다. 1961년에 출판된 그 책은 즉각적인 돌풍을 일으켰다.

**주요
업적**

When Child returned to America in the 1960s, she starred in one of the first cooking shows on US television, *The French Chef*. ⁵⁶There, she taught people how to make classic French dishes such as beef bourguignon at home. At the time, Americans considered French fare difficult to make and something they could only eat at fine dining establishments. Child's cheerful and authentic presentation style made certain that the show would remain on the air for a decade. It was

차일드가 1960년대에 미국으로 돌아왔을 때, 그녀는 미국 텔레비전의 최초 요리 프로그램 중 하나인 『프랑스 요리사』에 출연했다. ⁵⁶그곳에서, 그녀는 사람들에게 집에서 비프 부르기뇽과 같은 대표적인 프랑스 요리를 만드는 법을 가르쳤다. 그 당시, 미국인들은 프랑스 요리를 만들기 어렵고 고급 식당에서만 먹을 수 있는 것으로 여겼다. 차일드의 쾌활하면서도 진정성 있는 설명 방식은 그 프로그램이 10년 동안 방영을 지속할 것임을 확실히 했다. 그것은 피바디상과 에미상

recognized with prestigious television awards, such as a Peabody Award and an Emmy Award, for its entertainment value and educational content.

같이 명성 있는 텔레비전상으로 그것의 오락적 가치와 교육적 콘텐츠에 대해 인정받았다.

후기
업적
+
죽음

Child kept publishing cookbooks and making TV appearances through the 1990s, inspiring a generation of new cooks. In 1995, [57]she established the Julia Child Foundation, which continues to provide grants to non-profit organizations related to food. She died of kidney failure on August 13, 2004, at the age of 91.

차일드는 1990년대까지 계속해서 요리책을 출판하고 TV 출연을 했으며, 젊은 요리사 세대를 고무했다. 1995년에, [57]그녀는 줄리아 차일드 재단을 설립했고, 이것은 음식과 관련된 비영리 단체들에 계속해서 보조금을 제공하고 있다. 그녀는 2004년 8월 13일 91세의 나이에 신부전으로 사망했다.

어휘 | wealthy adj. 부유한 household n. 가정 excel v. 뛰어나다, 탁월하다 employ v. 고용하다 assistant n. 보조원 explosive n. 폭발물 set off phr. 터뜨리다 responsibility n. 책무, 책임 prepare v. 조제하다 repellent n. 퇴치제 enthusiastic adj. 열성적인 connoisseur n. 감정가, 전문가 prominent adj. 유명한 reception n. 반응, 평판 sensation n. 돌풍 star v. 출연하다 fare n. 요리 fine adj. 고급의 cheerful adj. 쾌활한 authentic adj. 진정성 있는 presentation n. 설명 prestigious adj. 명성 있는 appearance n. 출연 establish v. 설립하다 grant n. 보조금

---

53 특정세부사항   유명한 이유   난이도 ●●○

What is Julia Child best known for?

(a) **introducing French cooking to the American public**
(b) publishing the first English cookbook for an international audience
(c) hosting a television program about various countries' cuisines
(d) being the first American to appear on a French cooking show

줄리아 차일드는 무엇으로 가장 잘 알려져 있는가?

(a) **프랑스 요리를 미국 대중에게 소개한 것으로**
(b) 국제적인 독자를 위한 최초의 영어 요리책을 출판한 것으로
(c) 여러 나라의 음식에 관한 텔레비전 프로그램을 진행한 것으로
(d) 프랑스 요리 프로그램에 출연한 최초의 미국인으로

⟶ 지텔프 치트키

질문의 키워드 best known이 그대로 언급된 주변 내용을 주의 깊게 읽는다.

해설 | 1단락의 'best known for teaching US audiences how to make French cuisine for the first time'에서 줄리아 차일드는 최초로 미국 청중들에게 프랑스 요리를 만드는 방법을 가르쳐준 것으로 가장 잘 알려져 있다고 했다. 따라서 (a)가 정답이다.

Paraphrasing
US audiences 미국 청중들 → the American public 미국 대중
French cuisine 프랑스 요리 → French cooking 프랑스 요리

어휘 | host v. 진행하다

---

54 특정세부사항   When   난이도 ●●○

When did Child first get interested in food?

(a) when she moved to Paris

차일드는 언제 처음으로 음식에 관심을 가지게 되었는가?

(a) 파리로 이사했을 때

(b) **when she married her husband**
(c) when she ate at a French restaurant
(d) when she enrolled in cooking school

(b) 그녀의 남편과 결혼했을 때
(c) 프랑스 레스토랑에서 식사했을 때
(d) 요리 학교에 등록했을 때

지텔프 치트키

질문의 키워드 get interested가 develop ~ passion으로 paraphrasing되어 언급된 주변 내용을 주의 깊게 읽는다.

해설 | 4단락의 'Child did not develop a real passion for food until 1946 when she married Paul Child, an enthusiastic food connoisseur.'에서 차일드는 1946년에 열성적인 음식 감정가인 폴 차일드와 결혼하고 나서야 비로소 음식에 대한 진정한 열정을 키웠다고 했다. 따라서 (b)가 정답이다.

오답분석

(c) 4단락에서 파리에 있는 레스토랑에서의 식사가 프랑스 요리 수업을 듣고자 하는 차일드의 욕구를 불러일으켰다고 언급했지만, 이는 차일드가 이미 음식에 대한 열정을 키운 후이므로 오답이다.

---

55 추론 특정사실   난이도 ●●●

How did living in France most likely influence the content of Child's first book?

(a) by encouraging her to read recipes in French
(b) by making her well-known among the French people
(c) by allowing her to collaborate with other teachers
(d) by giving her the experience of working in publishing

프랑스에서 사는 것이 어떻게 차일드의 첫 번째 책의 내용에 영향을 미쳤던 것 같은가?

(a) 그녀가 프랑스어로 요리법을 읽도록 촉진함으로써
(b) 그녀를 프랑스 국민들 사이에서 유명하게 만듦으로써
(c) 그녀가 다른 강사들과 협력하게 함으로써
(d) 그녀에게 출판업에서 일하는 경험을 제공함으로써

지텔프 치트키

질문의 키워드 first book이 그대로 언급된 주변 내용을 주의 깊게 읽는다.

해설 | 5단락의 'she, along with fellow cooking teachers ~, spent the next decade creating the recipes that would form the basis of her first book, *Mastering the Art of French Cooking*'에서 차일드가 동료 요리 강사들과 함께 그녀의 첫 번째 책인 『프랑스 요리의 기술』의 토대를 이루는 요리법들을 고안하는 데 다음 10년을 보냈다고 한 것을 통해, 차일드가 프랑스에 살면서 만난 동료 요리 강사들과 협력한 것이 차일드의 첫 번째 책의 내용에 영향을 미쳤던 것임을 추론할 수 있다. 따라서 (c)가 정답이다.

어휘 | collaborate v. 협력하다 publishing n. 출판업

---

56 추론 특정사실   난이도 ●●○

What did *The French Chef* probably accomplish?

(a) It taught people to focus on the quality of ingredients.
(b) It showed how to make home-cooked versions of restaurant dishes.
(c) It won the first Emmy Award for a female broadcaster.
(d) It popularized educational television programming in the U.S.

『프랑스 요리사』는 무엇을 성취했던 것 같은가?

(a) 사람들에게 재료의 품질에 중점을 두도록 가르쳤다.
(b) 식당 음식의 가정에서 요리된 형태를 만드는 방법을 보여주었다.
(c) 여성 방송인에 대한 첫 에미상을 받았다.
(d) 미국에서 교육 텔레비전 프로그램의 편성을 대중화했다.

질문의 키워드 *The French Chef*가 그대로 언급된 주변 내용을 주의 깊게 읽는다.

해설 | 6단락의 'There, she taught people how to make classic French dishes ~ at home.'에서 차일드가 「프랑스 요리사」에서 사람들에게 집에서 대표적인 프랑스 요리를 만드는 법을 가르쳤다고 한 뒤, 'At the time, Americans considered French fare ~ something they could only eat at fine dining establishments.'에서 그 당시 미국인들은 프랑스 요리를 고급 식당에서만 먹을 수 있는 것으로 여겼다고 한 것을 통해, 「프랑스 요리사」가 성취했던 것은 식당 음식의 가정에서 요리된 형태를 만드는 방법을 보여 주었던 것이었음을 추론할 수 있다. 따라서 (b)가 정답이다.

오답분석

(c) 6단락에서 「프랑스 요리사」가 에미상을 받았다고는 언급했지만, 여성 방송인에 대한 첫 에미상이었는지는 언급되지 않았으므로 오답이다.

어휘 | ingredient n. 재료 broadcaster n. 방송인 popularize v. 대중화하다 programming n. 프로그램의 편성

---

57 특정세부사항 What   난이도 ●●○

According to the passage, what did Child do through her foundation?

(a) She gave cooking classes.
(b) She appeared in instructional cooking videos.
(c) She made contributions to charity groups.
(d) She released follow-ups to her cookbook.

지문에 따르면, 차일드는 그녀의 재단을 통해 무엇을 했는가?

(a) 요리 수업을 제공했다.
(b) 교육용 요리 영상들에 출연했다.
(c) 자선 단체들에 기부금을 냈다.
(d) 그녀의 요리책에 대한 속편들을 발간했다.

⊷○ 지텔프 치트키

질문의 키워드 foundation이 그대로 언급된 주변 내용을 주의 깊게 읽는다.

해설 | 7단락의 'she established the Julia Child Foundation, which continues to provide grants to non-profit organizations related to food'에서 차일드가 줄리아 차일드 재단을 설립했고, 이것은 음식과 관련된 비영리 단체들에 계속해서 보조금을 제공하고 있다고 했다. 따라서 (c)가 정답이다.

Paraphrasing
provide grants to non-profit organizations 비영리 단체들에 보조금을 제공하다 → made contributions to charity groups 자선 단체들에 기부금을 냈다

어휘 | instructional adj. 교육용의 make a contribution phr. 기부금을 내다 charity n. 자선 release v. 발간하다 follow-up n. 속편

---

58 어휘 유의어   난이도 ●○○

In the context of the passage, underline{particular} means _____.

(a) huge
(b) remarkable
(c) typical
(d) specific

지문의 문맥에서, 'particular'는 ~을 의미한다.

(a) 거대한
(b) 놀랄 만한
(c) 전형적인
(d) 특별한

밑줄 친 어휘의 유의어를 찾는 문제이므로, particular가 포함된 구절을 읽고 문맥을 파악한다.

해설 | 2단락의 'showed no particular interest'는 특별한 관심을 보이지 않았다는 뜻이므로, particular가 '특별한'이라는 의미로 사용된 것을 알 수 있다. 따라서 '특별한'이라는 같은 의미의 (d) specific이 정답이다.

59 어휘 유의어 난이도 ●●○

In the context of the passage, <u>sparked</u> means _____.

(a) **provoked**
(b) beamed
(c) issued
(d) revived

지문의 문맥에서, 'sparked'는 -을 의미한다.

(a) 불러일으켰다
(b) 발산했다
(c) 발표했다
(d) 소생시켰다

밑줄 친 어휘의 유의어를 찾는 문제이므로, sparked가 포함된 구절을 읽고 문맥을 파악한다.

해설 | 4단락의 'sparked Child's desire to take French cooking lessons'는 프랑스 요리 수업을 듣고자 하는 차일드의 욕구를 불러일으켰다는 뜻이므로, sparked가 '불러일으켰다'라는 의미로 사용된 것을 알 수 있다. 따라서 '불러일으켰다'라는 같은 의미의 (a) provoked가 정답이다.

PART 2 [60~66] 잡지 기사 계산 능력이 있는 두 종의 물고기

연구 결과

RESEARCHERS TRAIN FISH TO ADD AND SUBTRACT

연구원들이 물고기에게 덧셈과 뺄셈을 훈련시키다

연구 소개

A study at the Institute of Zoology in the University of Bonn has revealed that two species of fish can do simple math. Led by zoology professor Dr. Vera Schluessel, [60]the researchers showed that trained cichlids and stingrays have the ability to calculate sums and differences using the numbers one through five.

본 대학 동물학 연구소의 한 연구는 두 종의 물고기가 간단한 계산을 할 수 있다는 것을 밝혀냈다. 동물학 교수인 베라 쉬리셀 박사가 이끄는 [60]연구원들은 훈련받은 시클리드와 가오리가 1에서 5까지의 숫자를 사용하여 합과 차를 계산하는 능력을 가지고 있다는 것을 보여 줬다.

실험 방식

For the study, researchers used blue and yellow shapes to prompt the fish to add or subtract by one. [65]The shapes <u>ranged</u> in size from small to large, which made calculation more difficult. [61]To demonstrate their mathematical comprehension, the fish were expected to swim through a gate displaying one more or one less than the number of shapes on the card according to the color. Thus, if a researcher held up a card with four yellow shapes, the fish had to select a gate with three shapes.

이 연구를 위해, 연구원들은 물고기들이 1씩 더하거나 빼도록 유도하기 위해 파란색과 노란색의 도형들을 이용했다. [65]그 도형들은 작은 것부터 큰 것까지 크기가 다양했으며, 이는 계산을 더 어렵게 만들었다. [61]물고기들의 수학적 이해력을 증명하기 위해, 그것들은 색깔에 따라 카드에 있는 도형의 수보다 한 개 더 많거나 한 개 더 적은 수를 나타내는 문을 통과하기를 기대받았다. 따라서, 만약 연구원이 네 개의 노란색 도형이 있는 카드를 들고 있다면, 물고기는 세 개의 도형이 있는 문을 선택해야 했다.

실험 결과	Six cichlids and four stingrays successfully completed training and [62(c)]recognized specific colors as symbols for addition and subtraction. While [62(d)]cichlids learned faster than stingrays, and more cichlids carried out the task, [62(a)]the individual performances of stingrays exceeded those of cichlids. [62(b)]Cichlids achieved about a 78 percent and 69 percent correct answer rate for addition and subtraction, respectively. Meanwhile, [62(b)]stingrays were right about 94 percent and 89 percent of the time. Whenever [66]the fish <u>executed</u> a task correctly, they were rewarded with food.	여섯 마리의 시클리드와 네 마리의 가오리가 성공적으로 훈련을 완수했고 [62(c)]특정한 색깔들을 덧셈과 뺄셈의 상징으로 인식했다. [62(d)]시클리드가 가오리보다 더 빠르게 학습했고, 더 많은 시클리드가 그 임무를 수행했지만, [62(a)]가오리의 개별 성적이 시클리드의 성적을 능가했다. [62(b)]시클리드는 덧셈과 뺄셈에 대해 각각 약 78퍼센트와 69퍼센트의 정답률을 달성했다. 한편, [62(b)]가오리는 당시 약 94퍼센트와 89퍼센트만큼 정확했다. [66]물고기들이 임무를 정확하게 <u>수행할</u> 때마다, 그것들은 음식으로 보상받았다.
실험 결과의 의문점	The researchers were surprised by the results of the experiment, [63]as fish do not possess a cerebral cortex, which is the area of the brain responsible for complex reasoning. Moreover, according to Dr. Schluessel, it is odd that cichlids and stingrays have basic math skills because, unlike other species of fish, they do not rely on numbers when mating or laying eggs.	연구원들은 그 실험 결과에 놀랐는데, [63]물고기가 대뇌피질을 가지고 있지 않기 때문이며, 이것은 복잡한 추론을 담당하는 뇌의 영역이다. 게다가, 쉬리셀 박사에 따르면, 다른 종의 물고기와는 달리, 시클리드와 가오리는 짝짓기를 하거나 알을 낳을 때 숫자에 의존하지 않기 때문에 그것들이 기본적인 수학 능력을 갖추고 있다는 것은 특이한 것이다.
시사점	In general, the experiment suggests that the mathematical ability of fish is better than has long been assumed. [64]People have considered fish to be relatively unintelligent with a memory span of only a few seconds, but there is increasing evidence that their cognitive abilities have been grossly underestimated.	전반적으로, 그 실험은 물고기의 수학적 능력이 오랫동안 가정되었던 것보다 낫다는 것을 시사한다. [64]사람들은 물고기가 단지 몇 초의 기억 범위를 가지고 있어 비교적 우둔하다고 여겨 왔지만, 그것들의 인지 능력이 극도로 과소평가되어 왔다는 증거가 늘어나고 있다.

어휘 | subtract v. 빼다 reveal v. 밝혀내다 calculate v. 계산하다 prompt v. 유도하다 demonstrate v. 증명하다
comprehension n. 이해력 exceed v. 능가하다 respectively adv. 각각 reward v. 보상하다 possess v. 가지고 있다
complex adj. 복잡한 reasoning n. 추론 odd adj. 특이한, 이상한 suggest v. 시사하다 assume v. 가정하다
memory span phr. 기억 범위 evidence n. 증거 cognitive adj. 인지의 grossly adv. 극도로 underestimate v. 과소평가하다

---

60 특정세부사항   연구의 결과   난이도 ●●○

What did researchers find out about certain fish species?	연구원들은 특정 어종에 관해 무엇을 알아냈는가?
(a) that they can perceive up to five objects at a time (b) that they can use mathematics to track prey (c) that they can recognize words for numbers **(d) that they can perform basic calculations**	(a) 한 번에 최대 5개의 물체를 지각할 수 있다는 것 (b) 먹이를 쫓기 위해 수학을 사용할 수 있다는 것 (c) 숫자에 관한 단어들을 인지할 수 있다는 것 **(d) 기본적인 계산을 수행할 수 있다는 것**

──○ 지텔프 치트키

연구의 결과를 언급하는 지문의 초반을 주의 깊게 읽는다.

해설 | 1단락의 'the researchers showed that trained cichlids and stingrays have the ability to calculate sums and differences using the numbers one through five'에서 연구원들은 훈련받은 시클리드와 가오리가 1에서 5까지의 숫자를 사용하여 합과 차를 계산하는 능력을 가지고 있다는 것을 보여 줬다고 했다. 따라서 (d)가 정답이다.

Paraphrasing

ability to calculate 계산하는 능력 → can perform ~ calculations 계산을 수행할 수 있다

어휘 | perceive v. 지각하다 track v. 쫓다 prey n. 먹이

---

61 특정세부사항   How   난이도 ●●●

How did the fish demonstrate their understanding of the task?

(a) by swimming to a card displaying the previously seen color
(b) by selecting a picture featuring colorful objects
(c) by approaching a gate with identical geometric shapes
(d) by choosing an entrance marked with the correct number of figures

물고기는 임무에 대한 그들의 이해력을 어떻게 증명했는가?

(a) 이전에 본 색깔을 나타내는 카드로 헤엄침으로써
(b) 다채로운 물체들을 포함하는 그림을 선택함으로써
(c) 동일한 기하학적 모양들이 있는 문에 접근함으로써
(d) 도형의 올바른 수가 표시된 문을 선택함으로써

🔑 지텔프 치트키

질문의 키워드 demonstrate가 그대로 언급된 주변 내용을 주의 깊게 읽는다.

해설 | 2단락의 'To demonstrate their mathematical comprehension, the fish were expected to swim through a gate displaying one more or one less than the number of shapes on the card according to the color.'에서 물고기들의 수학적 이해력을 증명하기 위해 그것들은 색깔에 따라 카드에 있는 도형의 수보다 한 개 더 많거나 한 개 더 적은 수를 나타내는 문을 통과하기를 기대받았다고 했다. 따라서 (d)가 정답이다.

Paraphrasing

a gate displaying ~ the number of shapes 도형의 수를 나타내는 문 → an entrance marked with the ~ number of figures 도형의 수가 표시된 문

어휘 | approach v. 접근하다 identical adj. 동일한 geometric adj. 기하학적인 entrance n. 문, 입구 mark v. 표시하다 figure n. 도형

---

62 Not/True   Not 문제   난이도 ●●●

Which of the following is NOT an outcome of the study?

(a) Cichlids performed worse than stingrays overall.
(b) Both species were better at subtraction than addition.
(c) Both species exhibited an ability to make judgments.
(d) Not all of the fish learned at the same speed.

다음 중 연구의 결과가 아닌 것은 무엇인가?

(a) 전반적으로 시클리드가 가오리보다 성적이 더 나빴다.
(b) 두 종 모두 덧셈보다 뺄셈을 더 잘했다.
(c) 두 종 모두 판단을 내리는 능력을 보였다.
(d) 모든 물고기가 같은 속도로 학습하지는 않았다.

🔑 지텔프 치트키

질문의 키워드 outcome of the study와 관련된 주변 내용을 주의 깊게 읽고, 보기의 키워드와 지문 내용을 대조하며 언급되는 것을 하나씩 소거한다.

해설 | (b)는 3단락의 'Cichlids achieved about a 78 percent and 69 percent correct answer rate for addition and subtraction, respectively.'에서 시클리드가 덧셈과 뺄셈에 대해 각각 약 78퍼센트와 69퍼센트의 정답률을 달성했다고 한 뒤, 'stingrays were right about 94 percent and 89 percent of the time'에서 가오리는 약 94퍼센트와 89퍼센트만큼 정확했다고 했으므로 지문의 내용과 일치하지 않는다. 따라서 (b)가 정답이다.

오답분석

(a) 보기의 키워드 performed가 performances로 paraphrasing되어 언급된 3단락에서 가오리의 개별 성적이 시클리드의 성적을 능가했다고 언급되었다.

(c) 보기의 키워드 make judgments가 recognized로 paraphrasing되어 언급된 3단락에서 두 종 모두 특정한 색깔들을 덧셈과 뺄셈의 상징으로 인식했다고 언급되었다.

(d) 보기의 키워드 speed가 faster로 paraphrasing되어 언급된 3단락에서 시클리드가 가오리보다 더 빠르게 학습했다고 언급되었다.

어휘 | judgment n. 판단

---

63 특정세부사항   Why

난이도 ●●○

According to the article, why were the findings of the experiment unanticipated?

(a) because fish have an underdeveloped cerebral cortex
(b) because fish cease complex reasoning after mating
(c) because fish lack a part of an organ
(d) because fish do not count their eggs

기사에 따르면, 왜 그 실험 결과가 예상치 못한 것이었는가?

(a) 물고기는 덜 발달된 대뇌피질을 가지고 있기 때문에
(b) 물고기는 짝짓기 후에 복잡한 추론을 멈추기 때문에
(c) 물고기는 장기의 한 부분이 없기 때문에
(d) 물고기는 그들의 알을 세지 않기 때문에

지텔프 치트키

질문의 키워드 unanticipated가 surprised로 paraphrasing되어 언급된 주변 내용을 주의 깊게 읽는다.

해설 | 4단락의 'as fish do not possess a cerebral cortex, ~ the area of the brain responsible for complex reasoning'에서 물고기가 복잡한 추론을 담당하는 뇌의 영역인 대뇌 피질을 가지고 있지 않기 때문에 연구원들이 그 실험 결과에 놀랐다고 했다. 따라서 (c)가 정답이다.

Paraphrasing

the area of the brain 뇌의 영역 → a part of an organ 장기의 한 부분

어휘 | underdeveloped adj. 덜 발달된   cease v. 멈추다, 그만두다   organ n. 장기, 신체 기관

---

64 추론   특정사실

난이도 ●●○

What is most likely true about the mental capacity of fish?

(a) It exceeds people's expectations.
(b) It is surpassed by other small animals.
(c) It is restricted to counting capabilities.
(d) It correlates directly with memory span.

물고기의 정신 능력에 관해 사실인 것은 무엇인 것 같은가?

(a) 사람들의 예상을 뛰어넘는다.
(b) 다른 작은 동물들에 의해 능가된다.
(c) 계산 능력으로 제한된다.
(d) 기억 범위와 직접적인 관련이 있다.

지텔프 치트키

질문의 키워드 mental capacity가 cognitive abilities로 paraphrasing되어 언급된 주변 내용을 주의 깊게 읽는다.

해설 | 5단락의 'People have considered fish to be relatively unintelligent ~, but there is increasing evidence that their cognitive abilities have been grossly underestimated.'에서 사람들은 물고기가 비교적 우둔하다고 여겨 왔지만 그것들의 인지 능력이 극도로 과소평가되어 왔다는 증거가 늘어나고 있다고 한 것을 통해, 물고기의 정신 능력은 사람들의 예상을 뛰어넘는다는 것을 추론할 수 있다. 따라서 (a)가 정답이다.

어휘 | capacity n. 능력 expectation n. 예상 surpass v. 능가하다 restrict v. 제한하다 correlate v. 관련이 있다

65 어휘   유의어   난이도 ●●○

In the context of the passage, <u>ranged</u> means _____. (a) included **(b) varied** (c) secured (d) reached	지문의 문맥에서, 'ranged'는 -을 의미한다. (a) 포함했다 **(b) 다양했다** (c) 획득했다 (d) 이르렀다

⊸ 지텔프 치트키

밑줄 친 어휘의 유의어를 찾는 문제이므로, ranged가 포함된 구절을 읽고 문맥을 파악한다.

해설 | 2단락의 'The shapes ranged in size from small to large'는 도형들이 작은 것부터 큰 것까지 크기가 다양했다는 뜻이므로, ranged 가 '다양했다'라는 의미로 사용된 것을 알 수 있다. 따라서 '다양했다'라는 같은 의미의 (b) varied가 정답이다.

오답분석

(d) '이르다'라는 의미의 reach도 range의 사전적 유의어 중 하나이지만, reach는 장소나 목적지 등에 도달한다는 의미로 사용되므로 문맥에 어울리지 않아 오답이다.

66 어휘   유의어   난이도 ●○○

In the context of the passage, <u>executed</u> means _____. (a) gained (b) faced (c) ensured **(d) did**	지문의 문맥에서, 'executed'는 -을 의미한다. (a) 얻었다 (b) 직면했다 (c) 보장했다 **(d) 수행했다**

⊸ 지텔프 치트키

밑줄 친 어휘의 유의어를 찾는 문제이므로, executed가 포함된 구절을 읽고 문맥을 파악한다.

해설 | 3단락의 'the fish executed a task correctly'는 물고기들이 임무를 정확하게 수행했다는 뜻이므로, executed가 '수행했다'라는 의미로 사용된 것을 알 수 있다. 따라서 '수행했다'라는 같은 의미의 (d) did가 정답이다.

| 표제어 | **TOAST** | 건배 |

정의

⁶⁷A toast is a gesture in which people at a gathering raise their glass as a sign of honor or friendliness. Toasts are most commonly made with alcoholic beverages during meaningful events, such as weddings and birthdays.

건배의 기원

The exact origin of toasting is not known for certain. However, evidence of the practice can be found in many ancient cultures. The ancient Greeks, for example, poured out wine as a ritual offering to the gods and often drank to the health of others. ⁶⁸The convention is frequently described in works of ancient literature such as Homer's *The Odyssey*.

건배의 역할

The tradition of drinking to the health of others is thought to have arisen from concerns about poisoning, which was once a common way to eliminate rivals. ⁶⁹Taking the first sip of a drink after wishing someone well was a way of letting them know it was safe to consume it. Also, there are stories suggesting that clinking glasses together ⁷²<u>served</u> to build fellowship because this would cause the liquid from one glass to spill into the other.

새로운 역할의 등장

Toasting spread throughout the continent of Europe, becoming so popular that in the 17th century it was necessary to invent the role of the toastmaster. Toastmasters were skilled public speakers who ⁷³<u>oversaw</u> the practice of toasting at assemblies. ⁷⁰They made sure that no one spoke for too long and that everyone who wished to deliver a toast had the opportunity to do so.

오늘날 건배 풍습

Today, various nations around the world have developed their own toasting customs. Some countries in Northeast Asia, for instance, use phrases that sound similar to begin a toast. However, in practice, the toasts follow different rules of etiquette depending on the culture of origin. For the Chinese, those with junior status will lower their cups to their seniors to show respect when clinking glasses. In Korea, a glass is refilled only after it is emptied, whereas ⁷¹in Japan, the glass is continuously refilled so that it never becomes empty.

---

⁶⁷건배는 모임에서 사람들이 존경이나 친근함의 표시로 그들의 잔을 들어 올리는 행위이다. 건배는 결혼식과 생일과 같은 의미 있는 행사 동안 술과 함께 가장 흔히 이루어진다.

건배 행위의 정확한 기원은 확실히 알려져 있지 않다. 그러나, 그 관습의 증거는 많은 고대 문화에서 찾아볼 수 있다. 예를 들어, 고대 그리스인들은 신들을 향한 의식의 제물로서 술을 따랐고 종종 다른 사람들의 건강을 빌며 술을 마셨다. ⁶⁸그 관습은 호메로스의 『오디세이』와 같은 고대 문학 작품에서 자주 묘사된다.

다른 사람들의 건강을 빌며 술을 마시는 전통은 음독에 대한 우려에서 비롯된 것으로 생각되는데, 이것은 한때 경쟁자를 제거하는 흔한 방법이었다. ⁶⁹누군가의 축복을 기원한 후 술의 첫 한 모금을 마시는 것은 그것을 마셔도 안전하다는 것을 그들에게 알리는 방법이었다. 또한, 잔을 함께 부딪치는 것이 ⁷²유대감을 형성하는 역할을 했다고 제안하는 이야기들도 있는데 이는 술이 하나의 잔에서 다른 잔으로 쏟아지게 할 것이었기 때문이다.

건배 행위는 유럽 대륙 전역에 퍼졌고, 매우 대중적이게 되어서 17세기에는 토스트마스터라는 역할을 만드는 것이 필요했다. 토스트마스터는 모임에서 ⁷³건배 행위를 감독하는 숙련된 연설가였다. ⁷⁰그들은 어느 사람도 너무 오랫동안 말하지 않는 것과 건배의 말을 전하고 싶어 하는 모든 사람들이 그렇게 할 기회를 갖는 것을 확실히 했다.

오늘날, 전 세계의 다양한 국가들이 그들만의 건배 풍습을 발전시켰다. 예를 들어, 동북아시아의 몇몇 국가들은 건배를 시작하기 위해 비슷하게 들리는 구절을 사용한다. 하지만, 실제로, 건배는 그것이 시작된 문화에 따라 다른 예절 규칙을 따른다. 중국인의 경우, 후배 지위를 가진 사람들은 잔을 부딪칠 때 존경심을 표하기 위해 그들의 선배들을 향해 잔을 낮출 것이다. 한국에서는, 잔이 비워진 후에만 다시 채워지는 반면에, ⁷¹일본에서는, 잔이 절대 비지 않도록 계속해서 다시 채워진다.

어휘 | toast n. 건배, 건배의 말 gesture n. 행위, 몸짓 gathering n. 모임 raise v. 들어 올리다 meaningful adj. 의미 있는 origin n. 기원, 시작 ancient adj. 고대의 pour v. 따르다 ritual adj. 의식의; n. 의식 offering n. 제물 convention n. 관습 arise v. 비롯되다 concern n. 우려 poisoning n. 음독, 독살 eliminate v. 제거하다 clink v. 잔을 부딪치다 fellowship n. 유대감 spill v. 쏟아지다 toastmaster n. 토스트마스터(건배를 제의하는 사람) assembly n. 모임 custom n. 풍습 phrase n. 구절, 문구 etiquette n. 예절

TEST 1
TEST 2
TEST 3
TEST 4
TEST 5
TEST 6
TEST 7

67 특정세부사항   What   난이도 ●○○

According to the article, what do people do when they toast at an event?

(a) **express goodwill toward others**
(b) mark the beginning of a gathering
(c) encourage social drinking
(d) introduce a member of a group

기사에 따르면, 사람들은 행사에서 건배할 때 무엇을 하는가?

(a) **다른 사람들에게 친선을 표한다**
(b) 모임의 시작을 알린다
(c) 사교상의 음주를 장려한다
(d) 집단의 구성원을 소개한다

─○ 지텔프 치트키

질문의 키워드 event가 gathering으로 paraphrasing되어 언급된 주변 내용을 주의 깊게 읽는다.

해설 | 1단락의 'A toast is a gesture in which people at a gathering raise their glass as a sign of honor or friendliness.'에서 건배는 모임에서 사람들이 존경이나 친근함의 표시로 그들의 잔을 들어 올리는 행위라고 했다. 따라서 (a)가 정답이다.

Paraphrasing
a sign of ~ friendliness 친근함의 표시 → express goodwill 친선을 표하다

어휘 | goodwill n. 친선, 호의   mark v. 알리다

68 특정세부사항   What   난이도 ●●○

What is the evidence that toasting is an ancient practice?

(a) It is shown in old paintings.
(b) **It is written about in books.**
(c) It is named after a figure from history.
(d) It is performed in various religious rituals.

건배 행위가 고대의 관습이라는 증거는 무엇인가?

(a) 고대 그림들에 나타나 있다.
(b) **책에 쓰여 있다.**
(c) 역사 속 한 인물의 이름을 따서 명명되었다.
(d) 여러 종교의식에서 수행된다.

─○ 지텔프 치트키

질문의 키워드 ancient가 그대로 언급된 주변 내용을 주의 깊게 읽는다.

해설 | 2단락의 'The convention is frequently described in works of ancient literature such as Homer's *The Odyssey*.'에서 건배하는 관습은 호메로스의 『오디세이』와 같은 고대 문학 작품에서 자주 묘사된다고 했다. 따라서 (b)가 정답이다.

Paraphrasing
described in works of ~ literature 문학 작품에서 묘사되는 → written about in books 책에 쓰여 있는

어휘 | figure n. 인물   religious adj. 종교의

69 추론   특정사실   난이도 ●●○

Why most likely would someone take the first sip of a drink?

(a) to show appreciation for the host's generosity
(b) to improve a relationship with a rival
(c) **to prove the harmlessness of the beverage**

왜 누군가가 술의 첫 한 모금을 마실 것 같은가?

(a) 진행자의 관대함에 감사를 표하기 위해서
(b) 경쟁자와의 관계를 개선하기 위해서
(c) **음료의 무해성을 증명하기 위해서**

| (d) to tell a story about building fellowship | (d) 유대감을 형성하는 것에 관한 이야기를 하기 위해서 |

🔗 지텔프 치트키

질문의 키워드 first sip of a drink가 그대로 언급된 주변 내용을 주의 깊게 읽는다.

해설 | 3단락의 'Taking the first sip of a drink ~ was a way of letting them know it was safe to consume it.'에서 술의 첫 한 모금을 마시는 것은 그것을 마셔도 안전하다는 것을 알리는 방법이었다고 한 것을 통해, 누군가가 술의 첫 모금을 마시는 것은 음료의 무해함을 증명하기 위한 것임을 추론할 수 있다. 따라서 (c)가 정답이다.

어휘 | appreciation n. 감사 generosity n. 관대함 harmlessness n. 무해성

---

70 특정세부사항 How 난이도 ●●○

How did toastmasters fulfill their duties?	토스트마스터들은 어떻게 그들의 임무를 수행했는가?
(a) by planning regular gatherings	(a) 정기적인 모임을 계획함으로써
(b) by judging the quality of speeches	(b) 연설의 질을 판단함으로써
(c) by giving people a chance to speak	**(c) 사람들에게 말할 기회를 줌으로써**
(d) by preparing lessons about public speaking	(d) 연설에 관한 수업을 준비함으로써

🔗 지텔프 치트키

질문의 키워드 toastmasters가 그대로 언급된 주변 내용을 주의 깊게 읽는다.

해설 | 4단락의 'They made sure that ~ everyone who wished to deliver a toast had the opportunity to do so.'에서 토스트마스터들은 건배의 말을 전하고 싶어 하는 모든 사람들이 그렇게 할 기회를 가지는 것을 확실히 했다고 했다. 따라서 (c)가 정답이다.

Paraphrasing
deliver a toast 건배의 말을 전하다 → speak 말하다
the opportunity 기회 → a chance 기회

어휘 | fulfill v. 수행하다, 충족하다 regular adj. 정기적인

---

71 특정세부사항 When 난이도 ●○○

According to the passage, when should a glass be refilled in Japan?	지문에 따르면, 일본에서 잔은 언제 다시 채워져야 하는가?
(a) before it is given to a senior	(a) 선배에게 주어지기 전에
(b) when it is raised for a toast	(b) 건배를 위해 들어 올려질 때
(c) when it is lowered to express politeness	(c) 예의를 표하기 위해 낮춰졌을 때
(d) before it is completely drained	**(d) 완전히 비워지기 전에**

🔗 지텔프 치트키

질문의 키워드 Japan이 그대로 언급된 주변 내용을 주의 깊게 읽는다.

해설 | 5단락의 'in Japan, the glass is continuously refilled so that it never becomes empty'에서 일본에서는 잔이 절대 비지 않도

록 계속해서 다시 채워진다고 했다. 따라서 (d)가 정답이다.

Paraphrasing
it ~ becomes empty 비다 → it is completely drained 완전히 비워지다

어휘 | politeness n. 예의 drain v. 비우다

---

72 어휘   유의어   난이도 ●●○

In the context of the passage, <u>served</u> means _____ .

(a) **acted**
(b) offered
(c) believed
(d) provided

지문의 문맥에서, 'served'는 -을 의미한다.

(a) **역할을 했다**
(b) 권했다
(c) 믿었다
(d) 제공했다

━○ 지텔프 치트키

밑줄 친 어휘의 유의어를 찾는 문제이므로, served가 포함된 구절을 읽고 문맥을 파악한다.

해설 | 3단락의 'served to build fellowship'은 유대감을 형성하는 역할을 했다는 뜻이므로, served가 '역할을 했다'라는 의미로 사용된 것을 알 수 있다. 따라서 '역할을 했다'라는 같은 의미의 (a) acted가 정답이다.

오답분석

(d) '제공하다'라는 의미의 provide도 serve의 사전적 유의어 중 하나이지만, 잔을 함께 부딪치는 것이 유대감을 형성하는 역할을 했다는 의미가 되어야 적절하므로 문맥에 어울리지 않아 오답이다.

---

73 어휘   유의어   난이도 ●●○

In the context of the passage, <u>oversaw</u> means _____ .

(a) commanded
(b) **supervised**
(c) observed
(d) made

지문의 문맥에서, 'oversaw'는 -을 의미한다.

(a) 지휘했다
(b) **감독했다**
(c) 관찰했다
(d) 만들었다

━○ 지텔프 치트키

밑줄 친 어휘의 유의어를 찾는 문제이므로, oversaw가 포함된 구절을 읽고 문맥을 파악한다.

해설 | 4단락의 'oversaw the practice of toasting'은 건배 행위를 감독했다는 뜻이므로, oversaw가 '감독했다'라는 의미로 사용된 것을 알 수 있다. 따라서 '감독했다'라는 같은 의미의 (b) supervised가 정답이다.

오답분석

(a) '지휘하다'라는 의미의 command도 oversee의 사전적 유의어 중 하나이지만, command는 권위 있는 위치의 사람이 무엇을 명령하거나 지시하는 상황을 나타낼 때 쓰이므로 문맥에 어울리지 않아 오답이다.

수신인 정보

Edgar Agnello
Human Resources Director
Pierre Levine Museum
3390 E Lockett Rd
Flagstaff, AZ 86004

Dear Mr. Agnello:

편지의 목적: 입사 지원

[74]I am writing to apply for the position of head curator at the Pierre Levine Museum, which was advertised in the August issue of the museum's newsletter. I am currently working as an assistant curator at the Tobin Clegg Art Gallery in New Mexico, a role I have held for the last four years.

지원 동기 + 포부

[79]I am drawn to the museum not only because I would like to play a part in preserving Pierre Levine's artistic legacy but also because I admire the museum's many philanthropic and educational contributions to society. If chosen for the position, I promise [75]I will do everything I can to promote his creations and help the museum flourish.

자격 사항 + 경력

[76]I possess a bachelor's degree in fine arts and a master's degree in art history from Sutcliffe University. According to your ad, [76]these qualifications are your main criteria for the curator job. In addition, at the Tobin Clegg Art Gallery, I acquire new paintings and sculptures for the gallery and conduct research in preparation for exhibitions and publications. Moreover, I keep track of acquisition schedules and help [80]connect artists with collectors. I report directly to the head curator Mark Copeland, [77]whose letter of reference I have enclosed along with my résumé.

끝인사

My last day of work at the Tobin Clegg Art Gallery is September 5, and [78]I am permanently relocating to Arizona on September 15. I'd love the chance for an in-person interview with you once I am settled. Until then, I can be reached via e-mail at d.Cobbett@fastmail.com. I appreciate your consideration and look forward to hearing from you.

발신인 정보

Sincerely,
Diana Cobbett

Edgar Agnello
인사부장
Pierre Levine 미술관
동 로켓가 3390번지
86004 애리조나주 플래그스태프

Mr. Agnello께:

Pierre Levine 미술관의 [74]수석 큐레이터 직책에 지원하고자 편지를 쓰며, 이것은 미술관 소식지의 8월호에 광고되어 있었습니다. 저는 현재 뉴멕시코주에 있는 Tobin Clegg 미술관에서 보조 큐레이터로 일하고 있으며, 이는 제가 지난 4년 동안 맡아온 직무입니다.

[79]저는 그 미술관에 매료되었는데 이는 제가 Pierre Levine의 예술적 유산을 보존하는 데 이바지하고 싶을 뿐만 아니라 사회에 대한 미술관의 많은 자선적이고 교육적인 공헌을 존경하기 때문입니다. 만약 그 직책에 뽑힌다면, [75]저는 그의 작품들을 알리고 미술관이 번창하도록 돕기 위해 제가 할 수 있는 모든 것을 할 것을 약속드립니다.

[76]저는 Sutcliffe 대학의 미술학 학사와 미술사 석사 학위를 소지하고 있습니다. 귀사의 광고에 따르면, [76]이러한 자격들이 큐레이터 직무에 대한 귀사의 주요 기준입니다. 그뿐만 아니라, Tobin Clegg 미술관에서, 저는 미술관을 위한 새로운 그림과 조각품을 매입하고 전시와 간행물을 준비하며 연구를 수행합니다. 게다가, 저는 매입 일정을 파악하고 [80]예술가와 수집가를 연결하는 것을 돕습니다. 저는 수석 큐레이터인 Mark Copeland의 직속이며, [77]그의 추천서를 제 이력서와 함께 동봉했습니다.

Tobin Clegg 미술관에서의 제 마지막 근무 날은 9월 5일이고, [78]저는 9월 15일에 애리조나주로 영구 이주할 예정입니다. 제가 자리를 잡으면 귀하와 개인 면접의 기회를 얻고 싶습니다. 그때까지, 저는 이메일 d.Cobbett@fastmail.com을 통해 연락하실 수 있습니다. 귀하의 고려에 감사드리며 연락을 고대하고 있겠습니다.

Diana Cobbett 드림

어휘 | advertise v. 광고하다 newsletter n. 소식지 play a part phr. 이바지하다 preserve v. 보존하다 legacy n. 유산 admire v. 존경하다
philanthropic adj. 자선적인 contribution n. 공헌, 기여 promote v. 알리다, 홍보하다 creation n. 작품 flourish v. 번창하다
qualification n. 자격 criterion n. 기준 acquire v. 매입하다, 획득하다 publication n. 간행물 report v. 직속이다, 보고하다
enclose v. 동봉하다 permanently adv. 영구적으로, 영원히 relocate v. 이주하다 in-person interview phr. 개인 면접
settle v. 자리 잡게 하다 reach v. 연락하다 consideration n. 고려

74   주제/목적   편지의 목적   난이도 ●●○

What is the main purpose of the letter?

(a) to ask for assistance with a search for artwork
(b) to respond to an inquiry about an available position
(c) to submit an application for a job opening
(d) to ask about any employment opportunities

이 편지의 주된 목적은 무엇인가?

(a) 예술 작품 탐색에 도움을 요청하기 위해서
(b) 공석에 관한 문의에 답하기 위해서
(c) 채용 공고에 지원서를 제출하기 위해서
(d) 채용 기회에 관해 묻기 위해서

─○ 지텔프 치트키

지문의 초반을 주의 깊게 읽고 전체 맥락을 파악한다.

해설 | 1단락의 'I am writing to apply for the position of head curator'에서 Cobbett가 수석 큐레이터 직책에 지원하고자 편지를 쓴다고 한 뒤, 그녀의 입사 지원 동기와 자격 사항 등에 관한 내용이 이어지고 있다. 따라서 (c)가 정답이다.

Paraphrasing
apply 지원하다 → submit an application 지원서를 제출하다

어휘 | assistance n. 도움   inquiry n. 문의   submit v. 제출하다   application n. 지원서   job opening phr. 채용 공고
employment n. 채용, 고용

75   특정세부사항   How   난이도 ●●○

How does Cobbett think she can benefit the museum?

(a) by spreading awareness about an individual's work
(b) by organizing philanthropic events at the museum
(c) by contributing to an artist's collection
(d) by raising funds to expand the institution

Cobbett는 그녀가 어떻게 미술관에 도움이 될 수 있다고 생각하는가?

(a) 한 사람의 작품에 대한 인식을 널리 퍼뜨림으로써
(b) 미술관에서 자선 행사를 준비함으로써
(c) 한 예술가의 수집품에 기부함으로써
(d) 기관을 확장하기 위한 자금을 조달함으로써

─○ 지텔프 치트키

질문의 키워드 benefit가 help로 paraphrasing되어 언급된 주변 내용을 주의 깊게 읽는다.

해설 | 2단락의 'I will do everything I can to promote his creations and help the museum flourish'에서 Cobbett가 Pierre Levine의 작품들을 알리고 미술관이 번창하도록 돕기 위해 자신이 할 수 있는 모든 것을 할 것이라고 했다. 따라서 (a)가 정답이다.

Paraphrasing
promote ~ creations 작품들을 알리다 → spreading awareness about an individual's work 작품에 대한 인식을 널리 퍼뜨림

어휘 | awareness n. 인식   raise v. 조달하다   expand v. 확장하다   institution n. 기관

76   특정세부사항   How   난이도 ●●○

How does Cobbett fulfill the core requirements for the position?

(a) She is enrolled in a master's program.
(b) She possesses work experience at a museum.

Cobbett는 그 직책에 대한 핵심 요건들을 어떻게 충족하는가?

(a) 석사 과정에 등록되어 있다.
(b) 미술관에서 일한 경험이 있다.

(c) **She has the desired educational background.**

(d) She studies art history at a university.

(c) 요구되는 학력을 가지고 있다.

(d) 대학에서 미술사를 공부한다.

지텔프 치트키

질문의 키워드 core requirements가 main criteria로 paraphrasing되어 언급된 주변 내용을 주의 깊게 읽는다.

해설 | 3단락의 'I possess a bachelor's degree ~ and a master's degree ~ from Sutcliffe University.'에서 Cobbett가 Sutcliffe 대학의 학사와 석사 학위를 소지하고 있다고 한 뒤, 'these qualifications are your main criteria for the curator job'에서 이러한 자격들이 큐레이터 직무에 대한 Pierre Levine 미술관의 주요 기준이라고 했다. 따라서 (c)가 정답이다.

Paraphrasing

a bachelor's degree ~ and a master's degree 학사와 석사 학위 → educational background 학력

어휘 | educational background phr. 학력

---

77 추론 특정사실 난이도 ●●●

What can most likely be said about Mark Copeland?

(a) He is preparing for a major exhibition.

(b) He is unaware of Cobbett's resignation.

(c) He is leaving for a new position.

(d) He is supportive of Cobbett's future plans.

Mark Copeland에 관해 무엇이 말해질 수 있는 것 같은가?

(a) 대형 전시회를 준비하고 있다.

(b) Cobbett의 사직에 대해 알지 못한다.

(c) 새로운 직책을 위해 떠난다.

(d) Cobbett의 향후 계획을 지지한다.

지텔프 치트키

질문의 키워드 Mark Copeland가 그대로 언급된 주변 내용을 주의 깊게 읽는다.

해설 | 3단락의 'whose letter of reference I have enclosed along with my résumé'에서 Cobbett가 Mark Copeland의 추천서를 그녀의 이력서와 함께 동봉했다고 한 것을 통해, Mark Copeland는 일자리를 옮기고자 하는 Cobbett의 향후 계획을 지지하고 있음을 추론할 수 있다. 따라서 (d)가 정답이다.

어휘 | resignation n. 사직 supportive adj. 지지하는

---

78 추론 특정사실 난이도 ●●○

Why most likely does Cobbett mention her moving date?

(a) because she will terminate her employment on this date

(b) because she wants Agnello to contact her by this date

(c) because she is available for interviews before this date

(d) because she can meet Agnello after this date

왜 Cobbett가 그녀의 이사 날짜를 언급하는 것 같은가?

(a) 이 날짜에 그녀의 근무를 끝낼 것이기 때문에

(b) 이 날짜까지 Agnello가 그녀에게 연락하기를 원하기 때문에

(c) 이 날짜 이전에 면접이 가능하기 때문에

(d) 이 날짜 이후에 Agnello를 만날 수 있기 때문에

지텔프 치트키

질문의 키워드 moving이 relocating으로 paraphrasing되어 언급된 주변 내용을 주의 깊게 읽는다.

해설 | 4단락의 'I am ~ relocating to Arizona on September 15'에서 Cobbett가 9월 15일에 애리조나주로 이주할 예정이라고 한 뒤, 'I'd

---

love the chance for an in-person interview with you once I am settled.'에서 그녀가 자리를 잡으면 Agnello와 개인 면접의 기회를 얻고 싶다고 한 것을 통해, 이사 날짜 이후에 Agnello를 만날 수 있기 때문에 이사 날짜를 언급한 것임을 추론할 수 있다. 따라서 (d)가 정답이다.

어휘 | terminate v. 끝내다, 해지하다   contact v. 연락하다

---

79 어휘   유의어   난이도 ●●○

In the context of the passage, <u>drawn</u> means _____.

(a) carried
(b) attracted
(c) elicited
(d) dictated

지문의 문맥에서, 'drawn'은 -을 의미한다.

(a) 황홀한
(b) 매료된
(c) 유도된
(d) 영향을 받은

🔑 지텔프 치트키

밑줄 친 어휘의 유의어를 찾는 문제이므로, drawn이 포함된 구절을 읽고 문맥을 파악한다.

해설 | 2단락의 'I am drawn to the museum'은 그 미술관에 매료된다는 뜻이므로, drawn이 '매료된'이라는 의미로 사용된 것을 알 수 있다. 따라서 '매료된'이라는 같은 의미의 (b) attracted가 정답이다.

오답분석
(c) '유도해 내다'라는 의미의 elicit도 draw의 사전적 유의어 중 하나이지만, elicit는 대답이나 사실 등을 유도해 낸다는 의미이므로 문맥에 어울리지 않아 오답이다.

---

80 어휘   유의어   난이도 ●●○

In the context of the passage, <u>connect</u> means _____.

(a) associate
(b) engage
(c) assemble
(d) grow

지문의 문맥에서, 'connect'는 -을 의미한다.

(a) 관련시키다
(b) 사로잡다
(c) 모으다
(d) 발전시키다

🔑 지텔프 치트키

밑줄 친 어휘의 유의어를 찾는 문제이므로, connect가 포함된 구절을 읽고 문맥을 파악한다.

해설 | 3단락의 'connect artists with collectors'는 예술가와 수집가를 연결한다는 뜻이므로, connect가 '연결하다'라는 의미로 사용된 것을 알 수 있다. 따라서 '관련시키다'라는 비슷한 의미의 (a) associate가 정답이다.

TEST 3

정답·스크립트·해석·해설

GRAMMAR

LISTENING

READING & VOCABULARY

TEST 3 점수 확인하기

GRAMMAR _____ / 26 (점수 : _____ 점)
LISTENING _____ / 26 (점수 : _____ 점)
READING & VOCABULARY _____ / 28 (점수 : _____ 점)

TOTAL _____ / 80 (평균 점수 : _____ 점)

*각 영역 점수: 맞은 개수 × 3.75
*평균 점수: 각 영역 점수 합계 ÷ 3

정답 및 취약 유형 분석표

문제집 p.76

GRAMMAR

번호	정답	유형
01	b	시제
02	b	가정법
03	d	준동사
04	d	조동사
05	b	연결어
06	c	준동사
07	a	가정법
08	c	시제
09	a	준동사
10	b	조동사
11	d	관계사
12	b	시제
13	a	가정법
14	d	준동사
15	a	시제
16	d	가정법
17	c	연결어
18	c	조동사
19	d	가정법
20	d	시제
21	b	관계사
22	a	준동사
23	a	가정법
24	b	조동사
25	a	준동사
26	b	시제

LISTENING

PART	번호	정답	유형
PART 1	27	b	특정세부사항
	28	c	특정세부사항
	29	a	추론
	30	d	특정세부사항
	31	b	특정세부사항
	32	c	특정세부사항
	33	a	추론
PART 2	34	b	Not/True
	35	b	특정세부사항
	36	a	특정세부사항
	37	d	특정세부사항
	38	c	특정세부사항
	39	b	추론
PART 3	40	b	특정세부사항
	41	d	특정세부사항
	42	a	특정세부사항
	43	c	특정세부사항
	44	a	특정세부사항
	45	c	추론
PART 4	46	a	주제/목적
	47	d	특정세부사항
	48	d	특정세부사항
	49	b	특정세부사항
	50	c	추론
	51	c	특정세부사항
	52	a	특정세부사항

READING & VOCABULARY

PART	번호	정답	유형
PART 1	53	c	특정세부사항
	54	d	추론
	55	b	추론
	56	c	특정세부사항
	57	b	특정세부사항
	58	a	어휘
	59	d	어휘
PART 2	60	c	주제/목적
	61	a	특정세부사항
	62	d	추론
	63	b	특정세부사항
	64	b	특정세부사항
	65	c	어휘
	66	a	어휘
PART 3	67	b	특정세부사항
	68	c	Not/True
	69	d	추론
	70	d	추론
	71	a	특정세부사항
	72	c	어휘
	73	c	어휘
PART 4	74	c	주제/목적
	75	b	추론
	76	a	특정세부사항
	77	d	특정세부사항
	78	d	특정세부사항
	79	a	어휘
	80	b	어휘

유형	맞힌 개수
시제	/ 6
가정법	/ 6
준동사	/ 6
조동사	/ 4
연결어	/ 2
관계사	/ 2
TOTAL	/ 26

유형	맞힌 개수
주제/목적	/ 1
특정세부사항	/ 19
Not/True	/ 1
추론	/ 5
TOTAL	/ 26

유형	맞힌 개수
주제/목적	/ 2
특정세부사항	/ 11
Not/True	/ 1
추론	/ 6
어휘	/ 8
TOTAL	/ 28

GRAMMAR

01 시제   과거완료진행   난이도 ●○○

Today, the art program at Redwood High School officially shut down. When the administrators announced that it suffered from inadequate funding, some of the teachers admitted that they _____ for supplies with their own money for the last few months.

(a) were shopping
(b) had been shopping
(c) shopped
(d) would have shopped

오늘, Redwood 고등학교의 미술 프로그램이 공식적으로 종료되었다. 관리자들이 불충분한 자금으로 그것이 어려움을 겪고 있다고 발표했을 때, 교사들 중 일부는 지난 몇 달 동안 자신들의 돈으로 준비물을 구매해오고 있던 중이었다고 시인했다.

🔑 지텔프 치트키

'when + 과거 동사'와 'for + 기간 표현'이 함께 오면 과거완료진행 시제가 정답이다.

> 💡 과거완료진행과 자주 함께 쓰이는 시간 표현
> • before / when / since + 과거 동사 + (for + 기간 표현) ~하기 전에 / ~했을 때 / ~ 이래로 (~ 동안)
> • (for + 기간 표현) + (up) until + 과거 동사 (~ 동안) ~했을 때까지

해설 | 과거완료진행 시제와 함께 쓰이는 시간 표현 'when + 과거 동사'(When ~ announced)와 'for + 기간 표현'(for the last few months)이 있고, 문맥상 대과거(교사들 중 일부가 자신들의 돈으로 준비물을 구매하기 시작한 시점)부터 과거(관리자들이 불충분한 자금으로 미술 프로그램이 어려움을 겪고 있다고 발표한 시점)까지 몇 달 동안 계속해서 교사들이 자신들의 돈으로 준비물을 구매해오고 있던 중이었다는 의미가 되어야 자연스럽다. 따라서 과거완료진행 시제 (b) had been shopping이 정답이다.

오답분석
(a) 과거진행 시제는 특정 과거 시점에 한창 진행 중이었던 일을 나타내므로, 대과거에 시작해서 특정 과거 시점까지 계속해서 진행되고 있었던 일을 표현할 수 없어 오답이다.

어휘 | announce v. 발표하다 inadequate adj. 불충분한 admit v. 시인하다, 인정하다 supply n. 준비물, 물자

02 가정법   가정법 과거완료   난이도 ●●○

Sandra is disappointed that she could only afford to buy her brother a small present for his birthday. If she had developed the habit of saving her allowance, she _____ him a video game console.

(a) had gotten
(b) would have gotten
(c) would get
(d) will have gotten

Sandra는 그녀가 남동생의 생일에 겨우 작은 선물만 줄 수밖에 없다는 것이 실망스럽다. 만약 그녀가 용돈을 저축하는 습관을 길렀다면, 그녀는 그에게 비디오 게임기를 사 줬을 것이다.

🔑 지텔프 치트키

'if + had p.p.'가 있으면 'would/could + have p.p.'가 정답이다.

해커스 지텔프 최신기출유형 실전문제집 7회 (Level 2)

해설 | If절에 'had p.p.' 형태의 had developed가 있으므로, 주절에는 이와 짝을 이루어 가정법 과거완료를 만드는 'would(조동사 과거형) + have p.p.'가 와야 한다. 따라서 (b) would have gotten이 정답이다.

어휘 | disappointed adj. 실망스러운, 낙담한 afford v. 주다, 형편이 되다 allowance n. 용돈

---

03 준동사   동명사를 목적어로 취하는 동사   난이도 ●●○

Scott tried to finalize the design plans, but he couldn't focus on his work. After one of his miscalculations had caused a weeklong delay in his firm's bridge-building project, he started to dread _____ his work to the senior architect.

(a) to present
(b) having presented
(c) to be presenting
(d) presenting

Scott은 디자인 도면을 마무리 지으려고 노력했지만, 그는 일에 집중할 수 없었다. 그의 계산 착오 중 하나가 그의 회사의 교량 건설 프로젝트에 일주일간의 지연을 초래한 뒤, 그는 선임 건축가에게 그의 작업물을 보여 주는 것을 두려워하기 시작했다.

○── 지텔프 치트키

dread는 동명사를 목적어로 취한다.

> 💡 **동명사를 목적어로 취하는 빈출 동사**
> dread 두려워하다 avoid 피하다 imagine 상상하다 mind 개의하다 keep 계속하다 consider 고려하다 prevent 방지하다
> enjoy 즐기다 recommend 권장하다 risk 위험을 무릅쓰다 involve 포함하다

해설 | 빈칸 앞 동사 dread는 동명사를 목적어로 취하므로, 동명사 (d) presenting이 정답이다.

> 오답분석
> (b) having presented도 동명사이기는 하지만, 완료동명사(having presented)로 쓰일 경우 '두려워하는' 시점보다 '보여 주는' 시점이 앞선다는 것을 나타내므로 문맥에 적합하지 않아 오답이다.

어휘 | finalize v. 마무리 짓다 miscalculation n. 계산 착오 dread v. 두려워하다 architect n. 건축가 present v. 보여 주다, 발표하다

---

04 조동사   조동사 should 생략   난이도 ●●○

The city of Harrisburg has been having trouble with some local tour agencies that abandon tourists at random places. For visitors wishing to see the city, authorities suggest that they _____ the services of a reputable personal guide instead.

(a) secured
(b) are securing
(c) will secure
(d) secure

Harrisburg시는 관광객들을 아무 장소에나 두고 떠나는 몇몇 지역 여행사들로 인해 애를 먹고 있다. 이 도시를 보고 싶어 하는 방문객들을 위해, 당국은 그들이 대신 평판이 좋은 개인 가이드의 서비스를 확보해야 한다고 제안한다.

○── 지텔프 치트키

suggest 다음에는 that절에 동사원형이 온다.

해설 | 주절에 제안을 나타내는 동사 suggest가 있으므로 that절에는 '(should +) 동사원형'이 와야 한다. 따라서 동사원형 (d) secure가 정답이다.

어휘 | abandon v. 두고 떠나다 authority n. 당국, 관계자 reputable adj. 평판이 좋은 secure v. 확보하다

---

05 연결어   접속부사   난이도 ●●●

The writing structure of James Joyce's novel *Ulysses* is experimental, dense, and so confusing that most readers give up before concluding all 730 pages. _____, it is considered a masterpiece and Joyce's magnum opus.

(a) Eventually
(b) Nevertheless
(c) Therefore
(d) Similarly

제임스 조이스의 소설 『율리시스』의 글 구조는 실험적이고, 난해하며, 너무 혼란스러워서 대부분의 독자들은 730쪽 전체를 다 읽기도 전에 포기한다. 그럼에도 불구하고, 그것은 걸작이자 조이스의 대표작으로 여겨진다.

━○ 지텔프 치트키

'그럼에도 불구하고'라는 의미의 양보를 나타낼 때는 Nevertheless를 쓴다.

> ☼ 양보를 나타내는 빈출 접속부사
> Nevertheless 그럼에도 불구하고 Nonetheless 그럼에도 불구하고

해설 | 문맥상 대부분의 독자들이 제임스 조이스의 소설 『율리시스』를 다 읽기도 전에 포기하지만, 그럼에도 불구하고 그것은 걸작이자 조이스의 대표작으로 여겨진다는 의미가 되어야 자연스럽다. 따라서 '그럼에도 불구하고'라는 의미의 양보를 나타내는 접속부사 (b) Nevertheless가 정답이다.

오답분석

(a) Eventually는 '마침내', (c) Therefore는 '그러므로', (d) Similarly는 '비슷하게'라는 의미로, 문맥에 적합하지 않아 오답이다.

어휘 | structure n. 구조 experimental adj. 실험적인 dense adj. 난해한, 밀집한 confusing adj. 혼란스러운 masterpiece n. 걸작
magnum opus phr. 대표작

---

06 준동사   to 부정사의 부사 역할   난이도 ●●●

Many of Courtney's friends wondered why she rarely bought new clothes or electronic devices. She told them that she avoided these items _____ a minimalist lifestyle.

(a) maintaining
(b) to have maintained
(c) to maintain
(d) having maintained

Courtney의 많은 친구들은 왜 그녀가 새 옷이나 전자기기를 거의 사지 않는지 궁금해했다. 그녀는 그들에게 최소주의적인 생활 방식을 유지하기 위해 그녀가 이러한 물품들을 피했다고 말했다.

━○ 지텔프 치트키

'~하기 위해'라고 말할 때는 to 부정사를 쓴다.

해커스 지텔프 최신기출유형 실전문제집 7회 (Level 2)

07 가정법 가정법 과거완료

난이도 ●●○

My friend Helen entrusted her two poodles to the staff at an expensive pet hotel when she went to her uncle's farm for a month. I _____ her pets if I had known she was going out of town!

(a) would have looked after
(b) would look after
(c) had looked after
(d) looked after

내 친구 Helen은 그녀가 한 달 동안 그녀 삼촌의 농장에 갔을 때 그녀의 푸들 두 마리를 값비싼 애견 호텔의 직원에게 맡겼다. 만약 내가 그녀가 마을을 떠난다는 것을 알았었다면 나는 그녀의 반려동물들을 돌봤을 것이다!

─○ 지텔프 치트키

'if + had p.p.'가 있으면 'would/could + have p.p.'가 정답이다.

해설 | if절에 'had p.p.' 형태의 had known이 있으므로, 주절에는 이와 짝을 이루어 가정법 과거완료를 만드는 'would(조동사 과거형) + have p.p.'가 와야 한다. 따라서 (a) would have looked after가 정답이다.

어휘 | entrust v. 맡기다, 위탁하다 staff n. 직원 look after phr. ~을 돌보다

08 시제 현재완료진행

난이도 ●●○

Manchester City fans have taken to the streets. They want to show their appreciation for the league-winning squad that inspired them all season. Therefore, the supporters _____ in front of the stadium since early this morning.

(a) are gathering
(b) gather
(c) have been gathering
(d) will be gathering

맨체스터 시티의 팬들이 거리로 나왔다. 그들은 시즌 내내 그들에게 활기를 주었던 리그 우승 선수단에 감사의 뜻을 표하고 싶어 한다. 따라서, 팬들이 오늘 아침 일찍부터 경기장 앞으로 결집해오고 있는 중이다.

─○ 지텔프 치트키

'since + 과거 시점'이 있으면 현재완료진행 시제가 정답이다.

 ☼ 현재완료진행과 자주 함께 쓰이는 시간 표현
  • (ever) since + 과거 시점 + (for + 기간 표현) ~한 이래로 (줄곧) (~ 동안)
  • lately / for + 기간 표현 + now 최근에 / 현재 ~ 동안

해설 | 현재완료진행 시제와 함께 쓰이는 시간 표현 'since + 과거 시점'(since early this morning)이 있고, 문맥상 과거 시점인 오늘 아침 일찍부터 현재까지 계속해서 팬들이 경기장 앞으로 결집해오고 있는 중이라는 의미가 되어야 자연스럽다. 따라서 현재완료진행 시제 (c) have been gathering이 정답이다.

TEST 1
TEST 2
TEST 3
TEST 4
TEST 5
TEST 6
TEST 7

(a) 현재진행 시제는 특정 현재 시점에 한창 진행 중인 일을 나타내므로, 과거에 시작해서 현재 시점까지 계속해서 진행되고 있는 일을 표현할 수 없어 오답이다.

어휘 | appreciation n. 감사, 감상 squad n. 선수단 inspire v. 활기를 주다, 영감을 주다 supporter n. 팬, 지지자 stadium n. 경기장 gather v. 결집하다, 모이다

---

09 준동사 동명사를 목적어로 취하는 동사 난이도 ●●○

Shawn downloaded an incredibly effective application called Privacy Guard onto his laptop. It prevents _____ so he can protect the personal information that is stored on his computer.

(a) **being hacked**
(b) to be hacked
(c) having been hacked
(d) to have been hacked

Shawn은 그의 노트북에 Privacy Guard라고 불리는 엄청나게 효과적인 애플리케이션을 다운로드 했다. 그것은 그가 그의 컴퓨터에 저장되어 있는 신상 정보를 보호할 수 있도록 해킹당하는 것을 방지한다.

◦─○ 지텔프 치트키

prevent는 동명사를 목적어로 취한다.

해설 | 빈칸 앞 동사 prevent는 동명사를 목적어로 취하므로, 동명사 (a) being hacked가 정답이다.

오답분석
(c) having been hacked도 동명사이기는 하지만, 완료동명사(having been hacked)로 쓰일 경우 '방지하는' 시점보다 '해킹당하는' 시점이 앞선다는 것을 나타내므로 문맥에 적합하지 않아 오답이다.

어휘 | incredibly adv. 엄청나게 effective adj. 효과적인 prevent v. 방지하다, 예방하다 store v. 저장하다 hack v. 해킹하다

---

10 조동사 조동사 must 난이도 ●●○

Kellyanne was excited about lunch. She'd ordered her favorite curry and couldn't wait to dig in. But when she opened the bag, it was just an order of rice and roasted chicken. The driver _____ have delivered the wrong order.

(a) can
(b) **must**
(c) would
(d) should

Kellyanne은 점심으로 인해 들떴다. 그녀는 가장 좋아하는 카레를 주문했고 먹고 싶어서 견딜 수가 없었다. 하지만 그녀가 봉지를 열었을 때, 그것은 단지 밥과 구운 닭고기 주문 음식뿐이었다. 배달 기사가 잘못된 주문 음식을 전달했음이 틀림없다.

◦─○ 지텔프 치트키

'~했음이 틀림없다'라고 말할 때는 must have p.p.를 쓴다.

해설 | 문맥상 Kellyanne이 점심을 먹기 위해 봉지를 열었을 때 그녀가 주문한 카레가 아닌 밥과 구운 닭고기가 있었던 것으로 보아 배달 기사가

잘못된 주문 음식을 전달했음이 틀림없다는 의미가 되어야 자연스럽다. 따라서 'have p.p.'와 함께 쓰일 때 '~했음이 틀림없다'라는 의미의 과거에 대한 강한 확신을 나타내는 조동사 (b) must가 정답이다.

> 오답분석
> (d) 조동사 should는 'have p.p.'와 함께 쓰일 때 '~했어야 했다'라는 의미의 과거에 대한 후회/유감을 나타내므로 문맥에 적합하지 않아 오답이다.

어휘 | dig in phr. 꾹 참고 기다리다 roast v. (고기 등을) 굽다

---

11 관계사 주격 관계대명사 which 난이도 ●●○

Today, Michelle woke up before dawn and spent the whole morning baking for the family reunion. Fortunately, her efforts were not in vain because her treats, _____, were applauded by everyone.

(a) where they included pies and cakes
(b) what included pies and cakes
(c) that included pies and cakes
(d) which included pies and cakes

오늘, Michelle은 동이 트기 전에 일어나서 가족 모임을 위한 음식을 굽는 데 오전 시간을 다 보냈다. 다행히, 그녀의 간식이, 파이와 케이크를 포함했는데, 모두의 극찬을 받았기 때문에 그녀의 노력은 헛되지 않았다.

> **지텔프 치트키**
> 사물 선행사가 관계절 안에서 주어 역할을 하고, 빈칸 앞에 콤마(,)가 있으면 주격 관계대명사 which가 정답이다.

해설 | 사물 선행사 her treats를 받으면서 콤마(,) 뒤에 올 수 있는 주격 관계대명사가 필요하므로, (d) which included pies and cakes가 정답이다.

> 오답분석
> (c) 관계대명사 that도 사물 선행사를 받을 수 있지만, 콤마 뒤에 올 수 없으므로 오답이다.

어휘 | dawn n. 동이 틀 무렵, 새벽 bake v. (음식을) 굽다 reunion n. 모임, 동창회 fortunately adv. 다행히, 운이 좋게도 effort n. 노력 in vain phr. 헛된 treat n. 간식, 대접 applaud v. 극찬하다, 갈채를 보내다

---

12 시제 미래진행 난이도 ●●○

Professor Rogers took the semester off from teaching to dedicate all his time to finishing a paper for the October issue of an academic journal. At his current pace, however, he _____ it when graduates receive their diplomas next spring.

(a) will still write
(b) will still be writing
(c) has still written
(d) is still writing

Rogers 교수는 10월 호 학술지에 실릴 논문을 끝내는 데 그의 모든 시간을 바치고자 교직에 한 학기 휴직계를 냈다. 그의 현재 속도로는, 그러나, 내년 봄에 졸업생들이 그들의 졸업장을 받을 때 그는 그것을 여전히 쓰고 있는 중일 것이다.

TEST 1

TEST 2

TEST 3

TEST 4

TEST 5

TEST 6

TEST 7

해커스 지텔프 최신기출유형 실전문제집 7회 (Level 2)

'for + 기간 표현' 없이 'when + 현재 동사'와 특정 미래 시점을 나타내는 표현만 있으면 미래진행 시제가 정답이다.

> 💡 미래진행과 자주 함께 쓰이는 시간 표현
> - when / if + 현재 동사 ~할 때 / 만약 ~한다면
> - next + 시간 표현 다음 ~에
> - until / by + 미래 시점 ~까지
> - starting + 미래 시점 / tomorrow ~부터 / 내일

해설 | 현재 동사로 미래의 의미를 나타내는 시간의 부사절 'when + 현재 동사'(when ~ receive)와 미래진행 시제와 함께 쓰이는 시간 표현 next spring이 있고, 문맥상 미래 시점인 내년 봄에 졸업생들이 그들의 졸업장을 받을 때 Rogers 교수는 여전히 논문을 쓰고 있는 중일 것이라는 의미가 되어야 자연스럽다. 따라서 미래진행 시제 (b) will still be writing이 정답이다.

오답분석

(a) 미래 시제는 미래에 대한 단순한 약속, 제안, 예측을 나타내므로, 특정 미래 시점에 한창 진행되고 있을 일을 표현할 수 없어 오답이다.

어휘 | semester n. 학기 dedicate v. (시간·노력을) 바치다, 전념하다 pace n. 속도 receive v. 받다 diploma n. 졸업장

---

13 가정법 가정법 과거완료   난이도 ●●○

After much deliberation, I decided to stick with my old cell phone even though all my coworkers were raving about the latest model released by Strata. Had it featured a cleaner interface, I _____ the device without hesitation.

(a) would have purchased
(b) will have purchased
(c) would purchase
(d) have purchased

많은 고민 끝에, 비록 나의 모든 동료들이 Strata 사에 의해 출시된 최신 모델에 대해 극찬하고 있음에도 불구하고 나는 내 오래된 휴대 전화를 계속 사용하기로 결심했다. 그것이 더 깔끔한 사용자 환경을 포함했었다면, 나는 망설임 없이 그 기기를 구입했을 것이다.

Had p.p.가 있으면 'would/could + have p.p.'가 정답이다.

해설 | if가 생략되어 도치된 절에 'had p.p.' 형태의 Had ~ featured가 있으므로, 주절에는 이와 짝을 이루어 가정법 과거완료를 만드는 'would (조동사 과거형) + have p.p.'가 와야 한다. 따라서 (a) would have purchased가 정답이다. 참고로, 'Had it featured ~'는 'If it had featured ~'로 바꿔 쓸 수 있다.

어휘 | deliberation n. 고민, 심사숙고 stick with phr. ~을 계속 사용하다 rave v. 극찬하다, 열광하다 release v. 출시하다 feature v. (특별히) 포함하다, 특징으로 삼다 interface n. (소프트웨어의) 사용자 환경 device n. 기기, 장치 hesitation n. 망설임

---

14 준동사 to 부정사를 목적어로 취하는 동사   난이도 ●●○

Maria needed to cut back on her living expenses and figured that the best way to do it would be to stop eating out so often. As a result, she vowed _____ at home at least five days a week.

(a) cooking

Maria는 그녀의 생활비를 줄일 필요가 있었고 그것을 하는 가장 좋은 방법은 너무 자주 외식하는 일을 그만두는 것이라고 생각했다. 그 결과, 그녀는 적어도 일주일에 5일은 집에서 요리하겠다고 맹세했다.

(b) to be cooking
(c) having cooked
(d) to cook

vow는 to 부정사를 목적어로 취한다.

해설 | 빈칸 앞 동사 vow는 to 부정사를 목적어로 취하므로, to 부정사 (d) to cook이 정답이다.

어휘 | cut back on phr. ~을 줄이다 figure v. 생각하다 vow v. 맹세하다

---

15 시제   현재진행

난이도 ●○○

Romance novels have been the most popular genre in the book market for a decade, and the demand for such stories has been increasing. This explains why publishers _____ to put out books about love these days.

(a) are scrambling
(b) scrambled
(c) had scrambled
(d) will have scrambled

로맨스 소설은 10년 동안 도서 시장에서 가장 인기 있는 장르였고, 그러한 이야기에 대한 수요가 증가해오는 중이다. 이것은 왜 출판사들이 요즘 사랑에 관한 책들을 내놓기 위해 <u>앞다투고 있는 중인지</u>를 설명한다.

these days가 있으면 현재진행 시제가 정답이다.

> ☀ **현재진행과 자주 함께 쓰이는 시간 표현**
> • right now / now / currently / at the moment 바로 지금 / 지금 / 현재 / 바로 지금
> • these days / nowadays 요즘

해설 | 현재진행 시제와 함께 쓰이는 시간 표현 these days가 있고, 문맥상 말하고 있는 시점인 요즘에 로맨스 소설의 인기와 수요의 증가가 왜 출판사들이 사랑에 관한 책들을 내놓기 위해 앞다투고 있는 중인지를 설명한다는 의미가 되어야 자연스럽다. 따라서 현재진행 시제 (a) are scrambling이 정답이다.

어휘 | demand n. 수요 publisher n. 출판사 put out phr. 내놓다, 출판하다 scramble v. 앞다투다, 서로 밀치다

---

16 가정법   가정법 과거

난이도 ●●○

Paul's final exam consisted of one question that asked about the second law of thermodynamics, which he had overlooked when cramming the night before. If he were to take the test again, he _____ all of his study time on that principle.

(a) has concentrated
(b) would have concentrated

Paul의 기말고사는 열역학 제2 법칙에 관해 묻는 질문 한 개로 구성되어 있었는데, 그것은 그가 전날 밤에 벼락치기 공부를 할 때 간과했었던 것이었다. 만약 그가 시험을 다시 치른다면, 그는 그의 모든 공부 시간을 그 <u>원칙에 집중시킬 것이다.</u>

(c) concentrated
(d) would concentrate

지텔프 치트키

'if + were to + 동사원형'이 있으면 'would/could + 동사원형'이 정답이다.

해설 | If절에 과거 동사(were to take)가 있으므로, 주절에는 이와 짝을 이루어 가정법 과거를 만드는 'would(조동사 과거형) + 동사원형'이 와야 한다. 따라서 (d) would concentrate가 정답이다.

어휘 | consist of phr. ~으로 구성되다 thermodynamics n. 열역학 overlook v. 간과하다 cram v. 벼락치기 공부를 하다 principle n. 원칙
concentrate n. 집중시키다

---

17 연결어 전치사   난이도 ●●○

Exercise doesn't need to be done in a large time block to be beneficial to one's health. _____ working through your exercise routines all at once, you can break them up into multiple shorter sessions.

(a) In case of
(b) Despite
(c) Rather than
(d) Because of

개인의 건강에 도움이 되기 위해 운동이 꼭 큰 시간 단위로 되어야 할 필요는 없습니다. 당신의 운동 과정을 모두 한 번에 수행하기보다는, 당신은 그것들을 여러 개의 더 짧은 시간들로 쪼갤 수 있습니다.

지텔프 치트키

'~보다는'이라는 의미의 비교를 나타낼 때는 rather than을 쓴다.

> 💡 비교를 나타내는 빈출 전치사
> rather than ~보다는 other than ~과 다른

해설 | 빈칸 뒤에 working through your exercise routines라는 명사구가 있으므로 빈칸은 전치사 자리이다. 운동이 꼭 큰 시간 단위로 되어야 할 필요는 없다고 했으므로, 문맥상 운동 과정을 모두 한 번에 수행하기보다는 그것들을 여러 개의 더 짧은 시간들로 쪼갤 수 있다는 의미가 되어야 자연스럽다. 따라서 '~보다는'이라는 의미의 비교를 나타내는 전치사 (c) Rather than이 정답이다.

오답분석
(a) In case of는 '~의 경우', (b) Despite는 '~에도 불구하고', (d) Because of는 '~ 때문에'라는 의미로, 문맥에 적합하지 않아 오답이다.

어휘 | block n. 단위 beneficial adj. 도움이 되는, 이로운 routine n. 과정, 정해진 방식 break up phr. ~을 쪼개다, 나누다
session n. (특정한 활동을 위한) 시간

---

18 조동사 조동사 should 생략   난이도 ●●○

Due to rising energy costs, Thimble Creek Manufacturing is enacting new policies at its factories to curb electricity consumption. For example, it ordered that machines _____ when not in use.

상승하는 에너지 비용으로 인해, Thimble Creek 제조사는 전력 소비를 억제하고자 그것의 공장들에서 새로운 정책들을 시행하고 있다. 예를 들어, 그것은 기계가 사용되지 않을 때 <u>전기 공급이 끊겨야 한다</u>고 지시했다.

(a) are disconnected
(b) have been disconnecting
(c) be disconnected
(d) will be disconnected

🔑 지텔프 치트키

order 다음에는 that절에 동사원형이 온다.

해설 | 주절에 명령을 나타내는 동사 order가 있으므로 that절에는 '(should +) 동사원형'이 와야 한다. 따라서 동사원형 (c) be disconnected 가 정답이다.

어휘 | enact v. 시행하다 policy n. 정책 curb v. 억제하다 consumption n. 소비 disconnect v. (전기의) 공급을 끊다

---

19 가정법   혼합가정법   난이도 ●●●

I find it frustrating that our social media marketing team continues to release dull content that is full of grammatical errors. If we have hired a copy editor with more experience, we _____ this issue now.

(a) will not face
(b) would not have faced
(c) had not faced
(d) would not be facing

나는 우리 소셜 미디어 마케팅팀이 문법적 오류들로 가득 찬 따분한 콘텐츠를 계속해서 발표하는 것을 실망스럽게 여긴다. 만약 우리가 더 많은 경험을 가진 교열 편집자를 고용했었다면, 우리는 지금 이 문제에 <u>직면하고 있지 않을 것이다.</u>

🔑 지텔프 치트키

'if + had p.p.'와 현재 시간 표현이 있고, 과거 상황이 현재까지 영향을 미치면 'would/could + 동사원형'이 정답이다.

💡 혼합가정법
If + 주어 + had p.p., 주어 + would/could(조동사 과거형) + 동사원형 + 현재 시간 표현

해설 | If절에 'had p.p.' 형태의 had hired가 있으므로 보통의 경우라면 주절에는 이와 짝을 이루어 가정법 과거완료를 만드는 'would(조동사 과거형) + have p.p.'가 와야 한다. 그러나 주절에 현재 시간 표현 now가 있으므로, 과거 시점에 있었던 일이 현재까지 영향을 미치는 상황에서 현재 상황을 반대로 가정하고 있음을 알 수 있다. 따라서 주절에는 가정법 과거를 만드는 'would(조동사 과거형) + 동사원형'이 와야 하므로 (d) would not be facing이 정답이다. 참고로, 지텔프에는 간혹 혼합가정법이 출제되기도 하는데, 이 경우 보통 주절에 now와 같은 현재 시간 표현이 포함되어 있다.

어휘 | frustrating adj. 실망스러운, 좌절감을 주는 dull adj. 따분한, 재미없는 grammatical adj. 문법적인 copy editor phr. 교열 편집자 face v. 직면하다, 맞닥뜨리다

---

20 시제   과거진행   난이도 ●●○

Marcus, a volunteer firefighter, was the first to respond to the blaze at the Walker Building downtown. When the emergency report appeared on the news, he _____ to the building to make sure that people there had evacuated safely.

자원봉사 소방관인 Marcus는 시내에 있는 Walker 빌딩의 화재에 대응한 최초의 인물이었다. 뉴스에 긴급 보도가 나왔을 때, 그는 그곳에 있는 사람들이 안전하게 대피했다는 것을 확실히 하기 위해 건물로 <u>이미 향하고 있는 중이었다.</u>

(a) has already headed
(b) would already head
(c) already headed
(d) was already heading

TEST 1 TEST 2 **TEST 3** TEST 4 TEST 5 TEST 6 TEST 7

지텔프 치트키

'for + 기간 표현' 없이 'when + 과거 동사'만 있으면 과거진행 시제가 정답이다.

> 💡 **과거진행과 자주 함께 쓰이는 시간 표현**
> • when / while + 과거 동사 ~했을 때 / ~하던 도중에
> • last + 시간 표현 / yesterday 지난 ~에 / 어제

해설 | 과거진행 시제와 함께 쓰이는 시간 표현 'when + 과거 동사'(When ~ appeared)가 있고, 문맥상 뉴스에 Walker 빌딩의 화재에 관한 긴급 보도가 나왔을 때 Marcus는 건물로 이미 향하고 있는 중이었다는 의미가 되어야 자연스럽다. 따라서 과거진행 시제 (d) was already heading이 정답이다.

오답분석

(c) 특정 과거 시점에 한창 진행 중이었던 행동을 표현하기에는 과거 시제보다 과거진행 시제가 더 적절하므로, 과거 시제는 오답이다.

어휘 | volunteer n. 자원봉사 blaze n. 화재 downtown adj. 시내에 있는 appear v. 나오다, 나타나다 evacuate v. 대피하다 head v. 향하다

| **21** | **관계사** | 목적격 관계대명사 that | 난이도 ●○○ |

Emmett is confident about getting the programming job since he passed the skills evaluation test and progressed through three stages of interviews with different employees of Smart Software, including the CEO. The offer _____ may arrive this week.

(a) whom he has been looking forward to receiving
(b) that he has been looking forward to receiving
(c) what he has been looking forward to receiving
(d) when he has been looking forward to receiving it

Emmett는 기술 평가 시험을 통과했고 최고 경영자를 포함한 Smart Software 사의 다양한 직원들과 세 단계의 면접들을 진행했기 때문에 프로그래밍 일자리를 얻는 데 자신 있다. 그가 받기를 고대해온 제안은 이번 주에 도착할지도 모른다.

지텔프 치트키

사물 선행사가 관계절 안에서 목적어 역할을 하면 목적격 관계대명사 that이 정답이다.

해설 | 사물 선행사 The offer를 받으면서 보기의 관계절 내에서 동사 receiving의 목적어가 될 수 있는 목적격 관계대명사가 필요하므로, (b) that he has been looking forward to receiving이 정답이다.

어휘 | confident adj. 자신 있는, 확신하는 evaluation n. 평가 progress v. 진행하다, 진전하다 offer n. 제안 look forward to phr. ~을 고대하다

22 준동사   to 부정사의 관용적 표현   난이도 ●●○

Adela has been planning a summer trip to Hawaii for ages and finally flies out next weekend. However, when she checked the weather forecast, she saw that it was likely _____ for most of her time there.

(a) to rain
(b) to have rained
(c) raining
(d) having rained

Adela는 오랫동안 하와이로의 여름 여행을 계획해 왔고 마침내 다음 주말에 출국한다. 하지만, 그녀가 일기예보를 확인했을 때, 그녀는 그녀가 그곳에서 보내는 대부분의 시간 동안 비가 올 것 같다는 것을 알게 되었다.

○── 지텔프 치트키

'~할 것 같다'라고 말할 때는 'be likely + to 부정사'를 쓴다.

해설 | 빈칸 앞 형용사 likely는 'be likely + to 부정사'의 형태로 쓰여 '~할 것 같다'라는 관용적 의미를 나타낸다. 따라서 to 부정사 (a) to rain이 정답이다.

어휘 | for ages phr. 오랫동안   fly out phr. 출국하다, 비행기를 타고 떠나다   weather forecast phr. 일기예보

---

23 가정법   가정법 과거   난이도 ●●○

A lack of qualified teachers is a major factor affecting the quality of American schools. Indeed, few of those entering the workforce consider a career in education. If the nation's teachers were to receive higher compensation, the profession _____ more job seekers' attention.

(a) would grab
(b) has grabbed
(c) will grab
(d) would have grabbed

자격 있는 교사들의 부족은 미국 학교의 질에 영향을 미치는 주요 요인이다. 실제로, 노동 시장에 진입하는 사람들은 교육 분야의 직업을 거의 고려하지 않는다. 만약 그 나라의 교사들이 더 높은 보수를 받는다면, 그 직업은 더 많은 구직자들의 관심을 끌 것이다.

○── 지텔프 치트키

'if + were to + 동사원형'이 있으면 'would/could + 동사원형'이 정답이다.

해설 | If절에 과거 동사(were to receive)가 있으므로, 주절에는 이와 짝을 이루어 가정법 과거를 만드는 'would(조동사 과거형) + 동사원형'이 와야 한다. 따라서 (a) would grab이 정답이다.

어휘 | factor n. 요인   career n. 직업, 진로   compensation n. 보수, 보상   profession n. 직업   grab v. (관심을) 끌다

---

24 조동사   조동사 will   난이도 ●●●

Sonya, the manager at Super Shoe Depot, notified the staff that she will hold a training session on the store's new inventory system tomorrow at 10 a.m. She clarified that the

Super Shoe Depot 사의 관리자인 Sonya는 직원들에게 내일 오전 10시에 그녀가 매장의 새로운 재고 시스템에 대한 연수회를 열 것이라고 공지했다. 그녀는 이

meeting is not optional, so all employees _____ be in attendance.

(a) can
(b) will
(c) may
(d) might

모임은 선택적인 것이 아니므로, 모든 직원이 참석할 것임을 분명히 말했다.

📌 지텔프 치트키

'~할 것이다'라고 말할 때는 will을 쓴다.

해설 ┃ 문맥상 매장의 새로운 재고 시스템에 대한 연수회는 선택적인 것이 아니므로 Sonya는 모든 직원이 모임에 참석할 것임을 분명히 말했다는 의미가 되어야 자연스러우므로, '~할 것이다'를 뜻하면서 예정을 나타내는 조동사 (b) will이 정답이다.

어휘 ┃ notify v. 공지하다, 알리다   inventory n. 재고(품)   clarify v. 분명히 말하다   optional adj. 선택적인   be in attendance phr. 참석하다

---

25 준동사   동명사를 목적어로 취하는 동사   난이도 ●●○

Fran requested leave for Thursday to spend time with her old friend Addison who came from Louisiana. Because they both enjoy _____ modern art, they spent the entire day at the opening of the World Abstract Art Exhibition.

(a) viewing
(b) to view
(c) will view
(d) to have viewed

Fran은 루이지애나주에서 온 그녀의 오랜 친구 Addison과 시간을 보내기 위해 목요일에 휴가를 요청했다. 그들은 둘 다 현대 미술을 관람하는 것을 즐기기 때문에, 그들은 세계 추상 미술 전시회의 개막식에서 온종일 시간을 보냈다.

📌 지텔프 치트키

enjoy는 동명사를 목적어로 취한다.

해설 ┃ 빈칸 앞 동사 enjoy는 동명사를 목적어로 취하므로, 동명사 (a) viewing이 정답이다.

어휘 ┃ modern art phr. 현대 미술   opening n. 개막식   abstract adj. 추상적인   exhibition n. 전시회   view v. 관람하다, 보다

---

26 시제   미래완료진행   난이도 ●●○

The two presidential candidates strongly disagree about whether the country ought to accept more immigrants. By the end of the forthcoming election, they _____ this controversial issue publicly for over three months.

(a) have been debating
(b) will have been debating
(c) are debating
(d) will be debating

두 대통령 후보는 그 나라가 더 많은 이민자들을 받아들여야 하는지에 대해 강하게 의견이 엇갈린다. 다가오는 선거가 끝날 무렵이면, 그들은 3개월이 넘는 기간 동안 이 논란 많은 문제를 공개적으로 토론해오고 있는 중일 것이다.

'by + 미래 시점'과 'for + 기간 표현'이 함께 오면 미래완료진행 시제가 정답이다.

> 🔆 미래완료진행과 자주 함께 쓰이는 시간 표현
> • by the time / when / if + 현재 동사 + (for + 기간 표현) ~할 무렵이면 / ~할 때 / 만약 ~한다면 (~ 동안)
> • by / in + 미래 시점 + (for + 기간 표현) ~ 즈음에는 / ~에 (~ 동안)

해설 | 미래완료진행 시제와 함께 쓰이는 표현 'by + 미래 시점'(By the end of the forthcoming election)과 'for + 기간 표현'(for over three months)이 있고, 문맥상 미래 시점인 다가오는 선거가 끝날 무렵이면 두 대통령 후보가 3개월이 넘는 기간 동안 계속해서 논란 많은 문제를 공개적으로 토론해오고 있는 중일 것이라는 의미가 되어야 자연스럽다. 따라서 미래완료진행 시제 (b) will have been debating 이 정답이다.

오답분석

(d) 미래진행 시제는 특정 미래 시점에 진행 중일 일을 나타내므로, 과거 또는 현재에 시작해서 특정 미래 시점까지 계속해서 진행되고 있을 일을 표현할 수 없어 오답이다.

어휘 | presidential candidate phr. 대통령 후보 accept v. 받아들이다 immigrant n. 이민자 forthcoming adj. 다가오는 election n. 선거 controversial adj. 논란이 많은 publicly adv. 공개적으로 debate v. 토론하다, 논의하다

LISTENING

PART 1 [27~33]　일상 대화　바비큐 파티에 관한 두 이웃의 대화

안부 인사	F: Hi, Sam. ²⁷We missed you at the barbecue yesterday! M: Hello, Jane. What barbecue? I hadn't heard anything about it.
주제 제시: 바비큐 파티	F: During the summer our homeowners association holds barbecues at a different person's house. Yesterday was the first one this summer. Didn't you get the neighborhood newsletter? M: No. When I moved in earlier this month, I signed up for it, but I think it had already been sent out. I haven't received my first copy yet. F: Too bad. You and your family could have met some of our other neighbors. M: You're right about that. It sounds like ²⁸it would've been a perfect time to get to know some of the other people around here. Will there be another one?
바비큐 파티 일정	F: Yes. They're held monthly from June to August. I usually try to schedule them on the first Saturday of each month, but ²⁹sometimes they're on other days if there is something else planned at the center. All are listed on the calendar in the newsletter.
참가 비용	M: Great. I'll look for it when I get my first one. ³⁰Do we have to pay a fee to attend? F: No, not at all. ³⁰It's covered by the monthly homeowners' dues. The cost is added to the association's annual budget.
바비큐 파티 음식	M: I see. How exactly does it work? Does everyone bring their own food to cook, or is it provided? F: Well, hamburgers, hot dogs, and chicken are provided along with potato salad, baked beans, and other side dishes. However, attendees usually bring some kind of snack or dessert to share with everyone else. M: Wow! I bet you get to try a lot of interesting new foods that way. F: Yes. As you know, the neighborhood is very diverse. Some people prepare their favorite desserts from their home countries, and others bring back snacks from trips. You never know what you'll get, so it's kind of a food adventure.

여: 안녕하세요, Sam. ²⁷어제 바비큐 파티에서 저희는 당신을 보고 싶었어요!
남: 안녕하세요, Jane. 무슨 바비큐 파티요? 저는 그것에 관해 아무것도 듣지 못했어요.

여: 여름 동안 저희 입주자 협회는 각각 다른 사람의 집에서 바비큐 파티를 열어요. 어제가 올해 여름의 첫 번째 파티였어요. 동네 소식지를 받지 않으셨나요?
남: 아니요. 제가 이번 달 초에 이사 왔을 때, 그것을 신청했는데, 이미 발송됐던 것 같아요. 저는 아직 첫 번째 것을 받지 못했어요.
여: 아쉽네요. 당신과 당신 가족은 저희의 다른 이웃들 중 몇 명을 만날 수 있었을 거예요.
남: 그건 당신 말이 맞아요. ²⁸그것은 이곳 주변의 다른 사람들 몇 명과 친해질 수 있는 완벽한 시간이었을 것 같네요. 또 다른 파티가 있을까요?

여: 네. 그것들은 6월부터 8월까지 매월 열려요. 저는 보통 매월 첫 번째 토요일에 그것들의 일정을 잡으려고 하지만, ²⁹센터에 계획되어 있는 다른 무언가가 있는 경우에는 가끔 다른 날에 진행돼요. 모든 것이 소식지에 있는 달력에 기재되어 있어요.

남: 잘됐네요. 첫 번째 것을 받으면 그것을 찾아볼게요. ³⁰참석하기 위해 비용을 지불해야 하나요?
여: 아뇨, 전혀요. ³⁰그것은 입주자들의 월 회비로 충당돼요. 그 경비는 협회의 연간 예산에 추가되어 있어요.

남: 그렇군요. 정확히 어떻게 진행되는 건가요? 모든 사람들이 요리할 음식을 가지고 오나요, 아니면 제공되나요?
여: 음, 햄버거, 핫도그, 그리고 치킨은 감자샐러드, 구운 콩, 그리고 다른 반찬들과 함께 제공돼요. 하지만, 참석자들은 보통 다른 사람들과 나눠 먹기 위한 몇몇 종류의 간식이나 디저트를 가지고 와요.
남: 와! 그런 식으로 틀림없이 많은 흥미로운 새로운 음식들을 먹어볼 수 있겠네요.
여: 네. 당신도 아시다시피, 이웃들은 아주 다양해요. 어떤 사람들은 그들의 고국에서 그들이 가장 좋아하는 디저트를 준비해오기도 하고, 다른 사람들은 여행에서 간식을 가지고 오기도 해요. 당신이 무엇을 받을지 당신도 결코 알지 못하기 때문에, 그것은 일종의 음식 모험이에요.

	M: I can imagine. Did you prepare anything special yesterday? F: I didn't have time to make anything myself, so I stopped by the Lebanese bakery and ³¹picked up a dessert called *kanafeh*. I haven't had it since I was a child in Lebanon. Luckily, everyone at the barbecue loved it as much as I do. M: I'm sure they did! Are there any scheduled activities besides eating?	남: 상상이 되네요. 당신은 어제 특별한 무언가를 준비하셨나요? 여: 저는 무엇을 직접 만들 시간이 없어서, 레바논 빵집에 들러 ³¹크나페라는 이름의 디저트를 샀어요. 저는 레바논에서의 어린 시절 이후로 그것을 먹어본 적이 없어요. 다행히도, 바비큐 파티에 있던 모든 사람들이 저만큼 그것을 좋아했어요. 남: 분명히 그랬을 거예요! 식사 외에 예정된 활동들이 있나요?
바비큐 파티 활동	F: Of course! ³²The host prepares plenty of things to do, such as card games, board games, puzzles, or even a treasure hunt! M: I'm not good at any of those. I guess I could just watch. F: Ha-ha . . . Actually, none of us are really good at games. ³²It's just a way to amuse ourselves. M: That's good. I'm disappointed that I missed it now. It sounds like a lot of fun. F: It was. But there's always next month. M: That's true. I definitely want to make it to the next one.	여: 물론이죠! ³²주최자는 카드게임, 보드게임, 퍼즐, 또는 심지어 보물찾기와 같이 많은 할 거리를 준비해요! 남: 저는 그중 어떤 것도 잘하지 못해요. 저는 그냥 구경만 할 수 있겠네요. 여: 하하... 사실, 우리 중 게임을 정말 잘하는 사람은 아무도 없어요. ³²그것은 그저 우리 자신을 즐겁게 하는 방법이에요. 남: 다행이네요. 그것을 놓쳤다니 이제 속상하네요. 정말 재미있었을 것 같아요. 여: 그럼요. 하지만 항상 다음 달은 있으니까요. 남: 맞아요. 다음 파티에는 꼭 참석하고 싶어요.
여자가 다음에 할 일	F: Great. ³³I'm in charge of making the association calendar of events and I'm working on it now, so I'll let you know when it is. M: Thanks, Jane. That would be great. F: Don't mention it, Sam. It's the least I can do for our newest neighbor. M: I think I'm going to enjoy living in this community.	여: 좋아요. ³³제가 협회의 행사 일정표 제작을 담당하고 있고 지금 작업 중이니, 그것이 언제일지 알려드릴게요. 남: 고마워요, Jane. 그래 주시면 정말 좋을 것 같아요. 여: 별말씀을요, Sam. 이것은 새로 온 이웃을 위해 제가 할 수 있는 최소한의 일인걸요. 남: 저는 이 동네에 사는 것이 즐거울 것 같아요.

어휘 | homeowner[hóumòunər] 입주자　association[əsòusiéiʃən] 협회　newsletter[nú:zlètər] 소식지　monthly[mʌ́nθli] 매월, 다달이
fee[fi:] 비용　cover[kʌ́vər] 충당하다　due[du:] 회비　annual[ǽnjuəl] 연간의　budget[bʌ́dʒit] 예산　attendee[ətèndí:] 참석자
diverse[daivə́:rs] 다양한　adventure[ədvéntʃər] 모험, 체험　besides[bisáidz] ~ 외에　amuse[əmjú:z] 즐겁게 하다
disappointed[dìsəpɔ́intid] 속상한　be in charge of ~을 담당하다　community[kəmjú:nəti] 동네, 지역 사회

27　특정세부사항　What　난이도 ●○○

What did Jane do the day before the conversation?	Jane은 대화 전날 무엇을 했는가?
(a) She met Sam at a neighborhood meeting. **(b) She attended a local event for residents.** (c) She hosted a backyard party with her colleagues. (d) She joined a local association as an executive.	(a) 반상회에서 Sam을 만났다. **(b) 주민들을 위한 동네 행사에 참석했다.** (c) 그녀의 동료들과 함께 뒤뜰 파티를 주최했다. (d) 지역 협회에 운영진으로 가입했다.

━○ 지텔프 치트키

질문의 키워드 the day before가 yesterday로 paraphrasing되어 언급된 주변 내용을 주의 깊게 듣는다.

해설 | 여자가 'We missed you at the barbecue yesterday!'라며 어제 바비큐 파티에서 남자를 보고 싶었다고 했다. 따라서 (b)가 정답이다.

Paraphrasing

the barbecue 바비큐 파티 → a local event 동네 행사

어휘 | neighborhood meeting 반상회 executive [igzékjətiv] 운영진, 경영진

---

28 특정세부사항   What   난이도 ●●○

What does Sam think he could have done at the barbecue?	Sam은 그가 바비큐 파티에서 무엇을 할 수 있었을 것이라고 생각하는가?
(a) introduce himself to the organization	(a) 협회에 자신을 소개한다
(b) try new cooking techniques	(b) 새로운 요리 기술들을 시도한다
(c) become acquainted with new neighbors	**(c) 새로운 이웃들을 알게 된다**
(d) participate in some group activities	(d) 몇몇 단체 활동들에 참여한다

지텔프 치트키

질문의 키워드 could have done at the barbecue와 관련된 주변 내용을 주의 깊게 듣는다.

해설 | 남자가 'it would've been a perfect time to get to know ~ other people around here'라며 바비큐 파티가 이곳 주변의 다른 사람들 몇 명과 친해질 수 있는 완벽한 시간이었을 것이라고 했다. 따라서 (c)가 정답이다.

Paraphrasing

get to know ~ other people around here 이곳 주변의 사람들과 친해지다 → become acquainted with ~ neighbors 이웃들을 알게 되다

어휘 | acquaint [əkwéint] 알게 하다, 숙지하다

---

29 추론   특정사실   난이도 ●●○

Based on the conversation, how would Sam most likely learn about upcoming activities?	대화에 따르면, Sam은 앞으로 있을 활동들에 대해 어떻게 알게 될 것 같은가?
(a) by reading a neighborhood publication	**(a) 동네 간행물을 읽음으로써**
(b) by referring to an online calendar	(b) 온라인 달력을 참고함으로써
(c) by receiving a copy of an invitation	(c) 초대장 한 부를 받음으로써
(d) by signing up for a community website	(d) 지역 사회 웹 사이트에 가입함으로써

지텔프 치트키

질문의 키워드 upcoming activities가 something else planned로 paraphrasing되어 언급된 주변 내용을 주의 깊게 듣는다.

해설 | 여자가 'sometimes they're on other days if there is something else planned at the center'라며 센터에 계획되어 있는 다른 무언가가 있는 경우에는 바비큐 파티가 가끔 (첫 번째 토요일이 아닌) 다른 날에 진행된다고 한 뒤, 'All are listed on the calendar in the newsletter.'라며 모든 것이 소식지에 있는 달력에 기재되어 있다고 한 것을 통해, Sam은 동네 간행물을 읽음으로써 동네에서 앞으로 있을 활동들에 대해 알게 될 것임을 추론할 수 있다. 따라서 (a)가 정답이다.

어휘 | upcoming [ʌ́pkʌ̀miŋ] 앞으로 있을, 다가오는 publication [pʌ̀blikéiʃən] 간행물 refer [rifə́:r] 참고하다

30 특정세부사항 Why

Why is there no charge for the neighborhood barbecues?

(a) The fee is covered by a government grant.
(b) The gatherings are hosted in a public space.
(c) The gatherings are held by a charitable association.
(d) The fee is included in residents' payments.

동네 바비큐 파티에 왜 비용을 내지 않는가?

(a) 그 경비는 정부 보조금으로 충당된다.
(b) 그 모임들은 공공장소에서 개최된다.
(c) 그 모임들은 자선 단체에 의해 진행된다.
(d) 그 경비는 거주자들의 납부금에 포함되어 있다.

지텔프 치트키

질문의 키워드 charge가 fee로 paraphrasing되어 언급된 주변 내용을 주의 깊게 듣는다.

해설 | 남자가 'Do we have to pay a fee to attend?'라며 바비큐 파티에 참석하기 위해 비용을 지불해야 하는지를 묻자, 여자가 'It's covered by the monthly homeowners' dues.'라며 그 비용은 입주자들의 월 회비로 충당된다고 했다. 따라서 (d)가 정답이다.

Paraphrasing
homeowners' dues 입주자들의 회비 → residents' payments 거주자들의 납부금

어휘 | grant[grænt] 보조금 charitable[tʃǽrətəbəl] 자선의, 너그러운 payment[péimənt] 납부금, 지불금

---

31 특정세부사항 When

When was the last time Jane ate the dessert that she brought to the party?

(a) when she visited a Lebanese bakery
(b) when she lived in another country
(c) when she went to the last neighborhood event
(d) when she was on vacation abroad

Jane이 파티에 가지고 간 디저트를 마지막으로 먹은 것은 언제였는가?

(a) 레바논 빵집에 방문했을 때
(b) 다른 나라에 살았을 때
(c) 지난 동네 행사에 갔을 때
(d) 해외로 휴가를 갔을 때

지텔프 치트키

질문의 키워드 dessert ~ brought가 picked up ~ dessert로 paraphrasing되어 언급된 주변 내용을 주의 깊게 듣는다.

해설 | 여자가 'picked up a dessert called *kanafeh*'라며 바비큐 파티를 위해 크나페라는 이름의 디저트를 샀다고 한 뒤, 'I haven't had it since I was a child in Lebanon.'이라며 그녀가 레바논에서의 어린 시절 이후로 그것을 먹어본 적이 없다고 했다. 따라서 (b)가 정답이다.

Paraphrasing
Lebanon 레바논 → another country 다른 나라

오답분석
(a) 여자가 레바논 빵집에 들러 크나페라는 이름의 디저트를 샀다고는 언급했지만, 그 빵집에 방문했을 때 마지막으로 크나페를 먹었다고 한 것은 아니므로 오답이다.

---

32 특정세부사항 How

How do the barbecue attendees entertain themselves?

(a) by making special local dishes for each other

바비큐 파티 참가자들은 어떻게 그들 자신을 즐겁게 하는가?

(a) 서로를 위한 특별한 향토 음식을 만듦으로써

(b) by performing card tricks for the children
(c) by playing various kinds of games together
(d) by competing against one another in athletic events

(b) 아이들을 위해 카드 마술을 공연함으로써
(c) 함께 다양한 종류의 게임을 함으로써
(d) 체육 행사에서 서로 경쟁함으로써

◀─○ 지텔프 치트키

질문의 키워드 entertain이 amuse로 paraphrasing되어 언급된 주변 내용을 주의 깊게 듣는다.

해설 | 여자가 'The host prepares plenty of things to do, such as card games ~ or even a treasure hunt!'라며 주최자는 카드게임, 또는 심지어 보물찾기와 같이 많은 할 거리를 준비한다고 한 뒤, 'It's ~ a way to amuse ourselves.'라며 그것은 그들 자신을 즐겁게 하는 방법이라고 했다. 따라서 (c)가 정답이다.

어휘 | perform[pərfɔ́:rm] 공연하다, 수행하다 trick[trik] 마술 athletic[æθlétik] 체육의

TEST 1
TEST 2
TEST 3
TEST 4
TEST 5
TEST 6
TEST 7

---

33 추론   다음에 할 일   난이도 ●●●

What will Jane most likely do after the conversation?

(a) continue working on an agenda
(b) select a host for the next event
(c) send out invitations to a party
(d) contact a neighbor living next door

Jane은 대화 이후에 무엇을 할 것 같은가?

(a) 일정을 작업하는 것을 계속한다
(b) 다음 행사의 주최자를 선정한다
(c) 파티 초대장을 보낸다
(d) 옆집에 사는 이웃에게 연락한다

◀─○ 지텔프 치트키

다음에 할 일을 언급하는 후반을 주의 깊게 듣는다.

해설 | 여자가 'I'm in charge of making the association calendar of events and I'm working on it now, so I'll let you know when it is.'라며 그녀가 협회의 행사 일정표 제작을 담당하고 있고 지금 작업 중이므로, 남자에게 다음 바비큐 파티가 언제일지 알려주겠다고 한 것을 통해, Jane은 대화 이후에도 일정을 작업하는 것을 계속할 것임을 추론할 수 있다. 따라서 (a)가 정답이다.

어휘 | agenda[ədʒéndə] 일정, 안건 목록

PART 2[34~39] **발표 새로운 커뮤니티 센터 개관 홍보**

음성 바로 듣기

주제 제시: 센터 개관 홍보

Hello! I'm the general manager of the Ridge City Community Center and I'm excited to be here today to talk about our new facility. ³⁴⁽ᵃ⁾After two years of construction, ³⁴⁽ᵇ⁾the center will finally be open to the public starting this weekend. We hope it will be a positive place where everyone, ³⁴⁽ᶜ⁾regardless of age, feels welcome to come in and enjoy educational, recreational, social, and ecological activities.

For those of you who don't know, the community center ³⁴⁽ᵈ⁾is located next to Bellflower Park. This places

안녕하세요! 저는 Ridge City 커뮤니티 센터의 총괄 관리자이며 오늘 저희의 새로운 시설에 관해 이야기하기 위해 이곳에 오게 되어 기쁩니다. ³⁴⁽ᵃ⁾2년간의 공사 끝에, ³⁴⁽ᵇ⁾이번 주말부터 센터가 마침내 대중에게 개방될 예정입니다. 저희는 이곳이 누구나, ³⁴⁽ᶜ⁾나이에 상관없이, 자유롭게 방문하여 교육, 오락, 친목, 그리고 생태계 관련 활동들을 즐길 수 있는 긍정적인 장소이길 바랍니다.

잘 모르시는 분들을 위해, 커뮤니티 센터는 ³⁴⁽ᵈ⁾Bellflower 공원 옆에 위치해 있습니다. 이것은 저

us close to the elementary school and middle school and makes us an ideal hub for the neighborhood. The center will be open from 6 a.m. to 9 p.m. Monday through Saturday, and from 8 a.m. to 4 p.m. on Sundays.

The Ridge City Community Center has partnered with local schools to provide tutoring and academic support in our homework club. We are striving to create a welcoming environment with minimal distractions for children. [35]Skilled tutors will cover a range of topics, including mathematics, science, and language, which will allow students to receive mentoring and form new friendships.

In addition, a large number of recreational and non-academic classes will be offered to members of all ages. Taking a computer or cooking class is a great way to learn new skills. Or you may enroll in an art class if you want to try your hand at an unfamiliar hobby. Under a trained teacher, participants will be able to express their creativity through different types of crafts and projects. For example, [36]our pottery class will help keep their minds and bodies active, all while creating practical items.

The Ridge City Community Center will arrange social gatherings as well. Each morning, the main multi-purpose room will host Tea Time. This is a chance to come together and enjoy snacks along with warm beverages, such as coffee and tea. From trivia competitions to concerts, [37]different types of entertaining events will take place in this room at least once a month. When the multi-purpose room is not in use, it can be rented out for private events such as children's birthday parties or community meetings.

The center grounds will be the site of a public garden. Members will have access to garden plots where they can grow fresh organic food as well as colorful decorative plants. While gardeners are free to plant whatever they want, [38]the center politely encourages the growth of plants that are native to our geographic region and that will help attract beneficial butterflies and bees to the area. This is part of our commitment to making the community healthy and sustainable.

Use of the community garden and other facilities is included in the annual community center membership. Most of the classes are also available at no further cost, though there will be a supplementary fee for classes that require extra supplies, like cooking and art. We recommend that you register early as spots are limited.

희 센터를 초등학교 및 중학교와 가깝게 하고 이 동네의 이상적인 중심지로 만듭니다. 센터는 월요일부터 토요일까지는 오전 6시부터 오후 9시까지 문을 열 것이며, 일요일에는 오전 8시부터 오후 4시까지 문을 열 것입니다.

Ridge City 커뮤니티 센터는 저희의 공부 동아리에서 개인 교습과 학업 지원을 제공하기 위해 지역 학교들과 제휴했습니다. 저희는 아이들에게 방해 요소가 아주 적은 우호적인 환경을 만들기 위해 노력하고 있습니다. [35]숙련된 개인 교사들이 수학, 과학, 그리고 언어를 포함한 다양한 주제들을 다룰 것이며, 이는 학생들이 멘토링을 받고 새로운 우정을 형성할 수 있게 할 것입니다.

게다가, 모든 연령대의 회원들에게 다수의 오락 및 학문 외적인 수업이 제공될 것입니다. 컴퓨터 수업이나 요리 수업을 수강하는 것은 새로운 기술들을 배우는 좋은 방법입니다. 혹은 여러분이 생소한 취미를 시도해 보고 싶으시다면 미술 수업에 등록하실 수도 있습니다. 숙련된 강사 밑에서, 수강생들은 다양한 종류의 공예와 과제를 통해 그들의 창의성을 표현할 수 있을 것입니다. 예를 들어, [36]저희의 도자기 수업은 실용적인 물건들을 만들어 내는 동시에, 그들의 심신을 활발하게 유지하는 것을 도울 것입니다.

Ridge City 커뮤니티 센터는 친목 모임도 마련할 것입니다. 매일 아침에, 본관 다목적실에서 티타임을 열 것입니다. 이것은 모여서 커피와 차와 같은 따뜻한 음료와 함께 간식을 즐길 기회입니다. 일반 상식 대회부터 콘서트까지, [37]적어도 한 달에 한 번은 이 공간에서 다양한 종류의 오락 행사들이 진행될 것입니다. 다목적실이 사용되지 않을 때는, 어린이들의 생일 파티나 주민 모임과 같은 개인적인 행사를 위해 대여될 수 있습니다.

센터의 구내는 공공 텃밭의 부지가 될 것입니다. 회원들은 화려한 장식용 식물뿐만 아니라 신선한 유기농 식품을 기를 수 있는 텃밭의 땅을 이용하실 수 있을 것입니다. 정원을 가꾸는 분들이 원하는 것은 무엇이든 자유롭게 심으실 수 있긴 하지만, [38]센터는 우리의 지리학적 지역에 자생하고 이로운 나비들과 벌들을 이 지역에 끌어들이는 데 도움이 될 식물들의 재배를 정중히 권장해 드립니다. 이것은 지역 사회를 건강하고 지속 가능하게 만드는 것에 대한 저희 노력의 일환입니다.

공동체 텃밭과 기타 시설들의 이용은 커뮤니티 센터 연회비에 포함됩니다. 대부분의 수업들 또한 추가적인 비용 없이 이용하실 수 있지만, 요리나 미술과 같이 별도의 준비물을 필요로 하는 수업에는 추가 비용이 있을 것입니다. 자리가 한정되어 있으니 빨리 등록하시는 것을 추천해 드립니다.

끝인사

Thank you for your attention. I hope to see you at the Ridge City Community Center soon. Before you leave today, please take a brochure. [39]You can see pictures of the center, a full list of the amenities, and further details regarding membership fees and pricing for various activities. For any additional questions, please call the center's help desk during our operating hours.

경청해 주셔서 감사합니다. 조만간 Ridge City 커뮤니티 센터에서 여러분을 뵙기를 바랍니다. 오늘 가시기 전에, 안내 책자를 챙겨 가시기 바랍니다. [39]센터의 사진, 편의 시설의 전체 목록, 그리고 가입비와 다양한 활동들의 가격에 관한 자세한 정보를 확인하실 수 있습니다. 추가적인 문의 사항이 있으시면, 운영 시간 중에 센터의 안내 데스크에 전화 주시기 바랍니다.

어휘 | construction[kənstrʌ́kʃən] 공사 recreational[rèkriéiʃənəl] 오락의 ecological[ì:kəlá:dʒikəl] 생태계의 hub[hʌb] 중심지 partner[pá:rtnər] 제휴하다 minimal[mínəməl] 아주 적은 distraction[distrǽkʃən] 방해 요소 try one's hand at ~을 시도해 보다 craft[kræft] 공예 pottery[pá:təri] 도자기 trivia[tríviə] 일반 상식 organic[ɔ:rgǽnik] 유기농의 decorative[dékəreitiv] 장식용의 politely[pəláitli] 정중히 geographic[dʒì:əgrǽfik] 지리학적인 commitment[kəmítmənt] 노력 sustainable[səstéinəbəl] 지속 가능한 supplementary[sʌ̀pləméntəri] 추가의 brochure[brouʃúr] 안내 책자 amenity[əménəti] 편의 시설

34 Not/True   Not 문제   난이도 ●●○

Which statement is not true about the Ridge City Community Center?	Ridge City 커뮤니티 센터에 관해 사실이 아닌 진술은 무엇인가?
(a) It is completely built.	(a) 완공되었다.
(b) It is currently available for activities.	**(b) 현재 활동들이 이용 가능하다.**
(c) It is open to people of all ages.	(c) 모든 연령대의 사람들에게 열려 있다.
(d) It is located near a park.	(d) 공원 근처에 위치해 있다.

🔑 지텔프 치트키
보기의 키워드와 담화의 내용을 대조하며 듣는다.

해설 | (b)는 화자가 'the center will ~ be open to the public starting this weekend'라며 커뮤니티 센터가 이번 주말부터 대중에게 개방될 예정이라고 언급했으므로 담화의 내용과 일치하지 않는다. 따라서 (b)가 정답이다.

오답분석
(a) 화자가 2년간의 공사가 끝났다고 언급하였다.
(c) 화자가 누구나 나이에 상관없이 센터에 방문하여 활동들을 즐길 수 있다고 언급하였다.
(d) 화자가 커뮤니티 센터는 Bellflower 공원 옆에 위치해 있다고 언급하였다.

35 특정세부사항   What   난이도 ●●○

What can students do at the center's study club?	학생들은 센터의 공부 동아리에서 무엇을 할 수 있는가?
(a) They can learn how to be effective tutors.	(a) 효과적인 개인 교사가 되는 법을 배울 수 있다.
(b) They can study an array of subjects.	**(b) 다수의 과목들을 공부할 수 있다.**
(c) They can work with people from different regions.	(c) 다른 지역의 사람들과 협력할 수 있다.
(d) They can do community service.	(d) 지역 사회 봉사를 할 수 있다.

🔑 지텔프 치트키
질문의 키워드 study club이 homework club으로 paraphrasing되어 언급된 주변 내용을 주의 깊게 듣는다.

해설 | 화자가 'Skilled tutors will cover a range of topics, including mathematics, science, and language'라며 숙련된 개인 교사들이 수학, 과학, 그리고 언어를 포함한 다양한 주제들을 다룰 것이라고 했다. 따라서 (b)가 정답이다.

Paraphrasing
a range of topics 다양한 주제들 → an array of subjects 다수의 과목들

어휘 | community service 지역 사회 봉사

---

36 특정세부사항   Why   난이도 ●●○

According to the talk, why would a member take a course on pottery?

(a) **to make useful everyday objects**
(b) to improve their critical thinking ability
(c) to pick up new skills to use in the workplace
(d) to create cooking vessels of professional quality

담화에 따르면, 회원은 왜 도자기 수업을 수강할 것 같은가?

(a) **유용한 일상적인 물건들을 만들기 위해서**
(b) 비판적 사고 능력을 향상하기 위해서
(c) 직장에서 사용할 새로운 기술들을 습득하기 위해서
(d) 전문적인 품질의 요리용 용기들을 만들기 위해서

━━○ 지텔프 치트키

질문의 키워드 course on pottery가 pottery class로 paraphrasing되어 언급된 주변 내용을 주의 깊게 듣는다.

해설 | 화자가 'our pottery class will help keep their minds and bodies active, all while creating practical items'라며 도자기 수업은 실용적인 물건들을 만들어 내는 동시에, 수강생들의 심신을 활발하게 유지하는 것을 도울 것이라고 했다. 따라서 (a)가 정답이다.

Paraphrasing
creating practical items 실용적인 물건들을 만들어 내는 → make useful everyday objects 유용한 일상적인 물건들을 만들다

어휘 | course[kɔːrs] 수업, 강좌 pick up 습득하다 vessel[vésəl] 용기, 그릇

---

37 특정세부사항   What   난이도 ●○○

What are offered in the multi-purpose room of the center?

(a) performances by music students
(b) social media courses for new users
(c) celebrations for older individuals in the community
(d) **a wide variety of special monthly events**

센터의 다목적실에서 무엇이 제공되는가?

(a) 음악 학생들의 공연
(b) 신규 이용자들을 위한 소셜 미디어 강좌
(c) 지역 사회의 노인들을 위한 기념행사
(d) **매우 다양한 월례 특별 행사**

━━○ 지텔프 치트키

질문의 키워드 multi-purpose room이 그대로 언급된 주변 내용을 주의 깊게 듣는다.

해설 | 화자가 'different types of entertaining events will take place in this room at least once a month'라며 적어도 한 달에 한 번은 센터의 다목적실에서 다양한 종류의 오락 행사들이 진행될 것이라고 했다. 따라서 (d)가 정답이다.

Paraphrasing
different types of ~ events 다양한 종류의 행사들 → a wide variety of ~ events 매우 다양한 행사
once a month 한 달에 한 번 → monthly 월례의

어휘 | celebration[sèləbréiʃən] 기념행사

38   특정세부사항   Which

난이도 ●●●

Which kinds of plants are recommended in the community garden?

(a) plants that produce different colors
(b) plants that have medicinal uses
(c) plants that draw pollinating insects
(d) plants that are grown without chemicals

공동체 텃밭에서 어떤 종류의 식물들이 권장되는가?

(a) 여러 가지 색을 만들어 내는 식물들
(b) 약용으로 쓰이는 식물들
(c) 수분하는 곤충들을 끌어들이는 식물들
(d) 화학 물질 없이 자란 식물들

지텔프 치트키

질문의 키워드 community garden이 public garden으로 paraphrasing되어 언급된 주변 내용을 주의 깊게 듣는다.

해설 | 화자가 'the center ~ encourages the growth of plants ~ that will help attract beneficial butterflies and bees to the area'라며 센터는 이로운 나비들과 벌들을 그 지역에 끌어들이는 데 도움이 될 식물들의 재배를 권장한다고 했다. 따라서 (c)가 정답이다.

Paraphrasing

recommended 권장되는 → encourages 권장한다
attract ~ butterflies and bees 나비들과 벌들을 끌어들이다 → draw pollinating insects 수분하는 곤충들을 끌어들인다

오답분석
(a) 화자가 공공 텃밭에서 화려한 장식용 식물을 기를 수 있다고는 언급했지만, 그것의 재배를 권장한다고 한 것은 아니므로 오답이다.
(d) 화자가 공공 텃밭에서 유기농 식품을 기를 수 있다고는 언급했지만, 그것의 재배를 권장한다고 한 것은 아니므로 오답이다.

어휘 | medicinal[mədísənəl] 약의   pollinating[pá:ləneìtiŋ] 수분하는   chemical[kémikəl] 화학 물질

39   추론   특정사실

난이도 ●●●

Why might people read the community center's brochure?

(a) to view photographs of instructors
(b) to learn about the cost to join
(c) to read a list of frequently asked questions
(d) to see a schedule of events

사람들이 왜 커뮤니티 센터의 안내 책자를 읽을 것 같은가?

(a) 강사들의 사진을 보기 위해서
(b) 가입 비용에 관해 알기 위해서
(c) 자주 묻는 질문들의 목록을 읽기 위해서
(d) 행사들의 일정을 확인하기 위해서

지텔프 치트키

질문의 키워드 brochure가 그대로 언급된 주변 내용을 주의 깊게 듣는다.

해설 | 화자가 'You can see ~ further details regarding membership fees and pricing for various activities.'라며 안내 책자에서 가입비와 다양한 활동들의 가격에 관한 자세한 정보를 확인할 수 있다고 한 것을 통해, 사람들은 가입 비용에 관해 알기 위해서 안내 책자를 읽을 것임을 추론할 수 있다. 따라서 (b)가 정답이다.

Paraphrasing

membership fees 가입비 → the cost to join 가입 비용

어휘 | instructor[instrʌ́ktər] 강사   frequently[frí:kwəntli] 자주, 흔히

안부 인사	M: Hey, Charlotte. I heard that you opened a café. How's it going? F: Hi, Max. It's doing well, but ⁴⁰I'm stressed due to staffing problems. It's hard to find people to work nowadays.	남: 안녕, Charlotte. 네가 카페를 개업했다고 들었어. 어떻게 되어 가고 있어? 여: 안녕, Max. 잘 되고 있지만, ⁴⁰인력 문제로 스트레스를 받고 있어. 요즘 일할 사람을 찾기가 힘들어.
주제 제시: 장단점 비교	M: I've heard a lot of business owners complaining about that lately. But you need to have staff at your cafe. F: Yes, I do. I'm thinking about buying robotic servers to deal with the issue. M: That could be a good solution. I recently went to a restaurant that uses automated staff, and they were fast and efficient. What's stopping you from doing it? F: Well, I'm not sure if it's a smart plan. There are so many different things to consider. I can't make up my mind. M: I see. Why don't we talk through the advantages and disadvantages of robotic workers? That could help you decide one way or the other.	남: 최근에 많은 사업주들이 그것에 대해 불평하는 것을 들었어. 하지만 카페에 직원이 있어야 하잖아. 여: 응, 맞아. 그 문제를 해결하기 위해 로봇 종업원들을 구매할까 생각 중이야. 남: 그게 좋은 해결책이 될 수 있겠어. 최근에 자동화 직원을 사용하는 식당에 갔는데, 그것들은 빠르고 효율적이었어. 무엇이 네가 그것을 하는 걸 막고 있는 거야? 여: 글쎄, 나는 그게 현명한 계획인지 잘 모르겠어. 고려해야 할 것들이 너무 많아. 난 결정을 못 하겠어. 남: 그렇구나. 우리가 로봇 종업원들의 장단점에 대해 이야기해보는 건 어때? 그것은 네가 어느 쪽을 선택할지 결정하는 데 도움을 줄 수 있을 거야.
로봇 직원의 장점	F: That would be great. I think ⁴¹the biggest benefit of the robotic workers is that they're always on. They can work from the time the café opens until it closes. M: In addition, you don't have to worry about them getting sick or turning up late. F: Exactly. They never complain about doing their job ⁴²nor do they make trouble with other staff in the workplace. M: Ha-ha. That's true. ⁴²Without personalities, they wouldn't have emotional conflicts with others. Moreover, switching to automated workers would considerably lower staffing costs, wouldn't it? F: Yes. In small businesses like mine, salaries make up a large portion of the operating costs. If I didn't have to have as many workers, I could probably save a few hundred dollars a day. M: Wow! That's more than I expected. Using automated workers would greatly boost your profitability. Does it have any noticeable drawbacks?	여: 아주 좋아. 내 생각에 ⁴¹로봇 종업원들의 가장 큰 장점은 그것들이 항상 작동하고 있다는 점이야. 그것들은 카페가 문을 열 때부터 문을 닫을 때까지 일할 수 있지. 남: 게다가, 넌 그것들이 아프거나 늦게 도착하는 것에 대해 걱정할 필요가 없어. 여: 바로 그거야. 그것들은 일하는 것에 대해 불평하지도 않고 ⁴²현장에서 다른 직원들과 문제를 일으키지도 않아. 남: 하하. 맞아. ⁴²인격 없이는, 그것들은 다른 이들과 감정적인 갈등을 겪지 않을 거야. 또한, 자동화 종업원들로 전환하는 것은 인건비를 상당히 절감할 거야, 그렇지 않아? 여: 맞아. 내 것과 비슷한 소규모 사업체에서는, 급여가 운영비의 큰 부분을 차지해. 만약 내가 그렇게 많은 종업원들을 고용할 필요가 없다면, 아마도 하루에 몇백 달러를 절약할 수 있을 거야. 남: 와! 내가 예상했던 것 이상이야. 자동화 종업원을 사용하는 것은 네 수익성을 크게 향상시켜 줄 거야. 그것에는 주목할 만한 단점들이 있어?
	F: Definitely ⁴³the unreliability of the technology! Robots are still relatively new, so they might malfunction or require a lot of costly maintenance. M: Oh, my. That could cause you some problems. But wouldn't they have some kind of warranty? F: It's possible, but not guaranteed. But even if they do, they would be useless when out of service. I'd have	여: 확실히 ⁴³그 기술을 신뢰할 수 없다는 점이지! 로봇은 여전히 비교적 최근에 생겼기 때문에, 오작동을 일으키거나 많은 값비싼 유지보수를 필요로 할 수 있어. 남: 오, 이런. 그것이 너에게 문제를 초래할 수 있겠네. 하지만 그것들은 일종의 보증서가 있지 않아? 여: 있을 수도 있지만, 장담할 수는 없어. 하지만 있더라도, 고장이 나면 그것들은 소용없을 거야. 내게

로봇
직원의
단점

to have a backup plan, like temporary workers, which could be expensive. And, to make matters worse, if they can't be repaired, I'd have to buy replacements.

M: I guess you would need to plan for those things. We still haven't addressed their impact on customer service.

F: Hmm . . . That's right. [44]Since they don't have feelings, it would be impossible for them to form emotional bonds with guests.

M: Precisely. For many people, the personal touch of the staff is what keeps them coming back. [44]Trading a genuine human connection for mechanical efficiency could backfire.

F: Robots could store information about customers' habits and preferences, but that may seem cold and calculated rather than warm and inviting.

M: That is a serious concern. I don't think most people would want to have their morning coffee in a factory.

F: Yeah. People who visit cafés want a cozy environment, and the staff contributes to that. Robot workers might look too impersonal. I'm worried they would turn my customers off.

여자의
결정

M: I hadn't thought about that. You really do have a number of factors to weigh.

F: Yes, but I've made my choice. [45]The technology is just too untested and risky. I don't want to take any unnecessary chances with my new business.

M: I don't blame you. You've already got enough stress in your life.

F: That's exactly what I was thinking.

임시 종업원과 같은 대안이 있어야 하는데, 그것은 비용이 많이 들 수 있어. 그리고, 설상가상으로, 만약 그것들이 수리될 수 없다면, 나는 대체품들을 구매해야 할 거야.

남: 네가 그런 것들에 대한 계획을 세워야 할 것 같아. 우리는 아직 고객 서비스에 미치는 그것들의 영향을 다루지 않았어.

여: 흠... 맞아. [44]그것들은 감정이 없기 때문에, 그것들이 손님들과 감정적인 유대감을 형성하는 것은 불가능할 거야.

남: 그렇고말고. 많은 사람들에게 있어, 그들을 계속 다시 방문하게 하는 것은 직원들의 인간적인 접근이야. [44]진실된 인간관계와 기계의 효율성을 맞바꾸는 것은 역효과를 낳을 수 있어.

여: 로봇은 고객의 습관과 선호에 관한 정보를 저장할 수 있지만, 그것은 따뜻하고 매력적이기보다는 차갑고 계산적으로 보일 수 있어.

남: 그건 심각한 걱정거리다. 나는 대부분의 사람들이 공장에서 그들의 아침 커피를 마시고 싶어 하지 않을 거라고 생각해.

여: 맞아. 카페를 찾는 사람들은 친밀한 환경을 원하고, 직원들이 그것에 이바지해. 로봇 종업원들은 너무 냉담해 보일 수 있어. 나는 그것들이 내 고객들의 흥미를 잃게 할까 봐 걱정이야.

남: 난 그것에 대해서 생각해 보지 못했어. 네가 따져 볼 요소들이 정말 많구나.

여: 응, 하지만 난 결정을 내렸어. [45]그 기술은 너무 검증되지 않았고 위험해. 나는 내 새로운 사업에서 그 어떤 불필요한 위험도 감수하고 싶지 않아.

남: 그럴 만도 해. 너는 이미 네 삶에서 충분한 스트레스를 받고 있잖아.

여: 그게 바로 내가 생각하고 있던 거야.

어휘 | automate[ɔ́ːtəmeit] 자동화하다 turn up 도착하다, 나타나다 personality[pə̀ːrsənǽləti] 인격, 성격 emotional[imóuʃənəl] 감정적인 conflict[kɑ́ːnflikt] 갈등 switch[switʃ] 전환하다 portion[pɔ́ːrʃən] 부분 profitability[prὰːfətəbíləti] 수익성 noticeable[nóutəsəbəl] 주목할 만한 unreliability[ʌ̀nrilàiəbíləti] 신뢰할 수 없음 malfunction[mælfʌ́ŋkʃən] 오작동을 일으키다 maintenance[méintənəns] 유지보수 warranty[wɔ́ːrənti] 보증서 guarantee[gæ̀rəntíː] 장담하다 out of service 고장 난 backup plan 대안 temporary[témpəreri] 임시의 replacement[ripléismənt] 대체품 trade[treid] 맞바꾸다, 교환하다 genuine[dʒénjuin] 진실된, 진짜의 backfire[bǽkfàiər] 역효과를 낳다 cozy[kóuzi] 친밀한 turn off 흥미를 잃게 하다 weigh[wei] 따져 보다

---

40 특정세부사항 Why
난이도 ●○○

Why is Charlotte feeling anxious?

(a) because she wants to open a new business
(b) because she cannot find workers to hire
(c) because she cannot make her café successful
(d) because her staff has been complaining a lot

Charlotte는 왜 걱정하고 있는가?

(a) 새로운 사업을 시작하기를 원하기 때문에
(b) 고용할 종업원을 찾을 수 없기 때문에
(c) 그녀의 카페를 성공적으로 만들 수 없기 때문에
(d) 그녀의 직원이 많은 불평을 해오고 있었기 때문에

질문의 키워드 feeling anxious가 stressed로 paraphrasing되어 언급된 주변 내용을 주의 깊게 듣는다.

해설 | 여자가 'I'm stressed due to staffing problems'라며 인력 문제로 스트레스를 받고 있다고 한 뒤, 'It's hard to find people to work nowadays.'라며 요즘 일할 사람을 찾기가 힘들다고 했다. 따라서 (b)가 정답이다.

Paraphrasing
hard to find people to work 일할 사람을 찾기가 힘든 → cannot find workers to hire 고용할 종업원들을 찾을 수 없다

---

41 특정세부사항 장·단점   난이도 ●●○

What is the biggest advantage of using robot workers?	로봇 종업원들을 사용하는 것의 가장 큰 장점은 무엇인가?
(a) They can perform the work of multiple people.	(a) 여러 사람의 작업을 수행할 수 있다.
(b) They do not need worker's accident compensation insurance.	(b) 근로자의 재해 보상 보험이 필요하지 않다.
(c) They are always fast when they complete tasks.	(c) 작업을 완료할 때 항상 빠르다.
(d) They are ready to work at all times.	**(d) 언제든지 일할 준비가 되어 있다.**

질문의 키워드 using robot workers와 관련된 긍정적인 흐름을 파악한다.

해설 | 여자가 'the biggest benefit of the robotic workers is that they're always on'이라며 로봇 종업원들의 가장 큰 장점은 그것들이 항상 작동하고 있다는 점이라고 했다. 따라서 (d)가 정답이다.

Paraphrasing
always on 항상 작동하고 있는 → ready to work at all times 언제든지 일할 준비가 된

어휘 | compensation[kɑ̀ːmpənséiʃən] 보상 insurance[inʃúərəns] 보험

---

42 특정세부사항 How   난이도 ●●○

How does having robot staff reduce issues in the workplace?	로봇 직원을 두고 있는 것이 현장에서 어떻게 문제를 줄이는가?
(a) by avoiding causing problems with others	**(a) 다른 이들과 문제를 일으키는 것을 피함으로써**
(b) by having fewer visitors report poor experience	(b) 더 적은 손님들이 불만족스러운 경험을 보고하게 함으로써
(c) by helping resolve trouble between staff members	(c) 직원 간의 문제를 해결하도록 도움으로써
(d) by lessening stress on human workers	(d) 인간 종업원들의 스트레스를 줄임으로써

질문의 키워드 issues가 trouble로 paraphrasing되어 언급된 주변 내용을 주의 깊게 듣는다.

해설 | 여자가 'nor do they make trouble with other staff in the workplace'라며 로봇 직원들은 현장에서 다른 직원들과 문제를 일으키지 않는다고 하자, 남자가 'Without personalities, they wouldn't have emotional conflicts with others.'라며 인격 없이는 로봇 직원들이 다른 이들과 감정적인 갈등을 겪지 않을 것이라고 했다. 따라서 (a)가 정답이다.

Paraphrasing

nor ~ make trouble with other staff 다른 직원들과 문제를 일으키지도 않는다 → avoiding causing problems with others 다른 이들과 문제를 일으키는 것을 피함

---

43 특정세부사항 　What

난이도 ●●○

What makes robot workers unreliable?

(a) the time required to get a replacement
(b) the limited number of functions
(c) the possibility of a technology breakdown
(d) the lack of trained repair technicians

로봇 종업원들을 신뢰할 수 없게 하는 것은 무엇인가?

(a) 대체품을 구하는 데 필요한 시간
(b) 제한적인 기능의 수
(c) 기술 고장의 가능성
(d) 숙련된 수리 기술자들의 부족

─○ 지텔프 치트키

질문의 키워드 unreliable이 unreliability로 paraphrasing되어 언급된 주변 내용을 주의 깊게 듣는다.

해설 | 여자가 'the unreliability of the technology'라며 로봇 기술을 신뢰할 수 없다고 한 뒤, 'Robots are ~ new, so they might malfunction or require ~ maintenance.'라며 로봇이 최근에 생겼기 때문에 오작동을 일으키거나 유지보수를 필요로 할 수 있다고 했다. 따라서 (c)가 정답이다.

Paraphrasing

malfunction 오작동을 일으키다 → a technology breakdown 기술 고장

어휘 | breakdown [bréikdaun] 고장

---

44 특정세부사항 　Why

난이도 ●●○

Why does Charlotte think robots would have a negative effect on customer service?

(a) They cannot form personal connections with guests.
(b) Customers would have difficulty operating them.
(c) They would affect the restaurant's temperature.
(d) Customers cannot ask them questions.

왜 Charlotte는 로봇이 고객 서비스에 부정적인 영향을 미칠 것이라고 생각하는가?

(a) 손님들과 개인적인 관계를 형성할 수 없다.
(b) 고객들이 그것들을 조작하는 데 어려움을 겪을 것이다.
(c) 식당의 온도에 영향을 줄 것이다.
(d) 고객들이 그것들에게 질문할 수 없다.

─○ 지텔프 치트키

질문의 키워드 customer service가 그대로 언급된 주변 내용을 주의 깊게 듣는다.

해설 | 여자가 'Since they don't have feelings, it would be impossible for them to form emotional bonds with guests.'라며 로봇들은 감정이 없기 때문에 손님들과 감정적인 유대감을 형성하는 것은 불가능할 것이라고 하자, 남자가 'Trading a genuine human connection for mechanical efficiency could backfire.'라며 진실된 인간관계와 기계의 효율성을 맞바꾸는 것은 역효과를 낳을 수 있다고 했다. 따라서 (a)가 정답이다.

Paraphrasing

have a negative effect 부정적인 영향을 미치다 → backfire 역효과를 낳다
impossible ~ to form emotional bonds 감정적인 유대감을 형성하는 것이 불가능한 → cannot form personal connections 개인적인 관계를 형성할 수 없다

어휘 | temperature [témprətʃər] 온도

45 추론 다음에 할 일

Based on the conversation, what will Charlotte most likely do?

(a) install software updates on all of the computers in the café
(b) test the functionality of the new machinery
(c) continue to exclusively hire human workers
(d) reduce the size of her staff

대화에 따르면, Charlotte는 무엇을 할 것 같은가?

(a) 카페의 모든 컴퓨터에 소프트웨어 업데이트를 설치한다
(b) 새로운 기계의 기능성을 시험해 본다
(c) 계속해서 전적으로 인간 종업원만 고용한다
(d) 직원의 수를 줄인다

⊸ 지텔프 치트키

다음에 할 일을 언급하는 후반을 주의 깊게 듣는다.

해설 | 여자가 'The technology is ~ too untested and risky.'라며 로봇 기술은 너무 검증되지 않았고 위험하다고 한 뒤, 'I don't want to take any unnecessary chances with my new business.'라며 그녀의 새로운 사업에서 그 어떤 불필요한 위험도 감수하고 싶지 않다고 한 것을 통해, Charlotte는 로봇 직원이 아닌 인간 종업원만을 계속해서 고용할 것임을 추론할 수 있다. 따라서 (c)가 정답이다.

어휘 | functionality[fʌ̀ŋkʃənǽləti] 기능성   machinery[məʃíːnəri] 기계   exclusively[iksklúːsivli] 전적으로

PART 4 (46~52) 설명 운전면허를 취득하기 위한 6단계의 과정

음성 바로 듣기

인사 + 주제 제시

Good morning, everyone. Welcome to the Department of Motor Vehicles. I am the lead licensing clerk, and [46]I'm here to explain the basic process for getting a driver's license in California.

운전 면허의 필요성

[47]A license is important here as most of the state has a driving culture, so it is difficult to get around only by walking or using public transportation. But if you already have a license issued elsewhere, you may continue to use your current license for the duration of your visit. For those who are moving here, however, you will need to apply for a local license within 10 days of establishing residency.

1단계: 신청서 작성

The first thing that you'll need to do is fill out the driver's license application form. It asks for information such as your full legal name, address, and social security number. These details will be used to ensure your eligibility and will be printed on the license, so make sure that they are accurate.

The second step is to prove your identity and your residency in the state. To verify who you are, present a valid government-issued identification that matches your application's information. The most common of these are passports, birth certificates, residency cards, or driver's

좋은 아침입니다, 여러분. 차량 관리국에 오신 것을 환영합니다. 저는 면허 발부 책임 관리자이고, [46]캘리포니아주에서 운전면허를 취득하기 위한 기본적인 절차를 설명하기 위해 이곳에 왔습니다.

[47]주의 대부분이 운전하는 문화를 가지고 있기 때문에 이곳에서는 면허가 중요하고, 따라서 걷거나 대중교통을 이용하는 것만으로는 돌아다니기 어렵습니다. 하지만 만약 여러분이 이미 다른 곳에서 발급받은 면허를 가지고 계신다면, 여러분은 방문 기간 동안 현재의 면허를 계속 사용하실 수 있습니다. 하지만, 이곳으로 이사 오시는 분들의 경우, 거주 확정 후 10일 이내에 현지 면허를 신청하셔야 할 겁니다.

가장 먼저 하셔야 할 일은 운전면허 신청서를 작성하는 것입니다. 그것은 여러분의 법적 성명, 주소, 그리고 사회 보장 번호와 같은 정보를 요구합니다. 이러한 세부 사항들은 여러분의 자격을 확실히 하기 위해 사용될 것이며 면허증에 인쇄될 것이므로, 그것들이 정확한지 확인하시기 바랍니다.

두 번째 단계는 여러분의 신원과 주에서의 거주를 증명하는 것입니다. 여러분이 누구인지 입증하기 위해, 신청서상의 정보와 일치하는 유효한 정부 발급 신분증을 제시하세요. 가장 흔한 것들은 여권, 출생증명서, 거주증, 또는 다른 주의 운전면허증입니다. 또한,

2단계: 신분 및 거주 증명

licenses from other states. In addition, you'll need something to show you are a legal resident of California, such as a copy of the ownership papers or lease for your home. You could also provide a utility bill with your name and address on it. If you don't have any of the things I mentioned, [48]you can check the list by the door for other acceptable forms of identification or certificates of residence.

3단계: 시력 검사

Third, after your application package is accepted, you'll need to take a quick vision exam. You will be asked to read a chart of letters. [49]If you cannot read them without corrective lenses, you can use your glasses or contacts. However, this will result in a restriction being placed on your license, requiring you to wear them while driving.

4단계: 이론 시험

Fourth, you will need to take a test on driving theory. [50]Don't worry if you have trouble with English. The exam is currently available in seven other languages. The multiple-choice questions will evaluate your understanding of California driving laws, signs, and basic driving skills. Should you get more than eight of the 46 questions wrong, you must come back another day to retake the test.

5단계: 실기 시험

Once you pass the written exam, you will move on to the fifth step, which is the practical driving test. [51]This is the behind-the-wheel test where you drive with a DMV examiner who will give you verbal commands on what to do and where to drive. [51]The examiner will determine if you complete each command safely and properly.

6단계: 사진 및 지문 찍기

If you're given a passing score by the evaluator, you'll move on to the final step, having your photograph taken. This picture will be printed onto your license and registered in the national database along with your thumbprint. [52]This allows you to use your license as an official identification card.

끝인사

That's all there is to obtaining a driver's license here in California. Once you've finished these steps, you'll receive a license valid for five years. Now, if you have any questions, I will be at my desk near the main entrance for the next 30 minutes.

여러분이 캘리포니아주의 합법적 거주자라는 것을 보여 줄 수 있는 소유권 증명서의 사본이나 집 임대차 계약 사본과 같은 것이 필요할 것입니다. 여러분의 성명과 주소가 적힌 공과금 고지서를 제출하실 수도 있습니다. 제가 언급한 어떤 것도 가지고 있지 않으시다면, [48]문 옆에 있는 목록에서 기타 허용 가능한 신분증 혹은 거주 증명서 형식을 확인하실 수 있습니다.

셋째, 여러분의 모든 지원서가 승인되고 나면, 시간이 얼마 걸리지 않는 시력 검사를 받으셔야 할 것입니다. 여러분은 글자들이 있는 표를 읽으라고 요구받을 것입니다. [49]만약 여러분이 교정 렌즈 없이 그것들을 읽으실 수 없다면, 여러분의 안경이나 콘택트렌즈를 사용하실 수 있습니다. 그러나, 이것은 여러분의 면허에 제약을 두는 결과를 낳을 것이고, 여러분이 운전 중에 그것들을 착용하도록 규정할 것입니다.

넷째, 여러분은 운전 이론에 대한 시험을 치러야 할 것입니다. [50]만약 여러분이 영어에 어려움이 있더라도 걱정하지 마세요. 이 시험은 현재 7개 국어로 응시가 가능합니다. 객관식 문제들이 캘리포니아주의 운전 법규, 표지판, 그리고 기본적인 운전 기술에 대한 여러분의 이해도를 평가할 것입니다. 46개의 문제 중 8개 이상을 틀리신다면, 여러분은 시험을 다시 치르기 위해 다른 날에 다시 오셔야 합니다.

필기시험에 합격하시면, 여러분은 다섯 번째 단계로 넘어갈 것인데, 이는 실기 운전 시험입니다. 이것은 무엇을 해야 하고 어디로 운전해야 하는지에 대해 [51]여러분에게 구두 지시를 줄 차량 관리국의 검사관과 함께 운전하는 운전면허 실기 시험입니다. 검사관은 여러분이 각각의 지시를 안전하고 적절하게 완료하는지를 확인할 것입니다.

평가자로부터 합격 점수를 받으면, 여러분은 최종 단계로 넘어가실 것이고, 사진을 찍으실 겁니다. 이 사진은 여러분의 면허증에 인쇄되고 엄지손가락 지문과 함께 국가 데이터베이스에 등록될 것입니다. [52]이것은 여러분이 면허증을 공식적인 신분증으로 사용할 수 있게 합니다.

이곳 캘리포니아주에서 운전면허를 취득하는 것은 이것이 전부입니다. 이 단계들을 완료하시면, 여러분은 5년 동안 유효한 면허를 받으실 것입니다. 그럼, 질문이 있으시다면, 앞으로 30분 동안 제가 중앙 출입문 근처에 있는 책상에 있도록 하겠습니다.

어휘 | license [láisəns] 면허를 발부하다; 면허(증) **clerk** [klə:rk] 관리자, 직원 **process** [prá:ses] 절차, 과정 **issue** [íʃu:] 발급하다
establish [istæbliʃ] 확정하다 **residency** [rézədənsi] 거주 **eligibility** [èlidʒəbíləti] 자격, 적격성 **accurate** [ǽkjərət] 정확한
identity [aidéntəti] 신원, 신분 **valid** [vǽlid] 유효한 **certificate** [sərtífikət] 증명서 **lease** [li:s] 임대차 계약 **utility bill** 공과금 (고지서)
corrective [kəréktiv] 교정의 **restriction** [ristríkʃən] 제약 **evaluate** [ivǽljueit] 평가하다 **behind-the-wheel test** 운전면허 실기 시험
verbal [vɔ́:rbəl] 구두의 **command** [kəmǽnd] 지시, 명령 **thumbprint** [θʌ́mprint] 엄지손가락 지문

주제/목적　담화의 주제　　　　　　　　　　　　　　　　　난이도 ●●○

What is the talk all about?	담화는 무엇에 관한 것인가?
(a) the process to attain a state document	**(a) 주의 공식 서류를 획득하기 위한 과정**
(b) the way to get a business license	(b) 사업 면허를 취득하기 위한 방법
(c) the significance of establishing state residency	(c) 주에서의 거주 확정의 중요성
(d) the necessity of learning the basics of driving	(d) 운전의 기초를 배우는 것의 필요성

━○ 지텔프 치트키

담화의 주제를 언급하는 초반을 주의 깊게 듣고 전체 맥락을 파악한다.

해설 | 화자가 'I'm here to explain the basic process for getting a driver's license in California'라며 캘리포니아주에서 운전면허를 취득하기 위한 기본적인 절차를 설명하기 위해 이곳에 왔다고 한 뒤, 담화 전반에 걸쳐 주의 공식 서류인 운전면허를 획득하기 위한 과정을 설명하는 내용이 이어지고 있다. 따라서 (a)가 정답이다.

Paraphrasing
getting a ~ license in California 캘리포니아주에서 면허를 취득하는 것 → attain a state document 주의 공식 서류를 획득하다

어휘 | attain[ətéin] 획득하다　significance[signífikəns] 중요성　necessity[nəsésəti] 필요성

---

47 **특정세부사항**　What　　　　　　　　　　　　　　　　　난이도 ●○○

What makes it important to have a driver's license in California?	캘리포니아주에서 운전면허를 소지하는 것을 중요하게 만드는 것은 무엇인가?
(a) It can be used to prove U.S. citizenship.	(a) 미국 시민권을 증명하는 데 사용될 수 있다.
(b) The climate is too hot for walking.	(b) 기후가 걷기에 너무 덥다.
(c) It provides access to a discount on public transportation.	(c) 대중교통 할인을 받을 수 있는 기회를 제공한다.
(d) The state has a culture of personal automobile use.	**(d) 그 주가 개인 자동차 이용 문화를 가지고 있다.**

━○ 지텔프 치트키

질문의 키워드 important to have a ~ license가 A license is important로 paraphrasing되어 언급된 주변 내용을 주의 깊게 듣는다.

해설 | 화자가 'A license is important here as most of the state has a driving culture'라며 주의 대부분이 운전하는 문화를 가지고 있기 때문에 캘리포니아주에서는 면허가 중요하다고 했다. 따라서 (d)가 정답이다.

Paraphrasing
a driving culture 운전하는 문화 → a culture of personal automobile use 개인 자동차 이용 문화

---

48 **특정세부사항**　How　　　　　　　　　　　　　　　　　난이도 ●●○

How can listeners learn about additional types of allowable identification?	청자들은 허용되는 신분증의 다른 유형들에 대해 어떻게 알 수 있는가?
(a) by checking an application form	(a) 신청서를 확인함으로써
(b) by calling a government agency	(b) 정부 기관에 전화함으로써
(c) by writing to a state representative	(c) 주 대표에게 편지를 씀으로써

(d) by referring to a posted list

(d) 게시된 목록을 참고함으로써

━━○ 지텔프 치트키

질문의 키워드 allowable identification이 acceptable ~ identification으로 paraphrasing되어 언급된 주변 내용을 주의 깊게 듣는다.

해설 | 화자가 'you can check the list by the door for other acceptable forms of identification or certificates of residence'라며 문 옆에 있는 목록에서 기타 허용 가능한 신분증 형식을 확인할 수 있다고 했다. 따라서 (d)가 정답이다.

Paraphrasing
check the list 목록에서 확인하다 → referring to a ~ list 목록을 참고함

---

49 특정세부사항   When

난이도 ●●○

When will a restriction be applied to a driver's license?

(a) when the driver is unavailable for an eye exam
(b) when the vision test was passed with corrective eyewear
(c) when the application package was not submitted on time
(d) when the applicant plans to wear sunglasses while driving

운전면허에 언제 제약이 적용될 것인가?

(a) 운전자가 시력 검사를 받을 수 없을 때
(b) 교정 안경류를 착용하고 시력 검사에 합격했을 때
(c) 모든 신청서가 제시간에 제출되지 않았을 때
(d) 신청자가 운전 중에 선글라스를 착용할 계획일 때

━━○ 지텔프 치트키

질문의 키워드 restriction이 그대로 언급된 주변 내용을 주의 깊게 듣는다.

해설 | 화자가 'If you cannot read them without corrective lenses, you can use your glasses or contacts.'라며 만약 교정 렌즈 없이 이 글자들을 읽을 수 없다면 안경이나 콘택트렌즈를 사용할 수 있다고 한 뒤, 'However, this will result in a restriction being placed on your license'라며 그러나 이것은 면허에 제약을 두는 결과를 낳을 것이라고 했다. 따라서 (b)가 정답이다.

Paraphrasing
corrective lenses 교정 렌즈 → corrective eyewear 교정 안경류

---

50 추론   특정사실

난이도 ●●○

According to the talk, why might a person require another version of the test?

(a) because one cannot recognize the signs on it
(b) because one has trouble with multiple-choice questions
(c) because one is not comfortable with English
(d) because one gets more than eight answers wrong

담화에 따르면, 왜 어떤 사람은 다른 버전의 시험을 필요로 할 것 같은가?

(a) 그것에 있는 표시를 알아볼 수 없기 때문에
(b) 객관식 문제에 어려움을 겪기 때문에
(c) 영어가 편하지 않기 때문에
(d) 8개보다 많은 답을 틀리기 때문에

━━○ 지텔프 치트키

질문의 키워드 another version of the test가 exam ~ available in ~ other languages로 paraphrasing되어 언급된 주변 내용을 주의 깊게 듣는다.

해설 | 화자가 'Don't worry if you have trouble with English.'라며 영어에 어려움이 있더라도 걱정하지 말라고 한 뒤, 'The exam is currently available in seven other languages.'라며 이 시험은 현재 7개 국어로 응시가 가능하다고 한 것을 통해, 영어가 편하지 않

은 사람들에게 다른 언어로 된 버전의 시험이 필요할 것임을 추론할 수 있다. 따라서 (c)가 정답이다.

어휘 | comfortable[kʌ́mfərtəbəl] 편한, 쉽게 다룰 수 있는

---

51 **특정세부사항** What 난이도 ●●●

According to the speaker, what is a task of a DMV employee during the behind-the-wheel test?

(a) confirm that a vehicle meets safety standards
(b) check if a written examination was completed
(c) verify that spoken instructions are followed
(d) determine if a route was selected properly

화자에 따르면, 차량 관리국 직원이 운전면허 실기 시험 동안 해야 할 일은 무엇인가?

(a) 차량이 안전 기준을 충족하는지 확인한다
(b) 필기시험이 완료되었는지를 확인한다
(c) 구두로 내린 지시가 준수되는지를 확인한다
(d) 경로가 제대로 선택되었는지를 확인한다

지텔프 치트키

질문의 키워드 behind-the-wheel test가 그대로 언급된 주변 내용을 주의 깊게 듣는다.

해설 | 화자가 'This is the behind-the-wheel test where you drive with a DMV examiner who will give you verbal commands' 라며 운전면허 실기 시험은 구두 지시를 줄 차량 관리국의 검사관과 함께 운전하는 시험이라고 한 뒤, 'The examiner will determine if you complete each command safely and properly.'라며 검사관은 운전자가 각각의 지시를 안전하고 적절하게 완료하는지를 확인할 것이라고 했다. 따라서 (c)가 정답이다.

Paraphrasing
verbal commands 구두 지시 → spoken instructions 구두로 내린 지시

어휘 | confirm[kənfə́ːrm] 확인하다 standard[stǽndərd] 기준, 수준 examination[igzæ̀mənéiʃən] 시험 instruction[instrʌ́kʃən] 지시, 설명

---

52 **특정세부사항** What 난이도 ●●○

What is the purpose of having a photograph on a driver's license?

(a) so it serves as proof of identity
(b) so the owner can validate passing the test
(c) so the owner can renew it after its expiration
(d) so it matches records in a national database

운전면허증에 사진이 있는 목적은 무엇인가?

(a) 신분 증명 역할을 하게 하기 위해서
(b) 소지자가 시험에 합격한 것을 입증할 수 있게 하기 위해서
(c) 소지자가 만료 후 그것을 갱신할 수 있게 하기 위해서
(d) 국가 데이터베이스에 있는 기록과 일치하게 하기 위해서

지텔프 치트키

질문의 키워드 photograph가 그대로 언급된 주변 내용을 주의 깊게 듣는다.

해설 | 화자가 'This allows you to use your license as an official identification card.'라며 이것(사진이 면허증에 인쇄되고 국가 데이터베이스에 등록되는 것)은 면허증을 공식적인 신분증으로 사용할 수 있게 한다고 했다. 따라서 (a)가 정답이다.

Paraphrasing
use your license as an official identification card 면허증을 공식적인 신분증으로 사용하다 → serves as proof of identity 신분 증명 역할을 하다

어휘 | validate[vǽlədeit] 입증하다, 확인하다 renew[rinjúː] 갱신하다 expiration[èkspəréiʃən] 만료

READING & VOCABULARY

인물 이름

소개 + 유명한 이유

어린 시절 + 업적 시작 계기

경력의 변환점 + 초기 업적

주요 업적

ERIN JACKSON

Erin Jackson is an American speed skater, inline skater, and roller derby player. She is ⁵³famous for being the first Black woman to be awarded a gold medal in an individual Winter Olympic sport. She also became the first American woman to win a solo event since 2002 and a 500-meter race since 1994.

Erin Jackson was born on September 19, 1992 in Ocala, Florida to Tracy Jackson, a US Army veteran, and Rita Jackson, a pharmacy technician. Jackson was athletically gifted from a young age. ⁵⁴Inspired by the artistic techniques used by figure skater Michelle Kwan at the Olympics, she joined a local inline skating team at the age of 10.

Jackson transitioned to the ice in 2017 because, like other inline skaters before her, she ⁵⁸aspired to challenge herself at the highest level of speed skating. ⁵⁵After only four months, Jackson skated at the 2017 Olympic trials to see where she stood. To her disbelief, she was among the fastest skaters—coming in third in the 500-meter sprint—and qualified for the 2018 Winter Olympics. Two years later, at the 2020 World Single Distances Speed Skating Championships, she came in 0.6 seconds behind winner Nao Kodaira, whom she later beat in several World Cup races.

Jackson ⁵⁹improved her skills in preparation for the 2022 Winter Olympics and became the top-ranked 500-meter speed skater in the world. However, she fell and finished third at the US trials when she needed to be one of the top two finishers to be eligible for a spot. Fortunately, ⁵⁶her teammate Brittany Bowe, who finished first in the trial and was set to compete in other events, decided to give her spot in the 500-meter event to Jackson. On February 13, 2022, Jackson finished the race in 37.04 seconds, becoming the first Black woman to win a gold medal in any non-team winter competition at the Olympics. This was only five years after Jackson switched from inline skating to ice.

에린 잭슨

에린 잭슨은 미국의 스피드스케이팅 선수이자, 인라인스케이팅 선수이자, 롤러더비 선수이다. 그녀는 ⁵³동계 올림픽 개인 경기에서 금메달을 딴 최초의 흑인 여성으로 유명하다. 그녀는 또한 2002년 이후 개인 종목에서 우승하고 1994년 이후 500미터 경기에서 우승한 최초의 미국 여성이 되었다.

에린 잭슨은 1992년 9월 19일에 플로리다주 오칼라에서 미군 참전 용사 트레이시 잭슨과 약사 보조원 리타 잭슨 사이에서 태어났다. 잭슨은 어린 나이부터 운동에 재능이 있었다. ⁵⁴올림픽에서 피겨스케이팅 선수 미셸 콴이 사용한 예술적 기술들에 영감을 받아, 그녀는 10살 때 지역 인라인스케이팅팀에 합류했다.

잭슨은 2017년에 빙상으로 전환했는데 이는, 그녀 이전의 다른 인라인스케이팅 선수들처럼, 그녀도 스피드 스케이팅의 최고 단계에서 ⁵⁸스스로 도전하기를 열망했기 때문이다. ⁵⁵불과 4개월 후에, 잭슨은 자신의 위치를 확인하기 위해 2017년 올림픽 선발 대회에서 스케이트를 탔다. 믿기지 않게도, 500m 단거리 경기에서 3위를 차지하며 그녀는 가장 빠른 스케이팅 선수들 중 한 명이 되었고 2018년 동계 올림픽에 출전할 자격을 얻었다. 2년 뒤, 2020년 세계 종목별 스피드스케이팅 선수권대회에서, 그녀는 우승자 고다이라 나오에게 0.6초 뒤졌는데, 그녀를 잭슨이 이후에 여러 월드컵 경기에서 이겼다.

잭슨은 2022년 동계 올림픽을 준비하면서 ⁵⁹그녀의 기술들을 향상시켰고 세계 랭킹 1위의 500미터 스피드 스케이팅 선수가 되었다. 그러나, 그녀는 미국 대표 선수 선발 대회에서 넘어져 3위를 했는데 이는 출전 자리의 자격을 얻기 위해 상위 두 명의 주자 중 한 명이 되어야 했을 때였다. 운이 좋게도, ⁵⁶그녀의 동료 선수인 브리트니 보는, 그 대표 선수 선발 대회에서 1위로 들어왔고 다른 종목에 출전할 예정이었는데, 500미터 종목에서 그녀의 출전 자리를 잭슨에게 주기로 결정했다. 2022년 2월 13일에, 잭슨은 37.04초 만에 경기를 마쳤고, 올림픽의 동계 개인전 경기에서 금메달을 획득한 최초의 흑인 여성이 되었다. 이것은 잭슨이 인라인스케이팅에서 빙상 스케이팅으로 바꾼 지 불과 5년이 지난 후였다.

| 근황 | Since her victory, Jackson has become a partner of Edge Sports, a non-profit organization that [57]hopes to boost the participation of people of color in winter sports. She is collaborating with them to establish a chapter in Salt Lake City, Utah, where she is currently training for the 2026 Winter Olympics. | 그녀의 우승 이후, 잭슨은 에지 스포츠 사의 협력자가 되었는데, 이것은 [57]유색인종의 동계 스포츠 참여를 증진하고 싶어 하는 비영리 단체이다. 그녀는 유타주 솔트레이크시티에 지부를 설립하기 위해 그들과 협력하고 있는데, 그곳에서 그녀는 현재 2026년 동계 올림픽을 위해 훈련하고 있다. |

어휘 | individual adj. 개인의 veteran n. 참전 용사 pharmacy technician phr. 약사 보조원 athletically gifted phr. 운동에 재능이 있는 artistic adj. 예술적인 join v. 합류하다, 가입하다 transition v. 전환하다, 옮겨 가다 challenge v. 도전하다 trial n. (대표 선수) 선발 대회 disbelief n. 믿기지 않음, 불신감 sprint n. 단거리 경기 qualify v. 자격을 얻다 beat v. 이기다 eligible adj. 자격을 얻은 compete v. 출전하다, 경쟁하다 competition n. 경기 partner n. 협력자 non-profit adj. 비영리의 collaborate v. 협력하다 establish v. 설립하다, 수립하다 chapter n. 지부

---

53 특정세부사항 유명한 이유   난이도 ●○○

What is Erin Jackson best known for?	에린 잭슨은 무엇으로 가장 유명한가?
(a) holding an Olympic record for over 10 years	(a) 10년 이상 올림픽 기록을 보유한 것으로
(b) being the first American to medal in speed skating	(b) 스피드스케이팅에서 메달을 딴 최초의 미국인으로
(c) winning an individual gold medal as a Black woman	**(c) 흑인 여성으로서 개인전 금메달을 획득한 것으로**
(d) earning the most distinctions on the US skating team	(d) 미국 스케이팅팀에서 가장 많은 업적을 쌓은 것으로

○ 지텔프 치트키

질문의 키워드 best known for가 famous for로 paraphrasing되어 언급된 주변 내용을 주의 깊게 읽는다.

해설 | 1단락의 'famous for being the first Black woman to be awarded a gold medal in an individual Winter Olympic sport'에서 에린 잭슨은 동계 올림픽 개인 경기에서 금메달을 딴 최초의 흑인 여성으로 유명하다고 했다. 따라서 (c)가 정답이다.

Paraphrasing
be awarded a gold medal in an individual ~ sport 개인 경기에서 금메달을 따다 → winning an individual gold medal 개인전 금메달을 획득한 것

어휘 | hold v. 보유하다 medal v. 메달을 따다; n. 메달 earn v. 쌓다, 얻다 distinction n. 업적, 탁월함

---

54 추론 특정사실   난이도 ●●○

According to the article, what most likely prompted Jackson's interest in skating?	기사에 따르면, 무엇이 잭슨의 스케이팅에 대한 관심을 자극했던 것 같은가?
(a) the encouragement of her parents	(a) 그녀 부모님의 격려
(b) the hosting of the Olympics by her town	(b) 그녀가 사는 도시의 올림픽 개최
(c) the formation of a local skating team	(c) 지역 스케이팅팀의 형성
(d) the performance of an athlete	**(d) 한 운동선수의 공연**

○ 지텔프 치트키

질문의 키워드 prompted가 Inspired로 paraphrasing되어 언급된 주변 내용을 주의 깊게 읽는다.

해설 | 2단락의 'Inspired by the artistic techniques used by figure skater ~, she joined a local inline skating team at the age of 10.'에서 잭슨은 피겨스케이팅 선수가 사용한 예술적 기술들에 영감을 받아 10살 때 지역 인라인스케이팅팀에 합류했다고 한 것을 통해, 한 운동선수의 공연이 잭슨의 스케이팅에 대한 관심을 자극했던 것임을 추론할 수 있다. 따라서 (d)가 정답이다.

어휘 | prompt v. 자극하다 encouragement n. 격려 formation n. 형성, 구성

---

55 추론 특정사실
난이도 ●●●

Why was Jackson probably surprised by the result of the 2017 Olympic trials?

(a) because her previous achievements were not considered
(b) because she succeeded despite a lack of experience
(c) because her competitors looked down on former inline skaters
(d) because she did not expect to take part in the qualifying race so early

왜 잭슨은 2017년 올림픽 선발 대회의 결과에 놀랐던 것 같은가?

(a) 그녀의 이전 업적들이 고려되지 않았기 때문에
(b) 경험의 부족에도 불구하고 성과를 거두었기 때문에
(c) 그녀의 경쟁자들이 이전의 인라인스케이팅 선수들을 무시했기 때문에
(d) 예선전에 그렇게 일찍 참가할 것이라고 예상하지 못했기 때문에

지텔프 치트키

질문의 키워드 surprised가 disbelief로 paraphrasing되어 언급된 주변 내용을 주의 깊게 읽는다.

해설 | 3단락의 'After only four months, Jackson skated at the 2017 Olympic trials to see where she stood.'에서 불과 4개월 후에 잭슨이 2017년 올림픽 선발 대회에서 스케이트를 탔다고 한 뒤, 'To her disbelief, she ~ qualified for the 2018 Winter Olympics.'에서 믿기지 않게도 잭슨이 2018년 동계 올림픽에 출전할 자격을 얻었다고 한 것을 통해, 잭슨은 경험의 부족에도 불구하고 성과를 거두었기 때문에 2017년 올림픽 선발 대회의 결과에 놀랐던 것임을 추론할 수 있다. 따라서 (b)가 정답이다.

어휘 | previous adj. 이전의 achievement n. 업적 look down on phr. ~를 무시하다 qualifying race phr. 예선전

---

56 특정세부사항 How
난이도 ●●○

How did Jackson make it to the 2022 Olympics?

(a) by agreeing to participate in longer races
(b) by finishing in third place at the US trials
(c) by taking a fellow athlete's place in an event
(d) by becoming the world's top 500-meter speed skater

잭슨은 어떻게 2022년 올림픽에 참가했는가?

(a) 더 긴 경주에 참가하는 것을 수락함으로써
(b) 미국 대표 선수 선발 대회에서 3위를 함으로써
(c) 한 경기에서 동료 선수의 자리를 대신함으로써
(d) 세계 1위 500미터 스피드스케이팅 선수가 됨으로써

지텔프 치트키

질문의 키워드 2022 Olympics가 그대로 언급된 주변 내용을 주의 깊게 읽는다.

해설 | 4단락의 'her teammate Brittany Bowe ~ decided to give her spot in the 500-meter event to Jackson'에서 잭슨의 동료 선수인 브리트니 보가 500미터 종목에서 그녀의 출전 자리를 잭슨에게 주기로 결정했다고 했다. 따라서 (c)가 정답이다.

Paraphrasing

her teammate 동료 선수 → a fellow athlete 동료 선수
give her spot 그녀의 자리를 주다 → taking a ~ place 자리를 대신함

어휘 | make it phr. 참가하다, 진출하다 take one's place phr. ~의 자리를 대신하다 fellow n. 동료

What is the objective of Edge Sports?	에지 스포츠 사의 목표는 무엇인가?
(a) to use Jackson's celebrity status for exposure	(a) 대중의 관심을 끄는 일에 잭슨의 유명 인사 지위를 이용하는 것
(b) to increase ethnic diversity in a field dominated by white people	**(b) 백인이 우세한 분야에서 민족적 다양성을 증가시키는 것**
(c) to promote involvement in winter sports across the state of Utah	(c) 유타주 전역에서 동계 스포츠에 대한 참여를 촉진하는 것
(d) to sponsor Jackson at the 2026 Winter Olympics	(d) 2026년 동계 올림픽에서 잭슨을 후원하는 것

─○ 지텔프 치트키

질문의 키워드 Edge Sports가 그대로 언급된 주변 내용을 주의 깊게 읽는다.

해설 | 5단락의 'hopes to boost the participation of people of color in winter sports'에서 에지 스포츠 사는 유색인종의 동계 스포츠 참여를 증진하고 싶어 한다고 했다. 따라서 (b)가 정답이다.

어휘 | exposure n. 대중의 관심을 끄는 일 ethnic adj. 민족적 dominate v. 우세하다, 지배하다 involvement n. 참여 sponsor v. 후원하다

---

58 **어휘** 유의어 난이도 ●●○

In the context of the passage, aspired means _____.	지문의 문맥에서, 'aspired'는 –을 의미한다.
(a) desired	**(a) 열망했다**
(b) required	(b) 필요로 했다
(c) demanded	(c) 요구했다
(d) claimed	(d) 주장했다

─○ 지텔프 치트키

밑줄 친 어휘의 유의어를 찾는 문제이므로, aspired가 포함된 구절을 읽고 문맥을 파악한다.

해설 | 3단락의 'aspired to challenge herself'는 스스로 도전하기를 열망했다는 뜻이므로, aspired가 '열망했다'라는 의미로 사용된 것을 알 수 있다. 따라서 '열망했다'라는 같은 의미의 (a) desired가 정답이다.

---

59 **어휘** 유의어 난이도 ●●○

In the context of the passage, improved means _____.	지문의 문맥에서, 'improved'는 –을 의미한다.
(a) fortified	(a) 강화했다
(b) established	(b) 확립했다
(c) broadened	(c) 넓혔다
(d) developed	**(d) 발달시켰다**

─○ 지텔프 치트키

밑줄 친 어휘의 유의어를 찾는 문제이므로, improved가 포함된 구절을 읽고 문맥을 파악한다.

PART 2 (60~66) 잡지 기사   인간의 감정을 읽는 로봇의 개발

기사 제목	**[60]A ROBOT TO READ HUMAN EMOTIONS IS DEVELOPED**

[60]A ROBOT TO READ HUMAN EMOTIONS IS DEVELOPED

Pepper is a four-foot-tall humanoid robot that was introduced by SoftBank founder Masayoshi Son at a press conference on June 5, 2014. It has a tablet display on its chest and was [60]the world's first robot designed to read emotions. This machine was the result of cooperation with Aldebaran Robotics, which was acquired by the Japanese company SoftBank in 2012 for $100 million.

Pepper was equipped with technology that allowed it to [65]gauge people's emotions based on their tone of voice and facial expression. The more the robot interacted with humans, whether by making jokes, dancing, or communicating through its touchscreen, the more it understood about people. In fact, [61]everything each robot learned was uploaded to a cloud-based system that other units could access, meaning the robots quickly grasped how to act naturally.

Although Aldebaran had previously produced other robots including the Noa and Romeo models, SoftBank was new to this field prior to Pepper. Regardless, the creation of a robot possessing the ability to recognize feelings was consistent with the company's mission to better people's lives through technology. [62]When Pepper went on sale in Japan in 2015, priced at just under $2,000 per unit, 1,000 units sold out within a minute.

In addition to having been used in thousands of homes since then, Pepper was employed in offices, airports, restaurants, and banks. It performed a variety of functions including chatting with customers, offering menus, and making recommendations. Furthermore, in 2017, an international team received more than £2 million to fund [63]a project using Pepper robots to help elderly individuals in hospitals and assisted living facilities feel less lonely. The team hoped that Pepper could alleviate some of the pressure faced by staff and [66]complement existing care.

[60]인간의 감정을 읽는 로봇이 개발되다

페퍼는 소프트뱅크 사의 창업자 손 마사요시가 2014년 6월 5일에 기자회견에서 선보인 4피트 크기의 인간과 비슷한 로봇이다. 그것은 가슴에 태블릿 디스플레이를 가지고 있으며 [60]감정을 읽도록 설계된 세계 최초의 로봇이었다. 이 기계는 알데바란 로보틱스 사와의 협력의 결과물이었는데, 그것은 2012년에 1억 달러에 일본 기업 소프트뱅크 사에 의해 인수되었다.

페퍼는 목소리 톤과 표정에 기반하여 그것으로 하여금 [65]사람들의 감정을 판단할 수 있게 하는 기술을 탑재했다. 그 로봇이 농담을 하거나, 춤을 추거나, 터치 스크린을 통해 의사소통하며 인간과 더 많이 상호 작용할수록, 그것은 사람에 대해 더 잘 이해했다. 사실, [61]각 로봇이 학습한 모든 것은 다른 기기들이 접근할 수 있는 클라우드 기반 시스템에 업로드되었으며, 이는 로봇들이 자연스럽게 행동하는 법을 빠르게 파악했다는 것을 의미한다.

알데바란 사는 이전에 노아와 로미오 모델을 포함한 다른 로봇들을 생산했던 적이 있었지만, 소프트뱅크 사는 페퍼 이전까지는 이 분야가 처음이었다. 그럼에도 불구하고, 감정을 인식하는 능력을 갖춘 로봇의 창조는 기술을 사용하여 사람들의 삶을 개선하려는 그 회사의 임무와 일치했다. [62]페퍼가 2015년에 일본에서 판매되기 시작했을 때, 기기당 가격이 2,000달러 조금 안 되었는데, 1,000대의 기기가 1분 안에 매진되었다.

그때부터 수많은 가정에서 사용되어 온 것과 더불어, 페퍼는 사무실, 공항, 식당, 그리고 은행에서 사용되었다. 그것은 고객과 담소를 나누는 것, 메뉴를 제공하는 것, 그리고 추천을 하는 것을 포함하여 다양한 기능을 수행했다. 게다가, 2017년에, 한 국제 조직은 [63]병원 및 생활 보조 시설에 있는 노인들이 외로움을 덜 느끼도록 돕고자 페퍼 로봇을 사용하는 프로젝트에 자금을 대기 위해 2백만 파운드 이상을 받았다. 그 조직은 페퍼가 직원들이 받는 압박의 일부를 완화하고 [66]기존의 치료를 보완할 수 있기를 바랐다.

| 위기
+
향후
계획 | Nevertheless, despite Pepper's potential, SoftBank ceased production of the robot in June 2021, citing declining demand. In all, only 27,000 Pepper units were produced. According to industry sources familiar with Pepper's development, restarting production would be costly for the company. Instead, with its purchase of a 40 percent ownership stake in the industry leader AutoStore, [64]SoftBank is shifting its robotics strategy to focus on storage automation. | 그렇지만, 페퍼의 잠재력에도 불구하고, 소프트뱅크 사는 수요 감소를 이유로 들며, 2021년 6월에 그 로봇의 생산을 중단했다. 모두 합쳐, 겨우 27,000개의 페퍼가 생산되었다. 페퍼의 개발에 정통한 업계 소식통들에 따르면, 생산을 재개하는 것은 회사에 부담이 될 것이다. 대신, 업계 선두 주자인 오토스토어 사의 소유 지분 40퍼센트를 매입하면서, [64]소프트뱅크 사는 창고 자동화에 집중하기 위해 그것의 로봇 공학 전략을 바꾸고 있다. |

어휘ㅣ humanoid adj. 인간과 비슷한 introduce v. 선보이다, 소개하다 press conference phr. 기자회견 acquire v. 인수하다, 획득하다 equip v. 탑재하다, 갖추다 grasp v. 파악하다 consistent adj. 일치하는, 일관된 mission n. 임무 better v. 개선하다 employ v. 사용하다 assisted living facility phr. 생활 보조 시설 alleviate v. 완화하다, 경감하다 pressure n. 압박, 부담 potential n. 잠재력; adj. 잠재적인 cease v. 중단하다 cite v. 이유로 들다, 언급하다 declining adj. 감소하는 industry source phr. 업계 소식통 ownership n. 소유 stake n. 지분 robotics n. 로봇 공학 strategy n. 전략 automation n. 자동화

---

60 주제/목적 　기사의 주제 　　　　　　　　　　　　　　　　난이도 ●○○

What is the article mainly about?	기사의 주제는 무엇인가?
(a) a joint effort to improve artificial intelligence	(a) 인공지능을 향상시키기 위한 합동 노력
(b) the acquisition of a Japanese robotics firm	(b) 일본의 한 로봇 공학 회사의 인수
(c) a machine capable of understanding humans	**(c) 인간을 이해할 수 있는 기계**
(d) a tablet designed to enhance cooperation	(d) 협력을 증진하도록 설계된 태블릿

⊶◯ 지텔프 치트키

제목과 지문의 초반을 주의 깊게 읽고 전체 맥락을 파악한다.

해설ㅣ 기사의 제목 'A Robot to Read Human Emotions Is Developed'에서 인간의 감정을 읽는 로봇이 개발되었다고 했고, 1단락의 'the world's first robot designed to read emotions'에서 로봇 페퍼는 감정을 읽도록 설계된 세계 최초의 로봇이라고 한 뒤, 페퍼에 관한 세부 내용이 이어지고 있다. 따라서 (c)가 정답이다.

Paraphrasing
read human emotions 인간의 감정을 읽다 → understanding humans 인간을 이해하는

어휘ㅣ joint adj. 합동의, 공동의 artificial intelligence phr. 인공지능 capable adj. 할 수 있는

---

61 특정세부사항 　Why 　　　　　　　　　　　　　　　　　　난이도 ●●○

According to the article, why do Pepper units learn how to behave so quickly?	기사에 따르면, 페퍼 기기들은 왜 행동하는 법을 그렇게 빨리 배우는가?
(a) because they can access data uploaded online	**(a) 온라인에 업로드된 데이터에 접근할 수 있기 때문에**
(b) because they can recognize vocal tones with sensors	(b) 감지기로 목소리 톤을 인식할 수 있기 때문에
(c) because they are programmed to adjust to situations	(c) 상황에 적응하도록 설정되어 있기 때문에

(d) because they are equipped with advanced software

(d) 고급 소프트웨어를 탑재하고 있기 때문에

해설 | 2단락의 'everything each robot learned was uploaded to a cloud-based system ~, meaning the robots quickly grasped how to act naturally'에서 각 로봇이 학습한 모든 것은 클라우드 기반 시스템에 업로드되었으며, 이는 로봇들이 자연스럽게 행동하는 법을 빠르게 파악했다는 것을 의미한다고 했다. 따라서 (a)가 정답이다.

Paraphrasing

was uploaded to a cloud-based system 클라우드 기반 시스템에 업로드되었다 → uploaded online 온라인에 업로드된

오답분석
(b) 2단락에서 페퍼가 목소리 톤에 기반하여 그것으로 하여금 사람들의 감정을 판단할 수 있게 하는 기술을 탑재했다고는 했지만, 이것이 페퍼 기기들이 행동하는 법을 빨리 배우는 이유는 아니므로 오답이다.

어휘 | program v. 설정하다 adjust v. 적응하다 advanced adj. 고급의

---

62 추론 특정사실 난이도 ●●●

What can be said about Pepper's release in Japan?

(a) It was sold at a discounted price.
(b) It coincided with the sale of other robots.
(c) It created global demand for the technology.
(d) It was highly anticipated by the public.

페퍼의 일본에서의 출시에 관해 무엇이 말해질 수 있는가?

(a) 할인된 가격에 팔렸다.
(b) 다른 로봇들의 판매와 동시에 일어났다.
(c) 그 기술에 대한 세계적인 수요를 창출했다.
(d) 대중의 큰 기대를 받았다.

해설 | 3단락의 'When Pepper went on sale in Japan in 2015, ~ 1,000 units sold out within a minute.'에서 페퍼가 2015년에 일본에서 판매되기 시작했을 때 1,000대의 기기가 1분 안에 매진되었다고 한 것을 통해, 페퍼의 일본에서의 출시가 대중의 큰 기대를 받았다는 것을 추론할 수 있다. 따라서 (d)가 정답이다.

오답분석
(a) 3단락에서 페퍼가 일본에서 판매되기 시작했을 때 기기당 가격이 2,000달러 조금 안되었다고는 했지만, 이것이 할인된 가격인지는 언급되지 않았으므로 오답이다.

어휘 | coincide v. 동시에 일어나다 anticipate v. 기대하다, 예상하다

---

63 특정세부사항 Why 난이도 ●●○

Why were Pepper robots used in hospitals and assisted living facilities?

(a) to monitor elderly residents' bank accounts
(b) to assist individuals' psychological well-being

왜 페퍼 로봇은 병원과 생활 보조 시설에서 사용되었는가?

(a) 노인 거주자들의 은행 계좌를 관찰하기 위해서
(b) 사람들의 정신적 행복에 도움을 주기 위해서

(c) to help an international team of doctors

(d) to replace the original staff members

(c) 국제 의사 팀을 지원하기 위해서

(d) 기존의 직원들을 대체하기 위해서

지텔프 치트키

질문의 키워드 hospitals and assisted living facilities가 그대로 언급된 주변 내용을 주의 깊게 읽는다.

해설 | 4단락의 'a project using Pepper robots to help elderly individuals in hospitals and assisted living facilities feel less lonely'에서 한 프로젝트가 병원 및 생활 보조 시설에 있는 노인들이 외로움을 덜 느끼도록 돕고자 페퍼 로봇을 사용했다고 했다. 따라서 (b)가 정답이다.

Paraphrasing

help ~ feel less lonely 외로움을 덜 느끼도록 돕다 → assist ~ psychological well-being 정신적 행복에 도움을 주다

어휘 | psychological adj. 정신적인 well-being n. 행복, 안녕감 replace v. 대체하다

---

64 특정세부사항 How 난이도 ●●○

How does SoftBank plan to move forward with its business?

(a) by reengaging in the production of Pepper units

(b) by moving its attention to another area of robotics

(c) by ceasing robotic development in the near future

(d) by offering an ownership stake to an industry leader

소프트뱅크 사는 사업을 어떻게 진전시킬 계획인가?

(a) 페퍼 기기의 생산에 다시 개입함으로써

(b) 로봇 공학의 다른 분야로 관심을 옮김으로써

(c) 가까운 미래에 로봇 개발을 중단함으로써

(d) 업계 선두 주자에게 소유 지분을 제공함으로써

지텔프 치트키

질문의 키워드 plan이 strategy로 paraphrasing되어 언급된 주변 내용을 주의 깊게 읽는다.

해설 | 5단락의 'SoftBank is shifting its robotics strategy to focus on storage automation'에서 소프트뱅크 사는 창고의 자동화에 집중하기 위해 그것의 로봇 공학 전략을 바꾸고 있다고 했다. 따라서 (b)가 정답이다.

Paraphrasing

shifting its robotics strategy 로봇 공학 전략을 바꾸고 있는 → moving its attention to another area of robotics 로봇 공학의 다른 분야로 관심을 옮김

어휘 | reengage v. 다시 개입하다

---

65 어휘 유의어 난이도 ●●○

In the context of the passage, gauge means _____.

(a) collect

(b) reject

(c) assess

(d) quantify

지문의 문맥에서, 'gauge'는 -을 의미한다.

(a) 수집하다

(b) 거부하다

(c) 판단하다

(d) 수량화하다

밑줄 친 어휘의 유의어를 찾는 문제이므로, gauge가 포함된 구절을 읽고 문맥을 파악한다.

해설 | 2단락의 'gauge people's emotions'는 사람들의 감정을 판단한다는 뜻이므로, gauge가 '판단하다'라는 의미로 사용된 것을 알 수 있다. 따라서 '판단하다'라는 같은 의미의 (c) assess가 정답이다.

66 어휘 유의어 난이도 ●●○

In the context of the passage, underline{complement} means _____.

(a) **enhance**
(b) match
(c) instill
(d) complete

지문의 문맥에서, 'complement'는 -을 의미한다.

(a) **개선하다**
(b) 맞추다
(c) 주입하다
(d) 완료하다

밑줄 친 어휘의 유의어를 찾는 문제이므로, complement가 포함된 구절을 읽고 문맥을 파악한다.

해설 | 4단락의 'complement existing care'는 기존의 치료를 보완한다는 뜻이므로, complement가 '보완하다'라는 의미로 사용된 것을 알 수 있다. 따라서 '개선하다'라는 비슷한 의미의 (a) enhance가 정답이다.

PART 3[67~73] 지식 백과 데린쿠유 지하 도시의 기원 및 특징

표제어	**DERINKUYU UNDERGROUND CITY**	데린쿠유 지하 도시
정의	The Derinkuyu underground city is an ancient, multi-level settlement located in Cappadocia, Turkey, which was carved from naturally occurring structures. [67]Derinkuyu is notable because it extends 85 meters below the surface, making it the world's deepest subterranean city.	데린쿠유 지하 도시는 튀르키예 카파도키아에 위치한 고대 다층 주거지이며, 그곳은 자연적으로 생긴 구조물들을 깎아서 만들어졌다. [67]데린쿠유는 지면 아래 85미터까지 이르는 것으로 유명하며, 이는 그것을 세계에서 가장 깊은 지하 도시로 만든다.
생성 + 용도 변화	The creation of Derinkuyu, and [68(d)]the region's other underground settlements, was made possible by the area's geology. [68(a)]Prehistoric volcanic eruptions covered the landscape with ash, [68(b)]leaving formations of easy-to-carve rock. Initially, residents probably dug small underground rooms for food storage. [68(c)]As time passed, however, [72]these rooms were underline{expanded} and transformed into an intricate city which citizens could flee to in the event of invasion.	데린쿠유의 생성과, [68(d)]그 지역의 다른 지하 주거지들은 그 지역의 지질에 의해 가능해졌다. [68(a)]선사 시대의 화산 폭발들이 그 지역을 화산재로 뒤덮었으며, [68(b)]이는 조각하기 쉬운 암석층을 남겼다. 처음에, 거주인들은 아마도 음식 보관을 위해 작은 지하실들을 팠을 것이다. [68(c)]그러나, 시간이 흐르면서, [72]이 방들은 확장되었고 침략당할 경우에 시민들이 도망갈 수 있는 복잡한 도시로 변형되었다.
	The settlement could accommodate up to 20,000 people and their livestock. It also featured amenities	이 주거지는 최대 20,000명의 사람들과 그들의 가축을 수용할 수 있었다. 그것은 또한 예배당과 학교를

생활 환경	including chapels and schools. Ventilation chimneys distributed air throughout the city, while wells ensured a supply of water. Illumination, meanwhile, was done with torches.
기원	It is uncertain who built this secret city. Some think the Hittites constructed it in the 15th century BC as [73]they inhabited Cappadocia then and had many enemies. Others believe the Phrygians were responsible. In fact, the Phrygians overthrew the Hittites and dominated the region from the 12th to 6th centuries BC. [69]They are also known to have erected other sophisticated structures like the fortress at Gordion.
용도	Although there is no record of when the city was established, people continued to use it for centuries. Based on the discovery of artifacts, it was a place of refuge for citizens during the Arab-Byzantine wars. This is suggested by the heavy stone doors that closed from within and protected the city from potential threats. [70]A passage connecting the city to a distinct community called Kaymakli indicates the two groups may have been allies.
재발견	In 1923, the Greek Christian refugees who had made their home in Derinkuyu were forcibly returned to Greece. For the next 40 years, [71]the underground city remained undisturbed until a man carrying out repairs on his house knocked down a basement wall and accidentally found it. Then in 1969, Derinkuyu was partially opened to the public.

포함한 편의 시설들을 특징으로 삼았다. 환기 굴뚝은 도시 전체에 공기를 분산시켰고, 우물은 물의 공급을 보장했다. 한편, 불빛은 횃불로 이뤄졌다.

누가 이 비밀 도시를 건설했는지는 불확실하다. 어떤 사람들은 히타이트인들이 기원전 15세기에 그것을 건설했다고 생각하는데 이는 [73]그들이 그때 카파도키아에 거주했고 많은 적들이 있었기 때문이다. 다른 이들은 프리기아인들에게 책임이 있다고 믿는다. 실제로, 프리기아인들은 히타이트인들을 정복했고 기원전 12세기부터 6세기까지 그 지역을 지배했다. [69]그들은 고르디온에 있는 요새와 같은 다른 정교한 구조물들을 세웠던 것으로도 알려져 있다.

비록 그 도시가 언제 세워졌는지에 대한 기록은 없지만, 사람들은 수 세기 동안 그곳을 계속해서 사용했다. 유물들의 발견으로 미루어 볼 때, 이곳은 아랍-비잔틴 전쟁 당시에 시민들의 피난처였다. 이는 내부에서 닫혀 잠재적인 위협으로부터 도시를 보호했던 무거운 돌문들에 의해 암시된다. [70]그 도시를 카이마클리라고 불리는 별개의 공동체와 연결하는 통로는 두 집단이 동맹이었을 수도 있음을 나타낸다.

1923년에, 데린쿠유에서 가정을 꾸렸던 그리스의 기독교 난민들은 그리스로 강제로 돌려보내졌다. 이후 40년 동안, [71]그 지하 도시는 집을 수리하던 한 남자가 지하실 벽을 무너뜨리고 우연히 그곳을 발견하기 전까지 그 누구도 손대지 않은 채로 남아 있었다. 그 후 1969년에, 데린쿠유는 부분적으로 대중에게 공개되었다.

어휘 | settlement n. 주거지, 정착지 carve v. 깎아서 만들다, 조각하다 notable adj. 유명한, 주목할 만한 extend v. 이르다, 뻗다 subterranean adj. 지하의 geology n. 지질, 지질학 prehistoric adj. 선사 시대의 eruption n. 폭발 formation n. 층, 형성물 transform v. 변형시키다 intricate adj. 복잡한 flee v. 도망가다 invasion n. 침략 accommodate v. 수용하다 livestock n. 가축 chapel n. 예배당 ventilation n. 환기 chimney n. 굴뚝 distribute v. 분산시키다, 퍼뜨리다 illumination n. 불빛, 조명 overthrow v. 정복하다 erect v. 세우다 sophisticated adj. 정교한 fortress n. 요새 artifact n. 유물 refuge n. 피난 distinct adj. 별개의 ally n. 동맹 refugee n. 난민 undisturbed adj. 그 누구도 손대지 않은 basement n. 지하실 accidentally adv. 우연히

67	**특정세부사항**	What	난이도 ●●○

According to the article, what makes Derinkuyu noteworthy?

(a) its location in Turkey
(b) its great depth beneath the ground
(c) its multiple levels
(d) its construction from natural elements

기사에 따르면, 무엇이 데린쿠유를 주목할 만하게 만드는가?

(a) 튀르키예에서의 위치
(b) 굉장한 땅속 깊이
(c) 여러 개의 층
(d) 자연적인 요소들에 의한 구성

질문의 키워드 noteworthy가 notable로 paraphrasing되어 언급된 주변 내용을 주의 깊게 읽는다.

해설 | 1단락의 'Derinkuyu is notable because it extends 85 meters below the surface, making it the world's deepest subterranean city.'에서 데린쿠유는 지면 아래 85미터까지 이르는 것으로 유명하며, 이는 데린쿠유를 세계에서 가장 깊은 지하 도시로 만든다고 했다. 따라서 (b)가 정답이다.

Paraphrasing
below the surface 지면 아래 → beneath the ground 땅속
deepest 가장 깊은 → great depth 굉장한 깊이

어휘 | depth n. 깊이 element n. 요소, 성분

68 Not/True True 문제
난이도 ●●○

Which of the following is true about Derinkuyu?

(a) It was used to escape dangerous volcanic eruptions.
(b) Its chambers were carved from hard stones.
(c) Its purpose changed with the passage of time.
(d) It was the only settlement of its kind in the region.

다음 중 데린쿠유에 관해 사실인 것은 무엇인가?

(a) 위험한 화산 폭발을 피하기 위해 사용되었다.
(b) 내부의 공간들이 단단한 돌들을 깎아서 만들어졌다.
(c) 시간이 지남에 따라 목적이 변했다.
(d) 그 지역의 주거지들 중 유일한 종류의 것이었다.

지텔프 치트키

보기의 키워드와 지문 내용을 대조하며 읽는다.

해설 | (c)의 키워드인 passage of time이 time passed로 paraphrasing되어 언급된 2단락의 'As time passed, ~ these rooms were ~ transformed into an intricate city which citizens could flee to in the event of invasion.'에서 시간이 흐르면서 음식 보관을 위해 파졌던 방들은 침략당할 경우에 시민들이 도망갈 수 있는 복잡한 도시로 변형되었다고 했으므로 지문의 내용과 일치한다. 따라서 (c)가 정답이다.

오답분석
(a) 보기의 키워드 volcanic eruptions가 그대로 언급된 2단락에서 선사 시대의 화산 폭발들이 그 지역을 화산재로 뒤덮었다고는 했지만, 데린쿠유가 화산 폭발을 피하기 위해 사용되었는지는 언급되지 않았다.
(b) 보기의 키워드 stones가 rock으로 paraphrasing되어 언급된 2단락에서 선사 시대의 화산 폭발들이 조각하기 쉬운 암석층을 남겼다고 했으므로 지문의 내용과 일치하지 않는다.
(d) 보기의 키워드 region이 그대로 언급된 2단락에서 그 지역의 다른 지하 주거지들이 있었다고 했으므로 지문의 내용과 일치하지 않는다.

어휘 | escape v. 피하다, 도망치다 chamber n. 내부의 공간, 방

69 추론 특정사실
난이도 ●●●

Why most likely do some experts believe the Phrygians designed Derinkuyu?

(a) because they were in power longer than the Hittites
(b) because they reigned over the region in the 15th century BC

왜 일부 전문가들은 프리기아인들이 데린쿠유를 설계했다고 믿는 것 같은가?

(a) 히타이트인들보다 더 오래 권력을 잡고 있었기 때문에
(b) 기원전 15세기에 그 지역을 지배했기 때문에

(c) because they were constantly threatened by enemies

(d) because they built a complex fort in another area

(c) 적들로부터 끊임없이 위협을 받았기 때문에

(d) 다른 지역에 복잡한 요새를 지었기 때문에

⊶◯ 지텔프 치트키

질문의 키워드 Phrygians가 그대로 언급된 주변 내용을 주의 깊게 읽는다.

해설 | 4단락의 'They are also known to have erected other sophisticated structures like the fortress at Gordion.'에서 프리기 아인들은 고르디온에 있는 요새와 같은 다른 정교한 구조물들을 세운 것으로도 알려져 있다고 한 것을 통해, 프리기아인들이 다른 지역에 복 잡한 요새를 지었기 때문에 일부 전문가들은 그들이 데린쿠유를 설계했다고 믿는 것임을 추론할 수 있다. 따라서 (d)가 정답이다.

오답분석

(b) 4단락에서 기원전 15세기에 히타이트인들이 카파도키아에 거주했다고 했으므로 오답이다.

어휘 | reign v. 지배하다 constantly adv. 끊임없이 complex adj. 복잡한 fort n. 요새

---

70 추론 특정사실 난이도 ●●○

Why probably was there a passage between Derinkuyu and Kaymakli?

(a) to accommodate a higher refugee population
(b) to serve as an escape route in case of earthquakes
(c) to prevent livestock from running away
(d) to facilitate cooperation between the cities

왜 데린쿠유와 카이마클리 사이에 통로가 있었던 것 같은가?

(a) 더 많은 난민 인구를 수용하기 위해서
(b) 지진 발생 시 탈출 경로의 역할을 하기 위해서
(c) 가축이 달아나는 것을 막기 위해서
(d) 도시들 간의 협력을 촉진하기 위해서

⊶◯ 지텔프 치트키

질문의 키워드 Kaymakli가 그대로 언급된 주변 내용을 주의 깊게 읽는다.

해설 | 5단락의 'A passage connecting the city to ~ Kaymakli indicates the two groups may have been allies.'에서 데린쿠유 지하 도시를 카이마클리라고 불리는 공동체와 연결하는 통로는 두 집단이 동맹이었을 수도 있음을 나타낸다고 한 것을 통해, 데린쿠유와 카 이마클리 간의 협력을 촉진하기 위해서 두 도시 사이에 통로가 있었던 것임을 추론할 수 있다. 따라서 (d)가 정답이다.

어휘 | facilitate v. 촉진하다

---

71 특정세부사항 When 난이도 ●○○

When did Derinkuyu become accessible to the general public?

(a) after a home was renovated
(b) after refugees returned to their home nation
(c) after authorities inspected a disturbance
(d) after a tourist attraction was planned

데린쿠유는 언제 일반 대중에게 접근 가능해졌는가?

(a) 집이 수리된 후에
(b) 난민들이 그들의 본국으로 돌아간 후에
(c) 당국이 지각 변동을 점검한 후에
(d) 관광 명소가 설치된 후에

⊶◯ 지텔프 치트키

질문의 키워드 accessible to ~ public이 opened to ~ public으로 paraphrasing되어 언급된 주변 내용을 주의 깊게 읽는다.

해설 | 6단락의 'the underground city remained undisturbed until a man carrying out repairs on his house ~ accidentally found it'에서 데린쿠유 지하 도시는 집을 수리하던 한 남자가 우연히 그곳을 발견하기 전까지 그 누구도 손대지 않은 채로 남아 있었다고 한 뒤, 'Then in 1969, Derinkuyu was ~ opened to the public.'에서 그 후에 데린쿠유가 대중에게 공개되었다고 했다. 따라서 (a)가 정답이다.

Paraphrasing

carrying out repairs on his house 집을 수리하는 → a home was renovated 집이 수리되었다

어휘 | renovate v. 수리하다, 개조하다 inspect v. 점검하다 disturbance n. 지각 변동, 소란 tourist attraction phr. 관광 명소

---

72 어휘 · 유의어

난이도 ●●○

In the context of the passage, <u>expanded</u> means _____.

(a) limited
(b) amplified
(c) enlarged
(d) stretched

지문의 문맥에서, 'expanded'는 -을 의미한다.

(a) 제한된
(b) 증폭된
(c) 확장된
(d) 연장된

○— 지텔프 치트키

밑줄 친 어휘의 유의어를 찾는 문제이므로, expanded가 포함된 구절을 읽고 문맥을 파악한다.

해설 | 2단락의 'these rooms were expanded'는 이 방들이 확장되었다는 뜻이므로, expanded가 '확장된'이라는 의미로 사용된 것을 알 수 있다. 따라서 '확장된'이라는 같은 의미의 (c) enlarged가 정답이다.

오답분석

(b) '증폭시키다'라는 의미의 amplify는 주로 소리나 전류의 범위가 늘어나거나 커지는 경우에 사용하므로, 문맥에 어울리지 않아 오답이다.

---

73 어휘 유의어

난이도 ●●○

In the context of the passage, <u>inhabited</u> means _____.

(a) contained
(b) defended
(c) occupied
(d) fulfilled

지문의 문맥에서, 'inhabited'는 -을 의미한다.

(a) 포함했다
(b) 방어했다
(c) 거주했다
(d) 달성했다

○— 지텔프 치트키

밑줄 친 어휘의 유의어를 찾는 문제이므로, inhabited가 포함된 구절을 읽고 문맥을 파악한다.

해설 | 4단락의 'they inhabited Cappadocia then'은 그들이 그때 카파도키아에 거주했다는 뜻이므로, inhabited가 '거주했다'라는 의미로 사용된 것을 알 수 있다. 따라서 '거주했다'라는 같은 의미의 (c) occupied가 정답이다.

해커스 지텔프 최신기출유형 실전문제집 7회 (Level 2)

수신인 정보	Ms. Grace Adair 1414 Havenhurst Street West Hollywood, CA 90046 Dear Ms. Adair:	Ms. Grace Adair 헤이븐허스트가 1414번지 90046 캘리포니아주 웨스트 할리우드 Ms. Adair께:
편지의 목적: 심사위원 역할 제안	I am writing from MCW Studios to tell you about a new competition show called *Make Me a Star*. Like other shows in this genre, the participants will be amateurs hoping to be discovered. It will air on television and later be uploaded to MCW's social media channel. There will be various types of acts, some of which will feature music. Since this is your area of expertise, ⁷⁴we would like to know if you are interested in becoming a judge.	저는 MCW 스튜디오를 대표하여 「Make Me a Star」라는 이름의 새로운 경연 프로그램에 대해 알려 드리기 위해 편지를 씁니다. 이 장르의 다른 프로그램들처럼, 참가자들은 재능이 발견되기를 바라는 아마추어들일 것입니다. 그것은 텔레비전에서 방영될 것이고 추후에 MCW의 소셜 미디어 채널에 업로드될 것입니다. 다양한 종류의 공연들이 있을 것이고, 그중 일부는 음악을 포함할 것입니다. 이것은 귀하의 전문 분야이기 때문에, ⁷⁴저희는 귀하가 심사위원이 되는 것에 관심이 있는지를 알고 싶습니다.
제안 이유	⁷⁵Your successful career as a recording artist makes you ⁷⁹ideal for the role. While audiences mostly want to see contestants perform, they also tune in for the judges. I know ⁷⁵people will appreciate what you have to say.	⁷⁵귀하의 음반 예술가로서의 성공적인 경력은 귀하를 ⁷⁹그 역할에 이상적이게 만듭니다. 관객들은 주로 경연자들이 공연하는 것을 보고 싶어 하겠지만, 그들은 심사위원들 때문에 시청하기도 합니다. 저는 ⁷⁵사람들이 귀하의 의견을 높이 평가할 것이라는 것을 알고 있습니다.
역할 설명	The judges will observe the contestants carefully. ⁷⁶They will then vote for who will return in the show's next episode and who will leave. Throughout the process, the panel will comment on each act, ⁸⁰either giving criticism or praise. Essentially, ⁷⁷contestants will be eliminated until the season finale, when the winner and two runners-up will be chosen. You'd have to film two episodes a week from June to September and would be compensated accordingly.	심사위원들은 경연자들을 주의 깊게 지켜볼 것입니다. ⁷⁶그다음에 그들은 그 프로그램의 다음 편에서 누가 다시 나오고 누가 탈락할지를 투표할 것입니다. 전 과정에 걸쳐, 패널은 ⁸⁰비판이나 칭찬을 하면서, 각각의 공연에 대해 논평할 것입니다. 기본적으로, ⁷⁷경연자들은 시즌의 마지막 편까지 탈락될 것인데, 그때 우승자와 두 명의 준우승자가 선택될 것입니다. 귀하는 6월부터 9월까지 일주일에 두 편씩 촬영해야 할 것이며 그에 따라 보상을 받게 될 것입니다.
요청 + 끝인사	If this opportunity appeals to you, please call me at 533-4679 so we can set up an appointment to meet at MCW Studios. ⁷⁸Max Rasmussen, the show's creator, will be in attendance to discuss your duties more specifically.	이 기회가 마음에 드신다면, MCW 스튜디오에서 만날 약속을 잡을 수 있도록 533-4679로 전화 주십시오. ⁷⁸이 프로그램의 제작자인 Max Rasmussen이 귀하의 임무에 대해 더 구체적으로 상의하기 위해 자리에 참석할 것입니다.
발신인 정보	Sincerely, Darrel Cannon Head of Programming MCW Studios	Darrel Cannon 드림 프로그램 편성 책임자 MCW 스튜디오

어휘 | discover v. 재능을 발견하다, 발굴하다 air v. 방영되다 expertise n. 전문, 전문 지식 judge n. 심사위원 recording artist phr. 음반 예술가
contestant n. 경연자 tune in phr. 시청하다 appreciate v. 높이 평가하다, 진가를 알아보다 vote v. 투표하다 criticism n. 비판
essentially adv. 기본적으로 eliminate v. 탈락하다, 제거하다 runner-up n. 준우승자 compensate v. 보상하다, 보상금을 주다
accordingly adv. 그에 따라 appointment n. 약속 duty n. 임무, 업무

74 주제/목적　편지의 목적

Why did Darrel Cannon write a letter to Grace Adair?

(a) to invite her to be a contestant on a show
(b) to remark on her recent television appearance
(c) to present her with a part in a competition
(d) to ask her to play music of various genres on the air

왜 Darrel Cannon은 Grace Adair에게 편지를 썼는가?

(a) 한 프로그램의 경연자로 그녀를 초청하기 위해서
(b) 그녀의 최근 텔레비전 출연에 관해 논평하기 위해서
(c) 그녀에게 한 경연에서의 역할을 제시하기 위해서
(d) 그녀에게 방송에서 다양한 장르의 음악 연주를 부탁하기 위해서

⟴○ 지텔프 치트키

지문의 초반을 주의 깊게 읽고 전체 맥락을 파악한다.

해설 | 1단락의 'we would like to know if you are interested in becoming a judge'에서 Darrel Cannon이 Grace Adair에게 그녀가 심사위원이 되는 것에 관심이 있는지를 알고 싶다고 한 뒤, 심사위원 역할을 제안하는 이유와 그 역할에 관해 설명하는 내용이 이어지고 있다. 따라서 (c)가 정답이다.

어휘 | remark v. 논평하다　appearance n. 출연, 외모　part n. 역할, 배역

75 추론　특정사실

Why do competition show audiences probably want to see Grace Adair?

(a) because she has a positive personality
(b) because she is a renowned celebrity
(c) because she has released a new album
(d) because she is experienced as a judge

왜 경연 프로그램의 시청자들은 Grace Adair를 보고 싶어 하는 것 같은가?

(a) 긍정적인 성격을 가지고 있기 때문에
(b) 명망 있는 유명 인사이기 때문에
(c) 새 앨범을 발매했기 때문에
(d) 심사위원으로서 경험이 풍부하기 때문에

⟴○ 지텔프 치트키

질문의 키워드 audiences가 그대로 언급된 주변 내용을 주의 깊게 읽는다.

해설 | 2단락의 'Your successful career as a recording artist makes you ideal for the role.'에서 Grace Adair의 음반 예술가로서의 성공적인 경력은 그녀를 심사위원 역할에 이상적이게 만든다고 한 뒤, 'people will appreciate what you have to say'에서 사람들이 그녀의 의견을 높이 평가할 것이라고 한 것을 통해, Grace Adair가 명망 있는 유명 인사이기 때문에 경연 프로그램의 시청자들이 그녀를 보고 싶어 할 것임을 추론할 수 있다. 따라서 (b)가 정답이다.

어휘 | renowned adj. 명망 있는, 저명한　experienced adj. 경험이 풍부한, 능숙한

76 특정세부사항　When

When do contestants know if they will appear in the next episode?

(a) after the judges cast their ballots
(b) when they reach the end of an episode

경연자들은 언제 그들이 다음 편에 출연할지의 여부를 알 수 있는가?

(a) 심사위원들이 투표한 후에
(b) 그들이 한 편의 말미에 이를 때

(c) when the audience votes for them
(d) after they comment on each other

(c) 시청자가 그들에게 투표할 때
(d) 그들이 서로에 대해 논평한 후에

○― 지텔프 치트키

질문의 키워드 next episode가 그대로 언급된 주변 내용을 주의 깊게 읽는다.

해설 | 3단락의 'They will ~ vote for who will return in the show's next episode and who will leave.'에서 심사위원들이 그 프로그램의 다음 편에서 누가 다시 나오고 누가 탈락할지를 투표할 것이라고 했다. 따라서 (a)가 정답이다.

Paraphrasing
appear 출연하다 → return 다시 나오다
vote 투표하다 → cast their ballots 투표하다

어휘 | cast v. (표를) 던지다 ballot n. 투표 reach v. 이르다, 도달하다

---

77 특정세부사항 What   난이도 ●●●

What happens leading up to the last episode of the season?

(a) A contestant is chosen as the winner.
(b) A contestant receives a cash prize.
(c) Some participants compete in shorter rounds.
(d) Some participants are cut from the show.

시즌의 마지막 편에 이르기까지 무슨 일이 일어나는가?

(a) 한 경연자가 우승자로 선정된다.
(b) 한 경연자가 상금을 받는다.
(c) 일부 참가자들이 더 짧은 시합에서 경쟁한다.
(d) 일부 참가자들이 그 프로그램에서 제명된다.

○― 지텔프 치트키

질문의 키워드 last episode가 finale로 paraphrasing되어 언급된 주변 내용을 주의 깊게 읽는다.

해설 | 3단락의 'contestants will be eliminated until the season finale'에서 경연자들은 시즌의 마지막 편까지 탈락될 것이라고 했다. 따라서 (d)가 정답이다.

Paraphrasing
leading up to the last episode of the season 시즌의 마지막 편에 이르기까지 → until the season finale 시즌의 마지막 편까지
contestants will be eliminated 경연자들이 탈락될 것이다 → participants are cut 참가자들이 제명된다

오답분석
(a) 3단락에서 시즌 마지막 편에서 우승자가 선택된다고는 했지만, 이것은 시즌의 마지막 편에만 해당하는 일이며 마지막 편에 이르기까지 일어나는 일이 아니므로 오답이다.

어휘 | lead up to phr. ~에 이르다 cut v. 제명하다

---

78 특정세부사항 Why   난이도 ●●○

Why will Max Rasmussen attend a meeting?

(a) so he can discuss changes to a show
(b) so he can finalize a schedule with MCW Studios

왜 Max Rasmussen은 모임에 참석할 예정인가?

(a) 프로그램의 변경 사항에 대해 상의하기 위해서
(b) MCW 스튜디오와의 일정을 확정하기 위해서

(c) so he can see the results of an audience survey
(d) so he can talk about a project in detail

(c) 시청자 설문 조사의 결과를 확인하기 위해서
(d) 프로젝트에 대해 자세히 이야기하기 위해서

지텔프 치트키

질문의 키워드 Max Rasmussen이 그대로 언급된 주변 내용을 주의 깊게 읽는다.

해설 | 4단락의 'Max Rasmussen, the show's creator, will be in attendance to discuss your duties more specifically.'에서 이 프로그램의 제작자인 Max Rasmussen이 Grace Adair의 임무에 대해 더 구체적으로 상의하기 위해서 자리에 참석할 것이라고 했다. 따라서 (d)가 정답이다.

Paraphrasing
attend 참석하다 → be in attendance 자리에 참석하다
discuss ~ specifically 구체적으로 상의하다 → talk ~ in detail 자세히 이야기하다

어휘 | finalize v. 확정하다 survey n. 설문 조사

---

79 어휘 유의어
난이도 ●●○

In the context of the passage, <u>ideal</u> means _____.

(a) best
(b) serious
(c) specialized
(d) preferred

지문의 문맥에서, 'ideal'은 -을 의미한다.

(a) 최적의
(b) 진지한
(c) 전문적인
(d) 우선의

지텔프 치트키

밑줄 친 어휘의 유의어를 찾는 문제이므로, ideal이 포함된 구절을 읽고 문맥을 파악한다.

해설 | 2단락의 'ideal for the role'은 그 역할에 이상적이라는 뜻이므로, ideal이 '이상적인'이라는 의미로 사용된 것을 알 수 있다. 따라서 '최적의'라는 비슷한 의미의 (a) best가 정답이다.

---

80 어휘 유의어
난이도 ●●○

In the context of the passage, <u>praise</u> means _____.

(a) cheer
(b) acclaim
(c) devotion
(d) honor

지문의 문맥에서, 'praise'는 -을 의미한다.

(a) 환호
(b) 칭찬
(c) 헌신
(d) 영광

지텔프 치트키

밑줄 친 어휘의 유의어를 찾는 문제이므로, praise가 포함된 구절을 읽고 문맥을 파악한다.

해설 | 3단락의 'either giving criticism or praise'는 비판이나 칭찬을 한다는 뜻이므로, praise가 '칭찬'이라는 의미로 사용된 것을 알 수 있다. 따라서 '칭찬'이라는 같은 의미의 (b) acclaim이 정답이다.

TEST 4

정답·스크립트·해석·해설

GRAMMAR

LISTENING

READING & VOCABULARY

TEST 4 점수 확인하기

GRAMMAR _____ / 26 (점수 : _____ 점)
LISTENING _____ / 26 (점수 : _____ 점)
READING & VOCABULARY _____ / 28 (점수 : _____ 점)

TOTAL _____ / 80 (평균 점수 : _____ 점)

*각 영역 점수: 맞은 개수 × 3.75
*평균 점수: 각 영역 점수 합계 ÷ 3

GRAMMAR

번호	정답	유형
01	b	가정법
02	a	조동사
03	a	조동사
04	b	관계사
05	d	시제
06	c	준동사
07	d	가정법
08	a	시제
09	c	준동사
10	d	가정법
11	d	연결어
12	d	시제
13	c	준동사
14	a	조동사
15	b	시제
16	d	준동사
17	c	가정법
18	c	조동사
19	d	준동사
20	b	시제
21	a	연결어
22	c	관계사
23	a	가정법
24	c	시제
25	b	준동사
26	a	가정법

LISTENING

PART	번호	정답	유형
PART 1	27	c	특정세부사항
	28	d	특정세부사항
	29	a	특정세부사항
	30	d	특정세부사항
	31	b	특정세부사항
	32	d	추론
	33	b	추론
PART 2	34	a	특정세부사항
	35	b	특정세부사항
	36	d	특정세부사항
	37	a	특정세부사항
	38	c	Not/True
	39	b	추론
PART 3	40	b	특정세부사항
	41	c	특정세부사항
	42	d	추론
	43	b	특정세부사항
	44	a	특정세부사항
	45	d	추론
PART 4	46	c	특정세부사항
	47	c	특정세부사항
	48	a	추론
	49	b	특정세부사항
	50	c	특정세부사항
	51	a	특정세부사항
	52	a	추론

READING & VOCABULARY

PART	번호	정답	유형
PART 1	53	d	추론
	54	a	특정세부사항
	55	b	추론
	56	d	특정세부사항
	57	c	특정세부사항
	58	b	어휘
	59	d	어휘
PART 2	60	b	특정세부사항
	61	d	특정세부사항
	62	a	추론
	63	c	특정세부사항
	64	d	특정세부사항
	65	c	어휘
	66	a	어휘
PART 3	67	b	주제/목적
	68	a	특정세부사항
	69	d	추론
	70	b	특정세부사항
	71	c	특정세부사항
	72	b	어휘
	73	a	어휘
PART 4	74	d	추론
	75	c	특정세부사항
	76	a	특정세부사항
	77	c	추론
	78	c	특정세부사항
	79	b	어휘
	80	a	어휘

유형	맞힌 개수
시제	/ 6
가정법	/ 6
준동사	/ 6
조동사	/ 4
연결어	/ 2
관계사	/ 2
TOTAL	/ 26

유형	맞힌 개수
주제/목적	/ 0
특정세부사항	/ 18
Not/True	/ 1
추론	/ 7
TOTAL	/ 26

유형	맞힌 개수
주제/목적	/ 1
특정세부사항	/ 13
Not/True	/ 0
추론	/ 6
어휘	/ 8
TOTAL	/ 28

GRAMMAR

01   가정법   가정법 과거완료   난이도 ●●○

I'm sorry to say this, but I really must be going now. If I _____ about this get-together beforehand, I would have rescheduled my other engagement today.

(a) were told
(b) had been told
(c) am told
(d) would be told

이런 말씀 드려서 죄송하지만, 저는 이제 정말 가봐야겠습니다. 만약 제가 이 모임에 대해 미리 전달받았었다면, 저는 오늘 다른 약속의 일정을 변경했을 것입니다.

─○ 지텔프 치트키

if와 'would/could + have p.p.'가 있으면 had p.p.가 정답이다.

> ☼ 가정법 과거완료
> If + 주어 + had p.p., 주어 + would/could(조동사 과거형) + have p.p.

해설ㅣ 주절에 'would(조동사 과거형) + have p.p.' 형태의 would have rescheduled가 있으므로, If절에는 이와 짝을 이루어 가정법 과거완료를 만드는 과거완료 동사가 와야 한다. 따라서 (b) had been told가 정답이다.

어휘ㅣ get-together n. 모임   reschedule v. 일정을 변경하다   engagement n. 약속

02   조동사   조동사 should 생략   난이도 ●●○

The nuclear power plant in Bruno City had an accident that almost led to a massive radiation leak. Residents urged that the plant _____ to ensure that such a tragic incident would never happen.

(a) be shut down
(b) would be shut down
(c) has been shut down
(d) had been shut down

Bruno시에 있는 원자력 발전소에서 하마터면 대규모의 방사선 유출로 이어질 뻔한 사고가 발생했다. 주민들은 그러한 비극적인 사건이 절대 일어나지 않을 것을 확실히 하기 위해 그 시설이 폐쇄되어야 한다고 강력히 촉구했다.

─○ 지텔프 치트키

urge 다음에는 that절에 동사원형이 온다.

> ☼ 주장·요구·명령·제안을 나타내는 빈출 동사
> urge 강력히 촉구하다   recommend 권고하다   demand 요구하다   request 요청하다   suggest 제안하다   order 명령하다   ask 요청하다
> propose 제안하다   insist 주장하다   advise 권고하다

해설ㅣ 주절에 요구를 나타내는 동사 urge가 있으므로 that절에는 '(should +) 동사원형'이 와야 한다. 따라서 동사원형 (a) be shut down이 정답이다.

어휘ㅣ massive adj. 대규모의, 막대한   radiation n. 방사선   leak n. 유출   resident n. 주민   urge v. 강력히 촉구하다   ensure v. 확실히 하다   tragic adj. 비극적인   incident n. 사건

In times of inflation, consumers need to make an effort to differentiate between wants and needs. Once this is done, they _____ prioritize essential items when shopping and curtail unnecessary spending.

(a) should
(b) would
(c) could
(d) might

━○ 지텔프 치트키

'~해야 한다'라고 말할 때는 should를 쓴다.

인플레이션 시기에, 소비자들은 원하는 것과 필요한 것을 구별하기 위해 노력해야 한다. 이것이 완료되면, 그들은 쇼핑할 때 필수 품목들의 우선순위를 정하고 불필요한 지출을 줄여야 한다.

해설 | 문맥상 인플레이션 시기에 소비자들은 원하는 것과 필요한 것을 구별하기 위해 노력해야 하며, 이것이 완료되면 쇼핑할 때 필수 품목들의 우선순위를 정하고 불필요한 지출을 줄여야 한다는 의미가 되어야 자연스러우므로, '~해야 한다'를 뜻하면서 당위성을 나타내는 조동사 (a) should가 정답이다. 참고로, should와 must 모두 '~해야 한다'를 뜻하지만, should는 must보다 약한 어조로 충고나 권유를 할 때 쓴다.

어휘 | differentiate v. 구별하다   prioritize v. 우선순위를 정하다   essential adj. 필수의   curtail v. 줄이다

In psychology, the concept of introversion simply refers to a person's tendency to consider their inner thoughts over external factors. There are, however, plenty of introverts _____ to seek the safety of solitude.

(a) which are motivated by social anxiety
(b) who are motivated by social anxiety
(c) whom are motivated by social anxiety
(d) what are motivated by social anxiety

━○ 지텔프 치트키

사람 선행사가 관계절 안에서 주어 역할을 하면 주격 관계대명사 who가 정답이다.

심리학에서, 내향성의 개념은 그저 외부 요인들보다 내면의 생각들을 고려하는 한 사람의 성향을 나타낸다. 그러나, 고독의 안전성을 추구하도록 사회적 불안에 의해 자극받은 많은 내향적인 사람들이 있다.

해설 | 사람 선행사 plenty of introverts를 받으면서 보기의 관계절 내에서 동사 are motivated의 주어가 될 수 있는 주격 관계대명사가 필요하므로, (b) who are motivated by social anxiety가 정답이다.

어휘 | psychology n. 심리학   introversion n. 내향성   external adj. 외부의   introvert n. 내향적인 사람   seek v. 추구하다   solitude n. 고독   motivate v. 자극하다   anxiety n. 불안

Paul Thomas Anderson burst onto the scene in the 1990s with hits like *Magnolia*. He _____ consistently well-regarded films featuring a bold visual style and strong acting performances since then.

(a) would have directing
(b) had been directing
(c) was directing
(d) has been directing

폴 토마스 앤더슨은 1990년대에 「매그놀리아」와 같은 인기 작품들과 함께 영화계에 불쑥 등장했다. 그는 그때 이후로 과감한 영상미와 탄탄한 연기력을 특징으로 하는 꾸준히 호평받는 영화들을 <u>연출해오고 있는 중이다</u>.

─○ 지텔프 치트키

'since + 과거 시점'이 있으면 현재완료진행 시제가 정답이다.

해설 | 현재완료진행 시제와 함께 쓰이는 시간 표현 'since + 과거 시점'(since then)이 있고, 문맥상 폴 토마스 앤더슨이 영화계에 불쑥 등장한 과거 시점 이후로 현재까지 계속해서 과감한 영상미와 탄탄한 연기력을 특징으로 하는 꾸준히 호평받는 영화들을 연출해오고 있는 중이라는 의미가 되어야 자연스럽다. 따라서 현재완료진행 시제 (d) has been directing이 정답이다.

어휘 | burst v. 불쑥 등장하다   hit n. 인기 작품   consistently adv. 꾸준히, 일관되게   well-regarded adj. 호평받는, 잘 알려진   bold adj. 과감한 direct v. 연출하다, 감독하다

Apple is developing the first-ever fully autonomous vehicle that will require no input from a human driver. According to Apple analyst Ming-Chi Kuo, the company wishes _____ production by 2025 at the earliest.

(a) starting
(b) to be started
(c) to start
(d) will start

Apple 사는 인간 운전자의 투입을 필요로 하지 않은 최초의 완전 자율 주행 차량을 개발하고 있다. Apple 사의 분석가 귀밍치에 따르면, 그 회사는 빠르면 2025년쯤에 생산을 <u>시작하는 것을</u> 희망한다.

─○ 지텔프 치트키

wish는 to 부정사를 목적어로 취한다.

☀ to 부정사를 목적어로 취하는 빈출 동사
wish 희망하다   promise 약속하다   expect 예상하다   vow 맹세하다   plan 계획하다   decide 결정하다   hope 바라다   agree 동의하다 intend 계획하다   prepare 준비하다

해설 | 빈칸 앞 동사 wish는 to 부정사를 목적어로 취하므로, to 부정사 (c) to start가 정답이다.

어휘 | first-ever adj. 최초의   autonomous vehicle phr. 자율 주행 차량   input n. 투입, 입력   analyst n. 분석가   production n. 생산

Dr. Lamar mentioned that Hannah's vitamin D deficiency had been present for some time. If she had gotten a checkup in the last two years, she _____ what was causing her fatigue much sooner.

(a) would find out
(b) found out
(c) had found out
(d) would have found out

Dr. Lamar는 Hannah의 비타민 디 결핍이 한동안 존재해 왔다고 말했다. 만약 그녀가 지난 2년 안에 건강 검진을 받았었다면, 그녀는 무엇이 그녀의 피로를 유발하고 있는지 훨씬 더 빨리 <u>발견했을 것이다</u>.

━━○ 지텔프 치트키

'if + had p.p.'가 있으면 'would/could + have p.p.'가 정답이다.

해설 | If절에 'had p.p.' 형태의 had gotten이 있으므로, 주절에는 이와 짝을 이루어 가정법 과거완료를 만드는 'would(조동사 과거형) + have p.p.'가 와야 한다. 따라서 (d) would have found out이 정답이다.

어휘 | mention v. 말하다, 언급하다 deficiency n. 결핍 present adj. 존재하는 checkup n. 건강 검진 fatigue n. 피로

Please be quiet. The writing examination is in progress. The students _____ on the test as hard as they can, and even the slightest noise will disturb them.

(a) are currently focusing
(b) were currently focusing
(c) have currently focused
(d) will currently focus

조용히 해주세요. 필기시험이 진행 중입니다. 학생들은 <u>지금</u> 최대한 시험에 <u>집중하고 있는 중</u>이며, 아주 작은 소음조차도 그들을 방해할 것입니다.

━━○ 지텔프 치트키

보기에 currently가 있으면 현재진행 시제가 정답이다.

해설 | 보기에 현재진행 시제와 함께 쓰이는 시간 표현 currently가 있고, 문맥상 말하고 있는 현재 시점에 학생들이 최대한 시험에 집중하고 있는 중이라는 의미가 되어야 자연스럽다. 따라서 현재진행 시제 (a) are currently focusing이 정답이다.

어휘 | examination n. 시험, 조사 in progress phr. 진행 중인 disturb v. 방해하다

Joel moved from Los Angeles to Chicago with his family. While he likes his bigger room and the view from their house, he's worried about the winters because he has not experienced _____ extremely cold weather.

Joel은 그의 가족과 함께 로스앤젤레스에서 시카고로 이사했다. 그는 그의 더 큰 방과 그들의 집에서 보이는 풍경이 마음에 들지만, 극도로 추운 날씨에 <u>대처하는 것</u>을 경험한 적이 없기 때문에 그는 겨울에 대해 걱정하고 있다.

(a) being dealt with
(b) to deal with
(c) dealing with
(d) to have dealt with

experience는 동명사를 목적어로 취한다.

해설 | 빈칸 앞 동사 experience는 동명사를 목적어로 취하므로, 동명사 (c) dealing with가 정답이다.

어휘 | deal with phr. ~에 대처하다, ~을 처리하다

10 가정법 · 가정법 과거

난이도 ●●○

Olsen hurt his back moving a sofa, so the doctor told him to rest for three days. However, he has to return to work immediately. If there were someone in the office to fill in for him, he _____ the doctor's instructions.

(a) does not ignore
(b) would not have ignored
(c) will not ignore
(d) would not ignore

Olsen은 소파를 옮기다가 등허리를 다쳐서, 의사가 그에게 3일 동안 쉬라고 말했다. 그러나, 그는 즉시 업무에 복귀해야 한다. 만약 사무실에 그를 대신할 사람이 있다면, 그는 의사의 지시를 <u>무시하지 않을</u> 것이다.

'if + 과거 동사'가 있으면 'would/could + 동사원형'이 정답이다.

🔆 **가정법 과거**
If + 주어 + 과거 동사, 주어 + would/could(조동사 과거형) + 동사원형

해설 | If절에 과거 동사(were)가 있으므로, 주절에는 이와 짝을 이루어 가정법 과거를 만드는 'would(조동사 과거형) + 동사원형'이 와야 한다. 따라서 (d) would not ignore가 정답이다.

어휘 | back n. 등허리, 등 fill in for phr. ~를 대신하다 instruction n. 지시 ignore v. 무시하다

11 연결어 · 접속부사

난이도 ●●●

Former colleagues at Prime Financial say that the new CFO of Southern Bank is an impressive young executive with fresh ideas. _____, some investors warn that she has too little know-how to meet the demands of the role.

(a) Similarly
(b) Besides
(c) Instead
(d) On the other hand

Prime Financial 사의 예전 동료들은 Southern Bank 사의 신임 최고 재무 책임자가 참신한 아이디어들을 가진 인상적인 젊은 임원이라고 말한다. <u>반면에</u>, 일부 투자자들은 그녀가 그 역할의 요건을 충족하기에는 지나치게 적은 노하우를 가지고 있다고 경고한다.

'반면에'라는 의미의 대조를 나타낼 때는 On the other hand를 쓴다.

> 💡 대조를 나타내는 빈출 접속부사
> On the other hand 반면에 However 그러나 Otherwise 그렇지 않으면 In contrast 그에 반해

해설 | 빈칸 앞 문장은 Southern Bank 사의 신임 최고 재무 관리자의 예전 동료들이 그녀가 참신한 아이디어들을 가진 인상적인 젊은 임원이라고 말한다는 내용이고, 빈칸 뒤 문장은 일부 투자자들이 그녀가 최고 재무 책임자 역할의 요건을 충족하기에는 지나치게 적은 노하우를 가지고 있다고 경고한다는 대조적인 내용이다. 따라서 '반면에'라는 의미의 대조를 나타내는 접속부사 (d) On the other hand가 정답이다.

오답분석
(a) Similarly는 '비슷하게', (b) Besides는 '게다가', (c) Instead는 '대신에'라는 의미로, 문맥에 적합하지 않아 오답이다.

어휘 | former adj. 예전의 colleague n. 동료 CFO(chief financial officer) n. 최고 재무 책임자 impressive adj. 인상적인 investor n. 투자자 meet v. 충족하다 demand n. 요건, 요구

---

12 시제   과거완료진행   난이도 ●●○

Ms. Jenkins ordered Kenny to stay after the period was over to have a chat about proper classroom behavior. He _____ at his smartphone for 30 minutes, up until she finally got his attention.

(a) would have stared
(b) is staring
(c) has stared
(d) had been staring

Ms. Jenkins는 Kenny에게 올바른 학급 태도에 관해 대화를 나누기 위해 수업 시간이 끝난 후 남아 있으라고 지시했다. 그녀가 마침내 그의 주의를 끌 때까지, 그는 30분 동안 그의 스마트폰을 <u>응시해오고 있던 중이었다</u>.

'up until + 과거 동사'와 'for + 기간 표현'이 함께 오면 과거완료진행 시제가 정답이다.

해설 | 과거완료진행 시제와 함께 쓰이는 시간 표현 'for + 기간 표현'(for 30 minutes)과 'up until + 과거 동사'(up until ~ got)가 있고, 문맥상 대과거(Kenny가 스마트폰을 응시하기 시작한 시점)부터 과거(Ms. Jenkins가 마침내 Kenny의 주의를 끈 시점)까지 Kenny는 30분 동안 계속해서 그의 스마트폰을 응시해오고 있던 중이었다는 의미가 되어야 자연스럽다. 따라서 과거완료진행 시제 (d) had been staring이 정답이다.

어휘 | have a chat phr. 대화를 나누다 proper adj. 올바른 behavior n. 태도 up until prep. ~까지 stare v. 응시하다

---

13 준동사   to 부정사의 진주어 역할   난이도 ●●○

As cold fusion sounds like a shortcut to an unlimited supply of clean and safe energy, the idea will always seem appealing. Nevertheless, researchers have come to a consensus that it is impossible _____ a fusion reaction without a great deal of heat.

(a) generating

상온 핵융합은 깨끗하고 안전한 에너지의 무제한 공급으로의 지름길처럼 들리기 때문에, 이 개념은 항상 매력적으로 보일 것이다. 그럼에도 불구하고, 연구원들은 많은 양의 열 없이 핵융합 반응을 <u>일으키는 것</u>이 불가능하다는 합의에 이르렀다.

(b) having generated

(c) to generate

(d) to be generating

가주어 it이 있으면 to 부정사가 정답이다.

해설 | 빈칸 문장에 있는 that절의 주어 자리에 가주어 it이 있고 문맥상 '핵융합 반응을 일으키는 것이 불가능하다'라는 의미가 되어야 자연스러우므로, 빈칸에는 동사 is의 진주어인 '일으키는 것'이 와야 한다. 따라서 진주어 자리에 올 수 있는 to 부정사 (c) to generate가 정답이다.

어휘 | cold fusion phr. 상온 핵융합   shortcut n. 지름길   unlimited adj. 무제한의   appealing adj. 매력적인   consensus n. 합의, 의견 일치   generate v. 일으키다, 발생시키다

---

14 **조동사**   조동사 should 생략   난이도 ●●○

Parent-teacher conferences are important for establishing a clear communication channel that will ultimately benefit the children. Instructors ask that parents or guardians _____ any situations at home that might affect their child's conduct at school.

(a) report

(b) are reporting

(c) reported

(d) will report

학부모-교사 회의는 궁극적으로 아이들에게 도움이 될 명확한 의사소통 수단을 구축하는 데 중요하다. 교사들은 부모나 보호자들이 학교에서 아이의 행동에 영향을 미칠지도 모르는 가정에서의 그 어떤 상황도 알려야 한다고 요청한다.

---

ask 다음에는 that절에 동사원형이 온다.

해설 | 주절에 요구를 나타내는 동사 ask가 있으므로 that절에는 '(should +) 동사원형'이 와야 한다. 따라서 동사원형 (a) report가 정답이다.

어휘 | conference n. 회의   establish v. 구축하다   channel n. 수단, 경로   ultimately adv. 궁극적으로   benefit v. 도움이 되다   instructor n. 교사   guardian n. 보호자   conduct n. 행동

---

15 **시제**   미래진행   난이도 ●●○

Today, Naomi went for a 10-mile bike ride in the sweltering heat. She is supposed to have dinner with her friends at 5 p.m., but she is terribly exhausted. There's no doubt that she _____ on the couch tonight.

(a) was relaxing

(b) will be relaxing

(c) will have been relaxing

(d) has relaxed

오늘, Naomi는 찌는 듯한 더위 속에서 자전거를 타고 10마일을 달렸다. 그녀는 오후 5시에 친구들과 함께 저녁 식사를 하기로 되어 있지만, 그녀는 몹시 기진맥진하다. 그녀가 오늘 밤 소파에서 휴식을 취하고 있는 중일 것이라는 데는 의심의 여지가 없다.

'for + 기간 표현' 없이 특정 미래 시점을 나타내는 표현만 있으면 미래진행 시제가 정답이다.

해설 | 미래진행 시제와 함께 쓰이는 시간 표현 tonight이 있고, 문맥상 Naomi가 찌는 듯한 더위 속에서 자전거를 타고 10마일을 달린 후 몹시 기진맥진하기 때문에 오늘 밤 소파에서 휴식을 취하고 있는 중일 것이라는 의미가 되어야 자연스럽다. 따라서 미래진행 시제 (b) will be relaxing이 정답이다.

어휘 | sweltering adj. 찌는 듯한 be supposed to phr. ~하기로 되어 있다 exhausted adj. 기진맥진한 couch n. 소파

---

16 준동사　　동명사를 목적어로 취하는 동사　　　　　　　　　　난이도 ●●○

Elaine knew she had other viral marketing projects that should take priority. Still, she was unable to resist _____ her coworkers for a meeting about the new PR campaign. She reasoned that this was a chance to grow as an employee.

(a) to join
(b) to have joined
(c) being joined
(d) joining

Elaine은 우선 사항이 되어야 하는 다른 바이럴 마케팅 프로젝트들이 있다는 것을 알고 있었다. 그럼에도 불구하고, 그녀는 새로운 홍보 캠페인에 관한 회의를 위해 동료들과 <u>만나는 것</u>을 거부할 수 없었다. 그녀는 이것이 직원으로서 성장할 기회라고 판단했다.

resist는 동명사를 목적어로 취한다.

해설 | 빈칸 앞 동사 resist는 동명사를 목적어로 취하므로, 동명사 (d) joining이 정답이다.

어휘 | priority n. 우선 사항 resist v. 거부하다 PR(public relations) n. 홍보 reason v. 판단하다

---

17 가정법　　가정법 과거　　　　　　　　　　　　　　　　　　난이도 ●●○

Marta took a deep breath and raised her hand to volunteer to give her presentation first. Even if the thought of speaking in front of the whole class made her nervous, she _____ more anxious waiting until later.

(a) will only have felt
(b) only felt
(c) would only feel
(d) had only felt

Marta는 심호흡을 하고 먼저 발표하겠다고 자원하기 위해 손을 들어 올렸다. 설령 학급 전체 앞에서 연설할 생각이 그녀를 초조하게 만든다 해도, 나중까지 기다리면서 그녀는 불안함을 더 <u>느낄 뿐일 것이다</u>.

'if + 과거 동사'가 있으면 'would/could + 동사원형'이 정답이다.

해설 | if절에 과거 동사(made)가 있으므로, 주절에는 이와 짝을 이루어 가정법 과거를 만드는 'would(조동사 과거형) + 동사원형'이 와야 한다. 따라서 (c) would only feel이 정답이다.

어휘 | raise v. 들어 올리다 volunteer v. 자원하다 nervous adj. 초조한

In the past, Danny had always been the last person picked when he played basketball on the playground. But now that he _____ perform a picture-perfect dunk as a result of persistent practice, the other players want to be on his team.

(a) would
(b) should
(c) can
(d) will

과거에, Danny는 운동장에서 농구를 할 때 항상 마지막으로 선택받는 사람이었다. 그러나 꾸준한 연습의 결과로 그가 흠잡을 데 없이 완벽한 덩크 슛을 해 보일 수 있는 지금은, 다른 선수들이 그의 팀에 있고 싶어 한다.

◆━━○ 지텔프 치트키

'~할 수 있다'라고 말할 때는 can을 쓴다.

해설 | 문맥상 과거에는 Danny가 농구를 할 때 항상 마지막으로 선택받을 만큼 그와 같은 팀을 하고 싶어 하는 선수가 없었지만, 꾸준한 연습의 결과로 그가 흠잡을 데 없이 완벽한 덩크 슛을 해 보일 수 있는 지금은 다른 선수들이 그의 팀에 있고 싶어 한다는 의미가 되어야 자연스럽다. 따라서 '~할 수 있다'를 뜻하면서 능력을 나타내는 조동사 (c) can이 정답이다.

어휘 | picture-perfect adj. 흠잡을 데 없이 완벽한 persistent adj. 꾸준한

All newly hired staff members at Dresden Media participate in a three-hour orientation on their first day of work. They initially meet with the head of the personnel department, Ms. Reese, who gives a brief talk _____ the company's policies.

(a) to have explained
(b) having explained
(c) will explain
(d) to explain

Dresden Media 사에 새로 고용된 모든 직원들은 근무 첫날에 3시간 짜리 오리엔테이션에 참여한다. 그들은 처음에 인사과장인 Ms. Reese를 만나는데, 그녀는 회사의 정책들을 설명하기 위해 간단한 강연을 한다.

◆━━○ 지텔프 치트키

'~하기 위해'라고 말할 때는 to 부정사를 쓴다.

해설 | 빈칸 앞에 주어 역할을 하는 관계사(who), 동사(gives), 목적어(a brief talk)가 갖춰진 완전한 절이 있으므로, 빈칸 이하는 문장의 필수 성분이 아닌 수식어구이다. 따라서 목적을 나타내며 수식어구를 이끌 수 있는 to 부정사 (d) to explain이 정답이다.

어휘 | initially adv. 처음에 **personnel department** phr. 인사과 **brief** adj. 간단한

20 시제 과거진행

난이도 ●●○

Last Sunday morning, my friend Elliott was given two tickets to the Super Bowl, which started at 1 p.m. He decided to invite me, but he couldn't reach me on the phone. When he called, I _____ my lawn.

(a) would be mowing
(b) was mowing
(c) had mown
(d) mowed

지난 일요일 아침에, 내 친구 Elliott는 슈퍼볼 표 두 장을 얻었는데, 그것은 오후 1시에 시작했다. 그는 나를 초대하기로 결정했지만, 나에게 전화로 연락할 수 없었다. 그가 전화했을 때, 나는 <u>잔디를 깎고 있던 중이었다</u>.

지텔프 치트키

'for + 기간 표현' 없이 'when + 과거 동사'만 있으면 과거진행 시제가 정답이다.

해설 | 과거진행 시제와 함께 쓰이는 시간 표현 'when + 과거 동사'(When ~ called)가 있고, 문맥상 친구 Elliott가 전화했던 과거 시점에 잔디를 깎고 있던 중이었다는 의미가 되어야 자연스럽다. 따라서 과거진행 시제 (b) was mowing이 정답이다.

오답분석
(c) 과거완료 시제는 특정 과거 시점 이전에 일어난 대과거의 일을 나타내는 시제인데, 친구 Elliott가 전화한 일과 내가 잔디를 깎은 일은 동시에 일어난 일이므로 오답이다.

어휘 | reach v. 연락하다, 도착하다 lawn n. 잔디 mow v. 깎다, 베다

21 연결어 접속사

난이도 ●●●

Needing a pair of black shoes for a job interview, I asked my cousin if I could borrow hers. She agreed to lend them to me _____ I gave them back by the weekend because she wanted to wear them to a company dinner.

(a) as long as
(b) whereas
(c) so that
(d) unless

취업 면접을 위해 검은색 구두 한 켤레가 필요해서, 나는 사촌에게 그녀의 것을 빌릴 수 있는지를 물었다. 그녀는 그것을 신고 회사 회식에 가기를 원했기 때문에 내가 주말까지 그것을 <u>돌려주는 한</u> 빌려줄 것을 승낙했다.

지텔프 치트키

'~하는 한'이라는 의미의 조건을 나타낼 때는 as long as를 쓴다.

💡 조건을 나타내는 빈출 접속사
as long as ~하는 한 unless ~하지 않는 한 provided that ~이라는 조건으로 just in case ~한 경우에 한해서

해설 | 사촌이 검은색 구두를 신고 회사 회식에 가기를 원했기 때문에 주말까지 그것을 돌려주는 한 빌려줄 것을 승낙했다는 의미가 되어야 자연스럽다. 따라서 '~하는 한'이라는 의미의 조건을 나타내는 부사절 접속사 (a) as long as가 정답이다.

오답분석
(b) whereas는 '~인 반면', (c) so that은 '~할 수 있도록', (d) unless는 '~하지 않는 한'이라는 의미로, 문맥에 적합하지 않아 오답이다.

22 관계사 주격 관계대명사 that

난이도 ●●○

Ms. Leslie, the principal of Westwood High School, recently announced that funds had been set aside to expand the library's collection. Many of the books _____ were requested by students via a school survey.

(a) how they have been selected for purchase
(b) what have been selected for purchase
(c) that have been selected for purchase
(d) who have been selected for purchase

Westwood 고등학교의 교장인 Ms. Leslie는 도서관의 장서를 확장하기 위한 자금이 따로 마련되어 있다고 최근에 발표했다. 구매를 위해 선정된 많은 책들은 학교 설문 조사를 통해 학생들에 의해 요청되었다.

⚷ 지텔프 치트키

사물 선행사가 관계절 안에서 주어 역할을 하면 주격 관계대명사 that이 정답이다.

해설 | 사물 선행사 Many of the books를 받으면서 보기의 관계절 내에서 동사 have been selected의 주어가 될 수 있는 주격 관계대명사가 필요하므로, (c) that have been selected for purchase가 정답이다.

어휘 | principal n. 교장 set aside phr. 따로 마련하다, 확보하다 expand v. 확장하다 collection n. (도서관의) 장서 via prep. ~을 통해 select v. 선정하다

23 가정법 가정법 과거완료

난이도 ●●○

My teammate Norton often annoys me with his unsolicited advice. For example, he told me yesterday that if I had taken a different subway line, I _____ at work on time.

(a) could have arrived
(b) could arrive
(c) arrived
(d) will arrive

나의 팀 동료 Norton은 부탁하지 않은 충고로 종종 나를 짜증나게 한다. 예를 들어, 어제 그는 나에게 만약 내가 다른 지하철 노선을 탔었다면, 제시간에 회사에 도착할 수 있었을 것이라고 말했다.

⚷ 지텔프 치트키

'if + had p.p.'가 있으면 'would/could + have p.p.'가 정답이다.

해설 | if절에 'had p.p.' 형태의 had taken이 있으므로, 주절에는 이와 짝을 이루어 가정법 과거완료를 만드는 'could(조동사 과거형) + have p.p.'가 와야 한다. 따라서 (a) could have arrived가 정답이다.

어휘 | annoy v. 짜증나게 하다 unsolicited adj. 부탁하지 않은 advice n. 충고

24 시제 미래완료진행

난이도 ●●○

Mr. Connor is the longest-serving CEO in the history of Newport Restaurant Supplies. By the end of next month, he _____ the company for more than two decades, and he hopes to continue in his role for a few more years.

Mr. Connor는 Newport Restaurant Supplies 사의 역사상 가장 오래 근무한 최고 경영자이다. 다음 달 말 즈음에는, 그는 20년이 넘는 기간 동안 그 회사를 운영해오고 있는 중일 것이고, 그는 몇 년 더 자신의 역할을 계속하기를 희망한다.

(a) would have run
(b) is running
(c) will have been running
(d) will be running

지텔프 치트키

'by + 미래 시점'과 'for + 기간 표현'이 함께 오면 미래완료진행 시제가 정답이다.

해설 | 미래완료진행 시제와 함께 쓰이는 시간 표현 'by + 미래 시점'(By the end of next month)과 'for + 기간 표현'(for more than two decades)이 있고, 문맥상 미래 시점인 다음 달 말 즈음에는 Mr. Connor가 20년이 넘는 기간 동안 계속해서 Newport Restaurant Supplies 사를 운영해오고 있는 중일 것이라는 의미가 되어야 자연스럽다. 따라서 미래완료진행 시제 (c) will have been running이 정답이다.

오답분석

(d) 미래진행 시제는 특정 미래 시점에 한창 진행 중일 일을 나타내므로, 과거 또는 현재에 시작해서 특정 미래 시점까지 계속해서 진행되고 있을 일을 표현할 수 없어 오답이다.

어휘 | serve v. 근무하다

---

25 준동사 동명사를 목적어로 취하는 동사 난이도 ●●○

Although Tanya's little brother is having a hard time in university, she is no longer willing to give him suggestions for improving his grades. Why has she given up _____ to help him? It is because he never follows her counsel!

(a) to try
(b) trying
(c) to be trying
(d) having tried

Tanya의 남동생은 대학에서 힘든 시간을 보내고 있지만, 그녀는 더 이상 그에게 성적을 향상시키는 것에 관한 조언을 해줄 의향이 없다. 그녀는 왜 그를 도우려고 노력하는 것을 포기했을까? 왜냐하면 그가 결코 그녀의 조언을 따르지 않기 때문이다!

지텔프 치트키

give up은 동명사를 목적어로 취한다.

해설 | 빈칸 앞 동사 give up은 동명사를 목적어로 취하므로, 동명사 (b) trying이 정답이다.

오답분석

(d) having tried도 동명사이기는 하지만, 완료동명사(having tried)로 쓰일 경우 '포기하는' 시점보다 '노력하는' 시점이 앞선다는 것을 나타내므로 문맥에 적합하지 않다.

어휘 | be willing to phr. ~할 의향이 있다 suggestion n. 조언, 제안 counsel n. 조언, 충고

The sales director of Aspen Plastics has delayed Friday's seminar until next week. If it _____ as originally scheduled, several employees would be absent because they would be taking part in a workshop in another city.

(a) took place
(b) had taken place
(c) was taking place
(d) has taken place

Aspen Plastics 사의 영업부장은 금요일 세미나를 다음 주로 연기했다. 만약 그것이 원래 계획된 대로 개최된다면, 몇몇 직원들은 다른 도시에서 열리는 워크숍에 참석할 것이기 때문에 불참할 것이다.

───○ **지텔프 치트키**

if와 'would/could + 동사원형'이 있으면 과거 동사가 정답이다.

해설 | 주절에 'would(조동사 과거형) + 동사원형' 형태의 would be가 있으므로, If절에는 이와 짝을 이루어 가정법 과거를 만드는 과거 동사가 와야 한다. 따라서 (a) took place가 정답이다.

어휘 | delay v. 연기하다　absent adj. 불참한　take part in phr. ~에 참석하다　take place phr. 개최되다, 일어나다

안부 인사	M: Hey, Emma. [27]How was the last day of your summer internship?	남: 안녕, Emma. [27]네 여름 인턴십의 마지막 날은 어땠니?
주제 제시: 인턴십 경험	F: It was really nice, David. There was a farewell party for the interns. We enjoyed a big meal, took pictures, and talked about the next steps in our careers. M: You worked at an advertising agency, right? F: That's right. I worked as a copywriter at Nelson Promotions.	여: 정말 좋았어, David. 인턴들을 위한 송별회가 있었어. 우리는 푸짐한 식사를 즐기고, 사진을 찍고, 우리 진로의 다음 단계들에 관해 이야기를 나눴어. 남: 너는 광고 대행사에서 일했어, 그렇지? 여: 맞아. 나는 Nelson Promotions 사에서 카피라이터로 일했어.
직업 설명	M: Um . . . copywriter? I'm not familiar with that job. Can you tell me about it? F: A copywriter writes advertising copy for websites, social media posts, and anything else related to marketing. M: Advertising copy? I don't know what that is . . . F: Don't worry! Before my internship, I had never heard of it, either. Advertising copy is the text in an advertisement that convinces the reader to make a purchase. M: So, a copywriter thinks of the slogans that I see in advertisements? F: Exactly! And [28]having an effective slogan is very important. It makes people curious about the product or service, and this makes them more likely to buy it.	남: 음... 카피라이터? 난 그 직업에 대해 잘 몰라. 그것에 대해 말해 줄 수 있어? 여: 카피라이터는 웹 사이트, 소셜 미디어 게시물, 그리고 마케팅과 관련된 그 밖의 다른 것을 위한 광고 문안을 작성해. 남: 광고 문안? 난 그게 뭔지 모르겠어... 여: 걱정 마! 인턴십 전에는, 나도 그것을 들어본 적이 없었어. 광고 문안은 독자가 구매를 하도록 설득하는 광고 속 글귀야. 남: 그럼, 카피라이터가 내가 광고에서 보는 슬로건을 생각해 낸다는 거야? 여: 바로 그거야! 그리고 [28]효과적인 슬로건을 갖는 것은 매우 중요해. 그것은 사람들이 제품이나 서비스에 대해 궁금해하게 만들고, 이것은 그들이 그것을 구매할 가능성을 높이지.
필요 기술	M: That's cool. What sort of skills do you need to be a copywriter? F: Well, [29]you have to have excellent language skills. After all, [29]the job revolves around content that is interesting and free of grammatical errors. Most successful copywriters are also creative and resourceful.	남: 그거 멋지다. 카피라이터가 되려면 어떤 종류의 기술들이 필요하니? 여: 음, [29]뛰어난 언어 능력을 갖춰야 해. 결국, [29]그 직업은 흥미로우면서 문법적인 오류가 없는 콘텐츠를 중심으로 돌아가거든. 대부분의 성공적인 카피라이터들은 또한 창의적이고 임기응변에 능해.
담당 업무	M: That is the perfect job for you. What kinds of projects did you work on? F: I was assigned to a project for an interior design firm, and I also wrote some advertising copy for a medical equipment manufacturer. [30]I even helped make social media posts for a firm that specializes in arranging flights and accommodations for business travelers! M: That seems like a lot of work for an intern. Did you have any help?	남: 너에게 딱 맞는 직업이네. 넌 어떤 종류의 프로젝트를 했니? 여: 나는 인테리어 디자인 회사의 프로젝트에 배정됐고, 또한 의료 장비 제조업체를 위한 몇몇 광고 문안을 작성했어. [30]나는 심지어 업무상 출장자들을 위해 항공편과 숙소를 알선하는 것을 전문으로 하는 회사의 소셜 미디어 게시물을 만드는 것을 도왔어! 남: 한 명의 인턴이 하기엔 많은 일인 것 같아 보여. 넌 도움을 받았니?

멘토	F: I was mentored by a senior copywriter at the agency. She showed me how to be a competent copywriter. I learned to conduct research, interact with clients, and communicate with my team.	여: 나는 그 대행사에서 한 선임 카피라이터 분께 지도 받았어. 그녀는 나에게 유능한 카피라이터가 되는 방법을 가르쳐 주셨지. 나는 조사를 수행하고, 고 객들과 상호 작용하며, 내 팀과 소통하는 것을 배 웠어.
동료 인턴	M: Sounds like you had a great teacher. What were the other interns like? F: They were amazing. ³¹We always tried to help and encourage each other, so we became very close friends. We even ate lunch together every day!	남: 너에게 훌륭한 선생님이 있었던 것 같네. 다른 인 턴들은 어땠니? 여: 그들은 굉장했어. ³¹우리는 항상 서로를 돕고 격려 하려고 노력했고, 따라서 아주 친한 친구가 되었 어. 우리는 심지어 매일 점심도 함께 먹었지!
직업의 이점	M: It's always nice when colleagues get along. Do you think you want to be a copywriter now? F: Yes, I do. It's a challenging and exciting career. Not to mention ³²there is a special benefit that I truly like. M: What kind of benefit are you talking about? F: ³²Copywriters don't always have to work in an office. Some of the copywriters at the company work remotely. One person was even working from a beach in the Caribbean! M: Wow! Getting paid to go to the beach? Sounds wonderful to me. F: Me too! With a lot of hard work and a little luck, I'll be able to do that as well.	남: 동료들이 사이좋게 지내는 건 언제나 좋은 일이지. 너는 지금도 카피라이터가 되고 싶다고 생각해? 여: 응, 맞아. 그것은 도전적이고 흥미진진한 직업이야. 내가 정말 좋아하는 ³²특별한 이점이 있다는 것은 말할 것도 없고. 남: 어떤 종류의 이점을 말하는 거야? 여: ³²카피라이터들은 항상 사무실에서 일할 필요가 없어. 회사의 카피라이터들 중 일부는 원격으로 근무해. 한 사람은 심지어 카리브해의 해변에서 일하고 있었어! 남: 와! 해변에 가면서 돈을 받는 거야? 내게는 굉장하 게 들리는걸. 여: 나도 마찬가지야! 많은 노력과 약간의 행운이 있으 면, 나 역시 그렇게 할 수 있을 거야.
여자가 다음에 할 일	M: So, what will you do now that your internship is over? F: ³³I will try to find a permanent position in the industry. I have some work experience and I made connections at the company. In addition, my mentor wrote me a letter of recommendation too. M: I think you will be a great copywriter, Emma. Good luck with your applications! F: Thanks, David. ³³I'd better start working on my résumé!	남: 그래서, 이제 인턴십이 끝났으니 뭐 할 거야? 여: ³³나는 그 업계에서 정규직을 찾기 위해 노력할 거 야. 나는 업무 경험이 있고 회사에서 인맥을 쌓았 어. 게다가, 나의 멘토가 내게 추천서도 써 주셨어. 남: 난 네가 훌륭한 카피라이터가 될 거라고 생각해, Emma. 너의 지원에 행운을 빌어! 여: 고마워, David. ³³난 내 이력서 작성을 시작하는 게 좋겠어!

어휘 | farewell[fὲərwél] 송별 career[kərír] 진로, 직업 agency[éidʒənsi] 대행사 copywriter[kάːpiràitər] 카피라이터, 광고 문안가 advertisement[ædvərtáizmənt] 광고 convince[kənvíns] 설득하다 revolve[rivάːlv] ~을 중심으로 돌아가다 resourceful[risɔ́ːrsfəl] 임기응변에 능한 equipment[ikwípmənt] 장비 manufacturer[mǽnjəfǽktʃərər] 제조업체 specialize[spéʃəlaiz] 전문으로 하다 accommodation[əkὰːmədéiʃən] 숙소 mentor[méntɔːr] 지도하다 competent[kάːmpitənt] 유능한 challenging[tʃǽləndʒiŋ] 도전적인 remotely[rimóutli] 원격으로 permanent position 정규직 recommendation[rèkəmendéiʃən] 추천 application[æplikéiʃən] 지원 résumé[rézjumei] 이력서

27	**특정세부사항**	What	난이도 ●○○

What did David ask Emma?	David는 Emma에게 무엇을 물어봤는가?
(a) where she lived during the summer (b) when her internship would end **(c) how she enjoyed her final day at work**	(a) 그녀가 여름 동안 어디에서 살았는지 (b) 그녀의 인턴십이 언제 끝날지 **(c) 그녀가 직장에서의 마지막 날을 어떻게 즐겼는지**

(d) who attended the farewell party

(d) 누가 송별회에 참석했는지

지텔프 치트키

질문의 키워드 David ask Emma와 관련된 주변 내용을 주의 깊게 듣는다.

해설 | 남자가 'How was the last day of your summer internship?'이라며 여자에게 여름 인턴십의 마지막 날은 어땠는지를 물었다. 따라서 (c)가 정답이다.

Paraphrasing

the last day of your summer internship 여름 인턴십의 마지막 날 → her final day at work 직장에서의 마지막 날

---

28 특정세부사항 How   난이도 ●○○

How does an effective slogan increase the likelihood of a product or service being purchased?

(a) It reminds people of their needs.
(b) It helps people learn about its features.
(c) It makes advertisements easier to remember.
(d) It generates public interest in it.

효과적인 슬로건은 어떻게 제품이나 서비스가 구매될 가능성을 높이는가?

(a) 사람들에게 그것들의 필요를 상기시킨다.
(b) 사람들이 그것의 특징들을 익히도록 돕는다.
(c) 광고들을 기억하기 더 쉽게 만든다.
(d) 그것에 대중의 관심을 불러일으킨다.

지텔프 치트키

질문의 키워드 effective slogan이 그대로 언급된 주변 내용을 주의 깊게 듣는다.

해설 | 여자가 'having an effective slogan is very important'라며 효과적인 슬로건을 가지는 것이 매우 중요하다고 한 뒤, 'It makes people curious about the product or service, and this makes them more likely to buy it.'이라며 효과적인 슬로건은 사람들이 제품이나 서비스에 대해 궁금해하게 만들고, 이것은 그들이 그것(제품이나 서비스)을 구매할 가능성을 높인다고 했다. 따라서 (d)가 정답이다.

Paraphrasing

increase the likelihood of ~ being purchased 구매될 가능성을 높이다 → makes them more likely to buy it 그것을 구매할 가능성을 높인다

makes people curious 사람들이 궁금해하게 만든다 → generates public interest 대중의 관심을 불러일으킨다

어휘 | likelihood[láiklihud] 가능성 remind[rimáind] 상기시키다

---

29 특정세부사항 Why   난이도 ●●○

Why are strong language skills required for copywriters?

(a) because the writing must be technically correct
(b) because copy must be translated to other languages
(c) because they must develop interesting stories
(d) because they must produce reference materials

왜 카피라이터에게 강력한 언어 능력이 필요한가?

(a) 글이 기술적으로 정확해야 하기 때문에
(b) 문안이 다른 언어로들 번역되어야 하기 때문에
(c) 흥미로운 이야기들을 개발해야 하기 때문에
(d) 참고 자료들을 만들어야 하기 때문에

지텔프 치트키

질문의 키워드 strong language skills가 excellent language skills로 paraphrasing되어 언급된 주변 내용을 주의 깊게 듣는다.

해설 | 여자가 'you have to have excellent language skills'라며 카피라이터는 뛰어난 언어 능력을 갖추어야 한다고 한 뒤, 'the job revolves around content that is ~ free of grammatical errors'라며 그 직업은 문법적인 오류가 없는 콘텐츠를 중심으로 돌아간다고 했다. 따라서 (a)가 정답이다.

Paraphrasing

content 콘텐츠 → the writing 글

free of grammatical errors 문법적인 오류가 없는 → technically correct 기술적으로 정확한

어휘 | technically[téknikli] 기술적으로, 전문적으로 translate[trænsléit] 번역하다

---

30 특정세부사항 Which 난이도 ●●○

Which type of company did Emma work on a project for during her internship?	Emma는 인턴 기간 동안 어떤 종류의 회사를 위해 프로젝트를 수행했는가?
(a) a web design firm	(a) 웹 디자인 회사
(b) a medical clinic	(b) 병원
(c) a social media company	(c) 소셜 미디어 회사
(d) a travel agency	**(d) 여행사**

◦━○ 지텔프 치트키

질문의 키워드 project가 그대로 언급된 주변 내용을 주의 깊게 듣는다.

해설 | 여자가 'I ~ helped make social media posts for a firm that specializes in arranging flights and accommodations for business travelers!'라며 업무상 출장자들을 위해 항공편과 숙소를 알선하는 것을 전문으로 하는 회사의 소셜 미디어 게시물을 만드는 것을 도왔다고 했다. 따라서 (d)가 정답이다.

Paraphrasing

a firm that specializes in arranging flights and accommodations 항공편과 숙소를 알선하는 것을 전문으로 하는 회사 → a travel agency 여행사

오답분석

(c) 여자가 소셜 미디어 게시물을 만드는 것을 도왔다고 언급하기는 했지만, 소셜 미디어 회사를 위해 프로젝트를 수행했다고 한 것은 아니므로 오답이다.

어휘 | medical clinic 병원

---

31 특정세부사항 How 난이도 ●●○

How did Emma become friends with her fellow workers?	Emma는 어떻게 동료 직원들과 친구가 되었는가?
(a) by taking the same teacher's course	(a) 같은 교사의 강좌를 수강함으로써
(b) by supporting their efforts	**(b) 그들의 노력을 지지함으로써**
(c) by sharing the results of their research	(c) 그들의 조사 결과를 공유함으로써
(d) by communicating with the same clients	(d) 같은 고객들과 소통함으로써

◦━○ 지텔프 치트키

질문의 키워드 friends가 그대로 언급된 주변 내용을 주의 깊게 듣는다.

해설 | 여자가 'We always tried to help and encourage each other, so we became very close friends.'라며 그녀와 다른 동료 인턴들은 항상 서로를 돕고 격려하려고 노력했고, 따라서 아주 친한 친구가 되었다고 했다. 따라서 (b)가 정답이다.

Paraphrasing
help and encourage each other 서로를 돕고 격려하다 → supporting their efforts 노력을 지지함

어휘 | support[səpɔ́ːrt] 지지하다

---

32 추론 특정사실 난이도 ●●●

What is most likely a benefit that copywriters get?	카피라이터가 가지는 한 가지 이점은 무엇인 것 같은가?
(a) a high salary in the industry	(a) 업계에서의 높은 임금
(b) a schedule with long vacations	(b) 긴 휴가가 있는 일정
(c) the availability to select their own assignments	(c) 그들 자신의 업무를 선택할 수 있는 가능성
(d) the freedom to choose their work locations	**(d) 그들의 근무 장소를 선택할 수 있는 자유**

○ 지텔프 치트키

질문의 키워드 benefit이 그대로 언급된 주변 내용을 주의 깊게 듣는다.

해설 | 여자가 'there is a special benefit'이라며 카피라이터 직업의 특별한 이점이 있다고 한 뒤, 'Copywriters don't always have to work in an office.'라며 카피라이터들은 항상 사무실에서 일할 필요가 없다고 한 것을 통해, 카피라이터가 가지는 한 가지 이점은 근무 장소를 선택할 수 있는 자유임을 추론할 수 있다. 따라서 (d)가 정답이다.

어휘 | salary[sǽləri] 임금 assignment[əsáinmənt] 업무

---

33 추론 다음에 할 일 난이도 ●●○

Based on the conversation, what will Emma likely do in the near future?	대화에 따르면, Emma가 가까운 미래에 할 일은 무엇일 것 같은가?
(a) go on a trip to the Caribbean	(a) 카리브해로 여행을 간다
(b) apply for a job at an advertising agency	**(b) 광고 대행사의 일자리에 지원한다**
(c) ask her mentor for a reference letter	(c) 그녀의 멘토에게 추천서를 요청한다
(d) ask David about his work experience	(d) David에게 그의 업무 경험에 관해 묻는다

○ 지텔프 치트키

다음에 할 일을 언급하는 후반을 주의 깊게 듣는다.

해설 | 여자가 'I will try to find a permanent position in the industry.'라며 광고 업계에서 정규직을 찾기 위해 노력할 것이라고 한 뒤, 'I'd better start working on my résumé!'라며 자신의 이력서 작성을 시작하는 것이 좋겠다고 한 것을 통해, Emma가 광고 대행사의 일자리에 지원할 것임을 추론할 수 있다. 따라서 (b)가 정답이다.

어휘 | reference letter 추천서

<table>
<tr><td>주제
제시:
서비스
소개</td><td>Good afternoon, everyone! Isn't this the perfect weather to go on a picnic? Now, there is a new service to assist you in planning the picnic of your dreams! The Glam Squad Syndicate can help you enjoy outdoor living in a more elegant fashion. It's a new luxury picnic rental service right here in sunny Santa Barbara, California.</td></tr>
<tr><td>서비스
출시
배경</td><td>You may have heard of glamping, which has emerged recently as a popular leisure activity. Glamping, for those who are unfamiliar, is a style of camping that combines glamorous services with traditional camping. [34]The glamping trend inspired me to come up with a new outdoor experience designed specifically for residents of urban areas. I feel my customers deserve maximum comfort with minimal effort.</td></tr>
<tr><td>주요
혜택1:
냉난방
기구
제공</td><td>The Glam Squad Syndicate hosts picnics with a backcountry spirit without the inconvenience of being in the wilderness. [35]All of our events take place under tents equipped with heaters or cooling fans. That way, you can keep everyone warm in the winter and cool during the summer. When you choose The Glam Squad Syndicate, every season is perfect for an outdoor party!</td></tr>
<tr><td>주요
혜택2:
가구
및
장식품
제공</td><td>We know that when you are outdoors, you want to be just as comfortable as when you are indoors. That's why The Glam Squad Syndicate includes furniture and decorations with each of its picnic rentals. Our tables and chairs are made of the highest-quality wood. [36]If you really want to create a cozy atmosphere, you can request some of our fairy lamps instead of the lanterns we usually use to decorate the dining area.</td></tr>
<tr><td>주요
혜택3:
음식
제공</td><td>No picnic would be complete without delicious food. The Glam Squad Syndicate provides full catering services for our picnics. Our catering team is led by one of California's most popular chefs and serves an extensive menu that can be customized to your specific taste and dietary needs. [37]We have also partnered with a local bakery, so your guests can enjoy gourmet desserts. Of course, we outfit our picnic sites with proper food storage facilities to ensure that your food is safe.</td></tr>
<tr><td>주요
혜택4:
오락
활동</td><td>I think you will agree that a characteristic of all successful picnics is a wealth of recreational activities. The Glam Squad Syndicate gives Bluetooth sound systems and theater-quality projectors with portable screens for a thrilling experience. Your friends and family</td></tr>
</table>

좋은 오후입니다, 여러분! 소풍 가기 딱 좋은 날씨 아닌가요? 이제, 여러분이 꿈에 그리던 소풍을 계획하는 것을 도울 새로운 서비스가 있습니다! The Glam Squad Syndicate가 여러분이 더욱 우아한 방식으로 야외 생활을 즐기도록 도울 수 있습니다. 그것은 바로 여기 햇살 가득한 캘리포니아주 산타바버라에 있는 신규 고급 소풍 대여 서비스입니다.

여러분은 글램핑에 대해 들어 보셨을 텐데, 이것은 최근에 인기 있는 여가 활동으로 떠올랐습니다. 잘 모르시는 분들을 위해 말씀드리자면, 글램핑은 화려한 서비스와 전통적인 캠핑을 결합한 캠핑 방식입니다. [34]글램핑의 유행은 특히 도시 지역 거주자들을 위해 설계된 새로운 야외 활동을 창안하도록 제게 영감을 주었습니다. 저는 저희의 고객들이 최소한의 노력으로 최대한의 편안함을 누릴 자격이 있다고 생각합니다.

The Glam Squad Syndicate는 야생에 있는 것의 불편함이 없는 시골 분위기의 소풍을 주최합니다. [35]저희의 모든 행사들은 난방기 또는 냉각 팬을 갖춘 텐트 아래에서 진행됩니다. 그렇게 하면, 모두를 겨울에는 따뜻하게 그리고 여름에는 시원하게 유지할 수 있습니다. The Glam Squad Syndicate를 선택하시면, 모든 계절이 야외 파티에 적합할 것입니다!

여러분이 야외에 있을 때, 실내에 있을 때와 마찬가지로 편안하기를 원하신다는 것을 저희는 알고 있습니다. 이것이 바로 The Glam Squad Syndicate가 각각의 소풍 대여품들과 더불어 가구와 장식품들을 포함하는 이유입니다. 저희의 탁자와 의자는 최고 품질의 나무로 만들어졌습니다. [36]만약 여러분이 정말로 아늑한 분위기를 만들고 싶으시다면, 저희가 보통 식사 공간을 장식하는 데 사용하는 랜턴 대신에 꼬마전등 몇 개를 요청하실 수 있습니다.

맛있는 음식 없이는 그 어떤 소풍도 완벽하지 않을 것입니다. The Glam Squad Syndicate는 소풍을 위한 최고의 음식 출장 서비스를 제공합니다. 저희의 음식 출장 서비스 팀은 캘리포니아주에서 가장 인기 있는 요리사 중 한 명이 이끌고 있으며 여러분 개개인의 구체적인 취향과 식단 요구 사항에 맞춰질 수 있는 광범위한 메뉴를 제공합니다. [37]저희는 또한 지역 빵집과 제휴했고, 따라서 여러분의 손님들이 고급 디저트를 즐길 수 있습니다. 물론, 저희는 소풍 장소에 여러분 음식의 안전을 책임지는 적절한 식품 보관 시설을 갖추었습니다.

저는 모든 성공적인 소풍의 특징이 풍부한 오락 활동이라는 것에 여러분이 동의하실 것이라 생각합니다. The Glam Squad Syndicate는 아주 신나는 경험을 위해 블루투스 음향 시스템과 휴대용 스크린을 포함한 극장 수준의 프로젝터를 드립니다. 여러분의 친구들과

	will make unforgettable memories as they watch movies and dance to music.	가족은 영화를 보고 음악에 맞춰 춤을 추며 잊지 못할 추억들을 만들 것입니다.
주요 혜택5: 어린이 활동	The Glam Squad Syndicate has something for the kids too. Our children's picnic packages include an arts and crafts center where kids can ^{38(d)}construct model cabins, ^{38(b)}make fishing rods, or even ^{38(a)}assemble their own birdhouses. Some of the activities are so fun that the adults might want to do them with the kids. Not only that, we also prepare a special kid's menu featuring camping favorites such as hot dogs and s'mores.	The Glam Squad Syndicate에는 아이들을 위한 것 또한 있습니다. 저희의 어린이 소풍 패키지에는 어린이들이 ^{38(d)}모형 오두막을 짓거나, ^{38(b)}낚싯대를 만들거나, 심지어 ^{38(a)}그들 자신만의 새장을 조립할 수 있는 미술 공예 센터가 포함되어 있습니다. 몇몇 활동들은 너무 재미있어서 어른들이 아이들과 함께 그것들을 하고 싶어 할지도 모릅니다. 그뿐만 아니라, 저희는 핫도그와 스모어와 같은 캠핑 인기 메뉴를 특별히 포함하는 어린이 특선 메뉴도 마련합니다.
출시 기념 행사	To celebrate the launch of our service, The Glam Squad Syndicate is now offering a special promotion. ³⁹All customers who visit our website to make their first online reservation before May 22 will receive a ten percent discount on their booking. We'll also throw in a free drip coffee set for brewing the best coffee outdoors.	저희 서비스의 출시를 기념하기 위해서, The Glam Squad Syndicate는 지금 특별 행사를 제공하고 있습니다. ³⁹5월 22일 이전에 온라인으로 첫 예약을 하기 위해 저희의 웹 사이트를 방문하시는 모든 고객분들은 예약에 대해 10퍼센트 할인을 받으실 겁니다. 저희는 또한 야외에서 최고의 커피를 내릴 수 있는 무료 드립 커피 세트를 덤으로 드릴 예정입니다.
끝인사	So, if you need a break from the noise and crowds of the big city, but don't want to sacrifice elegance and glamour, do not hesitate to contact The Glam Squad Syndicate. We provide indoor comforts in an outdoor setting.	따라서, 대도시의 소음과 사람들로부터 휴식이 필요하지만, 우아함과 화려함을 포기하고 싶지 않으시다면, 주저하지 마시고 The Glam Squad Syndicate에 연락하십시오. 저희는 야외 환경에서 실내의 편안함을 선사합니다.

어휘 | fashion[fǽʃən] 방식 rental[réntəl] 대여 emerge[imə́rdʒ] 떠오르다, 나타나다 glamorous[glǽmərəs] 화려한 maximum[mǽksəməm] 최대한의 minimal[mínəməl] 최소한의 backcountry[bǽkkʌntri] 시골 spirit[spírit] 분위기 inconvenience[ìnkənvíːniəns] 불편함 wilderness[wíldərnəs] 야생, 황야 decoration[dèkəréiʃən] 장식품 cozy[kóuzi] 아늑한 catering service 음식 출장 서비스 extensive[iksténsiv] 광범위한 partner[pάːrtnər] 제휴하다 gourmet[gúrmei] 고급의 outfit[áutfit] 갖추다 recreational[rèkriéiʃənəl] 오락의 portable[pɔ́ːrtəbəl] 휴대용의 thrilling[θrílin] 아주 신나는 fishing rod 낚싯대 assemble[əsémbəl] 조립하다 feature[fíːtʃər] 특별히 포함하다 throw in 덤으로 주다 brew[bruː] (커피를) 내리다, 끓이다 sacrifice[sǽkrəfais] 포기하다

---

34 특정세부사항   What   난이도 ●●○

What inspired the speaker to start a picnic business?	화자가 소풍 사업을 시작하도록 영감을 준 것은 무엇인가?
(a) the popularity of a leisure activity	**(a) 한 여가 활동의 인기**
(b) the lack of outdoor space in urban areas	(b) 도시 지역의 야외 공간 부족
(c) a desire to spend more time outside	(c) 야외에서 더 많은 시간을 보내고자 하는 욕구
(d) an event held in Santa Barbara	(d) 산타바버라에서 개최된 한 행사

⟶○ 지텔프 치트키

질문의 키워드 inspired가 그대로 언급된 주변 내용을 주의 깊게 듣는다.

해설 | 화자가 'The glamping trend inspired me to come up with a new outdoor experience designed ~ for residents of urban areas.'라며 글램핑의 유행이 도시 지역 거주자들을 위해 설계된 새로운 야외 활동을 창안하도록 자신에게 영감을 주었다고 했다. 따라서 (a)가 정답이다.

---

35 특정세부사항   How   난이도 ●●○

How does The Glam Squad Syndicate ensure that picnics can be held in any season?

(a) It rents out clothes appropriate for the weather.
(b) It offers tools for controlling the temperature.
(c) It creates indoor backup plans for every picnic.
(d) It hosts parties in an area with a mild climate.

The Glam Squad Syndicate는 어떻게 소풍이 어떤 계절에도 열릴 수 있도록 보장하는가?

(a) 날씨에 적합한 옷을 빌려준다.
(b) 온도를 조절하기 위한 도구들을 제공한다.
(c) 모든 소풍에 대한 실내 대안을 마련한다.
(d) 온화한 기후의 지역에서 파티를 주최한다.

─○ 지텔프 치트키

질문의 키워드 be held가 take place로 paraphrasing되어 언급된 주변 내용을 주의 깊게 듣는다.

해설 | 화자가 'All ~ events take place under tents equipped with heaters or cooling fans.'라며 모든 행사들이 난방기 또는 냉각 팬을 갖춘 텐트 아래에서 진행된다고 한 뒤, 'That way, you can keep everyone warm in the winter and cool during the summer.'라며 그렇게 하면 모두를 겨울에는 따뜻하게 그리고 여름에는 시원하게 유지할 수 있다고 했다. 따라서 (b)가 정답이다.

Paraphrasing

heaters or cooling fans 난방기 또는 냉각 팬 → tools for controlling the temperature 온도를 조절하기 위한 도구들

어휘 | appropriate[əpróupriət] 적합한   mild[maild] 온화한   climate[kláimət] 기후

---

36 특정세부사항   How   난이도 ●●○

How can clients make their picnics cozier?

(a) by using outdoor furniture
(b) by setting up several lanterns around their tents
(c) by bringing a variety of snacks from home
(d) by asking for an alternative type of lighting

고객들은 어떻게 그들의 소풍을 더 아늑하게 만들 수 있는가?

(a) 실외용 가구를 사용함으로써
(b) 여러 개의 랜턴을 그들의 텐트 주위에 설치함으로써
(c) 다양한 간식을 집에서 가져옴으로써
(d) 다른 종류의 조명을 요청함으로써

─○ 지텔프 치트키

질문의 키워드 cozier가 cozy로 언급된 주변 내용을 주의 깊게 듣는다.

해설 | 화자가 'If you ~ want to create a cozy atmosphere, you can request ~ our fairy lamps instead of the lanterns we usually use to decorate the dining area.'라며 만약 아늑한 분위기를 만들고 싶다면 보통 식사 공간을 장식하는 데 사용하는 랜턴 대신에 꼬마전등을 요청할 수 있다고 했다. 따라서 (d)가 정답이다.

Paraphrasing

request ~ our fairy lamps instead of the lanterns 랜턴 대신 꼬마전등을 요청하다 → asking for an alternative type of lighting 다른 종류의 조명을 요청함

어휘 | lighting[láitiŋ] 조명

37 특정세부사항   Why

Why does The Glam Squad Syndicate work in partnership with a local bakery?

(a) to supply premium-quality desserts
(b) to provide gourmet bread for appetizers
(c) to keep the food fresher for longer
(d) to lower their catering service prices

The Glam Squad Syndicate는 왜 지역 빵집과 제휴하여 일하는가?

(a) 최고급 품질의 디저트를 제공하기 위해서
(b) 애피타이저로 고급 빵을 제공하기 위해서
(c) 식품을 더 오랫동안 보다 신선하게 유지하기 위해서
(d) 그들의 음식 출장 서비스 가격을 낮추기 위해서

⟲○ 지텔프 치트키

질문의 키워드 work in partnership이 partnered로 paraphrasing되어 언급된 주변 내용을 주의 깊게 듣는다.

해설 | 화자가 'We have ~ partnered with a local bakery, so your guests can enjoy gourmet desserts.'라며 The Glam Squad Syndicate가 지역 빵집과 제휴했고, 따라서 고객의 손님들이 고급 디저트를 즐길 수 있다고 했다. 따라서 (a)가 정답이다.

Paraphrasing
gourmet desserts 고급 디저트 → premium-quality desserts 최고급 품질의 디저트

---

38 Not/True   Not 문제

Which of the children's activities is not mentioned by the speaker?

(a) putting together houses for birds
(b) making a tool used to catch fish
(c) assembling structures out of sand
(d) building model accommodations

화자에 의해 언급되지 않은 어린이 활동은 무엇인가?

(a) 새장을 조립하는 것
(b) 물고기를 잡는 데 사용되는 도구를 만드는 것
(c) 모래로 구조물을 만드는 것
(d) 모형 숙소를 짓는 것

⟲○ 지텔프 치트키

질문의 키워드 children's activities가 children's picnic packages로 paraphrasing되어 언급된 주변 내용을 주의 깊게 들으며 언급되는 것을 하나씩 소거한다.

해설 | (c)는 언급되지 않았으므로, (c)가 정답이다.

　오답분석
(a) 화자가 어린이 소풍 패키지에 포함되어 있는 미술 공예 센터에서 새장을 조립할 수 있다고 언급하였다.
(b) 화자가 어린이 소풍 패키지에 포함되어 있는 미술 공예 센터에서 낚싯대를 만들 수 있다고 언급하였다.
(d) 화자가 어린이 소풍 패키지에 포함되어 있는 미술 공예 센터에서 모형 오두막을 지을 수 있다고 언급하였다.

---

39 추론   특정사실

What will customers most likely have to do to get a special discount?

(a) leave their first review on the website
(b) reserve the service over the Internet

고객들이 특별 할인을 받기 위해 무엇을 해야 할 것 같은가?

(a) 그들의 첫 리뷰를 웹 사이트에 남긴다
(b) 인터넷을 통해 서비스를 예약한다

| (c) submit a valid coupon | (c) 유효한 쿠폰을 제출한다 |
| (d) purchase a camping license | (d) 캠핑 허가증을 구매한다 |

━━○ 지텔프 치트키

질문의 키워드 discount가 그대로 언급된 주변 내용을 주의 깊게 듣는다.

해설 | 화자가 'All customers who visit our website to make their first online reservation ~ will receive a ten percent discount on their booking.'이라며 온라인으로 첫 예약을 하기 위해 The Glam Squad Syndicate의 웹 사이트를 방문하는 모든 고객들은 예약에 대해 10퍼센트 할인을 받을 것이라고 한 것을 통해, 고객들은 특별 할인을 받기 위해 인터넷을 통해 서비스를 예약해야 할 것임을 추론할 수 있다. 따라서 (b)가 정답이다.

Paraphrasing

make their ~ online reservation 온라인으로 예약하다 → reserve ~ over the Internet 인터넷을 통해 예약한다

어휘 | valid[vǽlid] 유효한 license[láisəns] 허가증, 면허증

PART 3⁽⁴⁰~⁴⁵⁾ 장단점 논의 대규모 학급과 소규모 학급의 장단점 비교

음성 바로 듣기

안부 인사	F: Hey, Shawn! What's new? M: Hi, Sarah. I'm preparing for summer school. ⁴⁰Have you decided if you will have a large class with many students or a small class with fewer students this year?
주제 제시: 장단점 비교	F: ⁴⁰I still haven't been able to make a final decision, so can you help me with my problem? M: Sure. Maybe going over the advantages and disadvantages of each class size will help you choose.
대규모 학급 장점	F: Great idea. How about we start with the advantages of large classes? M: Well, ⁴¹one positive thing is that the students can interact with a diverse group of peers. F: ⁴¹I think that would allow them to collaborate frequently with each other. M: Yes, and they would have many chances to cooperate with others and contribute to team projects. F: Good point. I remember reading that students in large classes learn to listen carefully to others' opinions and respect them. M: That's correct. By interacting with a greater number of students, they will understand how to clearly express their ideas and be more considerate of one another.
	F: I'll have to keep that in mind as I make my decision. Are there any disadvantages to having a large class?

여: 안녕하세요, Shawn! 잘 지내셨나요?
남: 안녕하세요, Sarah. 전 서머스쿨을 준비하고 있어요. ⁴⁰당신은 올해 학생 수가 많은 대규모 학급을 운영할 것인지 아니면 학생 수가 더 적은 소규모 학급을 운영할 것인지 결정하셨나요?

여: ⁴⁰아직도 최종 결정을 내리지 못하고 있는데, 제 문제를 도와주실 수 있나요?
남: 물론이죠. 어쩌면 각 학급 규모의 장단점을 살펴보는 것은 당신이 선택하는 데 도움이 될 거예요.

여: 좋은 생각이네요. 대규모 학급의 장점부터 시작하는 게 어때요?
남: 음, ⁴¹한 가지 긍정적인 점은 학생들이 다양한 또래 집단과 상호 작용할 수 있다는 것이에요.
여: ⁴¹그것은 그들이 서로 자주 협동하게 해 줄 것이라고 생각해요.
남: 네, 그리고 그들은 다른 사람들과 협력하고 팀 프로젝트에 기여할 많은 기회를 가질 거예요.
여: 좋은 지적이네요. 대규모 학급의 학생들은 다른 사람들의 의견을 주의 깊게 듣고 그것을 존중하는 법을 배운다고 읽었던 기억이 나요.
남: 맞아요. 더 많은 수의 학생들과 상호 작용함으로써, 그들은 그들의 생각을 명확하게 표현하고 서로를 더 배려하는 방법을 이해할 거예요.

여: 결정을 내릴 때 그것을 염두에 두어야겠어요. 대규모 학급을 운영하는 것에 단점이 있나요?

해커스 지텔프 최신기출유형 실전문제집 7회 (Level 2)

<table>
<tr>
<td rowspan="1">대규모
학급
단점</td>
<td>

M: Let me see. For one thing, [42]teachers may find it difficult to give an adequate amount of attention to each student. As more students are placed in a classroom, the teacher will have less and less time for each one.

F: Oh . . . Then, that must be why teachers who have large classes often report that they have a hard time with classroom management. It seems that as the size of the class grows, it becomes harder for the teacher to make sure everyone is behaving appropriately.

M: I've heard similar complaints from teachers. This is important because classroom management is directly related to the safety of students.

</td>
<td>

남: 글쎄요. 한 가지로, [42]교사들이 각 학생에게 충분한 양의 관심을 기울이는 것이 어렵다고 느낄 수 있어요. 한 학급에 더 많은 학생들이 배정될수록, 교사는 각 학생에게 점점 더 적은 시간을 갖게 될 거예요.

여: 오... 그럼, 그것이 분명 대규모 학급을 운영하는 교사들이 종종 학급 관리에 어려움을 겪는다고 전하는 이유일 거예요. 학급의 규모가 커질수록, 모두가 적절하게 행동하고 있는지 교사가 확인하는 것이 더 어려워지는 것 같네요.

남: 교사들로부터 비슷한 불평을 들은 적이 있어요. 학급 관리는 학생들의 안전과 직결되기 때문에 이것은 중요해요.

</td>
</tr>
<tr>
<td>소규모
학급
장점</td>
<td>

F: OK. Let's talk about small classes now.

M: Well, one major advantage is that students can receive plenty of individual care from the teacher.

F: That's true. [43]When teachers can spend time with students one on one, they do a better job of identifying the students' strengths and weaknesses.

M: Similarly, having a small number of students in the classroom allows the teacher to plan activities and lessons that are well suited to the students' particular capacities.

F: I agree. With a small class, the teacher can give each student exactly what they need. This is better than teaching one lesson to students who have different skill levels.

M: That's true. Customized lessons can be a great benefit to students by helping them stay engaged in the topic.

</td>
<td>

여: 알겠어요. 이제 소규모 학급에 관해 이야기해 보아요.

남: 음, 한 가지 주요 장점은 학생들이 교사로부터 개별적인 관심을 많이 받을 수 있다는 거예요.

여: 맞아요. [43]교사들이 학생들과 일대일로 시간을 보낼 수 있을 때, 그들은 학생들의 강점과 약점을 더 잘 파악해요.

남: 마찬가지로, 학급에 적은 수의 학생들이 있는 것은 교사가 학생들의 특정한 능력에 잘 맞는 활동과 수업을 계획할 수 있게 하죠.

여: 동의해요. 소규모 학급을 통해, 교사는 각 학생에게 그들이 필요한 것을 정확히 제공할 수 있어요. 이것은 각기 다른 능력 수준을 가진 학생들에게 단 하나의 교육 내용을 가르치는 것보다 더 좋아요.

남: 사실이에요. 맞춤형 수업은 그들이 주제에 계속 집중할 수 있도록 도움으로써 학생에게 큰 이득이 될 수 있어요.

</td>
</tr>
<tr>
<td>소규모
학급
단점</td>
<td>

F: That all sounds nice, but small classes must have some disadvantages, right?

M: They do. If there are fewer students in each class, then they will have fewer opportunities to contend with a variety of ideas.

F: You're right. Also, they will not be able to interact with classmates from different cultural backgrounds.

M: Exactly. This could put them at a disadvantage when it comes to their cognitive development. I've seen research that shows a significant connection between culturally diverse classrooms and gains in critical thinking skills.

F: That makes sense. [44]If students are surrounded by people with the same background, then they might become narrow-minded.

</td>
<td>

여: 다 좋은 것 같지만, 소규모 학급에도 단점이 있을 거예요, 그렇죠?

남: 있어요. 각 학급에 더 적은 수의 학생들이 있으면, 그들은 다양한 아이디어와 씨름할 기회가 줄어들 거예요.

여: 당신의 말이 맞아요. 또한, 그들은 다른 문화적 배경을 가진 급우들과 상호 작용할 수 없을 거예요.

남: 바로 그거예요. 이것은 그들의 인지 발달에 있어서 그들을 불리한 위치에 놓이게 할 수 있어요. 저는 문화적으로 다양한 학급과 비판적 사고 능력의 향상 사이의 유의미한 연관성을 보여주는 연구를 본 적이 있어요.

여: 일리가 있네요. [44]학생들이 같은 배경을 가진 사람들에게 둘러싸여 있으면, 그들은 편협해질지도 몰라요.

</td>
</tr>
</table>

M: You're probably right. Plus, that would make it difficult for them to participate in a global economy when they are older.	남: 당신 말이 맞을 거예요. 게다가, 그것은 그들이 나이가 들었을 때 세계 경제에 참여하기 어렵게 만들지도 몰라요.
F: Thank you for taking the time to discuss the pros and cons with me, Shawn.	여: 시간을 내어 저와 장단점을 논의해 주셔서 고마워요, Shawn.
M: My pleasure, Sarah. So, have you decided what kind of class you are going to have?	남: 별말씀을요, Sarah. 그럼, 어떤 종류의 학급을 운영할지 결정하셨나요?
F: I think so. Let's just say that ⁴⁵you won't hear me complaining about classroom management this summer!	여: 그런 것 같아요. ⁴⁵당신이 올해 여름에 제가 학급 관리에 대해 불평하는 것을 들을 일은 없을 것이라고 해 두죠!
M: Sounds like you've made the right choice. Good luck with your new class!	남: 당신이 옳은 선택을 한 것 같군요. 새로운 학급에 행운을 빕니다!

여자의 결정

어휘 | summer school 서머스쿨(여름 방학 동안에 일정한 학과나 실습을 목적으로 열리는 학교) diverse [daivə́ːrs] 다양한 peer [pir] 또래
collaborate [kəlǽbəreit] 협동하다 cooperate [kouáːpəreit] 협력하다 considerate [kənsídərət] 배려하는, 사려 깊은
adequate [ǽdikwət] 충분한, 적절한 complaint [kəmpléint] 불평 one on one 일대일로 identify [aidéntifai] 파악하다, 확인하다
capacity [kəpǽsəti] 능력 engage [ingéidʒ] 집중시키다 contend [kənténd] 씨름하다, 주장하다 significant [signífikənt] 유의미한, 중요한
surround [səráund] 둘러싸다, 에워싸다 narrow-minded 편협한

---

40 **특정세부사항** Why 난이도 ●○○

Why does Sarah ask Shawn for help?	Sarah는 왜 Shawn에게 도움을 요청하는가?
(a) She doesn't know where her classroom is.	(a) 그녀의 학급이 어디에 있는지를 모른다.
(b) She needs to choose the size of her class.	**(b) 그녀의 학급 규모를 선택해야 한다.**
(c) She wants to get information about her students.	(c) 그녀의 학생들에 대한 정보를 얻기를 원한다.
(d) She doesn't remember when the school year starts.	(d) 학년이 언제 시작하는지를 기억하지 못한다.

지텔프 치트키

질문의 키워드 help가 그대로 언급된 주변 내용을 주의 깊게 듣는다.

해설 | 남자가 'Have you decided if you will have a large class with many students or a small class with fewer students this year?'라며 여자에게 올해 학생 수가 많은 대규모 학급을 운영할 것인지 아니면 학생 수가 더 적은 소규모 학급을 운영할 것인지를 결정했는지 묻자, 여자가 'I still haven't been able to make a final decision, so can you help with my problem?'이라며 아직도 최종 결정을 내리지 못하고 있는데 그녀의 문제를 도와줄 수 있는지 물었다. 따라서 (b)가 정답이다.

Paraphrasing
make a ~ decision 결정을 내리다 → choose 선택하다

어휘 | school year 학년

---

41 **특정세부사항** 장·단점 난이도 ●●○

What is the advantage of having more students in a class?	한 학급에 더 많은 학생들이 있는 것의 장점은 무엇인가?

해커스 지텔프 최신기출유형 실전문제집 7회 (Level 2)

(a) They interact with the teacher more frequently.	(a) 교사와 더 자주 상호 작용한다.
(b) They meet a similar group of peers.	(b) 비슷한 또래 집단을 만난다.
(c) They have more chances to work together.	**(c) 협동할 기회가 더 많다.**
(d) They learn independently of each other.	(d) 서로 독립적으로 학습한다.

지텔프 치트키

질문의 키워드 having more students in a class와 관련된 긍정적인 흐름을 파악한다.

해설 | 남자가 'one positive thing is that the students can interact with a diverse group of peers'라며 대규모 학급의 한 가지 긍정적인 점은 학생들이 다양한 또래 집단과 상호 작용할 수 있다는 것이라고 하자, 여자가 'I think that would allow them to collaborate frequently with each other.'라며 대규모 학급은 학생들이 서로 자주 협동하게 해 줄 것이라고 생각한다고 했다. 따라서 (c)가 정답이다.

Paraphrasing
collaborate ~ with each other 서로 협동하다 → work together 협동하다

어휘 | independently [ìndəpéndəntli] 독립적으로

---

42 추론 특정사실 난이도 ●●●

What would a teacher in a large class most likely not do?	대규모 학급의 교사는 무엇을 하지 않을 것 같은가?
(a) struggle with classroom management	(a) 학급 관리에 어려움을 겪는다
(b) complain to other teachers about student behavior	(b) 학생 행동에 관해 다른 교사들에게 불평한다
(c) worry about the safety of students	(c) 학생들의 안전에 관해 걱정한다
(d) devote a similar amount of effort to each pupil	**(d) 각 학생에게 비슷한 양의 노력을 쏟는다**

지텔프 치트키

질문의 키워드 teacher in a large class와 관련된 주변 내용을 주의 깊게 듣는다.

해설 | 남자가 'teachers may find it difficult to give an adequate amount of attention to each student'라며 교사들이 각 학생에게 충분한 양의 관심을 기울이는 것이 어렵다고 느낄 수 있다고 한 것을 통해, 대규모 학급의 교사는 각 학생에게 비슷한 양의 노력을 쏟지 않을 것임을 추론할 수 있다. 따라서 (d)가 정답이다.

Paraphrasing
student 학생 → pupil 학생

어휘 | struggle [strʌ́gəl] 어려움을 겪다　devote [divóut] 쏟다, 바치다　pupil [pjúːpəl] 학생

---

43 특정세부사항 When 난이도 ●●○

When is it easier for a teacher to see a student's merits and faults?	교사는 언제 학생의 장단점을 더 쉽게 확인할 수 있는가?
(a) when activities are planned in advance	(a) 활동들이 사전에 계획되었을 때
(b) when teachers have individual time with students	**(b) 교사가 학생들과 개별적인 시간을 가질 때**
(c) when teachers organize group discussions	(c) 교사가 집단 토론을 준비할 때
(d) when the lessons are less difficult	(d) 교육 내용이 덜 어려울 때

●──○ 지텔프 치트키

질문의 키워드 merits and faults가 strengths and weaknesses로 paraphrasing되어 언급된 주변 내용을 주의 깊게 듣는다.

해설 | 여자가 'When teachers can spend time with students one on one, they do a better job of identifying the students' strengths and weaknesses.'라며 교사들이 학생들과 일대일로 시간을 보낼 수 있을 때 학생들의 강점과 약점을 더 잘 파악한다고 했다. 따라서 (b)가 정답이다.

Paraphrasing

spend time ~ one on one 일대일로 시간을 보내다 → have individual time 개별적인 시간을 가지다

어휘 | merit[mérit] 장점 fault[fɔːlt] 단점 in advance 사전에 individual[ìndəvídʒuəl] 개별적인 organize[ɔ́ːrɡənaiz] 준비하다, 조직하다

---

44 특정세부사항 How

난이도 ●●○

According to the conversation, how does lack of exposure to cultural diversity impact students?

(a) **by making them less receptive to unfamiliar concepts**

(b) by causing them to ignore background information

(c) by allowing them to change their point of view

(d) by encouraging them to be more open-minded

대화에 따르면, 문화적 다양성에 대한 노출의 부족이 학생들에게 어떻게 영향을 미치는가?

(a) **낯선 개념들에 덜 수용적이게 만듦으로써**

(b) 배경 정보를 무시하게 함으로써

(c) 그들의 관점을 바꿀 수 있도록 함으로써

(d) 더 편견이 없도록 장려함으로써

●──○ 지텔프 치트키

질문의 키워드 lack of exposure to cultural diversity가 surrounded by people with the same background로 paraphrasing 되어 언급된 주변 내용을 주의 깊게 듣는다.

해설 | 여자가 'If students are surrounded by people with the same background, then they might become narrow-minded.' 라며 학생들이 같은 배경을 가진 사람들에게 둘러싸여 있으면 편협해질지도 모른다고 했다. 따라서 (a)가 정답이다.

Paraphrasing

narrow-minded 편협한 → less receptive to unfamiliar concepts 낯선 개념들에 덜 수용적인

어휘 | receptive[riséptiv] 수용적인 open-minded 편견이 없는

---

45 추론 다음에 할 일

난이도 ●●○

Based on the conversation, what will Sarah probably do about her problem?

(a) teach a large number of students

(b) take breaks between classes

(c) learn how to manage large classes

(d) **have a class with fewer students**

대화에 따르면, Sarah는 그녀의 문제와 관련하여 무엇을 할 것 같은가?

(a) 많은 수의 학생들을 가르친다

(b) 수업 사이에 휴식을 취한다

(c) 대규모 학급을 관리하는 법을 배운다

(d) **학생 수가 더 적은 학급을 운영한다**

●──○ 지텔프 치트키

다음에 할 일을 언급하는 후반을 주의 깊게 듣는다.

해커스 지텔프 최신기출유형 실전문제집 7회 (Level 2)

PART 4 (46~52) 설명 건강한 아침 루틴을 형성하기 위한 6가지 조언

음성 바로 듣기

인사 + 주제 제시	Hello, everyone! I am the Vice President of Student Affairs, and I would like to welcome you to Chatwood University. [46]As you begin your life as a college student, you might feel overwhelmed by your new responsibilities. You know that the choices you make throughout the day contribute to your success, but you may not have given much thought to your morning routine. Today, I'm going to tell you how to develop a healthy one.	안녕하세요, 여러분! 저는 학생부의 부총장이며, 여러분이 Chatwood 대학에 오신 것을 환영합니다. [46]여러분이 대학생으로서의 생활을 시작하면서, 새로운 책임 때문에 부담을 느끼실지도 모릅니다. 여러분은 온종일 내리는 선택들이 여러분의 성공에 기여한다는 것을 알고 있지만, 아침 루틴에 대해서는 많은 생각을 하지 않았을지도 모릅니다. 오늘, 저는 여러분께 건강한 아침 루틴을 형성하는 방법을 알려 드리겠습니다.
조언1: 충분한 숙면	First, give sleep priority. Adults need between seven and nine hours of sleep to keep their bodies and minds functioning properly. In fact, lack of sleep can lead to cognitive decline, which is one thing college students should avoid. It is also well known that too little sleep increases the likelihood of suffering other health problems, such as diabetes and obesity. [47]If you are struggling to fall asleep, try to keep your room cool, quiet, and dark so that you can sleep with ease.	첫째, 수면에 우선순위를 부여하세요. 성인은 몸과 마음이 계속 제대로 기능하도록 유지하기 위해서 7시간에서 9시간 사이의 수면이 필요합니다. 실제로, 수면 부족은 인지 저하로 이어질 수 있으며, 이는 대학생이 피해야 할 한 가지입니다. 너무 적은 수면은 당뇨와 비만과 같은 다른 건강 문제들을 겪을 가능성을 높인다는 것 또한 잘 알려져 있습니다. [47]만약 여러분이 잠드는 데 어려움을 겪고 있다면, 편안히 잘 수 있도록 방을 시원하고, 조용하며, 어둡게 유지하려고 노력해 보세요.
조언2: 수분 섭취	Second, drink a tall glass of water. Hydrating shortly after waking up can promote alertness and improve your blood flow. If you're like me, you might be tempted to reach for a cup of coffee as soon as you open your eyes. However, that may not be a good idea. [48]Levels of the stress hormone cortisol tend to be high when we wake up and become higher due to caffeine. Prolonged exposure to elevated cortisol can weaken your immune system. So, have some water and wait a few hours before having your first cup of coffee.	둘째, 큰 잔으로 물을 마시세요. 기상 후 바로 수분을 공급하는 것은 주의력을 높이고 혈류를 개선할 수 있습니다. 만약 여러분이 저와 같다면, 눈을 뜨자마자 커피 한 잔에 손을 뻗고 싶은 유혹을 느끼실지도 모릅니다. 그러나, 그것은 좋은 생각이 아닐 수 있습니다. [48]스트레스 호르몬인 코르티솔의 수치는 잠에서 깨어났을 때 높은 경향이 있고 카페인으로 더 높아집니다. 상승된 코르티솔에 장기간 노출되는 것은 여러분의 면역 체계를 약화시킬 수 있습니다. 따라서, 물을 마시고 첫 커피 한 잔을 마시기 전에 몇 시간을 기다리세요.
조언3: 명상	Third, set aside time for meditation. [49]Research suggests that meditation reduces anxiety. It can also make it easier to focus during the day and to get a good night's sleep. Additionally, studies have found that meditation continues helping your brain function well even when you're not meditating. With benefits like that, mindfulness should be a part of everyone's daily life.	셋째, 명상을 위한 시간을 확보하세요. [49]연구는 명상이 불안을 감소시킨다고 제시합니다. 그것은 또한 낮에 집중하고 밤에 숙면하는 것을 더 수월하게 만듭니다. 게다가, 연구들은 명상이 여러분이 명상을 하지 않을 때조차도 뇌가 잘 기능하도록 계속해서 돕는다는 것을 발견했습니다. 이와 같은 이점들이 있으므로, 마음 챙김은 모든 사람의 일상생활의 일부가 되어야 합니다.
	Fourth, consider doing yoga in the morning. [50]Engaging in physical activity at the start of your day helps stimulate	넷째, 아침에 요가를 하는 것을 고려하세요. [50]하루를 시작할 때 신체 활동을 하는 것은 뇌의 해마를 자극

조언4: 아침 운동	the hippocampus in the brain, which increases memory, enhances self-esteem, and boosts creativity. Likewise, people who do morning workouts are more likely to feel energized for the rest of the day. You don't have to start training like a professional athlete, but you definitely want to include fitness in your morning routine. The positive effects will stay with you all day long.	하는 것에 도움이 되는데, 이는 기억력을 향상시키고, 자존감을 높이며, 창의력을 증진합니다. 마찬가지로, 아침 운동을 하는 사람들은 남은 하루 동안 활력을 느낄 가능성이 더 큽니다. 전문 운동선수처럼 훈련을 시작할 필요는 없지만, 여러분은 분명 여러분의 아침 루틴에 신체 단련을 포함해야 합니다. 긍정적인 효과는 온종일 여러분과 함께할 것입니다.
조언5: 마음 자극	Fifth, be sure to invigorate your mind. Mental exercise is just as important as physical exercise. Challenging your mind first thing in the morning is an effective way to prepare yourself to think of new ideas and solve problems later in the day. [51]There are many ways to do this, but consider writing a daily to-do list, listening to an educational podcast you enjoy, or working out a crossword puzzle.	다섯째, 반드시 마음에 활기를 불어넣으세요. 정신 운동은 신체 운동 못지않게 중요합니다. 아침에 가장 먼저 마음을 자극하는 것은 그날 오후에 새로운 아이디어를 떠올리고 문제를 해결하도록 여러분 자신을 준비시키는 효과적인 방법입니다. [51]이것을 하는 데는 많은 방법들이 있지만, 하루의 할 일 목록을 작성하거나, 여러분이 좋아하는 교육용 팟캐스트를 듣거나, 십자말풀이를 하는 것을 고려해 보세요.
조언6: 잠자리 정리	Finally, make your bed. This may sound like a trivial chore, but doing this small job can change your life in unexpected ways. [52]By making your bed every morning, you begin each day with an accomplishment. This will give you the encouragement you need to continue completing more tasks throughout the day. Moreover, according to sleep researchers, people who make their beds in the morning tend to sleep better at night.	마지막으로, 잠자리를 정리하세요. 이것은 사소한 잡일처럼 들릴지 모르지만, 이 작은 일을 하는 것이 여러분의 삶을 예상하지 못한 방식으로 바꿀 수 있습니다. [52]매일 아침 잠자리를 정리함으로써, 여러분은 하루를 성취로 시작할 것입니다. 이것은 온종일 더 많은 과업을 계속해서 완료하기 위해 여러분이 필요로 하는 격려를 제공할 것입니다. 게다가, 수면 연구원들에 따르면, 아침에 잠자리를 정리하는 사람들이 밤에 잠을 더 잘 자는 경향이 있습니다.
끝인사	Well, this ends my talk. Thank you for your time, and remember, once you've developed your own morning routine, you will be a better student and a happier person overall.	자, 이것으로 제 이야기를 마치겠습니다. 시간을 내주신 것에 감사드리며, 여러분 자신만의 아침 루틴을 형성했을 때, 여러분은 전반적으로 더 나은 학생 그리고 더 행복한 사람이 될 것임을 기억하십시오.

어휘 | overwhelmed[òuvərwélmd] 부담을 느끼는 priority[praiɔ́:rəti] 우선순위 diabetes[dàiəbí:tis] 당뇨 obesity[oubí:səti] 비만 hydrate[háidreit] 수분을 공급하다 alertness[ələ́:rtnis] 주의력 tempt[tempt] 유혹하다 prolonged[prəlɔ́:ŋd] 장기간의 elevate[éliveit] 상승시키다 weaken[wí:kən] 약화시키다 immune system 면역 체계 meditation[mèditéiʃən] 명상 mindfulness[máindfəlnəs] 마음 챙김 stimulate[stímjəleit] 자극하다 hippocampus[hìpəkǽmpəs] (대뇌 측두엽의) 해마 self-esteem 자존감 invigorate[invígəreit] 활기를 불어넣다 crossword puzzle 십자말풀이 make bed 잠자리를 정리하다 trivial[tríviəl] 사소한 chore[tʃɔːr] 잡일, 하기 싫은 일 accomplishment[əkɑ́:mpliʃmənt] 성취, 업적

---

46   특정세부사항   What

난이도 ●○○

What can cause college students to feel distressed?	대학생들이 괴로움을 느끼도록 야기할 수 있는 것은 무엇인가?
(a) the unwelcome feelings at school	(a) 학교에서 환영받지 않는 느낌
(b) the fear of making bad choices	(b) 잘못된 선택을 하는 것에 대한 두려움
(c) the new obligations they take on	**(c) 그들이 맡는 새로운 의무**
(d) the changes to their normal routine	(d) 그들의 일상 루틴의 변화

━○ 지텔프 치트키

질문의 키워드 feel distressed가 feel overwhelmed로 paraphrasing되어 언급된 주변 내용을 주의 깊게 듣는다.

해설 | 화자가 'As you begin your life as a college student, you might feel overwhelmed by ~ new responsibilities.'라며 대학생으로서의 생활을 시작하면서 새로운 책임 때문에 부담을 느낄지도 모른다고 했다. 따라서 (c)가 정답이다.

Paraphrasing
responsibilities 책임 → obligations 의무

어휘 | distressed[distrést] 괴로운 unwelcome[ʌnwélkəm] 환영받지 않는 obligation[ὰːbləɡéiʃən] 의무

---

47 특정세부사항   Why   난이도 ●●○

Why does the speaker tell people to keep their rooms in a certain condition?	화자는 왜 사람들에게 그들의 방을 특정 상태로 유지하라고 말하는가?
(a) to avoid falling asleep	(a) 잠이 드는 것을 피하기 위해서
(b) to help them stay organized	(b) 그들이 정돈된 상태를 유지할 수 있도록 돕기 위해서
(c) to improve the quality of their sleep	**(c) 그들의 수면의 질을 향상시키기 위해서**
(d) to prevent cognitive decline	(d) 인지 저하를 방지하기 위해서

⟶○ 지텔프 치트키

질문의 키워드 rooms가 room으로 언급된 주변 내용을 주의 깊게 듣는다.

해설 | 화자가 'If you are struggling to fall asleep, try to keep your room cool, quiet, and dark so that you can sleep with ease.'라며 만약 잠드는 데 어려움을 겪고 있다면 편안히 잘 수 있도록 방을 시원하고, 조용하며, 어둡게 유지하려고 노력해 보라고 했다. 따라서 (c)가 정답이다.

Paraphrasing
keep their rooms in a certain condition 방을 특정 상태로 유지하다 → keep your room cool, quiet, and dark 방을 시원하고, 조용하며, 어둡게 유지하다
sleep with ease 편안히 자다 → improve the quality of their sleep 수면의 질을 향상시키다

---

48 추론   특정사실   난이도 ●●●

Why is it probably a bad idea to drink coffee immediately upon awakening?	일어나자마자 바로 커피를 마시는 것이 왜 안 좋은 생각인 것 같은가?
(a) It may raise cortisol levels.	**(a) 코르티솔 수치를 높일 수 있다.**
(b) It causes damage to an empty stomach.	(b) 빈속에 해를 가한다.
(c) It may disrupt blood flow.	(c) 혈류를 방해할 수 있다.
(d) It slows the immune system's response time.	(d) 면역 체계의 반응 속도를 늦춘다.

⟶○ 지텔프 치트키

질문의 키워드 awakening이 wake up으로 paraphrasing되어 언급된 주변 내용을 주의 깊게 듣는다.

해설 | 화자가 'Levels of the stress hormone cortisol tend to be high when we wake up and become higher due to caffeine.'이라며 스트레스 호르몬인 코르티솔의 수치는 잠에서 깨어났을 때 높은 경향이 있고 카페인으로 더 높아진다고 한 것을 통해, 일어나자마자 바로 커피를 마시는 것이 안 좋은 생각인 이유는 그것이 코르티솔 수치를 높일 수 있기 때문임을 추론할 수 있다. 따라서 (a)가 정답이다.

Paraphrasing

Levels of ~ cortisol ~ become higher 코르티솔의 수치가 더 높아지다 → raise cortisol levels 코르티솔 수치를 높이다

어휘 | disrupt[disrʌ́pt] 방해하다

---

49 특정세부사항 What
난이도 ●●○

According to the speaker, what is the result of meditation?

(a) a better grasp on time management
(b) a lower degree of anxiety
(c) a higher capacity for problem solving
(d) an improved ability to wake up early

화자에 따르면, 명상의 결과는 무엇인가?

(a) 시간 관리에 대한 더 나은 이해
(b) 더 낮은 정도의 불안
(c) 더 높은 수준의 문제 해결 능력
(d) 향상된 일찍 일어나는 능력

○ 지텔프 치트키

질문의 키워드 meditation이 그대로 언급된 주변 내용을 주의 깊게 듣는다.

해설 | 화자가 'Research suggests that meditation reduces anxiety.'라며 연구는 명상이 불안을 감소시킨다고 제시한다고 했다. 따라서 (b)가 정답이다.

Paraphrasing

reduces anxiety 불안을 감소시킨다 → a lower degree of anxiety 더 낮은 정도의 불안

어휘 | grasp[græsp] 이해

---

50 특정세부사항 What
난이도 ●●○

What is a positive effect of morning exercise?

(a) It creates a routine activity to start the day.
(b) It boosts energy until the next day.
(c) It activates the memory structure in the brain.
(d) It enhances performance in professional settings.

아침 운동의 긍정적인 효과는 무엇인가?

(a) 하루를 시작하기 위한 일상적인 활동을 만든다.
(b) 다음날까지 에너지를 증가시킨다.
(c) 뇌의 기억 체계를 활성화한다.
(d) 전문적인 환경에서의 수행을 향상시킨다.

○ 지텔프 치트키

질문의 키워드 exercise가 physical activity로 paraphrasing되어 언급된 주변 내용을 주의 깊게 듣는다.

해설 | 화자가 'Engaging in physical activity at the start of your day helps stimulate the hippocampus in the brain, which increases memory'라며 하루를 시작할 때 신체 활동을 하는 것은 뇌의 해마를 자극하는 것에 도움이 되는데, 이는 기억력을 향상시킨다고 했다. 따라서 (c)가 정답이다.

Paraphrasing

increases memory 기억력을 향상시킨다 → activates the memory structure 기억 체계를 활성화한다

어휘 | activate[ǽktiveit] 활성화하다 performance[pərfɔ́ːrməns] 수행

Based on the talk, what is one way to stimulate the mind in the morning?

(a) **finish a challenging word game**
(b) watch an educational movie
(c) write a list of recent accomplishments
(d) produce a thought-provoking puzzle

담화에 따르면, 아침에 마음을 자극하는 한 가지 방법은 무엇인가?

(a) **도전적인 단어 게임을 완료한다**
(b) 교육적인 영화를 본다
(c) 최근의 성과 목록을 작성한다
(d) 사고를 자극하는 퍼즐을 만든다

─○ 지텔프 치트키

질문의 키워드 stimulate ~ mind가 Challenging ~ mind로 paraphrasing되어 언급된 주변 내용을 주의 깊게 듣는다.

해설 | 화자가 'There are many ways to do this, but consider ~ working out a crossword puzzle.'이라며 마음을 자극하는 데는 많은 방법들이 있지만 십자말풀이를 하는 것 등을 고려해 보라고 했다. 따라서 (a)가 정답이다.

Paraphrasing
working out a crossword puzzle 십자말풀이를 하는 것 → finish a ~ word game 단어 게임을 완료한다

어휘 | thought-provoking 사고를 자극하는

How most likely would college students accomplish more duties?

(a) **by finishing small things daily**
(b) by allowing extra time for sleep
(c) by encouraging each other
(d) by making their schedule predictable

대학생들이 어떻게 더 많은 과업을 완수할 것 같은가?

(a) **매일 작은 일을 끝냄으로써**
(b) 별도의 수면 시간을 허용함으로써
(c) 서로를 격려함으로써
(d) 그들의 일정을 예측할 수 있게 만듦으로써

─○ 지텔프 치트키

질문의 키워드 accomplish more duties가 completing more tasks로 paraphrasing되어 언급된 주변 내용을 주의 깊게 듣는다.

해설 | 화자가 'By making your bed every morning, you begin each day with an accomplishment.'라며 매일 아침 잠자리를 정리함으로써 대학생들이 하루를 성취로 시작할 것이라고 한 뒤, 'This will give you the encouragement you need to continue completing more tasks throughout the day.'라며 이것은 온종일 더 많은 과업을 계속해서 완료하기 위해 그들이 필요로 하는 격려를 제공할 것이라고 한 것을 통해, 매일 잠자리 정리와 같은 작은 일을 끝냄으로써 대학생들이 더 많은 과업을 완수할 것임을 추론할 수 있다. 따라서 (a)가 정답이다.

PART 1 [53~59] 인물의 일대기 나이키의 창업자 필 나이트

인물 이름

PHIL KNIGHT

소개 + 유명한 이유

Phil Knight is an American businessman best known for cofounding the multinational athletic footwear and apparel company Nike, Inc. with Bill Bowerman. Despite never owning a sports team or being a professional athlete, Knight has been called "the most powerful person in sports."

어린 시절

Phil Knight was born in Portland, Oregon, on February 24, 1938. His father William Knight, the publisher of the *Oregon Journal*, was strict with his son, [53]refusing to give him a job at his newspaper. Rather than becoming discouraged, Knight found a position at the rival paper the *Oregonian*. Around this time, Knight also developed a keen interest in running. He began running seven miles every morning and became a key member of his high school's track team.

업적 시작 계기

Knight attended the University of Oregon, where he competed for the school's track and field team. He was mentored by Bill Bowerman, a legendary coach who trained numerous champion athletes during his career. After graduating with a journalism degree in 1959, Knight pursued an MBA from Stanford University. [54]While writing a paper on the influence of Japanese imports, Knight started thinking about founding his own footwear business to sell Japanese running shoes.

초기 활동

Following his graduation, Knight [58]gained the rights to distribute the running shoe brand Tiger in America. [55]Knight mailed samples of the shoes to Bowerman, hoping he would buy some. In addition to making a purchase, Bowerman proposed that they become business partners. Together, they set up Blue Ribbon Sports on January 25, 1964.

주요 업적

In 1971, they did not renew their contract with Tiger and instead commenced designing their own products. The same year, they renamed the company Nike after the Greek goddess of victory and [59]unveiled the iconic "swoosh" logo. [56]As athletes began wearing its footwear at the Olympics, the company expanded rapidly. Throughout the 1980s and 1990s, Nike secured endorsements with some of the world's most famous

필 나이트

필 나이트는 빌 바우어만과 함께 다국적 운동화 및 의류 기업인 나이키 사를 공동 창립한 것으로 가장 잘 알려져 있는 미국 사업가이다. 스포츠 팀을 소유하거나 프로 운동선수였던 적이 없음에도 불구하고, 나이트는 '스포츠계에서 가장 영향력 있는 사람'으로 불려 왔다.

필 나이트는 1938년 2월 24일 오리건주 포틀랜드에서 태어났다. 「오리건 신문」의 출판인인 그의 아버지 윌리엄 나이트는 아들에게 엄격했고, [53]그의 신문사에서 아들에게 일자리를 주기를 거부했다. 낙담하는 대신에, 나이트는 경쟁 신문사인 「오리거니언」에서 일자리를 찾았다. 이 무렵, 나이트는 또한 달리기에 대한 뜨거운 관심을 키웠다. 그는 매일 아침에 7마일을 달리기 시작했고 그의 고등학교 육상팀의 주축 선수가 되었다.

나이트는 오리건 대학에 다녔고, 그곳에서 그는 그 학교의 육상 경기 팀을 위해 경기했다. 그는 경력 동안 수많은 챔피언 운동선수들을 훈련시킨 전설적인 코치 빌 바우어만에게 지도를 받았다. 1959년에 신문학 학위를 가지고 졸업한 후, 나이트는 스탠퍼드 대학에서 경영학 석사 학위를 취득했다. [54]일본 수입의 영향에 관한 논문을 쓰는 동안, 나이트는 일본 운동화를 판매하는 그 자신의 신발 사업체를 설립하는 것에 대해 고민하기 시작했다.

졸업 후에, 나이트는 운동화 브랜드인 타이거 사를 미국에서 [58]유통할 권한을 얻었다. [55]나이트는 바우어만에게 그 신발의 견본품들을 우편으로 보내면서, 그가 몇 켤레를 구매하기를 바랐다. 구매와 더불어, 바우어만은 그들이 사업 파트너가 되는 것을 제안했다. 함께, 그들은 1964년 1월 25일에 블루 리본 스포츠 사를 차렸다.

1971년에, 그들은 타이거 사와의 계약을 갱신하지 않았고 대신에 그들의 자체 제품들을 디자인하기 시작했다. 같은 해에, 그들은 그리스 승리의 여신의 이름을 따서 회사 이름을 나이키라고 바꾸었고 [59]상징적인 '부메랑' 로고를 공개했다. [56]운동선수들이 올림픽에서 그것의 신발을 착용하기 시작하면서, 그 회사는 빠르게 확장되었다. 1980년대와 1990년대 전반에 걸쳐, 나이키 사는 농구 선수 마이클 조던을 포함하여, 세계에서 가장 유명한 몇몇 운동선수들의 보증 광

athletes, including basketball player Michael Jordan. This increased the shoes' appeal among everyday sports enthusiasts. The company's "Just Do It" marketing campaign further amplified the exposure of the brand.

As of 2021, Knight's net worth was about $60.8 billion, and he has donated vast sums of money through the Philip H. Knight Charitable Foundation Trust since 1990. [57]Knight was inducted into the Oregon Sports Hall of Fame in 2000 for contributing approximately $230 million to the University of Oregon, thereby advancing athletics in the state. In 2021, the Naismith Memorial Basketball Hall of Fame recognized him for Nike's substantial backing of US basketball.

고를 확보했다. 이것은 생활 체육에 열심인 사람들 사이에서 그 신발의 매력을 증가시켰다. 그 회사의 'Just Do It(그냥 해봐)' 마케팅 캠페인은 그 브랜드의 노출을 더욱 확대했다.

2021년을 기준으로, 나이트의 순자산은 약 608억 달러였으며, 그는 1990년 이래로 필립 H. 나이트 위탁 자선 단체를 통해 막대한 금액을 기부해 왔다. [57]나이트는 오리건 대학에 약 2억 3,000만 달러를 기부한 것으로 2000년에 오리건주 스포츠 명예의 전당에 헌액되었으며, 그렇게 함으로써 그 주의 운동 경기를 발전시켰다. 2021년에, 네이스미스 기념 농구 명예의 전당은 미국 농구에 대한 나이키 사의 실질적인 지원에 대해 그의 공로를 인정했다.

어휘 | cofound v. 공동 창립하다 multinational adj. 다국적의 athletic footwear phr. 운동화 apparel n. 의류 publisher n. 출판인, 출판사 strict adj. 엄격한 keen adj. 뜨거운, 열정적인 legendary adj. 전설적인 pursue v. 취득하다, 추구하다 distribute v. 유통하다, 분배하다 renew v. 갱신하다 contract n. 계약 commence v. 시작하다 unveil v. 공개하다 expand v. 확장되다 secure v. 확보하다 endorsement n. (유명인에 의한 상품의) 보증 광고 enthusiast n. 열심인 사람, 애호가 amplify v. 확대하다, 증폭시키다 net worth phr. 순자산 donate v. 기부하다 induct v. 헌액하다, 입성하다 contribute v. 기부하다 substantial adj. 실질적인, 상당한 backing n. 지원

---

53 추론　특정사실　　　　난이도 ●●○

Which of the following is probably true about Knight during his early years?

(a) He was encouraged to become a journalist.
(b) He benefited from his father's business connections.
(c) He was an intern at a publishing company.
(d) He learned to be independent.

다음 중 어린 시절의 나이트에 관해 옳은 것은 무엇인 것 같은가?

(a) 기자가 되라고 권유를 받았다.
(b) 아버지의 거래처들로부터 이익을 얻었다.
(c) 출판사의 인턴이었다.
(d) 독립하는 법을 배웠다.

지텔프 치트키

질문의 키워드 his early years와 관련된 주변 내용을 주의 깊게 읽는다.

해설 | 2단락의 'refusing to give him a job at his newspaper'에서 나이트의 아버지는 그의 신문사에서 나이트에게 일자리를 주기를 거부했다고 한 뒤, 'Rather than becoming discouraged, Knight found a position at the rival paper the *Oregonian*.'에서 낙담하는 대신에 나이트는 경쟁 신문인 「오리거니언」에서 일자리를 찾았다고 한 것을 통해, 어린 시절의 나이트는 부모님의 도움을 받지 않고 독립하는 법을 배웠음을 추론할 수 있다. 따라서 (d)가 정답이다.

어휘 | encourage v. 권유하다 journalist n. 기자 benefit from phr. ~으로부터 이익을 얻다, ~의 도움을 받다

---

54 특정세부사항　What　　　　난이도 ●●●

What prompted Knight to start a footwear business?

(a) completing a university assignment

무엇이 나이트로 하여금 신발 사업을 시작하게 했는가?

(a) 대학 과제를 완료한 것

(b) running on a university's track team

(c) purchasing a pair of Japanese shoes

(d) finding out about the popularity of imported shoes

(b) 대학의 육상팀에서 달린 것

(c) 한 켤레의 일본 신발을 구입한 것

(d) 수입 신발의 인기에 대해 알게 된 것

─○ 지텔프 치트키

질문의 키워드 footwear business가 그대로 언급된 주변 내용을 주의 깊게 읽는다.

해설 | 3단락의 'While writing a paper on the influence of Japanese imports, Knight started thinking about founding his own footwear business to sell Japanese running shoes.'에서 나이트는 일본 수입의 영향에 관한 논문을 쓰는 동안 일본 운동화를 판매하는 그 자신의 신발 사업체를 설립하는 것에 대해 고민하기 시작했다고 했다. 따라서 (a)가 정답이다.

Paraphrasing

writing a paper 논문을 쓰는 → completing a university assignment 대학 과제를 완료한 것

---

55 추론   특정사실   난이도 ●●●

What can probably be said about Bill Bowerman?

(a) He bought shoes for the students he coached.

(b) He was impressed with the package he received.

(c) He had prior experience selling athletic footwear.

(d) He stopped coaching to go into business with Knight.

빌 바우어만에 관해 무엇이 말해질 수 있는 것 같은가?

(a) 그가 지도하는 학생들에게 신발을 사주었다.

(b) 그가 받은 소포에 감명을 받았다.

(c) 운동화를 판매한 사전 경험이 있었다.

(d) 나이트와 사업을 시작하기 위해 코칭을 그만두었다.

─○ 지텔프 치트키

질문의 키워드 Bowerman이 그대로 언급된 주변 내용을 주의 깊게 읽는다.

해설 | 4단락의 'Knight mailed samples of the shoes to Bowerman, hoping to he would buy some.'에서 나이트는 바우어만에게 신발의 견본품들을 우편으로 보내면서 그가 몇 켤레를 구매하기를 바랐다고 한 뒤, 'In addition to making a purchase, Bowerman proposed that they become business partners.'에서 구매와 더불어 바우어만은 나이트에게 그들이 사업 파트너가 되는 것을 제안했다고 한 것을 통해, 바우어만은 그가 받은 소포에 감명을 받았음을 추론할 수 있다. 따라서 (b)가 정답이다.

오답분석

(a) 4단락에서 바우어만이 나이트가 보낸 신발을 구매했다고는 했지만, 바우어만이 지도하는 학생들에게 사준 것인지는 언급되지 않았으므로 오답이다.

(d) 4단락에서 바우어만이 나이트에게 그들이 사업 파트너가 되는 것을 제안하여 함께 회사를 차렸다고는 했지만, 그가 나이트와 사업을 시작하기 위해 코칭을 그만두었는지는 언급되지 않았으므로 오답이다.

---

56 | 특정세부사항   When   난이도 ●●○

According to the article, when did Knight's company begin to grow fast?

(a) when he changed the name of the brand

(b) when his products were advertised through television commercials

기사에 따르면, 나이트의 회사는 언제 빠르게 성장하기 시작했는가?

(a) 브랜드의 이름을 바꿨을 때

(b) 그의 제품들이 텔레비전 광고를 통해 광고되었을 때

(c) after he added a new logo to his products

(d) after his shoes were worn at an international event

(c) 그의 제품들에 새로운 로고를 추가한 후에

(d) 그의 신발들이 국제적인 행사에서 착용된 후에

🔑 지텔프 치트키

질문의 키워드 grow fast가 expanded rapidly로 paraphrasing되어 언급된 주변 내용을 주의 깊게 읽는다.

해설 | 5단락의 'As athletes began wearing its footwear at the Olympics, the company expanded rapidly.'에서 운동선수들이 올림픽에서 나이트의 회사인 나이키 사의 신발을 착용하기 시작하면서 회사가 빠르게 확장되었다고 했다. 따라서 (d)가 정답이다.

Paraphrasing

the Olympics 올림픽 → an international event 국제적인 행사

어휘 | commercial n. 광고

---

57 특정세부사항   Why   난이도 ●●○

Why was Phil Knight honored in 2000?

(a) because he established a charitable foundation

(b) because his donation helped to finance US basketball

(c) because his funding improved sports in Oregon

(d) because he was the most famous graduate of his university

왜 필 나이트에게 2000년에 영예가 주어졌는가?

(a) 자선 단체를 설립했기 때문에

(b) 그의 기부가 미국 농구에 자금을 조달하는데 도움을 주었기 때문에

(c) 그의 기금이 오리건주에서 스포츠를 발전시켰기 때문에

(d) 그의 대학에서 가장 유명한 졸업생이었기 때문에

🔑 지텔프 치트키

질문의 키워드 honored in 2000가 inducted ~ in 2000로 paraphrasing되어 언급된 주변 내용을 주의 깊게 읽는다.

해설 | 6단락의 'Knight was inducted into the Oregon Sports Hall of Fame in 2000 for contributing approximately $230 million to the University of Oregon, thereby advancing athletics in the state.'에서 나이트는 오리건 대학에 약 2억 3,000만 달러를 기부한 것으로 2000년에 오리건주 스포츠 명예의 전당에 헌액되었으며, 그렇게 함으로써 오리건주의 운동 경기를 발전시켰다고 했다. 따라서 (c)가 정답이다.

Paraphrasing

advancing athletics in the state 그 주의 운동 경기를 발전시킨 → improved sports in Oregon 오리건주에서 스포츠를 발전시켰다

어휘 | finance v. 자금을 조달하다 funding n. 기금

---

58 어휘   유의어   난이도 ●○○

In the context of the passage, <u>gained</u> means _____.

(a) introduced

(b) obtained

(c) supported

(d) enlarged

지문의 문맥에서, 'gained'는 -을 의미한다.

(a) 도입했다

(b) 얻었다

(c) 지원했다

(d) 확장했다

해설 | 4단락의 'gained the rights to distribute'는 유통할 권한을 얻었다는 뜻이므로, gained가 '얻었다'라는 의미로 사용된 것을 알 수 있다. 따라서 '얻었다'라는 같은 의미의 (b) obtained가 정답이다.

---

59 어휘 유의어 난이도 ●●○

In the context of the passage, iconic means _____.	지문의 문맥에서, 'iconic'은 -을 의미한다.
(a) elaborate	(a) 정교한
(b) dramatic	(b) 극적인
(c) sensational	(c) 선풍적인
(d) well-known	**(d) 잘 알려진**

해설 | 5단락의 'unveiled the iconic "swoosh" logo'는 상징적인 '부메랑' 로고를 공개했다는 뜻이므로, iconic이 '상징적인'이라는 의미로 사용된 것을 알 수 있다. 따라서 '잘 알려진'이라는 비슷한 의미의 (d) well-known이 정답이다.

PART 2[60~66] 잡지 기사 녹지와 인지 능력의 연관성

	GREENERY MAY REDUCE DEPRESSION AND IMPROVE COGNITION	**녹지가 우울증을 줄이고 인지 능력을 향상시킬 수 있다**
연구 결과		
연구 소개	A new study has found that [60]living in cities with more vegetation could be linked to lower rates of depression and, by extension, higher cognitive function.	새로운 연구가 [60]식물이 더 많은 도시에 사는 것이 더 낮은 우울증 발병률과, 더 나아가, 더 높은 인지 기능과 연관되어 있을 수 있다는 것을 발견했다.
연구 방법	To begin the study, researchers led by Dr. Marcia Pescador Jimenez of the Boston University School of Public Health used a satellite image-based tool called the Normalized Difference Vegetation Index (NDVI). This allowed them to [65]estimate the amount of green space that could be found in selected residential neighborhoods. From 2014 to 2016, [61]they then tested the cognitive function of 13,595 women whose average age was 61.	연구를 시작하기 위해, 보스턴 대학 공중 보건과의 마르치아 페스카도르 히메네스 박사가 이끄는 연구원들은 정규 식생 지수(NDVI)라는 이름의 위성 이미지 기반 도구를 사용했다. 이것은 그들로 하여금 선택된 거주 지역들에서 발견될 수 있는 [65]녹지 공간의 양을 추정할 수 있게 했다. 2014년부터 2016년까지, [61]그러고 나서 그들은 평균 연령이 61세인 여성 13,595명의 인지 기능을 검사했다.
실험 결과	They established that while there were no differences in working memory, women in areas with more greenery had superior attention spans and faster mental processing speeds than those with less foliage. The researchers	그들은 작업 기억에는 차이가 없지만, 더 많은 녹지가 있는 지역의 여성들이 더 적은 수목이 있는 지역의 여성들보다 더 뛰어난 집중 시간과 더 빠른 정신적 처리 속도를 가지고 있다는 것을 밝혀냈다. 연구원들은 또한 대기 오염이나 신체 활동이 인지 기능에 일

also examined whether air pollution or physical activity played a role in cognitive function, and they ultimately determined that neither did.

조했는지를 조사했고, 결국 둘 다 그러지 않았다는 것을 알아냈다.

시사점

This study builds upon previous research that has shown that spending time in parks and community gardens is associated with lower levels of stress. This is important because [62]people who experience less stress in their day-to-day life are not as likely to suffer from depression, which is considered a risk factor for dementia.

이 연구는 공원과 공동체 텃밭에서 시간을 보내는 것이 더 낮은 수준의 스트레스와 관련이 있다는 것을 증명한 이전 연구를 기반으로 한다. 이것은 중요한데 왜냐하면 [62]일상생활에서 더 적은 스트레스를 받는 사람들은 우울증을 앓을 가능성이 적고, 그것(우울증)은 치매의 위험 요소로 간주되기 때문이다.

연구의 한계 + 극복 방법

Given the findings, Pescador Jimenez believes that it may be possible to improve the cognitive function of the population as a whole by adding more greenery to urban environments. However, [66]what types of vegetation could achieve this result is unknown as the NDVI is only able to detect the location of vegetation and not its variety. [63]She plans to use Google Street View images to discover which kinds of plants correlate with higher levels of cognitive health. Once discovered, this information could be valuable to city planners as they work with local governments to design green spaces for the benefit of citizens.

연구 결과를 고려할 때, 페스카도르 히메네스는 도시 환경에 더 많은 녹지를 추가함으로써 인구의 인지 기능을 전체적으로 향상시키는 것이 가능할 수도 있다고 믿는다. 그러나, NDVI는 식물의 다양성이 아닌 오직 위치만을 감지할 수 있기 때문에 [66]어떤 종류의 식물이 이러한 성과를 낼 수 있는지는 알려져 있지 않다. [63]그녀는 어떤 종류의 식물들이 더 높은 수준의 인지 건강과 연관성이 있는지 알아내기 위해 구글 스트리트 뷰의 이미지를 사용할 계획이다. 일단 밝혀지면, 도시 계획자들은 시민들의 혜택을 위한 녹지 공간들을 설계하기 위해 지방 정부와 협력하기 때문에 이 정보는 그들에게 가치가 있을 수 있다.

향후 연구 과제

Investigation into this topic is still ongoing, and the findings are not conclusive because the research subjects were primarily white. [64]To get a more comprehensive understanding of how the amount of green space in an urban area impacts cognitive function, the researchers believe other racial and ethnic groups must also be studied.

이 주제에 관한 조사는 여전히 진행 중이며, 연구 대상이 주로 백인들이었기 때문에 결과가 확실하지 않다. [64]도시 지역에 있는 녹지 공간의 양이 어떻게 인지 기능에 영향을 미치는지에 관한 더 포괄적인 이해를 얻기 위해, 연구원들은 다른 인종과 민족 집단들 또한 연구되어야 한다고 생각한다.

어휘 | greenery n. 녹지 depression n. 우울증 cognition n. 인지 능력 vegetation n. 식물, 초목 by extension phr. 더 나아가 cognitive adj. 인지의 satellite n. 위성 residential adj. 거주의 working memory phr. 작업 기억 superior adj. 더 뛰어난 foliage n. 수목, 잎 examine v. 조사하다 pollution n. 오염 play a role phr. 일조하다 associate v. 관련짓다 dementia n. 치매 detect v. 감지하다, 발견하다 correlate v. 연관성이 있다 investigation n. 조사 ongoing adj. 진행 중인 conclusive adj. 확실한, 결정적인 comprehensive adj. 포괄적인 racial adj. 인종의 ethnic adj. 민족의

60　**특정세부사항**　　연구의 결과　　　　　　　　　　　　　　　　　　　　난이도 ●●○

What did the study find out about cognitive ability?

(a) that it is impaired by intellectual disorders
(b) that exposure to green space can improve cognition
(c) that living in an urban area can negatively affect mental ability
(d) that it is positively correlated to depression rates

연구는 인지 능력에 관해 무엇을 알아냈는가?

(a) 그것이 지적 장애로 인해 손상된다는 것
(b) 녹지 공간에의 노출이 인지를 향상시킬 수 있다는 것
(c) 도시에 사는 것이 정신적 능력에 부정적인 영향을 미칠 수 있다는 것
(d) 그것이 우울증 발병률과 긍정적인 상관관계가 있다는 것

TEST 1
TEST 2
TEST 3
TEST 4
TEST 5
TEST 6
TEST 7

🔑 지텔프 치트키

연구의 결과를 언급하는 지문의 초반을 주의 깊게 읽는다.

해설 | 1단락의 'living in cities with more vegetation could be linked to ~ higher cognitive function'에서 식물이 더 많은 도시에 사는 것이 더 높은 인지 기능과 연관되어 있을 수 있다고 했다. 따라서 (b)가 정답이다.

Paraphrasing

living in cities with more vegetation 식물이 더 많은 도시에 사는 것 → exposure to green space 녹지 공간에의 노출
higher cognitive function 더 높은 인지 기능 → improve cognition 인지를 향상시키다

어휘 | intellectual adj. 지적인   disorder n. 장애

---

61 **특정세부사항**   How   난이도 ●●○

How did the researchers measure the figures after analyzing the green space in residential areas?

(a) They traveled to residential neighborhoods.
(b) They interviewed public health experts.
(c) They charted Boston's vegetation growth.
(d) They conducted mental ability exams.

연구원들은 거주 지역의 녹지 공간을 분석한 후에 그 수치를 어떻게 측정했는가?

(a) 주거 지역으로 이동했다.
(b) 공중 보건 전문가들을 인터뷰했다.
(c) 보스턴의 식물 성장을 기록했다.
(d) 정신적 능력 검사를 시행했다.

🔑 지텔프 치트키

질문의 키워드 analyzing ~ green space가 estimate ~ green space로 paraphrasing되어 언급된 주변 내용을 주의 깊게 읽는다.

해설 | 2단락의 'they then tested the cognitive function of 13,595 women whose average age was 61'에서 녹지 공간의 양을 추정하고 나서 연구원들은 평균 연령이 61세인 여성 13,595명의 인지 기능을 검사했다고 했다. 따라서 (d)가 정답이다.

Paraphrasing

tested the cognitive function 인지 기능을 검사했다 → conducted mental ability exams 정신적 능력 검사를 시행했다

어휘 | figure n. 수치   expert n. 전문가   chart v. 기록하다

---

62 **추론**   특정사실   난이도 ●●●

What do the researchers probably believe about women who experience daily stress?

(a) They are more inclined to develop age-related illness.
(b) They perform an inadequate amount of physical activity.
(c) They fail to take steps to manage their depression.
(d) They spend less time engaging in work activities.

연구원들은 매일 스트레스를 경험하는 여성들에 관해 무엇을 믿는 것 같은가?

(a) 나이와 관련된 질병이 더 잘 생기는 경향이 있다.
(b) 불충분한 양의 신체 활동을 한다.
(c) 그들의 우울증을 관리하기 위한 조치를 취하지 못한다.
(d) 직업 활동에 참여하는 데 시간을 덜 보낸다.

🔑 지텔프 치트키

질문의 키워드 daily stress가 stress in ~ day-to-day life로 paraphrasing되어 언급된 주변 내용을 주의 깊게 읽는다.

해설 | 4단락의 'people who experience less stress in their day-to-day life are not as likely to suffer from depression, which is considered a risk factor for dementia'에서 일상생활에서 더 적은 스트레스를 받는 사람들은 우울증을 앓을 가능성이 적고 우울증은 치매의 위험 요소로 간주된다고 한 것을 통해, 매일 스트레스를 경험하는 여성들은 나이와 관련된 질병이 더 잘 생기는 경향이 있다는 것을 추론할 수 있다. 따라서 (a)가 정답이다.

Paraphrasing

dementia 치매 → age-related illness 나이와 관련된 질병

어휘 | be inclined to phr. ~하는 경향이 있다 develop v. (병·문제가) 생기다 age-related adj. 나이와 관련된 inadequate adj. 불충분한

---

63 특정세부사항 Why

난이도 ●●○

Why does Pescador Jimenez intend to use Google Street View?

(a) to find out where the most vegetation is located in cities
(b) to discover areas where more trees can be planted
(c) to find what plants contribute to better mental function
(d) to determine which urban plant varieties are most common

페스카도르 히메네스는 왜 구글 스트리트 뷰를 사용하려고 하는가?

(a) 도시에서 식물이 가장 많이 있는 곳을 알아내기 위해서
(b) 더 많은 나무들이 심어질 수 있는 지역을 찾기 위해서
(c) 어떤 식물들이 더 나은 정신적 기능에 기여하는지 찾기 위해서
(d) 어떤 도시 식물 품종들이 가장 흔한지 알아내기 위해서

━○ 지텔프 치트키

질문의 키워드 Google Street View가 그대로 언급된 주변 내용을 주의 깊게 읽는다.

해설 | 5단락의 'She plans to use Google Street View images to discover which kinds of plants correlate with higher levels of cognitive health.'라며 페스카도르 히메네스는 어떤 종류의 식물들이 더 높은 수준의 인지 건강과 연관성이 있는지 알아내기 위해 구글 스트리트 뷰의 이미지를 사용할 계획이라고 했다. 따라서 (c)가 정답이다.

Paraphrasing

discover which kinds of plants correlate with ~ cognitive health 어떤 종류의 식물들이 인지 건강과 연관성이 있는지 알아내다 → find what plants contribute to ~ mental function 어떤 식물들이 정신적 기능에 기여하는지 찾다

어휘 | intend v. ~하려고 하다 common adj. 흔한, 일반적인

---

64 특정세부사항 How

난이도 ●●○

According to the article, how can the conclusions of the study be improved?

(a) by inspecting the amount of green space in different areas
(b) by studying women living outside urban environments
(c) by following up with the older subjects of the research
(d) by including a more diverse range of participants

기사에 따르면, 연구의 결과가 어떻게 개선될 수 있는가?

(a) 다른 지역에 있는 녹지 공간의 양을 조사함으로써
(b) 도시 환경 밖에 사는 여성들을 연구함으로써
(c) 나이가 더 많은 연구 대상자들을 탐구함으로써
(d) 더 다양한 범위의 참가자들을 포함함으로써

질문의 키워드 conclusions가 findings로 paraphrasing되어 언급된 주변 내용을 주의 깊게 읽는다.

해설 | 6단락의 'To get a more comprehensive understanding ~, the researchers believe other racial and ethnic groups must also be studied.'에서 더 포괄적인 이해를 얻기 위해 연구원들은 다른 인종과 민족 집단들 또한 연구되어야 한다고 생각한다고 했다. 따라서 (d)가 정답이다.

Paraphrasing

other racial and ethnic groups 다른 인종과 민족 집단들 → a ~ diverse range of participants 다양한 범위의 참가자들

어휘 | conclusion n. 결과 inspect v. 조사하다, 점검하다 diverse adj. 다양한 range n. 범위

---

65 어휘 유의어 난이도 ●●○

In the context of the passage, estimate means _____.

(a) review
(b) consider
(c) guess
(d) prove

지문의 문맥에서, 'estimate'는 -을 의미한다.

(a) 검토하다
(b) 고려하다
(c) 추정하다
(d) 증명하다

밑줄 친 어휘의 유의어를 찾는 문제이므로, estimate가 포함된 구절을 읽고 문맥을 파악한다.

해설 | 2단락의 'estimate the amount of green space'는 녹지 공간의 양을 추정한다는 뜻이므로, estimate가 '추정하다'라는 의미로 사용된 것을 알 수 있다. 따라서 '추정하다'라는 같은 의미의 (c) guess가 정답이다.

오답분석
(b) '고려하다'라는 의미의 consider도 estimate의 사전적 유의어 중 하나이지만, 문맥상 선택된 거주 지역들에서 발견될 수 있는 녹지 공간의 양을 연구원들이 추정한다는 의미가 되어야 적절하므로 문맥에 어울리지 않아 오답이다.

---

66 어휘 유의어 난이도 ●●○

In the context of the passage, result means _____.

(a) outcome
(b) triumph
(c) account
(d) reaction

지문의 문맥에서, 'result'는 -을 의미한다.

(a) 성과
(b) 승리
(c) 설명
(d) 반응

밑줄 친 어휘의 유의어를 찾는 문제이므로, result가 포함된 구절을 읽고 문맥을 파악한다.

해설 | 5단락의 'what types of vegetation could achieve this result is unknown'은 어떤 종류의 식물이 이러한 성과를 낼 수 있는지 알려져 있지 않다는 뜻이므로, result가 '성과'라는 의미로 사용된 것을 알 수 있다. 따라서 '성과'라는 같은 의미의 (a) outcome이 정답이다.

표제어	

GOLDENEYE 007

007 골든아이

정의

[67]GoldenEye 007 is a video game of the late 90s based on the 1995 James Bond film GoldenEye. It is considered revolutionary and frequently called one of the greatest video games of all time, both for its realism and for bringing first-person shooter games to home consoles.

[67]007 골든아이는 1995년 제임스 본드 영화 「007 골든아이」를 기반으로 한 90년대 후반의 비디오 게임이다. 그것은 혁신적인 것으로 여겨지며 역사상 최고의 비디오 게임 중 하나로 흔히 불리는데, 이는 그것의 사실성과 일인칭 사격 게임을 가정용 콘솔로 가져온 것 때문이다.

게임 제작 배경

Nintendo and British video game company Rare first began discussing GoldenEye 007 in November 1994. Earlier that year, Rare had made waves in the gaming world with its release of the highly successful Donkey Kong Country. As the game had been published for the Super Nintendo console, it was originally suggested that GoldenEye 007 be produced for the same platform. However, the game's director [68]Martin Hollis wanted to design the game for the Nintendo 64 console, which was still being worked on at the time.

닌텐도 사와 영국의 비디오 게임 회사인 레어 사는 1994년 11월에 007 골든아이에 대해 처음으로 논의하기 시작했다. 그해 초에, 레어 사는 매우 성공적인 동키콩 컨트리의 출시로 게임 세계에 열풍을 일으켰었다. 그 게임이 슈퍼 닌텐도 콘솔용으로 출시되었었기 때문에, 원래는 007 골든아이도 같은 플랫폼용으로 제작되어야 한다고 제안되었다. 하지만, 그 게임의 기획자인 [68]마틴 홀리스는 닌텐도64 콘솔용으로 그 게임을 설계하기를 원했는데, 그것은 당시에 아직 제작 중이었다.

게임 제작 과정

The development team, including character artist B. Jones and background artist Karl Hilton, visited the set of GoldenEye many times during the film's production. [69]Using [72]reference materials they garnered, Jones replicated the appearance of characters, while Hilton planned levels on the basis of locations in the film. Later, programmer Steve Ellies contributed to this massive hit by adding a multiplayer mode to the primarily single-player game. This allowed up to four players to compete against each other in several deathmatch scenarios.

캐릭터 아티스트 B. 존스와 배경 아티스트 칼 힐튼을 포함한 개발팀은 영화 제작 기간에 「007 골든아이」의 세트장을 여러 번 방문했다. [69/72]그들이 <u>수집한</u> 참조 자료를 사용하여, 존스는 캐릭터들의 모습을 복제한 반면, 힐튼은 영화 속 장소들을 기반으로 난이도를 구상했다. 이후에, 프로그래머인 스티브 엘리스가 본질적으로 일인용인 그 게임에 다인용 모드를 추가함으로써 이 엄청난 흥행에 기여했다. 이것은 최대 4명의 참가자가 여러 데스 매치 시나리오에서 서로에게 맞서 승부를 겨룰 수 있게 했다.

게임의 독특한 특징

GoldenEye 007 requires players to complete each level by fulfilling various objectives. These include rescuing hostages and destroying objects using a variety of weapons that the player can pick up from defeated enemies. The signature James Bond weapons available to use in the game appealed to players, with many feeling they created a sense of realism. The high-quality animations, special effects, and music were also praised. Meanwhile, [70]the multiplayer mode, three levels of difficulty, and unlockable secret levels and bonuses are cited as making the game more fun and replayable.

007 골든아이는 참가자들이 다양한 목표들을 달성함으로써 각 난이도를 완료하기를 요구한다. 이것들은 참가자가 패배한 적에게서 얻을 수 있는 다양한 무기들을 사용하여 인질들을 구하는 것과 물체들을 파괴하는 것을 포함한다. 게임에서 사용할 수 있는 대표적인 제임스 본드 무기들은 참가자들의 관심을 끌었는데, 많은 사람들은 그것들이 사실감을 자아낸다고 느꼈다. 질 높은 애니메이션, 특수 효과, 그리고 음악 또한 호평을 받았다. 한편, [70]다인용 모드, 3단계의 난이도, 그리고 잠금 해제가 가능한 비밀 단계 및 보너스들이 그 게임을 더 재미있고 다시 할 만하게 만드는 것으로 언급된다.

게임의 성공

[71]Expectations for GoldenEye 007 were low, as it was launched two years after the film on which it was based. However, [73]it was a <u>resounding</u> success. It received multiple awards and was the third-best-selling Nintendo 64 game ever, grossing $250 million worldwide.

[71]007 골든아이에 대한 기대는 낮았는데, 그것이 기반을 둔 영화가 나온 후 2년이 지나서 출시되었기 때문이었다. 그러나, [73]그것은 <u>굉장한</u> 성공을 거두었다. 그것은 여러 상을 받았고 역대 3번째로 많이 팔린 닌텐도64용 게임이었으며, 전 세계적으로 2억 5천만 달러의 수익을 올렸다.

어휘 | revolutionary adj. 혁신적인 realism n. 사실성, 사실주의 first-person adj. 일인칭의 console n. 콘솔, (게임) 기기 wave n. 열풍, 변화 originally adv. 원래 reference n. 참조 replicate v. 복제하다 massive adj. 엄청난 primarily adv. 본질적으로, 본래 deathmatch n. 데스 매치(컴퓨터 게임에서 패배자가 나올 때까지 계속하는 경기) fulfill v. 달성하다 objective n. 목표 hostage n. 인질 destroy v. 파괴하다 weapon n. 무기 defeated adj. 패배한 signature adj. 대표적인 praise v. 호평하다, 칭찬하다 unlockable adj. 잠금 해제가 가능한 cite v. 언급하다 replayable adj. 다시 할 만한 expectation n. 기대 gross v. 수익을 올리다

---

67 주제/목적 기사의 주제 난이도 ●○○

What is the article mainly about?

(a) the release of a video game console
(b) a game adapted from a film of the same title
(c) a script influenced by the James Bond series
(d) the birth of first-person shooter video games

기사의 주제는 무엇인가?

(a) 비디오 게임 콘솔의 출시
(b) 같은 제목의 영화로부터 각색된 게임
(c) 제임스 본드 시리즈에 의해 영향을 받은 대본
(d) 일인칭 사격 비디오 게임의 탄생

─○ 지텔프 치트키

지문의 초반을 주의 깊게 읽고 전체 맥락을 파악한다.

해설 | 1단락의 'GoldenEye 007 is a video game ~ based on the 1995 James Bond film GoldenEye.'에서 007 골든아이는 1995년 제임스 본드 영화 「007 골든아이」를 기반으로 한 비디오 게임이라고 한 뒤, 007 골든아이 게임에 관해 설명하는 내용이 이어지고 있다. 따라서 (b)가 정답이다.

어휘 | adapt v. 각색하다

---

68 특정세부사항 What 난이도 ●●○

What did Hollis aim to do when he was directing the game?

(a) create a game for a new device
(b) develop a brand-new video game platform
(c) improve his original gaming console
(d) make a version of Donkey Kong Country for Nintendo 64

홀리스는 게임을 기획할 때 무엇을 하는 것을 목표로 했는가?

(a) 새로운 장치를 위한 게임을 만드는 것
(b) 새로운 비디오 게임 플랫폼을 개발하는 것
(c) 그의 기존 게임 콘솔을 개선하는 것
(d) 닌텐도64용 동키콩 컨트리를 만드는 것

─○ 지텔프 치트키

질문의 키워드 Hollis가 그대로 언급된 주변 내용을 주의 깊게 읽는다.

해설 | 2단락의 'Martin Hollis wanted to design the game for the Nintendo 64 console, which was still being worked on at the time'이라며 마틴 홀리스는 닌텐도64 콘솔용으로 007 골든아이를 설계하기를 원했는데, 그것(닌텐도64 콘솔)은 당시에 아직 제작 중이었다고 했다. 따라서 (a)가 정답이다.

Paraphrasing
design the game 게임을 설계하다 → create a game 게임을 만들다
still being worked on at the time 당시에 아직 제작 중이었던 → new 새로운

어휘 | brand-new adj. 새로운

69 추론 　특정사실 난이도 ●●●

Why most likely did members of the development team visit the *GoldenEye* film set?

(a) to decide which characters to include in the game
(b) to get the rights to replicate scenes from the film
(c) to determine the best locations for deathmatch scenarios
(d) to have the game look as authentic as possible

개발팀의 구성원들이 왜 「007 골든아이」영화 세트장을 방문했던 것 같은가?

(a) 그 게임에 포함할 캐릭터들을 결정하기 위해서
(b) 영화의 장면들을 복제할 권한을 얻기 위해서
(c) 데스 매치 시나리오에 가장 알맞은 장소를 정하기 위해서
(d) 그 게임이 가능한 한 사실적으로 보이게 하기 위해서

─○ 지텔프 치트키

질문의 키워드 *GoldenEye* film set가 set of *GoldenEye*로 paraphrasing되어 언급된 주변 내용을 주의 깊게 읽는다.

해설 | 3단락의 'Using reference materials they garnered, Jones replicated the appearance of characters, while Hilton planned levels on the basis of locations in the film.'에서 개발팀이 「007 골든아이」의 세트장을 방문하여 수집한 참조 자료를 사용하여 존스는 캐릭터들의 모습을 복제한 반면, 힐튼은 영화 속 장소들을 기반으로 난이도를 구상했다고 한 것을 통해, 개발팀 구성원들이 007 골든아이가 가능한 한 사실적으로 보이게 하기 위해서 「007 골든아이」영화 세트장을 방문했던 것임을 추론할 수 있다. 따라서 (d)가 정답이다.

어휘 | authentic adj. 사실적인

---

70 특정세부사항 　Which 난이도 ●●○

According to the article, which of the following made users want to replay *GoldenEye 007*?

(a) the difficulty in completing objectives
(b) the ability to play with other people
(c) the chance to unlock secret weapons
(d) the high-quality soundtrack

기사에 따르면, 다음 중 사용자들로 하여금 007 골든아이를 다시 하고 싶게 만든 것은 무엇인가?

(a) 목표들을 달성하는 것의 난이도
(b) 다른 사람들과 게임을 하는 기능
(c) 비밀 무기들을 잠금 해제할 기회
(d) 질 높은 사운드트랙

─○ 지텔프 치트키

질문의 키워드 want to replay가 replayable로 언급된 주변 내용을 주의 깊게 읽는다.

해설 | 4단락의 'the multiplayer mode ~ and bonuses are cited as making the game ~ replayable'에서 다인용 모드 등이 007 골든아이를 다시 할 만하게 만드는 것으로 언급된다고 했다. 따라서 (b)가 정답이다.

Paraphrasing
the multiplayer mode 다인용 모드 → the ability to play with other people 다른 사람들과 게임을 하는 기능

---

71 특정세부사항 　Why 난이도 ●○○

Why were hopes for *GoldenEye 007* low?

(a) It was based on an unpopular series.
(b) It had to be remade multiple times.

왜 007 골든아이에 대한 기대가 낮았는가?

(a) 인기 없는 시리즈를 기반으로 했다.
(b) 여러 번 다시 만들어져야 했다.

(c) It came out a few years after the movie.

(d) It worked poorly on the Nintendo 64 console.

(c) 영화가 나온 후 몇 년이 지나서 출시되었다.

(d) 닌텐도64 콘솔용에서 제대로 작동하지 않았다.

지텔프 치트키

질문의 키워드 hopes가 Expectations로 paraphrasing되어 언급된 주변 내용을 주의 깊게 읽는다.

해설 | 5단락의 'Expectations for *GoldenEye 007* were low, as it was launched two years after the film on which it was based.'라며 007 골든아이에 대한 기대가 낮았는데, 그것이 기반을 둔 영화가 나온 후 2년이 지나서 출시되었기 때문이었다고 했다. 따라서 (c)가 정답이다.

Paraphrasing
was launched two years after the film 영화가 나온 후 2년이 지나서 출시되었다 → came out a few years after the movie 영화가 나온 후 몇 년이 지나서 출시되었다

어휘 | unpopular adj. 인기 없는

---

72 어휘 유의어 난이도 ●●○

In the context of the passage, garnered means _____.

(a) saved
(b) collected
(c) processed
(d) deposited

지문의 문맥에서, 'garnered'는 -을 의미한다.

(a) 저장했다
(b) 수집했다
(c) 가공했다
(d) 맡겼다

지텔프 치트키

밑줄 친 어휘의 유의어를 찾는 문제이므로, garnered가 포함된 구절을 읽고 문맥을 파악한다.

해설 | 3단락의 'reference materials they garnered'는 그들이 수집한 참조 자료라는 뜻이므로, garnered가 '수집했다'라는 의미로 사용된 것을 알 수 있다. 따라서 '수집했다'라는 같은 의미의 (b) collected가 정답이다.

---

73 어휘 유의어 난이도 ●●○

In the context of the passage, resounding means _____.

(a) major
(b) loud
(c) repetitive
(d) initial

지문의 문맥에서, 'resounding'은 -을 의미한다.

(a) 굉장한
(b) 시끄러운
(c) 반복적인
(d) 초기의

지텔프 치트키

밑줄 친 어휘의 유의어를 찾는 문제이므로, resounding이 포함된 구절을 읽고 문맥을 파악한다.

해설 | 5단락의 'it was a resounding success'는 그것이 굉장한 성공을 거두었다는 뜻이므로, resounding이 '굉장한'이라는 의미로 사용된 것을 알 수 있다. 따라서 '굉장한'이라는 같은 의미의 (a) major가 정답이다.

해커스 지텔프 최신기출유형 실전문제집 7회 (Level 2)

수신인 정보	Kerry Johnson Principal St. Jerome Middle School Dear Ms. Johnson,	Kerry Johnson 교장 St. Jerome 중학교 Ms. Johnson께,
편지의 목적: 감사 표시	I am writing to you as the chosen representative of the parents of St. Jerome students. We want to express our gratitude for the excellence you have shown as school principal. ⁷⁴We are particularly grateful for your recent decision to ⁷⁹start the school's athletics program.	저는 St. Jerome의 선출된 학부모 대표로서 이 편지를 씁니다. 저희는 귀하가 학교 교장으로서 보여주신 탁월함에 감사를 표하고 싶습니다. ⁷⁴ᐟ⁷⁹학교의 운동 경기 프로그램을 <u>시작하기</u>로 한 귀하의 최근 결정에 특히 감사드립니다.
예상 되는 긍정적 효과	The other parents and I agree that our children need greater opportunities to participate in sports. Too many of them are glued to their televisions, computers, and electronic devices most of the time. ⁷⁵Adding organized team sports to the school's extracurricular programs will not only help them get moving but also instill in them important traits such as leadership, teamwork, and sportsmanship. ⁷⁶We are also pleased with the selection of coaches, all of whom have impressive credentials.	다른 학부모님들과 저는 우리 아이들이 스포츠에 참여할 더 많은 기회를 필요로 한다는 데 동의합니다. 그들 중 너무 많은 아이들이 대부분의 시간 동안 텔레비전, 컴퓨터, 그리고 전자 기기에 열중해 있습니다. ⁷⁵학교의 비교과 프로그램에 조직적인 팀 스포츠를 추가하는 것은 그들이 몸을 움직이도록 도울 뿐만 아니라 그들에게 리더십, 팀워크, 그리고 스포츠 정신과 같은 중요한 특성들을 주입할 것입니다. ⁷⁶저희는 또한 코치의 선발에 대해 만족하는데, 그들 모두는 훌륭한 자격을 갖추고 있습니다.
학교 칭찬	St. Jerome has always been known for its exceptional academics. The fact that it now involves sports gives us confidence that our students will receive a more balanced education. Speaking personally, ⁷⁷I have had two other children attend St. Jerome since it opened and only wish that an initiative like this had been introduced sooner. ⁸⁰It is truly <u>encouraging</u> to see a meaningful effort to develop competitive student athletics.	St. Jerome은 항상 우수한 교과 과목들로 알려져 왔습니다. 그것이 이제 스포츠를 포함한다는 사실은 우리 학생들이 더욱 균형 잡힌 교육을 받을 것이라는 확신을 줍니다. 개인적으로 이야기하자면, ⁷⁷저는 개교 이래로 제 나머지 두 아이들을 St. Jerome에 다니게 했었는데 이와 같은 계획이 더 빨리 도입되었었기를 바랄 뿐입니다. 경쟁력 있는 학생 운동 경기들을 개발하기 위한 ⁸⁰<u>유의미한</u> 노력을 보는 것은 정말 <u>고무적</u>입니다.
끝인사	In closing, we are aware of the significant resources that incorporating team sports at St. Jerome will entail. Therefore, ⁷⁸we are prepared to offer any kind of assistance that the school might require when securing the gear needed for this program to be a success. We are at your disposal.	끝으로, 저희는 St. Jerome에 팀 스포츠를 포함시키는 것이 수반할 상당한 자원들에 대해 알고 있습니다. 따라서, ⁷⁸저희는 이 프로그램이 성공하기 위해 필요한 장비를 확보할 때 학교가 요구할 수 있는 모든 종류의 지원을 제공할 준비가 되어 있습니다. 저희는 귀하가 원하시는 대로 해드리겠습니다.
발신인 정보	Sincerely, Michael Davis	Michael Davis 드림

어휘 | representative n. 대표 gratitude n. 감사 grateful adj. 감사하는 be glued to phr. ~에 열중해 있다 team sports phr. 팀 스포츠(팀워크가 가장 중요한 요소가 되는 운동) extracurricular adj. 비교과의, 과외의 instill v. 주입하다 trait n. 특성 selection n. 선발 credential n. 자격 exceptional adj. 우수한, 뛰어난 academics n. 교과 과목들 confidence n. 확신, 자신감 initiative n. 계획 develop v. 육성하다 competitive adj. 경쟁력 있는 significant adj. 상당한 resource n. 자원 incorporate v. 포함시키다 entail n. 수반하다 assistance n. 지원, 도움 gear n. 장비 at one's disposal phr. ~가 원하는 대로 해주는

Why most likely is Michael Davis thanking Kerry Johnson in the letter?

(a) because she represented St. Jerome at an athletics event
(b) because she recommended an excellent school principal
(c) because she proposed a physical education program for parents
(d) because she recognized the importance of sports in education

왜 Michael Davis는 편지에서 Kerry Johnson에게 감사를 표하는 것 같은가?

(a) 그녀가 운동 경기 행사에서 St. Jerome을 대표했기 때문에
(b) 그녀가 훌륭한 학교 교장을 추천했기 때문에
(c) 그녀가 학부모들을 위한 체육 프로그램을 제안했기 때문에
(d) 그녀가 교육에서 스포츠의 중요성을 인정했기 때문에

지텔프 치트키

질문의 키워드 thanking이 grateful로 paraphrasing되어 언급된 주변 내용을 주의 깊게 읽는다.

해설 | 1단락의 'We are particularly grateful for your recent decision to start the school's athletics program.'에서 학교의 운동 경기 프로그램을 시작하기로 한 Kerry Johnson의 최근 결정에 특히 감사하다고 한 것을 통해, Kerry Johnson이 교육에서 스포츠의 중요성을 인정했기 때문에 Michael Davis가 감사를 표하는 것임을 추론할 수 있다. 따라서 (d)가 정답이다.

어휘 | physical education phr. 체육 recognize v. 인정하다, 인식하다

What effect do the parents anticipate the new school program will have?

(a) There will be an improvement in grades.
(b) Students will be better prepared for high school.
(c) Students will be less sedentary.
(d) The school's reputation will be enhanced.

학부모들은 새로운 학교 프로그램이 어떤 영향을 미칠 것이라고 예상하는가?

(a) 성적 향상이 있을 것이다.
(b) 학생들이 고등학교에 더 잘 대비할 것이다.
(c) 학생들이 덜 비활동적일 것이다.
(d) 학교의 명성이 높아질 것이다.

지텔프 치트키

질문의 키워드 school program이 school's ~ programs로 언급된 주변 내용을 주의 깊게 읽는다.

해설 | 2단락의 'Adding organized team sports to the school's extracurricular programs will ~ help them get moving'에서 학교의 비교과 프로그램에 조직적인 팀 스포츠를 추가하는 것은 그들(학생들)이 몸을 움직이도록 도울 것이라고 했다. 따라서 (c)가 정답이다.

Paraphrasing
get moving 몸을 움직이다 → less sedentary 덜 비활동적인

어휘 | anticipate v. 예상하다 sedentary adj. 비활동적인, 몸을 많이 움직이지 않는 reputation n. 명성

Which aspect of the selected coaches are parents pleased about?

학부모들은 선발된 코치들의 어떤 측면에 대해 만족하는가?

(a) **their strong professional qualifications**
(b) their history of teamwork
(c) their good displays of sportsmanship
(d) their superior leadership skills

(a) **쟁쟁한 전문적 자격**
(b) 팀워크의 이력
(c) 훌륭한 스포츠 정신 발휘
(d) 우수한 리더십 기술

지텔프 치트키

질문의 키워드 selected coaches가 selection of coaches로 paraphrasing되어 언급된 주변 내용을 주의 깊게 읽는다.

해설 | 2단락의 'We are ~ pleased with the selection of coaches, all of whom have impressive credentials.'에서 학부모들은 코치의 선발에 대해 만족하는데, 그들 모두는 훌륭한 자격을 갖추고 있다고 했다. 따라서 (a)가 정답이다.

Paraphrasing
impressive credentials 훌륭한 자격 → strong professional qualifications 쟁쟁한 전문적 자격

어휘 | qualification n. 자격 history n. 이력 display n. 발휘

---

77 추론 묘사

난이도 ●●●

How can St. Jerome Middle School most likely be described?

(a) It has never added extra subjects to its school curriculum.
(b) It is experiencing a decline in academic rankings.
(c) **It has never engaged in sports tournaments.**
(d) It is planning to initiate a leadership development course.

St. Jerome 중학교는 어떻게 묘사될 수 있을 것 같은가?

(a) 그것의 교육 과정에 추가 과목을 넣은 적이 한 번도 없다.
(b) 학업 순위의 하락을 겪고 있다.
(c) **스포츠 대회에 참여한 적이 한 번도 없다.**
(d) 리더십 개발 강좌를 시작하려고 계획하고 있다.

지텔프 치트키

질문의 키워드 St. Jerome이 그대로 언급된 주변 내용을 주의 깊게 읽는다.

해설 | 3단락의 'I have had ~ children attend St. Jerome since it opened and only wish that an initiative like this had been introduced sooner'에서 Michael은 개교 이래로 그의 아이들을 St. Jerome에 다니게 했었는데 학교의 비교과 프로그램에 팀 스포츠를 추가하는 지금의 계획이 더 빨리 도입되었었기를 바랄 뿐이라고 한 것을 통해, 지금까지 St. Jerome 중학교는 스포츠 대회에 참여한 적이 한 번도 없음을 추론할 수 있다. 따라서 (c)가 정답이다.

어휘 | curriculum n. 교육 과정 decline n. 하락 tournament n. 대회, 경기 initiate v. 시작하다

---

78 특정세부사항 How

난이도 ●●○

How are the parents of students prepared to support the school?

(a) by helping manage financial resources
(b) by disposing of old programs
(c) **by assisting to obtain sports equipment**
(d) by raising awareness of its needs

학부모들은 어떻게 학교를 지원할 준비가 되어 있는가?

(a) 재정 자원을 관리하는 것을 도움으로써
(b) 오래된 프로그램들을 없앰으로써
(c) **스포츠 장비를 구하는 것을 도움으로써**
(d) 그것의 요구 사항에 대한 인식을 높임으로써

지텔프 치트키

질문의 키워드 support가 offer ~ assistance로 paraphrasing되어 언급된 주변 내용을 주의 깊게 읽는다.

해설 | 4단락의 'we are prepared to offer ~ assistance that the school might require when securing the gear needed for this program to be a success'에서 학부모들은 학교의 운동 경기 프로그램이 성공하기 위해 필요한 장비를 확보할 때 학교가 요구할 수 있는 지원을 제공할 준비가 되어 있다고 했다. 따라서 (c)가 정답이다.

Paraphrasing

securing the gear 장비를 확보하는 → obtain ~ equipment 장비를 구하다

어휘 | financial adj. 재정의 dispose v. 없애다, 폐지하다 assist v. 돕다 obtain v. 구하다 awareness n. 인식

---

79 **어휘** 유의어   난이도 ●●○

In the context of the passage, <u>start</u> means _____.

(a) sponsor
(b) launch
(c) reform
(d) progress

지문의 문맥에서, 'start'는 -을 의미한다.

(a) 후원하다
(b) 시작하다
(c) 개선하다
(d) 진행하다

지텔프 치트키

밑줄 친 어휘의 유의어를 찾는 문제이므로, start가 포함된 구절을 읽고 문맥을 파악한다.

해설 | 1단락의 'start the school's athletics program'은 학교의 운동 경기 프로그램을 시작한다는 뜻이므로, start가 '시작하다'라는 의미로 사용된 것을 알 수 있다. 따라서 '시작하다'라는 같은 의미의 (b) launch가 정답이다.

---

80 **어휘** 유의어   난이도 ●●○

In the context of the passage, <u>encouraging</u> means _____.

(a) inspiring
(b) provoking
(c) beneficial
(d) fortunate

지문의 문맥에서, 'encouraging'은 -을 의미한다.

(a) 고무적인
(b) 자극적인
(c) 유익한
(d) 운이 좋은

지텔프 치트키

밑줄 친 어휘의 유의어를 찾는 문제이므로, encouraging이 포함된 구절을 읽고 문맥을 파악한다.

해설 | 3단락의 'It is truly encouraging to see a meaningful effort'는 유의미한 노력을 보는 것이 정말 고무적이라는 뜻이므로, encouraging이 '고무적인'이라는 의미로 사용된 것을 알 수 있다. 따라서 '고무적인'이라는 같은 의미의 (a) inspiring이 정답이다.

TEST 5

정답·스크립트·해석·해설

GRAMMAR

LISTENING

READING & VOCABULARY

TEST 5 점수 확인하기

GRAMMAR _____ / 26 (점수 : _____ 점)
LISTENING _____ / 26 (점수 : _____ 점)
READING & VOCABULARY _____ / 28 (점수 : _____ 점)

TOTAL _____ / 80 (평균 점수 : _____ 점)

*각 영역 점수: 맞은 개수 × 3.75
*평균 점수: 각 영역 점수 합계 ÷ 3

정답 및 취약 유형 분석표

자동 채점 및 성적 분석 서비스 ▶

문제집 p.124

GRAMMAR

번호	정답	유형
01	d	시제
02	a	준동사
03	b	연결어
04	a	준동사
05	a	조동사
06	b	가정법
07	c	시제
08	a	관계사
09	d	가정법
10	c	시제
11	c	조동사
12	b	준동사
13	d	시제
14	c	준동사
15	c	가정법
16	a	관계사
17	b	시제
18	a	조동사
19	d	가정법
20	c	연결어
21	a	준동사
22	b	가정법
23	b	시제
24	d	조동사
25	d	준동사
26	b	가정법

LISTENING

PART	번호	정답	유형
PART 1	27	b	특정세부사항
	28	d	특정세부사항
	29	b	특정세부사항
	30	a	추론
	31	c	특정세부사항
	32	b	특정세부사항
	33	a	추론
PART 2	34	c	주제/목적
	35	b	추론
	36	c	특정세부사항
	37	b	특정세부사항
	38	b	Not/True
	39	c	특정세부사항
PART 3	40	c	특정세부사항
	41	a	추론
	42	b	특정세부사항
	43	d	특정세부사항
	44	a	특정세부사항
	45	a	추론
PART 4	46	b	주제/목적
	47	a	특정세부사항
	48	b	특정세부사항
	49	c	추론
	50	b	특정세부사항
	51	a	특정세부사항
	52	d	특정세부사항

READING & VOCABULARY

PART	번호	정답	유형
PART 1	53	d	추론
	54	c	특정세부사항
	55	d	특정세부사항
	56	c	Not/True
	57	a	특정세부사항
	58	b	어휘
	59	a	어휘
PART 2	60	a	특정세부사항
	61	d	추론
	62	d	특정세부사항
	63	b	추론
	64	a	특정세부사항
	65	b	어휘
	66	c	어휘
PART 3	67	b	특정세부사항
	68	d	특정세부사항
	69	c	특정세부사항
	70	c	추론
	71	b	추론
	72	c	어휘
	73	a	어휘
PART 4	74	d	주제/목적
	75	a	특정세부사항
	76	b	특정세부사항
	77	b	추론
	78	d	특정세부사항
	79	c	어휘
	80	a	어휘

유형	맞힌 개수
시제	/ 6
가정법	/ 6
준동사	/ 6
조동사	/ 4
연결어	/ 2
관계사	/ 2
TOTAL	/ 26

유형	맞힌 개수
주제/목적	/ 2
특정세부사항	/ 17
Not/True	/ 1
추론	/ 6
TOTAL	/ 26

유형	맞힌 개수
주제/목적	/ 1
특정세부사항	/ 12
Not/True	/ 1
추론	/ 6
어휘	/ 8
TOTAL	/ 28

GRAMMAR

01 시제   미래진행

난이도 ●●○

Mr. Coyle, the CEO of the travel agency Sterling Destinations, has decided to move its headquarters to a new location. Starting next week, his company _____ out of an office building right across the street from the Newton Subway Station.

(a) has been operating
(b) operates
(c) is operating
(d) will be operating

Sterling Destinations 여행사의 최고 경영자인 Mr. Coyle은 그것의 본사를 새로운 장소로 이전하기로 결정했다. 다음 주부터, 그의 회사는 Newton 지하철역 바로 길 건너에 있는 사옥에서 운영되고 있는 중일 것이다.

──○ 지텔프 치트키

'for + 기간 표현' 없이 'starting + 미래 시점'만 있으면 미래진행 시제가 정답이다.

> 💡 **미래진행과 자주 함께 쓰이는 시간 표현**
> - when / if + 현재 동사 ~할 때 / 만약 ~한다면
> - next + 시간 표현 다음 ~에
> - until / by + 미래 시점 ~까지
> - starting + 미래 시점 / tomorrow ~부터 / 내일

해설 | 미래진행 시제와 함께 쓰이는 시간 표현 'starting + 미래 시점'(Starting next week)이 있고, 문맥상 Sterling Destinations 여행사의 최고 경영자가 그것의 본사를 새로운 장소로 이전하기로 결정하여 미래 시점인 다음 주부터 그의 회사가 새롭게 이전한 사옥에서 운영되고 있는 중일 것이라는 의미가 되어야 자연스럽다. 따라서 미래진행 시제 (d) will be operating이 정답이다.

어휘 | operate v. 운영되다, 가동되다

02 준동사   동명사를 목적어로 취하는 동사

난이도 ●●○

Dogwood Elementary School teacher Ms. Willis met with the principal to plan her class's upcoming field trip. They discussed _____ three hours at the National History Museum to give the children enough time to see all of the displays.

(a) spending
(b) to spend
(c) to be spending
(d) having spent

Dogwood 초등학교 교사인 Ms. Willis는 그녀가 맡은 학급의 곧 있을 현장 학습을 계획하기 위해 교장을 만났다. 그들은 아이들에게 모든 전시를 볼 충분한 시간을 주기 위해 국립 역사박물관에서 3시간을 보내는 것을 논의했다.

──○ 지텔프 치트키

discuss는 동명사를 목적어로 취한다.

> 💡 **동명사를 목적어로 취하는 빈출 동사**
> discuss 논의하다 avoid 피하다 imagine 상상하다 mind 개의하다 keep 계속하다 consider 고려하다 prevent 방지하다
> enjoy 즐기다 recommend 권장하다 risk 위험을 무릅쓰다 involve 포함하다

해설 | 빈칸 앞 동사 discuss는 동명사를 목적어로 취하므로, 동명사 (a) spending이 정답이다.

(d) having spent도 동명사이기는 하지만, 완료동명사(having spent)로 쓰일 경우 '논의한' 시점보다 '(시간을) 보내는' 시점이 앞선다는 것을 나타내므로 문맥에 적합하지 않아 오답이다.

어휘 | upcoming adj. 곧 있을, 다가오는   field trip phr. 현장 학습   display n. 전시

---

03 연결어   접속사

난이도 ●●●

Daniel was frustrated with his academic advisor's habit of taking a long time to reply to emails. He could not begin researching, let alone writing his dissertation, _____ she approved his topic.

(a) as soon as
(b) until
(c) after
(d) when

Daniel은 이메일에 답장하는 데 오랜 시간이 걸리는 지도 교수의 습관이 불만스러웠다. 그녀가 그의 주제를 승인할 때까지, 그는 논문을 쓰는 것은 고사하고, 조사하는 것조차 시작할 수 없었다.

──○ 지텔프 치트키

'~할 때까지'라는 의미의 시간을 나타낼 때는 until을 쓴다.

☆ 시간을 나타내는 빈출 접속사
until ~할 때까지   whenever ~할 때마다   while ~하는 동안   after ~한 이후에   before ~하기 전에

해설 | 문맥상 Daniel은 지도 교수가 그의 주제를 승인할 때까지 조사하는 것조차 시작할 수 없었다는 의미가 되어야 자연스럽다. 따라서 '~할 때까지'라는 의미의 시간을 나타내는 부사절 접속사 (b) until이 정답이다.

(a) as soon as는 '~하자마자', (c) after는 '~한 이후에', (d) when은 '~할 때'라는 의미로, 문맥에 적합하지 않아 오답이다.

어휘 | frustrated adj. 불만스러운   academic advisor phr. 지도 교수   let alone phr. ~은 고사하고   dissertation n. 논문   approve v. 승인하다

---

04 준동사   to 부정사의 형용사 역할

난이도 ●●○

When an individual visits a hospital because of an unidentified health problem, the doctor may arrange for a variety of medical tests. These provide the necessary information _____ the underlying cause of the patient's symptoms.

(a) to diagnose
(b) to be diagnosed
(c) diagnosing
(d) will diagnose

확인되지 않은 건강상의 문제 때문에 개인이 병원을 방문할 때, 의사는 여러 가지 건강 검진을 준비할 수도 있다. 이것들은 환자의 증상의 근본적인 원인을 진단할 필수 정보를 제공한다.

'~(해야) 할', '~하는'이라고 말할 때는 to 부정사를 쓴다.

해설 | 빈칸 앞에 명사(the necessary information)가 있고 문맥상 '근본적인 원인을 진단할 필수 정보'라는 의미가 되어야 자연스러우므로, 빈칸은 명사를 수식하는 형용사의 자리이다. 따라서 명사를 꾸며주는 형용사적 수식어구를 이끌 수 있는 to 부정사 (a) to diagnose가 정답이다.

어휘 | unidentified adj. 확인되지 않은 arrange v. 준비하다, 마련하다 underlying adj. 근본적인 symptom n. 증상

---

05 조동사 조동사 should 생략 난이도 ●○○

Mr. Weston, the chairperson of Lowden's public safety committee, is going to resign due to his deteriorating health. Considering Ms. Waters' contribution to the organization so far, he proposed that she _____ as his replacement.

(a) **serve**
(b) serves
(c) is serving
(d) will serve

Lowden시의 공공 안전 위원회 위원장인 Mr. Weston은 그의 악화되고 있는 건강 때문에 사임할 예정이다. 지금까지 이 조직에 대한 Ms. Waters의 공헌을 고려해 볼 때, 그는 그녀가 그의 후임자 역할을 해야 한다고 제안했다.

propose 다음에는 that절에 동사원형이 온다.

해설 | 주절에 제안을 나타내는 동사 propose가 있으므로 that절에는 '(should +) 동사원형'이 와야 한다. 따라서 동사원형 (a) serve가 정답이다.

어휘 | chairperson n. 위원장 resign v. 사임하다 deteriorate v. 악화되다 contribution n. 공헌 replacement n. 후임자

---

06 가정법 가정법 과거완료 난이도 ●●○

When Louisa paid for admission to the impressionist exhibition, she didn't notice the sign about the 20 percent discount for university students. Had she shown her student ID at the ticket booth, she _____ $2 on her ticket.

(a) had saved
(b) **could have saved**
(c) saved
(d) could save

Louisa가 인상파 화가 전시회에 입장료를 지불했을 때, 그녀는 대학생들을 위한 20퍼센트 할인에 관한 안내문을 알아채지 못했다. 그녀가 매표소에서 그녀의 학생증을 보여줬었다면, 그녀는 그녀의 입장권에 대해 2달러를 아낄 수 있었을 것이다.

Had p.p.가 있으면 'would/could + have p.p.'가 정답이다.

해설 | if가 생략되어 도치된 절에 'had p.p.' 형태의 Had ~ shown이 있으므로, 주절에는 이와 짝을 이루어 가정법 과거완료를 만드는 'could (조동사 과거형) + have p.p.'가 와야 한다. 따라서 (b) could have saved가 정답이다. 참고로, 'Had she shown ~'은 'If she had shown ~'으로 바꿔 쓸 수 있다.

어휘 | admission n. 입장료 impressionist n. 인상파 화가 ticket booth phr. 매표소

Despite his excellent academic record, Kyle is feeling uncertain about whether he will be accepted into Lethem University. He submitted his application, and he _____ a response from the school for the past month.

(a) would await
(b) is awaiting
(c) has been awaiting
(d) will have awaited

그의 뛰어난 학업 성적에도 불구하고, Kyle은 그가 Lethem 대학에 합격할지에 대해 불확실함을 느끼고 있다. 그는 지원서를 제출했고, 지난 한 달 동안 학교 측의 답변을 기다려오고 있는 중이다.

─○ 지텔프 치트키

'for the past + 기간 표현'이 있으면 현재완료진행 시제가 정답이다.

> 💡 현재완료진행과 자주 함께 쓰이는 시간 표현
> • (ever) since + 과거 시점 + (for + 기간 표현) ~한 이래로 (줄곧) (~ 동안)
> • lately / for + 기간 표현 + now 최근에 / 현재 ~ 동안

해설 | 현재완료진행 시제와 함께 쓰이는 시간 표현 'for the past + 기간 표현'(for the past month)이 있고, 문맥상 Kyle이 지원서를 제출한 뒤 지난 한 달 동안 계속해서 학교 측의 답변을 기다려오고 있는 중이라는 의미가 되어야 자연스럽다. 따라서 현재완료진행 시제 (c) has been awaiting이 정답이다.

보기 오답분석

(b) 현재진행 시제는 특정 현재 시점에 한창 진행 중인 일을 나타내므로, 과거에 시작해서 현재 시점까지 계속해서 진행되고 있는 일을 표현할 수 없어 오답이다.

어휘 | uncertain adj. 불확실한   submit v. 제출하다   application n. 지원서   response n. 답변

Amazing Adventure World is a popular tourist attraction that brings in many visitors from across the country. The amusement park, _____, includes Fun Scape, a roller coaster that reaches speeds of 65 miles per hour and features a 77-degree drop.

(a) which opened just last year
(b) when it opened just last year
(c) that opened just last year
(d) what opened just last year

Amazing Adventure World는 전국에서 온 많은 방문 객들을 불러들이는 인기 있는 관광 명소이다. 그 놀이 공원은, 바로 작년에 문을 열었는데, 시속 65마일에 달하며 77도 각도의 하강을 특징으로 하는 롤러코스터 인 Fun Scape를 포함한다.

─○ 지텔프 치트키

사물 선행사가 관계절 안에서 주어 역할을 하고, 빈칸 앞에 콤마(,)가 있으면 주격 관계대명사 which가 정답이다.

해설 | 사물 선행사 The amusement park를 받으면서 콤마(,) 뒤에 올 수 있는 주격 관계대명사가 필요하므로, (a) which opened just last year가 정답이다.

보기 오답분석

(c) 관계대명사 that도 사물 선행사를 받을 수 있지만, 콤마 뒤에 올 수 없으므로 오답이다.

09 가정법 가정법 과거   난이도 ●●○

Abigail became interested in learning Spanish after she joined a company that exports clothes to South America, but she doesn't have much time to study. If her work hours were reduced, she _____ in the language course offered at the Westlake Community Center.

(a) has enrolled
(b) would have enrolled
(c) enrolled
(d) would enroll

Abigail은 남미에 옷을 수출하는 회사에 입사한 후 스페인어를 배우는 것에 관심을 가지게 되었지만, 그녀는 공부할 시간이 많지 않다. 만약 그녀의 업무 시간이 줄어든다면, 그녀는 Westlake 커뮤니티 센터에서 제공되는 어학 강좌에 <u>등록할 것이다</u>.

○ 지텔프 치트키

'if + 과거 동사'가 있으면 'would/could + 동사원형'이 정답이다.

해설 | If절에 과거 동사(were reduced)가 있으므로, 주절에는 이와 짝을 이루어 가정법 과거를 만드는 'would(조동사 과거형) + 동사원형'이 와야 한다. 따라서 (d) would enroll이 정답이다.

어휘 | export v. 수출하다 enroll v. 등록하다

10 시제 과거완료진행   난이도 ●●○

Greg was relieved when his coworker helped him with his report. He _____ on it for five hours since he came to work that morning and knew that he couldn't finish it by the end of the day without assistance.

(a) labored
(b) would have labored
(c) had been laboring
(d) was laboring

Greg는 동료가 그의 보고서 작성을 도와주었을 때 안도했다. 그날 아침 직장에 온 이래로 그는 5시간 동안 그것에 애써오고 있던 중이었고 그가 도움 없이는 하루가 끝날 무렵까지 그것을 끝낼 수 없다는 것을 알았다.

○ 지텔프 치트키

'since + 과거 동사/시점'과 'for + 기간 표현'이 함께 오면 과거완료진행 시제가 정답이다.

> ☼ 과거완료진행과 자주 함께 쓰이는 시간 표현
> • before / when / since + 과거 동사 + (for + 기간 표현) ~하기 전에 / ~했을 때 / ~ 이래로 (~ 동안)
> • (for + 기간 표현) + (up) until + 과거 동사 (~ 동안) ~했을 때까지

해설 | 과거완료진행 시제와 함께 쓰이는 시간 표현 'for + 기간 표현'(for five hours)과 'since + 과거 동사/시점'(since ~ came ~ that morning)이 있고, 문맥상 Greg가 대과거(그날 아침 직장에 온 시점)부터 과거(동료가 그의 보고서 작성을 도와준 시점)까지 그것에 5시간 동안 계속해서 애써오고 있던 중이었다는 의미가 되어야 자연스럽다. 따라서 과거완료진행 시제 (c) had been laboring이 정답이다.

(d) 과거진행 시제는 특정 과거 시점에 한창 진행 중이었던 일을 나타내므로, 대과거에 시작해서 특정 과거 시점까지 계속해서 진행되고 있
었던 일을 표현할 수 없어 오답이다.

어휘 | relieved adj. 안도하는 assistance n. 도움 labor v. 애쓰다, 일을 하다

---

11 조동사   조동사 can   난이도 ●●○

Residents of the Burnside Apartments wonder when
the elevator will be repaired. The work is scheduled for
completion on Sunday, but the building manager says he
_____ definitely fix it by Friday because the problem
isn't very serious.

(a) must
(b) would
(c) can
(d) might

Burnside 아파트의 주민들은 엘리베이터가 언제 수
리될지 궁금해한다. 그 작업은 일요일에 완료될 예정
이지만, 건물 관리자는 문제가 아주 심각하지는 않기
때문에 그것을 금요일까지 확실하게 고칠 수 있다고
말한다.

지텔프 치트키

'~할 수 있다'라고 말할 때는 can을 쓴다.

해설 | 문맥상 Burnside 아파트의 건물 관리자는 엘리베이터 문제가 아주 심각하지는 않기 때문에 기존 완료 예정일인 일요일보다 빠른 금요일
까지 그것을 확실하게 고칠 수 있다고 말한다는 내용이 되어야 자연스럽다. 따라서 '~할 수 있다'를 뜻하면서 능력을 나타내는 조동사 (c) can
이 정답이다.

어휘 | resident n. 주민 wonder v. 궁금해하다 completion n. 완료 definitely adv. 확실하게

---

12 준동사   to 부정사를 목적어로 취하는 동사   난이도 ●○○

Attractive Automobiles would like to expand into new
markets in the following quarter. It plans _____ which
demographic groups would be most likely to purchase its
car cleaning services.

(a) researching
(b) to research
(c) to have researched
(d) having researched

Attractive 자동차사는 다음 분기에 새로운 시장으로
확장하기를 원한다. 그것은 어떤 인구층이 그것의 차
량 청소 서비스를 구매할 가능성이 가장 클지를 <u>조사</u>
<u>할</u> 계획이다.

지텔프 치트키

plan은 to 부정사를 목적어로 취한다.

해설 | 빈칸 앞 동사 plan은 to 부정사를 목적어로 취하므로, to 부정사 (b) to research가 정답이다.

(c) to have researched도 to 부정사이기는 하지만, 완료부정사(to have researched)로 쓰일 경우 '계획하는' 시점보다 '조사하는' 시점이 앞선다는 것을 나타내므로 문맥에 적합하지 않아 오답이다.

어휘 | expand v. 확장하다 quarter n. 분기 demographic adj. 인구의, 인구 통계학적인

---

13 시제 현재진행 난이도 ●●○

Nancy called her boss to tell him that she would be late. It snowed heavily last night, and she is worried about driving. At the moment, the streets _____ of snow by city workers, and she will leave her home as soon as they finish.

Nancy는 그녀의 상사에게 늦을 것 같다고 말하기 위해 전화했다. 어젯밤에 눈이 많이 내렸고, 그녀는 운전하는 것에 대해 걱정하고 있다. 바로 지금, 거리들은 시 근로자들에 의해 눈이 치워지고 있는 중이며, 그녀는 그들이 끝마치는 대로 집을 나설 것이다.

(a) will be cleared
(b) have been cleared
(c) were cleared
(d) are being cleared

지텔프 치트키

at the moment가 있으면 현재진행 시제가 정답이다.

> 💡 현재진행과 자주 함께 쓰이는 시간 표현
> • right now / now / currently / at the moment 바로 지금 / 지금 / 현재 / 바로 지금
> • these days / nowadays 요즘

해설 | 현재진행 시제와 함께 쓰이는 시간 표현 At the moment가 있고, 문맥상 말하고 있는 시점인 바로 지금 거리들은 시 근로자들에 의해 눈이 치워지고 있는 중이라는 의미가 되어야 자연스럽다. 따라서 현재진행 시제 (d) are being cleared가 정답이다.

어휘 | clear v. 치우다

---

14 준동사 동명사를 목적어로 취하는 동사 난이도 ●●○

The local government intends to renovate the city's parks. While many are excited about this development, some question how the administration can justify _____ taxes next year to pay for this project. It's no secret that inhabitants are suffering from the recession.

지방 정부는 그 도시의 공원들을 보수할 생각이다. 많은 사람들이 이 개발에 대해 들떠 있지만, 일부는 행정 당국이 이 프로젝트에 대한 비용을 지불하기 위해 내년에 세금을 올리는 것을 어떻게 정당화할 수 있을지에 관해 의문을 제기한다. 주민들이 불경기에 시달리고 있다는 것은 알려진 사실이다.

(a) to increase
(b) to have increased
(c) increasing
(d) will increase

지텔프 치트키

justify는 동명사를 목적어로 취한다.

해설 | 빈칸 앞 동사 justify는 동명사를 목적어로 취하므로, 동명사 (c) increasing이 정답이다.

어휘 | intend v. ~하려고 생각하다, 의도하다 renovate v. 보수하다 question v. 의문을 제기하다 justify v. 정당화하다 inhabitant n. 주민 recession n. 불경기

---

15 가정법 혼합가정법 난이도 ●●●

Gary was disappointed to hear that his history professor had rejected her students' request to push back the due date for the term paper. If the deadline had been extended, he _____ much less stress these days.

(a) is having
(b) has
(c) would have
(d) will have

Gary는 그의 역사 교수가 학기 말 과제의 제출 기한을 연기해 달라는 학생들의 요청을 거절했다는 소식을 듣고 실망했다. 만약 그 기한이 연장됐었다면, 그는 요즘 스트레스를 훨씬 덜 받을 것이다.

지텔프 치트키

'if + had p.p.'와 현재 시간 표현이 있고, 과거 상황이 현재까지 영향을 미치면 'would/could + 동사원형'이 정답이다.

해설 | If절에 'had p.p.' 형태의 had been extended가 있으므로, 보통의 경우라면 주절에는 이와 짝을 이루어 가정법 과거완료를 만드는 'would(조동사 과거형) + have p.p.'가 와야 한다. 그러나 주절에 현재 시간 표현 these days가 있으므로, 과거 시점에 있었던 일이 현재까지 영향을 미치는 상황에서 현재 상황을 반대로 가정하고 있음을 알 수 있다. 따라서 주절에는 가정법 과거를 만드는 'would(조동사 과거형) + 동사원형'이 와야 하므로, (c) would have가 정답이다. 참고로, 지텔프에는 간혹 혼합가정법이 출제되기도 하는데, 이 경우 보통 주절에 these days와 같은 현재 시간 표현이 포함되어 있다.

어휘 | request n. 요청 push back phr. 연기하다 due date phr. 제출 기한, 마감 기한 term paper phr. 학기 말 과제 extend v. 연장하다

---

16 관계사 관계부사 where 난이도 ●●○

Why do many independent stores in this area close during their first year of operation? Although there are a number of reasons, the most common is that these shops are set up in locations _____ to their potential consumers.

(a) where they are not conveniently accessible
(b) that they are not conveniently accessible
(c) when they are not conveniently accessible
(d) which they are not conveniently accessible

왜 이 지역의 많은 자영 점포들이 운영 첫해에 문을 닫는가? 여러 가지 이유들이 있지만, 가장 일반적인 이유는 이 가게들이 그것들의 잠재적 소비자들이 편리하게 접근할 수 없는 장소에 차려져 있다는 점이다.

지텔프 치트키

장소 선행사가 있고 관계사 뒤에 오는 절이 완전하면 관계부사 where가 정답이다.

해설 | 장소 선행사 locations를 받으면서 보기의 주어(they), 동사(are), 보어(accessible)를 갖춘 완전한 절을 이끌 수 있는 관계부사가 필요하므로, (a) where they are not conveniently accessible이 정답이다.

어휘 | independent adj. 자영의, 독립적인 potential adj. 잠재적인 accessible adj. 접근할 수 있는

---

17 시제　미래완료진행　난이도 ●●○

Ever since she started working at Wilson Marketing, Sally has never thought of changing jobs. If she signs another annual employment contract at the end of this month, she _____ a career there for eight years.

(a) is building
(b) will have been building
(c) has been building
(d) has built

Wilson Marketing 사에서 일을 시작한 이후로, Sally는 이직하는 것을 전혀 생각해 본 적이 없다. 만약 그녀가 이달 말에 또 한 번의 연간 고용 계약을 맺는다면, 그녀는 그곳에서 8년 동안 경력을 쌓아오고 있는 중일 것이다.

─○ 지텔프 치트키

'if + 현재 동사'와 'for + 기간 표현'이 함께 오면 미래완료진행 시제가 정답이다.

> ☀ 미래완료진행과 자주 함께 쓰이는 시간 표현
> • by the time / when / if + 현재 동사 + (for + 기간 표현) ~할 무렵이면 / ~할 때 / 만약 ~한다면 (~ 동안)
> • by / in + 미래 시점 + (for + 기간 표현) ~ 즈음에는 / ~에 (~ 동안)

해설 | 현재 동사로 미래의 의미를 나타내는 조건의 부사절 'if + 현재 동사'(If ~ signs)와 지속을 나타내는 'for + 기간 표현'(for eight years)이 있고, 문맥상 Sally가 또 한 번의 연간 고용 계약을 맺는 미래 시점에 그녀는 8년 동안 그곳에서 계속해서 경력을 쌓아오고 있는 중일 것이라는 의미가 되어야 자연스럽다. 따라서 미래완료진행 시제 (b) will have been building이 정답이다. 참고로, if는 미래진행 시제나 미래완료진행 시제 문제에서 간혹 조건의 부사절을 이끄는 접속사로 사용되기도 한다.

어휘 | annual adj. 연간의　sign a contract phr. 계약을 맺다

18 조동사　조동사 should 생략　난이도 ●●○

Austin was worried about how long it would take for his injured knee to heal. But he is almost fully recovered thanks to his doctor's suggestion that he _____ to assist with rehabilitation.

(a) exercise
(b) exercising
(c) exercised
(d) to exercise

Austin은 그의 다친 무릎이 낫기까지 얼마나 걸릴지 걱정했었다. 하지만 그는 재활을 도우려면 운동해야 한다는 주치의의 제안 덕분에 거의 완전히 회복되었다.

─○ 지텔프 치트키

suggestion 다음에는 that절에 동사원형이 온다.

> ☀ 주장·요구·명령·제안을 나타내는 빈출 명사
> suggestion 제안　desire 바람

해설 | 주절에 제안을 나타내는 명사 suggestion이 있으므로 that절에는 '(should +) 동사원형'이 와야 한다. 따라서 동사원형 (a) exercise가 정답이다.

어휘 | injured adj. 다친, 부상을 입은　heal v. 낫다, 치유되다　recover v. 회복하다　suggestion n. 제안　rehabilitation n. 재활

19 가정법 · 가정법 과거완료

It's not fair that I'm getting blamed for the failure of the advertising campaign! If management had followed my recommendation, we _____ the trouble of alienating the target audience entirely.

(a) will have avoided
(b) had avoided
(c) would avoid
(d) would have avoided

제가 그 광고 캠페인의 실패에 대해 비난을 받고 있는 것은 부당합니다! 만약 경영진이 저의 권고를 따랐었다면, 우리는 목표로 삼은 시청자를 완전히 멀어지게 만드는 문제를 피했을 것입니다.

🔑 지텔프 치트키

'if + had p.p.'가 있으면 'would/could + have p.p.'가 정답이다.

해설 | If절에 'had p.p.' 형태의 had followed가 있으므로, 주절에는 이와 짝을 이루어 가정법 과거완료를 만드는 'would(조동사 과거형) + have p.p.'가 와야 한다. 따라서 (d) would have avoided가 정답이다.

어휘 | fair adj. 타당한, 온당한 management n. 경영진 recommendation n. 권고 alienate v. 멀어지게 만들다 entirely adv. 완전히

---

20 연결어 · 접속부사

John spent three years working as a real estate agent for Happy House. _____, he prepared a business plan and secured a commercial loan for a small office. Now, he can open up his own agency.

(a) Therefore
(b) In fact
(c) Meanwhile
(d) In contrast

John은 Happy House 사의 부동산 중개인으로 일하면서 3년을 보냈다. 그동안에, 그는 사업 계획을 준비했고 작은 사무실을 위한 상업 대출을 받았다. 이제, 그는 자신의 중개소를 열 수 있다.

🔑 지텔프 치트키

'그동안에'라는 의미의 시간을 나타낼 때는 Meanwhile을 쓴다.

> 💡 시간을 나타내는 빈출 접속부사
> Meanwhile 그동안에 Later on 나중에 At the same time 그와 동시에

해설 | 빈칸 앞 문장은 John이 Happy House 사의 부동산 중개인으로 일하면서 3년을 보냈다는 내용이고, 빈칸 뒤 문장은 그가 사업 계획을 준비했고 작은 사무실을 위한 상업 대출을 받았다는 내용이다. 따라서 빈칸에는 하나의 일이 일어나고 있는 동안에 한편에서는 또 다른 일이 일어나고 있다는 내용을 만드는 연결어가 들어가야 자연스러우므로, '그동안에'라는 의미의 시간을 나타내는 접속부사 (c) Meanwhile이 정답이다.

오답분석
(a) Therefore는 '따라서', (b) In fact는 '사실은', (d) In contrast는 '그에 반해'라는 의미로, 문맥에 적합하지 않아 오답이다.

어휘 | real estate agent phr. 부동산 중개인 secure v. 받다, 확보하다 commercial adj. 상업의 loan n. 대출

21 준동사   to 부정사의 부사 역할   난이도 ●●○

Did you hear that Doug quit the school's baseball team? It turns out that he gave up all the other club activities he had been participating in _____ his time and attention to the theater group.

(a) **to devote**
(b) devoting
(c) having devoted
(d) to have devoted

너 Doug가 학교 야구부를 그만뒀다는 소식 들었니? 연극부에 그의 시간과 관심을 쏟기 위해 그가 참여해 오고 있던 다른 모든 동아리 활동들도 포기했다는 사실이 알려졌어.

🔑 지텔프 치트키

'~하기 위해'라고 말할 때는 to 부정사를 쓴다.

해설 | 빈칸 앞에 주어(he), 동사(gave up), 목적어(all the other club activities)가 갖춰진 완전한 절이 있으므로, 빈칸 이하는 문장의 필수 성분이 아닌 수식어구이다. 따라서 목적을 나타내며 수식어구를 이끌 수 있는 to 부정사 (a) to devote가 정답이다.

어휘 | quit v. 그만두다 turn out phr. 알려지다, 드러나다 give up phr. 포기하다 devote v. (돈·시간 등을) 쏟다, 바치다

22 가정법   가정법 과거   난이도 ●●○

Rebecca doesn't like her job at the restaurant, so she doesn't work very hard. If she _____ in an industry she had more passion for, she would perform her duties with a lot more effort.

(a) engages
(b) **engaged**
(c) has engaged
(d) had engaged

Rebecca는 식당에서의 그녀의 일을 좋아하지 않아서, 아주 열심히 일하지는 않는다. 만약 그녀가 더 열정을 가지고 있는 산업에 종사한다면, 그녀는 훨씬 더 많이 노력하여 그녀의 업무를 수행할 것이다.

🔑 지텔프 치트키

if와 'would/could + 동사원형'이 있으면 과거 동사가 정답이다.

해설 | 주절에 'would(조동사 과거형) + 동사원형' 형태의 would perform이 있으므로, If절에는 이와 짝을 이루어 가정법 과거를 만드는 과거 동사가 와야 한다. 따라서 (b) engaged가 정답이다.

어휘 | industry n. 산업 passion n. 열정 duty n. 업무, 임무 engage v. 종사하다

23 시제   과거진행   난이도 ●●○

I have mastered as many types of sports as I could over the years. But most of all, I have to say that I felt the fittest while I _____ for a marathon. Furthermore, I was indescribably happy when I completed the race.

나는 수년간 내가 할 수 있는 한 많은 종류의 스포츠를 섭렵해 왔다. 하지만 무엇보다도, 나는 마라톤을 위해 훈련하고 있던 동안에 가장 건강하다고 느꼈다고 말하고 싶다. 게다가, 나는 그 경주를 완주했을 때 형언할 수 없이 기뻤다.

해커스 지텔프 최신기출유형 실전문제집 7회 (Level 2)

(a) would train
(b) was training
(c) had trained
(d) am training

🔑 지텔프 치트키

'과거 동사 + while절'이 있으면 과거진행 시제가 정답이다.

💡 **과거진행과 자주 함께 쓰이는 시간 표현**
- when / while + 과거 동사 ~했을 때 / ~하던 도중에
- last + 시간 표현 / yesterday 지난 ~에 / 어제

해설 | 과거진행 시제와 함께 쓰이는 시간 표현 '과거 동사 + while절'(felt ~ while ~)이 있고, 문맥상 화자가 가장 건강하다고 느꼈던 과거 시점에 화자는 마라톤을 위해 훈련하고 있던 동안이었다는 의미가 되어야 자연스럽다. 따라서 과거진행 시제 (b) was training이 정답이다.

오답분석

(c) 과거완료 시제는 특정 과거 시점 이전에 일어난 대과거의 일을 나타내는 시제인데, 내가 마라톤을 위해 훈련한 일과 가장 건강하다고 느낀 일은 동시에 일어난 일이므로 오답이다.

어휘 | fit adj. 건강한 indescribably adv. 형언할 수 없이 train v. 훈련하다

---

24 조동사 조동사 must 난이도 ●●○

Prime Electronics has received multiple complaints from clients regarding late product deliveries. Though last-minute issues are sometimes inevitable, the company _____ send shipments by the expected time to maintain a good relationship with its customers.

Prime Electronics 사는 늦은 제품 배송과 관련하여 고객들로부터 많은 불만을 접수했다. 비록 막바지 문제들은 때때로 불가피할지라도, 그 회사가 고객들과 좋은 관계를 유지하기 위해서는 예정된 시간까지 배송물을 보내야 한다.

(a) would
(b) may
(c) can
(d) must

🔑 지텔프 치트키

'~해야 한다'라고 말할 때는 must를 쓴다.

해설 | 문맥상 Prime Electronics 사가 고객들과 좋은 관계를 유지하기 위해서는 예정된 시간까지 배송물을 보내야 한다는 의미가 되어야 자연스러우므로, '~해야 한다'를 뜻하면서 의무를 나타내는 조동사 (d) must가 정답이다. 참고로, must와 should 모두 '~해야 한다'를 뜻하지만, must는 should보다 강한 어조로 조언을 하거나 의무를 나타낼 때 쓴다.

어휘 | complaint n. 불만, 불평 last-minute adj. 막바지의 inevitable adj. 불가피한 shipment n. 배송물, 수송 maintain v. 유지하다

25 준동사 동명사를 목적어로 취하는 동사

It wasn't easy for Samantha to move out of the city. At first, she missed the convenience of enjoying cultural facilities at any time and having a shopping mall close at hand. However, she absolutely adores _____ in the countryside now.

(a) to have lived
(b) to live
(c) to be living
(d) living

Samantha에게 도시 밖으로 이사하는 일은 쉽지 않았다. 처음에, 그녀는 언제든지 문화 시설을 즐기는 것과 가까운 곳에 쇼핑몰이 있다는 것의 편리함이 그리웠다. 하지만, 그녀는 지금 시골에서 <u>사는 것을</u> 굉장히 좋아한다.

─○ 지텔프 치트키

adore는 동명사를 목적어로 취한다.

해설 | 빈칸 앞 동사 adore는 동명사를 목적어로 취하므로, 동명사 (d) living이 정답이다.

어휘 | facility n. 시설 close at hand phr. 가까운 곳에 absolutely adv. 굉장히, 전적으로 adore v. 좋아하다

26 가정법 가정법 과거완료

William couldn't believe that the school canceled the homecoming dance due to budget cuts. If the event had gone on as planned, he _____ his friends whom he graduated with last year.

(a) would see
(b) would have seen
(c) was seeing
(d) had seen

William은 예산 삭감으로 학교가 동창회 댄스파티를 취소했다는 것을 믿을 수 없었다. 만약 그 행사가 계획대로 진행되었더라면, 그는 작년에 같이 졸업한 그의 친구들을 <u>보았을 것이다.</u>

─○ 지텔프 치트키

'if + had p.p.'가 있으면 'would/could + have p.p.'가 정답이다.

해설 | If절에 'had p.p.' 형태의 had gone이 있으므로, 주절에는 이와 짝을 이루어 가정법 과거완료를 만드는 'would(조동사 과거형) + have p.p.'가 와야 한다. 따라서 (b) would have seen이 정답이다.

어휘 | cancel v. 취소하다 homecoming n. 동창회 budget n. 예산 graduate v. 졸업하다

LISTENING

음성 바로 듣기

안부 인사	F: Hi, Johnny. I got here as fast as I could. ²⁷What's the big announcement? M: Hey, Cathy. ²⁷My song is going to be featured in a new movie!	여: 안녕, Johnny. 나는 최대한 빨리 여기에 왔어. ²⁷중대한 발표 사항이 뭐야? 남: 안녕, Cathy. ²⁷내 노래가 신작 영화에 나올 거야!
주제 제시: 영화 음악 제작	F: Congratulations! Which song are you talking about? M: It's a lighthearted piece called "The Last Donut of the Day." ²⁸It'll be the theme for a hilarious film about a family bakery called *Just What I Kneaded*.	여: 축하해! 무슨 노래 말하는 거야? 남: 그것은 '오늘의 마지막 도넛'이라는 제목의 쾌활한 곡이야. 그것은 「내가 반죽해서 만든 바로 그것」이라는 제목의 가족 빵집에 관한 ²⁸아주 웃긴 영화의 주제곡이 될 거야.
영감을 얻는 방법	F: Sounds interesting. How do you come up with ideas for that kind of project? M: I always adhere to the same strategy regardless of the type of movie. ²⁹I consider the characters in the story and draw inspiration from them. F: I see. You mean, if the protagonist faces sadness and tragedy, you record somber and quiet sounds, right? M: Exactly. Since the family in this film is brimming with laughter and joy, I tried to capture their emotions with upbeat and lively music.	여: 재미있겠다. 넌 그런 종류의 프로젝트에 관한 아이디어를 어떻게 생각해 내? 남: 나는 영화의 종류에 상관없이 항상 같은 전략을 고수해. ²⁹나는 이야기 속의 인물들을 고찰하고 그들로부터 영감을 얻지. 여: 그렇구나. 네 말은, 만약 주인공이 슬픔과 비극에 직면한다면, 넌 침울하고 조용한 음악을 녹음한다는 뜻이지, 맞니? 남: 바로 그거야. 이 영화 속의 가족은 웃음과 기쁨으로 가득 차 있기 때문에, 난 흥겹고 활기찬 음악으로 그들의 감정을 담아내려고 노력했어.
음악 녹음 방법	F: That's fascinating. I know you write the songs by yourself, but does anyone help you in the studio? M: This time I hired live performers for the new song. The producers had an enormous budget, so no expense was spared. However, that isn't always the case. F: Oh, really? Then, how did you manage your previous recordings? M: ³⁰In the past, on independent films that didn't have much money, I had to rely on digital tools and software for everything. It was a relief to have professional musicians with real instruments on this project.	여: 그거 대단히 흥미롭구나. 네가 직접 곡을 쓴다는 건 알지만, 녹음실에서 누군가가 너를 도와주니? 남: 이번에는 신곡을 위해 라이브 연주자들을 고용했어. 제작자들이 막대한 예산을 가지고 있어서, 비용을 아끼지 않았거든. 하지만, 항상 그런 건 아니야. 여: 오, 정말? 그러면, 너의 이전 녹음들은 어떻게 해낸 거야? 남: ³⁰과거에, 돈이 많지 않았던 독립 영화에서는, 나는 모든 것을 디지털 도구와 소프트웨어에 의존해야 했어. 이번 프로젝트에는 실제 악기를 가진 전문 연주자들이 있어서 다행이었어.
	F: So, you told me about writing a song for a movie and recording it, but I'm curious about what happens between those two stages. M: I would love to go straight to the studio when I finish writing. Unfortunately, ³¹I need to have some crucial discussions with the director before recording can begin.	여: 그러면, 네가 영화를 위한 곡을 쓰고 녹음하는 것에 대해 내게 말해주었는데, 나는 그 두 단계 사이에 어떤 일이 일어나는지가 궁금해. 남: 나는 곡을 쓰는 것을 마치면 정말 곧장 작업실로 가고 싶어. 안타깝게도, ³¹난 녹음이 시작될 수 있기 전에 감독과 몇몇 중요한 논의를 해야 해.

작곡 관련 논의 절차

F: Hmm . . . I guess the two of you aren't always in perfect harmony.

M: On numerous occasions, I've thought that I had composed a masterpiece only to discover that the director hated it. Such a scenario can lead to some heated debates.

F: What happens when a song that you pitch is rejected?

M: When that occurs, I have to start again from the beginning. It's frustrating, but I try to remember that it's all part of the creative process.

남자의 향후 계획

F: I see. So, how will this project change your career? I'm sure everyone will want to work with you after this.

M: Actually, another director has already recruited me for an action movie set to be released next summer.

F: Next summer? That's more than a year away!

M: That's not as long as it sounds. There's a lot to do in that time. I've seen a few script excerpts, so I'll brainstorm some ideas.

F: ³²Will you write the lyrics first, or do you typically start with the music?

M: ³²I begin with a melody and go from there. Once the music is set, I write the words.

여자가 다음에 할 일

F: I can't wait to hear it. Can I get a preview before the movie comes out?

M: Of course, Cathy. I would love to get your opinion about the early recordings. ³³I even prepared some samples of the beat that you can listen to.

F: That's very exciting, Johnny! I've got a few minutes to spare now. ³³It would be great to hear what you've made.

여: 흠... 두 사람이 항상 완벽한 화합을 이루지는 못할 것 같아.

남: 많은 경우에, 나는 내가 걸작을 작곡했었다고 생각했지만 결국에는 감독이 그것을 마음에 안 들어 한다는 걸 깨달을 뿐이었어. 그러한 상황은 조금 격렬한 논쟁으로 이어질 수 있어.

여: 네가 내놓은 곡이 거부되면 어떻게 돼?

남: 그런 일이 일어날 때, 난 처음부터 다시 시작해야 해. 답답하지만, 나는 그것이 모두 창조적 과정의 일부라는 것을 기억하려고 노력해.

여: 그렇구나. 그럼, 이 프로젝트가 너의 경력을 어떻게 변화시킬까? 나는 이 일 이후에 모두가 너와 함께 일하고 싶어 할 거라고 확신해.

남: 사실, 다른 감독이 내년 여름에 개봉되기로 결정된 액션 영화에 이미 날 채용했어.

여: 내년 여름? 1년도 넘게 남았네!

남: 보이는 것만큼 그렇게 길지 않아. 그 시간에 할 일이 산더미야. 몇 개의 대본 발췌본을 봤으니, 몇 가지 아이디어를 브레인스토밍할 거야.

여: ³²가사를 먼저 쓸 거니, 아니면 보통 곡부터 시작해?

남: ³²난 멜로디부터 시작해서 거기서부터 이어가. 일단 곡이 준비되면, 나는 가사를 써.

여: 그걸 빨리 듣고 싶어. 영화가 나오기 전에 미리 들어봐도 될까?

남: 물론이지, Cathy. 초반 녹음에 대한 너의 의견을 얻고 싶어. ³³나는 심지어 네가 들어볼 수 있는 견본 비트를 몇 개 준비했어.

여: 정말 신나는 걸, Johnny! 난 지금 잠깐 여유가 있어. ³³네가 만든 것을 들어보면 정말 좋을 것 같아.

어휘 | announcement[ənáunsmənt] 발표 사항 lighthearted[làithá:rtid] 쾌활한, 근심이 없는 hilarious[hilériəs] 아주 웃긴
knead[ni:d] 반죽해서 만들다 adhere[ədhír] 고수하다 inspiration[ìnspəréiʃən] 영감 protagonist[proutǽgənist] 주인공
somber[sá:mbər] 침울한 brim[brim] 가득 차다 upbeat[ʌ́pbi:t] 흥겨운 enormous[inɔ́:rməs] 막대한 expense[ikspéns] 비용
instrument[ínstrəmənt] 악기 crucial[krú:ʃəl] 중요한, 결정적인 harmony[há:rməni] 화합, 일치 masterpiece[mǽstərpi:s] 걸작, 명작
debate[dibéit] 논쟁, 토론 pitch[pitʃ] (구매를 권하기 위해) 내놓다, 가락 recruit[rikrú:t] 채용하다, 모집하다 excerpt[éksərpt] 발췌본
lyric[lírik] 가사 typically[típikli] 보통, 일반적으로

---

27 **특정세부사항**   What   난이도 ●●○

What good news is Johnny telling Cathy?

(a) that his song will be featured in a commercial
(b) that his music will be in a film
(c) that his writing has won a songwriting award
(d) that his piece has been completed

Johnny는 Cathy에게 어떤 좋은 소식을 전하고 있는가?

(a) 그의 노래가 광고에 나올 것이라는 것
(b) 그의 음악이 영화에 나올 것이라는 것
(c) 그의 작품이 작곡상을 탔다는 것
(d) 그의 곡이 완성되었다는 것

질문의 키워드 news가 announcement로 paraphrasing되어 언급된 주변 내용을 주의 깊게 듣는다.

해설ㅣ 여자가 'What's the big announcement?'라며 중대한 발표 사항이 무엇인지를 묻자, 남자가 'My song is going to be featured in a new movie!'라며 그의 노래가 신작 영화에 나올 것이라고 했다. 따라서 (b)가 정답이다.

Paraphrasing
My song is going to be featured in a ~ movie 노래가 영화에 나올 것이다 → his music will be in a film 음악이 영화에 나올 것이다

어휘ㅣ commercial[kəmə́ːrʃəl] 광고

---

28 특정세부사항   What   난이도 ●○○

What genre of film is *Just What I Kneaded*?	「내가 반죽해서 만든 바로 그것」은 어떤 장르의 영화인가?
(a) a horror movie	(a) 공포 영화
(b) a romance movie	(b) 로맨스 영화
(c) a suspense movie	(c) 서스펜스 영화
(d) a comedy movie	**(d) 코미디 영화**

○ **지텔프 치트키**

질문의 키워드 *Just What I Kneaded*가 그대로 언급된 주변 내용을 주의 깊게 듣는다.

해설ㅣ 남자가 'It'll be the theme for a hilarious film'이라며 그의 곡이 아주 웃긴 영화의 주제곡이 될 것이라고 했다. 따라서 (d)가 정답이다.

Paraphrasing
a hilarious film 아주 웃긴 영화 → a comedy movie 코미디 영화

어휘ㅣ suspense[səspéns] 서스펜스, 긴장감

---

29 특정세부사항   How   난이도 ●●○

How does Johnny get inspired to write music for movies?	Johnny는 어떻게 영화 음악을 작곡하는 데 영감을 얻는가?
(a) by listening to somber music	(a) 침울한 음악을 들음으로써
(b) by studying the movie's characters	**(b) 영화의 등장인물들을 연구함으로써**
(c) by recording various sounds	(c) 다양한 소리를 녹음함으로써
(d) by looking at the faces of the actors	(d) 배우들의 얼굴을 살펴봄으로써

○ **지텔프 치트키**

질문의 키워드 inspired가 inspiration으로 언급된 주변 내용을 주의 깊게 듣는다.

해설ㅣ 남자가 'I consider the characters in the story and draw inspiration from them.'이라며 이야기 속의 인물들을 고찰하고 그들로부터 영감을 얻는다고 했다. 따라서 (b)가 정답이다.

Paraphrasing
get inspired 영감을 얻다 → draw inspiration 영감을 얻는다
consider the characters in the story 이야기 속의 인물들을 고찰하다 → studying the movie's characters 영화의 등장인물들을 연구함

Why most likely did Johnny record some of his previous songs with electronic instruments?

(a) **because it was expensive to use real instruments**
(b) because the tools sounded better
(c) because the software was more professional
(d) because it was easier to perform live

Johnny는 왜 전자 악기를 사용하여 그의 이전 노래 몇 곡을 녹음했던 것 같은가?

(a) **실제 악기를 사용하는 것이 비쌌기 때문에**
(b) 그 도구들의 소리가 더 좋았기 때문에
(c) 소프트웨어가 더 전문적이었기 때문에
(d) 라이브로 연주하는 것이 더 쉬웠기 때문에

지텔프 치트키

질문의 키워드 electronic instruments가 digital tools and software로 paraphrasing되어 언급된 주변 내용을 주의 깊게 듣는다.

해설 | 남자가 'In the past, on independent films that didn't have much money, I had to rely on digital tools and software for everything.'이라며 과거에 돈이 많지 않았던 독립 영화에서는 모든 것을 디지털 도구와 소프트웨어에 의존해야 했다고 한 것을 통해, 실제 악기를 사용하는 것이 비쌌기 때문에 전자 악기를 사용하여 그의 이전 노래 몇 곡을 녹음했던 것임을 추론할 수 있다. 따라서 (a)가 정답이다.

어휘 | electronic[ilèktrá:nik] 전자의 perform[pərfɔ́:rm] 연주하다

When does Johnny discuss a song with a film's director?

(a) when he finishes recording
(b) when he signs a contract
(c) **before he starts recording**
(d) before he finalizes his pitch

Johnny는 언제 영화의 감독과 음악에 관해 논의하는가?

(a) 녹음을 끝낼 때
(b) 계약을 맺을 때
(c) **녹음을 시작하기 전에**
(d) 그의 가락을 완성하기 전에

지텔프 치트키

질문의 키워드 discuss가 have ~ discussions로 paraphrasing되어 언급된 주변 내용을 주의 깊게 듣는다.

해설 | 남자가 'I need to have some crucial discussions with the director before recording can begin'이라며 녹음이 시작될 수 있기 전에 감독과 몇몇 중요한 논의를 해야 한다고 했다. 따라서 (c)가 정답이다.

Paraphrasing
before recording can begin 녹음이 시작될 수 있기 전에 → before he starts recording 녹음을 시작하기 전에

어휘 | contract[ká:ntrækt] 계약(서)

How does Johnny start composing a song?

(a) He thinks of the lyrics.
(b) **He comes up with the tune.**
(c) He talks to the producers.
(d) He selects excerpts from films.

Johnny는 어떻게 노래를 작곡하는 것을 시작하는가?

(a) 가사를 생각해 낸다.
(b) **선율을 떠올린다.**
(c) 제작자들과 이야기를 나눈다.
(d) 영화에서 발췌본을 선정한다.

해설 | 여자가 'Will you write the lyrics first, or do you typically start with the music?'이라며 가사를 먼저 쓸 것인지 아니면 보통 곡부터 시작하는지를 묻자, 남자가 'I begin with a melody'라며 멜로디부터 시작한다고 했다. 따라서 (b)가 정답이다.

Paraphrasing

start 시작하다 → begin 시작한다
a melody 멜로디 → the tune 선율

33	추론	다음에 할 일	난이도 ●●○

Based on the conversation, what will Cathy probably do next?	대화에 따르면, Cathy는 다음에 무엇을 할 것 같은가?
(a) She'll listen to music samples.	**(a) 견본 음악을 들을 것이다.**
(b) She'll watch a movie preview.	(b) 영화 예고편을 볼 것이다.
(c) She'll go to a recording studio.	(c) 녹음실에 갈 것이다.
(d) She'll meet with a songwriter.	(d) 작곡가를 만날 것이다.

해설 | 남자가 'I ~ prepared some samples of the beat that you can listen to.'라며 여자가 들어볼 수 있는 견본 비트를 몇 개 준비했다고 하자, 여자가 'It would be great to hear what you've made.'라며 남자가 만든 것을 들어보면 정말 좋을 것 같다고 한 것을 통해, Cathy가 Johnny가 만든 견본 음악을 들을 것임을 추론할 수 있다. 따라서 (a)가 정답이다.

Paraphrasing

samples of the beat 견본 비트 → music samples 견본 음악

PART 2 (34~39) 발표 새로운 사진 공유 애플리케이션 홍보

음성 바로 듣기

인사 + 앱 개발 배경	Good morning, everyone! Summertime is quickly approaching and so are our summer holidays. Many of us will be going on adventures and creating memories that we'll want to document. As a result, we will all be taking many pictures of exciting times with family and friends. But how can we share those photographs with others online?	좋은 아침입니다, 여러분! 여름철이 빠르게 다가오고 있으며 우리의 여름 연휴도 마찬가지입니다. 우리들 중 다수는 모험을 떠나고 기록하고 싶은 추억들을 만들 것입니다. 결과적으로, 우리는 모두 가족 및 친구들과 보내는 신나는 시간의 사진들을 많이 찍을 것입니다. 하지만 우리는 어떻게 그 사진들을 온라인상에서 다른 사람들과 공유할 수 있을까요?
주제 제시: 앱 출시	[34]With Nando Technology's new LibrePixel photo-sharing platform, you can easily manage your photos online no matter what device you take them with. Whether you use your phone, tablet, or any other device, getting your photos online and organized into easily	[34]Nando Technology 사의 새로운 LibrePixel 사진 공유 플랫폼을 사용하면, 여러분이 어떤 기기로 사진들을 찍든 그것들을 온라인상에서 쉽게 관리하실 수 있습니다. 여러분이 휴대전화, 태블릿, 혹은 다른 어느 기기를 사용하든, LibrePixel을 사용하면 사진들을 온

sharable albums is simple with LibrePixel!

The best thing about LibrePixel is that there is no limit to what kind of images you can share with the world. You are free to upload your photographs regardless of the file format that your device uses. Additionally, [35]LibrePixel displays your high-definition pictures without altering them with harsh compression algorithms. You will never have to use third-party conversion software before posting your pictures on our app, and [35]they'll always look exactly the same as they did when you first took them.

However, we know that some of your photographs could use a little improvement after you take them. That's why LibrePixel provides an easy-to-use photo editor with a huge selection of filters. Our team believes that everyone deserves to have high-quality photographs of all the important events in their lives. From simple corrections like red-eye reduction, color filtering, and collage creation to applying fun stickers, LibrePixel will let you add the perfect touch to your most cherished memories.

No photo-sharing service would be complete without a way to communicate with other users. Therefore, LibrePixel supports direct messaging. Our messaging function is totally encrypted, so nobody can peek at your conversations. The LibrePixel messenger also includes [36]a full emoji keyboard for those times when words can't capture how you feel.

The LibrePixel developers are committed to providing an open-source platform. This means that anyone can see how our app works. So, you can be certain that there is no unethical behavior behind the scenes. [37]Remaining open-source also encourages us to stay innovative. Anyone creative can improve our application by copying it, modifying it, and suggesting that their changes be included in the next update!

In addition, LibrePixel is, and always will be, an ad-free application. LibrePixel will never subject you to annoying advertisements. Removing unwanted and intrusive marketing [38(d)]saves memory on your computer and [38(a)]allows you to have a faster experience. With LibrePixel, [38(c)]you can edit and share your photos without being interrupted by requests to purchase products that you don't want.

라인으로 가져와 쉽게 공유할 수 있는 앨범에 정리하는 것이 간단합니다!

LibrePixel의 가장 좋은 점은 여러분이 세상과 공유할 수 있는 사진의 종류에 제한이 없다는 것입니다. 여러분의 기기가 사용하는 파일의 형식과 관계없이 사진을 자유롭게 업로드하실 수 있습니다. 게다가, [35]LibrePixel은 지나친 압축 알고리즘으로 여러분의 고화질 사진들을 왜곡하지 않고 그것들을 보여줍니다. 여러분은 사진들을 저희 앱에 게시하기 전에 제3의 변환 소프트웨어를 사용할 필요가 결코 없을 것이며, [35]그것들은 언제나 여러분이 처음 촬영했을 때와 다름없이 똑같이 보일 겁니다.

그러나, 여러분의 몇몇 사진들은 촬영 후에 약간의 개선이 필요할 수 있다는 것을 압니다. 그것이 바로 LibrePixel이 사용하기 쉬운 사진 편집기를 선택의 폭이 넓은 필터와 함께 제공하는 이유입니다. 저희 팀은 모든 사람들이 그들의 삶에서 모든 중요한 사건들의 고품질 사진들을 가질 자격이 있다고 생각합니다. 적목 현상 감소, 색깔 필터링, 그리고 콜라주 생성과 같은 간단한 수정에서부터 재미있는 스티커를 적용하는 것까지, LibrePixel은 여러분이 가장 소중히 여기는 기억들에 완벽한 마무리를 더하게 해 줄 것입니다.

다른 이용자들과 소통하는 방법 없이는 그 어떤 사진 공유 서비스도 완벽하지 않을 것입니다. 따라서, LibrePixel은 다이렉트 메시징을 지원합니다. 저희의 메시지 기능은 완전히 암호화되어 있어서, 아무도 여러분의 대화를 엿볼 수 없습니다. LibrePixel 메신저는 또한 [36]말로는 여러분의 기분을 담아낼 수 없을 때를 위해 풍부한 이모티콘 자판을 포함합니다.

LibrePixel 개발자들은 개방형 소스 플랫폼을 제공하는 데 전념하고 있습니다. 이것은 누구나 저희 앱이 어떻게 작동하는지를 볼 수 있다는 것을 의미합니다. 따라서, 여러분은 그 이면에 어떤 비윤리적인 행위도 없다는 것을 확신하실 수 있습니다. [37]개방형 소스로 남아있는 것은 또한 저희가 혁신을 유지할 수 있도록 장려합니다. 창의적인 사람이라면 누구나 그것(애플리케이션)을 복사하고, 수정하고, 그들의 변경 사항이 다음 업데이트에 포함될 것을 제안함으로써 저희 애플리케이션을 개선할 수 있습니다!

게다가, LibrePixel은 광고 없는 애플리케이션이고, 앞으로도 계속 그럴 것입니다. LibrePixel은 절대 여러분이 성가신 광고를 겪게 하지 않을 것입니다. 불필요하고 거슬리는 마케팅을 제거하는 것은 [38(d)]여러분 컴퓨터의 메모리를 절약하고 [38(a)]여러분이 더 빠른 경험을 하도록 할 것입니다. LibrePixel을 사용하면, 여러분은 원하지 않는 제품을 구매하라는 요청에 의해 [38(c)]방해받지 않고 사진을 편집하고 공유하실 수 있습니다.

<table>
<tr><td>3단계
구독</td><td>LibrePixel subscriptions will be available in three tiers. With the basic subscription, users can share up to 200 photos free of charge and use the basic editing features and stickers. For $5 per month, [39]users can upgrade to the Power-level subscription, which adds more advanced editing features and a 1,000-photograph limit. For those who want it all, the Pro-level subscription gives access to all of our services and unlimited photo posting, for only $10 per month.</td><td>LibrePixel 구독은 3가지 단계로 이용 가능할 것입니다. 기본 구독을 사용하면, 이용자들은 최대 200장의 사진을 무료로 공유하고 기본적인 편집 기능과 스티커를 사용할 수 있습니다. 월 5달러로, [39]이용자들은 파워 단계 구독으로 업그레이드할 수 있는데, 이것은 더 고급의 편집 기능과 1,000장의 사진 제한을 추가합니다. 이 모든 것을 원하는 분들을 위해, 프로 단계 구독은 단지 월 10달러에 당사의 모든 서비스와 무제한 사진 게시 기능을 이용할 수 있는 기회를 제공합니다.</td></tr>
<tr><td>끝인사</td><td>We want to welcome as many of you as possible to the LibrePixel family. For this reason, everyone who creates a LibrePixel account within the next 30 days will receive a one-month Pro-level subscription at no charge! Sign up today and start posting your pictures right away!</td><td>저희는 가능한 한 많은 여러분을 LibrePixel의 가족으로 맞이하고 싶습니다. 이런 이유로, 향후 30일 이내에 LibrePixel 계정을 만드시는 모든 분들은 무료로 1개월의 프로 단계 구독을 받으실 것입니다! 오늘 가입하시고 곧바로 사진을 게시하기 시작해보세요!</td></tr>
</table>

어휘 | document[dá:kjəmənt] 기록하다 organize[ɔ́:rgənaiz] 정리하다 high-definition 고화질의 compression[kəmpréʃən] 압축 conversion[kənvə́:rʒən] 변환 selection[səlékʃən] 선택 correction[kərékʃən] 수정 apply[əplái] 적용하다 touch[tʌtʃ] 마무리 cherish[tʃériʃ] 소중히 여기다 direct messaging 다이렉트 메시징(사람들끼리 비공개 메시지를 주고받는 행위) encrypt[inkrípt] 암호화하다 peek[pi:k] 엿보다 capture[kǽptʃər] 담아내다, 사로잡다 unethical[ʌnéθikəl] 비윤리적인 innovative[ínəvèitiv] 혁신적인 subject[sʌ́bdʒikt] 겪게 하다 intrusive[intrú:siv] 거슬리는 subscription[səbskrípʃən] 구독 tier[tir] 단계

---

34 주제/제목   담화의 주제   난이도 ●●○

What topic is the speaker mainly discussing?	화자가 주로 논하고 있는 주제는 무엇인가?
(a) a way to develop an application (b) a summer photo-sharing contest (c) **a new tool for managing pictures** (d) a simple market research strategy	(a) 애플리케이션을 개발하는 방법 (b) 여름 사진 공유 대회 (c) **사진들을 관리하는 새로운 도구** (d) 간단한 시장 조사 전략

➤ 지텔프 치트키

담화의 주제를 언급하는 초반을 주의 깊게 듣고 전체 맥락을 파악한다.

해설 | 화자가 'With Nando Technology's new LibrePixel photo-sharing platform, you can easily manage your photos online no matter what device you take them with.'이라며 Nando Technology 사의 새로운 LibrePixel 사진 공유 플랫폼을 사용하면 어떤 기기로 사진들을 찍든 그것들을 온라인상에서 쉽게 관리할 수 있다고 한 뒤, 담화 전반에 걸쳐 사진들을 관리하는 새로운 도구인 LibrePixel에 관해 설명하는 내용이 이어지고 있다. 따라서 (c)가 정답이다.

---

35 추론   특정사실   난이도 ●●●

What will most likely happen when photographs are uploaded to LibrePixel?	사진들이 LibrePixel에 업로드될 때 무슨 일이 일어날 것 같은가?
(a) They are approved by professional photo editors.	(a) 전문 사진 편집자들에 의해 승인된다.

(b) **They are posted in their original forms.**
(c) They are converted to a specific file format.
(d) They are scanned by an advanced algorithm.

(b) 그것들의 원본 형태로 게시된다.
(c) 특정한 파일 형식으로 변환된다.
(d) 고급 알고리즘에 의해 검토된다.

질문의 키워드 photographs ~ uploaded가 posting ~ pictures로 언급된 주변 내용을 주의 깊게 듣는다.

해설 | 화자가 'LibrePixel displays your high-definition pictures without altering them with harsh compression algorithms'라
며 LibrePixel은 지나친 압축 알고리즘으로 고화질 사진들을 왜곡하지 않고 보여준다고 한 뒤, 'they'll always look exactly the same
as they did when you first took them'이라며 사진들은 언제나 처음 촬영했을 때와 다름없이 똑같이 보일 것이라고 한 것을 통해, 사
진들이 LibrePixel에 업로드될 때 원본 형태로 게시될 것임을 추론할 수 있다. 따라서 (b)가 정답이다.

어휘 | convert[kənvə́:rt] 변환하다   scan[skæn] 검토하다, 조사하다

36 특정세부사항   Why   난이도 ●●○

According to the talk, why is using emojis useful for online conversations?

(a) because they are easily encrypted
(b) because they make chats more fun
(c) **because they express ideas that words cannot**
(d) because they connect users that speak different languages

담화에 따르면, 이모티콘을 사용하는 것이 왜 온라인 대화에 유용한가?

(a) 쉽게 암호화되기 때문에
(b) 대화를 더 재미있게 만들기 때문에
(c) **말로 할 수 없는 생각들을 표현하기 때문에**
(d) 다른 언어를 사용하는 이용자들을 연결해 주기 때문에

질문의 키워드 emojis가 emoji로 언급된 주변 내용을 주의 깊게 듣는다.

해설 | 화자가 'a full emoji keyboard for those times when words can't capture how you feel'이라며 풍부한 이모티콘 자판은 말로
는 이용자의 기분을 담아낼 수 없을 때를 위한 것이라고 했다. 따라서 (c)가 정답이다.

Paraphrasing
capture how you feel 기분을 담아내다 → express ideas that words cannot 말로 할 수 없는 생각들을 표현한다

어휘 | connect[kənékt] 연결하다

37 특정세부사항   What   난이도 ●●○

What do LibrePixel programmers do to remain cutting-edge?

(a) They hire creative software designers.
(b) **They allow anyone to edit the application.**
(c) They include tools to get feedback from users.
(d) They modify the service regularly.

LibrePixel의 프로그래머들은 첨단성을 유지하기 위해 무엇을 하는가?

(a) 창의적인 소프트웨어 설계자들을 고용한다.
(b) **누구나 애플리케이션을 수정할 수 있도록 허용한다.**
(c) 이용자들로부터 피드백을 받는 수단들을 포함한다.
(d) 정기적으로 서비스를 수정한다.

해커스 지텔프 최신기출유형 실전문제집 7회 (Level 2)

━━○ 지텔프 치트키

질문의 키워드 cutting-edge가 innovative로 paraphrasing되어 언급된 주변 내용을 주의 깊게 듣는다.

해설 | 화자가 'Remaining open-source ~ encourages us to stay innovative.'라며 개방형 소스로 남아 있는 것은 LibrePixel이 혁신을 유지할 수 있도록 장려한다고 한 뒤, 'Anyone creative can improve our application by ~ modifying it, and suggesting that their changes be included in the next update!'라며 창의적인 사람이라면 누구나 애플리케이션을 수정하고 그들의 변경 사항이 다음 업데이트에 포함될 것을 제안함으로써 애플리케이션을 개선할 수 있다고 했다. 따라서 (b)가 정답이다.

Paraphrasing
remain cutting-edge 첨단성을 유지하다 → stay innovative 계속 혁신적이다
modifying 수정하는 → edit 수정하다

어휘 | regularly[régjələrli] 정기적으로

---

38 | Not/True   Not 문제   난이도 ●●○

Which is not a benefit of using an ad-free service?	다음 중 광고 없는 서비스를 사용하는 것의 이점이 아닌 것은 무엇인가?
(a) having an app run more quickly	(a) 앱이 더 빨리 작동하도록 하는 것
(b) offering a personalized marketing platform	**(b) 맞춤형 마케팅 플랫폼을 제공하는 것**
(c) providing an uninterrupted user experience	(c) 방해받지 않는 사용자 경험을 제공하는 것
(d) reducing the overall memory usage	(d) 전반적인 메모리 사용량을 줄이는 것

━━○ 지텔프 치트키

질문의 키워드 ad-free가 그대로 언급된 주변 내용을 주의 깊게 들으며 언급되는 것을 하나씩 소거한다.

해설 | (b)는 언급되지 않았으므로, (b)가 정답이다.

> 오답분석
> (a) 화자가 불필요하고 거슬리는 마케팅을 제거하는 것은 이용자가 더 빠른 경험을 하도록 할 것이라고 언급하였다.
> (c) 화자가 광고 없는 LibrePixel을 사용하면 방해받지 않고 사진을 편집하고 공유할 수 있다고 언급하였다.
> (d) 화자가 불필요하고 거슬리는 마케팅을 제거하는 것은 이용자 컴퓨터의 메모리를 절약한다고 언급하였다.

어휘 | personalized[pə́ːrsənəlaizd] 맞춤형의

---

39 | 특정세부사항   Who   난이도 ●●○

Who will choose a Power-level subscription?	누가 파워 단계 구독을 선택할 것인가?
(a) those who need a limited number of stickers	(a) 제한된 수의 스티커가 필요한 사람들
(b) those who need all of the photo editing tools	(b) 모든 사진 편집 도구가 필요한 사람들
(c) those who will upload up to 1,000 photos	**(c) 사진을 최대 1,000장까지 업로드할 사람들**
(d) those who will pay a $10 monthly subscription fee	(d) 매달 10달러의 구독료를 지불할 사람들

━━○ 지텔프 치트키

질문의 키워드 Power-level subscription이 그대로 언급된 주변 내용을 주의 깊게 듣는다.

해설 | 화자가 'users can upgrade to the Power-level subscription, which adds ~ a 1,000-photograph limit'이라며 이용자들은 파워 단계 구독으로 업그레이드할 수 있는데, 이것은 1,000장의 사진 제한을 추가한다고 했다. 따라서 (c)가 정답이다.

Paraphrasing

a 1,000-photograph limit 1,000장의 사진 제한 → up to 1,000 photos 최대 1,000장의 사진

PART 3 (40~45) 장단점 논의 카페인 섭취의 장단점 비교

음성 바로 듣기

안부 인사	M: Good morning, Carol. ⁴⁰Thanks for making coffee for me this morning. F: You're welcome, Paul. I know you can't start the day without your first cup.
주제 제시: 장단점 비교	M: Actually, I've been considering giving up coffee to reduce my caffeine intake, but it's hard to make a decision. I can't disregard its benefits.
장점1: 심장 강화	F: What are the benefits? I don't know a lot about coffee. M: Well, studies have shown that drinking three to five caffeinated beverages daily can decrease the risk of heart failure. F: Oh, I think I remember reading about that. People who drank coffee every day were less likely to suffer from heart disease than those who didn't, right? M: That's correct. Researchers think that ⁴¹caffeine improves blood flow, which contributes to a stronger heart!
장점2: 체중 감량 촉진	F: That reminds me . . . ⁴²Doesn't caffeine also promote weight loss? M: I was just going to mention that! ⁴²Our body's ability to exhaust energy increases for several hours after having a caffeinated drink. F: Those are significant advantages. I can see why you'd be worried about giving up your daily coffee.
장점3: 각성 효과	M: Yes, but that's not all. Caffeine also has a stimulating effect on the central nervous system. As a result, drinking coffee can increase alertness and productivity. F: Oh, I guess that's the reason you feel more energetic after you have your coffee. It all sounds really good for you. Why would you be considering giving it up?
	M: Well . . . There are some downsides. For one, coffee can interfere with sleep. Evidence suggests that there is a connection between the intake of stimulants like caffeine and diminished sleep quality.

남: 좋은 아침이야, Carol. ⁴⁰오늘 아침에 나를 위해 커피를 만들어 줘서 고마워.

여: 천만에, Paul. 난 당신이 첫 잔 없이는 하루를 시작할 수 없다는 걸 알아.

남: 사실, 카페인 섭취를 줄이기 위해 커피를 끊는 것을 고려해 왔지만, 결정을 내리기가 어려워. 나는 그것의 이점을 무시할 수가 없어.

여: 이점이 뭔데? 난 커피에 대해 많이 알지는 않아.

남: 음, 연구들은 매일 카페인이 든 음료를 3잔에서 5잔을 마시는 것이 심장 기능 상실의 위험을 줄일 수 있다는 것을 나타내 왔어.

여: 오, 그것에 대해 읽은 기억이 나는 것 같아. 매일 커피를 마신 사람들은 그러지 않은 사람들보다 심장병을 앓을 가능성이 더 작았어, 그렇지?

남: 맞아. 연구원들은 ⁴¹카페인이 혈류를 개선하는데, 이것이 더 강한 심장에 기여한다고 생각해!

여: 그러고 보니 생각나네... ⁴²카페인이 체중 감량도 촉진하지 않아?

남: 내가 막 그 말을 하려던 참이었어! ⁴²카페인이 든 음료를 마신 후 몇 시간 동안 우리 몸의 에너지를 소모시키는 능력이 향상돼.

여: 그것들은 중요한 장점이네. 당신이 왜 매일 마시는 커피를 끊는 것에 대해 걱정하는지 알겠어.

남: 응, 근데 그게 다가 아니야. 카페인은 또한 중추 신경계에 각성 효과를 일으켜. 결과적으로, 커피를 마시는 것은 주의력과 생산성을 높일 수 있어.

여: 오, 그게 커피를 마시고 나면 당신이 더욱 활기를 느끼는 이유인 것 같네. 모든 게 당신한테 정말 유익한 것 같아. 왜 당신은 그걸 끊는 것을 고려하고 있는 거야?

남: 음... 몇 가지 단점이 있어. 우선, 커피는 수면을 방해할 수 있어. 증거 자료는 카페인과 같은 각성제의 섭취와 저하된 수면의 질 사이에 연관성이 있다는 것을 시사해.

TEST 1 TEST 2 TEST 3 TEST 4 **TEST 5** TEST 6 TEST 7

해커스 지텔프 최신기출유형 실전문제집 7회 (Level 2)

TEST 5 LISTENING 235

<table>
<tr>
<td>단점1:
수면
방해</td>
<td>

F: That is why [43]I don't drink coffee. It affects my sleep cycles, and I wake up more often when I do have coffee. That makes it harder to get enough rest.

M: Exactly. We shouldn't underestimate the importance of getting plenty of quality sleep. To make matters worse, drinking too much coffee can result in a caffeine addiction.
</td>
<td>

여: 그것이 [43]내가 커피를 마시지 않는 이유야. 그것은 나의 수면 주기에 영향을 미치고, 나는 커피를 마실 때 더 자주 잠에서 깨. 그것은 충분한 휴식을 취하는 것을 더 어렵게 만들어.

남: 바로 그거야. 우리는 충분한 양질의 수면을 취하는 것의 중요성을 과소평가해서는 안 돼. 설상가상으로, 커피를 너무 많이 마시는 것은 카페인 중독을 야기할 수 있어.
</td>
</tr>
<tr>
<td>단점2:
카페인
중독</td>
<td>

F: You mean your body will become dependent upon it the same way some people are addicted to alcohol and nicotine?

M: Yes. And like those others, [44]trying to get off caffeine can bring about symptoms of withdrawal, such as headache, fatigue, and depression. This makes it very hard to give it up.

F: Oh, my. It sounds like even though the caffeine in coffee can have a stimulating effect, it results in the opposite if you develop an unhealthy habit.
</td>
<td>

여: 당신 말은 알코올과 니코틴에 중독된 몇몇 사람들과 같은 방식으로 당신의 몸이 그것(카페인)에 의존하게 될 것이라는 뜻이야?

남: 맞아. 그리고 그런 다른 사람들처럼, [44]카페인을 끊으려고 하는 것은 두통, 피로, 그리고 우울증과 같은 금단 증상을 초래할 수 있어. 이것이 그것을 끊는 것을 몹시 어렵게 만들지.

여: 오, 이런. 비록 커피에 들어 있는 카페인이 각성 효과를 낼 수 있을지라도, 만약 당신이 건강하지 않은 습관을 형성하면 그 반대의 결과를 초래하는 것 같아.
</td>
</tr>
<tr>
<td>단점3:
혈압
상승</td>
<td>

M: Yes, but that's not the worst of it. Consuming too much caffeine can cause some health problems, specifically, high blood pressure and an increased heart rate.

F: I thought you said it was good for your heart. How can it be both good and bad?

M: It's all about how much you drink. Like most things in life, it's good in moderation, but overindulgence can lead to some problems.

F: Maybe that's something you should worry about then. When we went to the clinic for checkups before we left for our honeymoon, the doctor said your blood pressure was higher than normal. She suggested that we monitor it regularly.

M: I know. That was something that I've been thinking about. I should probably do everything I can to keep my blood pressure in check, including cutting out anything that will increase it.

F: I have to say that there's more to think about coffee than I initially realized. It makes sense that you're uncertain about quitting coffee.
</td>
<td>

남: 맞아, 하지만 그게 가장 나쁜 점이 아니야. 지나치게 많은 카페인을 섭취하는 것은 몇몇 건강 문제들, 특히, 고혈압과 증가된 심장 박동수를 야기할 수 있어.

여: 당신은 그게 심장에 좋다고 말한 줄 알았는데. 어떻게 그것이 좋기도 하고 나쁘기도 할 수 있지?

남: 얼마나 많이 마시는지가 중요해. 삶의 대부분의 것들과 마찬가지로, 적당한 건 좋지만, 과다 섭취는 몇 가지 문제들로 이어질 수 있어.

여: 그러면 아마도 그게 당신이 고민해야 할 점인 것 같네. 우리가 신혼여행을 떠나기 전에 건강 검진을 위해 병원에 갔을 때, 의사가 당신의 혈압이 평균보다 높다고 했잖아. 그녀는 우리가 그것을 정기적으로 검사할 것을 제안했어.

남: 알아. 그건 내가 생각해왔던 거였어. 난 그것을 증가시키는 것이라면 무엇이든지 그만두는 것을 포함해서, 혈압을 억제하기 위해 아마 내가 할 수 있는 모든 것을 해야 할 거야.

여: 정말이지 내가 처음에 인식했던 것보다 커피에 대해 생각해 볼 것들이 더 많네. 왜 당신이 커피를 끊는 것에 대해 갈피를 못 잡는지 이해가 돼.
</td>
</tr>
<tr>
<td>남자의
결정</td>
<td>

M: Absolutely. But this has been a really helpful conversation, Carol.

F: I'm glad I could help, Paul. Well, [45]have you arrived at a decision?

M: Yes, [45]I'll just try to drink less. Oh! Before I forget, I think we're all out of coffee beans now. Could you pick some up for me at the grocery store this afternoon? I want to finish mowing the lawn before sunset.
</td>
<td>

남: 물론이지. 하지만 이건 정말 도움이 되는 대화였어, Carol.

여: 내가 도움이 될 수 있어서 기뻐, Paul. 자, [45]결정을 내렸어?

남: 응, [45]나는 그냥 덜 마시도록 노력해 볼게. 오! 잊어버리기 전에, 이제 커피 원두가 다 떨어진 것 같아. 오늘 오후에 날 위해 식료품점에서 조금 사다 줄 수 있어? 난 해가 지기 전에 잔디를 깎는 것을 끝내고 싶어.
</td>
</tr>
</table>

어휘 | intake[ínteik] 섭취 disregard[dìsrigɑ́:rd] 무시하다 metabolism[mətǽbəlizəm] 신진대사 stimulating[stímjəleitiŋ] 각성하는, 자극하는 central nervous system 중추 신경계 interfere[ìntərfír] 방해하다 evidence[évídəns] 증거 (자료) stimulant[stímjələnt] 각성제 diminish[dəmíniʃ] 저하시키다 underestimate[ʌndəréstimeit] 과소평가하다 addiction[ədíkʃən] 중독 dependent[dipéndənt] 의존하는 withdrawal[wiðdrɔ́:əl] 금단 fatigue[fətí:g] 피로 depression[dipréʃən] 우울증 moderation[mɑ̀:dəréiʃən] 적당한 것 overindulgence[òuvərindʌ́ldʒəns] 과다 섭취 keep in check 억제하다, 방지하다

40 특정세부사항 What
난이도 ●○○

What did Carol do for Paul this morning?

(a) She bought a new coffee maker.
(b) She made a healthy meal.
(c) She prepared a caffeinated beverage.
(d) She washed a coffee cup.

Carol은 오늘 아침에 Paul을 위해 무엇을 했는가?

(a) 새로운 커피 기계를 샀다.
(b) 건강한 음식을 만들었다.
(c) 카페인이 든 음료를 준비했다.
(d) 커피잔을 씻었다.

━○ 지텔프 치트키

질문의 키워드 this morning이 그대로 언급된 주변 내용을 주의 깊게 듣는다.

해설 | 남자가 'Thanks for making coffee for me this morning.'이라며 여자에게 오늘 아침에 그를 위해 커피를 만들어 줘서 고맙다고 했다. 따라서 (c)가 정답이다.

Paraphrasing
making coffee 커피를 만들어 주는 → prepared a caffeinated beverage 카페인이 든 음료를 준비했다

41 추론 특정사실
난이도 ●●●

How most likely does consuming caffeine lower the risk of heart failure?

(a) It enhances blood circulation.
(b) It improves muscle strength.
(c) It reinforces the immune system.
(d) It eliminates a disease symptom.

카페인을 섭취하는 것이 어떻게 심장 기능 상실의 위험을 낮추는 것 같은가?

(a) 혈액 순환을 향상시킨다.
(b) 근력을 향상시킨다.
(c) 면역 체계를 강화한다.
(d) 질병의 증상을 없앤다.

━○ 지텔프 치트키

질문의 키워드 heart failure가 그대로 언급된 주변 내용을 주의 깊게 듣는다.

해설 | 남자가 'caffeine improves blood flow, which contributes to a stronger heart'라며 카페인은 혈류를 개선하는데, 이것이 더 강한 심장에 기여한다고 한 것을 통해, 카페인을 섭취하는 것이 혈액 순환을 향상시켜서 심장 기능 상실의 위험을 낮추는 것임을 추론할 수 있다. 따라서 (a)가 정답이다.

어휘 | circulation[sə̀:rkjəléiʃən] 순환 immune[imjú:n] 면역의 reinforce[rì:ənfɔ́:rs] 강화하다 eliminate[ilímineit] 없애다, 제거하다

How does caffeine increase the likelihood of losing weight?

(a) by decreasing the amount of sleep needed
(b) by improving the ability to burn calories briefly
(c) by providing extra energy for exercise
(d) by reducing feelings of tiredness

카페인은 어떻게 체중을 감량하는 것의 가능성을 증가시키는가?

(a) 필요한 수면의 양을 줄임으로써
(b) 칼로리를 연소시키는 능력을 잠시 향상시킴으로써
(c) 운동을 위한 추가적인 에너지를 제공함으로써
(d) 피로감을 줄임으로써

─○ 지텔프 치트키

질문의 키워드 losing weight가 weight loss로 paraphrasing되어 언급된 주변 내용을 주의 깊게 듣는다.

해설 | 여자가 'Doesn't caffeine ~ promote weight loss?'라며 카페인이 체중 감량을 촉진하지 않는지를 묻자, 남자가 'Our body's ability to exhaust energy increases for several hours after having a caffeinated drink.'라며 카페인이 든 음료를 마신 후 몇 시간 동안 몸의 에너지를 소모시키는 능력이 향상된다고 했다. 따라서 (b)가 정답이다.

Paraphrasing
Our body's ability to exhaust energy increases for several hours 몇 시간 동안 몸의 에너지를 소모시키는 능력이 향상된다 → improving the ability to burn calories briefly 칼로리를 연소시키는 능력을 잠시 향상시킴

어휘 | briefly[bríːfli] 잠시

Why does Carol avoid drinking coffee?

(a) It decreases appetite.
(b) It results in nervousness.
(c) It leads to extreme diet changes.
(d) It alters sleep patterns.

Carol은 왜 커피를 마시는 것을 피하는가?

(a) 식욕을 감소시킨다.
(b) 초조감을 야기한다.
(c) 지나친 식단 변화를 초래한다.
(d) 수면 패턴을 바꾼다.

─○ 지텔프 치트키

질문의 키워드 avoid drinking이 don't drink로 paraphrasing되어 언급된 주변 내용을 주의 깊게 듣는다.

해설 | 여자가 'I don't drink coffee'라며 커피를 마시지 않는다고 한 뒤, 'It affects my sleep cycles, and I wake up more often when I do have coffee.'라며 커피가 여자의 수면 주기에 영향을 미치고 커피를 마실 때 더 자주 잠에서 깬다고 했다. 따라서 (d)가 정답이다.

Paraphrasing
affects my sleep cycles 수면 주기에 영향을 미친다 → alters sleep patterns 수면 패턴을 바꾼다

어휘 | appetite[ǽpətait] 식욕 alter[ɔ́ːltər] 바꾸다

Why is it difficult for people addicted to caffeine to stop consuming it?

(a) because they may experience negative health issues

왜 카페인에 중독된 사람들은 그것을 섭취하는 것을 멈추는 것이 어려운가?

(a) 좋지 않은 건강 문제들을 경험할 수 있기 때문에

(b) because they might develop unhealthy habits

(c) because they may turn to alcohol

(d) because they might worry about a productivity decline

(b) 건강하지 않은 습관을 형성할 수 있기 때문에

(c) 술에 의존할 수 있기 때문에

(d) 생산력 감소에 대해 걱정할 수 있기 때문에

━○ 지텔프 치트키

질문의 키워드 stop이 get off로 paraphrasing되어 언급된 주변 내용을 주의 깊게 듣는다.

해설 | 남자가 'trying to get off caffeine can bring about symptoms of withdrawal, such as headache, fatigue, and depression'이라며 카페인을 끊으려고 하는 것은 두통, 피로, 그리고 우울증과 같은 금단 증상을 초래할 수 있다고 한 뒤, 'This makes it very hard to give it up.'이라며 이것이 카페인을 끊는 것을 몹시 어렵게 만든다고 했다. 따라서 (a)가 정답이다.

Paraphrasing

symptoms of withdrawal 금단 증상 → negative health issues 좋지 않은 건강 문제들

어휘 | turn to ~에 의존하다

---

45 추론 　 다음에 할 일 　 난이도 ●●○

What has Paul probably decided to do after the conversation?

(a) **cut down on his caffeine consumption**

(b) drive to the grocery store

(c) place an order for coffee beans online

(d) postpone his plan to mow the lawn

Paul은 대화 후에 무엇을 하기로 결정한 것 같은가?

(a) 그의 카페인 섭취를 줄인다

(b) 운전해서 식료품점에 간다

(c) 온라인으로 커피 원두를 주문한다

(d) 잔디를 깎으려는 그의 계획을 연기한다

━○ 지텔프 치트키

다음에 할 일을 언급하는 후반을 주의 깊게 듣는다.

해설 | 여자가 'have you arrived at a decision?'이라며 결정을 내렸는지를 묻자, 남자가 'I'll ~ try to drink less'라며 커피를 덜 마시도록 노력해 보겠다고 한 것을 통해, Paul은 카페인 섭취를 줄일 것임을 추론할 수 있다. 따라서 (a)가 정답이다.

어휘 | postpone [pouspóun] 연기하다

PART 4 (46~52) 　 설명 　 초를 만드는 6단계의 과정

음성 바로 듣기

인사 + 주제 제시

Good day, everyone! Thank you for coming to today's class. We all like doing craft projects and making customized gifts for those in our lives. As you may have guessed from the materials prepared for you, ⁴⁶I am going to teach you how to make your own candles.

Step one is choosing the perfect container. ⁴⁷You can be creative with your choice as long as the vessel is heat-resistant. Most things made of glass and ceramic will work great, while plastics and synthetics should be

좋은 하루입니다, 여러분! 오늘 수업에 와 주셔서 감사합니다. 우리는 모두 공예 작업을 하는 것과 우리의 삶 속 사람들을 위한 맞춤형 선물을 만드는 것을 좋아합니다. 여러분들을 위해 준비된 재료들에서 짐작하셨겠지만, ⁴⁶제가 여러분만의 초를 만드는 방법을 가르쳐드릴 것입니다.

첫 번째 단계는 최적의 용기를 선택하는 것입니다. ⁴⁷용기가 내열성이기만 하면 여러분은 선택에 있어 창의적이셔도 됩니다. 유리와 도자기로 만들어진 대부분의 것들은 괜찮겠지만, 플라스틱과 합성 물질은 피

avoided. Some readily available options are fruit jars, small bowls, or old vases. This can be a fine way to recycle items that might be lying around the house. Just make sure to clean the container thoroughly if you're planning to reuse it.

For step two, figure out how much wax you will need. Now, [48]this step won't be the same for everyone because it depends on the size of the container you have chosen. The easiest way to determine the correct amount is to fill your vessel with water and then transfer it to a measuring cup. You should note the measurement accurately since it is important for the next step.

Step three requires you to weigh and melt the wax. Bring some water to a boil and verify that your scale is at zero. Weigh 30 grams of wax for every 30 milliliters of the container's volume. Place the wax in a glass pitcher and set it in the simmering water. Stir it occasionally until it is completely melted. At this point, you'll have a liquid that looks a bit like olive oil. [49]It will be very hot, so be careful! Leave the melted wax in a safe place while you perform the next step.

Step four involves attaching the wick, [50]which will allow the candle to burn. Add a drop of hot glue to the metal part of the wick and press it firmly to the bottom of the container. It is important to keep your wick straight and stable so that it doesn't fall when you pour in the wax. An easy way to achieve this is to pierce a small hole in a piece of tape, pull the wick through the hole, and secure the tape to the sides.

Step five is to add the fragrance. Select your favorite essential oil and mix some of it in with the melted wax, which should have cooled slightly. You will have to do a little experimentation to find the ratio that is perfect for you. A good starting point is approximately 1 milliliter of perfume per 15 grams of wax. Keep in mind that [51]the scent will be weaker when the wax is dry because the oils evaporate and give off their aroma when heated.

The final step is to pour the wax to form the candles. You must consider the temperature of the melted wax. As a general rule, it is best to keep it around 55 degrees Celsius. [52]Pour it into a vessel in a slow and controlled manner to avoid making air bubbles since they can harm the appearance of your candle. Let it cool for 24 hours at room temperature.

해야 합니다. 쉽게 구할 수 있는 몇 개의 선택지로는 유리 과일 병, 작은 그릇, 혹은 오래된 꽃병이 있습니다. 이는 집안에 아무렇게나 놓여 있을지도 모르는 물건들을 재활용하는 좋은 방법일 수 있습니다. 용기를 재사용할 계획이시라면 반드시 그것을 완벽히 닦아 주시기 바랍니다.

두 번째 단계에서, 밀랍이 얼마나 많이 필요할지 계산하십시오. 이제, [48]이 단계는 여러분이 선택한 용기의 크기에 달려 있기 때문에 모든 사람에게 같지는 않을 것입니다. 정확한 양을 측정하는 가장 쉬운 방법은 용기를 물로 채운 다음 그것을 계량컵으로 옮기는 것입니다. 그 측정값은 다음 단계에서 중요하기 때문에 여러분은 그것을 정확하게 기록해 두셔야 합니다.

세 번째 단계는 여러분이 밀랍의 무게를 재고 녹이는 것을 요구합니다. 물을 조금 끓이고 저울이 0에 맞춰졌는지 확인하십시오. 용기 용량의 30밀리리터당 30그램의 왁스를 저울에 다십시오. 그 밀랍을 유리병에 넣고 그것을 끓이고 있는 물에 담그십시오. 그것이 완전히 녹을 때까지 이따금 저어주십시오. 이 시점에, 여러분에게는 다소 올리브유처럼 보이는 액체가 있을 것입니다. [49]그것은 매우 뜨거울 것이니, 조심하십시오! 다음 단계를 수행하는 동안 녹은 밀랍을 안전한 곳에 두십시오.

네 번째 단계는 심지를 부착하는 것을 포함하는데, [50]이것은 초가 타도록 할 것입니다. 심지의 금속 부분에 뜨거운 접착제 한 방울을 떨어트리고 용기의 바닥에 그것을 단단히 밀착시키십시오. 여러분이 밀랍을 부을 때 심지가 넘어지지 않도록 그것을 곧고 안정적이게 유지하는 것이 중요합니다. 이것을 해내는 쉬운 방법은 테이프 한 조각에 작은 구멍을 뚫고, 그 구멍을 통해 심지를 빼낸 다음, 테이프를 양쪽에 고정하는 것입니다.

다섯 번째 단계는 향을 첨가하는 것입니다. 여러분이 가장 좋아하는 방향유를 선택하고 그것 조금을 녹은 밀랍과 섞으시면 되는데, 이것(녹은 밀랍)은 약간 식었을 것입니다. 여러분은 자신에게 완벽한 비율을 찾기 위해 작은 실험을 해야 할 것입니다. 좋은 출발점은 밀랍 15그램당 약 1밀리리터의 향수입니다. [51]가열되면 향유가 증발하면서 향을 내보내기 때문에 밀랍이 말랐을 때는 향이 더 약할 것이라는 점을 명심하십시오.

마지막 단계는 초를 틀에 따라 만들어 내기 위해 밀랍을 붓는 것입니다. 여러분은 녹은 밀랍의 온도를 고려하셔야 합니다. 일반적으로, 그것을 약 섭씨 55도로 유지하는 게 가장 좋습니다. [52]기포가 초의 외양을 해칠 수 있기 때문에 그것들이 생기는 것을 피하도록 용기에 밀랍을 천천히 그리고 조심스러운 방식으로 부으십시오. 실온에서 그것을 24시간 동안 식도록 두십시오.

| 끝인사 | This process might feel overwhelming the first time, but don't lose your motivation. Remember, a candle is nothing more than an ignitable string in a flammable solid. Now that you know the basics of candle making, let's try to make one together. | 이 과정이 처음에는 벅차게 느껴지실 수 있지만, 의욕을 잃지 마십시오. 기억하십시오, 초는 가연성 고체 속에 있는 발화 가능한 하나의 끈에 지나지 않습니다. 이제 여러분은 초 만들기의 기본을 아셨으니, 우리 함께 초를 만들어 봅시다. |

어휘 | container[kəntéinər] 용기, 그릇 heat-resistant 내열성의 synthetic[sinθétik] 합성 물질; 합성의 figure out 계산하다 wax[wæks] 밀랍 verify[vérifai] 확인하다 volume[vá:ljəm] 용량, 부피 simmer[símər] 끓다 occasionally[əkéiʒənəli] 이따금 attach[ətǽtʃ] 부착하다 wick[wik] 심지 firmly[fə́:rmli] 단단히 pierce[pirs] 뚫다 secure[sikjúr] 고정하다 fragrance[fréigrəns] 향 essential oil 방향유(방향성 약용 식물에서 추출하는 치유 효능을 가진 천연 식물성 오일) experimentation[ikspèrəmentéiʃən] 실험 evaporate[ivǽpəreit] 증발하다 give off 내보내다, 발하다 ignitable[ignáitəbəl] 발화 가능한 flammable[flǽməbəl] 가연성의

---

46 주제/목적 담화의 주제

난이도 ●○○

What is the talk all about?

(a) how to choose appropriate gifts
(b) a do-it-yourself project
(c) how to make aromas for candles
(d) a home décor store

담화의 주제는 무엇인가?

(a) 알맞은 선물을 고르는 방법
(b) 손수 만드는 활동
(c) 초를 위한 향을 만드는 방법
(d) 실내 장식 매장

지텔프 치트키

담화의 주제를 언급하는 초반을 주의 깊게 듣고 전체 맥락을 파악한다.

해설 | 화자가 'I am going to teach you how to make your own candles'라며 자신만의 초를 만드는 방법을 가르쳐줄 것이라고 한 뒤, 담화 전반에 걸쳐 초를 손수 만드는 방법에 관해 설명하는 내용이 이어지고 있다. 따라서 (b)가 정답이다.

Paraphrasing
make your own candles 자신만의 초를 만들다 → a do-it-yourself project 손수 만드는 활동

어휘 | appropriate[əpróupriət] 알맞은, 적절한

---

47 특정세부사항 What

난이도 ●●●

What is a typical characteristic of containers for candles?

(a) They can tolerate high temperatures.
(b) They are made of recycled materials.
(c) They can be cleaned very easily.
(d) They incorporate synthetic substances.

초를 위한 용기의 일반적인 특징은 무엇인가?

(a) 높은 온도를 견딜 수 있다.
(b) 재활용된 물질로 만들어졌다.
(c) 아주 쉽게 세척될 수 있다.
(d) 합성 물질을 포함한다.

지텔프 치트키

질문의 키워드 containers가 vessel로 paraphrasing되어 언급된 주변 내용을 주의 깊게 듣는다.

해설 | 화자가 'You can be creative with your choice as long as the vessel is heat-resistant.'라며 용기가 내열성이기만 하면 초를 위한 용기 선택에 있어 창의적이어도 된다고 했다. 따라서 (a)가 정답이다.

해커스 지텔프 최신기출유형 실전문제집 7회 (Level 2)

Paraphrasing

heat-resistant 내열성의 → tolerate high temperatures 높은 온도를 견디다

오답분석

(b) 화자가 집안에 아무렇게나 놓여 있을지도 모르는 물건들을 초를 위한 용기로 재활용할 수 있다고 언급하기는 했지만, 이것이 초를 위한 용기의 일반적인 특징은 아니므로 오답이다.

어휘 | tolerate[tάːləreit] 견디다 incorporate[inkɔ́ːrpəreit] 포함하다

---

48 특정세부사항   Which

난이도 ●●○

Which factor determines the amount of wax needed?	필요한 밀랍의 양을 결정하는 요소는 무엇인가?
(a) the type of container **(b) the volume of the vessel** (c) the transfer rate of the water (d) the size of the measuring cup	(a) 용기의 종류 **(b) 용기의 용량** (c) 물의 이동 속도 (d) 계량컵의 크기

지텔프 치트키

질문의 키워드 amount of wax가 how much wax로 paraphrasing되어 언급된 주변 내용을 주의 깊게 듣는다.

해설 | 화자가 'this step won't be the same for everyone because it depends on the size of the container you have chosen' 이라며 밀랍이 얼마나 많이 필요할지를 계산하는 단계는 각자가 선택한 용기의 크기에 달려 있기 때문에 모든 사람에게 같지는 않을 것이라고 했다. 따라서 (b)가 정답이다.

Paraphrasing

the size of the container 용기의 크기 → the volume of the vessel 용기의 용량

---

49 추론   특정사실

난이도 ●●●

According to the talk, why most likely should the melted wax be stored safely?	담화에 따르면, 왜 녹은 밀랍이 안전하게 보관되어야 하는 것 같은가?
(a) because its structure needs time to solidify (b) because it can cause a glass vessel to break **(c) because its temperature can be dangerous** (d) because it must simmer for a long time	(a) 그것의 형태가 굳어지는 데 시간이 필요하기 때문에 (b) 유리 용기를 깨지게 할 수 있기 때문에 **(c) 그것의 온도가 위험할 수 있기 때문에** (d) 오랫동안 끓어야 하기 때문에

지텔프 치트키

질문의 키워드 safely가 safe로 언급된 주변 내용을 주의 깊게 듣는다.

해설 | 화자가 'It will be very hot, so be careful!'이라며 다소 올리브유처럼 보이는 액체인 녹은 밀랍이 매우 뜨거울 것이니 조심하라고 한 뒤, 'Leave the melted wax in a safe place while you perform the next step.'이라며 다음 단계를 수행하는 동안 녹은 밀랍을 안전한 곳에 두라고 한 것을 통해, 녹은 밀랍의 온도가 위험할 수 있기 때문에 안전하게 보관되어야 하는 것임을 추론할 수 있다. 따라서 (c)가 정답이다.

Paraphrasing

be stored safely 안전하게 보관되다 → Leave ~ in a safe place 안전한 곳에 두다

50 특정세부사항   What

난이도 ●●○

What is hot glue used for when making a candle?

(a) melting the candle's wax
(b) fastening the burning element
(c) preventing the wick from falling into the wax
(d) securing the candle in the container

초를 만들 때 뜨거운 접착제는 무엇에 사용되는가?

(a) 초의 밀랍을 녹이는 것
(b) 불타는 물질을 고정하는 것
(c) 심지가 밀랍에 빠지는 것으로부터 막는 것
(d) 초를 용기에 고정하는 것

─○ 지텔프 치트키

질문의 키워드 hot glue가 그대로 언급된 주변 내용을 주의 깊게 듣는다.

해설 | 화자가 'which will allow the candle to burn'이라며 심지는 초가 타도록 할 것이라고 한 뒤, 'Add a drop of hot glue to the metal part of the wick and press it firmly to the bottom of the container.'라며 심지의 금속 부분에 뜨거운 접착제 한 방울을 떨어트리고 용기의 바닥에 심지를 단단히 밀착시키라고 했다. 따라서 (b)가 정답이다.

Paraphrasing
the wick 심지 → the burning element 불타는 물질
press 밀착시키다 → fasten 고정하다

어휘 | fasten[fǽsən] 고정하다

51 특정세부사항   Why

난이도 ●●○

Why is there a change in scent after candle wax dries?

(a) because the fragrance is emitted by heated oil
(b) because the ratio of fragrance has changed
(c) because the temperature of the fragrance has cooled
(d) because the fragrance is mixed with the wax

왜 초 밀랍이 마른 후에 향에 변화가 있는가?

(a) 향이 가열된 오일에 의해 방출되기 때문에
(b) 향의 비율이 변했기 때문에
(c) 향의 온도가 내려갔기 때문에
(d) 향이 밀랍과 섞이기 때문에

─○ 지텔프 치트키

질문의 키워드 scent가 그대로 언급된 주변 내용을 주의 깊게 듣는다.

해설 | 화자가 'the scent will be weaker when the wax is dry because the oils ~ give off their aroma when heated'라며 향유가 가열되면 증발하면서 향을 내보내기 때문에 밀랍이 말랐을 때는 향이 더 약할 것이라고 했다. 따라서 (a)가 정답이다.

Paraphrasing
after candle wax dries 초 밀랍이 마른 후에 → when the wax is dry 밀랍이 말랐을 때
give off their aroma 향을 내보내다 → the fragrance is emitted 향이 방출된다

어휘 | emit[imít] 방출하다

해커스 지텔프 최신기출유형 실전문제집 7회 (Level 2)

When can the look of the candle be damaged?

(a) when it is cooled to room temperature
(b) when its temperature is over 55 degrees
(c) when it is dried in a slow manner
(d) when its vessel is filled too quickly

언제 초의 생김새가 손상될 수 있는가?

(a) 상온으로 식혀질 때
(b) 그것의 온도가 55도 이상일 때
(c) 천천히 말려질 때
(d) 그것의 용기가 너무 빨리 채워질 때

━━○ **지텔프 치트키**

질문의 키워드 look이 appearance로 paraphrasing되어 언급된 주변 내용을 주의 깊게 듣는다.

해설 ┃ 화자가 'Pour it into a vessel in a slow ~ manner to avoid making air bubbles since they can harm the appearance of your candle.'이라며 기포가 초의 외양을 해칠 수 있기 때문에 그것들이 생기는 것을 피하도록 용기에 밀랍을 천천히 부으라고 했다. 따라서 (d)가 정답이다.

Paraphrasing
the look of the candle be damaged 초의 생김새가 손상되는 → harm the appearance of your candle 초의 외양을 해치다

어휘 ┃ damage[dǽmidʒ] 손상시키다

READING & VOCABULARY

인물 이름	**AKON**	**에이콘**

인물
소개

Akon is a Senegalese-American singer, record producer, and entrepreneur known for combining his R&B-style vocals with hip-hop beats. He is the first solo artist to ever achieve the number one and number two spots simultaneously on the *Billboard* Hot 100.

에이콘은 그의 R&B 스타일 보컬과 힙합 비트를 결합한 것으로 알려져 있는 세네갈계 미국인 가수이자, 음반 제작자이자, 기업가이다. 그는 빌보드 핫 100에서 1위와 2위 자리를 동시에 달성한 최초의 솔로 아티스트이다.

어린
시절

Akon was born on April 16, 1973, in St. Louis, Missouri. [53]His father [58]Mor Thiam is a <u>celebrated</u> drummer, and his mother Kine Gueye Thiam is a dancer. Growing up in this environment, Akon was exposed to music from an early age. He learned to play five instruments including the guitar and the djembe, a traditional drum from West Africa. He lived in Dakar, Senegal until he was seven years old when his family returned to the US. There he heard hip-hop for the first time.

에이콘은 1973년 4월 16일에 미주리주의 세인트루이스에서 태어났다. [53]그의 아버지 [58]모르 티암은 <u>유명한</u> 드럼 연주자이고, 어머니 키네 게에 티암은 무용수이다. 이러한 환경에서 자라면서, 에이콘은 어린 나이부터 음악에 노출되었다. 그는 기타와 서아프리카의 전통 드럼인 젬베를 포함하여 5개의 악기를 연주하는 법을 배웠다. 그는 그의 가족이 미국으로 돌아온 7살까지 세네갈 다카르에서 살았다. 그곳(미국)에서 그는 처음으로 힙합을 들었다.

업적
시작
계기

As a young man, Akon became involved in car theft and faced legal issues. [54]While he was in jail, however, Akon rediscovered his interest in music and used the time to explore ideas for songs. Upon his release, he started recording tracks at home, and not long after, one of them was introduced to Devyne Stephens, the president of the record label Upfront Megatainment.

젊은 시절에, 에이콘은 자동차 절도 사건에 연루되었고 법적인 문제에 직면했다. [54]그러나, 감옥에 있는 동안, 에이콘은 음악에 대한 그의 흥미를 다시 발견했고 그 시간을 노래에 관한 아이디어를 탐구하는 데 사용했다. 출소하자마자, 그는 집에서 곡들을 녹음하기 시작했고, 얼마 지나지 않아, 그것들 중 하나가 업프런트 메가테인먼트 음반사의 대표인 데빈 스티븐스에게 전해졌다.

초기
활동

Stephens became Akon's friend and mentor, and Akon began producing songs at Stephens' studio. [55]His demo tape fell into the hands of an executive at SRC Records, and Akon was signed on as an artist shortly thereafter. *Trouble*, Akon's debut album, came out in 2004. It contained the lead single "Locked Up," which reached number 8 on the *Billboard* Hot 100. The album also featured "Lonely," which [59]became a worldwide <u>sensation</u> partially because it sampled Bobby Vinton's 1964 song "Mr. Lonely."

스티븐스는 에이콘의 친구이자 멘토가 되었고, 에이콘은 스티븐스의 작업실에서 곡을 제작하기 시작했다. [55]그의 데모 테이프는 SRC 레코드 사의 한 임원의 손에 넘어갔고, 에이콘은 그로부터 얼마 후에 아티스트로 계약되었다. 에이콘의 데뷔 앨범인 「Trouble」은 2004년에 발매되었다. 그것은 리드 싱글 'Locked Up'을 포함했는데, 그것은 빌보드 핫 100에서 8위에 올랐다. 그 앨범은 또한 'Lonely'를 포함했는데, 그것은 부분적으로는 바비 빈턴의 1964년 노래 'Mr. Lonely'를 샘플링했기 때문에 [59]세계적인 돌풍을 일으켰다.

주요
업적

Since then, Akon has issued four other albums and also [56(c)]signed countless successful musicians to his own record label. He collaborated with legendary figures like Michael Jackson and [56(b)]co-wrote popular songs including Lady Gaga's Grammy Award-nominated "Just Dance." [56(d)]He has won numerous awards such as Favorite Soul/R&B Male Artist at the American Music Awards and [56(a)]was ranked number 6 on *Billboard*'s

그 이후로, 에이콘은 4개의 다른 앨범을 발매했고 또한 [56(c)]수많은 성공적인 음악가들을 그의 음반사와 계약했다. 그는 마이클 잭슨과 같은 전설적인 인물들과 함께 작업했고 [56(b)]그래미상 후보에 오른 레이디 가가의 'Just Dance'를 포함하여 인기 있는 노래들을 공동 작곡했다. 아메리칸 뮤직 어워드에서 [56(d)]그는 소울/R&B 부문 최우수 남자가수상과 같은 수많은 상을 받았고 [56(a)]빌보드가 선정한 지난 10년간의 최고

list of Top Digital Song Artists of the decade.

Beyond his career in entertainment, Akon works to improve the lives of underprivileged young people in West Africa and the United States through the Konfidence Foundation, an organization he started with his mother. In 2014, he launched Akon Lighting Africa, [57]a project that has so far provided communities in 15 African countries with electricity via solar energy.

자선
활동

디지털 음악 아티스트 목록에서 6위를 차지했다.

연예계에서의 경력을 넘어, 에이콘은 컨피던스 재단을 통해 서아프리카와 미국의 불우한 청년들의 삶을 개선하기 위해 노력하고 있는데, 이 단체는 그의 어머니와 함께 시작한 것이다. 2014년에, 그는 에이콘 라이팅 아프리카를 시작했는데, [57]이 프로젝트는 현재까지 아프리카 15개국의 지역 사회에 태양 에너지에 의한 전기를 공급해 온 것이다.

어휘 | entrepreneur n. 기업가, 사업가 simultaneously adv. 동시에 instrument n. 악기 theft n. 절도 legal adj. 법적인 jail n. 감옥 explore v. 탐구하다, 살펴보다 executive n. 임원 worldwide adj. 세계적인 issue v. 발매하다 legendary adj. 전설적인 nominate v. 후보에 올리다 underprivileged adj. 불우한 launch v. 시작하다 electricity n. 전기 solar adj. 태양의, 태양열을 이용한

---

53 추론 특정사실   난이도 ●○○

How most likely did Akon's parents influence him?

(a) by inspiring him to travel the world
(b) by encouraging him to listen to hip-hop
(c) by introducing him to famous musicians
(d) by giving him an appreciation of music

에이콘의 부모는 어떻게 그에게 영향을 미쳤던 것 같은가?

(a) 그가 세계를 여행하도록 격려함으로써
(b) 그가 힙합을 듣도록 격려함으로써
(c) 그를 유명한 음악가들에게 소개함으로써
(d) 그에게 음악에 대한 이해를 제공함으로써

지텔프 치트키
질문의 키워드 parents가 father ~ and ~ mother로 paraphrasing되어 언급된 주변 내용을 주의 깊게 읽는다.

해설 | 2단락의 'His father ~ is a celebrated drummer, and his mother ~ is a dancer.'에서 에이콘의 아버지는 유명한 드럼 연주자이고 어머니는 무용수라고 한 뒤, 'Growing up in this environment, Akon was exposed to music from an early age.'에서 이러한 환경에서 자라면서 에이콘은 어린 나이부터 음악에 노출되었다고 한 것을 통해, 에이콘의 부모는 에이콘에게 음악에 대한 이해를 제공함으로써 그에게 영향을 미쳤던 것임을 추론할 수 있다. 따라서 (d)가 정답이다.

어휘 | inspire v. 격려하다 appreciation n. 이해

---

54 특정세부사항 How   난이도 ●●○

How did going to jail benefit Akon's career?

(a) It educated him about the law.
(b) He met the head of a record label.
(c) It rekindled his love for music-making.
(d) He made songs with other inmates.

감옥에 가는 것이 어떻게 에이콘의 경력에 도움이 되었는가?

(a) 그에게 법에 대해 가르쳤다.
(b) 그가 음반사의 대표를 만났다.
(c) 작곡에 대한 그의 사랑에 다시 불을 붙였다.
(d) 그가 다른 수감자들과 함께 노래를 만들었다.

지텔프 치트키
질문의 키워드 jail이 그대로 언급된 주변 내용을 주의 깊게 읽는다.

해설 | 3단락의 'While he was in jail, ~, Akon rediscovered his interest in music'에서 감옥에 있는 동안 에이콘은 음악에 대한 그의 흥미를 다시 발견했다고 했다. 따라서 (c)가 정답이다.

Paraphrasing

rediscovered his interest in music 음악에 대한 흥미를 다시 발견했다 → rekindled his love for music-making 작곡에 대한 사랑에 다시 불을 붙였다

오답분석

(b) 3단락에서 에이콘의 곡들 중 하나가 음반사의 대표인 데빈 스티븐스에게 전해졌다고는 했지만, 이는 에이콘이 출소한 이후에 일어난 일이므로 오답이다.

어휘 | educate v. 가르치다, 교육하다 rekindle v. 다시 불을 붙이다 inmate n. 수감자

---

55 특정세부사항 When 난이도 ●●○

When did Akon begin recording music for SRC Records?

(a) when his first single started to gain popularity in the US
(b) after he mentored an artist at the label
(c) when his first album became an international success
(d) after a music authority heard his samples

에이콘은 언제 SRC 레코드 사를 위해 음악을 녹음하기 시작했는가?

(a) 그의 첫 싱글이 미국에서 인기를 얻기 시작했을 때
(b) 그가 그 음반사에서 한 아티스트를 지도한 후에
(c) 그의 첫 앨범이 세계적인 성공을 거두었을 때
(d) 한 음악 권위자가 그의 샘플을 들은 후에

지텔프 치트키

질문의 키워드 SRC Records가 그대로 언급된 주변 내용을 주의 깊게 읽는다.

해설 | 4단락의 'His demo tape fell into the hands of an executive at SRC Records, and Akon was signed on as an artist shortly thereafter.'에서 에이콘의 데모 테이프가 SRC 레코드 사의 한 임원의 손에 넘어갔고 에이콘이 그로부터 얼마 후에 아티스트로 계약되었다고 했다. 따라서 (d)가 정답이다.

Paraphrasing

His demo tape 그의 데모 테이프 → his samples 그의 샘플
an executive at SRC Records SRC 레코드 사의 한 임원 → a music authority 한 음악 권위자

---

56 Not/True True 문제 난이도 ●●●

According to the article, what is true about Akon's record company?

(a) It became *Billboard*'s top label.
(b) It produced Grammy-winning songs.
(c) It represents popular acts.
(d) It develops Soul and R&B music.

기사에 따르면, 에이콘의 음반사에 관해 사실인 것은 무엇인가?

(a) 빌보드가 선정한 최고의 음반사가 되었다.
(b) 그래미상을 받은 노래들을 제작했다.
(c) 인기 있는 음악 공연자들을 대표한다.
(d) 소울과 R&B 음악을 발전시킨다.

지텔프 치트키

질문의 키워드 record company가 record label로 paraphrasing되어 언급된 주변 내용을 주의 깊게 읽고, 보기의 키워드와 지문 내용을 대조하며 읽는다.

해설 | (c)의 키워드인 popular acts가 successful musicians로 paraphrasing되어 언급된 5단락의 'signed countless successful musicians to his own record label'에서 에이콘은 수많은 성공적인 음악가들을 그의 음반사와 계약했다고 했으므로 지문의 내용과 일치한다. 따라서 (c)가 정답이다.

(a) 5단락에서 에이콘이 빌보드가 선정한 지난 10년간의 최고 디지털 음악 아티스트 목록에서 6위를 차지했다고는 했지만, 에이콘의 음반 사가 빌보드가 선정한 최고의 음반사가 되었는지는 언급되지 않았다.

(b) 보기의 키워드 Grammy가 그대로 언급된 5단락에서 에이콘이 그래미상 후보에 오른 레이디 가가의 노래를 공동 작곡했다고는 했지만, 에이콘의 음반사가 제작한 노래들이 그래미상을 받았는지는 언급되지 않았다.

(d) 보기의 키워드 Soul and R&B가 Soul/R&B로 언급된 5단락에서 에이콘이 소울/R&B 부문 최우수 남자가수상을 받았다고는 했지 만, 에이콘의 음반사가 소울과 R&B 음악을 발전시키는지는 언급되지 않았다.

어휘 | act n. 음악 공연자

---

57 특정세부사항   What
난이도 ●●○

What does Akon Lighting Africa do?	에이콘 라이팅 아프리카는 무엇을 하는가?
(a) supply energy to villages in Africa	**(a) 아프리카의 마을들에 에너지를 공급한다**
(b) spread awareness of renewable energy	(b) 재생 가능 에너지에 대한 인식을 확산시킨다
(c) replace traditional energy sources with solar panels	(c) 기존의 에너지원을 태양 전지판으로 대체한다
(d) provide youth in need with employment opportunities	(d) 가난한 청년들에게 취업 기회를 제공한다

지텔프 치트키

질문의 키워드 Akon Lighting Africa가 그대로 언급된 주변 내용을 주의 깊게 읽는다.

해설 | 6단락의 'a project that has ~ provided communities in 15 African countries with electricity via solar energy'에서 에 이콘 라이팅 아프리카 프로젝트는 아프리카 15개국의 지역 사회에 태양 에너지에 의한 전기를 공급해 온 것이라고 했다. 따라서 (a)가 정답 이다.

Paraphrasing

has ~ provided communities ~ with electricity 지역 사회에 전기를 공급해 왔다 → supply energy to villages 마을들에 에너지를 공급 하다

어휘 | renewable adj. 재생 가능한 replace v. 대체하다 panel n. 전지판 in need phr. 가난한, 궁핍한 employment n. 취업

---

58 어휘   유의어
난이도 ●●○

In the context of the passage, celebrated means _____.	지문의 문맥에서, 'celebrated'는 –을 의미한다.
(a) sophisticated	(a) 세련된
(b) distinguished	**(b) 유명한**
(c) noticeable	(c) 두드러진
(d) memorable	(d) 인상적인

지텔프 치트키

밑줄 친 어휘의 유의어를 찾는 문제이므로, celebrated가 포함된 구절을 읽고 문맥을 파악한다.

해설 | 2단락의 'Mor Thiam is a celebrated drummer'는 모르 티암이 유명한 드럼 연주자라는 뜻이므로, celebrated가 '유명한'이라는 의 미로 사용된 것을 알 수 있다. 따라서 '유명한'이라는 같은 의미의 (b) distinguished가 정답이다.

In the context of the passage, <u>sensation</u> means _____.

(a) hit
(b) impression
(c) impact
(d) sense

지문의 문맥에서, 'sensation'은 -을 의미한다.

(a) 대성공
(b) 인상
(c) 영향
(d) 감각

⊶○ 지텔프 치트키

밑줄 친 어휘의 유의어를 찾는 문제이므로, sensation이 포함된 구절을 읽고 문맥을 파악한다.

해설 | 4단락의 'became a worldwide sensation'은 세계적인 돌풍을 일으켰다는 뜻이므로, sensation이 '돌풍'이라는 의미로 사용된 것을 알 수 있다. 따라서 '대성공'이라는 비슷한 의미의 (a) hit가 정답이다.

오답분석

(d) '감각'이라는 의미의 sense도 sensation의 사전적 유의어 중 하나이지만, 문맥상 곡이 세계적인 돌풍을 일으켰다는 의미가 되어야 적절하므로 sensation이 '감각'이 아닌 '돌풍'이라는 의미로 사용된 것을 알 수 있다. 따라서 문맥에 어울리지 않아 오답이다.

PART 2[60~66] 잡지 기사 어그부츠의 재유행

기사 제목	

HOW UGGS MADE A COMEBACK

정의

The Ugg boot is a pull-on boot with fleece inside and a sheepskin exterior. It was a must-have item in the early 2000s and remained a wardrobe staple until the early 2010s when consumers started viewing them as unfashionable. In the 2020s, however, Uggs began making a comeback.

유래

[60]The style associated with Uggs originated in Australia. Boots similar to Uggs were worn during the 1920s by sheep shearers and during the 1960s by surfers for comfort and warmth. Entrepreneur Brian Smith helped popularize the footwear outside of Australia. In 1978, he established a California-based sheepskin boot company, which he trademarked "UGG." [61]Sheepskin boots had always been referred to as "uggs" in Australia as they were thought to be ugly and only used for utilitarian purposes, but registering the name officially connected Smith to this particular style of boot.

홍보 + 위기

In the 1990s, Smith began offering free Uggs to celebrities in the hope of gaining more exposure. By the early 2000s, famous American talk show host Oprah Winfrey was promoting them on her show and giving away hundreds of pairs. They were soon selling out,

어떻게 어그부츠가 다시 인기를 얻었는가

어그부츠는 양털로 된 내부와 양가죽으로 된 외관을 가진 잡아당겨 착용하는 부츠이다. 이것은 2000년대 초반에 옷장 속 기본 아이템이었고 소비자들이 그것들을 유행에 뒤떨어진 것으로 보기 시작한 2010년대 초반까지 계속 옷장 속 필수 품목이었다. 그러나, 2020년대에, 어그부츠가 다시 인기를 얻기 시작했다.

[60]어그부츠와 관련된 스타일은 호주에서 비롯되었다. 어그부츠와 비슷한 부츠들은 1920년대에 양털을 깎는 사람들에 의해 착용되었고 1960년대에는 편안함과 따뜻함을 위해 서퍼들에 의해 착용되었다. 사업가 브라이언 스미스가 그 신발을 호주 밖에서 대중화하는 데 도움을 주었다. 1978년에, 그는 캘리포니아주에 기반을 둔 양가죽 부츠 회사를 설립했고, 그것에 'UGG'라는 상표를 붙였다. [61]호주에서 양가죽 부츠는 못생긴 것으로 여겨지고 오직 실용적인 목적으로만 사용되었기 때문에 항상 '어그'라고 불렸었지만, 공식적으로 이 명칭을 등록하는 것은 스미스를 이 특정한 스타일의 부츠와 결부시켰다.

1990년대에, 스미스는 더 많이 알려질 것이라는 희망으로 유명 인사들에게 무료 어그부츠를 제공하기 시작했다. 2000년대 초쯤에, 유명한 미국 토크쇼의 진행자 오프라 윈프리는 그녀의 쇼에서 그것들을 홍보하고 수백 켤레를 무료로 나누어 주었다. 그것들은 곧 매진되었고, 온라인에서 가격이 200퍼센트 이상

with prices being marked up by over 200 percent online. But, as is the case with all trends, [62]the fervor eventually waned. Counterfeits entered the market, making the look less exclusive, and by 2010, they [65]were deemed too sloppy to be worn in public.

Though they fell out of fashion for a decade, Deckers Outdoor Corporation, which had purchased the company from Smith, expanded the Ugg product line while maintaining the footwear's comfortable aesthetic. By the 2020s, consumer demand for nostalgic items from the 1990s and early 2000s surged, which prompted a revival of the brand. Moreover, [63]since people were working from home due to the pandemic, comfort became more important than fashion.

Whether Uggs will ever [66]reach their former level of popularity among celebrities and the general public remains to be seen. However, given that [64]consumers today are placing more of an emphasis on the quality and longevity of goods and that Uggs are now available in various colors and styles, Uggs are likely to stay a part of the fashion landscape for the foreseeable future.

제품군
확장
+
재유행

현황

인상되었다. 하지만, 모든 유행이 그렇듯이, [62]그 열기는 결국 시들해졌다. 위조품들이 시장에 유입되었고, 이는 그 스타일을 덜 독점적이게 만들었으며, 2010년쯤에, 그것들은 공공장소에서 착용되기에 [65]너무 단정하지 못하다고 여겨졌다.

그것들은 비록 10년 동안 유행에서 뒤떨어졌지만, 데커스 아웃도어 코퍼레이션 사는, 스미스로부터 그 회사를 인수했었는데, 그 신발의 편안함을 주는 미적 가치관을 유지하면서 어그부츠의 제품군을 확장했다. 2020년대쯤에, 1990년대와 2000년대 초반의 향수를 불러일으키는 물건들에 대한 소비자 수요가 급증하였고, 이는 그 브랜드의 재유행을 촉발했다. 게다가, [63]사람들이 세계적인 유행병으로 인해 집에서 일하고 있었기 때문에, 편안함이 패션보다 더 중요해졌다.

유명 인사들과 일반 대중들 사이에서 어그부츠가 [66]이전 정도의 인기에 도달할지는 두고 볼 일이다. 하지만, [64]오늘날 소비자들이 상품의 품질과 수명에 더 많은 중점을 두고 있고 어그부츠가 현재 다양한 색상과 스타일로 제공된다는 것을 고려하면, 어그부츠가 가까운 미래 동안에는 계속 패션계의 한 부분으로 남아 있을 것 같다.

어휘 | fleece n. 양털 **wardrobe staple** phr. 옷장 속 기본 아이템, 유행을 타지 않는 품목 **originate** v. 비롯되다, 유래하다 **shearer** n. 깎는 사람 **trademark** v. 상표를 붙이다 **utilitarian** adj. 실용적인 **mark up** phr. 가격을 인상하다 **fervor** n. 열기 **wane** v. 시들해지다, 약해지다 **counterfeit** n. 위조품 **exclusive** adj. 독점적인 **sloppy** adj. 단정하지 못한 **aesthetic** n. 미적 가치관 **nostalgic** adj. 향수를 불러일으키는 **surge** v. 급증하다 **revival** n. 재유행, 부활 **longevity** n. 수명 **landscape** n. 계, 분야 **foreseeable** adj. 가까운

---

60 **특정세부사항** Which 난이도 ●○○

Which group first started wearing the Ugg-style of boot?

(a) those who got wool from sheep
(b) those who rode ocean waves
(c) those who had a sense of style
(d) those who lived in California

어떤 집단이 처음으로 어그 스타일의 부츠를 착용하기 시작했는가?

(a) 양의 털을 얻었던 사람들
(b) 바다의 파도를 탔던 사람들
(c) 스타일 감각이 있었던 사람들
(d) 캘리포니아주에 살았던 사람들

─○ 지텔프 치트키

질문의 키워드 first started가 originated로 paraphrasing되어 언급된 주변 내용을 주의 깊게 읽는다.

해설 | 2단락의 'The style associated with Uggs originated in Australia.'에서 어그부츠와 관련된 스타일이 호주에서 비롯되었다고 한 뒤, 'Boots similar to Uggs were worn during the 1920s by sheep shearers'에서 어그부츠와 비슷한 부츠들이 1920년대에 양털을 깎는 사람들에 의해 착용되었다고 했다. 따라서 (a)가 정답이다.

Paraphrasing
sheep shearers 양털을 깎는 사람들 → those who got wool from sheep 양의 털을 얻었던 사람들

TEST 1
TEST 2
TEST 3
TEST 4
TEST 5
TEST 6
TEST 7

61 추론 특정사실 난이도 ●●○

Where most likely does the term "ugg" come from?

(a) from a technique employed by Australian farmers
(b) from an expression denoting comfort
(c) from a trademark style of a company
(d) from an opinion about appearance

'어그'라는 용어는 어디에서 유래한 것 같은가?

(a) 호주 농부들에 의해 사용되는 한 기술로부터
(b) 편안함을 나타내는 한 표현으로부터
(c) 한 회사의 트레이드마크 스타일로부터
(d) 생김새에 대한 한 견해로부터

━○ 지텔프 치트키

질문의 키워드 "ugg"가 "uggs"로 언급된 주변 내용을 주의 깊게 읽는다.

해설┃ 2단락의 'Sheepskin boots had always been referred to as "uggs" ~ as they were thought to be ugly and only used for utilitarian purposes'에서 양가죽 부츠는 못생긴(ugly) 것으로 여겨졌기 때문에 항상 '어그'라고 불렸다고 한 것을 통해, 어그부츠의 생김새에 대한 한 견해로부터 '어그'라는 용어가 유래한 것임을 추론할 수 있다. 따라서 (d)가 정답이다.

어휘┃ employ v. 사용하다 denote v. 나타내다

62 특정세부사항 Why 난이도 ●●○

Why did the popularity of Uggs decrease?

(a) because their price went up dramatically
(b) because they stopped sales promotion activities
(c) because they were criticized by celebrities
(d) because their imitations became widely available

왜 어그부츠의 인기가 감소했는가?

(a) 그것들의 가격이 급격하게 올랐기 때문에
(b) 판촉 활동을 중단했기 때문에
(c) 유명 인사들로부터 비난받았기 때문에
(d) 그것들의 모조품이 널리 이용 가능해졌기 때문에

━○ 지텔프 치트키

질문의 키워드 popularity ~ decrease가 fervor ~ waned로 paraphrasing되어 언급된 주변 내용을 주의 깊게 읽는다.

해설┃ 3단락의 'the fervor eventually waned'에서 어그부츠에 대한 열기가 결국 시들해졌다고 한 뒤, 'Counterfeits entered the market, making the look less exclusive'에서 어그부츠의 위조품들이 시장에 유입되었고 이는 어그부츠의 스타일을 덜 독점적이게 만들었다고 했다. 따라서 (d)가 정답이다.

Paraphrasing
Counterfeits entered the market 위조품들이 시장에 유입되었다 → their imitations became widely available 모조품이 널리 이용 가능해졌다

오답분석
(a) 3단락에서 어그부츠의 가격이 인상되었다고는 했지만, 이것 때문에 어그부츠의 인기가 감소했다고 한 것은 아니므로 오답이다.

어휘┃ dramatically adv. 급격하게 criticize v. 비난하다 imitation n. 모조품

63 추론 특정사실 난이도 ●●●

What probably prompted consumers to reconsider Uggs during the pandemic?

(a) People were pleased with the expanded product offerings.

무엇이 세계적인 유행병 동안 소비자들이 어그부츠를 재고하도록 촉발했던 것 같은가?

(a) 사람들이 확장된 제품군 제공에 만족했다.

(b) **People prioritized comfort over style.**
(c) Uggs had completely changed their look.
(d) Uggs appeared in fashion advertisements.

(b) 사람들이 스타일보다 편안함을 우선시했다.
(c) 어그부츠가 겉모양을 완전히 바꿨다.
(d) 어그부츠가 패션 광고에 등장했다.

─○ 지텔프 치트키

질문의 키워드 pandemic이 그대로 언급된 주변 내용을 주의 깊게 읽는다.

해설 | 4단락의 'since people were working from home due to the pandemic, comfort became more important than fashion' 에서 사람들이 세계적인 유행병으로 인해 집에서 일하고 있었기 때문에 편안함이 패션보다 더 중요해졌다고 한 것을 통해, 세계적인 유행병 동안 소비자들이 스타일보다 편안함을 우선시했던 것이 어그부츠를 재고하도록 촉발했던 것임을 추론할 수 있다. 따라서 (b)가 정답이다.

Paraphrasing

comfort became more important than fashion 편안함이 패션보다 더 중요해졌다 → prioritized comfort over style 스타일보다 편안함을 우선시했다

오답분석

(a) 4단락에서 데커스 아웃도어 코퍼레이션 사가 어그부츠의 제품군을 확장했다고는 했지만, 사람들이 확장된 제품군 제공에 만족했는지 의 여부는 언급되지 않았으므로 오답이다.

---

64 특정세부사항 What
난이도 ●●○

According to the article, what do consumers value nowadays?

(a) **the durability of products**
(b) views of famous people
(c) diversity in product lines
(d) the recognition of brands

기사에 따르면, 요즘에 소비자들은 무엇을 중요시하 는가?

(a) **제품의 내구성**
(b) 유명한 사람들의 의견
(c) 제품군의 다양성
(d) 브랜드의 인지도

─○ 지텔프 치트키

질문의 키워드 consumers ~ nowadays가 consumers today로 paraphrasing되어 언급된 주변 내용을 주의 깊게 읽는다.

해설 | 5단락의 'consumers today are placing more of an emphasis on the ~ longevity of goods'에서 오늘날 소비자들이 상품의 수명에 더 많은 중점을 두고 있다고 했다. 따라서 (a)가 정답이다.

Paraphrasing

value 중요시하다 → placing ~ an emphasis 중점을 두는
the ~ longevity of goods 상품의 수명 → the durability of products 제품의 내구성

어휘 | value v. 중요시하다 durability n. 내구성 diversity n. 다양성 recognition n. 인지도

---

65 어휘 유의어
난이도 ●●○

In the context of the passage, deemed means _____.

(a) created
(b) **considered**

지문의 문맥에서, 'deemed'는 -을 의미한다.

(a) 형성된
(b) **여겨진**

(c) announced
(d) allowed

(c) 알려진
(d) 허용된

—○ 지텔프 치트키

밑줄 친 어휘의 유의어를 찾는 문제이므로, deemed가 포함된 구절을 읽고 문맥을 파악한다.

해설 | 3단락의 'were deemed too sloppy'는 너무 단정하지 못하다고 여겨졌다는 뜻이므로, deemed가 '여겨진'이라는 의미로 사용된 것을 알 수 있다. 따라서 '여겨진'이라는 같은 의미의 (b) considered가 정답이다.

66 어휘 유의어 난이도 ●●●

In the context of the passage, <u>level</u> means _____.

(a) stage
(b) force
(c) amount
(d) peak

지문의 문맥에서, 'level'은 -을 의미한다.

(a) 단계
(b) 힘
(c) 양
(d) 정점

—○ 지텔프 치트키

밑줄 친 어휘의 유의어를 찾는 문제이므로, level이 포함된 구절을 읽고 문맥을 파악한다.

해설 | 5단락의 'reach their former level of popularity'는 이전 정도의 인기에 도달한다는 뜻이므로, level이 '정도'라는 의미로 사용된 것을 알 수 있다. 따라서 '양'이라는 비슷한 의미의 (c) amount가 정답이다.

오답분석

(a) '단계'라는 의미의 stage도 level의 사전적 유의어 중 하나이지만, 문맥상 어그부츠가 이전 정도의 인기에 도달한다는 의미가 되어야 적절하므로 level이 '단계'가 아닌 '정도'라는 의미로 사용된 것을 알 수 있다. 따라서 문맥에 어울리지 않아 오답이다.

PART 3 [67~73] 지식 백과 제이가르니크 효과의 정의 및 적용

표제어	**ZEIGARNIK EFFECT**	**제이가르니크 효과**
정의	The Zeigarnik effect is the tendency for people to have better recall of unfinished tasks than completed ones. Named after Lithuanian-Soviet psychologist Bluma Zeigarnik, the effect was first observed in waiters who [67]were able to remember the pending orders but forgot them as soon as customers were served.	제이가르니크 효과는 사람들이 완료되지 않은 작업들을 완료된 것들보다 더 잘 기억하는 경향이다. 리투아니아계 소련인 심리학자 블루마 제이가르니크의 이름을 딴 이 효과는 [67]완료되지 않은 주문들은 기억할 수 있었지만 손님이 음식을 받자마자 곧 그것들을 잊어버린 종업원들에게서 처음 관찰되었다.
실험 내용	To back up her observation, Zeigarnik conducted experiments in 1927 with participants who were asked to work on short tasks like winding thread and constructing puzzles. [68]Half of the participants were allowed to start an undertaking but then were ordered to move on to the	그녀의 관찰 결과를 뒷받침하기 위해, 제이가르니크는 1927년에 실 감기와 퍼즐 조립하기와 같은 간단한 작업들을 하도록 요청받은 참가자들과 함께 실험을 수행했다. [68]참가자들 중 절반은 작업을 시작하도록 허락되었지만 그런 다음 [72]그들이 그것에 가장 몰두해 있

| | next one when [72]they were most <u>engrossed</u> in it. The other participants were not interrupted. When later asked to discuss the assignments, those who were stopped halfway recalled them twice as well as those who accomplished the objectives. | 었을 때 다음 것으로 넘어가라는 지시를 받았다. 다른 참가자들은 방해받지 않았다. 나중에 그 작업들에 대해 논의하라는 요청을 받았을 때, 도중에 제지당했던 사람들은 목표를 달성한 사람들보다 그것들을 두 배 더 잘 기억해 냈다. |

실험 결과

Zeigarnik concluded that [69]as people approach the culmination of a job at hand, cognitive tension increases. In this state, the brain will remember the discontinued activity until it is resolved. [69]Once completed, though, the strain is released and the pursuit fades from memory.

제이가르니크는 [69]사람들이 당면한 일의 완료에 가까워질수록, 인지적 긴장이 증가한다는 결론을 내렸다. 이 상태에서, 뇌는 해결될 때까지 그 중단된 활동을 기억할 것이다. [69]그러나, 일단 완료되면, 긴장은 풀어지고 그 일은 기억에서 사라진다.

적용1: 방송 편성 방식

The Zeigarnik effect can be applied in a number of ways. For instance, television writers know that [70]audiences are more likely to keep watching a show each week if an episode ends in a suspenseful way. Because a satisfying conclusion has not been reached, viewers recollect what happened until there is a resolution.

제이가르니크 효과는 여러 가지 방식으로 적용될 수 있다. 예를 들어, 텔레비전 작가들은 [70]에피소드가 긴장감 넘치는 방식으로 끝나면 시청자들이 매주 프로그램을 계속 시청할 가능성이 더 크다는 것을 알고 있다. [70]만족스러운 결론에 도달하지 않았기 때문에, 시청자들은 해답이 있을 때까지 무슨 일이 발생했는지를 회상한다.

적용2: 학습 방법

The Zeigarnik effect may also impact how people learn. If students split up their study sessions instead of going through all the material in one sitting, they will probably think about what they have already reviewed during their breaks. Furthermore, the effect could help people avoid procrastination in the sense that it is difficult to stop thinking about a chore once it has been started, increasing the likelihood of it getting finished.

제이가르니크 효과는 또한 사람들이 학습하는 방법에 영향을 미칠 수 있다. 만약 학생들이 한 번에 모든 자료를 검토하는 대신에 그들의 공부 시간을 나눈다면, 그들은 아마도 쉬는 시간에 그들이 이미 복습한 것에 대해 생각할 것이다. 더욱이, 그 효과는 일단 시작되면 과업에 대해 생각하는 것을 멈추기 어렵다는 점에서 사람들이 미루는 것을 피하도록 도울 수 있으며, 이는 그것이 완료될 가능성을 증가시킨다.

반박 연구

While subsequent studies [73]<u>support</u> Zeigarnik's findings, others refute them, suggesting that the effect cannot be reliably reproduced. [71]Researchers who believe this claim that the effect depends on factors that change with each individual. These include how motivated they are to complete the task and how difficult they perceive it to be.

이후의 연구들이 [73]제이가르니크의 연구 결과를 <u>뒷받침하는</u> 반면, 다른 것들은 그 효과가 확실하게 재현될 수 없다고 제시하며 반박한다. [71]이것을 믿는 연구자들은 그 효과가 각 개인에 따라 달라지는 요인들에 달려 있다고 주장한다. 이것들은 그들이 작업을 완료하는 것에 얼마나 동기 부여가 되어 있는지와 그것이 얼마나 어렵다고 인지하는지를 포함한다.

어휘 | tendency n. 경향 recall n. 기억; v. 기억해 내다 pending adj. 완료되지 않은 observation n. 관찰 결과, 관찰 wind v. 감다 construct v. 조립하다 undertaking n. 작업, 일 halfway adv. 도중에 objective n. 목표 conclude v. 결론을 내리다 culmination n. 완료, 정점 tension n. 긴장 discontinue v. 중단하다 resolve v. 해결하다 strain n. 긴장 pursuit n. 일, 근무 suspenseful adj. 긴장감 넘치는 recollect v. 회상하다, 기억해 내다 resolution n. 해답 in one sitting phr. 한 번에 procrastination n. 미루는 것, 지연 subsequent adj. 이후의 refute v. 반박하다 reliably adv. 확실하게 reproduce v. 재현하다

---

67 특정세부사항 What
난이도 ●○○

According to Bluma Zeigarnik's observations, what were the waiters able to do?

(a) They recalled the person who asked for the priciest dish.

블루마 제이가르니크의 관찰 결과에 따르면, 종업원들은 무엇을 할 수 있었는가?

(a) 가장 비싼 요리를 요구했던 사람을 기억해 냈다.

(b) They recollected the uncompleted requests of customers.

(c) They remembered the details of completed orders.

(d) They fulfilled the orders in a timely manner.

(b) 고객들의 완료되지 않은 요청들을 기억해 냈다.

(c) 완료된 주문들의 세부 사항을 기억했다.

(d) 주문을 적시에 수행했다.

지텔프 치트키

질문의 키워드 waiters가 그대로 언급된 주변 내용을 주의 깊게 읽는다.

해설 | 1단락의 'were able to remember the pending orders'에서 종업원들은 완료되지 않은 주문들을 기억할 수 있었다고 했다. 따라서 (b)가 정답이다.

Paraphrasing

remember the pending orders 완료되지 않은 주문들을 기억하다 → recollected the uncompleted requests of customers 고객들의 완료되지 않은 요청들을 기억해 냈다

어휘 | fulfill v. 수행하다 timely adj. 적시의, 시기적절한

---

68 특정세부사항   Which   난이도 ●●○

Which of the following was included in Zeigarnik's experiments?

(a) assessing the quality of the participants' work

(b) timing the speed of the completed tasks

(c) interrupting participants from recounting assignments

(d) preventing participants from finishing jobs

다음 중 제이가르니크의 실험에 포함되었던 것은 무엇인가?

(a) 참가자들의 작업 품질을 평가하는 것

(b) 완료된 작업들의 속도를 재는 것

(c) 참가자들이 임무에 관해 이야기하는 것을 방해하는 것

(d) 참가자들이 작업을 끝내는 것을 막는 것

지텔프 치트키

질문의 키워드 experiments가 그대로 언급된 주변 내용을 주의 깊게 읽는다.

해설 | 2단락의 'Half of the participants ~ were ordered to move on to the next one when they were most engrossed in it.'에서 참가자들 중 절반은 그들이 작업에 가장 몰두해 있었을 때 다음 것으로 넘어가라는 지시를 받았다고 했다. 따라서 (d)가 정답이다.

Paraphrasing

were ordered to move on to the next one when ~ most engrossed in it 그것에 가장 몰두해 있었을 때 다음 것으로 넘어가라는 지시를 받았다 → preventing ~ from finishing jobs 작업을 끝내는 것을 막는 것

어휘 | assess v. 평가하다 time v. 재다, 기록하다 recount v. 이야기하다, 열거하다

---

69 특정세부사항   How   난이도 ●●○

According to the article, how is mental tension relieved?

(a) by forgetting a paused task

(b) by recalling important memories

(c) by reaching an activity's conclusion

(d) by continuing to decrease cognitive load

기사에 따르면, 정신적 긴장감은 어떻게 완화되는가?

(a) 일시 중지된 작업을 잊어버림으로써

(b) 중요한 기억들을 회상함으로써

(c) 활동의 종결에 도달함으로써

(d) 인지 부하를 계속 감소시킴으로써

질문의 키워드 tension relieved가 strain ~ released로 paraphrasing되어 언급된 주변 내용을 주의 깊게 읽는다.

해설 | 3단락의 'as people approach the culmination of a job at hand, cognitive tension increases'에서 사람들이 당면한 일의 완료에 가까워질수록 인지적 긴장이 증가한다고 한 뒤, 'Once completed, though, the strain is released'에서 그러나 일단 완료되면 긴장은 풀어진다고 했다. 따라서 (c)가 정답이다.

Paraphrasing
completed 완료된 → reaching an activity's conclusion 활동의 종결에 도달함

어휘 | conclusion n. 종결, 결론 load n. 부하, 부담

---

70 추론 특정사실   난이도 ●●○

What probably explains why people watch weekly TV shows?	사람들이 매주 TV 프로그램들을 시청하는 이유를 설명하는 것은 무엇인 것 같은가?
(a) the extensive discussion among viewers	(a) 시청자들 사이의 광범위한 토론
(b) the satisfying endings featured in them	(b) 그것들에 포함된 만족스러운 결말
(c) the desire to see the solution to an issue	**(c) 문제에 대한 해결책을 보고 싶은 욕구**
(d) the willingness to keep up with series	(d) 시리즈를 놓치지 않으려는 의지

🔑 지텔프 치트키

질문의 키워드 watch weekly ~ shows가 watching a show each week로 paraphrasing되어 언급된 주변 내용을 주의 깊게 읽는다.

해설 | 4단락의 'audiences are more likely to keep watching a show each week if an episode ends in a suspenseful way'에서 에피소드가 긴장감 넘치는 방식으로 끝나면 시청자들이 매주 프로그램을 계속 시청할 가능성이 더 크다고 한 뒤, 'Because a satisfying conclusion has not been reached, viewers recollect what happened until there is a resolution.'에서 만족스러운 결론에 도달하지 않았기 때문에 시청자들은 해답이 있을 때까지 에피소드에서 무슨 일이 발생했는지를 회상한다고 한 것을 통해, 사람들이 문제에 대한 해결책을 보고 싶은 욕구 때문에 매주 TV 프로그램을 시청하는 것임을 추론할 수 있다. 따라서 (c)가 정답이다.

Paraphrasing
a resolution 해답 → the solution 해결책

어휘 | extensive adj. 광범위한 willingness n. 의지

---

71 추론 특정사실   난이도 ●●●

Why most likely do some researchers feel that Zeigarnik's experiments cannot be replicated?	왜 일부 연구자들은 제이가르니크의 실험이 되풀이될 수 없다고 생각하는 것 같은가?
(a) because participants find the tests difficult	(a) 참가자들이 시험을 어렵게 여기기 때문에
(b) because participants have different skill sets	**(b) 참가자들이 서로 다른 능력을 갖추고 있기 때문에**
(c) because the public is aware of their findings	(c) 대중이 그것의 결과를 알고 있기 때문에
(d) because the original tasks no longer motivate people	(d) 기존의 작업들이 더 이상 사람들에게 동기를 부여하지 않기 때문에

🔑 지텔프 치트키

질문의 키워드 replicated가 reproduced로 paraphrasing되어 언급된 주변 내용을 주의 깊게 읽는다.

해설 | 6단락의 'Researchers who believe this claim that the effect depends on factors that change with each individual.'에서 제이가르니크 효과가 확실하게 재현될 수 없다는 것을 믿는 연구자들이 그 효과가 각 개인에 따라 달라지는 요인들에 달려 있다고 주장한다고 한 뒤, 'These include ~ how difficult they perceive it to be.'에서 그 요인들은 그들이 작업이 얼마나 어렵다고 인지하는지를 포함한다고 한 것을 통해, 참가자들이 서로 다른 능력을 갖추고 있기 때문에 일부 연구자들은 제이가르니크의 실험이 되풀이될 수 없다고 생각하는 것임을 추론할 수 있다. 따라서 (b)가 정답이다.

어휘 | replicate v. 되풀이하다

72 어휘   유의어   난이도 ●●○

In the context of the passage, <u>engrossed</u> means _____.

(a) directed
(b) entailed
(c) absorbed
(d) attracted

지문의 문맥에서, 'engrossed'는 -을 의미한다.

(a) 규제된
(b) 수반된
(c) 몰두한
(d) 매료된

━○ 지텔프 치트키

밑줄 친 어휘의 유의어를 찾는 문제이므로, engrossed가 포함된 구절을 읽고 문맥을 파악한다.

해설 | 2단락의 'they were most engrossed in it'은 그들이 그것에 가장 몰두해 있었다는 뜻이므로, engrossed가 '몰두한'이라는 의미로 사용된 것을 알 수 있다. 따라서 '몰두한'이라는 같은 의미의 (c) absorbed가 정답이다.

73 어휘   유의어   난이도 ●●○

In the context of the passage, <u>support</u> means _____.

(a) endorse
(b) assist
(c) utilize
(d) cancel

지문의 문맥에서, 'support'는 -을 의미한다.

(a) 지지한다
(b) 돕는다
(c) 이용한다
(d) 무효화한다

━○ 지텔프 치트키

밑줄 친 어휘의 유의어를 찾는 문제이므로, support가 포함된 구절을 읽고 문맥을 파악한다.

해설 | 6단락의 'support Zeigarnik's findings'는 제이가르니크의 연구 결과를 뒷받침한다는 뜻이므로, support가 '뒷받침한다'라는 의미로 사용된 것을 알 수 있다. 따라서 '지지한다'라는 비슷한 의미의 (a) endorse가 정답이다.

오답분석
(b) '돕다'라는 의미의 assist도 support의 사전적 유의어 중 하나이지만, 문맥상 이후의 연구들이 제이가르니크의 연구 결과를 뒷받침한다는 의미가 되어야 적절하므로 문맥에 어울리지 않아 오답이다.

해커스 지텔프 최신기출유형 실전모의고사 7회 (Level 2)

수신인 정보	Andrew Pacheco Peacock Kitchen 174 Sandy Pines Road East Montpelier, VT 05651 Dear Mr. Pacheco:
편지의 목적: 유통 센터 홍보	[74]I'm pleased to inform you that we are opening our newest distribution center near your restaurant next Friday. Shephard Family Farm grows a wide variety of organic fruits and vegetables. In addition, we offer many other high-quality goods such as cheese, honey, and bread that you might be interested in using as ingredients at your establishment.
농장 소개	Shephard Family Farm began over 20 years ago with the mission to [79]minimize the distance food travels and encourage people to buy from local suppliers. As you are aware, sourcing food from outside the region or other countries negatively impacts the environment since [75]the fuel used in the transportation process adds to the overall carbon footprint.
혜택1: 빠른 배달	Furthermore, [76]fruits and vegetables begin losing nutrients not long after they are harvested. Therefore, eating produce that is transported thousands of miles over several days is not the healthiest option. [76]That's why we drop off all customer orders within two business days.
혜택2: 지속적 정보 제공	We are committed to [77]keeping our customers informed about what produce is available and discounted at our local retail partners through our monthly newsletter, *Shephard's Harvest*. That way, you can plan various seasonal menus throughout the year, [80]which I understand is especially important in the restaurant business.
끝인사	If you'd like to learn more about our farm, please visit our website at shephardfamilyfarm.com. [78]I would also be happy to come to your restaurant to speak with you in person and give you a catalog of our products and rates. If you would like this, please let me know a day and time that works for you.
발신인 정보	Best regards, Eileen Shephard Shephard Family Farm 1134 W Schultz Lane Rutland, VT 03581

Andrew Pacheco
Peacock Kitchen
샌디파인즈로 174번길
05651 버몬트주 이스트 몬트필리어

Mr. Pacheco께:

다음 주 금요일에 [74]귀하의 식당 근처에 저희의 새로운 유통 센터를 오픈할 예정임을 알리게 되어 기쁩니다. Shephard Family 농장은 매우 다양한 유기농 과일과 채소를 재배합니다. 또한, 저희는 치즈, 꿀, 그리고 빵과 같이 귀하가 식당에서 식자재로 사용하는 것에 관심이 있을 수 있는 많은 다른 고품질의 제품들을 제공합니다.

Shephard Family 농장은 20여 년 전에 [79]식품이 이동하는 거리를 줄이고 사람들이 지역의 공급업체로부터 구매하도록 장려하려는 사명을 가지고 시작되었습니다. 아시다시피, [75]운송 과정에서 사용되는 연료가 전체 탄소 발자국을 증가시키기 때문에 지역 밖에서 혹은 다른 나라로부터 식품을 조달하는 것은 환경에 부정적인 영향을 미칩니다.

게다가, [76]과일과 채소는 수확된 지 얼마 지나지 않아 영양분을 상실하기 시작합니다. 따라서, 수일에 걸쳐 수천 마일 운반되는 농산물을 먹는 것은 가장 건강한 선택지가 아닙니다. [76]그것이 저희가 영업일 기준 2일 이내에 모든 고객님들의 주문을 배달해 드리는 이유입니다.

저희는 [77]월간 소식지 『Shephard's Harvest』를 통해 저희의 지역 소매 협력 업체에서 어떤 농산물이 구매 가능하고 할인되는지 고객님들께 지속적으로 정보를 제공하는 것에 전념하고 있습니다. [77]그렇게 하면, 여러분이 1년 내내 다양한 계절 메뉴들을 기획하실 수 있는데, [80]이는 제가 알기로 외식업에서 특히 중요합니다.

저희 농장에 대해 더 알고 싶으시면, 저희의 웹 사이트 shephardfamilyfarm.com을 방문하시기 바랍니다. [78]저는 또한 귀하와 직접 이야기를 나누고 당사의 제품과 가격에 대한 카탈로그를 전달해 드리기 위해 귀하의 식당에 방문하면 좋을 것 같습니다. 괜찮으시다면, 편하신 날짜와 시간을 알려 주시기 바랍니다.

Eileen Shephard 드림
Shephard Family 농장
W 슈틀츠로 1134번지
03581 버몬트주 러틀랜드

어휘 | inform v. 알리다, 정보를 제공하다 distribution n. 유통, 분배 organic adj. 유기농의 establishment n. 식당, 기관 source v. 조달하다
carbon footprint phr. 탄소 발자국(상품을 생산·소비하는 과정에서 직간접적으로 발생하는 이산화 탄소의 총량) nutrient n. 영양분
harvest v. 수확하다 produce n. 농산물 drop off phr. 배달하다 newsletter n. 소식지 catalog n. 카탈로그, 일람

74 주제/목적   편지의 목적   난이도 ●○○

Why did Eileen Shephard write Andrew Pacheco a letter?	왜 Eileen Shephard는 Andrew Pacheco에게 편지를 썼는가?
(a) to congratulate him on starting a new business	(a) 그가 새로운 사업을 시작한 것을 축하하기 위해서
(b) to inquire about the food at his restaurant	(b) 그의 식당 음식에 대해 문의하기 위해서
(c) to follow up on an order	(c) 주문에 대한 후속 조치를 취하기 위해서
(d) to promote products to a potential client	**(d) 잠재 고객에게 제품들을 홍보하기 위해서**

—○ 지텔프 치트키

지문의 초반을 주의 깊게 읽고 전체 맥락을 파악한다.

해설 | 1단락의 'I'm pleased to inform you that we are opening our newest distribution center near your restaurant'에서 Eileen Shephard가 Andrew Pacheco에게 그의 식당 근처에 새로운 유통 센터를 오픈할 예정임을 알리게 되어 기쁘다고 한 뒤, Shephard Family 농장에서 제공하는 제품과 서비스에 관해 홍보하는 내용이 이어지고 있다. 따라서 (d)가 정답이다.

어휘 | inquire v. 문의하다 follow up phr. 후속 조치를 취하다 promote v. 홍보하다 potential adj. 잠재적인

75 특정세부사항   What   난이도 ●●○

According to the letter, what is the problem with non-local food?	편지에 따르면, 비현지 식품의 문제점은 무엇인가?
(a) Its shipping produces greenhouse gas emissions.	**(a) 그것의 운송이 온실가스 배출을 초래한다.**
(b) Its transportation costs vary depending on the region.	(b) 그것의 운송비가 지역에 따라 다르다.
(c) It is grown using environmentally irresponsible methods.	(c) 환경적으로 무책임한 방법을 사용하여 재배된다.
(d) It hinders the development of the local economy.	(d) 지역 경제의 발전을 저해한다.

—○ 지텔프 치트키

질문의 키워드 non-local이 outside the region으로 paraphrasing되어 언급된 주변 내용을 주의 깊게 읽는다.

해설 | 2단락의 'the fuel used in the transportation process adds to the overall carbon footprint'에서 식품의 운송 과정에서 사용되는 연료가 전체 탄소 발자국을 증가시킨다고 했다. 따라서 (a)가 정답이다.

Paraphrasing
the transportation 운송 → Its shipping 운송
adds to the overall carbon footprint 전체 탄소 발자국을 증가시킨다 → produces greenhouse gas emissions 온실가스 배출을 초래한다

어휘 | emission n. 배출 irresponsible adj. 무책임한 hinder v. 저해하다

해커스 지텔프 최신기출유형 실전문제집 7회 (Level 2)

Why does the Shephard Family Farm deliver produce within two business days?

(a) so customers continue to use the service
(b) so it can retain more of its nutritional value
(c) so it can stay ripe when it arrives
(d) so customers have time to explore order options

Shephard Family 농장은 왜 영업일 기준 2일 이내에 농산물을 배송하는가?

(a) 고객들이 그 서비스를 계속 이용하게 하기 위해서
(b) 더 많은 영양가를 유지할 수 있게 하기 위해서
(c) 도착할 때 익은 상태를 유지할 수 있게 하기 위해서
(d) 고객들이 주문 선택지들을 살펴볼 시간을 가질 수 있게 하기 위해서

지텔프 치트키

질문의 키워드 two business days가 그대로 언급된 주변 내용을 주의 깊게 읽는다.

해설 | 3단락의 'fruits and vegetables begin losing nutrients not long after they are harvested'에서 과일과 채소는 수확된 지 얼마 지나지 않아 영양분을 상실하기 시작한다고 한 뒤, 'That's why we drop off all customer orders within two business days.'에서 그것이 Shephard Family 농장이 영업일 기준 2일 이내에 모든 고객의 주문을 배달하는 이유라고 했다. 따라서 (b)가 정답이다.

Paraphrasing
nutrients 영양분 → nutritional value 영양가

What will Pacheco probably do if he reads the farm's publication?

(a) inform his customers where the goods come from
(b) use different ingredients depending on the time of the year
(c) enter into partnerships with other local businesses
(d) plan a menu that includes seasonal special discounts

Pacheco가 그 농장의 간행물을 읽으면 무엇을 할 것 같은가?

(a) 고객들에게 상품이 어디서 생산되었는지를 알린다
(b) 일 년 중 시기에 따라 다른 재료를 사용한다
(c) 다른 지역 사업체들과 제휴한다
(d) 계절에 따른 특별 할인을 포함한 메뉴를 기획한다

지텔프 치트키

질문의 키워드 publication이 newsletter로 paraphrasing되어 언급된 주변 내용을 주의 깊게 읽는다.

해설 | 4단락의 'keeping our customers informed ~ through our monthly newsletter, *Shephard's Harvest*'에서 월간 소식지를 통해 고객들에게 지속적으로 정보를 제공한다고 한 뒤, 'That way, you can plan various seasonal menus throughout the year'에서 그렇게 하면 고객들이 1년 내내 다양한 계절 메뉴들을 기획할 수 있다고 한 것을 통해, Pacheco가 Shephard Family 농장의 간행물을 읽으면 일 년 중 시기에 따라 다른 재료를 사용할 것임을 추론할 수 있다. 따라서 (b)가 정답이다.

어휘 | enter into partnership phr. 제휴하다, 협력하다

How can Pacheco find out about the products' prices?

(a) by going to the store's website
(b) by meeting with Shephard on her farm

Pacheco는 제품들의 가격을 어떻게 알 수 있는가?

(a) 그 가게의 웹 사이트에 접속함으로써
(b) Shephard와 그녀의 농장에서 만남으로써

(c) by viewing a catalog on the Internet
(d) by accepting Shephard's offer to visit him

(c) 인터넷에서 카탈로그를 봄으로써
(d) 그를 방문하겠다는 Shephard의 제안을 승낙함으로써

질문의 키워드 prices가 rates로 paraphrasing되어 언급된 주변 내용을 주의 깊게 읽는다.

해설 | 5단락의 'I would ~ be happy to come to your restaurant to ~ give you a catalog of our products and rates.'에서 Shephard는 농장의 제품과 가격에 대한 카탈로그를 전달하기 위해 Pacheco의 식당에 방문하면 좋을 것 같다고 했다. 따라서 (d)가 정답이다.

Paraphrasing
come to ~에 방문하다 → visit 방문하다

오답분석
(a) 5단락에서 Shephard Family 농장에 대해 더 알고 싶으면 농장의 웹 사이트를 방문하라고는 했지만, 웹 사이트에서 제품들의 가격을 알 수 있는지는 언급되지 않았으므로 오답이다.

---

79 어휘 유의어 난이도 ●●○

In the context of the passage, <u>minimize</u> means _____.

(a) control
(b) ease
(c) lessen
(d) degrade

지문의 문맥에서, 'minimize'는 -을 의미한다.

(a) 통제하다
(b) 완화하다
(c) 줄이다
(d) 저하시키다

밑줄 친 어휘의 유의어를 찾는 문제이므로, minimize가 포함된 구절을 읽고 문맥을 파악한다.

해설 | 2단락의 'minimize the distance food travels'는 식품이 이동하는 거리를 줄인다는 뜻이므로, minimize가 '줄이다'라는 의미로 사용된 것을 알 수 있다. 따라서 '줄이다'라는 같은 의미의 (c) lessen이 정답이다.

---

80 어휘 유의어 난이도 ●●○

In the context of the passage, <u>understand</u> means _____.

(a) grasp
(b) reserve
(c) settle
(d) admit

지문의 문맥에서, 'understand'는 -을 의미한다.

(a) 파악한다
(b) 보류한다
(c) 해결한다
(d) 인정한다

밑줄 친 어휘의 유의어를 찾는 문제이므로, understand가 포함된 구절을 읽고 문맥을 파악한다.

해설 | 4단락의 'which I understand is especially important in the restaurant business'는 이것이 화자가 알기로 외식업에서 특히 중요하다는 뜻이므로, understand가 '안다'라는 의미로 사용된 것을 알 수 있다. 따라서 '파악한다'라는 비슷한 의미의 (a) grasp가 정답이다.

TEST 6

정답·스크립트·해석·해설

GRAMMAR

LISTENING

READING & VOCABULARY

TEST 6 점수 확인하기

GRAMMAR _____ / 26 (점수 : _____ 점)
LISTENING _____ / 26 (점수 : _____ 점)
READING & VOCABULARY _____ / 28 (점수 : _____ 점)

TOTAL _____ / 80 (**평균 점수 :** _____ 점)

*각 영역 점수: 맞은 개수 × 3.75
*평균 점수: 각 영역 점수 합계 ÷ 3

정답 및 취약 유형 분석표

자동 채점 및 성적 분석 서비스 ▶

문제집 p.148

GRAMMAR

번호	정답	유형
01	c	준동사
02	d	시제
03	a	조동사
04	c	가정법
05	d	시제
06	c	준동사
07	c	가정법
08	b	관계사
09	a	준동사
10	c	시제
11	b	가정법
12	b	연결어
13	d	조동사
14	a	시제
15	c	가정법
16	d	준동사
17	b	연결어
18	a	시제
19	a	준동사
20	d	가정법
21	a	조동사
22	a	조동사
23	c	시제
24	b	준동사
25	d	가정법
26	c	관계사

유형	맞힌 개수
시제	/ 6
가정법	/ 6
준동사	/ 6
조동사	/ 4
연결어	/ 2
관계사	/ 2
TOTAL	/ 26

LISTENING

PART	번호	정답	유형
PART 1	27	c	특정세부사항
	28	b	특정세부사항
	29	b	Not/True
	30	a	특정세부사항
	31	d	특정세부사항
	32	d	특정세부사항
	33	a	추론
PART 2	34	b	주제/목적
	35	d	특정세부사항
	36	a	특정세부사항
	37	b	추론
	38	c	특정세부사항
	39	c	특정세부사항
PART 3	40	c	특정세부사항
	41	d	특정세부사항
	42	b	특정세부사항
	43	d	특정세부사항
	44	a	특정세부사항
	45	a	추론
PART 4	46	c	주제/목적
	47	a	특정세부사항
	48	d	추론
	49	c	특정세부사항
	50	b	특정세부사항
	51	b	추론
	52	a	특정세부사항

유형	맞힌 개수
주제/목적	/ 2
특정세부사항	/ 18
Not/True	/ 1
추론	/ 5
TOTAL	/ 26

READING & VOCABULARY

PART	번호	정답	유형
PART 1	53	a	특정세부사항
	54	d	특정세부사항
	55	d	추론
	56	a	특정세부사항
	57	b	Not/True
	58	c	어휘
	59	d	어휘
PART 2	60	c	주제/목적
	61	c	특정세부사항
	62	d	추론
	63	a	특정세부사항
	64	b	특정세부사항
	65	a	어휘
	66	d	어휘
PART 3	67	c	추론
	68	a	특정세부사항
	69	b	특정세부사항
	70	c	추론
	71	b	특정세부사항
	72	d	어휘
	73	b	어휘
PART 4	74	b	주제/목적
	75	c	특정세부사항
	76	b	추론
	77	d	특정세부사항
	78	a	특정세부사항
	79	c	어휘
	80	a	어휘

유형	맞힌 개수
주제/목적	/ 2
특정세부사항	/ 12
Not/True	/ 1
추론	/ 5
어휘	/ 8
TOTAL	/ 28

GRAMMAR

01 준동사　to 부정사를 목적어로 취하는 동사

난이도 ●○○

Perfect Programming's loss of revenue is affecting business operations. The board of directors recently decided _____ the development of its newest program until more funding could be secured.

(a) suspending
(b) to have suspended
(c) to suspend
(d) having suspended

Perfect Programming 사의 수익 감소가 사업 운영에 영향을 미치고 있다. 이사회는 최근에 더 많은 자금이 확보될 수 있을 때까지 그 회사의 최신 프로그램 개발을 <u>중단하기</u>로 결정했다.

지텔프 치트키

decide는 to 부정사를 목적어로 취한다.

> 💡 **to 부정사를 목적어로 취하는 빈출 동사**
> decide 결정하다　promise 약속하다　expect 예상하다　vow 맹세하다　wish 희망하다　plan 계획하다　hope 바라다　agree 동의하다
> intend 계획하다　prepare 준비하다

해설ㅣ 빈칸 앞 동사 decide는 to 부정사를 목적어로 취하므로, to 부정사 (c) to suspend가 정답이다.

> 오답분석
>
> (b) to have suspended도 to 부정사이기는 하지만, 완료부정사(to have suspended)로 쓰일 경우 '결정하는' 시점보다 '중단하는' 시점이 앞선다는 것을 나타내므로 문맥에 적합하지 않아 오답이다.

어휘ㅣ revenue n. 수익　operation n. 운영　board of directors phr. 이사회　secure v. 확보하다　suspend v. 중단하다

02 시제　미래완료진행

난이도 ●●○

Henry won a Paul Harrison Classical Music Scholarship and will start college next month. He began playing the violin at the age of five. When he finishes university, he _____ the violin for nearly 20 years.

(a) will be learning
(b) is learning
(c) had learned
(d) will have been learning

Henry는 Paul Harrison 클래식 음악 장학금을 받았고 다음 달에 대학 생활을 시작할 것이다. 그는 5살 때 바이올린을 연주하기 시작했다. 그가 대학을 마칠 때, 그는 거의 20년 동안 바이올린을 <u>배워오고 있는 중일 것이다</u>.

지텔프 치트키

'when + 현재 동사'와 'for + 기간 표현'이 함께 오면 미래완료진행 시제가 정답이다.

해설ㅣ 현재 동사로 미래의 의미를 나타내는 시간의 부사절 'when + 현재 동사'(When ~ finishes)와 지속을 나타내는 'for + 기간 표현'(for ~ 20 years)이 있고, 문맥상 Henry가 대학을 마치는 미래 시점에 거의 20년 동안 계속해서 바이올린을 배워오고 있는 중일 것이라는 의미가 되어야 자연스럽다. 따라서 미래완료진행 시제 (d) will have been learning이 정답이다.

해커스 지텔프 최신기출유형 실전문제집 7회 (Level 2)

(a) 미래진행 시제는 특정 미래 시점에 한창 진행 중일 일을 나타내므로, 과거 또는 현재에 시작해서 특정 미래 시점까지 계속해서 진행되고 있을 일을 표현할 수 없어 오답이다.

---

03 조동사 조동사 can 난이도 ●●○

Urban farming has surprisingly strong yields of high-quality vegetables. Although it is not practical in every neighborhood, pick-your-own crops from urban farms _____ become a viable alternative to store-bought products.

(a) **can**
(b) must
(c) would
(d) should

도시 농업은 놀랍도록 아주 많은 고품질의 채소 수확량을 얻는다. 비록 그것(도시 농업)이 모든 지역에서 현실적인 것은 아니지만, 도시 농장에서 소비자가 직접 수확하는 작물들은 가게에서 구매되는 상품들의 실행 가능한 대안이 될 <u>수 있다</u>.

지텔프 치트키

'~할 수 있다'라고 말할 때는 can을 쓴다.

해설 | 문맥상 비록 도시 농업이 모든 지역에서 현실적인 것은 아니지만, 도시 농장에서 소비자가 직접 수확하는 작물들은 가게에서 구매되는 상품들의 실행 가능한 대안이 될 수 있다는 의미가 되어야 자연스러우므로, '~할 수 있다'를 뜻하면서 가능성을 나타내는 조동사 (a) can이 정답이다.

어휘 | yield n. 수확량, 산출량 practical adj. 현실적인 pick-your-own adj. (농장에서) 소비자가 직접 수확하는 viable adj. 실행 가능한 alternative n. 대안 store-bought adj. 가게에서 구매되는

---

04 가정법 가정법 과거 난이도 ●●○

The environmental group is having a hard time getting people to accept their proposal for reducing fine dust. If they were able to decrease the cost of the plan, many members of the public _____ it.

(a) will welcome
(b) had welcomed
(c) **would welcome**
(d) would have welcomed

그 환경 단체는 미세 먼지를 저감하는 것에 대한 그들의 제안을 국민들이 수용하게 만드는 것에 어려움을 겪고 있다. 만약 그들이 그 계획의 비용을 줄일 수 있다면, 대중의 많은 일원들은 그것을 <u>기꺼이 받아들일 것이다</u>.

지텔프 치트키

'if + 과거 동사'가 있으면 'would/could + 동사원형'이 정답이다.

> ☼ 가정법 과거
> If + 주어 + 과거 동사, 주어 + would/could(조동사 과거형) + 동사원형

해설 | If절에 과거 동사(were)가 있으므로, 주절에는 이와 짝을 이루어 가정법 과거를 만드는 'would(조동사 과거형) + 동사원형'이 와야 한다. 따

라서 (c) would welcome이 정답이다.

어휘 | proposal n. 제안, 제의 reduce v. 저감하다 fine dust phr. 미세 먼지 welcome v. 기꺼이 받아들이다

---

05 시제 과거완료진행

난이도 ●●○

Trade is commencing again between the two Asian nations after an intense storm made sea travel dangerous. Cargo ships from both countries departed this morning and will arrive soon. Before the weather cleared today, goods _____ at each nation's ports.

(a) piled up
(b) were piling up
(c) have been piling up
(d) had been piling up

거센 폭풍이 해상 이동을 위험하게 만든 이후 두 아시아 국가 간의 무역이 다시 시작되고 있다. 양국의 화물선들이 오늘 아침에 출발하였고 곧 도착할 것이다. 오늘 날씨가 개기 전에, 각국의 항구에는 물품들이 쌓여오고 있던 중이었다.

⊸○ 지텔프 치트키

'before + 과거 동사'가 있으면 과거완료진행 시제가 정답이다.

해설 | 과거완료진행 시제와 함께 쓰이는 시간 표현 'before + 과거 동사'(Before ~ cleared)가 있고, 문맥상 대과거(두 아시아 국가 간의 무역이 다시 시작된 시점)부터 과거(오늘 날씨가 갠 시점)까지 각국의 항구에 물품들이 쌓여오고 있던 중이었다는 의미가 되어야 자연스럽다. 따라서 과거완료진행 시제 (d) had been piling up이 정답이다.

오답분석
(b) 과거진행 시제는 특정 과거 시점에 한창 진행 중이었던 일을 나타내므로, 대과거에 시작해서 특정 과거 시점까지 계속해서 진행되고 있었던 일을 표현할 수 없어 오답이다.

어휘 | trade n. 무역 commence v. 시작되다 intense adj. 거센 cargo n. (선박·비행기의) 화물 depart v. 출발하다 clear v. (날씨가) 개다 port n. 항구 pile up phr. 쌓이다

---

06 준동사 동명사를 목적어로 취하는 동사

난이도 ●●○

Grayson is a heavy sleeper and always struggles with getting up early in the morning. A classmate who noticed his frequent tardiness recommended _____ only for afternoon courses.

(a) to have registered
(b) having registered
(c) registering
(d) to register

Grayson은 잠귀가 어두운 사람이며 아침에 일찍 일어나는 것에 항상 어려움을 겪는다. 그의 잦은 지각을 알고 있던 한 급우는 오후 수업만 등록하는 것을 권장했다.

⊸○ 지텔프 치트키

recommend는 동명사를 목적어로 취한다.

해설 | 빈칸 앞 동사 recommend는 동명사를 목적어로 취하므로, 동명사 (c) registering이 정답이다.

(b) having registered도 동명사이기는 하지만, 완료동명사(having registered)로 쓰일 경우 '권장하는' 시점보다 '등록하는' 시점이 앞선다는 것을 나타내므로 문맥에 적합하지 않아 오답이다.

어휘ㅣ heavy sleeper phr. 잠귀가 어두운 사람 frequent adj. 잦은, 빈번한 tardiness n. 지각 recommend v. 권장하다 register v. 등록하다

---

07 가정법 가정법 과거완료 난이도 ●●○

A national newspaper is being criticized by the CEO of AFC Industries for publishing an ad that misspelled the company's name. The paper publicly apologized and said that it _____ the ad if its editors had caught the mistake in time.

(a) would not print
(b) did not print
(c) would not have printed
(d) has not printed

한 전국지가 회사 이름의 철자를 잘못 쓴 광고를 실은 것으로 인해 AFC 산업사의 최고 경영자로부터 비판받고 있다. 그 신문사는 공개적으로 사과했고 만약 편집자들이 늦지 않게 그 실수를 알아챘었다면 그 광고를 게재하지 않았을 것이라고 말했다.

⊶○ 지텔프 치트키

'if + had p.p.'가 있으면 'would/could + have p.p.'가 정답이다.

> ☀ **가정법 과거완료**
> If + 주어 + had p.p., 주어 + would/could(조동사 과거형) + have p.p.

해설ㅣ if절에 'had p.p.' 형태의 had caught가 있으므로, 주절에는 이와 짝을 이루어 가정법 과거완료를 만드는 'would(조동사 과거형) + have p.p.'가 와야 한다. 따라서 (c) would not have printed가 정답이다.

어휘ㅣ criticize v. 비판하다 misspell v. 철자를 잘못 쓰다 publicly adv. 공개적으로 apologize v. 사과하다 print v. (인쇄 매체에) 게재하다, 싣다

---

08 관계사 주격 관계대명사 which 난이도 ●●○

Jackson City has large green spaces open to the public. People of all ages enjoy strolls in these areas. The leafy trees, _____, are appreciated by residents worn out by the heat.

(a) what provide plenty of shade to passerbys
(b) which provide plenty of shade to passerbys
(c) that provide plenty of shade to passerbys
(d) where they provide plenty of shade to passerbys

Jackson 시에는 대중에게 개방된 넓은 녹지 공간이 있다. 모든 연령대의 사람들이 이 공간에서 산책을 즐긴다. 잎이 무성한 나무들은, 행인들에게 충분한 그늘을 제공하는데, 더위로 인해 몹시 지친 주민들에게 호평받고 있다.

⊶○ 지텔프 치트키

사물 선행사가 관계절 안에서 주어 역할을 하고, 빈칸 앞에 콤마(,)가 있으면 주격 관계대명사 which가 정답이다.

해설ㅣ 사물 선행사 The leafy trees를 받으면서 콤마(,) 뒤에 올 수 있는 주격 관계대명사가 필요하므로, (b) which provide plenty of shade to passerbys가 정답이다.

(c) 관계대명사 that도 사물 선행사를 받을 수 있지만, 콤마 뒤에 올 수 없으므로 오답이다.

어휘 | stroll n. 산책 leafy adj. 잎이 무성한 appreciate v. 호평하다, 고마워하다 be worn out phr. 몹시 지치다 shade n. 그늘
passerby n. 행인

---

09 준동사 동명사를 목적어로 취하는 동사   난이도 ●○○

The firm had prepared the final documents to complete the merger, but it was not ready to release the news. When asked by a local reporter, the corporation's lawyer denied _____ the deal.

(a) **being aware of**
(b) to be aware of
(c) to have been aware of
(d) will be aware of

그 회사는 합병을 완료하기 위한 최종 문서를 준비했었지만, 이 소식을 공개할 준비가 되지 않았다. 현지 기자로부터 질문을 받았을 때, 기업 측 변호사는 그 합의에 대해 알고 있다는 것을 부인했다.

지텔프 치트키

deny는 동명사를 목적어로 취한다.

해설 | 빈칸 앞 동사 deny는 동명사를 목적어로 취하므로, 동명사 (a) being aware of가 정답이다.

어휘 | document n. 문서 merger n. 합병 release v. 공개하다 corporation n. 기업, 회사 deny v. 부인하다

---

10 시제 현재완료진행   난이도 ●●○

Discovered by a team of French scientists, the new bacteria are larger than anyone thought possible. The researchers _____ other microbes in the region for several years now, and they are hoping to continue their research.

(a) are investigating
(b) investigate
(c) **have been investigating**
(d) will investigate

프랑스 과학자팀에 의해 발견된, 그 새로운 박테리아는 모두가 가능하다고 생각했던 것보다 더 크다. 연구원들은 현재 몇 년 동안 그 지역의 다른 미생물들을 조사해오고 있는 중이며, 그들은 연구를 계속해 나가기를 희망하고 있다.

지텔프 치트키

'for + 기간 표현 + now'가 있으면 현재완료진행 시제가 정답이다.

해설 | 현재완료진행 시제와 함께 쓰이는 시간 표현 'for + 기간 표현 + now'(for several years now)가 있고, 문맥상 연구원들이 현재 몇 년 동안 그 지역의 다른 미생물들을 계속해서 조사해오고 있는 중이라는 의미가 되어야 자연스럽다. 따라서 현재완료진행 시제 (c) have been investigating이 정답이다.

(a) 현재진행 시제는 특정 현재 시점에 한창 진행 중인 일을 나타내므로, 과거에 시작해서 현재 시점까지 계속해서 진행되고 있는 일을 표현할 수 없어 오답이다.

어휘 | microbe n. 미생물 investigate v. 조사하다

해커스 지텔프 최신기출유형 실전문제집 7회 (Level 2)

Marcus doesn't think his team manager is using the right approach for the new content creation project. She is making all the members work on everything. If Marcus were to take charge of the team, he _____ individual tasks according to each employee's capabilities.

(a) assigned
(b) would assign
(c) would have assigned
(d) had assigned

Marcus는 그의 팀 관리자가 새로운 콘텐츠 제작 프로젝트에 대해 올바른 접근 방식을 사용하고 있다고 생각하지 않는다. 그녀는 모든 구성원들로 하여금 모든 일을 하게 만들고 있다. 만약 Marcus가 팀을 담당한다면, 그는 각 직원의 능력에 따라 개별 업무를 할당할 것이다.

 지텔프 치트키

'if + were to + 동사원형'이 있으면 'would/could + 동사원형'이 정답이다.

☀ 가정법 과거(were to)
If + 주어 + were to + 동사원형, 주어 + would/could(조동사 과거형) + 동사원형

해설 | If절에 과거 동사(were to take charge)가 있으므로, 주절에는 이와 짝을 이루어 가정법 과거를 만드는 'would(조동사 과거형) + 동사원형'이 와야 한다. 따라서 (b) would assign이 정답이다.

어휘 | approach n. 접근 방식 take charge of phr. ~을 담당하다 capability n. 능력 assign v. 할당하다

Jessica finally heard back from the president of McMinnville Technologies. The executive stated that he was interested in the fintech application she has been developing. _____, he proposed meeting the very next day at the firm's headquarters.

(a) Nevertheless
(b) In fact
(c) Otherwise
(d) For example

Jessica는 마침내 McMinnville Technologies 사의 사장으로부터 회답을 받았다. 그 경영자는 그녀가 개발해오고 있는 핀테크 애플리케이션에 관심이 있다고 말했다. 실제로, 그는 바로 다음 날 그 회사의 본사에서 만나는 것을 제안했다.

지텔프 치트키

'실제로'라는 의미의 강조를 나타낼 때는 In fact를 쓴다.

☀ 강조를 나타내는 빈출 접속부사
In fact 실제로 In truth 사실은 In other words 즉, 다시 말해 Surprisingly 놀랍게도 Undoubtedly 의심할 여지 없이

해설 | 문맥상 McMinnville Technologies 사의 사장이 Jessica가 개발해오고 있는 핀테크 애플리케이션에 관심이 있다고 말했다는 앞 문장의 내용을 강조하여 '실제로, 그는 바로 다음 날 그 회사의 본사에서 만나는 것을 제안했다'라는 의미가 되어야 자연스럽다. 따라서 '실제로'라는 의미의 강조를 나타내는 접속부사 (b) In fact가 정답이다.

오답분석

(a) Nevertheless는 '그럼에도 불구하고', (c) Otherwise는 '그렇지 않으면', (d) For example은 '예를 들어'라는 의미로 문맥에 적합하지 않아 오답이다.

13 조동사   조동사 should 생략   난이도 ●●○

Kristi is writing down a list of things to consider before she moves. It is important that she _____ in a quiet area that is close to her workplace and has good restaurants since she doesn't cook often.

(a) dwelt
(b) will dwell
(c) dwells
(d) dwell

Kristi는 이사하기 전에 고려할 사항들의 목록을 작성하는 중이다. 그녀는 그녀의 직장에서 가깝고 그녀가 요리를 자주 하지 않기 때문에 좋은 식당들이 있는 조용한 지역에 <u>사는</u> 것이 중요하다.

─○ 지텔프 치트키

important 다음에는 that절에 동사원형이 온다.

☀ 주장·요구·명령·제안을 나타내는 빈출 형용사
  important 중요한   essential 필수적인   best 제일 좋은   necessary 필요한   mandatory 의무적인

해설 | 주절에 주장을 나타내는 형용사 important가 있으므로 that절에는 '(should +) 동사원형'이 와야 한다. 따라서 동사원형 (d) dwell이 정답이다.

어휘 | dwell v. 살다, 거주하다

14 시제   과거진행   난이도 ●●○

The Davis High School graduation ceremony was a disaster because the administrators planned it as an outdoor event without checking the weather forecast in advance. The students _____ up to the stage to receive their diplomas when it began to pour.

(a) were walking
(b) walk
(c) have walked
(d) would walk

관리자들이 사전에 일기 예보를 확인하지 않고 그것을 야외 행사로 계획했기 때문에 Davis 고등학교 졸업식은 엉망진창이었다. 비가 마구 쏟아지기 시작했을 때 학생들은 졸업장을 받기 위해 무대 위로 <u>걸어가고 있던 중이었다.</u>

─○ 지텔프 치트키

'for + 기간 표현' 없이 'when + 과거 동사'만 있으면 과거진행 시제가 정답이다.

해설 | 과거진행 시제와 함께 쓰이는 시간 표현 'when + 과거 동사'(when ~ began)가 있고, 문맥상 비가 마구 쏟아지기 시작했던 과거 시점에 학생들은 졸업장을 받기 위해 무대 위로 걸어가고 있던 중이었다는 의미가 되어야 자연스럽다. 따라서 과거진행 시제 (a) were walking이 정답이다.

어휘 | disaster n. 엉망진창, 재앙   forecast n. 예보   in advance phr. 사전에   diploma n. 졸업장   pour v. (비가) 마구 쏟아지다

15 가정법   가정법 과거완료   난이도 ●●○

Yesterday, Nina's daughter suddenly went into labor. Nina had just visited her last week, and she wasn't due for another month. If Nina _____ the time was near, she would have stayed longer before flying home.

(a) knew
(b) would have known
(c) had known
(d) would know

어제, Nina의 딸이 갑자기 진통을 시작했다. Nina는 지난주에 그녀를 막 방문했었고, 그녀는 앞으로 한 달 동안은 출산 예정일이 아니었다. 만약 Nina가 그 시간(출산일)이 임박했다는 것을 알았었다면, 그녀는 비행기를 타고 집으로 돌아오기 전에 더 오래 머물렀을 것이다.

━○ 지텔프 치트키

if와 'would/could + have p.p.'가 있으면 had p.p.가 정답이다.

해설 | 주절에 'would(조동사 과거형) + have p.p.' 형태의 would have stayed가 있으므로, If절에는 이와 짝을 이루어 가정법 과거완료를 만드는 과거완료 동사가 와야 한다. 따라서 (c) had known이 정답이다.

어휘 | go into labor phr. 진통을 시작하다   due adj. (출산이) 예정된

16 준동사   to 부정사의 부사 역할   난이도 ●●○

Fuller Airlines introduced an additional nonstop flight from Atlanta to Rome, which is great news for passengers who are tired of lengthy layovers. The airline added the route _____ new customers, particularly business travelers.

(a) having acquired
(b) to be acquiring
(c) acquiring
(d) to acquire

Fuller 항공사가 애틀랜타에서 로마로 가는 추가의 직항편을 발표했는데, 이것은 너무 긴 기착에 지친 승객들에게 아주 좋은 소식이다. 그 항공사는 신규 고객들, 특히 출장 여행자들을 유입하기 위해 그 노선을 추가했다.

━○ 지텔프 치트키

'~하기 위해'라고 말할 때는 to 부정사를 쓴다.

해설 | 빈칸 앞에 주어(The airline), 동사(added), 목적어(the route)가 갖춰진 완전한 절이 있으므로, 빈칸 이하는 문장의 필수 성분이 아닌 수식어구이다. 따라서 목적을 나타내며 수식어구를 이끌 수 있는 to 부정사 (d) to acquire가 정답이다.

어휘 | additional adj. 추가의   lengthy adj. 너무 긴, 지루한   layover n. 기착, 도중하차   acquire v. 유입하다, 얻다

17 연결어   접속사   난이도 ●●●

Most cats hate being immersed in water, but that's not the case for Cooper, a three-year-old Bengal cat. He loves to swim and follows his owner _____ she heads into the backyard to take a dip in the pool.

대부분의 고양이들은 물에 몸을 담그는 것을 싫어하지만, 3살 된 벵갈 고양이 Cooper의 경우는 아니다. 그는 수영하는 것을 좋아하고 그의 주인이 수영장에서 잠깐 수영하기 위해 뒤뜰로 향할 때마다 그녀를 따라간다.

(a) because
(b) whenever
(c) since
(d) unless

🔑 지텔프 치트키

'~할 때마다'라는 의미의 시간을 나타낼 때는 whenever를 쓴다.

💡 시간을 나타내는 빈출 접속사
    whenever ~할 때마다   until ~할 때까지   while ~하는 동안   after ~한 이후에   before ~하기 전에

해설 | 문맥상 벵갈 고양이 Cooper는 대부분의 고양이들과는 달리 수영하는 것을 좋아하며, 그의 주인이 수영장에서 잠깐 수영하기 위해 뒤뜰로 향할 때마다 그녀를 따라간다는 의미가 되어야 자연스럽다. 따라서 '~할 때마다'라는 의미의 시간을 나타내는 부사절 접속사 (b) whenever 가 정답이다.

오답분석
(a) because와 (c) since는 '~하기 때문에', (d) unless는 '~하지 않는 한'이라는 의미로, 문맥에 적합하지 않아 오답이다.

어휘 | immerse v. (몸을) 담그다, 몰두시키다   head v. 향하다, 가다   take a dip phr. 잠깐 수영하다

---

18   시제   미래진행   난이도 ●●○

During the school announcements this morning, the principal talked about the upcoming Shakespeare Festival. The school plans to have various events related to his plays, and the drama club _____ _Hamlet_ until the end of next week.

(a) will be performing
(b) was performing
(c) will have performed
(d) has performed

오늘 아침 학교 안내 방송 시간에, 교장 선생님이 다가오는 셰익스피어 축제에 관해 말씀하셨다. 학교는 그의 희곡들과 관련된 다양한 행사를 하려고 계획하고 있으며, 연극 동아리는 다음 주 말까지 「햄릿」을 공연하고 있는 중일 것이다.

🔑 지텔프 치트키

'for + 기간 표현' 없이 'until + 미래 시점'만 있으면 미래진행 시제가 정답이다.

해설 | 미래진행 시제와 함께 쓰이는 시간 표현 'until + 미래 시점'(until the end of next week)이 있고, 문맥상 미래 시점인 다음 주 말까지 연극 동아리는 「햄릿」을 공연하고 있는 중일 것이라는 의미가 되어야 자연스럽다. 따라서 미래진행 시제 (a) will be performing이 정답이다.

어휘 | announcement n. 안내 방송   upcoming adj. 다가오는   play n. 희곡, 연극

---

19   준동사   동명사를 목적어로 취하는 동사   난이도 ●●○

I have some exciting news! My boss doesn't want to risk _____ out on a potential partnership with a client in Vietnam, so he is sending me there on a business trip to close the deal.

제게 흥미로운 소식이 있어요! 저의 상사는 베트남에 있는 고객과의 잠재적인 제휴를 놓칠 위험을 무릅쓰고 싶지 않아 하기 때문에, 거래를 성사시키기 위해 저를 그곳으로 출장을 보낼 거예요.

(a) to miss
(b) missing
(c) having missed
(d) to have missed

━○ 지텔프 치트키

risk는 동명사를 목적어로 취한다.

해설┃ 빈칸 앞 동사 risk는 동명사를 목적어로 취하므로, 동명사 (b) missing이 정답이다.

> 오답분석
>
> (c) having missed도 동명사이기는 하지만, 완료동명사(having missed)로 쓰일 경우 '위험을 무릅쓰는' 시점보다 '(제휴를) 놓치는' 시점이 앞선다는 것을 나타내므로 문맥에 적합하지 않아 오답이다.

어휘┃ risk v. 위험을 무릅쓰다 partnership n. 제휴, 협력 close a deal phr. 거래를 성사시키다

---

20 가정법   가정법 과거완료   난이도 ●●○

Amanda was looking forward to making her first Thanksgiving dinner, but she ended up burning the turkey even though she adhered to her mother's directions carefully. Had she realized it was so difficult to cook a turkey properly, she _____ a precooked one.

(a) was buying
(b) would buy
(c) had bought
(d) would have bought

Amanda는 그녀의 첫 추수감사절 저녁 식사를 만드는 것을 기대하고 있었지만, 그녀 어머니의 지시를 주의 깊게 지켰음에도 불구하고 결국 칠면조를 태우고 말았다. 그녀가 칠면조를 제대로 요리하는 것이 매우 어렵다는 것을 알았었다면, 그녀는 미리 익혀 놓은 것을 샀을 것이다.

━○ 지텔프 치트키

Had p.p.가 있으면 'would/could + have p.p.'가 정답이다.

> ☀ 가정법 과거완료(도치)
> Had + 주어 + p.p., 주어 + would/could(조동사 과거형) + have p.p.

해설┃ if가 생략되어 도치된 절에 'had p.p.' 형태의 Had ~ realized가 있으므로, 주절에는 이와 짝을 이루어 가정법 과거완료를 만드는 'would(조동사 과거형) + have p.p.'가 와야 한다. 따라서 (d) would have bought가 정답이다. 참고로, 'Had she realized ~'는 'If she had realized ~'로 바꿔 쓸 수 있다.

어휘┃ adhere v. 지키다, 고수하다 direction n. 지시 properly adv. 제대로 precooked adj. 미리 익혀 놓은

---

21 조동사   조동사 must   난이도 ●●○

The city council is debating whether or not to approve funding for library renovations. The final decision is expected to be reached next Monday. Supporters of the

시의회는 도서관 보수 공사를 위한 자금을 승인할지 말지의 여부를 논의하고 있다. 최종 결정은 다음 주 월요일에 내려질 것으로 예상된다. 이 지출의 지지자들

expenditure claim that the facility _____ be remodeled because it is currently in terrible condition.

(a) **must**
(b) can
(c) would
(d) might

은 그 시설이 현재 너무 안 좋은 상태에 놓여 있기 때문에 개조되어<u>야 한다</u>고 주장한다.

해설 | 문맥상 도서관 보수 공사를 위한 자금 지출의 지지자들은 도서관 시설이 현재 너무 안 좋은 상태에 놓여 있기 때문에 개조되어야 한다고 주장한다는 의미가 되어야 자연스러우므로, '~해야 한다'를 뜻하면서 의무를 나타내는 조동사 (a) must가 정답이다. 참고로, must와 should 모두 '~해야 한다'를 뜻하지만, must는 should보다 강한 어조로 조언을 하거나 의무를 나타낼 때 쓴다.

어휘 | city council phr. 시의회 approve v. 승인하다 renovation n. 보수 공사 supporter n. 지지자 expenditure n. (공공 기금의) 지출 facility n. 시설 remodel v. 개조하다

22 조동사   조동사 should 생략

난이도 ●○○

The Rover High School principal had a meeting with parents about getting rid of school uniforms owing to a petition signed by the students. While some parents agreed with this idea, the majority insisted that uniforms _____ mandatory.

(a) **remain**
(b) are remaining
(c) had remained
(d) remained

Rover 고등학교의 교장은 학생들이 서명한 청원서 때문에 교복을 없애는 것에 관하여 학부모들과 회의를 했다. 몇몇 학부모들은 이 생각에 동의했지만, 대다수는 교복이 의무적인 것으로 <u>남아야 한다</u>고 주장했다.

해설 | 주절에 주장을 나타내는 동사 insist가 있으므로 that절에는 '(should +) 동사원형'이 와야 한다. 따라서 동사원형 (a) remain이 정답이다.

어휘 | get rid of phr. ~을 없애다 owing to prep. ~ 때문에 petition n. 청원서 majority n. 대다수 mandatory adj. 의무적인

TEST 1
TEST 2
TEST 3
TEST 4
TEST 5
TEST 6
TEST 7

해커스 지텔프 최신기출유형 실전문제집 7회 (Level 2)

23 시제 현재진행

Anthony was selected to sing the national anthem at the memorial service for Veterans Day, which is only a week away. He cannot meet us right now because he _____ the song.

(a) practices
(b) practiced
(c) is practicing
(d) has been practicing

Anthony는 재향 군인의 날 추도식에서 국가를 부르기로 선정되었으며, 그것은 일주일밖에 남지 않았다. 그는 그 노래를 <u>연습하고 있는 중이기</u> 때문에 지금 당장 우리를 만날 수 없다.

지텔프 치트키

right now가 있으면 현재진행 시제가 정답이다.

해설 | 현재진행 시제와 함께 쓰이는 시간 표현 right now가 있고, 문맥상 말하고 있는 현재 시점에 Anthony가 노래를 연습하고 있는 중이라는 의미가 되어야 자연스럽다. 따라서 현재진행 시제 (c) is practicing이 정답이다.

오답분석

(a) 현재 시제는 반복되는 일이나 습관, 일반적인 사실을 나타내므로, 현재 시점에 한창 진행 중인 일을 표현하기에는 현재진행 시제보다 부적절하므로 오답이다.

어휘 | national anthem phr. 국가 memorial service phr. 추도식 Veterans Day phr. 재향 군인의 날

24 준동사 to 부정사를 목적어로 취하는 동사

Cindy's boiler pipes froze during the snowstorm last night, so her house was very cold at dawn. She chose _____ a plumber before she left for work so that she wouldn't have to shiver in her bed tonight.

(a) calling
(b) to call
(c) to have called
(d) having called

어젯밤에 눈보라가 치는 동안 Cindy의 보일러 관이 얼어서, 새벽녘에 그녀의 집은 매우 추웠다. 그녀는 오늘 밤 그녀의 침대에서 떨 필요 없도록 일하러 나가기 전에 배관공을 <u>부르기로</u> 결정했다.

지텔프 치트키

choose는 to 부정사를 목적어로 취한다.

해설 | 빈칸 앞 동사 choose는 to 부정사를 목적어로 취하므로, to 부정사 (b) to call이 정답이다.

오답분석

(c) to have called도 to 부정사이기는 하지만, 완료부정사(to have called)로 쓰일 경우 '결정하는' 시점보다 '부르는' 시점이 앞선다는 것을 나타내므로 문맥에 적합하지 않아 오답이다.

어휘 | freeze v. 얼다 dawn n. 새벽녘 plumber n. 배관공 shiver v. 떨다

25 가정법　　가정법 과거완료

Steps away from the finish line of the marathon, Victoria fell to the ground with an abrupt muscle spasm. After the competition, she told her family that she would have been all right if she _____ more prior to the race.

(a) is stretching
(b) would stretch
(c) stretched
(d) had stretched

마라톤의 결승선을 몇 걸음 남겨 놓고, Victoria는 갑작스러운 근육 경련 때문에 땅바닥에 쓰러졌다. 경기가 끝난 후, 그녀는 가족에게 만약 그녀가 경주에 앞서 더 많이 <u>스트레칭을 했다면</u> 그녀는 괜찮았을 것이라고 말했다.

지텔프 치트키

if와 'would/could + have p.p.'가 있으면 had p.p.가 정답이다.

해설 | 주절에 'would(조동사 과거형) + have p.p.' 형태의 would have been이 있으므로, if절에는 이와 짝을 이루어 가정법 과거완료를 만드는 과거완료 동사가 와야 한다. 따라서 (d) had stretched가 정답이다.

어휘 | abrupt adj. 갑작스러운　spasm n. 경련, 발작

26 관계사　　목적격 관계대명사 whom

The model of the human psyche consisting of the id, ego, and super-ego was postulated by the famous neurologist Sigmund Freud. Freud, _____, emphasized the importance of the unconscious mind.

(a) what scholars credit with the development of psychoanalysis
(b) which scholars credit with the development of psychoanalysis
(c) whom scholars credit with the development of psychoanalysis
(d) who credited with the development of psychoanalysis scholars

이드, 자아, 초자아로 구성된 인간 정신 모델은 유명한 신경학자인 지크문트 프로이트에 의해 상정되었다. 프로이트는, 그에게 학자들이 정신 분석학의 발전<u>에 대한 공을 돌리는데</u>, 무의식적인 마음의 중요성을 강조했다.

지텔프 치트키

사람 선행사가 관계절 안에서 목적어 역할을 하고, 빈칸 앞에 콤마(,)가 있으면 목적격 관계대명사 whom이 정답이다.

해설 | 사람 선행사 Freud를 받으면서 콤마(,) 뒤에 와서 보기의 관계절 내에서 동사 credit의 목적어가 될 수 있는 목적격 관계대명사가 필요하므로, (c) whom scholars credit with the development of psychoanalysis가 정답이다.

어휘 | psyche n. 정신　consist of phr. ~으로 구성되다　id n. 이드(인간의 원시적·본능적 요소가 존재하는 무의식 부분)　postulate v. 상정하다
neurologist n. 신경학자　emphasize v. 강조하다　unconscious adj. 무의식적인　scholar n. 학자
credit A with B phr. A에게 B에 대한 공을 돌리다　psychoanalysis n. 정신 분석학

LISTENING

음성 바로 듣기

안부 인사	M: Hey, Linda! ²⁷I like your new cap. Where did you get it? F: Hey, Jack! ²⁷I bought it when I went to my first baseball game last Saturday.
주제 제시: 야구 경기 관람	M: Wow! What finally made you take a trip to the ballpark? F: I've wanted to go for a long time but never had the chance. Fortunately, ²⁸my coworker had an extra ticket to last weekend's game between the Cubs and the Dodgers. ²⁸She offered it to me, and I happily accepted! M: That's great. Tell me what it was like. I want to hear all of the details. F: ²⁹⁽ᵇ⁾It was very exciting! ²⁹⁽ᶜ⁾The energy inside of the stadium was indescribable. ²⁹⁽ᵈ⁾The fans were cheering and chanting. ²⁹⁽ᵃ⁾There's nothing else quite like it!
팬들 사이의 유대감	M: Yeah, you have to witness it yourself to understand. ³⁰Did you meet any new people there? F: Yes, I did. ³⁰I started chatting with the group in front of me between innings, and by the end of the game, we were friends. M: Ah, yes. There is a strong sense of fellowship between fans. How about the food?
경기장 음식	F: That was one of the best parts. I made certain to try everything on the menu. It's hard to think of anything more special than having a hot dog at a baseball game! M: Ha-ha . . . Yes, it's something everyone should experience. By the way, which team won?
야구가 흥미 로운 이유	F: Well, we were rooting for the Cubs, but the Dodgers won in the end. It was very close though. It was hard to predict who the winner would be until the last inning. ³¹Baseball is definitely more interesting than I thought. M: Oh, really? What do you mean by that? F: ³¹I had no idea there were so many complicated strategies and techniques involved. The pitcher used lots of different throwing styles, and the batters were great at directing the ball with diverse kinds of hits. There was never a dull moment!

남: 안녕, Linda! ²⁷네 새 모자가 마음에 드는걸. 그거 어디서 구했어?

여: 안녕, Jack! ²⁷지난주 토요일에 내 첫 야구 경기를 보러 갔을 때 그것을 샀어.

남: 와! 드디어 야구장에 가게 된 계기가 뭐야?

여: 오래전부터 가 보고 싶었는데 한 번도 기회가 없었어. 운 좋게도, 컵스와 다저스 간의 ²⁸지난 주말 경기의 여분 표를 내 직장 동료가 가지고 있었어. 그녀가 나에게 그것을 줬고, 나는 기쁘게 받았지!

남: 멋지다. 그것(경기)이 어땠는지 말해줘. 모든 세부 사항을 듣고 싶어.

여: ²⁹⁽ᵇ⁾그것은 매우 흥미진진했어! ²⁹⁽ᶜ⁾경기장 안의 에너지는 말로 표현할 수 없었어. ²⁹⁽ᵈ⁾팬들은 환호성을 지르고 노래했지. ²⁹⁽ᵃ⁾이것과 같은 건 어떠한 것도 없어!

남: 맞아, 이해하기 위해서는 직접 봐야 해. ³⁰그곳에서 새로운 사람들을 만났어?

여: 응, 만났어. ³⁰이닝 사이에 내 앞에 있는 사람들과 이야기를 나누기 시작했고, 경기가 끝날 때쯤에, 우린 친구가 됐어.

남: 아, 맞아. 팬들 사이에는 강한 유대감이 있지. 음식은 어땠니?

여: 그것은 가장 좋은 부분 중 하나였어. 나는 메뉴에 있는 모든 것을 먹어 보는 것을 확실히 했어. 야구장에서 핫도그를 먹는 것보다 더 특별한 것을 생각하기는 어렵지!

남: 하하... 맞아, 그것은 모두가 경험해 봐야 할 일이야. 그건 그렇고, 어느 팀이 이겼어?

여: 음, 우리는 컵스를 응원했지만, 결국 다저스가 이겼어. 그래도 아주 막상막하였어. 마지막 이닝까지 승자가 누구일지 예측하기 어려웠어. ³¹야구는 확실히 내가 생각했던 것보다 더 흥미로워.

남: 오, 정말? 그게 무슨 뜻이야?

여: ³¹나는 그렇게 많은 복잡한 전략들과 기술들이 수반되는지 몰랐어. 투수는 많은 다양한 투구 스타일을 사용했고, 타자들은 다양한 유형의 안타로 공을 다루는 데 능숙했어. 결코 따분한 순간이 없었어!

M: Did you see anyone in the stands catch a ball? Sometimes when the batter hits the ball, it goes over the fence and a lucky fan grabs it.

F: I did! ³²One came right in my direction, but I couldn't get it because I didn't have a glove. The person directly behind me caught it.

M: Oh, I see . . . That's too bad. I guess you will have to be better prepared next time you go out to the ballpark.

F: Yes. I've made it my goal to catch a foul ball or a home run ball. I want to walk out of the stadium with a little piece of baseball history!

M: Sounds like you're becoming a real fan. I'm glad you enjoyed your first game, Linda.

F: Thanks, Jack. I only wish I had done it sooner. Hey, you should come along sometime!

M: That sounds great. I'm also a big fan of the Cubs. Actually, ³³if you're interested, I have an extra ticket to next weekend's game.

F: ³³That would be wonderful. I was ready for another game as soon as we left the ballpark.

M: Wow . . . It seems like you've really gotten into it.

남: 관중석에 있는 누군가가 공을 잡는 것을 봤니? 때때로 타자가 공을 칠 때, 그것이 펜스를 넘어가서 운이 좋은 팬이 그걸 잡잖아.

여: 봤어! ³²공 하나가 딱 내 방향으로 왔지만, 난 글러브가 없어서 그것을 잡지 못했어. 내 바로 뒤에 있던 사람이 그것을 잡았지.

남: 오, 그렇구나... 유감이네. 다음에 야구장에 갈 때는 더 잘 준비해야 할 것 같네.

여: 응. 난 파울 볼이나 홈런 볼을 잡는 것을 내 목표로 삼았어. 야구 역사의 작은 조각을 가지고 경기장을 빠져나가고 싶어!

남: 네가 진정한 팬이 되어가고 있는 것 같구나. 너의 첫 경기를 즐겼다니 기뻐, Linda.

여: 고마워, Jack. 더 빨리 갔었다면 좋았을 텐데. 저기, 너도 조만간 같이 가자!

남: 좋아. 나도 컵스의 열렬한 팬이야. 사실, ³³네가 원한다면, 나는 다음 주말 경기의 여분 표가 있어.

여: ³³그거 정말 좋다. 나는 야구장을 나오는 순간부터 다른 경기에 갈 준비가 되어 있었어.

남: 와... 너 정말 그것에 흥미를 가지게 된 것 같네.

공을 잡을 기회

남녀가 다음에 할 일

어휘 | ballpark[bɔ́:lpɑːrk] 야구장 fortunately[fɔ́:rtʃənətli] 운 좋게도, 다행히도 coworker[kóuwə̀:rkər] 직장 동료 indescribable[ìndiskráibəbəl] 말로 표현할 수 없는 chant[tʃænt] 노래하다 witness[wítnəs] 보다 inning[íniŋ] 이닝, 회 fellowship[félouʃip] 유대감 root for ~을 응원하다 close[klouz] 막상막하인 predict[pridíkt] 예측하다 pitcher[pítʃər] 투수 batter[bǽtər] 타자 direct[dərékt] 다루다, 지휘하다 dull[dʌl] 따분한 stand[stænd] 관중석 get into ~에 흥미를 가지다

---

27 특정세부사항   When   난이도 ●○○

When did Linda purchase her hat?

(a) when she visited a shopping mall last weekend
(b) when she went to her first basketball game
(c) when she attended a recent sporting event
(d) when she traveled to the first ballfield ever built

Linda는 언제 그녀의 모자를 구입했는가?

(a) 지난주에 쇼핑몰에 방문했을 때
(b) 그녀의 첫 농구 경기를 보러 갔을 때
(c) 최근의 스포츠 경기를 관람했을 때
(d) 최초로 건설된 야구장에 갔을 때

◁━○ 지텔프 치트키

질문의 키워드 hat이 cap으로 paraphrasing되어 언급된 주변 내용을 주의 깊게 듣는다.

해설 | 남자가 'I like your new cap.'이라며 여자의 새 모자가 마음에 든다고 하자, 여자가 'I bought it when I went to my first baseball game last Saturday.'라며 지난주 토요일에 그녀의 첫 야구 경기를 보러 갔을 때 그것을 샀다고 했다. 따라서 (c)가 정답이다.

Paraphrasing
my ~ baseball game 야구 경기 → a ~ sporting event 스포츠 경기

어휘 | attend[əténd] 관람하다, 참석하다

What did Linda get from her colleague?

(a) a voucher for a free trip
(b) an extra ticket to a game
(c) an invitation to a special match
(d) a VIP coupon for an event

Linda가 그녀의 직장 동료로부터 무엇을 받았는가?

(a) 자유 여행 할인권
(b) 경기의 여분 입장권
(c) 특별 경기로의 초대장
(d) 행사의 VIP 쿠폰

─○ 지텔프 치트키

질문의 키워드 colleague가 coworker로 paraphrasing되어 언급된 주변 내용을 주의 깊게 듣는다.

해설 | 여자가 'my coworker had an extra ticket to last weekend's game'이라며 지난 주말 경기의 여분 표를 그녀의 직장 동료가 가지고 있었다고 한 뒤, 'She offered it to me, and I happily accepted!'라며 직장 동료가 그녀에게 그것을 주었고 그녀는 기쁘게 받았다고 했다. 따라서 (b)가 정답이다.

Paraphrasing
get 받다 → accepted 받았다

According to Linda, what is not true about watching a game at the ballpark?

(a) It does not compare to anything else.
(b) It is not very stimulating.
(c) It is difficult to describe the energy.
(d) It is full of loud noises.

Linda에 따르면, 야구장에서 경기를 보는 것에 관해 사실이 아닌 것은 무엇인가?

(a) 다른 어떤 것과도 비교되지 않는다.
(b) 그다지 자극적이지 않다.
(c) 에너지를 묘사하기 어렵다.
(d) 시끄러운 소리들로 가득 차 있다.

─○ 지텔프 치트키

질문의 키워드 watching a game at the ballpark와 관련된 주변 내용을 주의 깊게 들으며 언급되는 것을 하나씩 소거한다.

해설 | (b)는 여자가 'It was very exciting!'이라며 야구장에서 경기를 보는 것이 매우 흥미진진했다고 언급했으므로 대화의 내용과 일치하지 않는다. 따라서 (b)가 정답이다.

오답분석
(a) 여자가 야구장에서 경기를 보는 것과 같은 것은 어떠한 것도 없다고 언급하였다.
(c) 여자가 경기장 안의 에너지는 말로 표현할 수 없었다고 언급하였다.
(d) 여자가 팬들이 환호성을 지르고 노래했다고 언급하였다.

How did Linda make new friends at the stadium?

(a) by talking to neighboring people
(b) by using a chatting app between innings
(c) by meeting fellow fans after the game

Linda는 경기장에서 어떻게 새로운 친구들을 사귀었는가?

(a) 근처의 사람들과 이야기함으로써
(b) 이닝 사이에 채팅 앱을 사용함으로써
(c) 경기 후에 동료 팬들을 만남으로써

(d) by sharing food with those nearby

(d) 주변 사람들과 음식을 나누어 먹음으로써

질문의 키워드 friends가 그대로 언급된 주변 내용을 주의 깊게 듣는다.

해설 | 남자가 'Did you meet any new people there?'라며 경기장에서 새로운 사람들을 만났는지를 묻자, 여자가 'I started chatting with the group in front of me ~, and by the end of the game, we were friends.'라며 그녀의 앞에 있는 사람들과 이야기를 나누기 시작했고, 경기가 끝날 때쯤에 친구가 되었다고 했다. 따라서 (a)가 정답이다.

Paraphrasing
chatting with the group in front 앞에 있는 사람들과 이야기를 나누는 → talking to neighboring people 근처의 사람들과 이야기함

---

31 특정세부사항 Why
난이도 ●●○

Why did Linda find baseball more intriguing than she previously believed?

(a) because it is a high-scoring game
(b) because it involves constant changes
(c) because it produces unexpected results
(d) because it requires complex strategy

왜 Linda는 그녀가 이전에 생각했던 것보다 야구가 더 흥미롭다고 생각했는가?

(a) 득점이 많이 나는 경기이기 때문에
(b) 끊임없는 변화들을 수반하기 때문에
(c) 예상치 못한 결과를 낳기 때문에
(d) 복잡한 전략을 필요로 하기 때문에

질문의 키워드 intriguing이 interesting으로 paraphrasing되어 언급된 주변 내용을 주의 깊게 듣는다.

해설 | 여자가 'Baseball is ~ more interesting than I thought.'라며 야구가 생각했던 것보다 더 흥미롭다고 한 뒤, 'I had no idea there were so many complicated strategies and techniques involved.'라며 그렇게 많은 복잡한 전략들과 기술들이 수반되는지를 몰랐다고 했다. 따라서 (d)가 정답이다.

Paraphrasing
complicated strategies ~ involved 복잡한 전략들이 수반되는 → requires complex strategy 복잡한 전략을 필요로 한다

어휘 | intriguing[intríːgiŋ] 흥미로운 constant[kάːnstənt] 끊임없는

---

32 특정세부사항 Why
난이도 ●●○

Why was Linda unable to obtain the ball that flew to her?

(a) She wasn't facing the right direction.
(b) She didn't know it was allowed.
(c) She wasn't sitting in the correct section.
(d) She didn't have the proper equipment.

왜 Linda는 그녀에게 날아온 공을 얻을 수 없었는가?

(a) 적절한 방향을 향하고 있지 않았다.
(b) 그것이 허용되는지 몰랐다.
(c) 적절한 구역에 앉아 있지 않았다.
(d) 적합한 장비를 가지고 있지 않았다.

질문의 키워드 obtain이 get으로 paraphrasing되어 언급된 주변 내용을 주의 깊게 듣는다.

해설 | 여자가 'One came right in my direction, but I couldn't get it because I didn't have a glove.'라며 공 하나가 딱 그녀의 방향

으로 왔지만 글러브가 없어서 그것을 잡지 못했다고 했다. 따라서 (d)가 정답이다.

Paraphrasing
a glove 글러브 → the ~ equipment 장비

어휘 | face[feis] 향하다 correct[kərékt] 적절한 section[sékʃən] 구역 equipment[ikwípmənt] 장비

---

33 추론 　다음에 할 일 　　　　　　　　　　　　　　　　　　　　　　　　　난이도 ●●○

Based on the conversation, what will Jack most likely do next weekend?	대화에 따르면, Jack은 다음 주말에 무엇을 할 것 같은가?
(a) go to the ballpark with his friend	**(a) 그의 친구와 함께 야구장에 간다**
(b) join the Cubs' next training session	(b) 컵스의 다음 훈련에 참여한다
(c) view a ball game on television	(c) 텔레비전으로 야구 경기를 본다
(d) look for another baseball park	(d) 다른 야구장을 찾는다

━○ 지텔프 치트키

다음에 할 일을 언급하는 후반을 주의 깊게 듣는다.

해설 | 남자가 'if you're interested, I have an extra ticket to next weekend's game'이라며 여자가 원한다면 다음 주말 경기의 여분 표가 있다고 하자, 여자가 'That would be wonderful.'이라며 정말 좋다고 한 것을 통해, Jack이 다음 주말에 그의 친구인 Linda와 함께 야구장에 갈 것임을 추론할 수 있다. 따라서 (a)가 정답이다.

PART 2 (34~39) 　발표 　새로운 안락의자 홍보

음성 바로 듣기

주제 제시: 제품 홍보	Good morning, everybody! ³⁴I'm here today to introduce a newly designed reclining chair that will be the perfect addition to your home. I'd like to tell you all about the Lounge King, a new recliner that is handmade in Gary, Indiana.	좋은 아침입니다, 여러분! ³⁴저는 오늘 여러분의 집에 완벽한 추가물이 될 새로 고안된 안락의자를 소개하기 위해 왔습니다. 저는 Lounge King에 관한 모든 것을 여러분께 말씀드리고 싶은데, 이 새로운 안락의자는 인디애나주 게리시에서 수작업으로 만들어진 것입니다.
필요성 제기	At the end of a hectic day at work, don't you want a peaceful spot to put your feet up? Or maybe you've been overwhelmed with household chores all day and need some time for yourself. Well, we have a sensible and sophisticated reclining chair for you.	직장에서의 정신없이 바쁜 하루 끝에, 여러분은 발을 올려놓을 평화로운 장소를 원하시지 않나요? 혹은 어쩌면 여러분은 온종일 집안일에 압도되어 자기 자신을 위한 조금의 시간이 필요하실 수 있습니다. 자, 저희는 여러분을 위한 실용적이고도 세련된 안락의자를 가지고 있습니다.
장점1: 편안함	When you think about a recliner, what's the first word that comes to mind? Comfort! We created the Lounge King to be the ultimate in relaxation. The cushions are made of soft down that lets you sink into the chair while supporting your posture. The only drawback is that you might not want to get up!	안락의자에 관해 생각하실 때, 가장 먼저 떠오르는 단어가 무엇인가요? 편안함! 저흰 Lounge King이 휴식의 극치가 되도록 만들었습니다. 쿠션은 여러분의 자세를 지지해 주면서 여러분이 의자에 편안히 앉을 수 있게 해주는 부드러운 솜털로 만들어졌습니다. 유일한 단점은 여러분이 일어나고 싶지 않을 수도 있다는 겁니다!

Everyone wants to have attractive furniture in their home. ³⁵We are especially proud of the Lounge King's sleek and elegant look, which we got by combining lush fabrics, clean lines, and modern design. The Lounge King was designed to be smaller than the average recliner to avoid taking up too much space. It is available in six colors, ranging from dark brown to bright red.

When it comes to recliners, the reclining mechanism is a critical aspect. The Lounge King utilizes buttons to adjust the position of the back and the headrest. This is ideal because they eliminate the need for a hand lever. The Lounge King reclines to three different angles to accommodate all of your needs. Whether you're watching a movie or reading a book, you'll want to be sitting in the Lounge King.

Electronics touch every part of our lives, from work to recreation. That's why the Lounge King features three USB charging ports, allowing you to use your favorite technology conveniently. There is also a wireless charging spot for compatible devices. ³⁶The headrest has a Bluetooth sound system with two speakers built in. ³⁶This makes the Lounge King the perfect seat for a captivating cinema-like experience.

We have absolute confidence in the quality of the Lounge King. That's why ³⁷we offer a full five-year warranty against defects in materials and workmanship. If you face a problem, simply contact the store where you purchased your Lounge King and a representative will come out to inspect the chair. If the problem cannot be fixed on site, we will provide you with a replacement at no cost.

In addition to the peace of mind afforded by our generous warranty, you can also rest easy knowing that ³⁸the Lounge King is ethically made. We are committed to a green manufacturing process, so we use only recycled wood and environmentally friendly materials. This means we never use harsh chemicals or fire retardants as we strive to reduce carbon emissions at our production facilities. With this, you don't have to compromise your principles when you choose the Lounge King.

³⁹We want more people to learn about the Lounge King. That's why we are running a special promotion. If you invite five individuals to sign up for our monthly newsletter, then you will receive a ten percent discount and free shipping for your Lounge King. So, tell all your friends and place your order today.

모든 사람들은 그들의 집에 매력적인 가구를 두길 원합니다. ³⁵저희는 Lounge King의 매끈하고 우아한 외관이 특히 자랑스러운데, 저희는 이것을 고급 직물, 깔끔한 선, 그리고 현대적인 디자인을 결합하여 얻었습니다. Lounge King은 너무 많은 공간을 차지하지 않도록 하기 위해 일반적인 안락의자보다 더 작게 설계되었습니다. 그것은 짙은 갈색부터 선홍색까지 6가지 색상으로 구매 가능합니다.

안락의자에 있어서, 등받이가 뒤로 젖혀지는 메커니즘은 매우 중요한 측면입니다. Lounge King은 등받이와 머리 받침대의 위치를 조절하기 위해 버튼을 사용합니다. 이는 이상적인데 왜냐하면 그것들이 손잡이의 필요성을 없애기 때문입니다. Lounge King은 여러분의 모든 요구를 수용하기 위해 3개의 다른 각도로 기울어집니다. 영화를 보든 책을 읽든, 여러분은 Lounge King에 앉아 있고 싶으실 겁니다.

전자제품은 일에서부터 오락 활동까지 우리 삶의 모든 부분에 영향을 미칩니다. 그것이 바로 Lounge King이 3개의 USB 충전 단자를 특별히 포함하여, 여러분이 특히 원하시는 기술을 편리하게 사용할 수 있게 하는 이유입니다. 또한 호환 가능한 기기들을 위한 무선 충전 장소가 있습니다. 2개의 스피커가 내장된 ³⁶블루투스 음향 시스템이 머리 받침대에 있습니다. 이것은 Lounge King을 영화관 같은 매혹적인 경험을 위한 완벽한 좌석으로 만듭니다.

저희는 Lounge King의 품질에 대한 절대적인 확신이 있습니다. 그것이 바로 ³⁷소재와 기술의 결함에 대해 5년간의 완전한 품질 보증을 제공하는 이유입니다. 여러분이 문제에 직면할 때, 여러분이 Lounge King을 구매하셨던 매장에 연락하기만 하시면 담당자가 해당 의자를 점검하러 갈 것입니다. 현장에서 문제가 해결될 수 없는 경우, 저희는 여러분께 무상으로 대체품을 제공할 것입니다.

저희의 넉넉한 품질 보증이 가져다주는 마음의 평안에 더하여, 여러분은 또한 ³⁸Lounge King이 윤리적으로 만들어졌다는 것을 아시고 안심하실 수 있습니다. ³⁸저희는 친환경적인 제조 공정에 전념하고 있고, 따라서 재활용된 목재와 환경친화적인 소재들만 사용합니다. 이는 저희의 생산 시설에서 탄소 배출을 줄이기 위해 노력하기 때문에 저희가 유독한 화학 물질이나 방화제를 절대 사용하지 않는다는 것을 의미합니다. 이로써, Lounge King을 선택하실 때 여러분의 신조를 굽힐 필요가 없습니다.

³⁹저희는 더 많은 사람들이 Lounge King에 관해 알기를 원합니다. 그것이 저희가 특별 판촉 활동을 진행하고 있는 이유입니다. 저희의 월간 소식지를 신청하도록 5명을 초대하시면, Lounge King에 대한 10퍼센트 할인과 무료 배송을 받으실 겁니다. 그러니, 여러분의 모든 친구들에게 알리시고 오늘 주문하세요.

어휘 | reclining chair 안락의자(등받이와 발 받침이 조절되는 의자) hectic[héktik] 정신없이 바쁜 sensible[sénsəbəl] 실용적인
sophisticated[səfístikeitid] 세련된 ultimate[ʌ́ltəmət] 극치 down[daun] 솜털 posture[pá:stʃər] 자세 sleek[sli:k] 매끈한
lush[lʌʃ] 고급의, 풍부한 headrest[hédrest] 머리 받침대 accommodate[əká:mədeit] 수용하다 compatible[kəmpǽtəbəl] 호환 가능한
captivating[kǽptəveitiŋ] 매혹적인 absolute[ǽbsəlu:t] 절대적인 warranty[wɔ́:rənti] 품질 보증 harsh[ha:rʃ] 유독한
compromise[ká:mprəmaiz] 굽히다, 타협하다

---

34 주제/목적 담화의 목적 난이도 ●●○

What is the purpose of the talk?

(a) introducing a new houseware manufacturer
(b) promoting a piece of furniture
(c) advocating for the purchase of handmade goods
(d) discussing the home design industry

담화의 목적은 무엇인가?

(a) 새로운 가정용품 제조업체를 소개하는 것
(b) 가구 한 점을 홍보하는 것
(c) 수제품들의 구매를 옹호하는 것
(d) 주거 디자인 산업에 관해 토론하는 것

🔑 지텔프 치트키

담화의 목적을 언급하는 초반을 주의 깊게 듣고 전체 맥락을 파악한다.

해설 | 화자가 'I'm here today to introduce a ~ reclining chair that will be the perfect addition to your home.'이라며 새로 고안된 안락의자를 소개하기 위해 왔다고 한 뒤, 담화 전반에 걸쳐 새로운 안락의자인 Lounge King을 홍보하는 내용이 이어지고 있다. 따라서 (b)가 정답이다.

어휘 | houseware[háuswer] 가정용품 advocate[ǽdvəkeit] 옹호하다

---

35 특정세부사항 How 난이도 ●●○

How does the Lounge King achieve a stylish appearance?

(a) by selecting expensive components
(b) by forgoing multiple color options
(c) by applying minimal hardware
(d) by including contemporary style

Lounge King은 어떻게 멋진 외관을 구현하는가?

(a) 고가의 부품들을 선택함으로써
(b) 다양한 색상 선택지들을 포기함으로써
(c) 최소한의 기재를 사용함으로써
(d) 현대적인 스타일을 포함함으로써

🔑 지텔프 치트키

질문의 키워드 appearance가 look으로 paraphrasing되어 언급된 주변 내용을 주의 깊게 듣는다.

해설 | 화자가 'We are ~ proud of the Lounge King's sleek and elegant look, which we got by combining lush fabrics, clean lines, and modern design.'이라며 Lounge King의 매끈하고 우아한 외관이 자랑스러운데, 이것을 고급 직물, 깔끔한 선, 그리고 현대적인 디자인을 결합하여 얻었다고 했다. 따라서 (d)가 정답이다.

Paraphrasing
modern design 현대적인 디자인 → contemporary style 현대적인 스타일

어휘 | component[kəmpóunənt] 부품 forgo[fɔːrgóu] 포기하다 hardware[há:rdwer] 기재, 부품 contemporary[kəntémpəreri] 현대적인

36

특정세부사항   Why   난이도 ●●○

Why does the Lounge King come equipped with Bluetooth?

(a) to offer the acoustics of a theater
(b) to collect data from user experience
(c) because it cannot connect to certain devices directly
(d) because it does not have USB ports

왜 Lounge King은 블루투스가 장착되어 나오는가?

(a) 극장의 음향 효과를 제공하기 위해서
(b) 사용자 경험으로부터의 자료를 수집하기 위해서
(c) 특정 장치들과 직접 연결할 수 없기 때문에
(d) USB 단자가 없기 때문에

━○ 지텔프 치트키

질문의 키워드 Bluetooth가 그대로 언급된 주변 내용을 주의 깊게 듣는다.

해설 | 화자가 'The headrest has a Bluetooth sound system'이라며 블루투스 음향 시스템이 머리 받침대에 있다고 한 뒤, 'This makes the Lounge King the perfect seat for a captivating cinema-like experience.'라며 이것이 Lounge King을 영화관 같은 매혹적인 경험을 위한 완벽한 좌석으로 만든다고 했다. 따라서 (a)가 정답이다.

Paraphrasing
has a ~ sound system 음향 시스템이 있다 → offer the acoustics 음향 효과를 제공하다
cinema-like 영화관 같은 → a theater 극장

어휘 | acoustics[əkúːstiks] 음향 효과   collect[kəlékt] 수집하다

37

추론   특정사실   난이도 ●●●

What most likely would happen if a Lounge King malfunctioned after five years?

(a) The company would be unable to inspect the chair.
(b) The customer would be responsible for the repairs.
(c) The company would issue a refund for the repair cost.
(d) The customer would send it back to the manufacturer.

만약 Lounge King이 5년 후에 오작동을 일으킨다면 어떤 일이 일어날 것 같은가?

(a) 회사가 의자를 점검할 수 없을 것이다.
(b) 고객이 수리에 대한 책임을 질 것이다.
(c) 회사가 수리비를 환불해 줄 것이다.
(d) 고객이 그것을 제조업체로 다시 보낼 것이다.

━○ 지텔프 치트키

질문의 키워드 five years가 five-year로 언급된 주변 내용을 주의 깊게 듣는다.

해설 | 화자가 'we offer a full five-year warranty against defects in ~ workmanship'이라며 기술 등의 결함에 대해 5년간의 완전한 품질 보증을 제공한다고 한 것을 통해, Lounge King이 품질 보증 기간이 끝났을 5년 후에 오작동을 일으킨다면 고객이 수리에 대한 책임을 질 것임을 추론할 수 있다. 따라서 (b)가 정답이다.

38

특정세부사항   What   난이도 ●●○

What is an ethical feature of the Lounge King?

(a) limited use of fire retardants
(b) recycled cotton fabric
(c) sustainable manufacturing processes
(d) fair pay for factory employees

Lounge King의 윤리적 특징은 무엇인가?

(a) 방화제의 제한적 사용
(b) 재활용된 면직물
(c) 지속 가능한 제조 공정
(d) 공장 직원에 대한 적정한 급여

질문의 키워드 ethical이 ethically로 언급된 주변 내용을 주의 깊게 듣는다.

해설 | 화자가 'the Lounge King is ethically made'라며 Lounge King이 윤리적으로 만들어졌다고 한 뒤, 'We are committed to a green manufacturing process'라며 친환경적인 제조 공정에 전념하고 있다고 했다. 따라서 (c)가 정답이다.

Paraphrasing
green 친환경적인 → sustainable 지속 가능한

오답분석
(a) 화자가 Lounge King의 생산 시설에서 방화제를 절대 사용하지 않는다고 언급하였다.
(b) 화자가 재활용된 면직물이 아닌 재활용된 목재를 사용한다고 언급하였다.

어휘 | sustainable [səstéinəbəl] (환경 파괴 없이) 지속 가능한

---

39 특정세부사항 Who

난이도 ●●○

Who is the target of the company's promotion?	회사의 판촉 활동 대상은 누구인가?
(a) those who work in the home furnishings industry	(a) 가정용 가구 산업에 종사하는 사람들
(b) those who buy a lot of home decorations	(b) 집 장식품을 많이 구매하는 사람들
(c) those who are unfamiliar with the brand's new product	**(c) 그 브랜드의 신제품을 잘 모르는 사람들**
(d) those who subscribe to the newsletter	(d) 소식지를 구독하는 사람들

🔑 지텔프 치트키

질문의 키워드 promotion이 그대로 언급된 주변 내용을 주의 깊게 듣는다.

해설 | 화자가 'We want more people to learn about the Lounge King.'이라며 더 많은 사람들이 Lounge King에 관해 알기를 원한다고 한 뒤, 'That's why we are running a special promotion.'이라며 그것이 특별 판촉 활동을 진행하고 있는 이유라고 했다. 따라서 (c)가 정답이다.

Paraphrasing
the Lounge King Lounge King → the brand's new product 그 브랜드의 신제품

어휘 | furnishing [fɔ́ːrniʃiŋ] 가구

PART 3 [40~45] 장단점 논의 카메라로 촬영하는 것과 휴대전화로 촬영하는 것의 장단점 비교

음성 바로 듣기

안부 인사	M: Hi, Abby. Are you all set for the architecture tour? F: Hello, Justin. Yes, I'm ready to snap some great photos. ⁴⁰Are you going to use a camera or your mobile phone?	남: 안녕, Abby. 건축 투어 준비는 다 됐어? 여: 안녕, Justin. 응, 멋진 사진을 촬영할 준비가 됐어. ⁴⁰너는 카메라를 사용할 거니 아니면 너의 휴대전화를 사용할 거니?
주제 제시: 장단점 비교	M: ⁴⁰Since I can't decide, do you think you could help me out? F: No problem. Sometimes it's helpful to discuss the pros and cons of each one.	남: ⁴⁰내가 결정을 못 하겠으니, 네가 나를 좀 도와줄 수 있겠니? 여: 당연하지. 때때로 각각의 장단점을 토론하는 것이 도움이 돼.

카메라 촬영 장점	M: I like that idea. Let's start with the advantages of using a camera. F: Well, one major strength of cameras is their superior ability to zoom. [41]With a regular camera lens, you can capture fantastic images from far away. M: Hmmm . . . That's true. But, can't smartphones do the same thing these days? F: There have been a lot of advances in the capabilities of mobile phones in this area, but there's a big difference between hardware and software. [42]A smartphone uses software to crop the image to zoom in rather than a moving, physical lens attached to a regular camera. M: Oh, so it's just focusing in on one part of the image instead of actually getting a closer shot. [42]That must be why so many long-range photos on my phone are blurry. Are there any disadvantages?
카메라 촬영 단점	F: Cameras can be bulky and inconvenient to carry. After all, those lenses aren't small! And you often have to bring multiple ones for different situations and photograph types. M: Yeah, I usually see photographers with large bags of equipment. It's not as easy as simply keeping my smartphone in my pocket. F: That's right. Good lenses can be expensive, so you have to transport them carefully.
휴대 전화 촬영 장점	M: All right. How about the advantages of taking pictures with a smartphone? F: Well, they're much easier to use. Anyone can pick up a phone and snap great pictures. M: What you're saying is that to make the most out of a traditional camera, you need to know how they work. F: Exactly. It [43]requires technical knowledge of things like aperture, shutter speed, and ISO. M: That sounds difficult! I don't know much about those things. [43]Taking pictures with a smartphone sounds less complicated. F: Of course, you can easily take photos with a smartphone just by pointing and shooting, but to get really breathtaking shots you have to study how to use it first!
	M: That's true. But, there must be some drawbacks, right? F: Yeah. At sunrise or sunset, it's nearly impossible to get decent photos because of the lighting conditions. M: Really? Our architecture tour today starts in the afternoon and runs into the evening. We might not be able to get nice photos with our smartphones.

남: 그 생각 좋은걸. 카메라를 사용하는 것의 장점부터 시작해 보자.

여: 음, 카메라의 한 가지 주요 장점은 뛰어난 줌 기능이야. [41]일반 카메라 렌즈를 이용하여, 너는 멀리 떨어진 멋진 모습들을 촬영할 수 있어.

남: 흠… 그건 그래. 하지만, 요즘에는 스마트폰도 그렇게 할 수 있지 않아?

여: 이 분야에서 휴대전화의 기능에 많은 발전이 있었지만, 하드웨어와 소프트웨어 사이에는 큰 차이가 있어. [42]스마트폰은 줌 인을 위해 일반 카메라에 부착된 움직이는 물리적 렌즈 대신에 영상을 잘라 내는 소프트웨어를 사용해.

남: 오, 그럼 그것이 실제로 더 근접하게 촬영하지 않고 그저 영상의 한 부분에 초점을 맞추고 있는 거구나. [42]그게 내 휴대전화에 있는 아주 많은 장거리 사진들이 흐릿한 이유임이 틀림없어. 단점들도 있니?

여: 카메라는 부피가 크고 휴대하기 불편할 수 있어. 무엇보다, 그 렌즈들은 작지 않아! 그리고 종종 너는 다양한 상황들과 사진 종류들을 위해 여러 개를 가져와야 하지.

남: 응, 나는 장비가 든 큰 가방을 들고 다니는 사진사들을 흔히 봐. 그것은 단순히 스마트폰을 주머니에 넣고 다니는 것만큼 쉽지는 않지.

여: 맞아. 좋은 렌즈들은 비쌀 수 있어서, 그것들을 조심히 운반해야 해.

남: 알았어. 스마트폰으로 사진을 찍는 것의 장점은 어때?

여: 음, 그것들은 사용하기 훨씬 더 쉬워. 누구나 휴대전화를 들고 멋진 사진들을 찍을 수 있어.

남: 네 말은 전통 카메라를 최대한 활용하기 위해서는, 그것들이 어떻게 작동하는지를 알아야 한다는 거구나.

여: 바로 그거야. 그것은 조리개, 셔터 속도, 감도와 같은 것들에 관한 [43]기술적 지식을 필요로 해.

남: 어렵겠는걸! 나는 그런 것들에 관해 잘 몰라. [43]스마트폰으로 사진을 찍는 것이 덜 복잡해 보이네.

여: 물론, 그저 방향을 맞추고 촬영함으로써 너는 스마트폰으로 쉽게 사진을 찍을 수 있지만, 정말로 기막힌 사진을 찍기 위해서는 어떻게 그것을 사용하는지 먼저 공부해야 해!

남: 맞아. 하지만, 분명 단점도 있을 거야, 그렇지?

여: 응. 동틀 녘이나 해 질 녘에는, 조명 조건 때문에 괜찮은 사진들을 찍는 것이 거의 불가능해.

남: 정말? 오늘 우리의 건축 투어는 오후에 시작해서 저녁까지 진행돼. 우리는 스마트폰으로 멋진 사진들을 찍을 수 없을지도 몰라.

<table>
<tr>
<td>휴대
전화
촬영
단점</td>
<td>

F: Yes, that could be a problem. Also, [44]unless you're willing to invest in some aftermarket attachments, your smartphone probably restricts you to one lens. This is fine if you're snapping quick shots for social media, but it won't be enough for more professional-looking photos.

M: Oh, I've been taking my photography more seriously lately, so I want to be ready for a variety of scenarios.

F: Although AI light processing in phones has improved a lot in recent years, even untrained individuals can spot the difference between mobile photos and those taken with traditional cameras.

</td>
<td>

여: 응, 그게 문제가 될 수도 있어. 또한, [44]네가 부속품 시장의 몇몇 부가 장치에 투자할 의향이 없는 한, 네 스마트폰은 아마도 너를 한 개의 렌즈로 제한할 거야. 이것이 소셜 미디어를 위한 신속한 사진들을 찍을 때는 괜찮지만, 더 전문적으로 보이는 사진들을 위해서는 충분하지 않을 거야.

남: 오, 나는 요즘 내 촬영술을 더 진지하게 생각하고 있었고, 그래서 다양한 상황에 대비하고 싶어.

여: 최근에 휴대전화의 인공지능 빛 처리가 많이 개선되었지만, 숙련되지 않은 사람들조차 휴대전화 사진들과 전통 카메라로 찍은 사진들의 차이를 알아챌 수 있어.

</td>
</tr>
<tr>
<td>남자의
결정</td>
<td>

M: Okay. Thanks for talking about the pros and cons with me, Abby.

F: My pleasure, Justin. Have you made your decision now?

M: Yes. [45]I'd better pack some extra lenses in my bags for the tour because I want to take nicer photos.

F: I think that's probably the best choice.

</td>
<td>

남: 알았어. 나와 장단점에 관해 이야기해 줘서 고마워, Abby.

여: 천만에, Justin. 이제 결정을 내렸어?

남: 응. [45]나는 더 멋진 사진들을 찍고 싶기 때문에 투어를 위해 가방에 여분의 렌즈들을 챙기는 게 좋겠어.

여: 아마 그게 최선의 선택일 거라고 생각해.

</td>
</tr>
</table>

어휘ㅣ architecture[ɑ́ːrkiətektʃər] 건축 snap[snæp] 촬영하다, (사진을) 찍다 capture[kǽptʃər] 촬영하다 crop[krɑːp] 잘라 내다 attach[ətǽtʃ] 부착하다 long-range 장거리의 blurry[blə́ːri] 흐릿한 bulky[bʌ́lki] 부피가 큰 aperture[ǽpərtʃur] 조리개 breathtaking[bréθtèikiŋ] 기막힌, 숨이 막히는 decent[díːsənt] 괜찮은, 적절한 aftermarket[ǽftərmàːrkət] 부속품 시장 restrict[ristríkt] 제한하다 photography[fətɑ́ːɡrəfi] 촬영술, 사진 촬영 spot[spɑːt] 알아채다 pack[pæk] 챙기다

---

40 **특정세부사항**   What   난이도 ●○○

<table>
<tr>
<td>

What is Justin asking Abby about?

(a) how to buy a new camera
(b) how to charge his phone quickly
(c) what to use to take pictures
(d) what to prepare for the architecture tour

</td>
<td>

Justin은 Abby에게 무엇에 관해 묻고 있는가?

(a) 새 카메라를 사는 방법
(b) 그의 휴대전화를 빠르게 충전하는 방법
(c) 사진을 촬영하기 위해 무엇을 사용할지
(d) 건축 투어를 위해 무엇을 준비할지

</td>
</tr>
</table>

━○ 지텔프 치트키

질문의 키워드 Justin asking Abby와 관련된 주변 내용을 주의 깊게 듣는다.

해설ㅣ 여자가 'Are you going to use a camera or your mobile phone?'이라며 남자에게 카메라와 휴대전화 중 무엇을 사용할 것인지를 묻자, 남자가 'Since I can't decide, do you think you could help me out?'이라며 결정을 못 하겠으니 여자에게 도와줄 수 있는지를 물었다. 따라서 (c)가 정답이다.

Paraphrasing
snap ~ photos 사진을 촬영하다 → take pictures 사진을 촬영하다

What is an advantage of traditional cameras?

(a) They have physical buttons.
(b) They run advanced software.
(c) They transfer images to storage quickly.
(d) They work well from a distance.

전통 카메라의 장점은 무엇인가?

(a) 물리적 버튼이 있다.
(b) 고급 소프트웨어를 실행시킨다.
(c) 사진들을 기억 장치에 빠르게 전송한다.
(d) 멀리서 잘 작동한다.

◯ 지텔프 치트키

질문의 키워드 traditional cameras와 관련된 긍정적인 흐름을 파악한다.

해설 | 여자가 'With a regular camera lens, you can capture fantastic images from far away.'라며 일반 카메라 렌즈를 이용하여 멀리 떨어진 멋진 모습들을 촬영할 수 있다고 했다. 따라서 (d)가 정답이다.

Paraphrasing
from far away 멀리 떨어진 → from a distance 멀리서

Why does Justin have a lot of unclear photos?

(a) because his hands move too much
(b) because he uses a phone to zoom
(c) because his lens reflects light
(d) because he crops his shots himself

Justin은 왜 불명확한 사진들을 많이 가지고 있는가?

(a) 그의 손이 너무 많이 움직이기 때문에
(b) 줌을 하기 위해 휴대전화를 사용하기 때문에
(c) 그의 렌즈가 빛을 반사하기 때문에
(d) 그의 사진들을 스스로 잘라 내기 때문에

◯ 지텔프 치트키

질문의 키워드 unclear가 blurry로 paraphrasing되어 언급된 주변 내용을 주의 깊게 듣는다.

해설 | 여자가 'A smartphone uses software ~ to zoom in rather than a moving, physical lens attached to a regular camera.'라며 스마트폰은 줌 인을 위해 움직이는 물리적 렌즈 대신에 소프트웨어를 사용한다고 하자, 남자가 'That must be why so many ~ photos on my phone are blurry.'라며 그것이 그의 휴대전화에 있는 아주 많은 장거리 사진들이 흐릿한 이유임이 틀림없다고 했다. 따라서 (b)가 정답이다.

어휘 | reflect[riflékt] 반사하다

Why is it easier to take photos with a smartphone?

(a) It can take less time.
(b) It has a faster shutter speed.
(c) It can capture anything in the frame.
(d) It requires less prior knowledge.

왜 스마트폰으로 사진을 찍는 것이 더 쉬운가?

(a) 더 적은 시간이 걸릴 수 있다.
(b) 더 빠른 셔터 속도를 가진다.
(c) 프레임 안에 있는 모든 것을 찍을 수 있다.
(d) 더 적은 사전 지식이 필요하다.

질문의 키워드 easier가 less complicated로 paraphrasing되어 언급된 주변 내용을 주의 깊게 듣는다.

해설 | 여자가 'requires technical knowledge'라며 전통 카메라는 기술적 지식을 필요로 한다고 하자, 남자가 'Taking pictures with a smartphone sounds less complicated.'라며 스마트폰으로 사진을 찍는 것이 덜 복잡해 보인다고 했다. 따라서 (d)가 정답이다.

Paraphrasing
technical knowledge 기술적 지식 → prior knowledge 사전 지식

---

44 특정세부사항 How 난이도 ●●○

How can users overcome the constraints of a smartphone camera?

(a) **by purchasing an aftermarket accessory**
(b) by finding tips on social media sites
(c) by utilizing professional editing software
(d) by replacing the original lens

사용자들은 어떻게 스마트폰 카메라의 제약을 극복할 수 있는가?

(a) **부속품 시장의 부품을 구입함으로써**
(b) 소셜 미디어 사이트에서 정보를 찾음으로써
(c) 전문 편집 소프트웨어를 활용함으로써
(d) 기존의 렌즈를 교체함으로써

○ 지텔프 치트키

질문의 키워드 constraints가 restricts로 paraphrasing되어 언급된 주변 내용을 주의 깊게 듣는다.

해설 | 여자가 'unless you're willing to invest in ~ aftermarket attachments, your smartphone probably restricts you to one lens'라며 부속품 시장의 부가 장치에 투자할 의향이 없는 한, 스마트폰은 사용자들을 한 개의 렌즈로 제한할 것이라고 했다. 따라서 (a)가 정답이다.

Paraphrasing
invest in ~ aftermarket attachments 부속품 시장의 부가 장치에 투자하다 → purchasing an aftermarket accessory 부속품 시장의 부품을 구입함

어휘 | accessory [əksésəri] 부품

---

45 추론 다음에 할 일 난이도 ●●○

What has Justin probably decided to do?

(a) **bring a camera on his upcoming tour**
(b) employ a mobile phone for photography
(c) buy a better pack for his gear
(d) borrow lenses from his friend

Justin은 무엇을 하기로 결정한 것 같은가?

(a) **곧 있을 투어에 카메라를 가져간다**
(b) 사진 촬영을 위해 휴대전화를 사용한다
(c) 그의 장비를 위해 더 좋은 배낭을 산다
(d) 그의 친구에게서 렌즈를 빌린다

○ 지텔프 치트키

다음에 할 일을 언급하는 후반을 주의 깊게 듣는다.

해설 | 남자가 'I'd better pack some extra lenses in my bags for the tour because I want to take nicer photos.'라며 더 멋진 사진들을 찍고 싶기 때문에 투어를 위해 가방에 여분의 렌즈들을 챙기는 것이 좋겠다고 한 것을 통해, Justin은 촬영 기능이 더 좋고 다양한 상황들과 사진 종류들을 위해 여러 개의 렌즈가 필요한 카메라를 곧 있을 건축 투어에 가져갈 것임을 추론할 수 있다. 따라서 (a)가 정답이다.

인사 + 주제 제시

Welcome, everyone! As you know, competitive ballroom dancing continues to grow in popularity. A web-based organization is a great way to bring together dance enthusiasts around the globe. Today, [46]I'm going to tell you how to start your own online dancesport club.

조언1: 목표 회원 설정

First, you need to decide who your members will be. After all, the dancesport community is a diverse group. Do you want the club to be only for dancesport professionals? Or do you want to make it for amateurs and those with a general interest in the sport? Gearing the club toward professionals could result in a small group of elite dancers who will do well at competitions. On the other hand, you might get larger membership numbers by appealing to amateurs. [47]Understanding your purpose and target members will determine what materials you post on your site.

조언2: 회원 혜택 제시

Second, set out exactly what your online club will offer to its members. This can take many forms. Meeting the needs of many of your dancers may just involve uploading instructional videos that teach the basic ballroom dancing steps. However, [48]you may want to provide some advanced features for your members. These could be things like messaging services, interactive bulletin boards to post and discuss events, and even meetings held by videoconferencing.

조언3: 구조 및 요건 표명

Third, formally declare the club's structure and requirements. [49]Members will refer to these regulations to settle any disputes within the group that may arise in the future. You certainly should explain the membership criteria, define how the club will be managed and what is expected of your dancers. Stipulating things such as attendance and competition obligations will help your members integrate with the broader dancesport community. Also, outline the amendment process. It will give your organization the ability to adapt to new circumstances.

조언4: 규칙 명시

Fourth, explicitly state what happens if members act inappropriately or fail to meet their responsibilities. Unfortunately, not everyone will behave perfectly all the time. [50]You'll need to set up rules to ensure that everyone is safe and comfortable. This is especially important in order to protect the online privacy of participants. You'll want to include penalties for those who violate the policies. These could range in severity

환영합니다, 여러분! 아시다시피, 경기용 사교댄스는 계속해서 인기를 얻고 있습니다. 인터넷 기반 단체는 전 세계의 댄스광들을 모을 수 있는 아주 좋은 방법입니다. 오늘, [46]저는 여러분만의 온라인 댄스스포츠 동호회를 시작하는 방법을 알려 드릴 것입니다.

첫째로, 누가 여러분의 회원이 될지 결정해야 합니다. 어쨌든, 댄스스포츠 커뮤니티는 다양한 집단입니다. 그 동호회가 오직 댄스스포츠 전문가들을 위한 것이기를 원하십니까? 아니면 그것을 아마추어들과 그 스포츠에 일반적인 관심이 있는 사람들을 위해 만들기를 원하십니까? 동호회를 전문가들에 적합하도록 만드는 것은 대회에서 좋은 성적을 거둘 소수의 엘리트 댄서 집단으로 이어질 수 있습니다. 반면에, 여러분은 아마추어들의 관심을 호소함으로써 더 많은 회원 수를 얻을 수 있습니다. [47]여러분의 목적과 목표 회원들을 아는 것은 여러분의 사이트에 어떤 자료를 게시할지를 결정할 것입니다.

둘째로, 여러분의 온라인 동호회가 회원들에게 무엇을 제공할 것인지를 분명히 제시하십시오. 이것은 여러 가지 형태를 띨 수 있습니다. 여러분의 댄서들 중 많은 이들의 요구를 충족시키는 것은 그저 사교댄스의 기본적인 스텝을 가르치는 교육용 동영상들을 게시하는 것을 포함할 수도 있습니다. 그러나, [48]여러분은 회원들에게 몇 가지 고급 기능들을 제공하고 싶으실 수도 있습니다. 이것들은 문자 서비스, 행사를 게시하고 논의할 수 있는 대화형 게시판, 그리고 심지어는 화상으로 개최되는 회의와 같은 것들이 될 수 있습니다.

셋째로, 동호회의 구조와 요건들을 공식적으로 표명하십시오. [49]회원들은 미래에 발생할지도 모르는 집단 내의 분쟁을 해결하기 위해 이 규정을 참고할 것입니다. 여러분은 반드시 회원 기준을 설명하고, 동호회가 어떻게 운영될 것이며 여러분의 댄서들에게 무엇이 요구되는지를 정의해야 합니다. 출석 및 대회 참가 의무와 같은 사항들을 규정하는 것은 회원들로 하여금 더 광범위한 댄스스포츠 커뮤니티와 융합되도록 도울 것입니다. 또한, 개정 과정을 약술하십시오. 그것은 여러분의 조직이 새로운 환경에 적응하는 능력을 줄 것입니다.

넷째로, 회원들이 부적절하게 행동하거나 그들의 책임을 다하지 못할 경우 어떤 일이 일어날지 명시하십시오. 안타깝게도, 모든 사람이 항상 완벽하게 행동하지는 않을 것입니다. [50]여러분은 모든 사람이 안전하고 편안하도록 보장하기 위해 규칙을 마련해야 할 것입니다. 이것은 참여자들의 온라인 개인 정보를 보호하기 위해 특히 중요합니다. 여러분은 정책을 위반하는 사람들에 대한 징계를 포함해야 할 것입니다. 이것들은 일시적 권리 정지에서 퇴출에 이르기까지

from temporary suspension to expulsion. No matter what you decide, don't forget to explain the steps for removing members.

Fifth, fund your organization. The club can't function without capital. In addition to the administrative costs of running a club, a dancesport club often has other expenses that must be paid, such as entrance fees for competitions. Some of these will be covered by membership dues, but it may be necessary to seek out sponsorship. Luckily, [51]with the popularity of competitive dancing, many local businesses may be keen to help out. In return, you may have to include their advertisements on the website or in official materials.

Finally, plan dance events. [52]Announce the specific dates and agendas for events in online sports publications so that the public can learn about and become interested in them. This is also a fine way to attract new members, as events will give sign-up opportunities to individuals who are curious about your organization. You may offer free lessons that teach the basics of dancesport as well to get people to sign up for paid classes.

Thank you for listening! By following the advice that you have heard here today, you can launch an amazing dancesport club.

강도가 다양할 수 있습니다. 어떤 결정을 내리든, 회원을 퇴출하는 것에 대한 단계들을 설명하는 것을 잊지 마십시오.

다섯째로, 조직에 자금을 지원하십시오. 동호회는 자본 없이는 기능할 수 없습니다. 동호회를 운영하는 것에 드는 관리비 외에도, 댄스스포츠 동호회는 대회 출전 비용과 같이 반드시 지불되어야 하는 여러 비용들이 종종 있습니다. 이것들 중 일부는 회비로 충당될 것이지만, 후원자를 찾을 필요가 있을 수도 있습니다. 다행히도, [51]경기용 댄스가 인기를 끌면서, 많은 지역 사업체들이 도움을 주고 싶어 할지도 모릅니다. 그 대가로, 여러분은 웹 사이트나 공식 자료에 그것들(지역 사업체들)의 광고를 포함해야 할지도 모릅니다.

마지막으로, 댄스 행사들을 계획하십시오. [52]대중이 그것들에 대해 알고 관심을 가질 수 있도록 온라인 스포츠 간행물에 행사들의 구체적인 날짜와 일정을 발표하십시오. 이것은 새로운 회원들을 끌어들이는 좋은 방법이기도 한데, 이는 행사들이 여러분의 단체에 대해 궁금해하는 사람들에게 가입 기회를 줄 것이기 때문입니다. 사람들이 유료 수업에 등록하도록 하기 위해 여러분은 댄스스포츠의 기초를 가르치는 무료 수업도 제공하실 수 있습니다.

들어 주셔서 감사합니다! 여러분이 오늘 여기서 들은 조언을 따르시면, 여러분은 멋진 댄스스포츠 동호회를 시작하실 수 있습니다.

어휘 | ballroom dancing 사교댄스 gear[gir] 적합하도록 만들다 instructional[instrʌ́kʃənəl] 교육용의 interactive[ìntərǽktiv] 대화형의 bulletin board 게시판 declare[diklέr] 표명하다 criterion[kraitíəriən] 기준 stipulate[stípjəleit] 규정하다 outline[áutlain] 약술하다 amendment[əméndmənt] 개정 adapt[ədǽpt] 적응하다 explicitly[iksplísitli] 명확하게 violate[váiəleit] 위반하다 severity[səvérəti] 강도, 심각성 temporary[témpəreri] 일시적인 suspension[səspénʃən] 권리 정지 expulsion[ikspʌ́lʃən] 퇴출 cover[kʌ́vər] 충당하다 keen[kiːn] ~하고 싶어 하는

46 주제/목적   담화의 주제   난이도 ●○○

What is the talk all about?

(a) how to host a private website
(b) the benefits of ballroom dancing
(c) how to found a dance organization
(d) the popularity of a web-based group

담화의 주제는 무엇인가?

(a) 개인 웹 사이트를 관리하는 방법
(b) 사교댄스의 이점들
(c) 댄스 단체를 설립하는 방법
(d) 인터넷 기반 단체의 인기

🔑 지텔프 치트키

담화의 주제를 언급하는 초반을 주의 깊게 듣고 전체 맥락을 파악한다.

해설 | 화자가 'I'm going to tell you how to start your own online dancesport club'이라며 온라인 댄스스포츠 동호회를 시작하는 방법을 알려 줄 것이라고 한 뒤, 담화 전반에 걸쳐 온라인 댄스스포츠 동호회를 설립하는 방법에 관한 내용이 이어지고 있다. 따라서 (c)가 정답이다.

Paraphrasing

how to start your own ~ dancesport club 자신만의 댄스스포츠 동호회를 시작하는 방법 → how to found a dance organization 댄스 단체를 설립하는 방법

어휘 | host[houst] 관리하다

---

47 특정세부사항   How

난이도 ●●○

How does deciding upon target members affect an online group?

(a) **It dictates the type of information posted.**
(b) It increases the public's interest in the group.
(c) It gives members a sense of purpose.
(d) It makes the group seem more professional.

목표 회원을 결정하는 것이 어떻게 온라인 단체에 영향을 미치는가?

(a) **게시되는 정보의 유형을 결정한다.**
(b) 그 단체에 대한 대중의 관심을 증가시킨다.
(c) 회원들에게 목표 의식을 준다.
(d) 그 단체를 더 전문적으로 보이게 한다.

지텔프 치트키

질문의 키워드 target members가 그대로 언급된 주변 내용을 주의 깊게 듣는다.

해설 | 화자가 'Understanding ~ target members will determine what materials you post on your site.'라며 목표 회원들을 아는 것은 사이트에 어떤 자료를 게시할지를 결정할 것이라고 했다. 따라서 (a)가 정답이다.

Paraphrasing

determine what materials you post 어떤 자료를 게시할지를 결정하다 → dictates the type of information posted 게시되는 정보의 유형을 결정한다

어휘 | dictate[díkteit] 결정하다, 좌우하다

---

48 추론   특정사실

난이도 ●●●

Why most likely would more advanced features be added to the website?

(a) so the members can receive discounts
(b) to help dancers become experts
(c) to encourage more people to join the club
(d) **so the members can communicate easily**

왜 웹 사이트에 더 많은 고급 기능들이 추가될 것 같은가?

(a) 회원들이 할인을 받을 수 있도록 하기 위해서
(b) 댄서들이 전문가가 되도록 돕기 위해서
(c) 더 많은 사람들이 동호회에 가입하도록 장려하기 위해서
(d) **회원들이 수월하게 소통할 수 있도록 하기 위해서**

지텔프 치트키

질문의 키워드 advanced features가 그대로 언급된 주변 내용을 주의 깊게 듣는다.

해설 | 화자가 'you may want to provide some advanced features for your members'라며 회원들에게 몇 가지 고급 기능들을 제공하고 싶을 수도 있다고 한 뒤, 'These could be things like messaging services, interactive bulletin boards ~, and even meetings held by videoconferencing.'이라며 이것들은 문자 서비스, 대화형 게시판, 그리고 심지어는 화상으로 개최되는 회의와 같은 것들이 될 수 있다고 한 것을 통해, 회원들이 수월하게 소통할 수 있도록 하기 위해서 웹 사이트에 더 많은 고급 기능들이 추가될 것임을 추론할 수 있다. 따라서 (d)가 정답이다.

특정세부사항   When   난이도 ●●○

When will members refer to the guidelines? (a) when they decide the purpose of the group (b) when they outline the amendment process **(c) when they address internal conflicts** (d) when they produce a difficult dance	회원들은 언제 지침을 참고할 것인가? (a) 단체의 목적을 결정할 때 (b) 개정 과정을 약술할 때 **(c) 내부 갈등을 다룰 때** (d) 어려운 춤을 창작할 때

━○ 지텔프 치트키

질문의 키워드 guidelines가 regulations로 paraphrasing되어 언급된 주변 내용을 주의 깊게 듣는다.

해설 | 화자가 'Members will refer to these regulations to settle any disputes within the group that may arise in the future.' 라며 회원들은 미래에 발생할지도 모르는 집단 내의 분쟁을 해결하기 위해서 규정을 참고할 것이라고 했다. 따라서 (c)가 정답이다.

Paraphrasing
settle any disputes within the group 집단 내의 분쟁을 해결하다 → **address internal conflicts** 내부 갈등을 다루다

---

50 **특정세부사항**   What   난이도 ●●○

What action should be taken to ensure members' safety and comfort? (a) limiting the number of members per class **(b) establishing a set of behavioral standards** (c) creating a strict reputation in the community (d) forming a powerful rules committee	회원들의 안전과 편안함을 보장하기 위해 어떤 행동 이 취해져야 하는가? (a) 수업 당 회원 수를 제한하는 것 **(b) 일련의 행동 기준을 수립하는 것** (c) 커뮤니티에서 강력한 평판을 만드는 것 (d) 강대한 의사 운영 위원회를 형성하는 것

━○ 지텔프 치트키

질문의 키워드 safety and comfort가 safe and comfortable로 언급된 주변 내용을 주의 깊게 듣는다.

해설 | 화자가 'You'll need to set up rules to ensure that everyone is safe and comfortable.'이라며 모든 사람이 안전하고 편안하도 록 보장하기 위해서 규칙을 마련해야 할 것이라고 했다. 따라서 (b)가 정답이다.

Paraphrasing
set up rules 규칙을 마련하다 → **establishing a set of behavioral standards** 일련의 행동 기준을 수립하는 것

어휘 | standard[stǽndərd] 기준 reputation[règpjətéiʃən] 평판 rules committee 의사 운영 위원회

---

51 **추론**   **특정사실**   난이도 ●●○

Why may local companies be willing to offer financial support to the club? (a) to sponsor a local competition **(b) to promote their businesses** (c) to gain access to foreign markets	왜 지역 업체들이 그 동호회에 재정적인 지원을 제공 할 의향이 있을 수도 있는가? (a) 지역 대회를 후원하기 위해서 **(b) 그들의 사업체를 홍보하기 위해서** (c) 해외 시장에 접근하기 위해서

(d) to have dancers in advertisements

(d) 광고에 댄서들을 포함시키기 위해서

지텔프 치트키

질문의 키워드 local companies가 local businesses로 paraphrasing되어 언급된 주변 내용을 주의 깊게 듣는다.

해설 | 화자가 'with the popularity of competitive dancing, many local businesses may be keen to help out'이라며 경기용 댄스가 인기를 끌면서 많은 지역 사업체들이 도움을 주고 싶어 할지도 모른다고 한 뒤, 'In return, you may have to include their advertisements on the website or in official materials.'라며 그 대가로 웹 사이트나 공식 자료에 그것들(지역 사업체들)의 광고를 포함해야 할지도 모른다고 한 것을 통해, 지역 업체들이 그들의 사업체를 홍보하기 위해서 재정적인 지원을 제공할 의향이 있을 것임을 추론할 수 있다. 따라서 (b)가 정답이다.

52　특정세부사항　How

난이도 ●●○

How can online dancesport clubs increase membership?

(a) **by making more people aware of their events**
(b) by lowering the prices of classes permanently
(c) by giving opportunities for beginners to perform
(d) by reaching out to individuals through social media

어떻게 온라인 댄스스포츠 동호회들은 회원 수를 증가시킬 수 있는가?

(a) **더 많은 사람들이 그것들의 행사에 대해 알게 함으로써**
(b) 수업료를 영구적으로 인하함으로써
(c) 초보자들에게 공연할 기회를 제공함으로써
(d) 소셜 미디어를 통해 사람들에게 접근함으로써

지텔프 치트키

질문의 키워드 increase membership이 attract new members로 paraphrasing되어 언급된 주변 내용을 주의 깊게 듣는다.

해설 | 화자가 'Announce the specific dates and agendas for events in online sports publications so that the public can learn about and become interested in them.'이라며 대중이 댄스 행사들에 대해 알고 관심을 가질 수 있도록 온라인 스포츠 간행물에 행사들의 구체적인 날짜와 일정을 발표하라고 한 뒤, 'This is ~ a fine way to attract new members'라며 이것은 새로운 회원들을 끌어들이는 좋은 방법이라고 했다. 따라서 (a)가 정답이다.

Paraphrasing
the public ~ learn 대중이 알다 → more people aware 더 많은 사람들이 아는

어휘 | lower[lóuər] 인하하다　permanently[pə́:rmənəntli] 영구적으로

PART 1 (53~59) 인물의 일대기 필즈상을 수상한 최초의 여성 수학자 마리암 미르자하니

인물 이름	**MARYAM MIRZAKHANI**

MARYAM MIRZAKHANI

Maryam Mirzakhani was a prominent Iranian mathematician and Stanford University professor. She is [53]best known as the first Iranian and the only woman thus far to be awarded the Fields Medal, which is akin to a Nobel Prize as it is the highest honor a mathematician can receive.

Mirzakhani was born on May 12, 1977 in Tehran, Iran, to parents Ahmad Mirzakhani and Zahra Haghighi. She initially wanted to become a writer. [54]She was not interested in mathematics due to a teacher's comment about her lack of talent in the subject, which shattered her confidence. It wasn't until another teacher later encouraged her that [58]she decided to pursue math seriously. Participating in the International Mathematical Olympiad as a high school student in 1994, she was the first Iranian girl to win a gold medal. The following year, she achieved a perfect score in the same competition.

After studying mathematics at Sharif University of Technology, she earned a PhD from Harvard University, where she was recognized as an influential mathematician for her thesis titled *Simple Geodesics on Hyperbolic Surfaces and Volume of the Moduli Space of Curves*. [55]Her thesis provided a new proof of the Witten conjecture on quantum gravity, which had long troubled mathematicians.

Mirzakhani continued focusing on the dynamics of moduli space after she became a professor at Stanford University in 2009. In 2014, [56]Mirzakhani proved that complex geodesics in moduli space are regular rather than irregular. She made this breakthrough with mathematician Alex Eskin of the University of Chicago, with whom she had started working in 2006.

The International Mathematical Union presented Mirzakhani with the Fields Medal in Seoul, South Korea in 2014 for her contributions to the theory of moduli spaces of Riemann surfaces. In an interview, she said that she herself hoped to inspire other women to go after successful careers in science and mathematics.

인물 이름 / 인물 소개 + 유명한 이유 / 어린 시절 + 업적 시작 계기 / 초기 업적 / 주요 업적 / 필즈상 수상

마리암 미르자하니

마리암 미르자하니는 저명한 이란 수학자이자 스탠퍼드 대학교 교수였다. 그녀는 [53]지금까지 필즈상을 수상한 최초의 이란인이자 유일한 여성으로 가장 잘 알려져 있는데, 이것은 수학자가 받을 수 있는 최고의 영예로 노벨상과 유사하다.

미르자하니는 부모 아흐마드 미르자하니와 자흐라 하지지 사이에서, 1977년 5월 12일에 이란의 테헤란 주에서 태어났다. 그녀는 원래 작가가 되기를 원했다. [54]그녀는 수학에 관심이 없었는데 이는 그녀가 그 과목에 재능이 없다는 한 교사의 언급 때문이었으며, 이것은 그녀의 자신감을 꺾었다. 또 다른 교사가 나중에 그녀를 격려하고 나서야 [58]그녀는 진지하게 수학을 공부하기로 결심했다. 1994년에 고등학생으로 국제 수학 올림피아드에 참가한 그녀는 금메달을 딴 최초의 이란 여학생이었다. 다음 해, 그녀는 같은 대회에서 만점을 달성했다.

샤리프 공과대학에서 수학을 공부한 후, 그녀는 하버드 대학에서 박사 학위를 취득했고, 그곳에서 그녀는 「쌍곡 곡면상의 단순한 측지선과 곡선들로 이루어진 모듈라이 공간의 부피」라는 제목의 논문으로 영향력 있는 수학자로서 인정받았다. [55]그녀의 논문은 양자 중력에 관한 위튼의 추측의 새로운 증명을 제시했는데, 이것은 오랫동안 수학자들을 애먹였었다.

미르자하니는 2009년에 스탠퍼드 대학의 교수가 된 후에도 모듈라이 공간의 동역학에 계속 집중했다. 2014년에, [56]미르자하니는 모듈라이 공간의 복잡한 측지선이 불규칙적이지 않고 규칙적이라는 것을 증명했다. 그녀는 시카고 대학의 수학자 알렉스 에스킨과 함께 이 획기적 발전을 이루어 냈는데, 그와 그녀는 2006년에 함께 일하기 시작했었다.

국제 수학 연맹은 2014년에 대한민국의 서울에서 리만 곡면의 모듈라이 공간 이론에 기여한 공로로 미르자하니에게 필즈상을 수여했다. 한 인터뷰에서, 그녀는 그녀 자신이 다른 여성들로 하여금 과학과 수학 분야에서 성공적인 경력을 쌓도록 고무하기를 바란다고 말했다.

말년
+
죽음

While [59]this was a <u>considerable</u> honor as she was the first woman to receive the famed medal, Mirzakhani won many other distinctions as well, including [57(c)]being admitted as a member of the Paris Academy of Sciences and the American Philosophical Society in 2015. After [57(a)]a four-year struggle against breast cancer, Mirzakhani died on July 14, 2017, at the age of 40. [57(d)]She is remembered today as a modest person whose enthusiasm and perseverance were unmatched.

그녀가 그 유명한 상을 받은 최초의 여성이었다는 점에서 [59]이것은 상당한 영광이었지만, 미르자하니는 그 밖에도 2015년에 [57(c)]파리 과학 아카데미와 미국 철학 학회의 회원으로 받아들여진 것을 포함하여 많은 영예들을 얻기도 했다. [57(a)]4년간의 유방암 투병 끝에, 미르자하니는 2017년 7월 14일에 40세의 나이로 사망하였다. [57(d)]그녀는 오늘날 열정과 끈기가 타의 추종을 불허하는 겸손한 사람으로 기억된다.

어휘 | prominent adj. 저명한 award v. 수여하다 akin adj. 유사한 honor n. 영예, 영광 initially adv. 원래, 처음에 shatter v. 꺾다, 산산조각 내다 influential adj. 영향력이 있는 thesis n. 논문 proof n. 증명, 증거 conjecture n. 추측 quantum n. 양자 trouble v. 애먹이다, 괴롭히다 dynamics n. 동역학 regular adj. 규칙적인 breakthrough n. 획기적 발전 present v. 수여하다 famed adj. 유명한 distinction n. 영예 admit v. 받아들이다 modest adj. 겸손한 enthusiasm n. 열정 perseverance n. 끈기 unmatched adj. 타의 추종을 불허하는

---

53 특정세부사항   유명한 이유   난이도 ●●○

What is Maryam Mirzakhani most famous for?

(a) **being the first woman to win a prestigious award**
(b) being the first Iranian to become a professor at an esteemed university
(c) teaching mathematics at a renowned Iranian educational institution
(d) getting a Nobel Prize for her work in mathematics

마리암 미르자하니는 무엇으로 가장 유명한가?

(a) 권위 있는 상을 받은 최초의 여성으로
(b) 존경받는 대학의 교수가 된 최초의 이란인으로
(c) 이란의 유명한 교육기관에서 수학을 가르친 것으로
(d) 수학에서의 업적에 대해 노벨상을 받은 것으로

지텔프 치트키

질문의 키워드 most famous for가 best known as로 paraphrasing되어 언급된 주변 내용을 주의 깊게 읽는다.

해설 | 1단락의 'best known as the first Iranian and the only woman ~ to be awarded the Fields Medal, which is ~ the highest honor a mathematician can receive'에서 마리암 미르자하니는 지금까지 수학자가 받을 수 있는 최고의 영예인 필즈상을 수상한 최초의 이란인이자 유일한 여성으로 가장 잘 알려져 있다고 했다. 따라서 (a)가 정답이다.

Paraphrasing
be awarded 수상하다 → win 받다
the highest honor 최고의 영예 → a prestigious award 권위 있는 상

어휘 | prestigious adj. 권위 있는 esteemed adj. 존경받는 renowned adj. 유명한

---

54 특정세부사항   Why   난이도 ●●○

Why was Mirzakhani indifferent to mathematics at first?

(a) because her parents pressured her to master the subject
(b) because she dreamed of becoming a writing instructor

왜 미르자하니는 처음에 수학에 관심이 없었는가?

(a) 부모가 그 과목을 숙달하라고 그녀를 압박했기 때문에
(b) 작문 강사가 되는 것을 꿈꿨기 때문에

(c) because she participated in other academic competitions

(d) because an educator pointed out her insufficient ability

(c) 다른 경시대회들에 참가했기 때문에

(d) 한 교사가 그녀의 부족한 능력을 지적했기 때문에

지텔프 치트키

질문의 키워드 indifferent가 not interested로 paraphrasing되어 언급된 주변 내용을 주의 깊게 읽는다.

해설 | 2단락의 'She was not interested in mathematics due to a teacher's comment about her lack of talent in the subject'에서 미르자하니는 그녀가 수학에 재능이 없다는 한 교사의 언급 때문에 수학에 관심이 없었다고 했다. 따라서 (d)가 정답이다.

Paraphrasing

a teacher's comment about her lack of talent 재능이 없다는 한 교사의 언급 → an educator pointed out her insufficient ability 한 교사가 부족한 능력을 지적했다

어휘 | indifferent adj. 관심이 없는 pressure v. 압박하다 insufficient adj. 부족한, 부적당한

---

55 추론   묘사   난이도 ●●●

What best describes the Witten conjecture before Mirzakhani's proof?

(a) It had provided groundbreaking data on gravity.
(b) It had proven the existence of simple geodesics.
(c) It had been influential in the field of technology.
(d) It had lacked the information to be confirmed.

미르자하니의 증명 전 위튼의 추측을 가장 잘 묘사하는 것은 무엇인가?

(a) 중력에 관한 획기적인 자료를 제공했다.
(b) 단순한 측지선의 존재를 증명했다.
(c) 기술 분야에서 영향력이 있었다.
(d) 입증되기에는 정보가 부족했다.

지텔프 치트키

질문의 키워드 Witten conjecture가 그대로 언급된 주변 내용을 주의 깊게 읽는다.

해설 | 3단락의 'Her thesis provided a new proof of the Witten conjecture ~, which had long troubled mathematicians.'에서 미르자하니의 논문이 양자 중력에 관한 위튼의 추측의 새로운 증명을 제시했는데, 그 추측이 오랫동안 수학자들을 애먹였었다고 한 것을 통해, 미르자하니의 증명 전 위튼의 추측은 입증되기에는 정보가 부족했음을 추론할 수 있다. 따라서 (d)가 정답이다.

> **오답분석**
> (a) 3단락에서 위튼의 추측이 양자 중력에 관한 것이라고는 했지만, 이것이 중력에 관한 획기적인 자료를 제공했는지는 언급되지 않았으므로 오답이다.

어휘 | groundbreaking adj. 획기적인 existence n. 존재 confirm v. 입증하다, 확인하다

---

56 특정세부사항   When   난이도 ●●○

When did Mirzakhani prove an important fact about complex geodesics?

(a) when she collaborated with another scholar
(b) when she attended the University of Chicago
(c) when Eskin made a discovery concerning geodesics
(d) when Eskin started studying moduli space

미르자하니는 언제 복잡한 측지선에 관한 중요한 사실을 증명했는가?

(a) 다른 학자와 협력했을 때
(b) 시카고 대학에 다녔을 때
(c) 에스킨이 측지선에 관한 발견을 했을 때
(d) 에스킨이 모듈라이 공간을 연구하기 시작했을 때

질문의 키워드 complex geodesics가 그대로 언급된 주변 내용을 주의 깊게 읽는다.

해설 | 4단락의 'Mirzakhani proved that complex geodesics in moduli space are regular than irregular'에서 미르자하니가 모듈라이 공간의 복잡한 측지선이 불규칙적이지 않고 규칙적이라는 것을 증명했다고 한 뒤, 'She made this breakthrough with mathematician Alex Eskin of the University of Chicago'에서 미르자하니는 시카고 대학의 수학자 알렉스 에스킨과 함께 이 획기적인 발전을 이루어 냈다고 했다. 따라서 (a)가 정답이다.

Paraphrasing
mathematician 수학자 → another scholar 학자

어휘 | collaborate v. 협력하다　concerning prep. ~에 관한

---

57 ｜ Not/True　Not 문제　　난이도 ●●○

Which of the following is NOT true about the later years of Mirzakhani's life?

(a) She contracted a deadly disease.
(b) She funded cancer research in Paris.
(c) She became a member of various scholarly organizations.
(d) She earned a reputation for being passionate.

다음 중 미르자하니의 말년에 관해 사실이 아닌 것은 무엇인가?

(a) 치명적인 병에 걸렸다.
(b) 파리에서 암 연구에 자금을 지원했다.
(c) 다양한 학술 단체의 회원이 되었다.
(d) 열정적이라는 평판을 얻었다.

질문의 키워드 later years와 관련된 지문의 후반을 주의 깊게 읽고, 보기의 키워드와 지문 내용을 대조하며 언급되는 것을 하나씩 소거한다.

해설 | (b)는 지문에 언급되지 않았으므로, (b)가 정답이다.

오답분석
(a) 보기의 키워드 disease가 cancer로 paraphrasing되어 언급된 6단락에서 미르자하니가 4년간의 유방암 투병 끝에 사망했다고 언급되었다.
(c) 보기의 키워드 became a member가 admitted as a member로 paraphrasing되어 언급된 6단락에서 미르자하니가 파리 과학 아카데미와 미국 철학 학회의 회원으로 받아들여졌다고 언급되었다.
(d) 보기의 키워드 passionate가 enthusiasm으로 paraphrasing되어 언급된 6단락에서 미르자하니가 오늘날 열정과 끈기가 타의 추종을 불허하는 겸손한 사람으로 기억된다고 언급되었다.

어휘 | contract v. (병에) 걸리다　scholarly adj. 학술의　passionate adj. 열정적인

---

58 ｜ 어휘　유의어　　난이도 ●●○

In the context of the passage, seriously means _____.

(a) inevitably
(b) honestly
(c) intently
(d) rightly

지문의 문맥에서, 'seriously'는 -을 의미한다.

(a) 필연적으로
(b) 정직하게
(c) 열심히
(d) 올바르게

밑줄 친 어휘의 유의어를 찾는 문제이므로, seriously가 포함된 구절을 읽고 문맥을 파악한다.

해설 | 2단락의 'she decided to pursue math seriously'는 그녀가 진지하게 수학을 공부하기로 결심했다는 뜻이므로, seriously가 '진지하게'라는 의미로 사용된 것을 알 수 있다. 따라서 '열심히'라는 비슷한 의미의 (c) intently가 정답이다.

---

59 어휘   유의어   난이도 ●○○

In the context of the passage, <u>considerable</u> means _____.	지문의 문맥에서, 'considerable'은 -을 의미한다.
(a) considerate	(a) 신중한
(b) necessary	(b) 필요한
(c) critical	(c) 중요한
(d) large	**(d) 상당한**

밑줄 친 어휘의 유의어를 찾는 문제이므로, considerable이 포함된 구절을 읽고 문맥을 파악한다.

해설 | 6단락의 'this was a considerable honor'는 이것이 상당한 영광이었다는 뜻이므로, considerable이 '상당한'이라는 의미로 사용된 것을 알 수 있다. 따라서 '상당한'이라는 같은 의미의 (d) large가 정답이다.

PART 2 (60~66) 잡지 기사   환경을 파괴하는 아보카도 농사

기사 제목	**60AVOCADO: THE "GREEN GOLD" DESTROYING THE PLANET**	**60아보카도: 지구를 파괴하는 '녹색 황금'**
아보 카도 생산지	The United States revoked a ban on the import of Mexican avocados in 1997, beginning what is now seemingly an obsession with the fruit. Since then, the Mexican state of Michoacán, the largest avocado producer in the world, has kept up with demand. However, 60Michoacán is currently facing resource depletion, extreme weather, soil degradation, and biodiversity loss.	미국은 1997년에 멕시코산 아보카도의 수입 금지를 철회했으며, 지금은 그 과일에 대해 집착처럼 보이는 것을 시작했다. 그 이후로, 세계 최대의 아보카도 생산지인 멕시코 미초아칸주가 수요를 따라잡고 있다. 그러나, 60미초아칸주는 현재 자원 고갈, 기상 이변, 토양 악화, 그리고 생물 다양성 손실에 직면하고 있다.
아보 카도 생산 수익	Producing 80 percent of Mexico's avocados, the state is dependent on this fruit, which creates job opportunities in the region, generating about $3.1 billion annually for the nation. 61Given how vital its continued success is to the state, where 50.9 percent of people have an income below the poverty line, it is no wonder that there is little regard for the environmental damage it inflicts.	멕시코산 아보카도의 80퍼센트를 생산하는 그 주는 이 과일에 의존적인데, 이것은 그 지역에서 고용 기회를 창출하고, 연간 약 31억 달러를 국가에 벌어들인다. 6150.9퍼센트의 사람들이 빈곤선 이하의 소득을 가지고 있는 그 주에 그것의 지속적인 성공이 얼마나 중요한지를 생각하면, 그것(아보카도)이 가하는 환경적 피해에 대한 관심이 거의 없는 것은 놀랄 일이 아니다.

환경 파괴 원인

[65]Large-scale deforestation has <u>passed</u> in the name of the lucrative industry. Because avocado trees require lots of sunlight to grow, taller trees nearby have been cut down. Furthermore, profit-seeking avocado producers are abusing a law designed to protect forest land. [62]The law states that the land can be used for commercial agriculture only if it is lost to fire. However, avocado producers are burning it down instead of waiting for a forest fire caused by a natural event or an accident. The loss of forest land has depleted the soil of nutrients and led to habitat loss resulting in a decrease in biodiversity.

환경 파괴 결과

The weather in Michoacán has become hotter and drier, and hurricanes are more intense due to the reduction of forested land. In addition, [63]the region is at a higher risk of earthquakes stemming from the frequent drilling of wells for agricultural water. In 2020, avocado farms drew approximately 9.5 billion liters of water a day from underground reservoirs, putting them in danger of being drained.

시사점 + 해결책

However, those involved in avocado production are not entirely responsible for the environmental damage. [64]The strong demand for the fruit means that consumers are also at fault. To [66]put an end to the <u>rampant</u> destruction, solutions such as expanding sustainable farming practices and revisions to trade agreements are being discussed.

[65]대규모 삼림 벌채는 수익성이 좋은 산업이라는 명목으로 발생해 왔다. 아보카도 나무들은 자라기 위해 많은 햇빛을 필요로 하기 때문에, 근처의 큰 나무들이 잘려 나갔다. 게다가, 이익을 추구하는 아보카도 생산자들은 삼림 지대를 보호하기 위해 고안된 법을 남용하고 있다. [62]그 법은 그 지대가 화재로 소실된 경우에만 상업적 농업에 사용될 수 있다고 명시한다. 그러나, 아보카도 생산자들은 자연 발생적인 사건이나 사고에 의해 야기된 산불을 기다리는 것 대신 그것을 태워버리고 있다. 삼림 지대의 손실은 토양에서 영양분을 고갈시켰고 생물 다양성의 감소로 이어지는 서식지 감소를 야기했다.

미초아칸주의 날씨는 더 더워지고 건조해졌으며, 삼림 지대의 감소 때문에 허리케인은 더 격렬해지고 있다. 또한, [63]그 지역은 농업용수를 위한 잦은 우물 굴착으로 인해 지진의 위험이 더 크다. 2020년에, 아보카도 농장들은 지하 저수지들에서 하루에 약 95억 리터의 물을 끌어왔으며, 그것들을(지하 저수지들을) 고갈될 위험에 처하게 했다.

하지만, 아보카도 생산에 관련된 사람들이 환경 파괴에 전적으로 책임이 있는 것은 아니다. [64]그 과일에 대한 높은 수요는 소비자들에게도 책임이 있다는 것을 의미한다. [66]걷잡을 수 없는 파괴를 종식시키기 위해, 지속 가능한 농업 관행의 확대와 무역 협정 개정과 같은 해결책들이 논의되고 있다.

어휘 | revoke v. 철회하다, 폐지하다 import n. 수입 obsession n. 집착 keep up with phr. ~을 따라잡다 demand n. 수요 resource n. 자원 depletion n. 고갈 degradation n. 악화 biodiversity n. 생물 다양성 dependent adj. 의존적인 poverty line phr. 빈곤선(최저한도의 생활을 유지하는 데 필요한 수입 수준) regard n. 관심, 고려 inflict v. (괴로움 등을) 가하다 deforestation n. 삼림 벌채 in the name of phr. ~이라는 명목으로 lucrative adj. 수익성이 좋은 profit-seeking adj. 이익을 추구하는 abuse v. 남용하다 commercial adj. 상업적인 agriculture n. 농업 habitat n. 서식지 reduction n. 감소 stem v. 기인하다 drilling n. 굴착 reservoir n. 저수지 drain v. 고갈시키다 fault n. 책임

---

60 | **주제/목적** | 기사의 주제 | 난이도 ●○○

What is the article mainly about?

(a) the negative effects of avocado consumption on health
(b) the cause of the rising demand for avocados
(c) the environmental impact of avocado farming
(d) the removal of a ban on avocado imports

기사의 주제는 무엇인가?

(a) 아보카도 섭취가 건강에 미치는 부정적인 영향
(b) 아보카도 수요 증가의 원인
(c) 아보카도 농사가 환경에 미치는 영향
(d) 아보카도 수입 금지의 해제

━○ 지텔프 치트키

제목과 지문의 초반을 주의 깊게 읽고 전체 맥락을 파악한다.

해설 | 기사의 제목 'Avocado: the "Green Gold" Destroying the Planet'에서 아보카도가 지구를 파괴하는 '녹색 황금'이라고 언급하였다. 그다음에, 1단락의 'Michoacán is currently facing resource depletion, extreme weather, soil degradation, and biodiversity loss'에서 세계 최대의 아보카도 생산지인 미초아칸주는 현재 자원 고갈, 기상 이변, 토양 악화, 그리고 생물 다양성 손실에 직면하고 있다고 한 뒤, 아보카도 농사가 환경에 미치는 영향에 관한 세부 내용이 이어지고 있다. 따라서 (c)가 정답이다.

어휘 | consumption n. 섭취, 소비   removal n. 해제, 제거

---

61 특정세부사항   Which   난이도 ●●○

According to the article, which is the result of the ongoing prosperity of the avocado industry?

(a) Avocados are being grown in other parts of the nation.
(b) Residents of Michoacán are becoming very rich.
(c) Residents of Michoacán are ignoring the ecological consequences.
(d) Avocados are getting more expensive in Mexico.

기사에 따르면, 아보카도 산업의 계속되는 성공에 따른 결과는 무엇인가?

(a) 아보카도가 국가의 다른 지역에서 재배되고 있다.
(b) 미초아칸주 주민들이 매우 부유해지고 있다.
(c) 미초아칸주 주민들이 생태학적 결과들을 무시하고 있다.
(d) 아보카도가 멕시코에서 점점 더 비싸지고 있다.

지텔프 치트키

질문의 키워드 ongoing prosperity가 continued success로 paraphrasing되어 언급된 주변 내용을 주의 깊게 읽는다.

해설 | 2단락의 'Given how vital its continued success is to the state, ~, it is no wonder that there is little regard for the environmental damage it inflicts.'에서 미초아칸주에 아보카도의 지속적인 성공이 얼마나 중요한지를 생각하면 아보카도가 가하는 환경적 피해에 대한 관심이 거의 없는 것은 놀랄 일이 아니라고 했다. 따라서 (c)가 정답이다.

Paraphrasing
little regard for the environmental damage 환경적 피해에 대한 관심이 거의 없는 → ignoring the ecological consequences 생태학적 결과들을 무시하는

어휘 | prosperity n. 성공, 번영   ecological adj. 생태학적

---

62 추론   특정사실   난이도 ●●●

What can probably be said about avocado producers?

(a) that they have their farmland legally protected
(b) that they are planting avocado trees within dense forests
(c) that they have changed a law regarding the use of forest land
(d) that they are exploiting a gap in some legislation

아보카도 생산자들에 관해 무엇이 말해질 수 있을 것 같은가?

(a) 그들의 농지를 법적으로 보호받게 한다는 것
(b) 울창한 숲에 아보카도 나무를 심고 있다는 것
(c) 삼림 지대 사용에 관한 법을 바꿨다는 것
(d) 일부 법률의 빈틈을 이용하고 있다는 것

지텔프 치트키

질문의 키워드 avocado producers가 그대로 언급된 주변 내용을 주의 깊게 읽는다.

해설 | 3단락의 'The law states that the land can be used ~ only if it is lost to fire.'에서 삼림 지대를 보호하기 위해 고안된 법이 삼림 지대는 화재로 소실된 경우에만 상업적 농업에 사용될 수 있다고 명시한다고 한 뒤, 'However, avocado producers are burning it down instead of waiting for a forest fire caused by a natural event or an accident.'에서 그러나 아보카도 생산자들은 자연

발생적인 사건이나 사고에 의해 야기된 산불을 기다리는 것 대신에 그 지대를 태워버리고 있다고 한 것을 통해, 아보카도 생산자들은 법률의 빈틈을 이용하고 있다는 것을 추론할 수 있다. 따라서 (d)가 정답이다.

어휘 | legally adv. 법적으로 dense adj. 울창한 exploit v. 이용하다 gap n. 빈틈 legislation n. 법률

---

63 특정세부사항　　Why　　　　　　　　　　　　　　　　　　난이도 ●●○

Why has the chance of natural disasters increased in Michoacán?

(a) because the land is being excavated often
(b) because the temperature has decreased significantly
(c) because there is little water left in surface-level reservoirs
(d) because there is not as much wildlife due to deforestation

왜 미초아칸주에서 자연재해의 가능성이 커졌는가?

(a) 땅이 자주 굴착되고 있기 때문에
(b) 기온이 크게 떨어졌기 때문에
(c) 지면 위의 저수지에 물이 거의 남아있지 않기 때문에
(d) 삼림 벌채로 인해 야생 동물이 많이 없기 때문에

─○ 지텔프 치트키

질문의 키워드 natural disasters가 earthquakes로 paraphrasing되어 언급된 주변 내용을 주의 깊게 읽는다.

해설 | 4단락의 'the region is at a higher risk of earthquakes stemming from the frequent drilling of wells for agricultural water'에서 미초아칸주는 농업용수를 위한 잦은 우물 굴착으로 인해 지진의 위험이 더 크다고 했다. 따라서 (a)가 정답이다.

Paraphrasing
the chance of natural disasters increased 자연재해의 가능성이 커졌다 → at a higher risk of earthquakes 지진의 위험이 더 큰
the frequent drilling 잦은 굴착 → excavated often 자주 굴착되는

어휘 | excavate v. 굴착하다, 파다 significantly adv. 크게, 상당히

---

64 특정세부사항　　How　　　　　　　　　　　　　　　　　　난이도 ●●○

How are buyers responsible for the environmental destruction in Michoacán?

(a) They promote the benefits of avocados.
(b) They encourage the production of avocados.
(c) They neglect to demand sustainable farming methods.
(d) They violate amendments to trade agreements.

소비자들은 미초아칸주의 환경 파괴에 어떻게 책임이 있는가?

(a) 아보카도의 이점을 홍보한다.
(b) 아보카도의 생산을 부추긴다.
(c) 지속 가능한 농경 방법 요구를 도외시한다.
(d) 무역 협정의 수정 사항을 위반한다.

─○ 지텔프 치트키

질문의 키워드 buyers가 consumers로 paraphrasing되어 언급된 주변 내용을 주의 깊게 읽는다.

해설 | 5단락의 'The strong demand for the fruit means that consumers are also at fault.'에서 아보카도에 대한 높은 수요는 소비자들에게도 책임이 있다는 것을 의미한다고 했다. 따라서 (b)가 정답이다.

Paraphrasing
The strong demand 높은 수요 → encourage the production 생산을 부추긴다

어휘 | neglect v. 도외시하다, 방치하다

In the context of the passage, <u>passed</u> means _____.

(a) occurred
(b) delivered
(c) approved
(d) succeeded

지문의 문맥에서, 'passed'는 -을 의미한다.

(a) 발생한
(b) 전달한
(c) 승인한
(d) 성공한

○━ 지텔프 치트키

밑줄 친 어휘의 유의어를 찾는 문제이므로, passed가 포함된 구절을 읽고 문맥을 파악한다.

해설 | 3단락의 'Large-scale deforestation has passed in the name of the lucrative industry.'는 대규모 산림 벌채가 수익성이 좋은 산업이라는 명목으로 발생해 왔다는 뜻이므로, passed가 '발생한'이라는 의미로 사용된 것을 알 수 있다. 따라서 '발생한'이라는 같은 의미의 (a) occurred가 정답이다.

오답분석

(b) '전달하다'라는 의미의 deliver도 pass의 사전적 유의어 중 하나이지만, 문맥상 대규모 산림 벌채가 발생해 왔다는 의미가 되어야 적절하므로 오답이다.

---

66 **어휘** 유의어 난이도 ●●○

In the context of the passage, <u>rampant</u> means _____.

(a) lavish
(b) robust
(c) prolonged
(d) uncontrolled

지문의 문맥에서, 'rampant'는 -을 의미한다.

(a) 풍성한
(b) 탄탄한
(c) 장기적인
(d) 제어되지 않는

○━ 지텔프 치트키

밑줄 친 어휘의 유의어를 찾는 문제이므로, rampant가 포함된 구절을 읽고 문맥을 파악한다.

해설 | 5단락의 'put an end to the rampant destruction'은 걷잡을 수 없는 파괴를 종식시킨다는 뜻이므로, rampant가 '걷잡을 수 없는'이라는 의미로 사용된 것을 알 수 있다. 따라서 '제어되지 않는'이라는 비슷한 의미의 (d) uncontrolled가 정답이다.

PART 3 [67~73] 지식 백과 더스트볼의 원인과 영향

표제어	**DUST BOWL**	더스트볼
정의	The Dust Bowl refers to a series of severe droughts and dust storms that took place in the Great Plains region of the United States during the 1930s. Its impact on the environment, the economy, and people was catastrophic and had long-lasting consequences.	더스트볼은 1930년대에 미국의 대초원 지대에서 발생했던 일련의 극심한 가뭄과 황사를 가리킨다. 환경, 경제, 그리고 사람들에 미친 그것의 영향은 재앙적이었고 오래 지속되는 결과를 가져왔다.

In the decades prior to the Dust Bowl, migrants had been drawn to the Great Plains by legislation that promoted the settlement of the American West. [67]They had no experience with the unique ecology and climate of the region, which are characterized by infrequent rain and high winds. Farmers therefore relied on [72]methods they previously used to <u>cultivate</u> crops. [67]This included digging up the native prairie grass before planting crops in the loose topsoil.

[68]When the droughts arrived in the summer of 1931, the crops died and the dry topsoil blew away. This created thick dust storms that blocked out the sun and blanketed everything, rendering the land useless for farming. It is estimated that during the most devastating drought, which took place between 1934 and 1935, the region lost as much as 1.2 billion tons of soil.

Unable to produce food or earn an income, [69]many families went bankrupt and had to leave their land. Approximately 2.5 million poverty-stricken people left states affected by the Dust Bowl in search of work. However, high unemployment resulting from the Great Depression made finding a job difficult. Many moved into homeless camps, where they continued to go hungry.

The establishment of the Soil Conservation Service by the Roosevelt administration helped cease soil erosion in the Great Plains, which had previously produced most of America's food supply. This service taught farmers agricultural techniques that would restore the land's fertility. [70]For agreeing to [73]<u>observe</u> the new approach in order to help address the nationwide hunger crisis, farmers were subsidized by the government.

Today, scientists speculate that temperature increases caused by climate change could lead to more droughts in the Great Plains. Despite this, agricultural crops will continue to be produced as irrigation is available via the Ogallala Aquifer. However, [71]industrial farming operations are depleting the water within it faster than it can be replenished. When it runs out, the region may face another Dust Bowl.

더스트볼 이전 수십 년 동안, 이민자들은 미국 서부의 정착을 촉진하는 법률에 따라 대초원으로 유인되었다. [67]그들은 그 지대의 독특한 생태와 기후에 대한 경험이 없었는데, 그것은 드물게 내리는 비와 강하게 부는 바람으로 특징지어진다. 농부들은 따라서 [72]작물을 재배하기 위해 그들이 이전에 사용했던 방법들에 의존했다. 이것은 푸석푸석한 겉흙에 농작물을 심기 전에 [67]대초원의 야생초를 땅에서 파내는 것을 포함했다.

[68]가뭄이 1931년 여름에 도래했을 때, 농작물들이 죽고 메마른 겉흙이 흩날렸다. 이것은 태양을 가리고 모든 것을 뒤덮는 짙은 황사를 만들어 냈고, 그 지대를 농사에 쓸모 없게 만들었다. 1934년과 1935년 사이에 발생한 가장 파괴적인 가뭄 동안, 그 지대는 거의 12억 톤의 토양을 잃었던 것으로 추정된다.

식량을 생산하거나 수입을 올릴 수 없었기 때문에, [69]많은 가정들은 파산했고 그들의 지역을 떠나야 했다. 가난에 시달린 250만여 명의 사람들이 일거리를 찾기 위해 더스트볼의 영향을 받은 주를 떠났다. 그러나, 대공황으로 인한 높은 실업률이 직장을 얻는 것을 어렵게 만들었다. 많은 사람들이 노숙자 수용소로 이동했고, 그곳에서 그들은 계속해서 굶주렸다.

루스벨트 정권에 의한 토양보존사무국의 설립은 대초원에서의 토양 침식을 중단하는 데 도움을 주었는데, 이곳은 이전에 미국의 식량 공급의 대부분을 생산해 왔었다. 이 사무국은 농부들에게 땅의 비옥함을 회복시킬 농업 기술들을 가르쳤다. [70]전국적인 기아 위기의 해결을 돕고자 [73]새로운 접근법을 따르는 데 동의함에 따라, 농부들은 정부로부터 보조금을 받았다.

오늘날, 과학자들은 기후 변화에 의해 야기된 기온 상승이 대초원에 더 많은 가뭄을 초래할 수 있다고 추측하고 있다. 그럼에도 불구하고, 오갈라라 대수층을 통해 관개가 가능하기 때문에 농작물은 계속해서 생산될 것이다. 그러나, [71]공업적 농장 운영은 그것이 다시 채워질 수 있는 것보다 더 빨리 그 안의 물을 고갈시키고 있다. 그것이 고갈되면, 그 지대는 또 다른 더스트볼에 직면할지도 모른다.

어휘 | drought n. 가뭄 dust storm phr. 황사 catastrophic adj. 재앙적인 settlement n. 정착 ecology n. 생태, 생태학 characterize v. 특징짓다 infrequent adj. 드문 prairie n. 대초원 loose adj. 푸석푸석한, 헐거운 topsoil n. 겉흙, 표토 blanket v. 뒤덮다 render v. (어떤 상태가 되게) 만들다 devastating adj. 파괴적인 bankrupt adj. 파산한 poverty-stricken adj. 가난에 시달리는 unemployment n. 실업률 Great Depression phr. 대공황 homeless n. 노숙자 establishment n. 설립 conservation n. 보존 administration n. 정권, 행정부 erosion n. 침식 fertility n. 비옥함 hunger n. 기아 subsidize v. 보조금을 주다 speculate v. 추측하다 irrigation n. 관개 aquifer n. 대수층(지하수가 있는 지층) replenish v. 다시 채우다

Why most likely did people not realize the effect of removing the native grass? (a) because they had no experience of farming (b) because they were used to significant amounts of rain **(c) because they were unfamiliar with the region** (d) because they thought the wind would not affect the soil	왜 사람들은 야생초를 제거하는 것의 결과를 몰랐던 것 같은가? (a) 농사 경험이 없었기 때문에 (b) 상당한 양의 비에 익숙했기 때문에 **(c) 그 지대에 익숙하지 않았기 때문에** (d) 바람이 토양에 영향을 주지 않을 것이라고 생각 했기 때문에

⊶○ 지텔프 치트키

질문의 키워드 removing the native grass가 digging up the native ~ grass로 paraphrasing되어 언급된 주변 내용을 주의 깊게 읽는다.

해설 | 2단락의 'They had no experience with the unique ecology and climate of the region'에서 이민자들은 미국 서부 지대의 독 특한 생태와 기후에 대한 경험이 없었다고 한 뒤, 'This included digging up the native prairie grass'에서 이것(농부들이 작물을 재 배하기 위해 이전에 사용했던 방법)이 대초원의 야생초를 땅에서 파내는 것을 포함했다고 한 것을 통해, 이민자들은 그 지대에 익숙하지 않 았기 때문에 야생초를 제거하는 것의 결과를 몰랐던 것임을 추론할 수 있다. 따라서 (c)가 정답이다.

오답분석

(b) 2단락에서 이민자들이 드물게 내리는 비로 특징지어지는 미국 서부 지대의 기후에 대한 경험이 없었다고는 했지만, 그들이 상당한 양의 비에 익숙했는지는 언급되지 않았으므로 오답이다.

According to the passage, what brought along the sandstorms? **(a) the beginning of a period of little rainfall** (b) the most severe drought in the history of the region (c) the loss of more than a billion tons of soil (d) the destruction of the land as a result of fire	지문에 따르면, 무엇이 모래 폭풍을 야기했는가? **(a) 강우량이 거의 없는 기간의 시작** (b) 그 지대의 역사상 가장 극심한 가뭄 (c) 10억 톤 이상의 토양 손실 (d) 화재로 인한 지대의 파괴

⊶○ 지텔프 치트키

질문의 키워드 sandstorms가 dust storms로 paraphrasing되어 언급된 주변 내용을 주의 깊게 읽는다.

해설 | 3단락의 'When the droughts arrived ~, the crops died and the dry topsoil blew away.'에서 가뭄이 도래했을 때 농작물들이 죽고 메마른 겉흙이 흩날렸다고 한 뒤, 'This created thick dust storms that ~ blanketed everything'에서 이것이 모든 것을 뒤덮 는 짙은 황사를 만들어 냈다고 했다. 따라서 (a)가 정답이다.

Paraphrasing
the droughts arrived 가뭄이 도래했다 → the beginning of a period of little rainfall 강우량이 거의 없는 기간의 시작

오답분석

(b) 3단락에서 그 지대의 가장 파괴적인 가뭄은 1934년과 1935년 사이에 발생했다고 했으며, 모래 폭풍을 야기한 것은 1931년에 도래한 가 뭄이므로 오답이다.

(c) 3단락에서 그 지대가 거의 12억 톤의 토양을 잃었던 것으로 추정된다고는 했지만, 이것은 모래 폭풍을 야기한 원인이 아닌 결과이므로 오답이다.

어휘 | rainfall n. 강우량

69 특정세부사항 When

난이도 ●●○

When did people impacted by the Dust Bowl leave their homes?

(a) when out-of-state jobs became available
(b) after they encountered financial ruin
(c) when homeless camps began to open
(d) after the Great Depression ended

더스트볼의 영향을 받은 사람들은 언제 그들의 거주지를 떠났는가?

(a) 다른 주의 직업을 가질 수 있게 되었을 때
(b) 재정상의 파멸을 직면한 후에
(c) 노숙자 수용소가 열리기 시작했을 때
(d) 대공황이 끝난 후에

지텔프 치트키

질문의 키워드 leave ~ homes가 leave ~ land로 paraphrasing되어 언급된 주변 내용을 주의 깊게 읽는다.

해설 | 4단락의 'many families went bankrupt and had to leave their land'에서 많은 가정들은 파산했고 그들의 지역을 떠나야 했다고 했다. 따라서 (b)가 정답이다.

Paraphrasing
went bankrupt 파산했다 → encountered financial ruin 재정상의 파멸을 직면했다

어휘 | encounter v. 직면하다 ruin n. 파멸

70 추론 특정사실

난이도 ●●○

Why probably were farmers in the Great Plains provided with monetary support?

(a) The government wanted to prevent starvation in other nations.
(b) The farmers were still using outdated agricultural tools.
(c) The government wanted to increase food supplies in the country.
(d) The farmers were asked to plant new types of crops.

왜 대초원의 농부들은 재정적 지원을 제공받았던 것 같은가?

(a) 정부가 여타 국가의 기아를 막기를 원했다.
(b) 농부들이 여전히 구식 농기구를 사용하고 있었다.
(c) 정부가 국가의 식량 공급을 늘리기를 원했다.
(d) 농부들이 새로운 종류의 작물을 심을 것을 요청받았다.

지텔프 치트키

질문의 키워드 financial support가 subsidized로 paraphrasing되어 언급된 주변 내용을 주의 깊게 읽는다.

해설 | 5단락의 'For agreeing to observe the new approach in order to help address the nationwide hunger crisis, farmers were subsidized by the government.'에서 전국적인 기아 위기의 해결을 돕고자 새로운 접근법을 따르는 데 동의함에 따라 농부들이 정부로부터 보조금을 받았다고 한 것을 통해, 정부가 국가의 식량 공급을 늘리기를 원했기 때문에 농부들이 재정적 지원을 제공받았던 것임을 추론할 수 있다. 따라서 (c)가 정답이다.

어휘 | monetary adj. 재정적인, 금전의 starvation n. 기아 outdated adj. 구식의

What do experts believe might happen to the Ogallala Aquifer?

(a) It will rely on industrial farming operations.
(b) It will be emptied from the overuse of water.
(c) It will be lost after the next Dust Bowl.
(d) It will dry up because of climate change.

전문가들은 오갈라라 대수층에 무슨 일이 일어날 수 있다고 생각하는가?

(a) 공업적 농장 운영에 의존할 것이다.
(b) 물의 남용으로 인해 비워질 것이다.
(c) 다음 더스트볼 이후에 사라질 것이다.
(d) 기후 변화 때문에 마를 것이다.

●─○ 지텔프 치트키

질문의 키워드 Ogallala Aquifer가 그대로 언급된 주변 내용을 주의 깊게 읽는다.

해설 | 6단락의 'industrial farming operations are depleting the water within it faster than it can be replenished'에서 공업적 농장 운영은 오갈라라 대수층이 다시 채워질 수 있는 것보다 더 빨리 그 안의 물을 고갈시키고 있다고 한 뒤, 'When it runs out, the region may face another Dust Bowl.'에서 그것이 고갈되면 그 지대는 또 다른 더스트볼에 직면할지도 모른다고 했다. 따라서 (b)가 정답이다.

Paraphrasing
depleting the water ~ faster than it can be replenished 다시 채워질 수 있는 것보다 더 빨리 물을 고갈시키는 → the overuse of water 물의 남용
runs out 고갈되다 → be emptied 비워지는

어휘 | overuse n. 남용

In the context of the passage, cultivate means _____.

(a) nurture
(b) enrich
(c) support
(d) grow

지문의 문맥에서, 'cultivate'는 -을 의미한다.

(a) 양육하다
(b) 풍성하게 하다
(c) 지지하다
(d) 재배하다

●─○ 지텔프 치트키

밑줄 친 어휘의 유의어를 찾는 문제이므로, cultivate가 포함된 구절을 읽고 문맥을 파악한다.

해설 | 2단락의 'methods they ~ used to cultivate crops'는 작물을 재배하기 위해 사용했던 방법들이라는 뜻이므로, cultivate가 '재배하다'라는 의미로 사용된 것을 알 수 있다. 따라서 '재배하다'라는 같은 의미의 (d) grow가 정답이다.

오답분석
(a) '양육하다'라는 의미의 nurture도 cultivate의 사전적 유의어 중 하나이지만, nurture는 교육이나 훈련 등을 통해 보살피고 양육한다는 의미로 주로 사람과 함께 사용된다. 따라서 문맥상 적절하지 않아 오답이다.

In the context of the passage, <u>observe</u> means _____.

(a) detect
(b) practice
(c) monitor
(d) examine

지문의 문맥에서, 'observe'는 -을 의미한다.

(a) 탐지하다
(b) 준수하다
(c) 감시하다
(d) 조사하다

━○ 지텔프 치트키

밑줄 친 어휘의 유의어를 찾는 문제이므로, observe가 포함된 구절을 읽고 문맥을 파악한다.

해설 | 5단락의 'observe the new approach'는 새로운 접근법을 따른다는 뜻이므로, observe가 '따르다'라는 의미로 사용된 것을 알 수 있다. 따라서 '준수하다'라는 비슷한 의미의 (b) practice가 정답이다.

오답분석

(c) '감시하다'라는 의미의 monitor도 observe의 사전적 유의어 중 하나이지만, 문맥상 농부들이 새로운 접근법을 따른다는 의미가 되어야 적절하므로 오답이다.

PART 4 (74~80) 비즈니스 편지 물류 회사의 일자리를 제안하는 편지

수신인 정보

Diane Orville
Chesapeake, Virginia

Dear Ms. Orville:

편지의 목적: 일자리 제안

Following your recent interview and the verification of your work references, 74we are delighted to offer you the position of account executive within the sales and marketing department. As discussed, you will serve as a link between Shipspeed Logistics and its corporate clients. Your job will be to guarantee that 79our relationships with them are <u>fruitful</u>.

보수

For this position, your annual salary will be $58,000 before taxes, 75with the possibility of an annual bonus subject to performance. You will also be entitled to our standard compensation package, which includes health insurance, 20 days of paid leave, and optional access to a pension plan.

복지

76After your first year of successful employment, you will be allowed to convert unused leave days into cash, attend professional training seminars off-site, and work remotely. You will also be given more opportunities for career advancement.

Diane Orville
체서피크시, 버지니아주

Ms. Orville께:

귀하의 최근 인터뷰와 업무 자료 확인 후에, 74귀하에게 영업 및 마케팅 부서 내 고객 회계 주임 직위를 제안드리게 되어 기쁩니다. 논의된 바와 같이, 귀하는 Shipspeed 물류사와 기업 고객들 간의 연결고리 역할을 하게 될 것입니다. 79그들과의 관계가 생산적이도록 보장하는 것이 귀하의 업무가 될 것입니다.

이 직위의 경우, 귀하의 연봉은 세전 58,000달러일 것이며, 75연간 상여금의 기회는 실적에 달려 있습니다. 또한 귀하에게 당사의 표준 보수를 받을 자격이 주어질 것이며, 이것은 건강보험, 유급휴가 20일, 그리고 연금 제도의 선택적 이용을 포함합니다.

76성공적인 입사 1년이 지나면, 귀하는 미사용된 휴가를 현금으로 전환하시고, 외부의 직업 교육 세미나에 참석하시고, 원격으로 근무하실 수 있습니다. 또한 귀하에게 더 많은 승진 기회가 주어질 것입니다.

<table>
<tr><td>계약
조건</td><td>Should you accept, your first day of work will be on June 4 at our head office in Norfolk, Virginia. ⁷⁷There will be a three-month trial period during which your job performance will be closely evaluated. Your hours will be from 8 a.m. to 5 p.m. daily from Monday to Friday. Occasional travel and overtime work may be required when your regular employment period begins.</td><td>수락하신다면, 귀하의 출근 첫날은 6월 4일에 버지니아주 노퍽시에 있는 저희 본사에서 있을 것입니다. ⁷⁷귀하의 업무 수행 능력이 면밀하게 평가될 3개월의 수습 기간이 있을 것입니다. 귀하의 업무 시간은 월요일부터 금요일까지 매일 오전 8시에서 오후 5시까지일 것입니다. 정규 고용 기간이 시작되면 가끔의 출장과 초과 근무가 요구될 수 있습니다.</td></tr>
<tr><td>회신
요청
+
끝인사</td><td>⁷⁸Please sign the enclosed response form and return it to me by May 1 to signify your acceptance. If you have any questions, do not hesitate to contact me at wmeek@shipspeed.com. We ⁸⁰look forward to <u>welcoming</u> you as the newest member of our company.</td><td>⁷⁸수락을 알리시려면 5월 1일까지 동봉된 회신 문서에 서명하여 저에게 돌려보내 주시기 바랍니다. 문의 사항이 있으시면, 주저하지 마시고 wmeek@shipspeed.com으로 제게 연락하십시오. 당사의 ⁸⁰새로운 구성원으로 귀하를 <u>맞이하기</u>를 기대하고 있겠습니다.</td></tr>
<tr><td>발신인
정보</td><td>Sincerely,
Walter Meek
Human Resources Manager
Shipspeed Logistics</td><td>Walter Meek 드림
인사 담당자
Shipspeed 물류사</td></tr>
</table>

어휘 | verification n. 확인 reference n. (참고) 자료 delighted adj. 기쁜 account executive phr. 고객 회계 주임 corporate adj. 기업의 annual salary phr. 연봉 subject to phr. ~에 달려 있는 entitle v. 자격을 주다 standard adj. 표준의 compensation package phr. 보수 insurance n. 보험 optional adj. 선택적인 pension plan phr. 연금 제도 employment n. 입사, 일자리 convert v. 전환하다 remotely adv. 원격으로 career advancement phr. 승진 trial period phr. 수습 기간 evaluate v. 평가하다 occasional adj. 가끔의 enclosed adj. 동봉된 form n. 문서, 서식 용지 signify v. 알리다, 나타내다

---

74 주제/목적   편지의 목적   난이도 ●○○

Why did Walter Meek write a letter to Diane Orville?	왜 Walter Meek는 Diane Orville에게 편지를 썼는가?
(a) to confirm a scheduled interview **(b) to make an offer of employment** (c) to clarify a job description (d) to introduce a corporate client	(a) 예정된 면접을 확정하기 위해서 **(b) 일자리를 제안하기 위해서** (c) 직무 설명을 명확하게 하기 위해서 (d) 기업 고객을 소개하기 위해서

지텔프 치트키

지문의 초반을 주의 깊게 읽고 전체 맥락을 파악한다.

해설 | 1단락의 'we are delighted to offer you the position of account executive within the sales and marketing department'에서 Walter Meek가 Diane Orville에게 영업 및 마케팅 부서 내 고객 회계 주임 직위를 제안하게 되어 기쁘다고 한 뒤, 그 직위의 보수와 계약 조건 등을 설명하는 내용이 이어지고 있다. 따라서 (b)가 정답이다.

어휘 | description n. 설명, 묘사 clarify v. 명확하게 하다

TEST 1
TEST 2
TEST 3
TEST 4
TEST 5
TEST 6
TEST 7

75 특정세부사항　　　How　　　　　　　　　　　　　　　난이도 ●●○

According to the letter, how can Diane Orville earn extra money?

(a) by securing her own health insurance
(b) by opting out of a pension plan
(c) by carrying out her job satisfactorily
(d) by working additional hours

편지에 따르면, Diane Orville은 어떻게 추가적인 수입을 얻을 수 있는가?

(a) 그녀 자신의 건강 보험을 확보함으로써
(b) 연금 제도를 해지함으로써
(c) 업무를 훌륭히 수행함으로써
(d) 초과 근무를 함으로써

─○ 지텔프 치트키

질문의 키워드 extra money가 bonus로 paraphrasing되어 언급된 주변 내용을 주의 깊게 읽는다.

해설 | 2단락의 'with the possibility of an annual bonus subject to performance'에서 연간 상여금의 기회는 실적에 달려 있다고 했다. 따라서 (c)가 정답이다.

Paraphrasing
performance 실적 → carrying out her job satisfactorily 업무를 훌륭히 수행함

어휘 | opt out phr. 해지하다, 빠져 나오다　satisfactorily adv. 훌륭히

76 추론　　　특정사실　　　　　　　　　　　　　　　난이도 ●●○

Based on the letter, what does an employee probably need to do to qualify for remote work?

(a) submit a formal request
(b) complete a year of labor
(c) participate in a training seminar
(d) advance to an executive position

편지에 따르면, 직원은 원격 근무 자격을 얻기 위해서 무엇을 해야 하는 것 같은가?

(a) 공식 요청서를 제출한다
(b) 1년의 근무를 완료한다
(c) 교육 세미나에 참여한다
(d) 이사 직위로 승진한다

─○ 지텔프 치트키

질문의 키워드 remote work가 work remotely로 paraphrasing되어 언급된 주변 내용을 주의 깊게 읽는다.

해설 | 3단락의 'After your first year of successful employment, you will be allowed to ~ work remotely.'에서 성공적인 입사 1년이 지나면 원격으로 근무할 수 있다고 한 것을 통해, 직원이 원격 근무 자격을 얻기 위해서 1년의 근무를 완료해야 할 것임을 추론할 수 있다. 따라서 (b)가 정답이다.

어휘 | qualify v. 자격을 얻다　submit v. 제출하다　request n. 요청서, 요청　advance v. 승진하다

77 특정세부사항　　　What　　　　　　　　　　　　　　　난이도 ●○○

What will happen during Orville's initial period of work?

(a) She will attend a brief orientation.
(b) She will work shorter hours than usual.
(c) She will travel to a business event.

Orville의 초기 근무 기간 동안 무슨 일이 발생할 것인가?

(a) 간단한 오리엔테이션에 참석할 것이다.
(b) 평소보다 짧은 시간 동안 일할 것이다.
(c) 비즈니스 행사에 방문할 것이다.

해커스 지텔프 최신기출유형 실전문제집 7회 (Level 2)

(d) She will be carefully reviewed.

(d) 꼼꼼히 평가될 것이다.

지텔프 치트키

질문의 키워드 initial period가 trial period로 paraphrasing되어 언급된 주변 내용을 주의 깊게 읽는다.

해설 | 4단락의 'There will be a ~ trial period during which your job performance will be closely evaluated.'에서 Orville의 업무 수행 능력이 면밀하게 평가될 수습 기간이 있을 것이라고 했다. 따라서 (d)가 정답이다.

Paraphrasing
closely evaluated 면밀하게 평가되는 → carefully reviewed 꼼꼼히 평가되는

---

78 특정세부사항 How
난이도 ●●○

How is Orville asked to respond to the letter?

(a) by sending back a document
(b) by preparing a list of questions
(c) by signing a contract electronically
(d) by placing a call to a department

Orville은 편지에 어떻게 응답하라고 요청받는가?

(a) 서류를 돌려보냄으로써
(b) 질문 목록을 준비함으로써
(c) 전자 계약서에 서명함으로써
(d) 부서에 전화함으로써

지텔프 치트키

질문의 키워드 respond가 response로 언급된 주변 내용을 주의 깊게 읽는다.

해설 | 5단락의 'Please sign the enclosed response form and return it to me ~ to signify your acceptance.'에서 Meek는 Orville에게 수락을 알리려면 동봉된 회신 문서에 서명하여 자신에게 돌려보내 달라고 했다. 따라서 (a)가 정답이다.

Paraphrasing
the ~ form 문서 → a document 서류
return 돌려보내다 → sending back 돌려보냄

어휘 | contract n. 계약서, 계약   electronically adv. 전자적으로

---

79 어휘 유의어
난이도 ●●○

In the context of the passage, fruitful means _____.

(a) fortunate
(b) promising
(c) productive
(d) efficient

지문의 문맥에서, 'fruitful'은 -을 의미한다.

(a) 운이 좋은
(b) 유망한
(c) 생산적인
(d) 효율적인

지텔프 치트키

밑줄 친 어휘의 유의어를 찾는 문제이므로, fruitful이 포함된 구절을 읽고 문맥을 파악한다.

해설 | 1단락의 'our relationships with them are fruitful'은 그들과의 관계가 생산적이라는 뜻이므로, fruitful이 '생산적인'이라는 의미로 사용된 것을 알 수 있다. 따라서 '생산적인'이라는 같은 의미의 (c) productive가 정답이다.

In the context of the passage, <u>welcoming</u> means _____.

(a) accepting
(b) releasing
(c) persuading
(d) entertaining

지문의 문맥에서, 'welcoming'은 -을 의미한다.

(a) 받아들이기
(b) 놓아주기
(c) 설득하기
(d) 즐겁게 해주기

───○ 지텔프 치트키

밑줄 친 어휘의 유의어를 찾는 문제이므로, welcoming이 포함된 구절을 읽고 문맥을 파악한다.

해설 | 5단락의 'look forward to welcoming you as the newest member'는 새로운 구성원으로 맞이하기를 기대하고 있겠다는 뜻이므로, welcoming이 '맞이하기'라는 의미로 사용된 것을 알 수 있다. 따라서 '받아들이기'라는 비슷한 의미의 (a) accepting이 정답이다.

TEST 7

정답·스크립트·해석·해설

GRAMMAR

LISTENING

READING & VOCABULARY

TEST 7 점수 확인하기

GRAMMAR _____ / 26 (점수 : _____ 점)
LISTENING _____ / 26 (점수 : _____ 점)
READING & VOCABULARY _____ / 28 (점수 : _____ 점)

TOTAL _____ / 80 (평균 점수 : _____ 점)

*각 영역 점수: 맞은 개수 × 3.75
*평균 점수: 각 영역 점수 합계 ÷ 3

정답 및 취약 유형 분석표

자동 채점 및 성적 분석 서비스 ▶

문제집 p.172

GRAMMAR

번호	정답	유형
01	a	연결어
02	d	시제
03	b	가정법
04	b	준동사
05	c	시제
06	d	관계사
07	c	시제
08	c	가정법
09	a	조동사
10	d	조동사
11	a	가정법
12	b	준동사
13	d	연결어
14	c	시제
15	b	조동사
16	a	가정법
17	a	준동사
18	c	가정법
19	d	준동사
20	b	관계사
21	c	준동사
22	c	시제
23	d	준동사
24	a	조동사
25	c	가정법
26	b	시제

유형	맞힌 개수
시제	/ 6
가정법	/ 6
준동사	/ 6
조동사	/ 4
연결어	/ 2
관계사	/ 2
TOTAL	/ 26

LISTENING

PART	번호	정답	유형
PART 1	27	d	특정세부사항
	28	b	추론
	29	a	특정세부사항
	30	b	특정세부사항
	31	c	특정세부사항
	32	b	특정세부사항
	33	b	추론
PART 2	34	d	특정세부사항
	35	c	추론
	36	a	특정세부사항
	37	a	특정세부사항
	38	c	특정세부사항
	39	d	특정세부사항
	40	b	특정세부사항
PART 3	41	c	Not/True
	42	d	추론
	43	a	특정세부사항
	44	c	특정세부사항
	45	d	추론
PART 4	46	a	주제/목적
	47	b	특정세부사항
	48	d	특정세부사항
	49	b	특정세부사항
	50	a	특정세부사항
	51	c	특정세부사항
	52	d	추론

유형	맞힌 개수
주제/목적	/ 1
특정세부사항	/ 18
Not/True	/ 1
추론	/ 6
TOTAL	/ 26

READING & VOCABULARY

PART	번호	정답	유형
PART 1	53	a	특정세부사항
	54	a	Not/True
	55	c	추론
	56	b	특정세부사항
	57	a	특정세부사항
	58	d	어휘
	59	d	어휘
PART 2	60	b	특정세부사항
	61	c	추론
	62	d	추론
	63	b	특정세부사항
	64	a	특정세부사항
	65	c	어휘
	66	a	어휘
PART 3	67	b	특정세부사항
	68	b	특정세부사항
	69	d	특정세부사항
	70	c	추론
	71	a	특정세부사항
	72	d	어휘
	73	c	어휘
PART 4	74	c	주제/목적
	75	b	특정세부사항
	76	c	특정세부사항
	77	d	특정세부사항
	78	a	추론
	79	b	어휘
	80	d	어휘

유형	맞힌 개수
주제/목적	/ 1
특정세부사항	/ 13
Not/True	/ 1
추론	/ 5
어휘	/ 8
TOTAL	/ 28

GRAMMAR

01 연결어 접속사
난이도 ●●○

Of the almost 7,000 languages in the world, nearly half are at risk of vanishing. Endangered languages are crucial to understanding the cultures of indigenous groups, _____ efforts are being made to preserve these dialects through audio recordings and other methods.

(a) so
(b) but
(c) since
(d) while

세계의 약 7,000개의 언어들 중, 거의 절반이 사라질 위험에 처해 있다. 멸종 위기에 처한 언어들은 토착 집단의 문화를 이해하는 데 매우 중요하므로, 음성 녹음과 다른 방법들을 통해 이러한 방언들을 보존하려는 노력이 이루어지고 있다.

⟶○ 지텔프 치트키

'~하므로'라는 의미의 결과를 나타낼 때는 so를 쓴다.

> ☼ 결과를 나타내는 빈출 접속사
> so ~하므로 so that ~할 수 있도록

해설 | 빈칸 앞 절은 '멸종 위기에 처한 언어들은 토착 집단의 문화를 이해하는 데 매우 중요하다'는 내용이고, 빈칸 뒤 절은 멸종 위기에 처한 언어들이 매우 중요한 것이 원인이 되어 발생하는 결과(방언들을 보존하려는 노력이 이루어짐)에 대한 내용이다. 따라서 '~하므로'라는 의미의 결과를 나타내는 등위 접속사 (a) so가 정답이다.

오답분석
(b) but은 '~이지만', (c) since는 '~하기 때문에', (d) while은 '~이긴 하지만'이라는 의미로, 문맥에 적합하지 않아 오답이다.

어휘 | vanish v. 사라지다 endangered adj. 멸종 위기에 처한 crucial adj. 매우 중요한 indigenous adj. 토착의 preserve v. 보존하다 dialect n. 방언, 사투리

02 시제 현재진행
난이도 ●●○

Digital Design Incorporated experimented with a remote work system last year and discovered that workers were generally more productive at home. As a result, most employees _____ their tasks from home on a full-time basis nowadays.

(a) will conduct
(b) have conducted
(c) conducted
(d) are conducting

Digital Design 주식회사는 작년에 원격 작업 시스템을 실험했고 근로자들이 일반적으로 집에서 더 생산적이라는 것을 발견했다. 그 결과, 대부분의 직원들이 요즘에는 집에서 풀타임으로 그들의 업무를 수행하고 있는 중이다.

TEST 1 TEST 2 TEST 3 TEST 4 TEST 5 TEST 6 TEST 7

> 💡 현재진행과 자주 함께 쓰이는 시간 표현
> • right now / now / currently / at the moment 바로 지금 / 지금 / 현재 / 바로 지금
> • these days / nowadays 요즘

해설 | 현재진행 시제와 함께 쓰이는 시간 표현 nowadays가 있고, 문맥상 대부분의 직원들이 요즘에는 집에서 그들의 업무를 수행하고 있는 중이라는 의미가 되어야 자연스럽다. 따라서 현재진행 시제 (d) are conducting이 정답이다.

어휘 | Incorporated adj. 주식회사 experiment v. 실험하다 remote adj. 원격의 productive adj. 생산적인 task n. 업무, 과제 on a full-time basis phr. 풀타임으로 conduct v. 수행하다, 행동하다

---

03 가정법 가정법 과거완료 난이도 ●●○

Dawson missed his daughter's school play as he had put off an assignment and had to work late to finish it, which upset his wife greatly. If he had managed his time more carefully, he _____ the performance.

(a) had attended
(b) could have attended
(c) could attend
(d) was attending

Dawson은 일을 미뤄서 그것을 끝내기 위해 늦게까지 근무해야 했기 때문에 딸의 학교 연극을 놓쳤고, 이것은 그의 아내를 대단히 속상하게 만들었다. 만약 그가 그의 시간을 더 신중하게 관리했었다면, 그는 공연에 참석할 수 있었을 것이다.

해설 | If절에 'had p.p.' 형태의 had managed가 있으므로, 주절에는 이와 짝을 이루어 가정법 과거완료를 만드는 'could(조동사 과거형) + have p.p.'가 와야 한다. 따라서 (b) could have attended가 정답이다.

어휘 | put off phr. (시간·날짜를) 미루다 assignment n. 일, 과제 upset v. 속상하게 만들다 attend v. 참석하다

---

04 준동사 동명사의 관용적 표현 난이도 ●●○

Steve was angry because the school bully kept calling him names. He was about to punch the bully when his friend Jenna stopped him, saying it was not worth _____. She told him that using violence would just cause more problems.

(a) will fight over
(b) fighting over
(c) to fight over
(d) having fought over

Steve는 학교 불량배가 그를 계속 욕했기 때문에 화가 났다. 그의 친구 Jenna가 그것은 싸울 가치가 없다고 말하며 그를 막았을 때 그는 불량배를 막 주먹으로 치려던 참이었다. 그녀는 그에게 폭력을 사용하는 것은 그저 더 많은 문제들을 일으킬 뿐이라고 이야기했다.

'~할 가치가 있다'라고 말할 때는 'be worth + 동명사'를 쓴다.

해설 | 빈칸 앞 형용사 worth는 'be worth + 동명사'의 형태로 쓰여 '~할 가치가 있다'라는 관용적 의미를 나타낸다. 따라서 동명사 (b) fighting over가 정답이다.

어휘 | bully n. 불량배, 괴롭히는 사람 call names phr. 욕하다, 험담하다 be about to phr. 막 ~하려는 참이다 punch v. 주먹으로 치다 violence n. 폭력, 폭행

---

05 시제 현재완료진행 난이도 ●●○

Coach Cartwright announced that the rookie player would be in the starting lineup. She _____ rapidly ever since she joined the team, and he feels that she can perform better than many of the veteran players.

(a) improves
(b) is improving
(c) has been improving
(d) will have been improving

Cartwright 감독은 그 신인 선수가 선발 라인업에 있을 것이라고 발표했다. 그녀는 팀에 합류한 이래로 줄곧 빠르게 발전해오고 있는 중이고, 그는 그녀가 많은 베테랑 선수들보다 더 잘 해낼 수 있다고 생각한다.

'ever since + 과거 동사'가 있으면 현재완료진행 시제가 정답이다.

> 💡 **현재완료진행과 자주 함께 쓰이는 시간 표현**
> • (ever) since + 과거 시점 + (for + 기간 표현) ~한 이래로 (줄곧) (~ 동안)
> • lately / for + 기간 표현 + now 최근에 / 현재 ~ 동안

해설 | 현재완료진행 시제와 함께 쓰이는 시간 표현 'ever since + 과거 동사'(ever since ~ joined)가 있고, 문맥상 신인 선수가 팀에 합류한 과거 시점부터 현재까지 계속해서 빠르게 발전해오고 있는 중이라는 의미가 되어야 자연스럽다. 따라서 현재완료진행 시제 (c) has been improving이 정답이다.

> 오답분석
> (b) 현재진행 시제는 특정 현재 시점에 한창 진행 중인 일을 나타내므로, 과거에 시작해서 현재 시점까지 계속해서 진행되고 있는 일을 표현할 수 없어 오답이다.

어휘 | announce v. 발표하다 rookie n. 신인 선수, 초심자

---

06 관계사 관계부사 when 난이도 ●●○

For the first 32 years of his life, Thomas Davenport was known as a blacksmith, not an inventor. However, that all changed in 1837 _____ for the first-ever electric motor.

(a) where he received an American patent
(b) that he received an American patent
(c) which he received an American patent

그의 인생 초반 32년 동안, 토마스 대본포트는 발명가가 아닌 대장장이로 알려져 있었다. 그러나, 최초의 전기 모터로 그가 미국 특허권을 받았던 때인 1837년에 그 모든 것이 바뀌었다.

(d) when he received an American patent

시간 선행사가 있고 관계사 뒤에 오는 절이 완전하면 관계부사 when이 정답이다.

해설 | 시간 선행사 1837을 받으면서 보기의 주어(he), 동사(received), 목적어(an American patent)를 갖춘 완전한 절을 이끌 수 있는 관계 부사가 필요하므로, (d) when he received an American patent가 정답이다.

어휘 | blacksmith n. 대장장이 inventor n. 발명가 first-ever adj. 최초의 patent n. 특허권

---

07 시제 미래완료진행 난이도 ●●○

I heard that my favorite artist, Brandt Lars, will display his latest paintings at the Lyman Gallery. By the time the exhibit opens later this year, he _____ art for more than six decades!

(a) has been creating
(b) will be creating
(c) will have been creating
(d) is creating

나는 내가 가장 좋아하는 화가인 Brandt Lars가 Lyman 미술관에서 그의 최신작 그림들을 전시할 것 이라고 들었다. 올해 말에 그 전시회가 열릴 무렵이 면, 그는 60년이 넘는 기간 동안 예술을 <u>창조해오고 있는 중일 것이다</u>!

'by the time + 현재 동사'와 'for + 기간 표현'이 함께 오면 미래완료진행 시제가 정답이다.

> ☀ 미래완료진행과 자주 함께 쓰이는 시간 표현
> • by the time / when / if + 현재 동사 + (for + 기간 표현) ~할 무렵이면 / ~할 때 / 만약 ~한다면 (~ 동안)
> • by / in + 미래 시점 + (for + 기간 표현) ~즈음에는 / ~에 (~ 동안)

해설 | 현재 동사로 미래의 의미를 나타내는 시간의 부사절 'by the time + 현재 동사'(By the time ~ opens)가 사용되었고, 미래완료진행 시 제와 함께 쓰이는 시간 표현 later this year와 'for + 기간 표현'(for more than six decades)이 있다. 또한, 문맥상 미래 시점인 올해 말에 Brandt Lars의 전시회가 열릴 무렵이면 그는 60년이 넘는 기간 동안 계속해서 예술을 창조해오고 있는 중일 것이라는 의미가 되어야 자연스럽다. 따라서 미래완료진행 시제 (c) will have been creating이 정답이다.

오답분석
(b) 미래진행 시제는 특정 미래 시점에 한창 진행 중일 일을 나타내므로, 과거 또는 현재에 시작해서 특정 미래 시점까지 계속해서 진행되 고 있을 일을 표현할 수 없어 오답이다.

어휘 | exhibit n. 전시회 decade n. 10년

---

08 가정법 가정법 과거 난이도 ●●○

Olivia's friends are always trying to get her to go out on her days off, but she prefers to spend time alone. If it were up to her, she _____ home watching movies every weekend.

Olivia의 친구들은 그녀가 쉬는 날이면 항상 그녀를 밖 에 나가게 하려고 노력하고 있지만, 그녀는 혼자 시 간을 보내는 것을 선호한다. 만약 선택권이 그녀에게 달려 있다면, 그녀는 주말마다 영화를 보며 집에 <u>머 물 것이다</u>.

(a) will stay
(b) has stayed
(c) would stay
(d) would have stayed

TEST 1

○── 지텔프 치트키

'if + 과거 동사'가 있으면 'would/could + 동사원형'이 정답이다.

해설 | If절에 과거 동사(were)가 있으므로, 주절에는 이와 짝을 이루어 가정법 과거를 만드는 'would(조동사 과거형) + 동사원형'이 와야 한다. 따라서 (c) would stay가 정답이다.

어휘 | day off phr. (근무·일을) 쉬는 날 prefer v. 선호하다 be up to phr. (선택권·결정권이) ~에게 달려 있다

---

09 조동사 　조동사 should 생략　　　　　난이도 ●○○

Awesome Outfits was planning to make a video that would play automatically on its website. Yet, the marketing director advised that the company _____ in this manner, since most of their target consumers find these types of ads intrusive.

(a) not advertise
(b) is not advertising
(c) will not advertise
(d) does not advertise

Awesome Outfits 사는 그것의 웹 사이트에서 자동으로 재생될 영상을 제작할 계획이었다. 그러나, 마케팅 이사는 그들의 목표 고객들 대부분은 이러한 종류의 광고들을 거슬린다고 여기기 때문에, 회사가 이 방식으로 광고하지 말아야 한다고 조언했다.

○── 지텔프 치트키

advise 다음에는 that절에 동사원형이 온다.

해설 | 주절에 제안을 나타내는 동사 advise가 있으므로 that절에는 '(should +) 동사원형'이 와야 한다. 따라서 동사원형 (a) not advertise가 정답이다.

어휘 | automatically adv. 자동으로 target n. 목표, 대상 consumer n. 고객, 소비자 intrusive adj. 거슬리는 advertise v. 광고하다

---

10 조동사 　조동사 might　　　　　난이도 ●●●

Luther's bicycle is a high-end model and is one of his most prized possessions. Even though he trusts his friends, he never lets them ride his bike because they _____ damage it by accident.

(a) will
(b) should
(c) shall
(d) might

Luther의 자전거는 고급 모델이며 그가 가장 아끼는 소유물 중 하나이다. 비록 그가 그의 친구들을 믿을지라도, 그들이 실수로 그것을 훼손할지도 모르기 때문에 그는 절대 그들이 그의 자전거를 타지 못하게 한다.

TEST 2　TEST 3　TEST 4　TEST 5　TEST 6　TEST 7

해커스 지텔프 최신기출유형 실전문제집 7회 (Level 2)

'~할지도 모른다'라고 말할 때는 might를 쓴다.

해설 | 문맥상 비록 Luther가 그의 친구들을 믿을지라도 그들이 실수로 그가 아끼는 자전거를 훼손할지도 모르기 때문에 그는 절대 그들이 그것을 타지 못하게 한다는 의미가 되어야 자연스럽고, 실제로는 자전거가 훼손되지 않은 상황에서 일어날지도 모르는 일을 추측하고 있으므로 '~할지도 모른다'를 뜻하면서 약한 추측을 나타내는 조동사 (d) might가 정답이다. 참고로, might와 may 모두 '~할지도 모른다'를 뜻하지만, might는 may보다 일어날 가능성이 더 작은 경우에 쓴다.

어휘 | high-end adj. 고급의 prized adj. 아끼는, 귀중한 possession n. 소유물, 소지품 trust v. 믿다, 신뢰하다 damage v. 훼손하다 by accident phr. 실수로

---

11 가정법　　가정법 과거　　　　　　　　　　난이도 ●●○

This watercolor was only painted seven years ago, but some of the colors are already fading. The painting _____ in such poor condition if the museum took better care of it.

(a) would not be
(b) had not been
(c) would have not been
(d) will not be

이 수채화는 고작 7년 전에 그려졌지만, 색상 일부가 벌써 바래고 있다. 만약 박물관이 그것을 더 잘 관리한다면 그림의 상태가 그렇게 나빠지는 <u>않을 것이다</u>.

'if + 과거 동사'가 있으면 'would/could + 동사원형'이 정답이다.

해설 | if절에 과거 동사(took)가 있으므로, 주절에는 이와 짝을 이루어 가정법 과거를 만드는 'would(조동사 과거형) + 동사원형'이 와야 한다. 따라서 (a) would not be가 정답이다.

어휘 | watercolor n. 수채화 fade v. 바래다, 희미해지다 take care of phr. ~을 관리하다, 돌보다

---

12 준동사　　to 부정사를 목적격 보어로 취하는 동사　　　　난이도 ●●●

The ownership association has voted to expand the apartment complex's fitness center. In order to cover the cost of the renovations, residents will be required _____ an additional $20 per month in condominium fees.

(a) paying
(b) to pay
(c) to have paid
(d) having paid

소유권 조합이 아파트 단지의 피트니스 센터를 확장하기로 가결했다. 개조 비용을 충당하기 위해, 거주자들은 아파트 관리비에서 매달 추가 20달러를 <u>내도록</u> 요구될 것이다.

require는 to 부정사를 목적격 보어로 취한다.

해설 | 빈칸 앞 동사 require는 'require + 목적어 + 목적격 보어'의 형태로 쓰일 때 to 부정사를 목적격 보어로 취하여, '-에게 ~하도록 요구하다'라는 의미로 사용된다. 따라서 to 부정사 (b) to pay가 정답이다. 참고로, 'residents will be required to pay'는 'require(동사) + residents(목적어) + to pay(목적격 보어)'에서 변형된 수동태 구문이다.

(c) to have paid도 to 부정사이기는 하지만, 완료부정사(to have paid)로 쓰일 경우 '요구되는' 시점보다 '(추가 20달러를) 내는' 시점이 앞선다는 것을 나타내므로 문맥에 적합하지 않아 오답이다.

어휘 | ownership n. 소유권 association n. 조합, 협회 vote v. 가결하다, 투표하다 complex n. (건물) 단지 cover v. (비용을) 충당하다 renovation n. 개조, 보수 condominium n. 아파트

13 연결어 접속부사 난이도 ●●●

Parents love their children and want to give them everything, but this often leads to a fear of saying no. They believe a "no" will harm the relationship. _____, they are afraid of angering their children or falling out with them.

(a) However
(b) Instead
(c) Regardless
(d) **Moreover**

부모들은 그들의 아이들을 사랑하고 그들에게 모든 것을 주고 싶어 하지만, 이것은 종종 거절하는 것에 대한 두려움으로 이어진다. 그들은 '안 돼'가 관계를 해칠 것이라고 믿는다. 게다가, 그들은 아이들을 화나게 하거나 그들과 사이가 틀어질까 봐 걱정한다.

지텔프 치트키

'게다가'라는 의미의 첨언을 나타낼 때는 Moreover를 쓴다.

💡 첨언을 나타내는 빈출 접속부사
Moreover 게다가 Besides 게다가 Also 또한

해설 | 빈칸 앞 문장은 부모들이 아이들에게 '안 돼'라고 하는 것이 관계를 해칠 것이라고 믿는다는 내용이고, 빈칸 뒤 문장은 부모들이 아이들을 화나게 하거나 그들과 사이가 틀어질까 봐 걱정한다는 내용으로 앞 문장에서 말한 것에 부가적인 내용을 덧붙여 설명하고 있다. 따라서 '게다가'라는 의미의 첨언을 나타내는 접속부사 (d) Moreover가 정답이다.

오답분석
(a) However는 '그러나', (b) Instead는 '대신에', (c) Regardless는 '개의치 않고'라는 의미로, 문맥에 적합하지 않아 오답이다.

어휘 | fear n. 두려움, 공포 harm v. 해치다 fall out with phr. ~와 사이가 틀어지다

14 시제 미래진행 난이도 ●●○

On account of the holiday, the postal service was suspended from Thursday to Sunday. This most likely means that next Monday postal workers _____ mail when their regular shifts end. Fortunately, they can collect overtime pay.

(a) were still distributing

연휴이기 때문에, 목요일부터 일요일까지 우편 서비스가 중단되었다. 이것은 아마도 다음 주 월요일에 우체부들은 그들의 정규 근무 시간이 끝날 때도 우편물을 여전히 배달하고 있는 중일 것임을 의미한다. 다행히, 그들은 초과 근무 수당을 받을 수 있다.

TEST 7 GRAMMAR **323**

(b) will still distribute

(c) will still be distributing

(d) have still distributed

🔑 지텔프 치트키

'for + 기간 표현' 없이 'when + 현재 동사'만 있으면 미래진행 시제가 정답이다.

💡 미래진행과 자주 함께 쓰이는 시간 표현

- when / if + 현재 동사 ~할 때 / 만약 ~한다면
- next + 시간 표현 다음 ~에
- until / by + 미래 시점 ~까지
- starting + 미래 시점 / tomorrow ~부터 / 내일

해설 | 현재 동사로 미래의 의미를 나타내는 시간의 부사절 'when + 현재 동사'(when ~ end)와 미래진행 시제와 함께 쓰이는 시간 표현 next Monday가 있고, 문맥상 미래 시점인 다음 주 월요일에 우체부들은 그들의 정규 근무 시간이 끝날 때도 우편물을 여전히 배달하고 있는 중일 것이라는 의미가 되어야 자연스럽다. 따라서 미래진행 시제 (c) will still be distributing이 정답이다.

오답분석
(b) 미래 시제는 미래에 대한 단순한 약속, 제안, 예측을 나타내므로, 특정 미래 시점에 한창 진행되고 있을 일을 표현할 수 없어 오답이다.

어휘 | postal adj. 우편의 suspend v. 중단하다 regular adj. 정규의, 규칙적인 shift n. 근무 시간 distribute v. (우편물·신문을) 배달하다

---

15 조동사   조동사 must   난이도 ●●○

Repusafe Financial experienced a security breach when hackers accessed its servers yesterday. The enterprise uses an outdated system that is more than a decade old. It _____ update to a newer one or else another attack is sure to occur.

(a) can

(b) must

(c) will

(d) might

Repusafe 금융사는 어제 해커들이 그것의 서버에 접속했을 때 보안 침입을 겪었다. 그 기업은 10년 이상 된 구식 시스템을 사용한다. 그것은 더 새로운 시스템으로 업데이트해야 하며 그렇지 않으면 분명히 또 다른 공격이 발생할 것이다.

🔑 지텔프 치트키

'~해야 한다'라고 말할 때는 must를 쓴다.

해설 | 문맥상 해커들에 의한 또 다른 보안 침입 공격이 발생하지 않도록 기업이 구식 시스템을 더 새로운 시스템으로 업데이트해야 한다는 의미가 되어야 자연스러우므로, '~해야 한다'를 뜻하면서 의무를 나타내는 조동사 (b) must가 정답이다. 참고로, must와 should 모두 '~해야 한다'를 뜻하지만, must는 should보다 강한 어조로 조언을 하거나 의무를 나타낼 때 쓴다.

어휘 | security n. 보안, 경비 breach n. 침입, 침해 access v. 접속하다 enterprise n. 기업, 회사 outdated adj. 구식의 occur v. 발생하다

When Gabriella picked zoology as her major, she didn't realize how many chemistry and math classes she would have to take. If she had been aware of these course requirements, she _____ to study something else.

(a) **would have chosen**
(b) would choose
(c) was choosing
(d) has chosen

Gabriella가 동물학을 전공으로 선택했을 때, 그녀는 그녀가 얼마나 많은 화학 강의들과 수학 강의들을 들어야 하는지 깨닫지 못했다. 만약 그녀가 이러한 강좌 필수 요건을 알고 있었다면, 그녀는 다른 것을 공부하기로 <u>결정했을 것이다</u>.

─○ 지텔프 치트키

'if + had p.p.'가 있으면 'would/could + have p.p.'가 정답이다.

해설 | If절에 'had p.p.' 형태의 had been이 있으므로, 주절에는 이와 짝을 이루어 가정법 과거완료를 만드는 'would(조동사 과거형) + have p.p.'가 와야 한다. 따라서 (a) would have chosen이 정답이다.

어휘 | zoology n. 동물학   chemistry n. 화학   be aware of phr. ~을 알다   course n. 강좌, 강의

Oscar's colleagues recommended that he use a professional cleaning service since he is too lazy to do housework. He objected because he dislikes _____ strangers into his house.

(a) **letting**
(b) to let
(c) to have let
(d) having let

Oscar의 동료들은 그가 집안일 하는 것을 너무 귀찮아하기 때문에 전문적인 청소 서비스를 이용할 것을 추천했다. 그는 낯선 사람들을 그의 집에 <u>들이는 것</u>을 싫어하기 때문에 반대했다.

─○ 지텔프 치트키

dislike는 동명사를 목적어로 취한다.

☀ 동명사를 목적어로 취하는 빈출 동사
dislike 싫어하다   avoid 피하다   imagine 상상하다   mind 개의하다   keep 계속하다   consider 고려하다   prevent 방지하다
enjoy 즐기다   recommend 권장하다   risk 위험을 무릅쓰다   involve 포함하다

해설 | 빈칸 앞 동사 dislike는 동명사를 목적어로 취하므로, 동명사 (a) letting이 정답이다.

오답분석

(d) having let도 동명사이기는 하지만, 완료동명사(having let)로 쓰일 경우 '싫어하는' 시점보다 '(낯선 사람들을) 들이는' 시점이 앞선다는 것을 나타내므로 문맥에 적합하지 않아 오답이다.

어휘 | housework n. 집안일, 가사   object v. 반대하다   stranger n. 낯선 사람

18 가정법 가정법 과거 난이도 ●●○

Although we don't notice it, the Earth spins at a speed of roughly 1,000 miles per hour. If the planet were to suddenly stop turning, anything not firmly attached to the ground _____ into the atmosphere.

(a) flies off
(b) will fly off
(c) would fly off
(d) is flying off

비록 우리가 그것을 의식하지는 못하지만, 지구는 대략 시간당 1,000마일의 속도로 회전한다. 만약 지구가 갑자기 도는 것을 멈춘다면, 땅에 단단히 부착되지 않은 것은 대기로 <u>날아가 버릴 것이다.</u>

──○ 지텔프 치트키

'if + were to + 동사원형'이 있으면 'would/could + 동사원형'이 정답이다.

해설| If절에 과거 동사(were to ~ stop)가 있으므로, 주절에는 이와 짝을 이루어 가정법 과거를 만드는 'would(조동사 과거형) + 동사원형'이 와야 한다. 따라서 (c) would fly off가 정답이다.

어휘| notice v. 의식하다 spin v. 회전하다 roughly adv. 대략, 거의 the planet phr. 지구 firmly adv. 단단히 attach v. 부착하다, 붙이다 atmosphere n. 대기 fly off phr. 날아가 버리다

---

19 준동사 to 부정사의 형용사 역할 난이도 ●●○

It was becoming obvious that Becky wasn't going to make it to the airport in time for her flight. She still had two bags _____ before she could call a taxi.

(a) packing
(b) having packed
(c) to have packed
(d) to pack

Becky가 그녀의 항공편 시간에 맞춰 공항에 도착하지 못할 것이라는 점이 분명해지고 있었다. 그녀가 택시를 부를 수 있기 전에 그녀는 아직도 <u>싸야 할</u> 2개의 가방들이 있었다.

──○ 지텔프 치트키

'~(해야) 할', '~하는'이라고 말할 때는 to 부정사를 쓴다.

해설| 빈칸 앞에 명사(bags)가 있고 문맥상 '싸야 할 가방들'이라는 의미가 되어야 자연스러우므로, 빈칸은 명사를 수식하는 형용사 자리이다. 따라서 명사를 꾸며주는 형용사적 수식어구를 이끌 수 있는 to 부정사 (d) to pack이 정답이다.

어휘| obvious adj. 분명한 flight n. 항공편, 항공기 pack v. (짐을) 싸다, 꾸리다

---

20 관계사 주격 관계대명사 which 난이도 ●●○

According to the World Health Organization, only one infectious disease has ever been completely eradicated. Smallpox, _____ during the late 1970s, officially achieved this distinction in 1980.

세계보건기구에 따르면, 지금까지 오직 한 가지 전염병만이 완전히 근절되었다. 천연두는, 1970년대 후반에 아프리카에서 마지막으로 알려진 사례가 있는데, 1980년에 공식적으로 이 영예를 획득했다.

(a) that had its last known case in Africa

(b) which had its last known case in Africa

(c) how it had its last known case in Africa

(d) who had its last known case in Africa

◆─○ 지텔프 치트키

사물 선행사가 관계절 안에서 주어 역할을 하고, 빈칸 앞에 콤마(,)가 있으면 주격 관계대명사 which가 정답이다.

해설 | 사물 선행사 Smallpox를 받으면서 콤마(,) 뒤에 올 수 있는 주격 관계대명사가 필요하므로, (b) which had its last known case in Africa가 정답이다.

> **오답분석**
>
> (a) 관계대명사 that도 사물 선행사를 받을 수 있지만, 콤마 뒤에 올 수 없으므로 오답이다.

어휘 | World Health Organization(WHO) phr. 세계보건기구 infectious adj. 전염되는 disease n. 병 eradicate v. 근절하다 smallpox n. 천연두 distinction n. 영예, 명예

21 준동사   동명사를 목적어로 취하는 동사   난이도 ●●○

Journalists are finding it tougher to document stories these days due to a lack of confidence in the press. Good reporting involves _____ trust from sources who have inside information, but many people worry that their stories will not be reported accurately.

(a) to earn

(b) to have earned

(c) earning

(d) earn

기자들은 언론에 대한 신뢰 부족 탓에 근래에 보도 내용을 기록하기가 더 어렵다고 생각하고 있다. 좋은 보도는 내부 정보를 가진 정보원으로부터 신임을 얻는 것을 포함하지만, 많은 사람들은 그들의 이야기가 정확하게 보도되지 않을 것이라고 걱정한다.

◆─○ 지텔프 치트키

involve는 동명사를 목적어로 취한다.

해설 | 빈칸 앞 동사 involve는 동명사를 목적어로 취하므로, 동명사 (c) earning이 정답이다.

어휘 | journalist n. 기자 tough adj. 어려운, 힘든 document v. 기록하다 story n. (신문·텔레비전 등의) 보도 내용, 이야기 confidence n. 신뢰 press n. 언론 earn v. 얻다

22 시제   과거완료진행   난이도 ●●○

Boston Rams fans were devastated to learn that Carl Ewing would be moving to a different team. Ewing _____ for the Rams for 14 years until he opted to take his talents to the New York Flames.

(a) competes

Boston Rams의 팬들은 Carl Ewing이 다른 팀으로 이적할 것이라는 사실을 알고 엄청난 충격을 받았다. Ewing은 그의 재능을 New York Flames에 가져가기로 택했을 때까지 14년 동안 Rams를 위해 경쟁해오고 있던 중이었다.

(b) has competed

(c) had been competing

(d) has been competing

'until + 과거 동사'와 'for + 기간 표현'이 함께 오면 과거완료진행 시제가 정답이다.

> ☀ **과거완료진행과 자주 함께 쓰이는 시간 표현**
> • before / when / since + 과거 동사 + (for + 기간 표현) ~하기 전에 / ~했을 때 / ~ 이래로 (~ 동안)
> • (for + 기간 표현) + (up) until + 과거 동사 (~ 동안) ~했을 때까지

해설 | 과거완료진행 시제와 함께 쓰이는 시간 표현 'for + 기간 표현'(for 14 years)과 'until + 과거 동사'(until ~ opted)가 있고, 문맥상 대과거 (Boston Rams를 위해 경쟁하기 시작했던 시점)부터 과거(다른 팀으로 이적하기로 택한 시점)까지 Ewing이 Rams를 위해 14년 동안 계속해서 경쟁해오고 있던 중이었다는 의미가 되어야 자연스럽다. 따라서 과거완료진행 시제 (c) had been competing이 정답이다.

어휘 | devastated adj. 엄청난 충격을 받은　opt v. 택하다　talent n. 재능　compete v. 경쟁하다, 겨루다

---

23 준동사　to 부정사를 목적어로 취하는 동사　난이도 ●○○

Julia is writing a list of goals for her summer break. In addition to frequent exercise and hanging out with friends, she hopes _____ at least five works of literature.

(a) reading
(b) having read
(c) to have read
(d) to read

Julia는 그녀의 여름 방학 목표 목록을 작성하고 있다. 잦은 운동과 친구들과 함께 시간을 보내는 것 외에도, 그녀는 적어도 5편의 문학 작품을 읽기를 희망한다.

hope는 to 부정사를 목적어로 취한다.

해설 | 빈칸 앞 동사 hope는 to 부정사를 목적어로 취하므로, to 부정사 (d) to read가 정답이다.

> 오답분석
> (c) to have read도 to 부정사이기는 하지만, 완료부정사(to have read)로 쓰일 경우 '희망하는' 시점보다 '읽는' 시점이 앞선다는 것을 나타내므로 문맥에 적합하지 않아 오답이다.

어휘 | in addition to phr. ~ 외에도, ~에 더하여　hang out with phr. ~와 함께 시간을 보내다　literature n. 문학

---

24 조동사　조동사 should 생략　난이도 ●●○

Riverside College aims to restructure its education model to increase class engagement. To accomplish this, experts on the school's steering committee state that it's necessary that the faculty _____ students more in the learning process.

Riverside 대학은 수업 참여도를 높이기 위해 그것의 교육 모형을 개편하는 것을 목표로 한다. 이것을 달성하기 위해, 그 학교 운영 위원회의 전문가들은 교수진이 학생들을 학습 과정에 더 많이 참여시켜야 하는 것이 필요하다고 말한다.

(a) involve
(b) has involved
(c) will involve
(d) involves

necessary 다음에는 that절에 동사원형이 온다.

해설 | 주절에 주장을 나타내는 형용사 necessary가 있으므로 that절에는 '(should +) 동사원형'이 와야 한다. 따라서 동사원형 (a) involve가 정답이다.

어휘 | aim v. 목표로 하다   restructure v. 개편하다   engagement n. 참여도   accomplish v. 달성하다, 성취하다
steering committee phr. 운영 위원회   faculty n. 교수진

---

25 가정법   가정법 과거완료   난이도 ●●○

Few investors doubted SkyTek's legitimacy when the firm was valued at $10 billion in 2020. But if they _____ its technological claims more closely, they probably would not have purchased a single stock.

2020년에 SkyTek 사가 100억 달러로 평가되었을 때 그 회사의 정통성을 의심하는 투자자는 거의 없었다. 그러나 만약 그들이 그것의 기술적인 주장을 더 자세히 <u>조사했었다면</u>, 그들은 아마 단 하나의 주식도 사지 않았을 것이다.

(a) were inspecting
(b) inspected
(c) had inspected
(d) would inspect

if와 'would/could + have p.p.'가 있으면 had p.p.가 정답이다.

해설 | 주절에 'would(조동사 과거형) + have p.p.' 형태의 would ~ have purchased가 있으므로, if절에는 이와 짝을 이루어 가정법 과거완료를 만드는 과거완료 동사가 와야 한다. 따라서 (c) had inspected가 정답이다.

어휘 | investor n. 투자자   doubt v. 의심하다   legitimacy n. 정통성, 합법성   value v. 평가하다   stock n. 주식   inspect v. 조사하다, 점검하다

---

26 시제   과거진행   난이도 ●●○

It was a beautiful Saturday afternoon, and Lucy was enjoying relaxing in her room. She _____ whether or not to take a walk outside when her friend Alyssa called to invite her to a barbecue.

아름다운 토요일 오후였고, Lucy는 그녀의 방에서 휴식을 취하는 것을 즐기고 있었다. 그녀의 친구 Alyssa가 그녀를 바비큐 파티에 초대하기 위해 전화했을 때 그녀는 밖에서 산책을 할지 말지 <u>고민하고 있던 중이었다.</u>

(a) considered
(b) was considering
(c) is considering
(d) has considered

'for + 기간 표현' 없이 'when + 과거 동사'만 있으면 과거진행 시제가 정답이다.

> ☼ **과거진행과 자주 함께 쓰이는 시간 표현**
> • when / while + 과거 동사 ~했을 때 / ~하던 도중에
> • last + 시간 표현 / yesterday 지난 ~에 / 어제

해설 ┃ 과거진행 시제와 함께 쓰이는 시간 표현 'when + 과거 동사'(when ~ called)가 있고, 문맥상 과거 시점인 토요일 오후에 Lucy의 친구 Alyssa가 그녀에게 전화했을 때 Lucy는 밖에서 산책을 할지 말지 고민하고 있던 중이었다는 의미가 되어야 자연스럽다. 따라서 과거진행 시제 (b) was considering이 정답이다.

[오답분석]
(a) 특정 과거 시점에 한창 진행 중이었던 행동을 표현하기에는 과거 시제보다 과거진행 시제가 더 적절하므로, 과거 시제는 오답이다.

어휘 ┃ consider v. 고민하다, 생각하다

LISTENING

PART 1^(27~33)　**일상 대화**　개 산책 서비스에 관한 두 친구의 대화

음성 바로 듣기

안부 인사	M: Hi, Gretchen. I heard that you are starting a new job. Congratulations! You must be very excited.
주제 제시: 개 산책 서비스 이용	F: Thanks, Joseph. I am, but ²⁷I'm a little worried too. My dog Baxter has never been left alone all day before. I'm not sure how he'll do. M: ²⁸Didn't he stay by himself while you were in school? F: No. I had a few roommates, so there was usually someone around to be with him. And ²⁸I scheduled breaks between my classes so I had time to run home. M: Oh, I see. That could be a problem. What are you going to do? F: I'm considering employing a dog walking service. I've never used one before, though.
문제1: 겁이 많은 성격	M: If you hire a professional service, I'm sure its staff will do a good job. F: You're probably right. But ²⁹Baxter is kind of timid. I fear that he might be uncomfortable with a stranger coming into the house and trying to approach him.
대책1: 주인과 함께 산책	M: Hmm . . . Maybe you could have them start coming before you begin your job. ³⁰Walk Baxter a few times together so he could get used to the new walker. F: That's a great idea. ³⁰That would also let me show the walker where I usually take Baxter on his walks and which toys he likes to play with. M: That's true. Getting to know the walker beforehand would put you at ease. Is that the only thing holding you back?
문제2: 비용	F: There are some others. The biggest one is the cost. I've looked at some services, and the average cost is $20 or more per walk. M: Wow! I didn't know that they charged so much for the service. Is there anything you could do for a better rate? F: Well, there is one that I found that is $10 per walk. But it's a group walk. ³¹Baxter gets scared of larger dogs sometimes, so I don't know if that is a good option for him.

남: 안녕, Gretchen. 나는 네가 새로운 일을 시작한다고 들었어. 축하해! 너 정말 신나겠구나.

여: 고마워, Joseph. 맞아, 하지만 ²⁷나는 조금 걱정되기도 해. 내 강아지 Baxter는 이전에 온종일 혼자 남겨진 적이 없었어. 난 그가 어떻게 할지 잘 모르겠어.

남: ²⁸네가 학교에 있었을 때 그는 혼자 있지 않았어?

여: 아니야. 나는 몇 명의 룸메이트가 있었고, 그래서 보통 그와 함께 있을 사람이 주변에 있었어. 그리고 ²⁸난 집에 잠깐 다녀올 시간이 있도록 수업들 사이에 휴식 시간을 계획해 두었어.

남: 오, 그렇구나. 그게 문제가 될 수 있겠다. 어떻게 할 거야?

여: 개 산책 서비스를 이용하는 것을 고려 중이야. 하지만 난 그것을 전에 이용해 본 적이 없어.

남: 만약 네가 전문 서비스를 이용한다면, 그것의 직원들이 일을 잘 해낼 거라고 난 확신해.

여: 네 말이 맞을지도 몰라. 하지만 ²⁹Baxter는 약간 겁이 많아. 나는 그가 낯선 사람이 집에 들어와서 그에게 다가가려고 하는 것을 불편해할까 봐 걱정돼.

남: 흠... 네가 일을 시작하기 전에 그들이 방문하는 것을 시작하도록 하면 좋을 것 같아. ³⁰Baxter가 새로운 산책시키는 사람에게 익숙해질 수 있도록 함께 몇 번 산책해 봐.

여: 아주 좋은 생각이야. ³⁰그것은 또한 산책 시에 내가 보통 Baxter를 데리고 가는 곳과 그가 무슨 장난감들을 가지고 놀기 좋아하는지를 산책시키는 사람에게 보여줄 수 있게 할 거야.

남: 맞아. 산책시키는 사람에 대해 미리 알게 되는 것은 네 마음을 편하게 할 거야. 그게 널 망설이게 만드는 유일한 것이니?

여: 다른 것들도 있어. 가장 큰 것은 비용이야. 몇몇 서비스를 살펴봤는데, 평균 비용이 산책 1회당 20달러 이상이야.

남: 와! 그들이 그 서비스에 그렇게 많은 요금을 청구하는지 몰랐어. 더 싼 요금을 위해 네가 할 수 있는 일이 있어?

여: 음, 내가 찾은 것 중에 산책 1회당 10달러인 게 있어. 하지만 그건 그룹 산책이야. ³¹Baxter는 때때로 큰 개들을 무서워해서, 그것이 그에게 좋은 선택지인지 모르겠어.

대책2: 그룹 산책	M: You should call the company and discuss it. They might be able to organize a group that only includes smaller dogs. When my mother used a dog walking service for her poodle, it exclusively worked with miniature breeds.	남: 그 회사에 전화해서 그것을 의논해 봐. 그들은 작은 개들만 포함하는 그룹을 준비해줄 수 있을지도 몰라. 우리 엄마가 그녀의 푸들을 위해 개 산책 서비스를 이용했을 때, 그것은 오로지 소형 품종들을 대상으로 했어.
그룹 산책 장점	F: If that's the case, then it would be perfect. I bet Baxter would love playing with a bunch of small dogs too. M: It would also be better exercise for him than just walking to the park and back because they could play together and run around for a while. F: I was thinking the same thing. And ³²it might be good for him to burn off some energy during the day. Otherwise, he'll be really stressed and act out when I get home from work in the evening. Besides, it'll stop him from getting bored. M: I hadn't thought of that. I'm sure that just having some time to be out of the house will have a positive effect on his behavior.	여: 만약 그렇다면, 그건 완벽하겠다. Baxter도 많은 작은 개들과 노는 걸 좋아할 거라고 확신해. 남: 그들은 잠시 동안 함께 놀고 뛰어다닐 수 있기 때문에 그것은 또한 공원까지 그저 왔다 갔다 하는 것보다 그에게 더 나은 운동일 거야. 여: 나도 같은 생각을 하고 있었어. 그리고 ³²낮에 약간의 에너지를 소모하는 것이 그에게 좋을 수 있어. 그렇지 않으면, 내가 저녁에 퇴근하고 집에 올 때 그는 너무 스트레스를 받아서 말썽을 피울 거야. 게다가, 그것은 그가 지루해지는 것을 막을 거야. 남: 그건 미처 생각하지 못했어. 집 밖에서 보내는 시간을 갖는 것만으로도 그의 행동에 긍정적인 영향을 미칠 거라고 확신해.
여자의 결정	F: Yes, I think so too. ³³I guess I'll just go ahead and give the cheaper agency a call. M: I think you're making the right decision.	여: 응, 나도 그렇게 생각해. ³³나는 그냥 곧바로 더 저렴한 업체에 전화 해야겠어. 남: 난 네가 옳은 결정을 하고 있다고 생각해.

어휘 | schedule[skédʒul] (일정을) 계획하다 run[rʌn] 잠깐 다녀오다 hire[hair] 이용하다, 고용하다 timid[tímid] 겁이 많은 approach[əpróutʃ] 다가가다 get used to ~에 익숙해지다 put at ease 마음을 편하게 하다, 안심시키다 hold back 망설이게 만들다 charge[tʃɑːrdʒ] 요금을 청구하다 organize[ɔ́ːrɡənaiz] 준비하다 exclusively[iksklúːsivli] 오로지 a bunch of 많은, 다수의 otherwise[ʌ́ðərwaiz] 그렇지 않으면 act out 말썽을 피우다

---

27 특정세부사항   What   난이도 ●○○

What is Gretchen's concern?	Gretchen의 걱정거리는 무엇인가?
(a) She is scared to work with dogs. (b) She is starting a new job. (c) She has never lived by herself. **(d) She has to leave her pet alone.**	(a) 개와 함께 일하는 것을 무서워한다. (b) 새로운 일을 시작할 것이다. (c) 그녀 혼자 살아 본 적이 없다. **(d) 그녀의 반려동물을 혼자 두어야 한다.**

◄────○ 지텔프 치트키

질문의 키워드 concern이 worried로 paraphrasing되어 언급된 주변 내용을 주의 깊게 듣는다.

해설 | 여자가 'I'm a little worried too'라며 조금 걱정되기도 한다고 한 뒤, 'My dog ~ has never been left alone all day before.'라며 그녀의 강아지는 이전에 온종일 혼자 남겨진 적이 없었다고 했다. 따라서 (d)가 정답이다.

오답분석
(b) 여자가 새로운 일을 시작한다고는 언급하였지만, 그것이 그녀의 걱정거리라고 한 것은 아니므로 오답이다.

어휘 | concern[kənsə́ːrn] 걱정거리

Why most likely did Gretchen plan breaks between her classes?

(a) to give herself a chance to rest during the day
(b) to be able to take better care of her dog
(c) to have time to work out at the school gym
(d) to visit her roommates before they went to school

왜 Gretchen은 수업들 사이에 휴식 시간을 계획했던 것 같은가?

(a) 그녀 자신에게 낮에 쉴 기회를 주기 위해서
(b) 그녀의 개를 더 잘 돌볼 수 있기 위해서
(c) 학교 체육관에서 운동할 시간을 가지기 위해서
(d) 룸메이트들이 학교에 가기 전에 그들을 방문하기 위해서

─○ 지텔프 치트키

질문의 키워드 plan breaks가 scheduled breaks로 paraphrasing되어 언급된 주변 내용을 주의 깊게 듣는다.

해설 | 남자가 'Didn't he stay by himself while you were in school?'이라며 여자가 학교에 있었을 때 그녀의 강아지 Baxter가 혼자 있지 않았는지를 묻자, 여자가 'I scheduled breaks between my classes so I had time to run home'이라며 집에 잠깐 다녀올 시간이 있도록 수업들 사이에 휴식 시간을 계획해 두었다고 한 것을 통해, 여자가 그녀의 개를 더 잘 돌볼 수 있기 위해서 수업들 사이에 휴식 시간을 계획했던 것임을 추론할 수 있다. 따라서 (b)가 정답이다.

Why is Gretchen hesitant about hiring a dog walker despite their professionalism?

(a) Her dog is shy around new people.
(b) She doesn't want anyone in her house.
(c) She can't trust an untested service.
(d) Her dog is afraid of going outside.

왜 Gretchen은 그들의 전문성에도 불구하고 개를 산책시키는 사람을 고용하는 것을 망설이는가?

(a) 그녀의 개는 처음 보는 사람들 앞에서 겁이 많다.
(b) 그녀는 그녀의 집에 아무도 들이고 싶지 않다.
(c) 그녀는 검증되지 않은 서비스를 믿을 수 없다.
(d) 그녀의 개는 밖에 나가는 것을 두려워한다.

─○ 지텔프 치트키

질문의 키워드 professionalism이 professional로 paraphrasing되어 언급된 주변 내용을 주의 깊게 듣는다.

해설 | 여자가 'Baxter is kind of timid'라며 Baxter가 약간 겁이 많다고 한 뒤, 'I fear that he might be uncomfortable with a stranger coming into the house and trying to approach him.'이라며 Baxter가 낯선 사람이 집에 들어와서 그에게 다가가려고 하는 것을 불편해할까 봐 걱정된다고 했다. 따라서 (a)가 정답이다.

Paraphrasing
timid 겁이 많은 → shy 겁이 많은
a stranger 낯선 사람 → new people 처음 보는 사람들

어휘 | shy [ʃai] 겁이 많은

According to the conversation, how can the new walker get familiar with the dog?

(a) by buying him new toys to play with

대화에 따르면, 새로운 산책시키는 사람은 어떻게 개와 친해질 수 있는가?

(a) 그에게 가지고 놀 새 장난감들을 사줌으로써

(b) **by taking him on his normal walking route**
(c) by bringing him to the walker's house beforehand
(d) by going with him to dog parks

(b) 그를 그의 일상적인 산책 경로로 데려감으로써
(c) 그를 산책시키는 사람의 집에 미리 데려감으로써
(d) 그와 함께 개 공원에 감으로써

질문의 키워드 get familiar with가 get used to로 paraphrasing되어 언급된 주변 내용을 주의 깊게 듣는다.

해설 | 남자가 'Walk Baxter ~ together so he could get used to the new walker.'라며 Baxter가 새로운 산책시키는 사람에게 익숙해질 수 있도록 함께 산책해 보라고 하자, 여자가 'That would ~ let me show the walker where I usually take Baxter on his walks and which toys he likes to play with.'라며 그것은 산책 시에 그녀가 보통 Baxter를 데리고 가는 곳과 그가 무슨 장난감들을 가지고 놀기 좋아하는지를 산책시키는 사람에게 보여줄 수 있게 할 것이라고 했다. 따라서 (b)가 정답이다.

Paraphrasing
where I usually take Baxter on his walks 산책 시에 보통 데리고 가는 곳 → his normal walking route 일상적인 산책 경로

어휘 | route[ruːt] 경로

---

31 **특정세부사항**   What   난이도 ●●○

What is the reason that Gretchen feels unsure of the cheaper option?

(a) the duration of the walks being offered
(b) the number of dogs on the walk
(c) **the size of the other dogs**
(d) the schedule of the service

Gretchen이 더 저렴한 선택지에 대해 확신하지 못하는 이유는 무엇인가?

(a) 제공되는 산책의 시간
(b) 산책하는 개들의 수
(c) **다른 개들의 크기**
(d) 서비스의 일정

질문의 키워드 option이 그대로 언급된 주변 내용을 주의 깊게 듣는다.

해설 | 여자가 'Baxter gets scared of larger dogs ~, so I don't know if that is a good option for him.'이라며 Baxter가 큰 개들을 무서워해서 더 저렴한 선택지인 그룹 산책이 그에게 좋은 선택지인지 모르겠다고 했다. 따라서 (c)가 정답이다.

Paraphrasing
larger dogs 큰 개들 → the size of ~ dogs 개들의 크기

어휘 | duration[djuréiʃən] (지속) 시간

---

32 **특정세부사항**   How   난이도 ●●○

How would a group walk service prevent the dog from being too stressed?

(a) by walking along a longer path in the park
(b) **by working off excess energy before the evening**
(c) by interacting with a variety of unfamiliar people
(d) by staying out of the house later in the afternoon

그룹 산책 서비스는 어떻게 개가 지나치게 스트레스 받는 것을 막을 수 있는가?

(a) 공원에서 더 긴 산책로를 산책함으로써
(b) **저녁 전에 과도한 에너지를 소모함으로써**
(c) 여러 낯선 사람들과 상호 작용함으로써
(d) 늦은 오후에 집 밖에 있음으로써

해설 | 여자가 'it might be good for him to burn off some energy during the day'라며 낮에 약간의 에너지를 소모하는 것이 Baxter에게 좋을 수 있다고 한 뒤, 'Otherwise, he'll be really stressed ~ when I get home from work in the evening.'이라며 그렇지 않으면 그녀가 저녁에 퇴근하고 집에 올 때 Baxter는 너무 스트레스를 받을 것이라고 했다. 따라서 (b)가 정답이다.

Paraphrasing

burn off ~ energy 에너지를 소모하다 → working off ~ energy 에너지를 소모함

어휘 | work off 소모하다, 해소하다   excess[iksés] 과도한, 초과의

---

33 추론   다음에 할 일   난이도 ●●●

What will Gretchen most likely do after the conversation?

(a) try to make her workday shorter than it is
(b) inquire about a size-specific group for her pet
(c) ask a business to offer a service discount
(d) begin training to be a professional dog walker

대화 이후에 Gretchen이 할 일은 무엇일 것 같은가?

(a) 그녀의 근무 시간을 지금보다 더 짧게 만들려고 노력한다
(b) 그녀의 반려동물을 위해 특정한 크기의 그룹에 관해 문의한다
(c) 업체에 서비스 할인을 제공해 줄 것을 요청한다
(d) 전문적인 개 산책시키는 사람이 되기 위해 훈련을 시작한다

해설 | 여자가 'I guess I'll just go ahead and give the cheaper agency a call.'이라며 그냥 곧바로 더 저렴한 업체에 전화 해야겠다고 한 것을 통해, Gretchen은 그녀의 반려동물을 위해 더 저렴한 요금의 그룹 산책을 제공하는 업체에 전화해서 특정한 크기의 그룹에 관해 문의할 것임을 추론할 수 있다. 따라서 (b)가 정답이다.

어휘 | workday[wə́ːrkdei] 근무 시간, 근무일

PART 2[34~39] 발표   디저트 축제 홍보

음성 바로 듣기

| 주제 제시: 축제 홍보 | Greetings, everyone! I am the lead coordinator for the Sweet Summer Dessert Festival. I'm thrilled to be here today to tell you about this exciting event. It will take place from 1 p.m. to 5 p.m. next Saturday at the downtown expo center. | 안녕하세요, 여러분! 저는 Sweet Summer 디저트 축제의 대표 진행 담당자입니다. 저는 이 흥미로운 행사에 관해 여러분께 알려드리기 위해 오늘 이 자리에 서게 되어 매우 기쁩니다. 그것은 다음 주 토요일 오후 1시부터 오후 5시까지 시내에 있는 엑스포 센터에서 진행될 예정입니다. |
| 축제 소개 | [34]The Sweet Summer Dessert Festival began as a way for local bakeries and online businesses to introduce their sweet creations to the citizens of our city. Now, the festival celebrates the advances in the art of dessert-making. This festival is where a number of delicious | [34]Sweet Summer 디저트 축제는 지역 제과점들과 온라인 사업체들이 그들의 달콤한 작품들을 저희 도시의 시민분들께 소개해 드리기 위한 방법으로 시작되었습니다. 이제, 그 축제는 디저트 제조 기술의 발전을 축하합니다. 이 축제는 여러 가지의 맛있는 맛, 독 |

flavors, unique textures, and beautiful presentations can be experienced for the first time.

This is the festival's fourth year and it promises to be the biggest one yet. Thanks to our generous sponsors, we were able to rent the expo center. It is the largest venue we've ever had, and it will allow for a record number of vendors to serve sweet treats.

Speaking of treats, the fair will have every dessert imaginable. Our vendors will be offering puddings, pies, chocolates, baked goods, churros, and more. For those with special dietary needs, there will be alternatives available, such as vegan selections. Moreover, [35]food trucks, serving everything from tacos to hot dogs, will be parked just outside in case you need a break from all the sweet items.

The Sweet Summer Dessert Festival is also a celebration of the season. So it will show off dessert stands featuring locally grown fruit, which taste the freshest in summer. Customized ice cream and handmade cakes will incorporate in-season fruits including peaches, watermelons, and grapes.

We will be hosting our first-ever cookie contest as well. Ten local pastry shops will compete to see who has the best cookie in town. Participants are free to make any type of cookie, from macarons and wafers to traditional biscuits like chocolate chip and oatmeal raisin cookies. [36]The best part is that the visitors will choose the champion. Guests will try samples of the cookies and judge them based on taste, creativity, and presentation. The winning baker will earn a cash prize and a new Kitchen Master mixer.

We will also have prizes available for the guests. Purchasing an admission ticket will automatically enter you into the festival raffle, which is held hourly. [37]You'll have the chance to take home boxes of free treats and festival merchandise, such as t-shirts, hats, and stickers. In addition, there will be an opportunity to win a gift certificate from a local vendor and a dessert cooking class from The Sugar Plum Fairies bakery.

The desserts are included in the price of the entrance ticket. When you arrive at the venue, you will receive 30 sample vouchers, which can be exchanged for desserts inside the festival. Don't feel pressured to consume all 30 treats on the spot. Upon entry, [38]you will be given a box so you can bring sweets home with you.

특한 식감, 그리고 아름다운 외양이 처음으로 경험될 수 있는 곳입니다.

올해는 그 축제의 4번째 해이며 지금까지 중 가장 큰 축제가 될 것 같습니다. 저희의 너그러운 후원자분들 덕분에, 저희는 엑스포 센터를 빌릴 수 있었습니다. 그것은 저희가 빌렸던 곳 중 가장 큰 행사장이고, 기록적인 수의 판매업체들이 달콤한 간식을 제공할 수 있게 할 것입니다.

간식에 관해서 말씀드리자면, 이 축제에는 상상할 수 있는 모든 디저트가 있을 것입니다. 저희의 판매업체들은 푸딩, 파이, 초콜릿, 구운 식품, 추로스 등을 제공할 것입니다. 특별한 식이 요건을 가진 분들을 위해, 채식 선택지와 같은 이용 가능한 대안들이 있을 것입니다. 게다가, [35]여러분이 모든 달콤한 것들로부터 휴식이 필요할 경우를 대비해서, 타코에서 핫도그에 이르기까지 모든 것을 제공하는, 푸드트럭들이 바로 밖에 세워져 있을 것입니다.

Sweet Summer 디저트 축제는 그 계절의 축전이기도 합니다. 따라서 그것은 지역에서 재배된 과일을 특색으로 하는 디저트 가판대를 내세울 것이며, 그것(지역에서 재배된 과일)은 여름에 가장 맛이 신선합니다. 개개인의 요구에 맞춘 아이스크림과 수제 케이크는 복숭아, 수박, 그리고 포도를 비롯한 제철 과일을 포함할 것입니다.

저희는 또한 사상 최초로 쿠키 대회를 개최할 것입니다. 10개의 지역 제과점들이 이 도시에서 누가 가장 맛있는 쿠키를 가지고 있는지 알아내기 위해 경쟁할 것입니다. 참가자들은 마카롱과 웨이퍼에서부터 초콜릿 칩과 오트밀 건포도 쿠키와 같은 전통적인 비스킷에 이르기까지, 어떤 종류의 쿠키든지 자유롭게 만들수 있습니다. [36]가장 좋은 점은 방문객들이 우승자를 선택할 것이라는 점입니다. 손님들은 쿠키의 샘플들을 먹어보고 맛, 창의성, 그리고 외양을 바탕으로 그것들을 평가할 겁니다. 우승한 제과점은 상금과 Kitchen Master 사의 새로운 믹서기를 받을 것입니다.

저희에게는 또한 손님들이 얻을 수 있는 상품들이 있을 것입니다. 입장권을 구매하는 것은 여러분을 자동으로 축제 추첨에 응모시키는데, 이것은 매시간 진행됩니다. [37]여러분에게 무료 간식들과 티셔츠, 모자, 그리고 스티커와 같은 축제 상품이 담긴 상자를 집에 가져갈 기회가 있을 겁니다. 이 밖에도, 지역 판매업체의 상품권과 The Sugar Plum Fairies 제과점의 디저트 만들기 수업을 받을 기회가 있을 것입니다.

디저트는 입장권의 가격에 포함되어 있습니다. 행사장에 도착하시면, 여러분은 30장의 샘플 교환권을 받으실 것이며, 이것은 축제 내에서 디저트와 교환될 수 있습니다. 현장에서 30가지 간식을 모두 먹어야 한다는 부담을 느끼지 마세요. 입장 시, [38]여러분은 집에 간식을 가지고 갈 수 있도록 상자를 받으실 겁니다.

입장권은 오직 온라인으로만 사전에 구매될 수 있다는 것을 참고하시기 바랍니다. Sweet Summer 디저트 축제에 참석하시고 싶으신 분들은, 지금 앞쪽 탁자로 와주십시오. ³⁹저희가 QR 코드를 게시해 두었습니다. 그것들 중 하나를 스캔하는 것은 여러분을 행사 웹 페이지로 데려다줄 것이며, 그곳에서 여러분의 축제 자리를 예약하실 수 있습니다.

어휘 | coordinator[kouɔ́ːrdəneitər] 진행 담당자 **texture**[tékstʃər] 식감, 질감 **presentation**[prìːzentéiʃən] 외양 **generous**[dʒénərəs] 너그러운 **sponsor**[spɑ́ːnsər] 후원자 **venue**[vénjuː] 행사장, 공연장 **vendor**[véndər] 판매업체 **imaginable**[imǽdʒənəbəl] 상상할 수 있는 **alternative**[ɔːltə́ːrnətiv] 대안 **celebration**[sèləbréiʃən] 축전 **stand**[stǽnd] 가판대 **raisin**[réizən] 건포도 **raffle**[rǽfəl] 추첨 **merchandise**[mə́ːrtʃəndaiz] 상품 **gift certificate** 상품권 **reserve**[rizə́ːrv] 예약하다

---

34 특정세부사항　What　　　　　　　　　　　　　난이도 ●●○

What was the original purpose of the festival?	축제의 본래 목적은 무엇이었는가?
(a) to celebrate the expansion of the urban business community	(a) 도시 사업 공동체의 확장을 축하하기 위해서
(b) to experiment with an array of cooking techniques	(b) 다수의 요리 기술들을 실험하기 위해서
(c) to unveil a newly renovated downtown music venue	(c) 새롭게 개조된 시내의 음악 공연장을 공개하기 위해서
(d) to showcase desserts to local residents for the first time	**(d) 지역 주민들에게 처음으로 디저트들을 선보이기 위해서**

─○ 지텔프 치트키

질문의 키워드 original purpose가 began as로 paraphrasing되어 언급된 주변 내용을 주의 깊게 듣는다.

해설 | 화자가 'The Sweet Summer Dessert Festival began as a way for local bakeries ~ to introduce their sweet creations to the citizens of our city.'라며 Sweet Summer 디저트 축제는 지역 제과점들이 그들의 달콤한 작품들을 도시의 시민들에게 소개하기 위한 방법으로 시작되었다고 했다. 따라서 (d)가 정답이다.

Paraphrasing
introduce their sweet creations to the citizens 시민들에게 달콤한 작품들을 소개하다 → showcase desserts to local residents 지역 주민들에게 디저트들을 선보이다

어휘 | expansion[ikspǽnʃən] 확장 **an array of** 다수의

---

35 추론　특정사실　　　　　　　　　　　　　　난이도 ●●●

Why would people most likely visit the food trucks outside the venue?	사람들은 왜 행사장 밖에 있는 푸드트럭을 방문할 것 같은가?
(a) so they can try one of the vegan recipes	(a) 채식 요리법들 중 한 가지를 시도해 볼 수 있도록
(b) so they can follow a dietary requirement	(b) 식이 요건을 따를 수 있도록
(c) so they can eat foods other than dessert	**(c) 디저트 외에 다른 음식들을 먹을 수 있도록**
(d) so they can order different kinds of chocolate	(d) 다양한 종류의 초콜릿을 주문할 수 있도록

질문의 키워드 food trucks가 그대로 언급된 주변 내용을 주의 깊게 듣는다.

해설 | 화자가 'food trucks, serving everything from tacos to hot dogs, will be parked just outside in case you need a break from all the sweet items'라며 모든 달콤한 것들로부터 휴식이 필요할 경우를 대비해서 타코에서 핫도그에 이르기까지 모든 것을 제공하는 푸드트럭들이 바로 밖에 세워져 있을 것이라고 한 것을 통해, 사람들은 디저트 외에 다른 음식들을 먹기 위해 행사장 밖에 있는 푸드트럭을 방문할 것임을 추론할 수 있다. 따라서 (c)가 정답이다.

오답분석
(b) 화자가 특별한 식이 요건을 가진 사람들을 위해 채식 선택지와 같은 이용 가능한 대안들이 있을 것이라고는 언급하였지만, 이는 푸드트럭이 아닌 축제의 디저트 판매업체들이 제공하는 것이므로 오답이다.

어휘 | recipe [résəpi] 요리법

---

36 특정세부사항 How · · · 난이도 ●●○

How will the winner of the cookie competition be chosen?

(a) The festival goers are going to evaluate the contestants' creations.
(b) The competitors will each cast a vote for the highest-quality one.
(c) The victors from previous contests will pick their favorite entries.
(d) The bakers will determine the most creative one.

쿠키 대회의 우승자는 어떻게 선발될 것인가?

(a) 축제에 가는 사람들이 참가자들의 작품들을 평가할 것이다.
(b) 경쟁자들이 최고 품질의 것에 각각 한 표씩 투표할 것이다.
(c) 이전 대회의 우승자들이 가장 마음에 드는 출품작을 뽑을 것이다.
(d) 제빵사들이 가장 창의적인 것을 결정할 것이다.

질문의 키워드 winner가 champion으로 paraphrasing되어 언급된 주변 내용을 주의 깊게 듣는다.

해설 | 화자가 'The best part is that the visitors will choose the champion.'이라며 쿠키 대회의 가장 좋은 점은 방문객들이 우승자를 선택할 것이라는 점이라고 한 뒤, 'Guests will try samples of the cookies and judge them based on ~ presentation.'이라며 손님들이 쿠키의 샘플들을 먹어보고 외양 등을 바탕으로 그것들을 평가할 것이라고 했다. 따라서 (a)가 정답이다.

Paraphrasing
the cookie competition 쿠키 대회 → our ~ cookie contest 쿠키 대회
judge 평가하다 → evaluate 평가하다

어휘 | victor [víktər] 우승자 entry [éntri] 출품작, 참가작

---

37 특정세부사항 What · · · 난이도 ●●○

What is one of the prizes that people can receive from the raffle?

(a) the event's souvenir products
(b) a free ticket for the following year's event
(c) the opportunity to meet the vendors

사람들이 추첨을 통해 받을 수 있는 상품들 중 한 가지는 무엇인가?

(a) 행사의 기념품들
(b) 다음 해 행사의 무료 티켓
(c) 판매업체들을 만날 기회

(d) a discount certificate for a cooking class | (d) 요리 수업의 할인권

지텔프 치트키

질문의 키워드 raffle이 그대로 언급된 주변 내용을 주의 깊게 듣는다.

해설 | 화자가 'You'll have the chance to take home boxes of free treats and festival merchandise, such as t-shirts, hats, and stickers.'라며 손님들에게 축제 추첨을 통해 무료 간식들과 티셔츠, 모자, 그리고 스티커와 같은 축제 상품이 담긴 상자를 집에 가져갈 기회가 있을 것이라고 했다. 따라서 (a)가 정답이다.

Paraphrasing
festival merchandise 축제 상품 → the event's souvenir products 행사의 기념품들

오답분석
(d) 화자가 축제 추첨을 통해 디저트 만들기 수업을 받을 기회가 있을 것이라고는 언급하였지만, 요리 수업의 할인권을 제공한다고 한 것은 아니므로 오답이다.

어휘 | souvenir[súːvənir] 기념품

---

38 특정세부사항 How | 난이도 ●●○

How can festival guests take desserts home with them?	축제 손님들은 어떻게 디저트들을 집에 가져갈 수 있는가?
(a) by buying the most expensive admission ticket	(a) 가장 비싼 입장권을 구매함으로써
(b) by bringing a box from their home	(b) 그들의 집에서 상자를 가져옴으로써
(c) by storing them in the provided container	**(c) 그것들을 제공된 용기에 보관함으로써**
(d) by receiving extra samples from vendors	(d) 판매업체들로부터 추가 샘플을 받음으로써

지텔프 치트키

질문의 키워드 take desserts home이 bring sweets home으로 paraphrasing되어 언급된 주변 내용을 주의 깊게 듣는다.

해설 | 화자가 'you will be given a box so you can bring sweets home with you'라며 손님들이 집에 간식을 가지고 갈 수 있도록 상자를 받을 것이라고 했다. 따라서 (c)가 정답이다.

Paraphrasing
be given a box 상자를 받다 → the provided container 제공된 용기

---

39 특정세부사항 What | 난이도 ●●○

What are the QR codes at the front table for?	앞쪽 탁자에 있는 QR 코드는 무엇을 위한 것인가?
(a) reserving spots for vendors in advance	(a) 판매업체들을 위한 자리를 사전에 예약하는 것
(b) learning driving directions to the site's location	(b) 현장 위치까지의 주행 방향을 익히는 것
(c) posting reviews of the event on a message board	(c) 게시판에 행사의 후기를 게시하는 것
(d) registering online to participate in a festival	**(d) 축제에 참가하기 위해 온라인으로 등록하는 것**

지텔프 치트키

질문의 키워드 QR codes가 그대로 언급된 주변 내용을 주의 깊게 듣는다.

해설 | 화자가 'We have posted QR codes.'라며 QR 코드를 게시해 두었다고 한 뒤, 'Scanning one of them will take you to the event webpage, where you can reserve your spot at the festival.'이라며 그것들 중 하나를 스캔하는 것은 사람들을 행사 웹페이지로 데려다줄 것이며, 그곳에서 축제 자리를 예약할 수 있다고 했다. 따라서 (d)가 정답이다.

Paraphrasing
reserve your spot 자리를 예약하다 → registering ~ to participate 참가하기 위해 등록하는 것

어휘 | direction [dərékʃən] 방향, 길

PART 3 (40~45) 장단점 논의 가족 나들이 장소로서 농장과 천문대의 장단점 비교

음성 바로 듣기

주제 제시: 장단점 비교	M: Hey, Sarah. ⁴⁰I've come up with some plans for our family outing this weekend. I was thinking we should bring the kids to a farm or observatory. F: Those are great options, David. They would like either one because they're both fun and educational. M: Exactly! That's why I'm having trouble choosing. F: Maybe we should discuss the pros and cons of each. That'll make it easier to pick one. How about we start with the farm? What do you think is the best reason for going to the farm?	남: 있잖아, Sarah. ⁴⁰내가 이번 주말 우리의 가족 나들이를 위한 몇 가지 계획을 세웠어. 난 우리가 아이들을 농장이나 천문대에 데려가야겠다고 생각하고 있어. 여: 그것들은 좋은 선택지들이야, David. 둘 다 재미있고 교육적이기 때문에 그들은 어느 것이든 좋아할 거야. 남: 맞아! 그게 내가 선택하는 데 어려움을 겪는 이유야. 여: 우리가 각각의 장단점에 관해 의논해 보는 게 좋겠어. 그게 한 가지를 고르는 것을 더 쉽게 만들 거야. 농장부터 시작하는 게 어때? 당신은 농장에 가는 가장 좋은 이유가 뭐라고 생각해?
농장 장점1: 지식 습득	M: There are a lot of things to learn on a farm. ⁴¹⁽ᵃ⁾/⁽ᵇ⁾Our children can acquire knowledge about growing plants and taking care of animals. ⁴¹⁽ᵈ⁾They can also see where food comes from.	남: 농장에서는 배울 것들이 많아. ⁴¹⁽ᵃ⁾/⁽ᵇ⁾우리의 아이들은 식물을 기르고 동물을 돌보는 것에 관한 지식을 얻을 수 있어. ⁴¹⁽ᵈ⁾그들은 또한 음식이 어디에서 오는지도 확인할 수 있지.
농장 장점2: 상호작용적 경험	F: Don't you think they might get bored if the only thing they're doing is learning? M: No, not at all. It's about the interactive experience as well. They would get to play with the animals or pick some fruits and vegetables themselves. If we're lucky, they could even get the chance to take a ride on a tractor.	여: 아이들이 하는 유일한 것이 배우는 것뿐이라면 그들이 지루해할 거라고 생각하지 않아? 남: 아니, 전혀 그렇지 않아. 그것은 상호작용적 경험에 관한 것이기도 해. 그들은 동물들과 놀거나 과일과 채소를 직접 따게 될 거야. 만약 우리가 운이 좋으면, 그들은 심지어 트랙터를 탈 기회도 얻을 수 있을 거야.
농장 단점	F: They would definitely enjoy that. But if the farm trip is so great, what's keeping you from choosing it? M: It has a few drawbacks. For one, the kids might be scared of the large animals there. But ⁴²most importantly, there are other dangers to consider. For example, the animals are unpredictable, and it's easy to get hurt by the farm equipment. It's also a lot messier. The kids would likely get really dirty and ruin their clothes.	여: 그들은 분명 그것을 즐길 거야. 하지만 만약 농장 여행이 그렇게 굉장하다면, 무엇이 당신이 그것을 선택하지 못하게 하는 거야? 남: 그것에는 몇 가지 단점이 있어. 우선, 아이들은 그곳에 있는 큰 동물들을 무서워할지도 몰라. 하지만 ⁴²가장 중요한 것은, 고려해야 할 다른 위험 요소들이 있다는 거야. 예를 들어, 동물들은 예측할 수 없고, 농기구에 의해 다치기 쉬워. 그것은 또한 훨씬 더 지저분해. 아이들은 틀림없이 아주 더러워지고 그들의 옷을 엉망으로 만들 거야.
	F: I see. Then what are the pros of going to the observatory?	여: 그렇구나. 그럼 천문대에 가는 것의 장점은 뭐야?

천문대 장점1: 안전성	M: Well, unlike the farm, we wouldn't have to worry about their safety. It's indoors and the activities are risk-free.	남: 음, 농장과는 달리, 우린 그들(아이들)의 안전에 대해 걱정할 필요가 없을 거야. 그것은 실내에 있고 활동들이 위험하지 않아.
	F: I get that, but that doesn't seem like the most compelling reason.	여: 이해해, 하지만 그게 가장 설득력 있는 이유는 아닌 것 같아.
천문대 장점2: 우주에 관한 올바른 지식 제공	M: That's not the only one. Our children would love it since they're both into space these days. They'd be excited to see the stars and the surface of the moon with their own eyes.	남: 그것뿐만이 아니야. 우리의 아이들은 요즘 우주에 빠져 있기 때문에 그들 둘 다 그것을 좋아할 거야. 그들은 그들 자신의 눈으로 별들과 달의 표면을 보는 것에 신나 할 거야.
	F: You're right. ⁴³They've been obsessed with outer space since we watched that movie about people living on Mars.	여: 당신 말이 맞아. ⁴³그들은 우리가 화성에 사는 사람들에 관한 영화를 본 이후로 우주에 사로잡혀 있지.
	M: That's what I'm saying. It would be nice for them to learn the reality, though. Most of their understanding is based on science fiction. Besides, with the importance of space in the future, it's better for them to start learning about it now.	남: 내 말이 그 말이야. 하지만 현실을 배우는 것이 그들에게 좋을 거야. 그들의 지식 대부분이 공상 과학 소설에 기반을 두고 있잖아. 더군다나, 훗날 우주의 중요성을 생각하면, 그들이 지금부터 그것에 관해 배우기 시작하는 게 더 좋아.
	F: Ha-ha. Yes, they do have some silly ideas about it now. What are the cons of going to the observatory?	여: 하하. 맞아, 그들은 지금으로서는 그것에 관해 엉뚱한 생각들을 가지고 있어. 천문대에 가는 것의 단점은 뭐야?
천문대 단점1: 가족 활동의 부재	M: The biggest one is that it's less family-oriented. If we go to the observatory, we won't have the opportunity to do activities as a family. Most of the activities will be led by a guide.	남: 가장 큰 것은 그것이 덜 가족 중심적이라는 거야. 만약 우리가 천문대에 간다면, 우리는 가족 단위로 활동할 기회가 없을 거야. 대부분의 활동들은 안내자에 의해 주도될 거야.
	F: I understand. I'm sure there are still some things that we'd be able to do together.	여: 잘 알겠어. 난 그래도 우리가 함께 할 수 있는 몇 개의 것들이 있다고 확신해.
천문대 단점2: 이동 거리	M: Probably, but I'm worried about the trip itself, too. The observatory is farther away. ⁴⁴It would take three hours to get there. A long car trip might annoy them.	남: 아마 있겠지, 하지만 난 이동 자체도 걱정이야. 천문대는 더 멀리 있어. ⁴⁴그곳에 가는 데 3시간이 걸릴 거야. 긴 자동차 이동은 그들을 짜증 나게 할 수도 있지.
	F: Oh, yeah. They sometimes get cranky even when we're driving around town.	여: 오, 맞아. 그들은 가끔 우리가 차를 타고 동네를 돌아다닐 때조차 짜증을 내잖아.
	M: That's what I was thinking too. It might spoil the whole outing.	남: 그게 나 역시 생각하고 있었던 거야. 그게 나들이 전체를 망칠지도 몰라.
남녀의 결정	F: After going through the options, are you leaning towards one?	여: 선택지들을 살펴보고 나니, 당신은 한쪽으로 마음이 기울고 있어?
	M: Yes. ⁴⁵I'm thinking we would all rather have a more hands-on learning experience. What do you think?	남: 응. ⁴⁵난 우리 모두가 더 체험 위주인 학습 경험을 하는 것이 차라리 낫다고 생각하고 있어. 당신은 어떻게 생각해?
	F: ⁴⁵I agree. That would probably be a better choice.	여: ⁴⁵나도 동의해. 그게 아마도 더 나은 선택일 거야.

어휘 | outing[áutiŋ] 나들이, 소풍 observatory[əbzɔ́:rvətɔ:ri] 천문대 educational[èdʒəkéiʃənəl] 교육적인 acquire[əkwáir] 얻다, 획득하다
unpredictable[ʌnpridíktəbəl] 예측할 수 없는 equipment[ikwípmənt] 기구 messy[mési] 지저분한 ruin[rú:in] 엉망으로 만들다
compelling[kəmpéliŋ] 설득력 있는 silly[síli] 엉뚱한 annoy[ənɔ́i] 짜증 나게 하다 cranky[krǽŋki] 짜증을 내는 spoil[spɔil] 망치다
lean[li:n] (마음이) 기울다 hands-on 체험 위주인

What are Sarah and David considering doing with their family?

(a) moving to a nearby farm for their children's health
(b) going on a weekend journey that is beneficial to kids
(c) visiting their family members who live on rural farms
(d) participating in a professional education program

Sarah와 David는 가족과 무엇을 할 것을 고려하고 있는가?

(a) 그들의 아이들의 건강을 위해 근처 농장으로 이사하는 것
(b) 아이들에게 유익한 주말여행을 가는 것
(c) 시골 농장에 사는 그들의 가족 구성원들을 방문하는 것
(d) 전문 교육 프로그램에 참여하는 것

━O 지텔프 치트키

질문의 키워드 family가 그대로 언급된 주변 내용을 주의 깊게 듣는다.

해설 | 남자가 'I've come up with some plans for our family outing this weekend.'라며 여자에게 이번 주말 가족 나들이를 위한 몇 가지 계획을 세웠다고 했다. 따라서 (b)가 정답이다.

Paraphrasing
our ~ outing this weekend 이번 주말 나들이 → a weekend journey 주말여행

Which of the following is not mentioned as a topic that can be learned at a farm?

(a) information on growing plants
(b) how to look after animals
(c) how to fix tractors
(d) the origin of food

다음 중 농장에서 배울 수 있는 주제로 언급되지 않은 것은 무엇인가?

(a) 식물을 키우는 것에 관한 정보
(b) 동물을 돌보는 방법
(c) 트랙터를 수리하는 방법
(d) 음식의 기원

━O 지텔프 치트키

질문의 키워드 learned at a farm이 learn on a farm으로 paraphrasing되어 언급된 주변 내용을 주의 깊게 들으며 언급되는 것을 하나씩 소거한다.

해설 | (c)는 언급되지 않았으므로, (c)가 정답이다.

오답분석
(a) 남자가 농장에서 아이들이 식물을 기르는 것에 관한 지식을 얻을 수 있다고 언급하였다.
(b) 남자가 농장에서 아이들이 동물을 돌보는 것에 관한 지식을 얻을 수 있다고 언급하였다.
(d) 남자가 농장에서 아이들이 음식이 어디에서 오는지를 확인할 수 있다고 언급하였다.

어휘 | look after ~을 돌보다 origin[ɔ́:ridʒin] 기원

What most likely does David consider the biggest con of visiting a farm?

David가 농장을 방문하는 것의 가장 큰 단점이라고 여기는 것은 무엇인 것 같은가?

(a) The kids don't like touching plants.
(b) It lacks sufficient indoor spaces for activities.
(c) The kids fear the larger animals.
(d) It comes with a risk of physical injury.

(a) 아이들이 식물을 만지는 것을 좋아하지 않는다.
(b) 활동들을 위한 충분한 실내 공간이 부족하다.
(c) 아이들이 큰 동물들을 무서워한다.
(d) 신체적 부상의 위험을 동반한다.

─○ 지텔프 치트키

질문의 키워드 visiting a farm과 관련된 부정적인 흐름을 파악한다.

해설 | 남자가 'most importantly, there are other dangers to consider'라며 가장 중요한 것은 고려해야 할 다른 위험 요소들이 있다는 것이라고 한 뒤, 'For example, ~ it's easy to get hurt by the farm equipment.'라며 그 예로 아이들이 농기구에 의해 다치기 쉽다고 한 것을 통해, David는 신체적 부상의 위험을 동반하는 것이 농장을 방문하는 것의 가장 큰 단점이라고 여기는 것임을 추론할 수 있다. 따라서 (d)가 정답이다.

Paraphrasing
get hurt 다치다 → physical injury 신체적 부상

오답분석
(c) 남자가 아이들이 큰 동물들을 무서워할지도 모른다고는 언급하였지만, 이것이 농장을 방문하는 것의 가장 큰 단점이라고 한 것은 아니므로 오답이다.

어휘 | injury [índʒəri] 부상

43 특정세부사항 How   난이도 ●●○

How did the couple's children become interested in space?
부부의 아이들은 어떻게 우주에 관심이 생겼는가?

(a) They saw a film that took place on another planet.
(b) They visited a famous observatory that had moon rocks.
(c) They watched a shooting star through a telescope.
(d) They took a science class during summer school.

(a) 다른 행성에서 일어난 영화를 보았다.
(b) 월석이 있는 유명한 천문대를 방문했다.
(c) 망원경을 통해 별똥별을 관찰했다.
(d) 하계학교 동안 과학 수업을 수강했다.

─○ 지텔프 치트키

질문의 키워드 interested가 obsessed로 paraphrasing되어 언급된 주변 내용을 주의 깊게 듣는다.

해설 | 여자가 'They've been obsessed with outer space since we watched that movie about people living on Mars.'라며 부부의 아이들이 화성에 사는 사람들에 관한 영화를 본 이후로 우주에 사로잡혀 있다고 했다. 따라서 (a)가 정답이다.

Paraphrasing
watched that movie about people living on Mars 화성에 사는 사람들에 관한 영화를 보았다 → saw a film that took place on another planet 다른 행성에서 일어난 영화를 보았다

44 특정세부사항 Why   난이도 ●●○

Why does David think a three-hour car trip is a problem?
David는 왜 3시간 동안의 자동차 이동이 문제라고 생각하는가?

(a) because the kids would prefer to go on an outing closer to home
(a) 아이들이 집에서 가까운 나들이를 가는 것을 선호할 것이기 때문에

(b) because it costs a lot due to the large increase in gasoline prices	(b) 휘발유 가격의 큰 상승으로 인해 비용이 많이 들기 때문에
(c) because the kids could become irritated	**(c) 아이들이 짜증이 날 수 있기 때문에**
(d) because it could be a waste of time	(d) 시간 낭비가 될 수 있기 때문에

지텔프 치트키

질문의 키워드 three-hour가 three hours로 언급된 주변 내용을 주의 깊게 듣는다.

해설 | 남자가 'It would take three hours to get there.'라며 천문대까지 가는 데 3시간이 걸릴 것이라고 한 뒤, 'A long car trip might annoy them.'이라며 긴 자동차 이동은 아이들을 짜증 나게 할 수도 있다고 했다. 따라서 (c)가 정답이다.

Paraphrasing

annoy them 그들을 짜증 나게 하다 → the kids ~ become irritated 아이들이 짜증이 나다

어휘 | irritated[íriteitid] 짜증이 난　waste[weist] 낭비

---

45 추론　다음에 할 일　　　　　　　　　　　　　난이도 ●●○

What have David and Sarah probably decided to do after the conversation?	David와 Sarah는 대화 이후에 무엇을 하기로 결정한 것 같은가?
(a) book a trip to the observatory	(a) 천문대로의 나들이를 예약한다
(b) make a hotel reservation	(b) 호텔을 예약한다
(c) go through the options again	(c) 선택지들을 다시 검토한다
(d) make a visit to the farm	**(d) 농장을 방문한다**

지텔프 치트키

다음에 할 일을 언급하는 후반을 주의 깊게 듣는다.

해설 | 남자가 'I'm thinking we would all rather have a more hands-on learning experience.'라며 더 체험 위주인 학습 경험을 하는 것이 차라리 낫다고 생각하고 있다고 하자, 여자가 'I agree.'라며 동의한다고 한 것을 통해, David와 Sarah는 동물들과 놀거나 과일과 채소를 직접 따는 등의 상호적 경험을 할 수 있는 농장을 방문하기로 결정한 것임을 추론할 수 있다. 따라서 (d)가 정답이다.

PART 4 [46~52]　설명　표절 예방을 위한 5가지 조언

음성 바로 듣기

| 인사 + 주제 제시 | Hello, students. I am the dean of Stonehaven University's Journalism and Media Studies Department, and I've been asked to speak to you about plagiarism. Plagiarism refers to using another person's ideas or work as your own without crediting the source. In my experience, most cases of this occur due to carelessness. Therefore, [46]I'm here to provide a couple of tips to help you avoid unintentional plagiarism. | 안녕하세요, 학생 여러분. 저는 Stonehaven 대학의 언론 및 미디어 연구과의 학장이고, 표절에 관해 여러분께 강연해 달라는 요청을 받았습니다. 표절은 자료의 출처를 밝히지 않고 다른 사람의 아이디어나 저작물을 자신의 것처럼 사용하는 것을 말합니다. 제 경험상, 이런 경우의 대부분은 부주의로 인해 발생합니다. 따라서, [46]저는 의도하지 않은 표절을 피하는 데 도움이 되는 몇 가지 조언을 제공해 드리려고 왔습니다. |

First, give yourself plenty of time to research and work on your assignment. Students who put off their papers will have a hard time finishing by the deadline. [47]In a rush, it's not surprising that these learners copy sections from other literature or forget to properly list their sources. Therefore, it is important to make full use of the available time to plan your research and take careful notes when outlining your project. Staying organized should prevent plagiarism caused by working too quickly.

Second, gather a large number of resources to learn about the topic. Whether digital or physical, reading many different sources will give you a comprehensive understanding of your topic. By considering various viewpoints, you will be better positioned to develop your own ideas on the matter. Conversely, using only one or two resources as the basis for your assignment increases the chances of plagiarism, since you're more likely to copy an idea. [48]If you are struggling to find sources, ask your professor or visit the library. Our campus librarians will be more than happy to direct you to the books or online journals you need.

Third, don't forget to cite your work and prepare a bibliography. Any finding, concept, or idea that you did not originally create must be mentioned in the paper's endnotes. If you repeat another author's work, put the phrase or sentence in quotes. Some students have committed accidental plagiarism because they incorrectly cited their source. To avoid this, follow the style guide required for your assignment. [49]This information can be found in the school's online reference library or on your class syllabus.

Fourth, paraphrase properly. Paraphrasing does not mean simply switching out a few words of the original text. Good paraphrasing shows that you understand the author's idea and are restating it in your own words. But even when expressed with your own phrasing, the content still doesn't belong to you. Thus, all paraphrased sections in your assignment must be referenced as well. Also, while paraphrasing is a valuable technique, [50]be careful not to overuse it. When evaluating your understanding of a subject, professors will have little interest in the thoughts of another author.

Finally, conduct a plagiarism check of your work. Even the most thorough students make mistakes, so it's best to have an objective, machine-based program examine

---

첫째, 여러분 자신에게 과제를 연구하고 작업할 충분한 시간을 주십시오. 과제를 미루는 학생들은 기한까지 끝마치는 것에 어려움을 겪을 겁니다. [47]서두르면, 이러한 학습자들이 다른 문헌의 일부를 베끼거나 출처를 제대로 기재하는 것을 잊어버리는 것은 놀라운 일이 아닙니다. 따라서, 프로젝트의 개요를 짤 때 조사 계획을 세우기 위해 이용 가능한 시간을 충분히 활용하고 꼼꼼히 메모하는 것이 중요합니다. 체계화된 상태를 유지하는 것은 지나치게 서둘러 일하는 것에서 야기되는 표절을 방지할 것입니다.

둘째, 해당 주제에 대해 학습하기 위해 많은 자료를 수집하십시오. 디지털이든 물리적이든, 많은 다양한 자료를 읽는 것은 여러분께 주제에 대한 포괄적인 이해를 제공할 것입니다. 다양한 관점들을 고려함으로써, 여러분은 그 주제에 대해 여러분 자신의 생각을 발전시킬 더 좋은 위치에 있게 될 것입니다. 반대로, 여러분 과제의 근거로 한두 개의 자료만 사용하는 것은 표절의 가능성을 증가시키는데, 이는 여러분이 아이디어를 베낄 확률이 높아지기 때문입니다. [48]만약 여러분이 자료를 찾는 데 어려움을 겪고 있다면, 교수님께 여쭤보거나 도서관에 방문하십시오. 우리 교내 사서분들은 여러분이 필요로 하는 책이나 온라인 저널로 여러분을 안내하는 것을 더할 나위 없이 기뻐할 것입니다.

셋째, 여러분의 저작물의 출처를 표시하고 참고 문헌 목록을 작성하는 것을 잊지 마십시오. 여러분이 독창적으로 창조해 내지 않은 연구 결과나, 개념, 혹은 생각은 반드시 보고서의 각주에 언급되어야 합니다. 만약 여러분이 다른 저자의 저작물을 그대로 옮겨 사용한다면, 그 구절이나 문장에 따옴표를 붙이십시오. 일부 학생들이 출처를 잘못 표시하여 뜻하지 않은 표절을 저지른 적이 있습니다. 이것을 방지하기 위해, 여러분의 과제에 요구되는 양식 지침서를 따르십시오. [49]이 정보는 학교의 온라인 문헌 도서관이나 여러분의 수업 요강에서 찾으실 수 있습니다.

넷째, 적절히 패러프레이즈하십시오. 패러프레이징은 단순히 원문의 단어 몇 개를 바꾸는 것을 의미하는 것이 아닙니다. 훌륭한 패러프레이징은 여러분이 저자의 생각을 이해하고 그것을 여러분 자신만의 말로 다시 표현하고 있다는 것을 보여 줍니다. 하지만 여러분 자신만의 말로 표현될지라도, 그 내용은 여전히 여러분의 것이 아닙니다. 따라서, 여러분의 과제에서 패러프레이징된 모든 부분들 역시 참조 표시가 달려야 합니다. 또한, 패러프레이징은 유용한 기술이지만, [50]그것을 남용하지 않도록 주의하십시오. 과목에 대한 여러분의 이해도를 평가할 때, 교수님들은 다른 저자의 생각에는 거의 관심이 없을 겁니다.

마지막으로, 여러분의 저작물에 대한 표절 검사를 실시하십시오. 가장 꼼꼼한 학생들조차도 실수를 하기 때문에, 객관적인 기계 기반의 프로그램이 표절에

어휘 | dean[diːn] 학장 plagiarism[pléidʒərìzəm] 표절 credit[krédit] 밝히다 source[sɔːrs] (자료의) 출처 unintentional[ʌ̀ninténʃənəl] 의도하지 않은 put off 미루다 viewpoint[vjúːpɔ̀int] 관점 basis[béisis] 근거 bibliography[bìbliáːɡrəfi] 참고 문헌 목록 originally[ərídʒənəli] 독창적으로 endnote[éndnout] 각주 quote[kwout] 따옴표, 인용문 accidental[æ̀ksədéntl] 뜻하지 않은 paraphrase[pǽrəfrèiz] 패러프레이즈하다(다른 말로 바꾸어 표현하다) overuse[òuvərjúːz] 남용하다 evaluate[ivǽljueit] 평가하다 objective[əbdʒéktiv] 객관적인 severity[səvérəti] 심각성 offense[əféns] 위법 행위 probation[proubéiʃən] 근신 expel[ikspél] 퇴학시키다

---

46 주제/목적   담화의 주제   난이도 ●○○

What topic is the speaker mainly discussing?	화자가 주로 논의하고 있는 주제는 무엇인가?
(a) how to avoid using another person's work (b) personal opinions about plagiarism (c) how to get an author's permission (d) different types of plagiarism in college	**(a) 다른 사람의 저작물을 사용하는 것을 피하는 방법** (b) 표절에 대한 개인적인 의견 (c) 저자의 허가를 얻는 방법 (d) 대학 내 다양한 종류의 표절

⟲ 지텔프 치트키

담화의 주제를 언급하는 초반을 주의 깊게 듣고 전체 맥락을 파악한다.

해설 | 화자가 'I'm here to provide a couple of tips to help you avoid unintentional plagiarism'이라며 의도하지 않은 표절을 피하는 데 도움이 되는 몇 가지 조언을 제공하려고 왔다고 한 뒤, 담화 전반에 걸쳐 다른 사람의 저작물을 사용하는 것을 피하는 방법에 관한 내용이 이어지고 있다. 따라서 (a)가 정답이다.

Paraphrasing

avoid ~ plagiarism 표절을 피하다 → avoid using another person's work 다른 사람의 저작물을 사용하는 것을 피하다

---

47 특정세부사항   What   난이도 ●●○

According to the talk, what is the problem with hurrying an assignment?	담화에 따르면, 과제를 서두르는 것에 대한 문제는 무엇인가?

(a) It makes it easier to forget important information.
(b) It leads to poorly cited papers.
(c) It diminishes the writing quality.
(d) It causes more grammar mistakes.

(a) 중요한 정보를 더 잊기 쉽게 만든다.
(b) 출처가 어설프게 밝혀진 보고서를 초래한다.
(c) 글의 질을 떨어뜨린다.
(d) 더 많은 문법 오류를 야기한다.

⊷◯ 지텔프 치트키

질문의 키워드 hurrying이 rush로 paraphrasing되어 언급된 주변 내용을 주의 깊게 듣는다.

해설 | 화자가 'In a rush, it's not surprising that these learners ~ forget to properly list their sources.'라며 서두르면 이러한(과제를 미루는) 학습자들이 출처를 제대로 기재하는 것을 잊어버리는 것은 놀라운 일이 아니라고 했다. 따라서 (b)가 정답이다.

Paraphrasing
forget to properly list their sources 출처를 제대로 기재하는 것을 잊어버린다 → poorly cited papers 출처가 어설프게 밝혀진 보고서

어휘 | diminish[dəmíniʃ] 떨어뜨리다

---

48 특정세부사항   When   난이도 ●●◯

When should students approach a campus librarian?

(a) when they find it hard to meet their professors
(b) when they fail to understand a topic
(c) when they need additional views
(d) when they have difficulty locating resources

학생들은 언제 교내 사서에게 접근해야 하는가?

(a) 그들의 교수들을 만나는 것이 어렵다고 느낄 때
(b) 주제를 이해하지 못할 때
(c) 추가적인 관점들이 필요할 때
(d) 자료를 찾아내는 데 어려움이 있을 때

⊷◯ 지텔프 치트키

질문의 키워드 librarian이 librarians로 언급된 주변 내용을 주의 깊게 듣는다.

해설 | 화자가 'If you are struggling to find sources, ~ visit the library.'라며 만약 자료를 찾는 데 어려움을 겪고 있다면 도서관에 방문하라고 한 뒤, 'Our campus librarians will ~ direct you to the books or online journals you need.'라며 교내 사서들은 학생들이 필요로 하는 책이나 온라인 저널로 그들을 안내할 것이라고 했다. 따라서 (d)가 정답이다.

Paraphrasing
struggling to find sources 자료를 찾는 데 어려움을 겪고 있는 → have difficulty locating resources 자료를 찾아내는 데 어려움이 있다

어휘 | locate[lóukeit] 찾아내다

---

49 특정세부사항   How   난이도 ●●◯

How can students find the relevant style guide for their assignment?

(a) by referring to the endnotes in the syllabus
(b) by searching the university's online library
(c) by contacting other students in their class
(d) by copying the quotes from the source material

학생들은 그들의 과제와 관련된 양식 지침서를 어떻게 찾을 수 있는가?

(a) 강의 요강에 있는 각주를 참고함으로써
(b) 대학교의 온라인 도서관을 살펴봄으로써
(c) 그들 학급의 다른 학생들에게 연락함으로써
(d) 원본 자료의 인용문들을 베낌으로써

해설 | 화자가 'This information can be found in the school's online reference library or on your class syllabus.'라며 과제에 요구되는 양식 지침서의 정보는 학교의 온라인 문헌 도서관이나 수업 요강에서 찾을 수 있다고 했다. 따라서 (b)가 정답이다.

Paraphrasing

the relevant style guide for their assignment 과제와 관련된 양식 지침서 → the style guide required for your assignment 과제에 요구되는 양식 지침서
the school's online ~ library 학교의 온라인 도서관 → the university's online library 대학교의 온라인 도서관

어휘 | relevant[réləvənt] 관련된, 적합한

---

50 특정세부사항   Why   난이도 ●●●

According to the speaker, why should paraphrasing not be used too frequently?	화자에 따르면, 왜 패러프레이징이 너무 자주 사용되어서는 안 되는가?
(a) because professors are unconcerned with an outsider's ideas	**(a) 교수들이 제삼자의 생각에 관심이 없기 때문에**
(b) because professors cannot evaluate works in a detached way	(b) 교수들이 저작물들을 공정한 방식으로 평가할 수 없기 때문에
(c) because it cannot convey complete comprehension	(c) 그것이 완전한 이해를 전달할 수 없기 때문에
(d) because it degrades the quality of a work	(d) 그것이 저작물의 질을 저하시키기 때문에

해설 | 화자가 'be careful not to overuse it'이라며 패러프레이징을 남용하지 않도록 주의하라고 한 뒤, 'When evaluating your understanding ~, professors will have little interest in the thoughts of another author.'라며 과목에 대한 학생들의 이해도를 평가할 때 교수들은 다른 저자의 생각에는 거의 관심이 없을 것이라고 했다. 따라서 (a)가 정답이다.

Paraphrasing

have little interest in the thoughts of another author 다른 저자의 생각에 거의 관심이 없다 → unconcerned with an outsider's ideas 제삼자의 생각에 관심이 없는

어휘 | unconcerned[ʌ̀nkənsə́ːrnd] 관심이 없는 outsider[autsáidər] 제삼자, 외부인 detached[ditǽtʃt] 공정한 convey[kənvéi] 전달하다 degrade[digréid] 저하시키다

---

51 특정세부사항   What   난이도 ●●○

What does the speaker suggest doing to ensure that student work is free of an error?	화자는 학생들의 저작물에 오류가 없다는 것을 확실히 하기 위해 무엇을 할 것을 제안하는가?
(a) use the best plagiarism checker available online	(a) 온라인상에서 이용 가능한 최고의 표절 검사 프로그램을 사용한다
(b) have an objective person thoroughly examine their work	(b) 객관적인 사람에게 그들의 저작물을 꼼꼼히 검사하게 한다

(c) **employ more than one Internet-based checking program**

(d) review the citations before submitting the work

(c) 한 개 이상의 인터넷 기반 검사 프로그램을 사용한다

(d) 저작물을 제출하기 전에 인용문들을 검토한다

🔑 지텔프 치트키

질문의 키워드 free of an error가 free of ~ errors로 언급된 주변 내용을 주의 깊게 듣는다.

해설 | 화자가 'I personally recommend running your work through multiple checkers'라며 여러 검사 프로그램에 저작물을 돌려 보는 것을 추천한다고 한 뒤, 'This can ensure that ~ your work is free of citation errors.'라며 이것은 저작물에 인용 오류가 없다는 것을 확실히 할 수 있다고 했다. 따라서 (c)가 정답이다.

Paraphrasing

multiple checkers 여러 검사 프로그램 → more than one ~ checking program 한 개 이상의 검사 프로그램

---

52 추론 　특정사실　　　　　　　　　　　　　　　　　　　　　　　　난이도 ●●○

Why would students most likely make email contact with the speaker?

(a) to share their experiences with academic probation
(b) to ask about the consequences of plagiarism
(c) to receive notifications for future talks
(d) **to obtain an overview of the discussion**

왜 학생들이 화자와 이메일로 연락을 할 것 같은가?

(a) 그들의 학사 경고 경험을 공유하기 위해서
(b) 표절의 대가에 관해 묻기 위해서
(c) 향후 담화에 대한 알림을 받기 위해서
(d) **논의의 개요를 얻기 위해서**

🔑 지텔프 치트키

질문의 키워드 email이 그대로 언급된 주변 내용을 주의 깊게 듣는다.

해설 | 화자가 'I will be sending out a summary of what we discussed today.'라며 오늘 논의한 내용의 요약본을 보내 줄 것이라고 한 뒤, 'If you're interested, please ~ leave your ~ email address.'라며 관심이 있다면 이메일 주소를 남겨 달라고 한 것을 통해, 학생들이 논의의 개요를 얻기 위해서 화자와 이메일로 연락을 할 것임을 추론할 수 있다. 따라서 (d)가 정답이다.

Paraphrasing

a summary of what we discussed 논의한 내용의 요약본 → an overview of the discussion 논의의 개요

어휘 | academic probation 학사 경고　consequence[ká:nsəkwəns] 대가, 결과　notification[nòutifikéiʃən] 알림　overview[óuvərvjuː] 개요

READING & VOCABULARY

ARTHUR READ

Arthur Read is the main character of the educational animated children's television series *Arthur*. It is based on the book series by Marc Brown, an American writer and illustrator. The series lasted for 25 seasons, making it the second longest-running animated series ever in the United States. [53]It deals primarily with real-life issues that affect children and families. Arthur Read is listed as number 26 in *TV Guide*'s 50 greatest cartoon characters of all time.

Arthur is a light brown aardvark with small ears and brown glasses. He [58]is most commonly <u>portrayed</u> as [54(b)]wearing a yellow sweater over a white collared shirt, blue jeans, and red and white sneakers. [54(a)]Arthur lives in Elwood City with his parents David and Jane, two younger sisters—a four-year-old nicknamed D.W. and an infant named Kate—and his dog Pal. He is a third-grade student in Mr. Ratburn's class at Lakewood Elementary School. In his free time, [54(d)]Arthur loves to read and [54(c)]hang out with his classmates, including his best friend Buster Baxter.

Arthur cares a lot about what his peers think of him. Like the celebrities he admires, he wants to be popular. In [59]a conscious <u>effort</u> to gain favor with his fellow schoolmates, he sometimes laughs enthusiastically at their jokes, even when he doesn't understand them. His yearning for popularity stems from the fact that he was often teased when he was younger. For example, [55]before getting glasses, he was made fun of by other students while playing basketball because he couldn't catch the ball.

While generally mild-mannered, Arthur lets his frustrations show from time to time. [56]His annoyance is usually caused by his sister D.W., who has a habit of waking him up, interrupting his homework, and fighting with him over the television remote control. Despite this, Arthur for the most part tries his best to ignore D.W.'s irritating behavior and even begrudgingly does nice things for her at the request of his parents.

아서 리드

아서 리드는 교육용 만화 영화로 된 어린이 텔레비전 시리즈인 「아서」의 주인공이다. 그것은 미국인 작가이자 삽화가인 마크 브라운이 쓴 책 시리즈에 바탕을 두고 있다. 그 시리즈는 25번의 시즌 동안 계속되었고, 그것을 지금까지 미국에서 두 번째로 오래 방영된 만화 영화 시리즈로 만들었다. [53]그것은 아이들과 가족들에게 영향을 미치는 실생활의 문제들을 주로 다룬다. 아서 리드는 「TV Guide」의 역대 최고의 만화 캐릭터 50위 중 26위에 올랐다.

아서는 귀가 작고 갈색 안경을 쓴 옅은 갈색의 땅돼지이다. 그는 [54(b)]흰색 깃의 셔츠 위에 노란색 스웨터를 입고, 청바지를 입으며, 빨간색과 흰색으로 된 운동화를 신은 모습으로 [58]가장 흔히 묘사된다. [54(a)]아서는 그의 부모님인 데이비드와 제인, 두 명의 여동생—D.W.라는 별명을 가진 네 살짜리 아이와 케이트라는 이름의 아기—그리고 그의 강아지 팔과 함께 엘우드 시티에 산다. 그는 레이크우드 초등학교에서 래트번 선생님 반의 3학년 학생이다. 자유 시간에, [54(d)]아서는 책을 읽는 것과 [54(c)]그의 가장 친한 친구인 버스터 백스터를 포함한 그의 반 친구들과 노는 것을 좋아한다.

아서는 그의 친구들이 그를 어떻게 생각하는지에 대해 매우 신경 쓴다. 그가 동경하는 연예인들처럼, 그는 인기 있고 싶어 한다. 그의 같은 학교 친구들의 [59]환심을 사기 위한 의식적인 <u>노력</u>으로, 그는 그들을 이해하지 못할 때조차도, 때때로 그들의 농담에 열성적으로 웃는다. 그의 인기에 대한 갈망은 그가 더 어렸을 때 자주 놀림을 당했다는 사실에서 비롯된다. 예를 들어, [55]안경을 맞추기 전에, 그는 공을 잡지 못해서 농구를 하는 동안 다른 학생들에게 놀림을 받았다.

대체로 온순하지만, 아서는 이따금 그의 불만을 내색하기도 한다. [56]그의 짜증은 보통 그의 여동생 D.W.에 의해 야기되는데, 그녀는 그를 잠에서 깨우고, 그의 숙제를 방해하며, 텔레비전 리모컨을 두고 그와 싸우는 경향이 있다. 이것에도 불구하고, 아서는 대개 D.W.의 거슬리는 행동을 무시하려고 최선을 다하며 심지어 그의 부모님의 요청에 따라 마지못해 그녀를 위해 좋은 일들을 한다.

| 근황 | Arthur grows up to become an author. [57]His childhood experiences and adventures with his friends and family in Elwood City help spawn a graphic novel, which earns him success as a professional writer. While the TV original series ended in 2022, fans of the show will be able to enjoy new content, as more episodes are expected to be released on an educational video platform. | 아서는 자라서 작가가 된다. [57]엘우드 시티에서 그의 친구들 및 가족과의 어린 시절 경험과 모험은 만화 소설을 만드는 데 도움을 주며, 이는 그가 전문 작가로서 성공을 거두게 한다. TV 원작 시리즈는 2022년에 끝났지만, 그 프로그램의 팬들은 새로운 콘텐츠를 즐길 수 있을 것인데, 이는 교육용 영상 플랫폼에 더 많은 에피소드들이 공개될 것으로 예상되기 때문이다. |

어휘 | animated adj. 만화 영화로 된 illustrator n. 삽화가 deal with phr. ~을 다루다 primarily adv. 주로 aardvark n. 땅돼지 peer n. 친구, 또래 admire v. 동경하다 conscious adj. 의식적인 favor n. 환심, 호감 fellow n. 친구, 동료 enthusiastically adv. 열성적으로 yearning n. 갈망 stem v. 비롯되다, 기인하다 tease v. 놀리다 mild-mannered adj. 온순한 frustration n. 불만, 좌절감 from time to time phr. 이따금, 때때로 annoyance n. 짜증 for the most part phr. 대개, 보통 begrudgingly adv. 마지못해 spawn v. 만들다, 낳다 graphic novel phr. 만화 소설

---

53 특정세부사항 What
난이도 ●○○

What is the subject of the TV show *Arthur*?

(a) problems that have an effect on real families
(b) the life of an American author
(c) techniques that are used for illustrations
(d) the education of young children

TV 프로그램 「아서」의 주제는 무엇인가?

(a) 실제 가족들에게 영향을 미치는 문제들
(b) 미국인 작가의 일생
(c) 삽화에 사용되는 기술들
(d) 어린아이들의 교육

◆─○ 지텔프 치트키

질문의 키워드 TV show *Arthur*가 television series *Arthur*로 paraphrasing되어 언급된 주변 내용을 주의 깊게 읽는다.

해설 | 1단락의 'It deals primarily with real-life issues that affect children and families.'에서 「아서」는 아이들과 가족들에게 영향을 미치는 실생활의 문제들을 주로 다룬다고 했다. 따라서 (a)가 정답이다.

Paraphrasing
real-life issues that affect ~ families 가족들에게 영향을 미치는 실생활의 문제들 → problems that have an effect on real families 실제 가족들에게 영향을 미치는 문제들

---

54 Not/True Not 문제
난이도 ●●○

Which of the following is NOT true about Arthur's life?

(a) He is the youngest child in his family.
(b) He dresses mostly in a layered outfit.
(c) He is in the same class as his best friend.
(d) He has a passion for books.

다음 중 아서의 삶에 관해 사실이 아닌 것은 무엇인가?

(a) 그의 가족 중에서 막내이다.
(b) 주로 겹쳐 입는 옷을 입는다.
(c) 그의 가장 친한 친구와 같은 반이다.
(d) 책에 대한 열정을 가지고 있다.

◆─○ 지텔프 치트키

질문의 키워드 Arthur's life와 관련된 주변 내용을 주의 깊게 읽고, 보기의 키워드와 지문 내용을 대조하며 언급되는 것을 하나씩 소거한다.

해설 | (a)는 2단락의 'Arthur lives ~ with ~, two younger sisters ~ and his dog Pal.'에서 아서는 두 명의 여동생과 함께 산다고 언급되

었으므로, 아서가 그의 가족 중에서 막내라는 것은 지문의 내용과 일치하지 않는다. 따라서 (a)가 정답이다.

> **오답분석**
>
> (b) 보기의 키워드 a layered outfit이 wearing ~ over로 paraphrasing되어 언급된 2단락에서 아서가 흰색 깃의 셔츠 위에 노란색 스웨터를 입는다고 언급되었다.
>
> (c) 보기의 키워드 best friend가 그대로 언급된 2단락에서 아서의 가장 친한 친구가 그의 반 친구들에 포함된다고 언급되었다.
>
> (d) 보기의 키워드 a passion for books가 loves to read로 paraphrasing되어 언급된 2단락에서 아서가 책을 읽는 것을 좋아한다고 언급되었다.

어휘 | outfit n. 옷, 복장 passion n. 열정

---

55 추론 특정사실 난이도 ●●○

Why most likely was Arthur bad at playing basketball?	왜 아서는 농구를 잘하지 못했던 것 같은가?
(a) because he had no friends to practice with	(a) 함께 연습할 친구가 없었기 때문에
(b) because he was not interested in sports	(b) 스포츠에 관심이 없었기 때문에
(c) because he had terrible eyesight	**(c) 시력이 좋지 않았기 때문에**
(d) because he was shorter than other players	(d) 다른 선수들보다 키가 작았기 때문에

> **━○ 지텔프 치트키**
>
> 질문의 키워드 playing basketball이 그대로 언급된 주변 내용을 주의 깊게 읽는다.

해설 | 3단락의 'before getting glasses, he was made fun of by other students while playing basketball because he couldn't catch the ball'에서 안경을 맞추기 전에 아서는 공을 잡지 못해서 농구를 하는 동안 다른 학생들에게 놀림을 받았다고 한 것을 통해, 아서가 시력이 좋지 않았기 때문에 농구를 잘하지 못했던 것임을 추론할 수 있다. 따라서 (c)가 정답이다.

어휘 | eyesight n. 시력

---

56 특정세부사항 What 난이도 ●●○

What does D.W. do that bothers Arthur?	D.W.는 무엇을 해서 아서를 짜증 나게 하는가?
(a) She wishes to control him.	(a) 그를 통제하기를 원한다.
(b) She disturbs his study time.	**(b) 그의 공부 시간을 방해한다.**
(c) She watches TV too loudly.	(c) TV를 너무 큰 소리로 본다.
(d) She wakes up late at times.	(d) 가끔 늦게 일어난다.

> **━○ 지텔프 치트키**
>
> 질문의 키워드 bothers가 annoyance로 paraphrasing되어 언급된 주변 내용을 주의 깊게 읽는다.

해설 | 4단락의 'His annoyance is usually caused by his sister D.W., who has a habit of ~ interrupting his homework, and fighting with him over the television remote control.'에서 아서의 짜증은 보통 그의 여동생 D.W.에 의해 야기되는데, 그녀는 그의 숙제를 방해하는 등의 경향이 있다고 했다. 따라서 (b)가 정답이다.

> **Paraphrasing**
>
> interrupting his homework 숙제를 방해하는 → disturbs his study time 공부 시간을 방해한다

어휘 | bother v. 짜증 나게 하다, 괴롭히다 disturb v. 방해하다

How did Arthur achieve success as an author?

(a) by writing about his younger days
(b) by turning his stories into educational videos
(c) by collaborating with a professional writer
(d) by describing adventures with new friends

아서는 작가로서 어떻게 성공을 거두었는가?

(a) 그의 어린 시절에 관해 글을 씀으로써
(b) 그의 이야기를 교육용 영상들로 만듦으로써
(c) 전문 작가와 공동으로 작업함으로써
(d) 새로운 친구들과의 모험을 서술함으로써

──○ 지텔프 치트키

질문의 키워드 achieve success가 earns ~ success로 paraphrasing되어 언급된 주변 내용을 주의 깊게 읽는다.

해설 | 5단락의 'His childhood experiences and adventures ~ help spawn a graphic novel, which earns him success as a professional writer.'에서 아서의 어린 시절 경험과 모험이 만화 소설을 만드는 데 도움을 주며, 이는 그가 전문 작가로서 성공을 거두게 한다고 했다. 따라서 (a)가 정답이다.

Paraphrasing
an author 작가 → a ~ writer 작가
His childhood 어린 시절 → his younger days 어린 시절

오답분석
(d) 5단락에서 친구들과의 어린 시절 경험과 모험이 아서가 만화 소설을 만드는 데 도움을 준다고는 했지만, 새로운 친구들과의 모험이라고 한 것은 아니므로 오답이다.

어휘 | turn into phr. ~으로 만들다, ~이 되게 하다   collaborate v. 공동으로 작업하다

---

58 어휘   유의어   난이도 ●●○

In the context of the passage, portrayed means _____.

(a) imitated
(b) interpreted
(c) remembered
(d) rendered

지문의 문맥에서, 'portrayed'는 -을 의미한다.

(a) 모방되는
(b) 해석되는
(c) 기억되는
(d) 묘사되는

──○ 지텔프 치트키

밑줄 친 어휘의 유의어를 찾는 문제이므로, portrayed가 포함된 구절을 읽고 문맥을 파악한다.

해설 | 2단락의 'He is most commonly portrayed'는 아서 리드가 가장 흔히 묘사된다는 뜻이므로, portrayed가 '묘사되는'이라는 의미로 사용된 것을 알 수 있다. 따라서 '묘사되는'이라는 같은 의미의 (d) rendered가 정답이다.

오답분석
(b) '해석하다'라는 의미의 interpret는 무언가의 뜻이나 의미를 설명하거나 해석하는 경우에 사용하므로, 문맥에 어울리지 않아 오답이다.

해커스 지텔프 최신기출유형 실전문제집 7회 (Level 2)

59 어휘   유의어

In the context of the passage, <u>effort</u> means _____.

(a) desire
(b) trial
(c) contribution
(d) endeavor

지문의 문맥에서, 'effort'는 -을 의미한다.

(a) 욕망
(b) 시도
(c) 기여
(d) 노력

◁─○ 지텔프 치트키

밑줄 친 어휘의 유의어를 찾는 문제이므로, effort가 포함된 구절을 읽고 문맥을 파악한다.

해설 | 3단락의 'a conscious effort to gain favor'는 환심을 사기 위한 의식적인 노력이라는 뜻이므로, effort가 '노력'이라는 의미로 사용된 것을 알 수 있다. 따라서 '노력'이라는 같은 의미의 (d) endeavor가 정답이다.

PART 2[60~66]   잡지 기사   재정적 압박이 구매 만족도에 미치는 영향

연구 결과	**PEOPLE UNDER FINANCIAL STRESS REPORT LOWER PURCHASE HAPPINESS**

PEOPLE UNDER FINANCIAL STRESS REPORT LOWER PURCHASE HAPPINESS

연구 소개

A study published in the *Journal of Consumer Research* found that people's financial stress is related to "purchase happiness," which describes how satisfied a person is with a transaction.

연구 내용

Researchers from Duke University's Fuqua School of Business [65]completed over 40 separate studies that evaluated people's understanding of their financial well-being and recent purchases. [60]The results showed that people subject to financial constraints registered far lower levels of purchase happiness. This condition was evident regardless of whether a person bought an article of clothing, a piece of technology like a computer, or a vacation.

요인1: 물가 상승

In addition, [61]since the study measured how wealthy people believe themselves to be rather than their actual wealth, low purchase happiness was observed across different income levels. Perceptions of wealth were adversely impacted by growing price inflation throughout multiple economic sectors, including housing, energy, and consumer goods.

요인2: 기회 비용

The researchers also revealed that low purchase happiness was closely correlated with notions surrounding opportunity cost. [62]Opportunity cost represents the potential benefits that shoppers could

재정적 압박에 시달리는 사람들이 더 낮은 구매 만족도를 보고한다

「소비자 연구 저널」에 발표된 한 연구는 사람들의 재정적 압박이 '구매 만족도'와 관련이 있다는 것을 발견했는데, 이것은 사람이 얼마나 거래에 만족하는지를 설명한다.

듀크 대학의 후쿠아 경영 대학원의 연구원들은 재정적인 형편과 최근의 구매에 대한 사람들의 이해도를 평가하는 [65]40개 이상의 개별 연구를 완료했다. [60]그 결과는 재정적 제약을 겪기 쉬운 사람들이 훨씬 더 낮은 구매 만족도를 나타낸다는 것을 보여주었다. 이 조건은 사람이 의류 한 벌을 사든, 컴퓨터와 같은 기술 한 가지를 사든, 혹은 휴가를 사든 상관없이 명백했다.

게다가, [61]그 연구는 사람들의 실제 재산보다는 그들이 스스로를 얼마나 부유하게 생각하는지를 측정했기 때문에, 다양한 소득 수준에 걸쳐 낮은 구매 만족도가 관찰되었다. 부에 대한 인식은 주택, 에너지, 그리고 소비재를 포함한 여러 경제 부문에 걸친 물가 상승의 확대에 의해 부정적인 영향을 받았다.

연구원들은 또한 낮은 구매 만족도가 기회비용을 둘러싼 개념과 밀접하게 관련되어 있다는 것을 밝혔다. [62]기회비용은 만약 구매자들이 그들 돈의 다른 쓰임새를 발견했었다면 누릴 수 있었을 잠재적인 이득

have enjoyed if they had found other uses for their money. Due to financial pressure, people weighed opportunity costs more heavily, which caused them to harbor a greater sense of "buyer's remorse."

According to the study, feelings of dissatisfaction lead to a rise in negative customer reviews. The researchers examined online reviews for over 850 restaurants across the United States. Then, they took data collected from surveys and detected the zip codes in which residents experience financial stress. They found that restaurants in cities where people reported the highest financial stress tended to have a higher number of negative reviews. As [66]these reviews accumulate, [63]they pose risks for retailers who depend on positive reviews for sales, pushing them to find alternative approaches to receiving feedback.

Overall, the report strongly indicates that a perceived sense of low wealth, and not the actual level of prosperity, limits people's purchasing options and makes them less happy with their acquisitions. It supplements a growing body of research that is answering questions about the relationship between money and happiness. [64]Future research will examine other factors, such as product quality and customer service, that influence purchase satisfaction.

을 의미한다. 재정적인 압박 때문에, 사람들은 기회비용을 더 많이 따져 보았고, 이는 그들로 하여금 '구매자의 후회'의 감정을 더 많이 품게 했다.

그 연구에 따르면, 불만족의 감정은 부정적인 고객 후기의 증가로 이어진다. 연구원들은 미국 전역에 걸쳐 850개 이상의 식당에 대한 온라인 후기를 조사했다. 그런 다음, 그들은 설문 조사에서 수집된 데이터를 가져와 거주자들이 재정적 압박을 겪고 있는 곳의 우편 번호를 알아냈다. 그들은 사람들이 가장 높은 재정적 압박을 보고한 도시의 식당들이 더 많은 수의 부정적인 후기를 경험하는 경향이 있는 것을 발견했다. [66]이러한 후기들이 쌓이면, [63]그것들은 매출을 위해 긍정적인 후기에 의존하는 소매업자들에게 위험이 되고, 그들이 피드백을 받을 대안적인 방법들을 찾도록 압력을 가한다.

전반적으로, 그 연구 보고는, 실제 부의 수준이 아니라, 지각된 낮은 부에 대한 인식이 사람들의 구매 선택지를 제한하고 그들이 구입한 것에 대해 덜 만족하게 만든다는 것을 명확히 보여준다. 그것은 돈과 행복의 관계에 관한 질문에 해답을 찾는 중인 증가하는 일련의 연구들을 보완한다. [64]향후 연구는, 제품 품질과 고객 서비스와 같이, 구매 만족도에 영향을 미치는 다른 요소들을 조사할 것이다.

연구 결과의 영향

시사점 + 향후 연구 과제

해커스 지텔프 최신기출유형 실전문제집 7회 (Level 2)

어휘 | financial adj. 재정적인　stress n. 압박　transaction n. 거래　well-being n. 형편, 행복　subject adj. 겪기 쉬운　constraint n. 제약
register v. (감정을) 나타내다　evident adj. 명백한　measure v. 측정하다　perception n. 인식　inflation n. 상승　notion n. 개념
opportunity cost phr. 기회비용　pressure n. 압박　weigh v. 따져 보다　harbor v. (생각·감정을) 품다　remorse n. 후회
dissatisfaction n. 불만족　examine v. 조사하다　perceive v. 지각하다　prosperity n. 부, 번영　acquisition n. 구입한 것
supplement v. 보완하다

60　특정세부사항　When

난이도 ●●○

When are people less satisfied with their consumption?

(a) when the items are expensive
(b) when they have insufficient funds
(c) when companies sell inferior products
(d) when they buy unnecessary merchandise

사람들은 언제 그들의 소비에 덜 만족하는가?

(a) 물건들이 비쌀 때
(b) 불충분한 자금을 가지고 있을 때
(c) 회사가 품질이 나쁜 제품들을 팔 때
(d) 불필요한 상품을 살 때

━○ 지텔프 치트키

질문의 키워드 less satisfied가 lower levels of ~ happiness로 paraphrasing되어 언급된 주변 내용을 주의 깊게 읽는다.

해설 | 2단락의 'The results showed that people subject to financial constraints registered far lower levels of purchase happiness.'에서 연구의 결과는 재정적 제약을 겪기 쉬운 사람들이 훨씬 더 낮은 구매 만족도를 나타낸다는 것을 보여주었다고 했다. 따라서 (b)가 정답이다.

어휘 | consumption n. 소비 insufficient adj. 불충분한 inferior adj. 품질이 나쁜 merchandise n. 상품

---

61 추론 특정사실   난이도 ●●●

Why most likely were people across different income levels affected by the same condition?

(a) They compared themselves to wealthier individuals.
(b) They tracked their wealth using inaccurate indicators.
(c) They based their status on a subjective measure.
(d) They bought products that rose in price uniformly.

왜 다양한 소득 수준의 사람들이 동일한 상태에 의해 영향을 받았던 것 같은가?

(a) 그들 자신을 더 부유한 사람들과 비교했다.
(b) 부정확한 지표를 사용하여 그들의 재산을 조사했다.
(c) 그들 상태의 근거를 주관적인 척도에 두었다.
(d) 획일적으로 가격이 오른 제품들을 샀다.

지텔프 치트키

질문의 키워드 across different income levels가 그대로 언급된 주변 내용을 주의 깊게 읽는다.

해설 | 3단락의 'since the study measured how wealthy people believe themselves to be ~, low purchase happiness was observed across different income levels'에서 그 연구가 사람들이 스스로를 얼마나 부유하게 생각하는지를 측정했기 때문에 다양한 소득 수준에 걸쳐 낮은 구매 만족도가 관찰되었다고 한 것을 통해, 각기 다른 소득 수준의 사람들이 그들 상태의 근거를 주관적인 척도에 두었기 때문에 낮은 구매 만족도라는 동일한 상태에 의해 영향을 받았던 것임을 추론할 수 있다. 따라서 (c)가 정답이다.

어휘 | inaccurate adj. 부정확한 indicator n. 지표 subjective adj. 주관적인 measure n. 척도 uniformly adv. 획일적으로

---

62 추론 특정사실   난이도 ●●○

According to the article, when would consumers consider opportunity costs?

(a) when they think they must maintain loyalty to one shop
(b) when they feel pressured to conclude transactions
(c) when they buy products that cost more than their actual worth
(d) when they believe they could have made a better decision

기사에 따르면, 소비자들은 언제 기회비용을 고려할 것 같은가?

(a) 한 가게에 대한 충성심을 유지해야 한다고 생각할 때
(b) 거래를 종결해야 한다는 압박감을 느낄 때
(c) 실제 가치보다 더 비싼 제품을 살 때
(d) 더 나은 결정을 할 수 있었다고 생각할 때

지텔프 치트키

질문의 키워드 opportunity costs가 그대로 언급된 주변 내용을 주의 깊게 읽는다.

해설 | 4단락의 'Opportunity cost represents the potential benefits that shoppers could have enjoyed if they had found other uses for their money.'에서 기회비용은 만약 구매자들이 그들 돈의 다른 쓰임새를 발견했었다면 누릴 수 있었을 잠재적인 이득을 의미한다고 한 것을 통해, 소비자들은 그들이 더 나은 결정을 할 수 있었다고 생각할 때 기회비용을 고려할 것임을 추론할 수 있다. 따라서 (d)가 정답이다.

어휘 | loyalty n. 충성심 conclude v. 종결하다, 체결하다

What action will companies that value customer reviews take?

(a) invest resources to improve the guest experience
(b) adjust their methods to solicit customer comments
(c) list client remarks on a larger number of review sites
(d) relocate to more prosperous cities

고객 후기를 중시하는 기업들은 어떤 조치를 취할 것인가?

(a) 고객 경험을 개선하기 위해 자원을 투자한다
(b) 고객의 의견을 요청하는 그들의 방법을 조정한다
(c) 고객의 의견을 더 많은 수의 후기 사이트들에 올린다
(d) 더 번영한 도시로 이전한다

─○ 지텔프 치트키

질문의 키워드 value ~ reviews가 depend on ~ reviews로 paraphrasing되어 언급된 주변 내용을 주의 깊게 읽는다.

해설 | 5단락의 'they pose risks for retailers who depend on positive reviews for sales, pushing them to find alternative approaches to receiving feedback'에서 부정적인 후기들이 매출을 위해 긍정적인 후기에 의존하는 소매업자들에게 위험이 되고, 그들이 피드백을 받을 대안적인 방법들을 찾도록 압력을 가한다고 했다. 따라서 (b)가 정답이다.

Paraphrasing
find alternative approaches to receiving feedback 피드백을 받을 대안적인 방법들을 찾다 → adjust their methods to solicit customer comments 고객의 의견을 요청하는 방법을 조정한다

어휘 | solicit v. 요청하다, 구하려고 하다   remark n. 의견, 말   relocate v. 이전하다   prosperous adj. 번영한

What will upcoming analysis focus on?

(a) additional drivers of consumer happiness
(b) changing attitudes toward personal finances
(c) the correlation of money with life satisfaction
(d) the contribution of customer service to sales

향후 분석은 무엇에 초점을 맞출 것인가?

(a) 소비자 만족의 추가적인 원인들
(b) 개인의 재정 상태에 대한 변화하는 태도
(c) 돈과 삶의 만족도 간의 상관관계
(d) 매출에 대한 고객 서비스의 기여도

─○ 지텔프 치트키

질문의 키워드 upcoming analysis가 Future research로 paraphrasing되어 언급된 주변 내용을 주의 깊게 읽는다.

해설 | 6단락의 'Future research will examine other factors, ~, that influence purchase satisfaction.'에서 향후 연구는 구매 만족도에 영향을 미치는 다른 요소들을 조사할 것이라고 했다. 따라서 (a)가 정답이다.

Paraphrasing
other factors, ~, that influence purchase satisfaction 구매 만족도에 영향을 미치는 다른 요소들 → additional drivers of consumer happiness 소비자 만족의 추가적인 원인들

어휘 | driver n. 원인, 동인

In the context of the passage, underline{completed} means _____.

(a) prepared

지문의 문맥에서, 'completed'는 -을 의미한다.

(a) 준비했다

(b) submitted

(c) finished

(d) monitored

(b) 제출했다

(c) 완료했다

(d) 관찰했다

━○ 지텔프 치트키

밑줄 친 어휘의 유의어를 찾는 문제이므로, completed가 포함된 구절을 읽고 문맥을 파악한다.

해설 | 2단락의 'completed over 40 separate studies'는 40개 이상의 개별 연구를 완료했다는 뜻이므로, completed가 '완료했다'라는 의미로 사용된 것을 알 수 있다. 따라서 '완료했다'라는 같은 의미의 (c) finished가 정답이다.

---

66 어휘   유의어   난이도 ●●●

In the context of the passage, <u>accumulate</u> means _____.

(a) gather

(b) unite

(c) extend

(d) develop

지문의 문맥에서, 'accumulate'는 -을 의미한다.

(a) 쌓인다

(b) 결합한다

(c) 연장한다

(d) 개발한다

━○ 지텔프 치트키

밑줄 친 어휘의 유의어를 찾는 문제이므로, accumulate가 포함된 구절을 읽고 문맥을 파악한다.

해설 | 5단락의 'these reviews accumulate'는 이러한 후기들이 쌓인다는 뜻이므로, accumulate가 '쌓인다'라는 의미로 사용된 것을 알 수 있다. 따라서 '쌓인다'라는 같은 의미의 (a) gather가 정답이다.

PART 3 (67~73)   지식 백과   쇠똥구리의 특징과 역할

표제어	**DUNG BEETLE**
	쇠똥구리

정의	Dung beetles are insects that utilize the feces of animals for food and reproduction. They live in deserts, grasslands, and forests, and can be found almost everywhere on earth.	쇠똥구리는 식량과 번식을 위해 동물의 배설물을 이용하는 곤충이다. 그것들은 사막, 초원, 그리고 숲에서 서식하며, 지구상의 거의 모든 곳에서 발견될 수 있다.
공통 특징	All dung beetles share a number of physical characteristics. Both males and females have large, horn-like structures on their heads or upper bodies as well as powerful front legs. [67]The males use these to fight each other for mates, whereas the females employ them to keep others away from their dung. Dung beetles also have long flight wings that are protected by hardened outer wings called *elytra*. These increase lift and allow them to [72]travel great distances when they detect manure with their antennae.	모든 쇠똥구리는 많은 신체적 특징들을 공유한다. 수컷과 암컷 둘 다 강력한 앞다리뿐만 아니라 머리 또는 상체에 크고, 뿔처럼 생긴 구조물도 가지고 있다. [67]수컷은 짝을 얻기 위해 서로 싸울 때 이것들을 사용하는 반면에, 암컷은 다른 동물들이 그것들의 똥으로부터 멀리 떨어지게 하기 위해 그것들(앞다리와 뿔처럼 생긴 구조물)을 사용한다. 쇠똥구리는 또한 '엘리트라'라는 이름의 단단한 겉날개에 의해 보호되는 긴 비행 날개를 가지고 있다. 이것들은 떠오르는 힘을 증가시키고 그것들이 더듬이로 거름을 탐지할 때 [72]먼 거리를 <u>이동할</u> 수 있게 한다.

분류
+
집단별
특징

[68]Depending on what dung beetles do with animal feces, they are classified into three groups: dwellers, tunnelers, and rollers. Dwellers lay their eggs on top of manure, with their larvae hatching and feeding there, while tunnelers burrow into the ground, taking pieces of the nearby excrement into the tunnels as needed. Rollers shape dung into a ball and push it to another location, where they use it as a food source and a place to breed. Rollers are known to use the band of light produced by clusters of stars as they transfer their perfectly round balls. [69]By aligning themselves with it, they can proceed in a straight line and avoid getting lost.

환경적
역할

Dung beetles [73]play a vital role in the environment. They improve soil quality by digging tunnels and burying feces. [70]They also inadvertently aid in the dispersal of seeds present in dung as they roam around. In agriculture, dung beetles are used by farmers to dispose of large amounts of livestock manure. Because these droppings are breeding grounds for pests, the beetles reduce pest populations that would otherwise harm farm animals.

연구
가치

Finally, dung beetles are regarded as organisms [71]whose status in an environment is examined to determine the overall health of an ecosystem. They are widely used in ecological research monitoring the year-to-year changes to plant and animal life within nature.

[68]쇠똥구리가 동물의 배설물로 무엇을 하는지에 따라, 그것들은 세 집단으로 분류되는데, 이는 거주하는 쇠똥구리, 굴을 파는 쇠똥구리, 그리고 똥을 굴리는 쇠똥구리이다. 거주하는 쇠똥구리는 거름 위에 알을 낳고, 그곳에서 그것들의 유충이 부화하고 먹이를 먹는 반면에, 굴을 파는 쇠똥구리는 땅속으로 파고들며, 필요에 따라 근처의 배설물 덩어리들을 굴로 가져간다. 똥을 굴리는 쇠똥구리는 똥을 공 모양으로 만들고 그것을 다른 장소로 밀고 나가는데, 그곳에서 그것들은 식량원과 번식 장소로 그것(똥)을 사용한다. 똥을 굴리는 쇠똥구리는 완벽하게 둥근 자신들의 공을 옮길 때 성단에 의해 생성된 빛의 띠를 이용하는 것으로 알려져 있다. [69]이것에 그것들 자신을 일직선으로 맞춤으로써, 그것들(똥을 굴리는 쇠똥구리)은 똑바로 나아가고 길을 잃는 것을 피할 수 있다.

쇠똥구리는 환경에서 [73]필수적인 역할을 한다. 그것들은 굴을 파고 배설물을 묻음으로써 토양의 질을 향상시킨다. [70]그것들은 또한 이리저리 돌아다니면서 뜻하지 않게 똥에 있는 씨앗의 분산을 돕는다. 농업에서, 쇠똥구리는 많은 양의 가축 배설물을 처리하기 위해 농부들에 의해 사용된다. 이 배설물들은 해충의 번식지이기 때문에, 쇠똥구리는 반대 상황이라면 가축들을 해칠 수도 있는 해충의 개체 수를 줄인다.

마지막으로, 쇠똥구리는 [71]생태계의 전반적인 건강성을 알아내기 위해 환경에서의 그것들의 상태가 조사되는 유기체로 여겨진다. 그것들은 자연 속 식물과 동물의 연도별 변화들을 관찰하는 생태학 연구에 널리 사용된다.

어휘 | dung n. 똥, 배설물 feces n. 배설물 reproduction n. 번식 mate n. 짝 hardened adj. 단단한 lift n. 떠오르는 힘; v. 들어 올리다 manure n. 거름, 배설물 classify v. 분류하다 lay v. 낳다 larvae n. 유충 hatch v. 부화하다 burrow v. 파고들다 excrement n. 배설물 breed v. 번식하다 transfer v. 옮기다 align v. 일직선으로 맞추다 proceed v. 나아가다 bury v. 묻다 inadvertently adv. 뜻하지 않게, 우연히 aid v. 돕다 dispersal n. 분산 roam v. 돌아다니다 dispose v. 처리하다 livestock n. 가축 dropping n. 배설물 pest n. 해충 population n. 개체 수 organism n. 유기체 ecological adj. 생태학의

---

67 **특정세부사항**   What   난이도 ●○○

What do male dung beetles use their horns for?

(a) to protect their dung balls
(b) to challenge others for partners
(c) to dig long tunnels for mates
(d) to detect fresh manure sources

수컷 쇠똥구리는 그것들의 뿔을 무엇을 위해 사용하는가?

(a) 그것들의 똥으로 된 공을 보호하기 위해서
(b) 짝을 얻기 위해 다른 쇠똥구리들과 겨루기 위해서
(c) 짝을 얻기 위해 긴 굴을 파기 위해서
(d) 신선한 거름의 공급원을 탐지하기 위해서

─○ 지텔프 치트키

질문의 키워드 male이 males로 언급된 주변 내용을 주의 깊게 읽는다.

해설 | 2단락의 'The males use these to fight each other for mates'에서 수컷은 짝을 얻기 위해 서로 싸울 때 앞다리와 뿔처럼 생긴 ㅡ
물을 사용한다고 했다. 따라서 (b)가 정답이다.

Paraphrasing

fight each other for mates 짝을 얻기 위해 서로 싸우다 → challenge others for partners 짝을 얻기 위해 다른 쇠똥구리들과 겨루다

오답분석

(d) 2단락에서 쇠똥구리는 더듬이로 거름을 탐지한다고 했으므로 오답이다.

---

68 특정세부사항   Which

난이도 ●●○

Which of the following distinguishes the different types of dung beetles?

(a) their methods of obtaining dung
(b) their use of the dung they find
(c) their means of transporting dung
(d) their disposal of the dung they find

다음 중 쇠똥구리의 각기 다른 종류를 구별짓는 것은 무엇인가?

(a) 그것들의 배설물을 획득하는 방법들
(b) 그것들이 발견한 배설물의 사용법
(c) 그것들의 배설물을 옮기는 수단
(d) 그것들이 발견한 배설물의 처분

─○ 지텔프 치트키

질문의 키워드 distinguishes가 classified로 paraphrasing되어 언급된 주변 내용을 주의 깊게 읽는다.

해설 | 3단락의 'Depending on what dung beetles do with animal feces, they are classified into three groups'에서 쇠똥구리가
동물의 배설물로 무엇을 하는지에 따라 세 집단으로 분류된다고 했다. 따라서 (b)가 정답이다.

Paraphrasing

what dung beetles do with animal feces 동물의 배설물로 무엇을 하는지 → their use of the dung 배설물의 사용법

어휘 | obtain v. 획득하다 disposal n. 처분, 처리

---

69 특정세부사항   How

난이도 ●●○

How do rollers navigate while moving a ball of dung?

(a) by using their antennae to detect smells
(b) by observing prominent landmarks
(c) by rolling feces into a perfect sphere
(d) by orienting themselves with starlight

똥을 굴리는 쇠똥구리는 똥으로 된 공을 옮기는 동안
어떻게 길을 찾는가?

(a) 냄새를 탐지하기 위해 그것들의 더듬이를 사용함
　　으로써
(b) 눈에 띄는 지형지물들을 관찰함으로써
(c) 배설물을 완벽한 구 모양으로 굴림으로써
(d) 별빛으로 그것들 자신의 위치를 확인함으로써

─○ 지텔프 치트키

질문의 키워드 navigate가 avoid getting lost로 paraphrasing되어 언급된 주변 내용을 주의 깊게 읽는다.

해설 | 3단락의 'By aligning themselves with it, they can proceed in a straight line and avoid getting lost.'에서 똥을 굴리는 쇠
똥구리는 성단에 의해 생성된 빛의 띠에 그것들 자신을 일직선으로 맞춤으로써 똑바로 나아가고 길을 잃는 것을 피할 수 있다고 했다. 따라서
(d)가 정답이다.

Paraphrasing

the band of light produced by clusters of stars 성단에 의해 생성된 빛의 띠 → starlight 별빛

오답분석

(c) 3단락에서 똥을 굴리는 쇠똥구리는 똥을 공 모양으로 만들며 그 공이 완벽하게 둥글다고는 했지만, 이것이 똥을 굴리는 쇠똥구리가 길을 찾는 방법은 아니므로 오답이다.

어휘 | prominent adj. 눈에 띄는   landmark n. (주요) 지형지물   orient v. 자신의 위치를 확인하다

---

70 추론   특정사실   난이도 ●●●

When most likely do dung beetles help plants grow in other areas?

(a) when they burrow underground to create home
(b) when they disperse their own waste
(c) when they transport feces to new locations
(d) when they consume animal manure on farms

언제 쇠똥구리가 다른 지역에서 식물들이 자라는 것을 돕는 것 같은가?

(a) 집을 만들기 위해 땅속에 굴을 팔 때
(b) 그것들 자신의 배설물을 퍼뜨릴 때
(c) 새로운 장소로 배설물을 운반할 때
(d) 농장에 있는 동물의 배설물을 먹을 때

○ **지텔프 치트키**

질문의 키워드 help plants grow in other areas가 aid in the dispersal of seeds로 paraphrasing되어 언급된 주변 내용을 주의 깊게 읽는다.

해설 | 4단락의 'They ~ inadvertently aid in the dispersal of seeds present in dung as they roam around.'에서 쇠똥구리는 이리저리 돌아다니면서 뜻하지 않게 똥에 있는 씨앗의 분산을 돕는다고 한 것을 통해, 쇠똥구리가 새로운 장소로 배설물을 운반할 때 다른 지역에서 식물들이 자라는 것을 돕는 것임을 추론할 수 있다. 따라서 (c)가 정답이다.

오답분석

(b) 3단락에서 똥을 굴리는 쇠똥구리가 똥을 공 모양으로 만들고 그것을 다른 장소로 밀고 나간다고는 했지만, 그것들 자신의 배설물이 아닌 동물의 배설물로 만드는 것이므로 오답이다.

---

71 특정세부사항   What   난이도 ●●○

According to the article, what can researchers learn by studying dung beetles?

(a) the condition of a natural environment
(b) the causes of extreme natural disasters
(c) the status of humans in an ecosystem
(d) the impact of changes in livestock diets

기사에 따르면, 연구원들은 쇠똥구리를 연구함으로써 무엇을 알 수 있는가?

(a) 자연환경의 상태
(b) 극심한 자연재해의 원인들
(c) 생태계에서 인간의 지위
(d) 가축의 사료 변화가 미치는 영향

○ **지텔프 치트키**

질문의 키워드 studying이 examined로 paraphrasing되어 언급된 주변 내용을 주의 깊게 읽는다.

해설 | 5단락의 'whose status in an environment is examined to determine the overall health of an ecosystem'에서 생태계의 전반적인 건강성을 알아내기 위해 환경에서의 쇠똥구리의 상태가 조사된다고 했다. 따라서 (a)가 정답이다.

해커스 지텔프 최신기출유형 실전문제집 7회 (Level 2)

Paraphrasing

the ~ health of an ecosystem 생태계의 건강성 → the condition of a natural environment 자연환경의 상태

어휘 | extreme adj. 극심한

---

72 어휘   유의어   난이도 ●○○

In the context of the passage, <u>travel</u> means _____.

(a) retain
(b) convert
(c) locate
(d) move

지문의 문맥에서, 'travel'은 -을 의미한다.

(a) 유지하다
(b) 전환하다
(c) 찾아내다
(d) 이동하다

—○ 지텔프 치트키

밑줄 친 어휘의 유의어를 찾는 문제이므로, travel이 포함된 구절을 읽고 문맥을 파악한다.

해설 | 2단락의 'travel great distances'는 먼 거리를 이동한다는 뜻이므로, travel이 '이동하다'라는 의미로 사용된 것을 알 수 있다. 따라서 '이동하다'라는 같은 의미의 (d) move가 정답이다.

---

73 어휘   유의어   난이도 ●●○

In the context of the passage, <u>vital</u> means _____.

(a) vibrant
(b) unique
(c) essential
(d) best

지문의 문맥에서, 'vital'은 -을 의미한다.

(a) 활기찬
(b) 독특한
(c) 필수적인
(d) 최고의

—○ 지텔프 치트키

밑줄 친 어휘의 유의어를 찾는 문제이므로, vital이 포함된 구절을 읽고 문맥을 파악한다.

해설 | 4단락의 'play a vital role'은 필수적인 역할을 한다는 뜻이므로, vital이 '필수적인'이라는 의미로 사용된 것을 알 수 있다. 따라서 '필수적인'이라는 같은 의미의 (c) essential이 정답이다.

오답분석

(a) '활기찬'이라는 의미의 vibrant도 vital의 사전적 유의어 중 하나이지만, 문맥상 쇠똥구리가 환경에서 필수적인 역할을 한다는 의미가 되어야 적절하므로 문맥에 어울리지 않아 오답이다.

수신인 정보

Ronald Brewster
President
Brewster Construction

Dear Mr. Brewster:

편지의 목적: 장소 변경 공지

I eagerly anticipate seeing you at our upcoming charity golf tournament, "Home in One." However, [74]please be informed that the event will no longer be taking place at the Chandler Creek Golf Resort but at the Mesa Ranch Golf Course instead.

장소 변경 이유

[75]The management at Chandler Creek recently told us that they are closing earlier than planned to undertake important rehabilitation work. Meanwhile, [79]Mesa Ranch has <u>confirmed</u> availability for the same date of Saturday, September 8.

변경 사항1: 만찬 + 휴식 장소

As a result of this change, we have had to make other adjustments as well. First, [76]the appreciation dinner for corporate sponsors is being moved inside. Since the outdoor veranda at Mesa Ranch is booked for a private event, [76]we will use its main ballroom instead. Furthermore, the change of venue means that we will not be able to use hotel rooms. Therefore, we will be setting up a large, air-conditioned tent for VIP guests to relax in.

변경 사항2: 비용 절감

On a more positive note, catering and equipment rental costs are now significantly lower. For that reason, [77]our executive committee is proposing that we add the excess funds to the event's charitable proceeds. They may be used alternatively to supplement cash prizes for the putting contest and raffle. [77]We are looking forward to hearing your feedback on this matter. As you know, prizes have already been arranged for the winners of the golf tournaments. These include holiday packages, discount offers, and computing devices.

끝인사

I hope that none of these changes causes you inconvenience. For other inquiries, you may contact our communications department at 602-657-6424. Thank you again for your support. This event will go a long way toward helping us [80]<u>realize</u> the mission of "Home in One," [78]which is to provide affordable housing for all.

발신인 정보

Yours truly,
Wendy Simon
Communications director
Heart Homes, Inc.

Ronald Brewster
회장
Brewster 건설사

Mr. Brewster께:

저희의 다가오는 자선 골프 대회 'Home in One'에서 귀하를 뵙기를 간절히 고대하고 있습니다. 그러나, [74]이 행사는 더 이상 Chandler Creek 골프 리조트가 아닌 Mesa Ranch 골프장에서 대신 진행될 것이라는 점을 알아 두시기를 바랍니다.

[75]Chandler Creek의 경영진은 최근에 저희에게 그들이 중요한 복구 작업을 시작하기 위해 계획했던 것보다 일찍 문을 닫을 것이라고 말했습니다. 한편, 같은 날짜인 9월 8일 토요일에 [79]Mesa Ranch는 이용이 가능하다는 것을 <u>확인해</u> 주었습니다.

이러한 변동의 결과로서, 저희는 다른 조정도 해야 했습니다. 우선, [76]기업 후원자들을 위한 감사 만찬이 내부로 옮겨질 것입니다. Mesa Ranch의 야외 베란다가 개인 행사를 위해 예약되어 있기 때문에, [76]저희는 대신에 그곳의 가장 큰 무도회장을 이용할 예정입니다. 그뿐만 아니라, 장소의 변경은 저희가 호텔 방을 사용할 수 없을 것이라는 사실을 의미합니다. 따라서, 저희는 VIP 손님들이 편히 쉬실 수 있도록 넓고 에어컨이 있는 텐트를 설치할 것입니다.

조금 더 긍정적인 관점에서, 출장 뷔페 비용과 장비 대여 비용이 이제 상당히 더 저렴합니다. 그러한 이유로, [77]저희의 집행 위원회는 여분의 자금을 행사의 자선 수익금에 보태는 것을 제안하고 있습니다. 그것들은 대신에 퍼팅 대회 및 추첨을 위한 상금을 보충하기 위해 사용될 수 있습니다. [77]저희는 이 문제에 대한 귀하의 의견을 듣기를 기대하고 있겠습니다. 아시다시피, 골프 대회의 우승자를 위한 상품들은 이미 준비되어 있습니다. 이것들은 휴가 패키지, 할인 혜택, 그리고 컴퓨터 기기를 포함합니다.

이러한 변경 사항 중 그 어떤 것도 귀하께 불편을 끼치지 않기를 바랍니다. 다른 문의 사항이 있으신 경우, 602-657-6424로 저희의 커뮤니케이션 부서에 연락하시면 됩니다. 귀하의 성원에 다시 한번 감사드립니다. 이 행사는 [78]모두에게 저렴한 주택을 공급하려는 'Home in One'의 [80]<u>사명을 실현하는</u> 데 있어 저희에게 큰 도움을 줄 것입니다.

Wendy Simon 드림
커뮤니케이션 부서장
Heart Homes 주식회사

어휘 | eagerly adv. 간절히 anticipate v. 고대하다, 기대하다 upcoming adj. 다가오는, 곧 있을 charity n. 자선
management n. 경영, 경영진 undertake v. 시작하다 rehabilitation n. 복구 adjustment n. 조정 corporate adj. 기업의
ballroom n. 무도회장 charitable adj. 자선의 proceeds n. 수익금 alternatively adv. 대신에 arrange v. 준비하다
go a long way phr. 큰 도움이 되다 affordable adj. 저렴한

---

74 주제/목적　편지의 목적　　　　　　　　　　　　　　　　　　난이도 ●○○

Why did Wendy Simon write Ronald Brewster a letter?	Wendy Simon은 왜 Ronald Brewster에게 편지를 썼는가?
(a) to request a different meeting time	(a) 다른 회의 시간을 요청하기 위해서
(b) to ask for contributions for an event	(b) 행사를 위한 기부금을 요청하기 위해서
(c) to mention a change of location	**(c) 장소의 변경을 언급하기 위해서**
(d) to cancel an upcoming appointment	(d) 다가오는 약속을 취소하기 위해서

◉─○ 지텔프 치트키

지문의 초반을 주의 깊게 읽고 전체 맥락을 파악한다.

해설 | 1단락의 'please be informed that the event will no longer be taking place at the Chandler Creek Golf Resort but at the Mesa Ranch Golf Course instead'에서 행사는 더 이상 Chandler Creek 골프 리조트가 아닌 Mesa Ranch 골프장에서 대신 진행될 것이라는 점을 알아 두라고 한 뒤, 장소의 변경으로 인해 달라진 점들을 안내하는 내용이 이어지고 있다. 따라서 (c)가 정답이다.

어휘 | contribution n. 기부금

---

75 특정세부사항　　Why　　　　　　　　　　　　　　　　　　난이도 ●●○

Why is Chandler Creek unavailable for the event?	Chandler Creek은 왜 행사에 이용될 수 없는가?
(a) It will be going out of business shortly.	(a) 곧 영업을 종료할 것이다.
(b) It is starting repairs sooner than expected.	**(b) 예상보다 빨리 수리를 시작할 것이다.**
(c) It is undergoing an alteration to its management.	(c) 그것의 경영에 변화를 겪고 있다.
(d) It will host a social occasion on the same day.	(d) 같은 날에 사교 행사를 주최할 것이다.

◉─○ 지텔프 치트키

질문의 키워드 unavailable이 closing으로 paraphrasing되어 언급된 주변 내용을 주의 깊게 읽는다.

해설 | 2단락의 'The management at Chandler Creek ~ told us that they are closing earlier than planned to undertake important rehabilitation work.'에서 Chandler Creek의 경영진은 중요한 복구 작업을 시작하기 위해 계획했던 것보다 일찍 문을 닫을 것이라고 말했다고 했다. 따라서 (b)가 정답이다.

Paraphrasing
earlier than planned 계획했던 것보다 일찍 → sooner than expected 예상보다 빨리
undertake ~ rehabilitation work 복구 작업을 시작하다 → starting repairs 수리를 시작하는

어휘 | go out of business phr. 영업을 종료하다 undergo v. 겪다 alteration n. 변화 occasion n. 행사

특정세부사항　Where

난이도 ●●○

Where will a meal for the benefactors take place?

(a) in a VIP lounge area
(b) in a hotel conference center
(c) in an indoor event room
(d) in an air-conditioned tent

후원자들을 위한 식사는 어디에서 진행될 것인가?

(a) VIP 라운지 구역에서
(b) 호텔 회의장에서
(c) 실내 행사장에서
(d) 에어컨이 있는 텐트에서

━○ 지텔프 치트키

질문의 키워드 meal for ~ benefactors가 dinner for ~ sponsors로 paraphrasing되어 언급된 주변 내용을 주의 깊게 읽는다.

해설 | 3단락의 'the appreciation dinner for corporate sponsors is being moved inside'에서 기업 후원자들을 위한 감사 만찬이 내부로 옮겨질 것이라고 한 뒤, 'we will use its main ballroom instead'에서 대신에 Mesa Ranch의 가장 큰 무도회장을 이용할 예정이라고 했다. 따라서 (c)가 정답이다.

Paraphrasing
its ~ ballroom 무도회장 → an indoor event room 실내 행사장

오답분석
(d) 3단락에서 VIP 손님들이 편히 쉴 수 있도록 넓고 에어컨이 있는 텐트가 설치될 것이라고는 했지만, 이곳에서 후원자들을 위한 식사가 진행되는 것은 아니므로 오답이다.

어휘 | benefactor n. 후원자

77　특정세부사항　What

난이도 ●●○

What does Simon expect Brewster to do about the committee's proposal?

(a) contribute to the size of the donation
(b) review the list of contest prizes
(c) reconsider the catering options
(d) comment on the use of extra funds

Simon은 Brewster가 위원회의 제안에 대해 무엇을 하기를 기대하는가?

(a) 기부금의 규모에 기여한다
(b) 대회 상품들의 목록을 검토한다
(c) 출장 뷔페 선택지들을 재고한다
(d) 여분의 자금 사용에 관한 의견을 말한다

━○ 지텔프 치트키

질문의 키워드 committee ~ proposing이 committee's proposal로 paraphrasing되어 언급된 주변 내용을 주의 깊게 읽는다.

해설 | 4단락의 'our executive committee is proposing that we add the excess funds to the event's charitable proceeds'에서 'Home in One'의 집행 위원회는 여분의 자금을 행사의 자선 수익금에 보태는 것을 제안하고 있다고 한 뒤, 'We are looking forward to hearing your feedback on this matter.'에서 이 문제에 대한 Brewster의 의견을 듣기를 기대하고 있겠다고 했다. 따라서 (d)가 정답이다.

Paraphrasing
the excess funds 여분의 자금 → extra funds 여분의 자금
your feedback 피드백 → comment 의견을 말하다

What most likely is the goal of the fundraising event? | 모금 행사의 목표는 무엇인 것 같은가?

(a) **helping individuals find inexpensive places to live**
(b) thanking a developer for providing affordable housing
(c) marketing products to practitioners of golf
(d) raising money for the acquisition of a new property

(a) **사람들이 저렴한 거처를 찾는 것을 돕는 것**
(b) 저렴한 주택을 제공하는 것에 대해 개발업자에게 감사를 표하는 것
(c) 골프 연습생들에게 제품들을 홍보하는 것
(d) 새 부동산 취득을 위해 자금을 모으는 것

○ **지텔프 치트키**
　질문의 키워드 goal이 mission으로 paraphrasing되어 언급된 주변 내용을 주의 깊게 읽는다.

해설 | 5단락의 'which is to provide affordable housing for all'에서 'Home in One'의 사명은 모두에게 저렴한 주택을 공급하는 것이라고 한 것을 통해, 모금 행사의 목표는 사람들이 저렴한 거처를 찾는 것을 돕는 것임을 추론할 수 있다. 따라서 (a)가 정답이다.

　Paraphrasing
　affordable housing 저렴한 주택 → inexpensive places to live 저렴한 거처

어휘 | practitioner n. 연습생　raise v. (자금 등을) 모으다　property n. 부동산

---

79 어휘　유의어　　　　　　　　　　　　　　　　　　　　　　　　　　난이도 ●●○

In the context of the passage, <u>confirmed</u> means _____. | 지문의 문맥에서, 'confirmed'는 -을 의미한다.

(a) selected
(b) **verified**
(c) explained
(d) proved

(a) 선택했다
(b) **확인했다**
(c) 설명했다
(d) 증명했다

○ **지텔프 치트키**
　밑줄 친 어휘의 유의어를 찾는 문제이므로, confirmed가 포함된 구절을 읽고 문맥을 파악한다.

해설 | 2단락의 'Mesa Ranch has confirmed availability'는 Mesa Ranch는 이용이 가능하다는 것을 확인해 주었다는 뜻이므로, confirmed가 '확인해 주었다'라는 의미로 사용된 것을 알 수 있다. 따라서 '확인했다'라는 비슷한 의미의 (b) verified가 정답이다.

---

80 어휘　유의어　　　　　　　　　　　　　　　　　　　　　　　　　　난이도 ●●○

In the context of the passage, <u>realize</u> means _____. | 지문의 문맥에서, 'realize'는 -을 의미한다.

(a) identify
(b) discover
(c) understand
(d) **fulfill**

(a) 확인하다
(b) 깨닫다
(c) 이해하다
(d) **실현하다**

○ **지텔프 치트키**
　밑줄 친 어휘의 유의어를 찾는 문제이므로, realize가 포함된 구절을 읽고 문맥을 파악한다.

해설 | 5단락의 'realize the mission'은 사명을 실현한다는 뜻이므로, realize가 '실현하다'라는 의미로 사용된 것을 알 수 있다. 따라서 '실현하다'라는 같은 의미의 (d) fulfill이 정답이다.

오답분석

(b) '깨닫다'라는 의미의 discover도 realize의 사전적 유의어 중 하나이지만, 문맥상 모두에게 저렴한 주택을 공급하려는 'Home in One'의 사명을 실현한다는 의미가 되어야 적절하므로 문맥에 어울리지 않아 오답이다.

TEST 1

TEST 2

TEST 3

TEST 4

TEST 5

TEST 6

TEST 7

해커스 지텔프 최신기출유형 실전문제집 7회 (Level 2)

MEMO

해커스
지텔프
Level 2
최신기출 유형
실전 문제집 7회

초판 4쇄 발행 2024년 9월 19일

초판 1쇄 발행 2022년 10월 28일

지은이	해커스 어학연구소
펴낸곳	㈜해커스 어학연구소
펴낸이	해커스 어학연구소 출판팀

주소	서울특별시 서초구 강남대로61길 23 ㈜해커스 어학연구소
고객센터	02-537-5000
교재 관련 문의	publishing@hackers.com
동영상강의	HackersIngang.com

ISBN	978-89-6542-522-9 (13740)
Serial Number	01-04-01

외국어인강 1위,
해커스인강 HackersIngang.com

해커스인강

· 효과적인 지텔프 청취 학습을 돕는 **무료 문제풀이 MP3**
· 교재의 핵심 어휘를 복습할 수 있는 **무료 지텔프 기출 단어암기장**
· 내 점수와 백분위를 확인하는 **무료 자동 채점 및 성적 분석 서비스**
· 시험 전 꼭 봐야 할 **"딱 한 장에 담은 지텔프 문법 총정리"** 무료 강의

영어 전문 포털,
해커스영어 Hackers.co.kr

해커스영어

· 무료 **지텔프 단기 고득점 비법 강의**
· 무료 **지텔프/공무원/세무사/회계사 시험정보 및 학습자료**